Teacher Guidebook
Level B

A Reason For Spelling ® Teacher's Guidebook - Level B
Copyright ©2012 by The Concerned Group, Inc.

ISBN#: 0-936785-28-4
TL#: SPTGB2012

Published by The Concerned Group, Inc.
P.O. Box 1000, 700 East Granite, Siloam Springs, AR 72761

Publisher: Russ L. Potter, II • Project Director: Kristin Potter
Senior Editor: Bill Morelan • Layout and Design: Mark Decker
Copy Editor: Mary Alice Hill • Story Editor: Tricia Schnell
Proofreaders: Daniel Swatsenberg, Rachel Tucker

Created by MOE Studio, Inc.
Authors: Rebecca Burton, Eva Hill, Leah Knowlton, Kay Sutherland
Black and White Illustrations: James McCullough
Colorization for Student Edition: Mark Decker
Design and Layout: Greg Hauth • Project Leader: Greg Sutherland

Printed in the United States of America

For more information about *A Reason For Spelling*,® *A Reason For Handwriting*,®
A Reason For Science® and *A Reason For Guided Reading*®
go to: *www.AReasonFor.com*

Contents:

Acknowledgments:

Field Test Participants:

Virginia Allen, East Rockaway, New York • Mrs. Christine Baker, Belleville, Pennsylvania • Judy M. Banks, Carmichael, California • Darya Birch, San Clemente, California • Mari Anne Burns, Baton Rouge, Louisiana • Karen Dafflitto, St. Louis, Missouri • Kristen J. Dorsett, Prescott, Arizona • Ms. Laura Guerrera, East Rockaway, New York • Mrs. Anne Gutierrez, San Antonio, Texas • Jeanette O. Kappel, Winstead, Minnesota • Sharon K. Kobilka, San Antonio, Texas • Connie Kozitza, Winsted, Minnesota • Vivian I. Sawyer, Carmichael, California • Harold W. Souther, San Antonio, Texas • Cleo F. Staples, Auburn, California • Suezy Tucker, Auburn, California • Martha Woodbury, Los Angeles, California

Placement Tests

In order to evaluate readiness and accurately meet individual student need, a simple placement test is recommended at the beginning of each school year.

Step 1: *Administer the test*

(Say) Number your paper from one to twenty. I will say the word once, use the word in a sentence, then say the word again. Write a word beside each number on your paper.

(Allow ample time and carefully monitor progress.)

Step 2: *Evaluate the corrected tests using the following criteria.*

If the student correctly spells 17 to 20 words:
• Assign the student to Level B program
• Encourage the student to work independently
• Assign Challenge Activities
• Select and assign several Other Word Forms to spell and test

If the student correctly spells 8 to 16 words:
• Assign the student to Level B program
• Allow opportunities to work independently
• Offer Challenge Activities

If the student correctly spells 0 to 7 words:
• Administer Level A placement test
• Based on results, you may choose to:
 a) Assign student to Level A Worktext, or
 b) Assign student to Level B, but use regular lessons without Challenge Activities
• Encourage completion of all Phonics Activities

Placement Test Level A

1. man — The **man** is tall.
2. red — I like my **red** hat.
3. not — We did **not** go to the park.
4. big — This **big** dog barks a lot.
5. run — They will **run** in the race.
6. him — This gift is for **him**.
7. ball — The **ball** is yellow.
8. top — We hiked to the **top** of the hill.
9. day — It is a sunny **day**.
10. ride — I will **ride** my bike in the parade.
11. go — The green light means **go**.
12. ten — I have **ten** fingers.
13. look — **Look** at the funny clown.
14. boy — The **boy** kicked the ball.
15. mother — My **mother** is baking bread.
16. for — The flowers are **for** you.
17. blue — The sky looks **blue** today.
18. her — Did you tell **her** about Jesus?
19. tell — **Tell** your friend to come in.
20. and — You **and** I will ride at the park.

Placement Test Level B

1. hat — I bought a new **hat**.
2. men — The **men** are working hard.
3. into — The frog jumped **into** the pond.
4. box — We have a **box** of toys.
5. must — They **must** be tired.
6. late — She will be **late** for school.
7. keep — I **keep** wishing it was my birthday.
8. hope — I **hope** you turned in your paper.
9. today — **Today** is my birthday.
10. car — The **car** is shiny and clean.
11. like — I **like** to play outside.
12. bird — The **bird** hops across the yard.
13. books — He has some **books** to read.
14. food — This **food** is very good.
15. round — The world is **round**.
16. toy — The **toy** is for him.
17. dish — The **dish** has fruit in it.
18. back — Let's come **back** tomorrow.
19. think — I **think** this is a fun game.
20. done — Are you **done** reading that story?

Day One

Literature Connection - Each week begins with a Scripture verse, followed by a theme story that develops the principles found in that verse. Topic and description are provided to inform the teacher of the story content. Some teachers may choose to use this theme story for the Monday morning devotional. (A CD version of the story is also available.)

Discussion Time *(optional)* - Discussion questions follow each story, giving the teacher the opportunity to evaluate student understanding, and to encourage students to apply the values found in the Scripture to their own lives.

Day One (cont.)

Preview - The test — study — test sequence begins with this pre-test which primarily uses sentences related to the story. Research has shown that immediate correction by the student — under teacher supervision — is one of the best ways to learn to spell. Optional challenge words are marked with a star to help meet enrichment needs.

Say *(bubble graphic)* - Instructions to the students that are to be read aloud by the teacher are marked with the Say symbol for easy identification.

Progress chart *(chart graphic)* - Students may record their Preview scores for later comparison against their Posttest scores.

Take a Minute *(clock graphic)* - Simple instructions are provided for committing to memory the Scripture verses upon which the stories are based.

Challenge *(star graphic)* - These words are provided for better spellers. Challenge activities are marked with a star for easy identification.

Level **B** Introduction

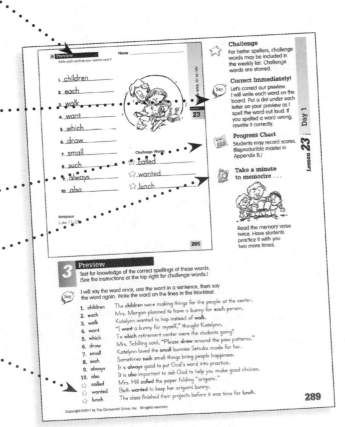

Day One (cont.)

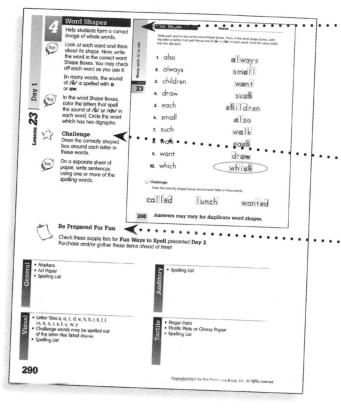

Word Shapes - The use of "Shape Boxes" is a research-based method that helps students form a correct visual image of each spelling word. An additional exercise is provided to enhance student identification of spelling patterns and thus strengthen phonemic awareness.

Challenge *(star graphic)* - These words are provided for better spellers. All challenge activities are marked with a star for easy identification.

Be Prepared for Fun *(list graphic)* - For teacher convenience, a weekly supply list is provided for "Fun Ways to Spell" on Day 1. Supplies for the "General" activity are readily available in most classrooms. Other categories may require minimal extra planning.

Day Two

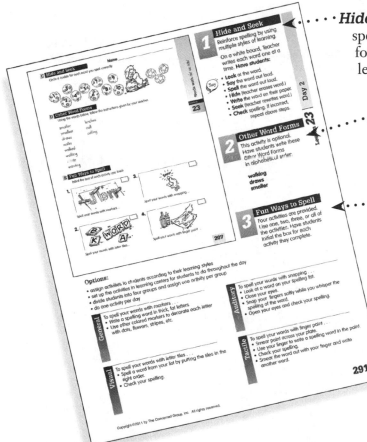

Hide & Seek - Another research-proven method of spelling instruction, Hide & Seek is highly effective for dealing with multiple intelligences and varying learning styles.

Other Word Forms *(optional)* - A variety of activities allow students to become familiar with other forms of the week's spelling words.

Fun Ways to Spell - Four options are offered each week. In addition to a "General" activity, "Auditory," "Tactile," and "Visual" options are provided for students with different learning styles. Suggestions are also given for adapting these activities to various classroom settings.

Introduction | Level **B**

v

Day Three

Language Arts Activity - Research studies show that meaningful, practical use of spelling words helps students become more familiar with the words they are studying. The weekly Language Arts activity is designed to offer practice in this area.

Take a Minute - Reminders to commit Scripture verses to memory are provided periodically.

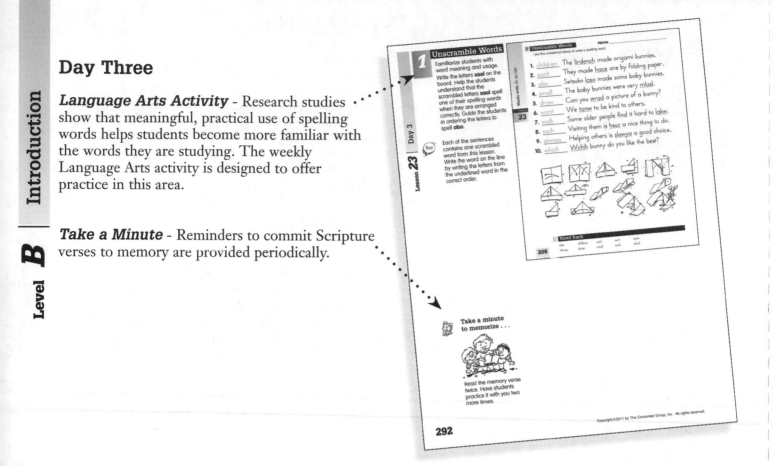

Day Four

Dictation - Students write dictated words to complete sentences. This strengthens their word usage and context skills. Previously taught spelling words are also included in this activity, providing maintenance of spelling skills.

Proofreading - Proofreading allows students to become familiar with the format of standardized tests as they mark misspelled words. Proofreading is also a critical skill that can be incorporated in students' own writing.

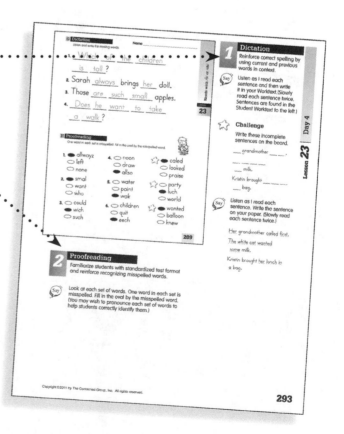

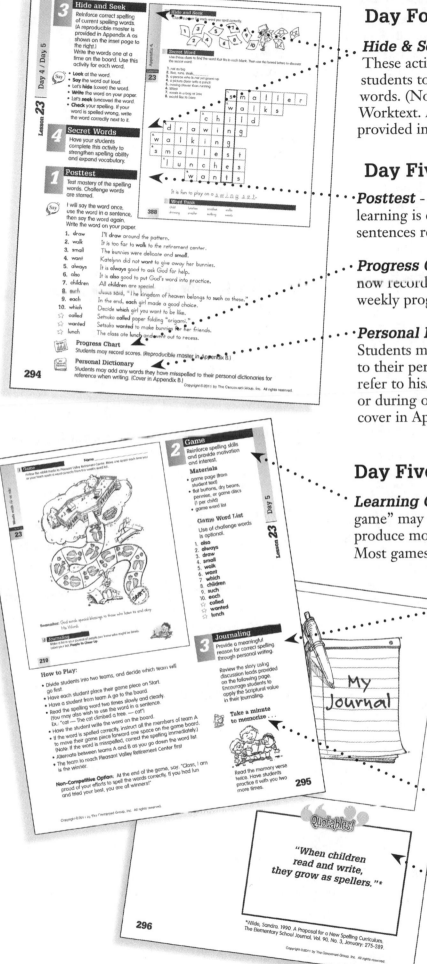

Day Four (cont.)

Hide & Seek/Other Word Forms (*optional*) -
These activities provide additional opportunity for students to practice other forms of their spelling words. (Note: These pages are not in the Student Worktext. A reproducible master for each week is provided in Appendix A.)

Day Five

Posttest - The test — study — test sequence of learning is completed with the posttest. Again, most sentences relate to the theme story.

Progress Chart (*chart graphic*) - Students may now record their posttest scores to evaluate their weekly progress.

Personal Dictionary (*dictionary graphic*) -
Students may add any words they have misspelled to their personal dictionaries. Each student may refer to his/her custom dictionary while journaling or during other writing activities. (Reproducible cover in Appendix B.)

Day Five (cont.)

Learning Game (*optional*) - The weekly "board game" may be used to reinforce spelling skills and produce motivation and interest in good spelling. Most games can be played multiple times.

Journal Entry - The underlying goal of spelling instruction is to create better writers! This weekly journaling activity allows students to apply their spelling skills in a meaningful way, while encouraging them to make the featured value their own. Guided discussion questions are provided to assist in reviewing the value taught by the story.

Take a Minute - Reminders to commit Scripture verses to memory are provided periodically.

Quotables! - Quotes from the comprehensive spelling research provide helpful insights for the teacher.

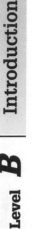

Introduction

Level B

A Reason For Spelling® emphasizes a balance between spelling skills, application, and student enjoyment. In short, it is designed to be both meaningful and fun! Each level promotes successful classroom practices while incorporating the following research findings:

Research Findings:

Application:

Daily Practice. A daily period of teacher-directed spelling activities based on meaningful content greatly enhances student proficiency in spelling.

Daily lessons in *A Reason For Spelling*® provide systematic development of spelling skills with a focus on Scripture verses and values.

Spelling Lists. The most productive spelling lists feature developmentally-appropriate words of highest frequency in writing.

Through daily lessons, challenge words, and other word forms, *A Reason For Spelling*® focuses on the high-frequency words children and adults use in daily writing.

Test—Study—Test. Effective educational programs are built on the learning model of "Test — Study — Test."

A Reason For Spelling® follows a weekly pretest/posttest format, and also includes a cumulative review for each unit.

Accurate Feedback. Pretest and proofreading results are crucial in helping students identify words that require their special attention.

Regular pretests and proofreading activities in *A Reason For Spelling*® help students identify words requiring their special attention.

Visual Imaging. Learning to spell a word involves forming a correct visual image of the whole word, rather than visualizing syllables or parts.

Every lesson in *A Reason For Spelling*® features word-shape grids to help students form a correct visual image of each spelling word.

Study Procedures. The most effective word-study procedures involve visual, auditory, and tactile modalities.

A Reason For Spelling® uses the "look, say, hide, write, seek, check" method as a primary teaching tool.

Learning Games. Well-designed games motivate student interest and lead to spelling independence.

A Reason For Spelling® includes a wide variety of spelling games at each instructional level.

Self-Correction. Student focus, accomplished through such activities as self-correction of pretests, is an essential strategy for spelling mastery at every grade and ability level.

Teacher directed self-correction of pretests and reviews is encouraged throughout *A Reason For Spelling*®.

Regular Application. Frequent opportunities to use spelling words in everyday writing contribute significantly to the maintenance of spelling ability.

A Reason For Spelling® provides opportunities for journaling in each lesson to promote the use of assigned spelling words in personal writing.

Research Bibliography

Cohen, Leo A. 1969. *Evaluating Structural Analysis Methods Used in Spelling Books*. Doctoral Thesis, Boston University.

Davis, Zephaniah T. 1987. Upper Grades Spelling Instruction: What Difference Does It Make? *English Journal*, March: 100-101.

Dolch, E.W. 1936. A Basic Sight Vocabulary. *The Elementary School Journal*, Vol. 36: 456-460.

Downing, John, Robert M. Coughlin and Gene Rich. 1986. Children's Invented Spellings in the Classroom. *The Elementary School Journal*, Vol. 86, No. 3, January: 295-303.

Fiderer, Adele. 1995. *Practical Assessments for Literature-Based Reading Classrooms*. New York: Scholastic Professional Books.

Fitzsimmons, Robert J., and Bradley M. Loomer. 1980. *Spelling: The Research Basis*. Iowa City: The University of Iowa.

Gardner, Howard. 1993. *Multiple Intelligences: The Theory in Practice*. New York: Basic-Books.

Gentry, J. Richard. 1997. *My Kid Can't Spell*. Portsmouth, NH: Heinemann Educational Books.

Gentry, J. Richard and Jean Wallace Gillet. 1993. *Teaching Kids to Spell*. Portsmouth, NH: Heinemann Educational Books.

Gentry, J. Richard. 1985. You Can Analyze Developmental Spelling-And Here's How To Do It! *Early Years K-8*, May:1-4.

Goswami, Usha. 1991. Learning about Spelling Sequences: The Role of Onsets and Rimes in Analogies in Reading. *Child Development*, 62, 1110-1123.

Graves, Donald H. 1977. Research Update: Spelling Texts and Structural Analysis Methods. *Language Arts 54* January: 86-90.

Harp, Bill. 1988. When the Principal Asks, "Why Are Your Kids Giving Each Other Spelling Tests?" *Reading Teacher*, Vol. 41, No. 7, March: 702-704.

Hoffman, Stevie and Nancy Knipping. 1988. Spelling Revisited: The Child's Way. *Childhood Education*, June: 284-287.

Horn, Ernest. 1926. *A Basic Writing Vocabulary: 10,000 Frequently Used Words in Writing*. Monograph First Series, No. 4. Iowa City: The University of Iowa.

Horn, Thomas. 1946. *The Effect of the Corrected Test on Learning to Spell*. Master's Thesis, The University of Iowa.

Horsky, Gregory Alexander. 1974. *A Study of the Perception of Letters and Basic Sight Vocabulary Words of Fourth and Fifth Grade Children*. Doctoral Thesis, The University of Iowa.

Lacey, Cheryl. 1994. *Moving On In Spelling*. Jefferson City, Missouri: Scholastic.

Lutz, Elaine. 1986. ERIC/RCS Report: Invented Spelling and Spelling Development. *Language Arts*, Vol. 63, No. 7, November: 742-744.

Marino, Jacqueline L. 1978. *Children's Use of Phonetic, Graphemic, and Morphophonemic Cues in a Spelling Task*. Doctoral Thesis, State University of New York at Albany.

Morris, Darrell, Laurie Nelson and Jan Perney. 1986. Exploring the Concept of 'Spelling Instructional Level' Through the Analysis of Error-Types. *The Elementary School Journal*, Vol. 87, No. 2, 195-197.

Nicholson, Tom and Sumner Schachter. 1979. Spelling Skill and Teaching Practice-Putting Them Back Together Again. *Language Arts*, Vol. 56, No. 7, October: 804-809.

Rothman, Barbara. 1997. *Practical Phonics Strategies to Build Beginning Reading and Writing Skills*. Medina, Washington: Institute for Educational Developmental.

Scott, Jill E. 1994. Spelling for Readers and Writers. *The Reading Teacher*, Vol. 48, No. 2, October: 188-190.

Simmons, Janice L. 1978. *The Relationship Between an Instructional Level in Spelling and the Instructional Level in Reading Among Elementary School Children*. Doctoral Thesis, University of Northern Colorado.

Templeton, Shane. 1986. Synthesis of Research on the Learning and Teaching of Spelling. *Educational Leadership*, March: 73-78.

Tireman, L.S. 1927. *The Value of Marking Hard Spots in Spelling*. Doctoral Thesis, University of Iowa.

Toch, Thomas. 1992. Nu Waz for Kidz tu Lern Rdn, Rtn. *U.S. News & World Report*, September 14: 75-76.

Wagstaff, Janiel M. *Phonics That Work! New Strategies for the Reading/Writing Classroom*. Jefferson City, Missouri: Scholastic.

Watson, Alan J. 1988. Developmental Spelling: A Word Categorizing Instructional Experiment. *Journal of Educational Research*, Vol. 82, No. 2, November/December: 82-88.

Webster's New American Dictionary. 1995. New York: Merriam-Webster Inc.

Wilde, Sandra. 1990. A Proposal for a New Spelling Curriculum. *The Elementary School Journal*, Vol. 90, No. 3, January: 275-289.

English Second Language (ESL)

Effective teachers are always sensitive to the special spelling challenges faced by ESL students. While it is not practical to provide specific guidelines for every situation where the teacher may encounter students with limited English proficiency, the following general guidelines for two of the most prominent cultural groups (Asian & Hispanic) may prove helpful.

alphabet Many Asian languages have a significantly different kind of alphabet and students may need considerable practice recognizing English letters and sounds.

vowels Some Asian languages do not have certain English vowel sounds. Speakers often substitute other sounds. Spanish vowels have a single sound: *a* as in *ball*, *e* as in *eight*, *i* as in *ski*, *o* as in *over*, *u* as in *rule*. The Spanish *a* is spelled *e*, *e* is spelled *i* or *y*, and *i* is often spelled *ai* or *ay*.

ô The variety of *ô* spellings may cause some problems for Spanish-speaking students.

ü, ú The *ú* sound does not occur in Spanish, and may cause problems.

ou This sound is spelled *au* in Spanish.

r This sound does not exist in Spanish. Many Asian languages do not have words ending with *r*.

b, d, h, j Spanish and Asian speakers often confuse the sounds of *b / d* and *h / j*.

ge, gi, j In Spanish, *ge*, *gi*, and *j* most closely resemble the English *h*.

l, f Many Asian languages do not have these sounds.

k, q The letter *k* does not exist in Spanish, but the sound *k* is spelled with either *c* or *qu*. The letter *q* always occurs with *ue* or *ui*.

p, g In most Asian languages, the consonants *p* and *g* do not exist.

v In Spanish, the letter *v* is pronounced *b*.

w There are no Spanish-originated words with the letter *w*.

y In Spanish, *y* is spelled *ll*.

x, z In Spanish, *x* is never used in the final position. There is no letter or sound for *z*.

ch, sh The Spanish language does not have the sound *sh*. Spellers often substitute *ch*. Many Asian languages do not contain *sh* or *ch*.

wh, th The initial *wh* and *th* sounds do not exist in most Spanish and some Asian languages. The Spanish *d*, however, is sometimes pronounced almost like the *th*.

kn This sound may be difficult for both Spanish and Asian spellers.

s clusters Spanish clusters that begin with s are always preceded by the vowels *a* or *e*. The most common clusters that will cause problems are *sc*, *sk*, *sl*, *sm*, *sn*, *sp*, *sq*, *st*, and *sw*. Many of these do not occur in Asian languages.

pl, fl, tr, fr, dr These sounds are used in Spanish, but may not be present in some Asian languages.

ng, nk, nt, nd Many Asian languages don't have *ng*, *nk*, *nt*, or *nd*. Spanish doesn't include the *ng* ending.

silent letters The only silent letter in Spanish is *h*. Silent consonants such as those in *mb*, *lk*, and *gh* do not occur in Spanish or Asian languages.

double consonants The only double consonants in Spanish are *cc*, *ll*, and *rr*.

ed In Spanish, the suffix *ed* is pronounced aid. This can be very confusing, especially when the *ed* has the soft *t* sound as in *dropped*.

plurals Spanish rules for adding plurals are: For words ending in a vowel, add *s*. For words ending in a consonant, add *es*. This may cause confusion both in pronunciation and spelling of English words.

contractions Only two contractions are used in Spanish: *a el* becomes *al*, and *de el* becomes *del*. Apostrophes do not exist.

syllables Many Asian languages consist entirely of one and two syllable words. Thus, many longer English words are often confusing.

Spelling Generalizations

In the English language, spelling cannot be taught primarily by rules or generalizations. It's a complex language that has evolved from many other languages and therefore contains many irregularities. There are exceptions to almost all spelling rules.

Research, however, indicates that some generalizations are of value in teaching children to spell. These generalizations have few exceptions and apply to a large number of words. Familiarity with these spelling rules can be helpful to many learners. In addition, generalizations that deal with adding suffixes to words can be quite valuable in expanding a student's ability to spell other word forms.

The following generalizations may prove to be helpful:

- The letter *q* is always followed by *u*.

- Every syllable contains a vowel. *Y* can also serve as a vowel.

- Words that end in silent *e*:
  . . . drop the *e* when adding a suffix beginning with a vowel. (live, living)
  . . . keep the *e* when adding a suffix beginning with a consonant. (time, timely)

- Words that end in *y*:
  . . . are not changed when adding suffixes if the *y* is preceded by a vowel. (say, saying)
  . . . change the *y* to *i* when adding suffixes if the *y* is preceded by a consonant, unless the suffix begins with *i*. (try, tried, trying)

- When *ei* or *ie* are used in a word, the *i* usually comes before the *e* except when they make the *a* sound, or follow after a *c*. (believe, eight, ceiling)

- Words ending in one consonant preceded by a single vowel usually double the final consonant when adding a suffix beginning with a vowel. (begin, beginning)

- Words ending with the sounds made by *x*, *s*, *sh*, and *ch* add the suffix *es* to form plurals or change tense. (mix, mixes)

- Proper nouns and most proper adjectives begin with capital letters.

Multiple Intelligences

In recognition of the multiple intelligences theory, *A Reason For Spelling*® provides activities to meet the varied needs of your students. (See "Fun Ways to Spell," and "Hide & Seek.")

Scripture Translation

Each weekly lesson in *A Reason For Spelling*® begins with Scripture verse. This is followed by a contemporary theme story designed to bring out key values found in the verse.

Teachers are strongly encouraged to introduce each lesson by reading the "Theme Text" aloud (or have a student read the verse aloud). This helps set the stage for principles and values students will be focusing on that week.

Scripture verses used in *A Reason For Spelling*® are similar in most translations, allowing teachers to use the Scripture translation their school prefers, without affecting academic content.

XI

Personal Spelling Dictionary

A great way to encourage students' spelling awareness is to help them develop and maintain their own Personal Spelling Dictionary at their desk to refer to when writing. This can be either a spiral-bound or loose-leaf notebook with a few pages designated for each letter of the alphabet. Throughout the school year, encourage students to constantly add words to their Personal Spelling Dictionary, not only from spelling class, but from other classes as well. These should include words a student finds difficult to spell, as well as words of particular interest (reproducible cover in Appendix B).

Word Walls

Another excellent method of promoting spelling awareness in your classroom is to create a word wall. This wall (often a large bulletin board) contains commonly used words and words of special interest to students. The classroom word wall becomes a permanent reference list that students may refer to as they read and write.

Words may be arranged in a variety of ways. Some examples include traditional alphabetical order; groups such as math words, weather words, color words; or alphabetically by the first letter of the targeted vowel schemes. For example:

A	E	I	O	U
gate	eaten	bit	fabulous	fun
tar	dread	like	skeleton	fur
	her	tonight		bubble

Some words could even have picture or context clues added. Sample words from word families being studied, or interesting words students want to know how to spell are added throughout the year. Students should be reminded not to simply copy the words from the wall, but to look at the word needed, then write it from memory — or write the word they are having difficulty with, then check it against the word wall.

Games can be played using the word wall as well.
- Rhyming Words: Ask students to find a word that "begins with G and rhymes with rod."

- Sentence Sense: Write the letter l on the board, then say "Look for a word that begins with an l and fits this sentence: I _ _ _ _ Jesus."

- Chant & Clap: Chant the spelling words, clapping for each vowel or consonant.

- Dictate & Write: Dictate a sentence for students to write using words found only on the wall.

- Read My Mind:

(Say) I am thinking of one of the words on the wall. It has _____ letters. It begins with _____.
The vowel is _____. It fits in this sentence: _____.

Flip Folders

The Flip Folder is a great way for students to use the research-based, time-tested "Look — Hide — Write — Seek — Check" method to learn spelling words. They may do this activity on their own or with a partner.

On the front of a standard file folder, make two cuts to create three flaps (see diagram below). On a separate piece of paper, have students make three columns, then write the words they need to study in the first column. Now have students slide the paper into the folder so that the words are under the first flap.

(Say)
- Open Flap 1 and **Look** at the first word.
- Now **Hide** the word by closing the flap.
- Open Flap 2 and **Write** the word in the middle column.
- Open Flaps 1 & 2 and **Seek** the word to . . .
- **Check** your spelling. If the word is misspelled . . .
- Open Flap 3 and **Write** the word correctly in the third column.

Inventive Spelling/Journaling

The goal of *A Reason For Spelling*® is to create proficient and self-reliant spellers and writers. By combining inventive spelling (through journaling) with formal spelling instruction, an excellent environment is created for students to develop into expert spellers (reproducible Journal cover in Appendix B).

As children learn to spell, they go through several stages. The move from one stage to another is gradual even though students may spell from more than one stage at one time. Just as a toddler who is talking in complete sentences doesn't suddenly regress to babbling, so students tend to remain relatively stable within and between stages. Recognized stages of spelling development include:

Precognitive Stage: Children use symbols from the alphabet for writing words, but letters are random and do not correspond to sound. (eagle = dfbrt; eighty = acbp)

Semiphonetic Stage: Children understand and consistently represent sounds with letters. Spellings are often abbreviated representing only the initial and/or final sounds. (eagle = e; eighty = a)

Phonetic Stage: Students in this stage spell words like they sound. The speller perceives and represents every sound in a word, though spellings may be unconventional. (eagle = egl; eighty = aty)

Transitional Stage: Students think about how words appear visually. Spelling patterns are apparent. Spellings exhibit customs of English spelling such as vowels in every syllable, correct e-marker and vowel digraph patterns, inflectional endings, and frequent English letter sequences. (eagle = egul; eighty = eightee)

Conventional Stage: This stage develops over years of word study and writing. Correct spelling has different instructional levels. Correct spelling for a group of words that can be spelled by the average third grader would be "third-grade level correct" spelling. (eagle = eagle; eighty = eighty)

An effective way to help students transition through the stages is to edit their first drafts, then talk with them about corrections. Discuss why changes are necessary. Encourage students to rewrite journal entries so others can read them easily. Display student work whenever possible. Teach students that invented spelling makes it easier for the writer, but that revision to standard spelling is a courtesy to the reader.

XIII

Level B | Introduction

Word lists in *A Reason For Spelling*® are based on frequency of use in student and adult writing; frequency of use in reading materials; spelling difficulty; and grade level familiarity.

Studies used in the development of these lists include: *Dolch Basic Sight Vocabulary* (a list of 220 high-frequency words); *The American Heritage Word Frequency Book* (a study of word frequency in print materials for grades three through nine); *Starter Words* (the 190 most frequently used words in children's writing, school materials, and adult print materials); and *A Basic Vocabulary of Elementary School Children.*

These standard references were extensively cross-checked with other respected studies (Gates; Horn; Greene & Loomer; Harris & Jacobson). It is significant to note that very few differences were found among these sources.

For teacher convenience, lesson numbers follow each word, and challenge words are indicated by a star.

Level-A

about-19	dad-1	he's-11☆	much-12	sit-4
above-22☆	day-13	help-2☆	my-16	six-26
add-1☆	did-4	hen-17	next-2☆	small-9☆
after-23	dig-4	her-24	nice-14	so-16
all-9	digit-28☆	hid-4	no-16	some-22
am-7	do-21	hide-14	none-22☆	soon-21☆
an-1	dog-3	him-8	not-3	south-19☆
and-7	down-19	his-8	now-19	still-4☆
are-24	draw-9☆	hit-4	number-26☆	stop-12
as-23	drop-12☆	hop-12	odd-3☆	such-12☆
ask-1☆	each-11☆	how-19	of-22	sum-6☆
at-1	eat-11	hug-6	off-3	take-13
away-13	enjoy-22☆	ice-14	on-3	talk-9☆
back-7☆	fall-9	if-8	one-26	tall-28
ball-9	feet-11	in-8	or-24	tell-2
bed-2	few-28	into-8☆	orange-27☆	ten-17
begin-8☆	finish-8☆	is-8	our-19	than-18☆
best-2☆	first-24☆	it-4	out-19	thank-1☆
big-4	five-26	jaw-9	pencil-17☆	that-23
black-27	for-24	joy-22	penny-17☆	the-18
blue-27	four-26	just-6☆	pink-27	them-18
books-21☆	frog-3☆	kid-4☆	plan-7☆	then-17
box-3☆	from-22	kind-14☆	play-13	there-18
boy-22	fun-6	know-16☆	pray-13☆	these-18☆
brown-27	funny-6☆	land-7	purple-27☆	they-18
bug-6	get-2	law-9	put-21	thick-28☆
but-12	girl-24	let-2	quit-4☆	thin-28☆
by-16	glad-7	line-14☆	ran-1	thing-18
call-9	go-16	little-28	red-2	think-18☆
came-13☆	God-3	long-28	ride-14	this-18
can-1	going-16☆	look-21	round-19☆	three-26
cat-1	good-21	Lord-24☆	run-6	time-14
cent-17	got-3	love-22	said-23	to-21
circle-24☆	grade-13☆	made-13	sand-7	tooth-21☆
clock-12☆	grand-7☆	make-13	saw-9	top-12
color-27☆	green-27	man-1	school-21	town-19
come-22	had-7	many-28	see-11	try-16
cot-12	hand-7	may-13	send-17	two-26
count-26☆	happy-23	me-11	sentence-17☆	up-6
cup-6	has-23	mom-3	seven-26	us-6
cut-12	hasn't-23☆	more-28	she-11	vowel-19☆
	have-23☆	most-16☆	short-28	was-23
	he-11	mother-24	side-14	wasn't-23☆

Level-B

we-11	bubble-5☆	frog-4	
we'll-11☆	buy-9	full-19	
well-2	cake-7	funny-29	
went-17	called-23☆	game-7	
when-17	came-7	gate-7	
white-27	camp-1	gave-7	
why-16	candy-26	give-3	
wide-14	car-14	gone-4	
will-8	card-14	grade-7	
win-8	care-15☆	grand-26	
with-18	child-9☆	grass-29	
write-14☆	children-23	great-7☆	
yellow-27	circle-16	grow-11	
yes-2	city-17☆	guess-29	
you-21	clean-8	gym-3☆	
your-24	clock-27	hang-27	
zero-26☆	cloud-21☆	hard-14	
	cold-10	hat-1	
above-5	color-16	have-1	
add-1	could-19	he's-8	
again-2☆	count-21	head-2	
air-15	cow-21	hear-19	
along-27☆	crown-21☆	heard-16☆	
also-23	cry-9	heart-14☆	
always-23	dark-14	help-2	
another-28	dear-19	here-19	
any-17	different-29☆	high-9☆	
apple-1☆	digit-3	hold-10	
arm-14	dinner-29☆	holy-17	
around-21	dish-25	home-10	
ask-1	does-5	hope-10	
asked-1☆	don't-10☆	horse-22	
baby-17	done-5	house-21	
back-27	door-22	I'm-9	
bake-7	dot-4	important-22☆	
balloon-20☆	draw-23	index-26☆	
band-26	dress-29	Indian-26	
barn-14	drop-4	into-3	
bath-1☆	dry-9	its-3	
be-8	duck-27	Jesus-8☆	
bear-15	each-23	job-4☆	
because-3☆	ear-19	jump-5	
been-3	east-8	just-5	
before-22☆	easy-17☆	keep-8	
begin-3	end-26	kid-3	
bell-29	enjoy-22	kind-26	
below-11☆	even-8	knew-20☆	
bend-26	ever-2	know-11	
beside-15☆	every-17	large-14☆	
best-2	eye-15	last-1	
better-29	family-17	late-7	
between-8☆	far-14	left-2	
Bible-9☆	farm-14	leg-2	
bird-16	fast-1	letter-29☆	
birthday-13☆	father-28☆	light-9	
blind-26	find-26	like-15	
block-27☆	fine-15	line-15	
blow-11	finish-25	live-3	
boat-10	fire-15	looked-19☆	
books-19	first-16	Lord-22	
both-28	fish-25	lost-4	
bow-21	flower-21☆	lot-4	
box-4	fly-9	low-11	
boys-22	food-20	lunch-23☆	
break-7☆	forgot-4☆	map-1	
bring-27	form-22	men-2	
brother-28☆	found-21	might-9	
	friend-26☆	milk-27	

XIV

mitten-29
most-10
mowing-11☆
must-5
name-7
nest-2
never-2☆
new-20
next-2
night-9
noise-22
none-5
noon-20
number-5
obey-7☆
odd-4
often-4
old-10
once-5☆
only-17
orange-22
other-28
over-10☆
own-11
page-7
paint-13
part-14
party-14☆
pay-13
penny-17
people-8
plan-1
plays-13
pond-26
praise-13☆
pray-13
print-5
pull-29
purple-16
quit-3
rabbit-29
rain-13
read-8
ready-17
right-9
road-10
roll-10
room-20
round-21
row-11
say-13
second-26☆
sentence-2☆
set-2
shelf-25☆
shoe-25
shoes-25☆
shop-25
short-25☆
should-25
show-25
shut-25
sick-27
sing-27
sister-3
sleep-8☆
slow-11
small-23

snow-11
snowman-11☆
soft-4
something-27☆
sometimes-5☆
soon-20
sound-21
south-21
stay-13
stayed-13☆
still-29
stood-19☆
store-22
story-17
study-17☆
such-23
sum-5
talk-27
than-1
thank-28
their-15
these-28
thick-28
thin-28
think-28
third-16☆
those-28
thought-28
through-20☆
throw-11
tie-9
today-13
together-28☆
told-10
tomorrow-4☆
too-20
took-19
tooth-20
tow-11
toy-22
train-13
tree-8
truck-27
under-16
until-3☆
use-20
very-17
voice-22☆
vowel-21
walk-23
want-23
wanted-23☆
wash-25
water-16
way-13
we'll-8
were-16
what-5
where-15
which-23
while-15☆
who-20
wish-25
wood-19
word-16
work-16
world-16☆

would-19
write-15
wrote-10☆
yard-14
year-19☆
zoo-20

Level-C

able-27
address-8
afraid-16
ago-20
airport-23
alarm-25
allow-22
alone-20
amount-22
angel-13
angry-17
answer-1
anyhow-22
apart-25
April-27
argue-25
army-25
artist-25
asleep-14
August-21
aunt-9
autumn-21
awake-16
bark-25
began-1
behind-9
belong-9
berry-1
bicycle-19
body-1
boot-31
boss-14
bother-3
bottle-27
bought-21
bread-5
bright-11
broke-5
brook-29
brought-21
bump-9
burn-28
bushes-29
busy-17
butter-8
buzz-2
cactus-2
cage-13
candle-27
careful-15
carry-17
cattle-27
caught-11
cause-21
center-26
certain-14
chair-3
chalk-11
change-3
charge-25

cheek-3
cheese-3
cherry-3
chest-1
chill-1
choose-31
circus-14
classroom-8
clay-4
close-4
cloth-4
clothes-11
clown-22
collar-2
cookie-29
copy-15
corner-23
course-23
cover-15
crash-10
crayon-5
creek-17
crop-2
cross-5
crowd-22
date-16
daughter-21
deaf-2
December-26
deep-17
die-19
dirt-28
dollar-26
doubt-22
drank-9
drew-31
driver-26
drown-22
eagle-27
early-28
earn-28
earth-10
edge-13
eight-16
February-17
felt-2
field-17
fight-19
flag-4
flame-4
flash-4
flew-31
float-20
floor-23
follow-20
football-29
forget-23
fork-15
fort-23
fought-21
fourth-23
fresh-10
Friday-19
front-1
fruit-31
gas-14
gift-1
giraffe-13

glass-4
glove-4
goes-20
gold-20
good-bye-29
grab-5
grandfather-9
grandmother-9
gray-5
ground-22
group-31
half-11
hall-21
hammer-26
handle-27
happen-8
hatch-10
heavy-17
held-1
hello-2
herd-28
honey-17
hood-29
hook-29
horn-23
hour-22
huge-13
hurry-28
husband-9
ink-9
January-13
jar-13
jealous-13
jolly-13
judge-13
jug-13
juice-13
July-13
June-13
kept-15
key-15
kick-10
knee-11
knot-11
ladder-8
lady-16
lamb-2
later-26
lay-16
learn-28
leave-17
less-14
lesson-8
lie-19
life-19
lift-1
list-1
loose-31
loud-22
made-16
mail-16
March-25
mark-25
market-25
marry-17
match-10
meal-17
mean-17

merry-8
metal-27
middle-27
million-8
mirror-26
Monday-9
moon-31
mouse-22
mouth-22
nearby-19
neck-10
needle-27
neighbor-11
neighborhood-29
north-3
notebook-29
November-26
October-15
open-20
order-23
owe-20
pants-2
paper-16
park-25
pass-14
paw-21
person-28
pick-1
place-4
plain-4
plane-16
plant-4
please-4
plow-22
plus-4
pool-31
poor-23
porch-10
pour-23
power-22
prayer-5
price-5
prize-5
proud-5
pulley-29
puppy-1
push-29
queen-15
quick-15
quiet-15
quilt-15
quite-15
race-14
rack-15
rage-13
rake-15
ranch-10
raw-21
really-8
remember-26
return-28
ripe-19
river-26
rode-20
rope-20
rubber-8
ruler-31

rush-10
sack-10
saddle-27
sail-16
salt-21
sandwich-10
sang-9
Saturday-28
save-14
score-23
scrap-7
scratch-7
scream-7
screen-7
scrub-7
search-28
sell-14
September-28
serve-28
seventh-14
sew-20
shade-16
shampoo-31
shark-25
sharp-25
shock-3
shook-29
shout-22
shown-20
shy-19
sidewalk-11
sight-11
sign-19
silver-26
since-14
skate-5
skin-5
skip-5
sleeve-4
slice-4
smart-25
smell-8
smile-19
smooth-31
soap-14
song-21
sore-23
sorry-14
spell-5
spend-5
splash-10
spoke-20
sport-23
spread-7
spring-7
sprinkle-27
squirrel-27
stamp-9
start-25
stiff-2
storm-23
straight-7
strange-7
straw-7
stream-7
street-7
string-7
strong-7

sudden-8
sugar-26
suit-31
summer-26
Sunday-2
sunny-8
supper-8
sweet-14
switch-10
table-16
taught-21
teacher-10
team-17
telephone-20
test-1
thankful-3
thirteen-3
thirty-28
though-11
threw-7
thumb-11
Thursday-3
tight-19
tiny-19
toast-20
track-15
travel-27
truth-31
Tuesday-31
turtle-27
twelve-2
twenty-17
unhappy-8
upon-21
visit-1
wagon-2
wait-16
wall-21
Wednesday-11
weigh-16
west-2
whale-3
wheat-3
whether-3
whip-3
whole-11
wild-19
wind-9
window-2
wing-9
wipe-19
wolf-29
woman-29
wonder-26
wool-29
wore-23
worse-28
wrap-11
young-9

Curriculum Objectives

Literature Connection
To increase comprehension and vocabulary development through a value-based story.

Discussion Time
To check understanding of the story and encourage personal value development.

Pretest
To test for knowledge of correct spellings of current spelling words.

Word Shapes
To help students form a correct visual image of whole words.

Hide & Seek
To reinforce correct spelling of current spelling words

Other Word Forms
To strengthen spelling ability and expand vocabulary.

Fun Ways to Spell
To reinforce correct spelling of current words with activities that appeal to varying learning styles.

Dictation
To reinforce using current and previous spelling words in context.

Proofreading
To reinforce recognition of misspelled words, and to familiarize students with standardized test format.

Language Arts Activity
To familiarize students with word meaning and usage.

Posttest
To test mastery of the current spelling words.

Learning Game
To reinforce correct spelling of test words.

Challenge Activities
To provide more advanced spellers with the opportunity to master more difficult words.

Journaling
To provide a meaningful reason for correct spelling through personal writing.

Unit Tests
To test mastery of the correct spelling of the words from each unit.

Unit Challenge Tests
To test more advanced spellers' mastery of the correct spellings of the challenge words from each unit.

Certificate
To provide opportunity for parents or guardians to encourage and assess their child's progress.

Parent Letter
To provide the parent or guardian with the spelling word lists for the next unit.

Phonics Units (Levels A and B only)
To provide a supplement for promoting phonemic awareness, and a review of basic phonic skills.

Common Spelling Patterns

The following list of sounds and spelling patterns will help you easily identify words with similar patterns.

Sounds	Sample Words	Sounds	Sample Words
a	**a**sk, h**a**t	ō	**o**ld, b**oa**t, h**oe**, gl**o**be, bl**ow**
ā	**a**pron, l**a**te, m**ai**l, pl**ay**	ô	t**a**lk, c**au**se, dr**aw**, s**o**ft, th**ou**ght
ä	f**a**ther, p**a**rt, h**ea**rt	ôr	st**o**ry, m**o**re, w**a**rd, f**ou**r
âr	aw**a**re, f**ai**r, b**ea**r, th**ere**	oi	p**oi**nt, b**oy**
b	**b**erry, a**b**le, scru**b**	ou	ab**ou**t, pl**ow**
ch	**ch**eese, bun**ch**, la**tch**, na**t**ure	p	**p**lan, re**p**ly, sna**p**, su**pp**ly
d	**d**og, la**dd**er	r	**r**an, me**rr**y, mo**r**e, **wr**ite
e	b**e**d, h**ea**vy, s**ai**d	s	**s**ay, gue**ss**, **sc**ent, pri**c**e, **c**ity
ē	sh**e**, h**ea**t, fr**ee**, ni**e**ce, k**ey**	sh	**sh**ip, ca**sh**, mi**ss**ion, ma**ch**ine, spe**c**ial,
f	**f**ish, loa**f**, o**ff**, enou**gh**, pro**ph**et		va**c**ation
g	**g**ive, for**g**ot, shru**g**	t	**t**en, pu**t**, bu**tt**er, creas**ed**
h	**h**as, any**h**ow, **wh**ole	th	**th**in, e**th**nic, wi**th**
wh	**wh**ine, **wh**ich	th	**th**em, wor**th**y, smoo**th**
i	d**i**g, g**y**m	u	c**u**p, d**o**ne, wh**a**t, y**ou**ng
ī	f**i**nd, p**ie**, m**i**ce, tr**y**	ū	h**u**man, y**ou**, t**u**ne
îr	cl**ea**r, d**ee**r, p**ie**rce, c**e**real, h**ere**	ü	cl**ue**, d**o**, s**oo**n, fr**ui**t
j	**j**ust, en**j**oy, **g**erm, hu**g**e, bu**dg**e	u̇	t**oo**k, sh**ou**ld, p**u**sh
k	**k**eep, hoo**k**, sti**ck**, s**ch**ool, **c**an	ûr	**ea**rn, st**e**rn, f**i**rst, w**o**rk, Th**u**rsday
l	**l**eft, Ju**l**y, hau**l**, fu**ll**y, te**ll**	v	**v**isit, a**v**oid, arri**v**e
m	**m**eal, cal**m**, cli**mb**,	w	**w**ash, drive**w**ay
	co**mm**on, hy**mn**	y	**y**oung, famil**i**ar
n	**n**ice, fu**n**, tu**nn**el, **kn**ow	z	la**z**y, ja**zz**, pri**z**e, rai**s**e, rein**s**, e**x**ample
ng	alo**ng**, bri**ng**ing, tha**n**k	zh	mea**s**ure, ero**s**ion
o	n**o**t, p**o**nd, w**a**tch	ə	**a**bove, wat**e**r, anim**a**l, gall**o**n, thank**fu**l

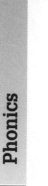

1 | Warm-Up

Arrange the Alphabet

Materials
• Several sets of alphabet cards

Preparation
Shuffle sets of alphabet cards so they are not sequential.

How to Play:
Hand 4 non-sequential alphabet cards to each student. Instruct each student to arrange their cards in alphabetical order on their desk. When a student successfully completes the task, hand them 5 cards to arrange. Continue as desired, increasing the number of cards each time.

A | **Poetry Connection**

Name _____

The Universe God Made
God made a lot of round things
Like the earth and shining stars,
The sun, and moon, and planets:
Venus, Mercury, Saturn, Mars.

He hung them all up in the sky
To show His love and care;
So when I see their shining light
I know that God is there.

Fill in the letter that comes between the given letters.

1. a _b_ c   x _y_ z   t _u_ v
2. j _k_ l   k _l_ m   n _o_ p
3. v _w_ x   m _n_ o   d _e_ f
4. e _f_ g   b _c_ d   p _q_ r
5. g _h_ i   s _t_ u   h _i_ j
6. q _r_ s   w _x_ y   c _d_ e

Write the letter that comes before and after the given letter.

7. _b_ c _d_   _v_ w _x_   _r_ s _t_
8. _p_ q _r_   _d_ e _f_   _u_ v _w_
9. _g_ h _i_   _x_ y _z_   _s_ t _u_
10. _n_ o _p_   _j_ k _l_   _l_ m _n_

Alphabetical Order

Day **1**

3

---

2 | Poetry Connection

Have students follow along as you read the poem. Explain that not only are the earth, moon, and planets round, but they also travel around the sun. You may need to explain that stars are round balls of burning gases, and do not actually have points the way we draw them.

3 | Activity Page 3

Objective:
To review the alphabet and alphabetical order

 Say At the top of your page, fill in the letter that comes between the given letters. At the bottom of your page, write the letter that comes before and after the given letter.

B Phonics

Name _____

Write the words from each group in ABC order.

1. fire   apple
   ball   ball
   apple   circle
   circle   dime
   dime   earth
   earth   fire

2. heaven   God
   Jupiter   heaven
   God   ice
   light   Jupiter
   keep   keep
   ice   light

3. quarter   moon
   Orion   night
   night   Orion
   moon   planets
   planets   quarter
   round   round

4. want   stars
   stars   telescope
   zenith   universe
   Venus   Venus
   universe want
   telescope zenith

4

Activity Page 4

Objective:
To review alphabetical order

(Say) Write the words from each group in ABC order.

1 Warm-Up

Beanbag Beginnings

Materials

• Six shoe-boxes

Preparation

Using the letters **M, N, V, W, Y,** and **Z**, label each box with a letter. Line up the six boxes in a row.

How to Play:

Have students take turns tossing a beanbag into a box. They will name the letter on the box that the beanbag lands in and say a word that begins with that letter. Continue as long as there is time or interest.

A ▸ **Poetry Connection**

Name _____

Slanted and Straight

The roof of our house slants this way and that,
It sits up on top like a party hat.
The walls of our house are tall and straight.
They're built very strong to hold up the weight.
The floor of our house is level and flat,
So things will stay put—I'm thankful for that!

Say the name of each picture. Write the letter for the beginning sound to complete each name.

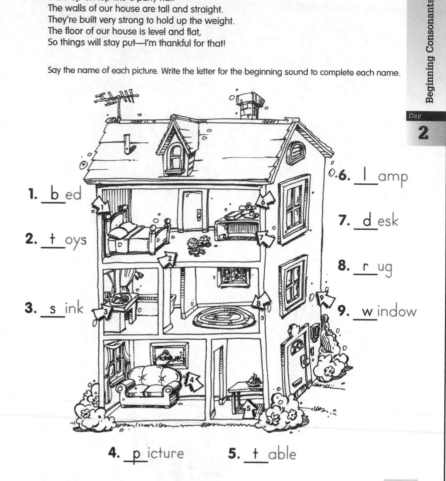

1. <u>b</u> ed

2. <u>t</u> oys

3. <u>s</u> ink

6. <u>l</u> amp

7. <u>d</u> esk

8. <u>r</u> ug

9. <u>w</u> indow

4. <u>p</u> icture   **5.** <u>t</u> able

5

2 Poetry Connection

Have students follow along as you read the poem. Think of other things that slant such as a tent, ice cream cone, teepee, pine tree, etc. Think of letters that have slanted lines in them and write them on the board. (**A, K, k, M, N, R, V, v, W, w, X, x, Y, y, Z, z**) Now, think of letters with tall, straight lines and add them to the list on the board. (**B, b, D, d, E, F, H, h, I, K, k, L, l, M, N, P, R, T**)

3 Activity Page 5

Objective:

To review beginning consonant sounds

(Say) Look at each numbered object in the house. Say the name of each picture. Write the letter for the beginning sound to complete each name.

4

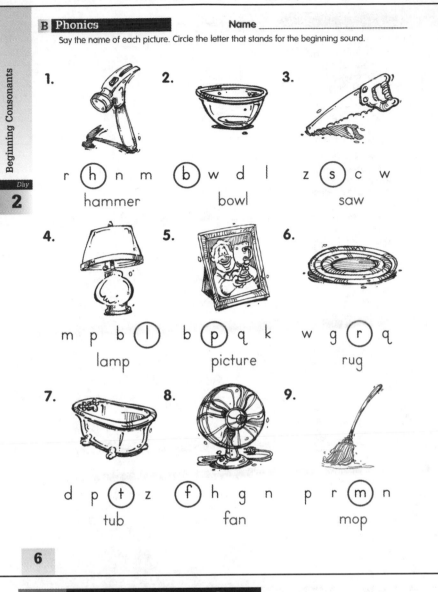

Name _____

Say the name of each picture. Circle the letter that stands for the beginning sound.

Beginning Consonants

Day 2

1. r (h) n m
hammer

2. (b) w d l
bowl

3. z (s) c w
saw

4. m p b (l)
lamp

5. b (p) q k
picture

6. w g (r) q
rug

7. d p (t) z
tub

8. (f) h g n
fan

9. p r (m) n
mop

6

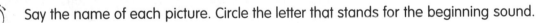

Activity Page 6

4

Objective:

To review beginning consonant sounds

(Say) Say the name of each picture. Circle the letter that stands for the beginning sound.

5

1 Warm-Up

Going on a Trip

Materials
• None

Preparation
None

How to Play:
Tell the students that today they are going on a trip. They may take only things that begin with the sound of **/b/**, **/d/**, **/g/**, **/p/**, or **/q/**. The first student might say, "I am going on a trip and I'm going to take a ball." The student can name anything that begins with the letter b. The next student thinks of a new b word to take on the trip. He might say, "I am going on a trip and I'm going to take a banana." Each student will try to take a new thing, but the word must begin with **/b/**. As soon as a student misses by not being able to think of another thing that begins with **/b/**, start taking things that begin with **/d/**. Continue until you have used each letter and all the students have had a turn.

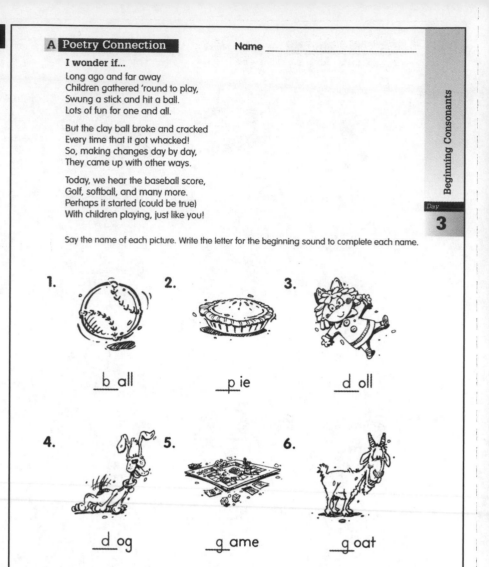

A Poetry Connection

Name _____

I wonder if...
Long ago and far away
Children gathered 'round to play,
Swung a stick and hit a ball.
Lots of fun for one and all.

But the clay ball broke and cracked
Every time that it got whacked!
So, making changes day by day,
They came up with other ways.

Today, we hear the baseball score,
Golf, softball, and many more.
Perhaps it started (could be true)
With children playing, just like you!

Say the name of each picture. Write the letter for the beginning sound to complete each name.

1. b_all

2. p_ie

3. d_oll

4. d_og

5. g_ame

6. g_oat

7

2 Poetry Connection

Have students follow along as you read the poem. Think of other games that are played using something round like a ball such as marbles, basketball, soccer, tennis, ping-pong, jacks, etc. (Other games may be common where you live.) Think of letters that include a ball shape or a ball and stick. Write these on the board. (**a, b, d, g, o, p, q**)

3 Activity Page 7

Objective:
To review the beginning consonant sounds of **/b/**, **/d/**, **/g/**, and **/p/**

 Say

Say the name of each picture. Write the letter for the beginning sound to complete each name.

B Phonics

Name _____

Say the name of each picture. Write the uppercase and lowercase partner letters for the beginning sound.

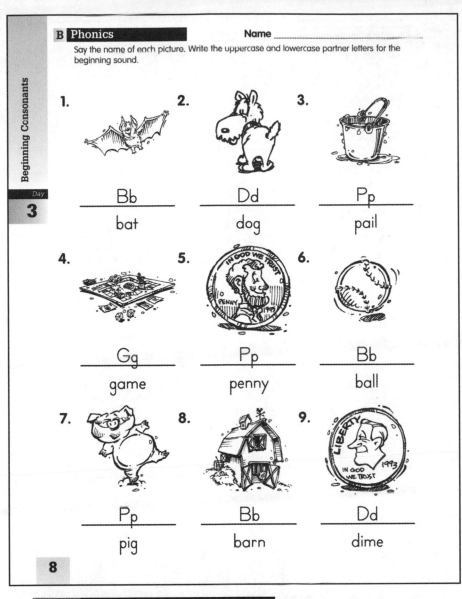

1.	2.	3.
Bb	Dd	Pp
bat	dog	pail
4.	5.	6.
Gg	Pp	Bb
game	penny	ball
7.	8.	9.
Pp	Bb	Dd
pig	barn	dime

8

Activity Page 8

Objective:

To review the beginning consonant sounds of **/b/**, **/d/**, **/g/**, and **/p/**

 Say the name of each picture. Write the uppercase and lowercase partner letters for the beginning sound.

1 | Warm-Up

Find the End

Materials
- Picture cards of objects whose names end with a consonant
- Small box

Preparation
Put the picture cards in a box.

How to Play:
Deliver the box to a student and ask them to select a card. Have the student hold up the card, say the name of the picture, and identify the ending sound. Let the student deliver the box to someone else and repeat the activity. Continue until all the students have had a turn.

A | Poetry Connection   Name _____

Baby Toes
When I was a baby, small as could be,
Mom counted my fingers and toes.
She made up a song, to sing just for me,
And this is the way it goes…

One, two,—three, four, five…
Little bees buzzing out of the hive,
Five, four,—three, two, one…
Better look out, 'cause here they come!

Say the name of each picture. Write the letter for the ending sound to complete each name.

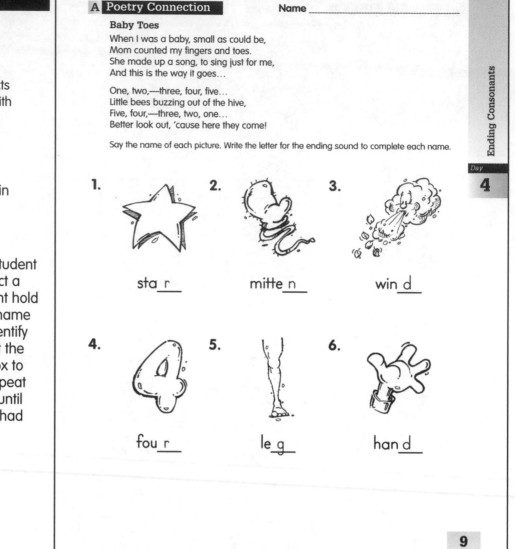

1. sta _r_

2. mitte _n_

3. win _d_

4. fou _r_

5. le _g_

6. han _d_

9

2 | Poetry Connection

Have students follow along as you read the poem. Talk about things that come in 2's - wings, mittens; 3's - traffic lights, wheels on a tricycle; 4's - legs on a chair, corners in a room; and 5's - fingers, points on a star, etc.

3 | Activity Page 9

Objective:
To review ending consonant sounds

(Say) Say the name of each picture. Write the letter for the ending sound to complete each name.

8

B Phonics   Name _____

Say the name of each picture. Write the letter for the ending sound.

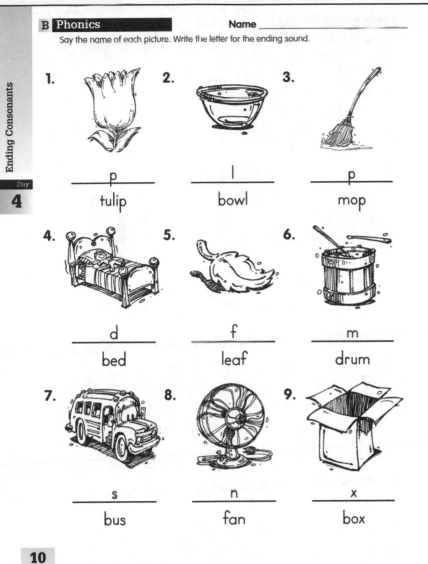

1.
p
tulip

2.
l
bowl

3.
p
mop

4.
d
bed

5.
f
leaf

6.
m
drum

7.
s
bus

8.
n
fan

9.
x
box

10

4 **Activity Page 10**

Objective:

To review ending consonant sounds

Say) Say the name of each picture. Write the letter for the ending sound.

1 Warm-Up

A Sound in Seven

Materials
• A card with the number seven on it

Preparation
Have students sit in a circle.

How to Play:
Show students the card with a seven on it and ask them what sound they hear in the middle of seven. Explain that you will pass the seven around the circle and count to seven. The seventh student will be holding the seven and should name something with a consonant sound in the middle, and name the letter that stands for that sound. Continue until all the students have had a turn.

Growing Pains

When I was just six, age seven looked fine.
When seven, I longed to be eight!
And now that I'm eight, I just want to be nine,
For I know being nine would be great.

When I get to ten, I'll almost be grown!
But Dad says when I'm a man,
I'll wish for the day when I was a boy
So be glad for the age that I am!

Say the name of each picture. Find the picture whose name will best complete each sentence. Write the middle letter to complete each name.

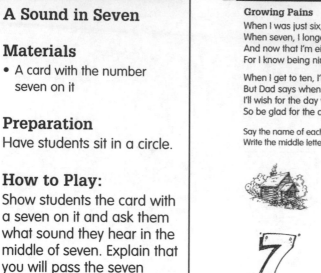

1. She had six le_m_ons for the pie.
2. That ti_g_er is big!
3. I ate se_v_en nuts.
4. The ca_m_el is brown.
5. Pull the red wa_g_on.
6. Did you see eight legs on the spi_d_er?
7. We can go to the ca_b_in.
8. This is my ra_d_io.

11

---

2 Poetry Connection

Have students follow along as you read the poem. Ask the students what they have each year to celebrate that they are a year older. You may ask for examples of their favorite birthday celebrations. Ask if anyone is impatient to be older. Encourage them to enjoy the age they are right now.

---

3 Activity Page 11

Objective:
To review medial consonant sounds

 Say the name of each picture. Find the picture whose name will best complete each sentence. Write the middle letter to complete each name.

B Phonics

Name _____

Say the name of each picture. Write the letter for the consonant sound you hear in the middle of each word.

1. b
rabbit

2. l
balloon

3. t
mitten

4. m
hammer

5. p
zipper

6. t
kitten

7. x
boxes

8. l
tulip

9. n
peanut

12

Activity Page 12

Objective:

To review medial consonant sounds

Say) Say the name of each picture. Write the letter for the consonant sound you hear in the middle of each word.

1 Warm-Up

Pop, Goes the Otter

Materials
• None

Preparation
None

How to Play:
Recite the phrase **Pop, Goes The Weasel** together. If students are unfamiliar with the song, you may like to sing it for them. Explain that another animal in the weasel family is the otter. Change the phrase to **Pop, Goes The Otter**. Write a word that has the sound of short **/a/** or **/o/** on the board. Have a student say the word, identify the vowel sound, then sing the phrase, replacing the word **pop** with the word on the board. You may want to use these words:

back, bang, catch, chop, clop, dodge, drop, fast, flash, flop, grab, gone, hop, jab, nod, paddle, slap, snap, stomp, stop

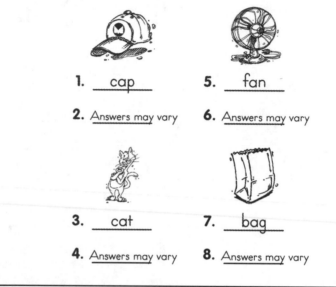

A **Poetry Connection**   Name _____

Otters at Play

Alphie and Dan were otter "best friends"
That lived by a lake in the woods,
At the top of a mountain that everyone called,
  "I'd-Climb-To-The-Top-If-I-Could."

Now, Alphie and Dan always played chase,
And wrestled and tickled and hid.
One day they were rolling and having such fun,
Straight down to the bottom they slid!

They couldn't climb up to get back to their home.
Going that way would take until dawn!
Then, they spotted a limber pine growing near by,
Bent it down, held it fast, and climbed on.

"Here we go," Danny cried, with a lopsided grin,
Alphie laughed, "We'll sure land with a plop!"
And when they let go... well, that tall, taut tree,
Sailed them up and right back to the top!

Say the name of each picture, and write the name on the first line. On the next line, write a word that rhymes with it.

1. __cap__   5. __fan__

2. Answers may vary   6. Answers may vary

3. __cat__   7. __bag__

4. Answers may vary   8. Answers may vary

13

2 Poetry Connection

Have students follow along as you read the poem. Define the word **taut**. Briefly discuss otters and their habits and habitat. Explain to students that the sound of **/a/** is usually spelled with **a**. (Exception: laughed) The sound of **/o/** can be spelled several ways, including **o** and **aw**. Write these spellings on the board. Have students find a word in the poem for each spelling pattern. (otter, top, dawn, etc.)

3 Activity Page 13

Objective:
To review the sound of **/a/**
To review rhyming words

(Say) Say the name of each picture, and write the name on the first line. On the next line, write a word that rhymes with it.

12

B Phonics

Name _____

Circle the word that names each picture.

1. (hot) pot fox

2. doll (otter) top

3. box (log) rock

4. cob cot (fox)

5. (pot) lot rob

6. mob (mop) top

7. log just (jog)

8. tip pot (top)

9. (dog) hog done

14

Activity Page 14

4

Objective:

To review the sound of **/o/**

Say Circle the word that names each picture.

13

1 Warm-Up

Grandma's Garden

Materials
• None

Preparation
None

How to Play:
Tell the students that today they are going to visit Grandma's garden. She only grows things with the sound of **/e/**. Invite them to listen carefully to each question and tell you about the visit to Grandma's garden.

1. Do we get to visit for five, or seven days? **(seven)**
2. Does Grandma grow more vegetables, or flowers? **(vegetables)**
3. Is she growing peppers, or onions? **(peppers)**
4. Do we find carrots, or celery? **(celery)**
5. Are those heads of lettuce, or cabbage? **(lettuce)**
6. Did she grow zucchini, or yellow squash? **(yellow squash)**
7. Are the pumpkins, or melons ready to pick? **(melons)**
8. Are the ripe tomatoes green, or red? **(red)**
9. Does she have berries, or grapes? **(berries)**
10. Is the tree shading her yard a maple, or an elm? **(elm)**
11. Is there a nest, or a swing in the tree? **(nest)**

A ▌**Poetry Connection**

Name _____

Deeds of Kindness
Every act of kindness,
Every word and deed,
Plants within someone's heart
A tiny, happy seed.

The seed begins to blossom,
To send down roots and grow.
Soon happiness is passed along
To everyone you know.

Circle the word that best completes each sentence and write it on the line.

1. Jen shared her blue ___pen___ .
   red   (pen)   best
2. Ted will ride on the green ___sled___ .
   (sled)   bed   desk
3. Mom ___fed___ the hens some corn.
   vet   pen   (fed)
4. We gave the ___red___ flowers to Grandma.
   (red)   bet   peg
5. The ___tent___ was the right size for Ben.
   get   held   (tent)
6. Tell Tom to ___help___ Dad.
   peck   led   (help)
7. I sat at a friend's ___desk___ .
   nest   (desk)   rest

The Sound of /e/

Day 7

15

---

2 Poetry Connection

Have students follow along as you read the poem. Define the word deed. Invite the students to share examples of times someone has been kind to them. Ask them how it made them feel.

3 Activity Page 15

Objective:
To review the sound of **/e/**

(Say) Read each sentence. Circle the word that best completes each sentence and write it on the line.

14

The Sound of /e/

Day 7

B Phonics

Name _____

Circle the word that names each picture.

1. (hen) hand pen

2. fed met (nest)

3. net web (bed)

4. peck (sled) vet

5. log (leg) lid

6. pan (pen) pond

7. (belt) bend bell

8. bed west (web)

9. tent (jet) peg

16

Activity Page 16

4

Objective:

To review the sound of **/e/**

Say Circle the word that names each picture.

15

1 Warm-Up

Put "i" in the Pocket

Materials
- Paper
- Scraps of fabric, ribbon
- Buttons

Preparation
None

How to Play:
Have students fold up the bottom of a sheet of paper and glue it along the edges to form a pocket. If there is time, they may like to decorate their pocket with fabric patches, buttons, or scraps of ribbon. On separate pieces of paper, have students draw and label pictures of things with the sound of /i/ and place the pictures in their pocket. Continue as long as there is time or interest.

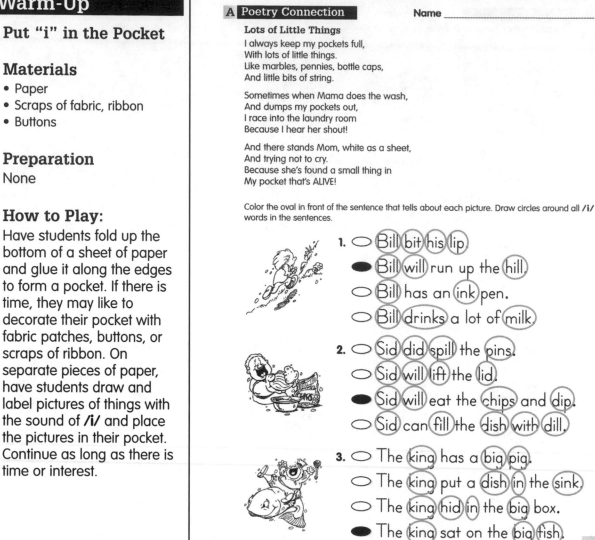

A Poetry Connection

Name _____

Lots of Little Things
I always keep my pockets full,
With lots of little things.
Like marbles, pennies, bottle caps,
And little bits of string.

Sometimes when Mama does the wash,
And dumps my pockets out,
I race into the laundry room
Because I hear her shout!

And there stands Mom, white as a sheet,
And trying not to cry.
Because she's found a small thing in
My pocket that's ALIVE!

Color the oval in front of the sentence that tells about each picture. Draw circles around all /i/ words in the sentences.

1. ○ Bill bit his lip.
   ● Bill will run up the hill.
   ○ Bill has an ink pen.
   ○ Bill drinks a lot of milk.

2. ○ Sid did spill the pins.
   ○ Sid will lift the lid.
   ● Sid will eat the chips and dip.
   ○ Sid can fill the dish with dill.

3. ○ The king has a big pig.
   ○ The king put a dish in the sink.
   ○ The king hid in the big box.
   ● The king sat on the big fish.

17

2 Poetry Connection

Have students follow along as you read the poem. Ask them if they like to put things in their pockets, and if so, what sorts of things. See if any of your students have anything special in their pockets right now.

3 Activity Page 17

Objective:
To review the sound of /i/

(Say) Color the oval in front of the sentence that tells about each picture. Circle each /i/ word in the sentences.

B Phonics

Name _____

Write the word that names each picture by filling in the missing letters.

The Sound of /i/

Day **8**

1. p i g

2. p i n

3. f i s h

4. l i p s

5. s i x

6. b i b

7. g i f t

8. w i g

9. h i l l

18

4 Activity Page 18

Objective:

To review words with the sound of **/i/**

(Say) Write the word that names each picture by filling in the missing letters.

1 Warm-Up

When Do "U" Jump?

Materials
• None

Preparation
Have students stand beside their desks.

How to Play:
Tell the students that you are going to say some words. They should listen carefully for words that have the sound of **/u/**. When they hear a word that has the sound of **/u/**, they should jump up. If the word does not contain the sound of **/u/**, they should stand still. You may want to use these words:

bug, cub, dog, duck, fox, hug, lock, mop, nut, pop, rug, sun

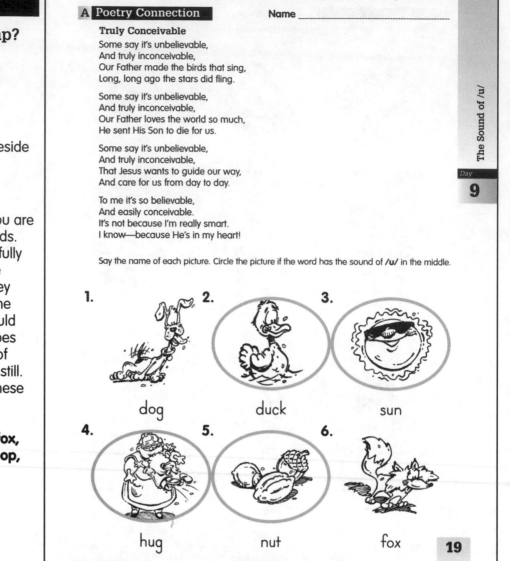

A **Poetry Connection**

Name _____

Truly Conceivable
Some say it's unbelievable,
And truly inconceivable,
Our Father made the birds that sing,
Long, long ago the stars did fling.

Some say it's unbelievable,
And truly inconceivable,
Our Father loves the world so much,
He sent His Son to die for us.

Some say it's unbelievable,
And truly inconceivable,
That Jesus wants to guide our way,
And care for us from day to day.

To me it's so believable,
And easily conceivable.
It's not because I'm really smart.
I know—because He's in my heart!

Say the name of each picture. Circle the picture if the word has the sound of /u/ in the middle.

1. dog   2. duck   3. sun
4. hug   5. nut   6. fox

The Sound of /u/

Day **9**

19

2 Poetry Connection

Have students follow along as you read the poem. Define inconceivable. Ask the students to name something that God made which they think is really amazing and special.

3 Activity Page 19

Objective:
To review the sound of **/u/**

(Say) Say the name of each picture. Circle the picture if the word has the sound of **/u/** in the middle.

Circle the word that best completes each sentence and write it on the line.

1. I had a ___cup___ of milk.

(cup)   bag

2. He saw a black ___bug___ on the wall.

bus   (bug)

3. Russ can ___jump___ and run.

net   (jump)

4. The dog sat on the ___rug___.

(rug)   run

5. Did she ___cut___ her leg?

(cut)   as

6. That white duck cannot ___run___ fast.

cap   (run)

7. I like red ___gum___ the best.

six   (gum)

8. Was it ___fun___ to ride the bike?

(fun)   kit

9. We sat in the hot ___sun___.

big   (sun)

10. I gave my mom a big ___hug___.

(hug)   hill

20

Activity Page 20

4

Objective:

To review the sound of **/u/**

(Say) Circle the word that best completes each sentence and write it on the line.

1 Warm-Up

The "G" Game

Materials
- None

Preparation
Divide students into two teams.

How to Play:
Instruct one team to stand when you say a word with the sound of /j/. The other team should stand when you say a word with the sound of /g/. You may want to use these words:

dog, age, goat, game, gentle, good, page, germs, gift, giraffe, gym, garden, general, goose, gum, giant, ginger, pig

---

A Poetry Connection

Name _____

Bubble Gum

I really do love chewing gum.
Blowing bubbles is lots of fun.
I chew gum quiet, chew it loud.
I chew alone, or in a crowd.

I chew it fast, I chew it slow,
But either way, one thing I know:
That when the flavor's gone at last,
I'll throw my gum into the trash.

For I know gum is fun to chew,
But not to find upon your shoe!
'Cause in my mouth it's soft and chewy,
But on the sidewalk, gross and gooey.

And so this promise I have made,
And with this promise I have stayed:
My chewing gum will not be found
Upon the sidewalk, street, or ground!

Say the name of each picture. Circle the picture if the word has the sound of /g/.

1. cage
2. egg
3. giraffe
4. goat
5. goose
6. gum

Hard and Soft g

Day **10**

21

---

2 Poetry Connection

Have students follow along as you read the poem. Ask them to raise their hands if they like to chew gum. Invite them to tell you what some of their favorite flavors are. Remind your students that they should always throw their gum in the trash can when they are done.

3 Activity Page 21

Objective:
To review the sounds of /g/ and /j/

Say) Say the name of each picture. Circle the picture if the word has the sound of /g/.

B Phonics

Name _____

Say each word. If it has the sound of /j/, write it in the top column. If the word has the sound of /g/, write it in the bottom column.

Soft g /j/

1. _____ age _____
2. _____ cage _____
3. _____ gem _____
4. _____ giant _____
5. _____ gym _____
6. _____ stage _____
7. _____ wage _____

Hard g /g/

8. _____ gave _____
9. _____ God _____
10. _____ goes _____
11. _____ good _____
12. _____ goose _____
13. _____ tag _____
14. _____ wagon _____

Word Bank

age	gave	giant	goes	goose	stage	wagon
cage	gem	God	good	gym	tag	wage

22

---

4 Activity Page 22

Objective:

To review the sounds of **/g/** and **/j/**

Say — Say each word. If it has the sound of **/j/**, write it in the top column. If the word has the sound of **/g/**, write it in the bottom column.

1 Warm-Up

Cats and Mice

Materials
• Class list for score keeping

Preparation
Have students sit in a circle.

How to Play:
Tell students you will point to one of them and say a word containing the letter **c**, then start counting "1-2-3 ...." The student you point to must put up both hands to form mice ears if the word has the sound of **/s/**, or use their fingers to make cat whiskers if it has the sound of **/k/**. The number you are on when their hands are in place is their score. Write the score beside their name on the paper. The student with the lowest score is the winner. You may want to use these words:

cat, mice, city, cold, fence, cart, cent, come, cut, center, cake, rice, cocoa, certain

---

Mice in the Night

One night my mom went down the stairs,
And in the kitchen saw a pair
Of mice behind the plastic bin
She keeps the new potatoes in.

My mother gave a dreadful wail,
Then grabbed a bag and let it sail.
It flew—then landed with such fury
That the mice began to scurry.

Then Dad ran into the kitchen,
He lost his balance, and started slippin'
Because the floor was slick as ice—
My mom had thrown a bag of rice!

So now Dad has a broken arm,
Because of the "night mice" alarm.
If Mom ever sees more mice,
She'll grab a broom instead of rice!

Say the name of each picture. Circle the picture if the word has the sound of /k/.

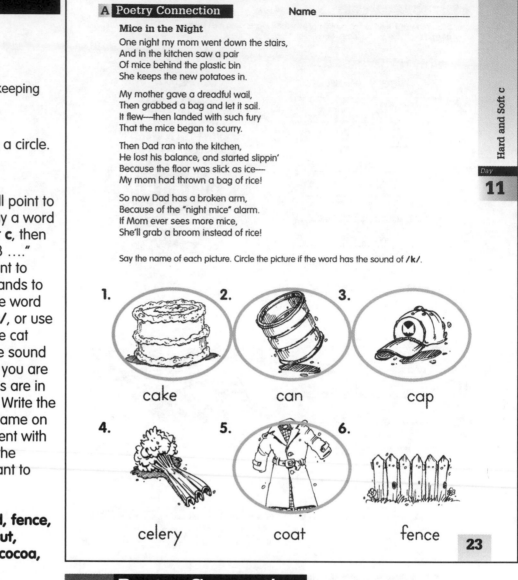

1. cake
2. can
3. cap
4. celery
5. coat
6. fence

Hard and Soft c

Day **11**

23

---

2 Poetry Connection

Have students follow along as you read the poem. Ask if they are afraid of mice or have a pet mouse. Explain to students that the sound of **/s/** can be spelled several ways, including **ce** or **s**. Write these spellings on the board. Have students find a word in the poem for each spelling pattern. (saw, mice, etc.) The letter **c** usually has the sound of **/s/** when followed by **e** or **i**.

3 Activity Page 23

Objective:
To review the sounds of **/k/** and **/s/**

Say) Say the name of each picture. Circle the picture if the word has the sound of **/k/**.

B Phonics   Name _____

Circle the word that best completes each sentence and write it on the line.

1. The dog was ___nice___ to me.
    (nice)   face

2. Mike put the ___can___ in the bag.
    (can)   race

3. Mom made a ___lace___ cap for my doll.
    mice   (lace)

4. I like ___rice___ with milk.
    cement   (rice)

5. You can bake a ___cake___ for Dad.
    (cake)   fence

6. This red ___coat___ is too big for me.
    celery   (coat)

7. Joe and Tom will run the ___race___ .
    (race)   rice

8. Please light the ___candles___ on the cake.
    candies   (candles)

9. Dad said not to climb the ___fence___ .
    (fence)   fact

10. We went to see the ___circus___ .
    (circus)   circles

Hard and Soft c

Day **11**

24

4 Activity Page 24

Objective:

To review the sounds of **/k/** and **/s/**

Say   Circle the word that best completes each sentence and write it on the line.

1 Warm-Up

Partner Compounds

Materials
- List of compound words for each pair of students (optional)

Preparation
Divide class into pairs of students.

How to Play:
Player 1 will say the first part of a compound word, such as dog. Player 2 will reply with the second part, such as wood or house. You may like to give player 1 a list of compound words to get started. You may want to use these words:

afternoon, airplane, airport, anyone, anything, backpack, barnyard, bedroom, chalkboard, classroom, everyone, everything, fireman, football, grandfather, homework, newspaper, notebook, rainbow, raincoat, sidewalk, somewhere

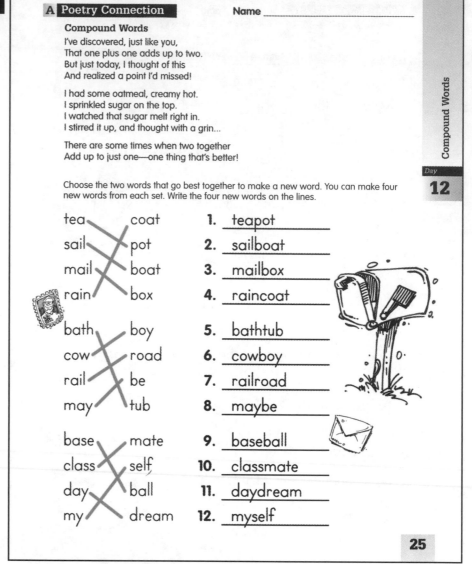

A | Poetry Connection

Name _____

Compound Words

I've discovered, just like you,
That one plus one adds up to two.
But just today, I thought of this
And realized a point I'd missed!

I had some oatmeal, creamy hot.
I sprinkled sugar on the top.
I watched that sugar melt right in.
I stirred it up, and thought with a grin...

There are some times when two together
Add up to just one—one thing that's better!

Choose the two words that go best together to make a new word. You can make four new words from each set. Write the four new words on the lines.

tea — coat	1. teapot
sail — pot	2. sailboat
mail — boat	3. mailbox
rain — box	4. raincoat
bath — boy	5. bathtub
cow — road	6. cowboy
rail — be	7. railroad
may — tub	8. maybe
base — mate	9. baseball
class — self	10. classmate
day — ball	11. daydream
my — dream	12. myself

Compound Words — Day 12

25

2 Poetry Connection

Have students follow along as you read the poem. Invite them to raise their hands if they like oatmeal. Ask students to give examples of other things they like to mix in their hot cereal. Show them that oat and meal are two words that have been put together to make a compound word.

3 Activity Page 25

Objective:
To review and write compound words

(Say) Choose two words that can go together to make a new word. Write each new word on the lines.

B Phonics   Name _____

Put each set of words together to make a new word. Write the word on the line, then read the sentence.

1. oat+meal   I like __oatmeal__ with brown sugar.

2. pan+cake   Mom puts butter on each __pancake__.

3. cup+cake   May I have a __cupcake__?

4. sea+weed   There is __seaweed__ on the sand.

5. base+ball   Will you play __baseball__ next spring?

6. pea+nut   We gave a __peanut__ to the monkey.

7. rain+coat   Did you wear a __raincoat__?

8. dog+house   We helped Dad build a __doghouse__.

9. blue+berry   Is this __blueberry__ ripe?

10. mail+box   Take this letter to the __mailbox__.

11. foot+ball   We like to play __football__.

12. bath+tub   Mom made me wash in the __bathtub__.

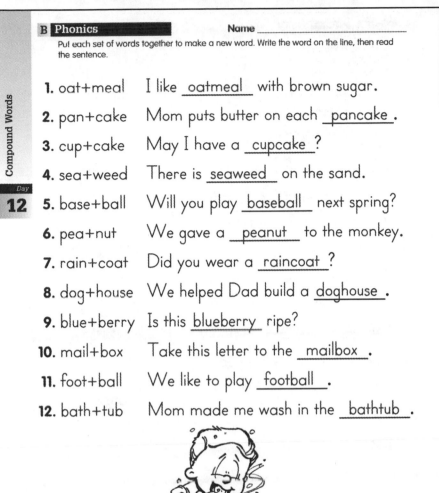

26

---

4 **Activity Page 26**

Objective:

To review compound words

Say)   Put each set of words together to make a new word. Write the word on the line then read the sentence.

1 Warm-Up

Buy a Cluster

Materials
• None

Preparation
None

How to Play:
Tell the students that today they are planning a shopping list. They may buy only things that have final consonant clusters. The first student might say, "I am going to buy a lamp." The student can name anything that ends with a consonant cluster. The teacher or student may write it on the board. The next student thinks of a new word to write. He might say, "I am going to buy a skunk." Each student will try to buy a new thing, but the word must end with a consonant cluster. Continue until all the students have had a turn.

A Poetry Connection

Name _____

Right or Wrong

Right or wrong, right or wrong.
Sometimes its hard to know
Whether something's right or wrong,
Or which way we should go.

But when we make bad choices
And ask God to forgive,
He loves to take away our sin
And show us how to live.

Name one of God's gifts to answer these riddles. Each answer is a word with a final cluster.

1. I am an animal God made.
   You do not like to have me around.
   I am a __skunk__.

2. Cows eat grass to make this.
   I am something to drink.
   I am __milk__.

3. Turtles and frogs live near me.
   I am a good home for fish.
   I am a __pond__.

4. Birds build this in a tree.
   I am a home for their babies.
   I am a __nest__.

Word Bank
milk   nest   pond   skunk

27

Final Clusters · Day 13

---

2 Poetry Connection

Have students follow along as you read the poem. Explain that God loves to give us gifts — some that we can see and others that we cannot see. Talk about gifts we cannot see such as forgiveness, salvation, love, joy, and help to make good choices. Now, talk about gifts we can see such as parents, food, homes, pets, friends.

3 Activity Page 27

Objective:
To review final clusters

 See if you can name one of God's gifts to answer these riddles. Each answer is a word with a final cluster.

26

B Phonics

Name _____

Say the name of each picture. Write the final cluster to complete each word.

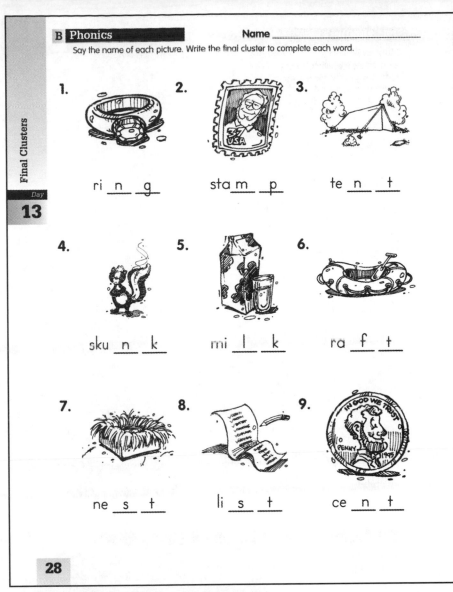

1. ri _n_ _g_

2. sta _m_ _p_

3. te _n_ _t_

4. sku _n_ _k_

5. mi _l_ _k_

6. ra _f_ _t_

7. ne _s_ _t_

8. li _s_ _t_

9. ce _n_ _t_

28

Activity Page 28

4

Objective:

To review final clusters

Say · Say the name of each picture. Write the final cluster to complete each word.

1 Warm-Up

Read the Mail

Materials
- 3"x5" cards
- Envelopes
- Small box

Preparation
Write words with the sound of /ā/ or /ē/ on 3"x5" cards. Put one card in each envelope. Put the envelopes in the box.

How to Play:
Deliver the box to a student. The student will take an envelope from the box and read the word on the card. They may then deliver the box to another student. Continue until all the mail has been read.

A Poetry Connection

Name _____

Rainy Day

This morning's weather? We have rain!
I'm staring out the window pane
And wondering what to do.

I guess that I could bake a cake,
Or make a purple play dough snake,
Or read a book or two.

I guess I could watch for the mail,
Or make a paper boat to sail,
Or build with sticks and glue.

But maybe, maybe if I wait,
The rain will start to dissipate,
And the sun will shine right through.

Then if Mother says, "Okay,"
I'll run right outside and play
And find a friend or two.

Find the word that best completes each sentence and write it on the line.

1. Kate ___made___ a cake for Mom.
2. Steve can hike to the ___cave___.
3. Dave put the ___mail___ in the box.
4. We cannot ___stay___ up late.
5. ___Rake___ the leaves into a pile.
6. Kay ___paid___ the man for the grapes.
7. Put these roses in a ___vase___.
8. What is his ___name___?

Word Bank

cave	mail	paid	stay
made	name	rake	vase

29

---

2 Poetry Connection

Have students follow along as you read the poem. Ask them if they enjoy rainy days sometimes. Let them give some examples of their favorite rainy-day activities. You may like to explain that the sound of /ā/ can be spelled several ways, including **ai**, **a-e**, or **ay**. Write these spellings on the board and have students find a word in the poem for each spelling pattern. (rain, pane, play, etc.)

3 Activity Page 29

Objective:
To review the sound of /ā/

 Find the word that best completes each sentence and write it on the line.

B Phonics

Name _____

Write the word that names each picture by filling in the missing vowels.

1. f _e_ _e_ t

2. j _e_ _e_ p

3. g _a_ m _e_

4. t _e_ _e_ th

5. tr _e_ _e_

6. r _a_ _i_ n

7. c _a_ k _e_

8. s _a_ _i_ l

9. sn _a_ k _e_

Word Bank

cake	game	rain	snake	tree
feet	jeep	sail	teeth	

30

---

4 **Activity Page 30**

Objective:

To review the sounds of **/ā/** and **/ē/**

(Say) Write the word that names each picture by filling in the missing vowels.

29

1 Warm-Up

Great Grape Clusters

Materials

• None

Preparation

Write the letters **br**, **cr**, **dr**, **fr**, **gr**, **pr** and **tr** on the board. Draw a vertical line to divide the board into two sections.

How to Play:

Tell the students that each team will be drawing a bunch of grapes. Have teams take turns thinking of words that begin with an **r** cluster. They may come to the board, add a grape to their bunch and write the **r** cluster they used, on the grape. Continue until all the students have had a turn.

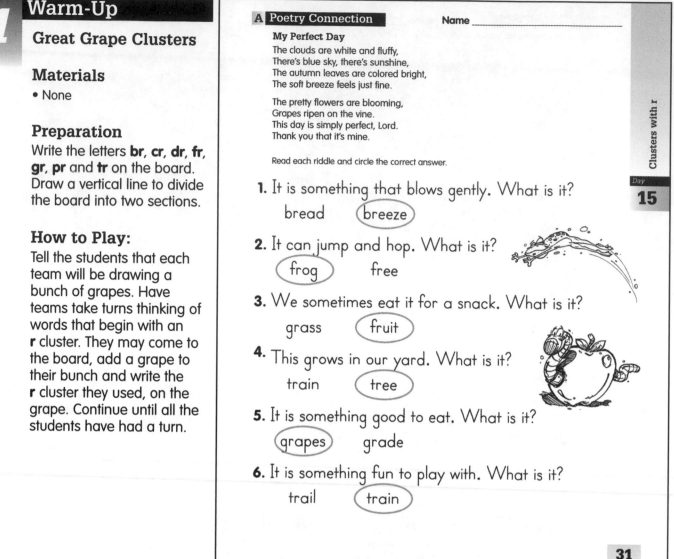

A ▏Poetry Connection   Name _____

My Perfect Day
The clouds are white and fluffy,
There's blue sky, there's sunshine,
The autumn leaves are colored bright,
The soft breeze feels just fine.

The pretty flowers are blooming,
Grapes ripen on the vine.
This day is simply perfect, Lord.
Thank you that it's mine.

Read each riddle and circle the correct answer.

1. It is something that blows gently. What is it?
  bread   (breeze)

2. It can jump and hop. What is it?
  (frog)   free

3. We sometimes eat it for a snack. What is it?
  grass   (fruit)

4. This grows in our yard. What is it?
  train   (tree)

5. It is something good to eat. What is it?
  (grapes)   grade

6. It is something fun to play with. What is it?
  trail   (train)

Clusters with r

Day
15

31

2 Poetry Connection

Have students follow along as you read the poem. Ask them which season this poem describes. Invite them to name other things about the fall that they especially enjoy.

3 Activity Page 31

Objective:

To review **r** clusters

 Read each riddle and circle the correct answer.

B Phonics

Circle the word that names each picture.

Name _____

1.   (grapes) grades

2.   trust (truck)

3.   from (frog)

4.   drive (drum)

5.   (tree) trim

6.   (train) trade

Find the r cluster in each word and write the cluster letters on the line.

1.   grapes
      _____gr_____

2.   truck
      _____tr_____

3.   train
      _____tr_____

4.   drink
      _____dr_____

5.   drum
      _____dr_____

6.   dress
      _____dr_____

7.   brick
      _____br_____

8.   branch
      _____br_____

9.   crowd
      _____cr_____

32

Activity Page 32

4

Objective:

To review **r** clusters

(Say) Circle the word that names each picture. At the bottom, find the **r** cluster in each word and write the cluster letters on the line.

1 Warm-Up

Stand for What's True

Materials
• None

Preparation
None

How to Play:
Read the statements to the students.
If it is a true statement, they may stand.
If the statement is false, they should sit down.

1. An ice cube will warm up your soup. **(F)**
2. You usually eat juice with a spoon. **(F)**
3. You should return a book when it is due. **(T)**
4. It is rude to sing a tune in the shower. **(F)**
5. A clue helps you solve a riddle. **(T)**
6. A dune is a huge pile of sand. **(T)**
7. A mule makes a good pupil in school. **(F)**
8. An inner tube can be used to float on. **(T)**
9. Prunes are a fruit that taste good with glue. **(F)**
10. Humans catch the flu. **(T)**

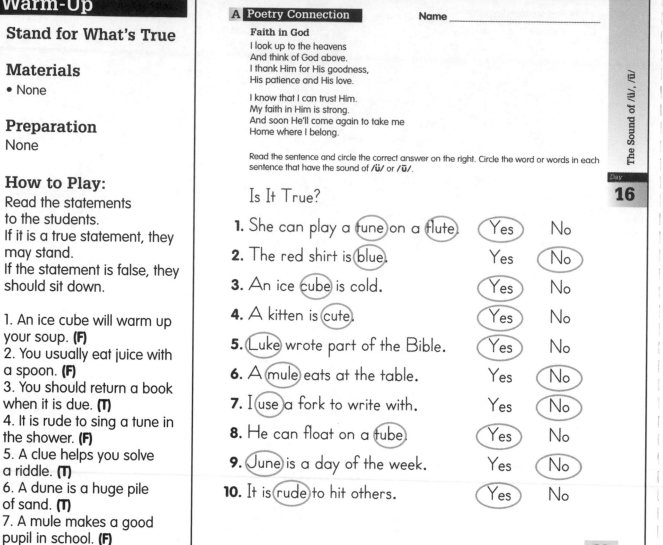

A Poetry Connection

Name _____

Faith in God
I look up to the heavens
And think of God above.
I thank Him for His goodness,
His patience and His love.

I know that I can trust Him.
My faith in Him is strong.
And soon He'll come again to take me
Home where I belong.

Read the sentence and circle the correct answer on the right. Circle the word or words in each sentence that have the sound of /ü/ or /ū/.

Is It True?

1. She can play a tune on a flute. Yes No
2. The red shirt is blue. Yes No
3. An ice cube is cold. Yes No
4. A kitten is cute. Yes No
5. Luke wrote part of the Bible. Yes No
6. A mule eats at the table. Yes No
7. I use a fork to write with. Yes No
8. He can float on a tube. Yes No
9. June is a day of the week. Yes No
10. It is rude to hit others. Yes No

33

2 Poetry Connection

Have students follow along as you read the poem. Invite them to tell some things our parents teach us that help us become better people. Talk about what faith means. Discuss things that we believe about God and heaven because our parents have taught us, or given us the opportunity to learn, such as through Christian education, taking us to church, family worship, etc.

3 Activity Page 33

Objective:
To review the sound of /ü/ or /ū/

Say

Read the sentence and circle the correct answer on the right. Circle the word or words in each sentence that have the sound of /ü/ or /ū/.

32

B Phonics   Name _____

Circle the words from the Word Bank in the puzzle.

The Sound of /ü/, /ū/

Day **16**

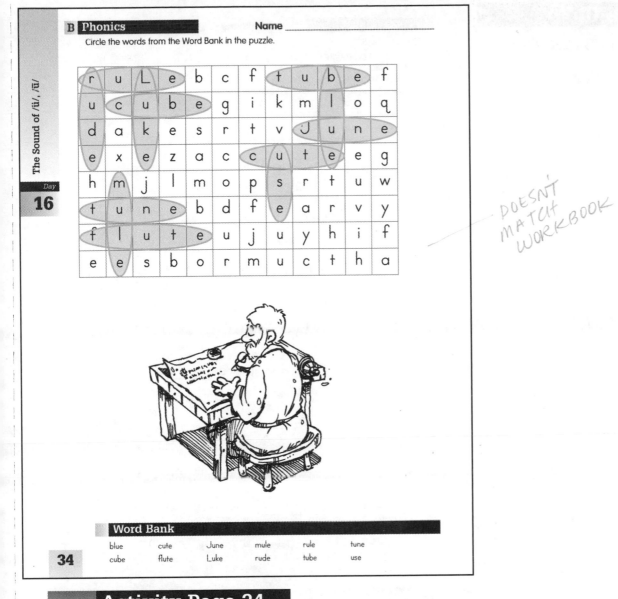

DOESN'T MATCH WORKBOOK

Word Bank					
blue	cute	June	mule	rule	tune
cube	flute	Luke	rude	tube	use

34

Activity Page 34

Objective:
To review the sound of **/ü/** or **/ū/**

Say   Circle the words from the Word Bank in the puzzle.

1 Warm-Up

Presto Change-O!

Materials
• None

Preparation
Write the following words on the board: **drive**, **mild**, **mile**, **pile**, **quite**, **ride**, **ripe**, **rise**, **spike**, **strike**, **tie**, **tire**, **write**

How to Play:
Have students take turns coming to the board. They should say the word, replace the **i** with an **o**, then say the new word they made. Continue until all the words are used.

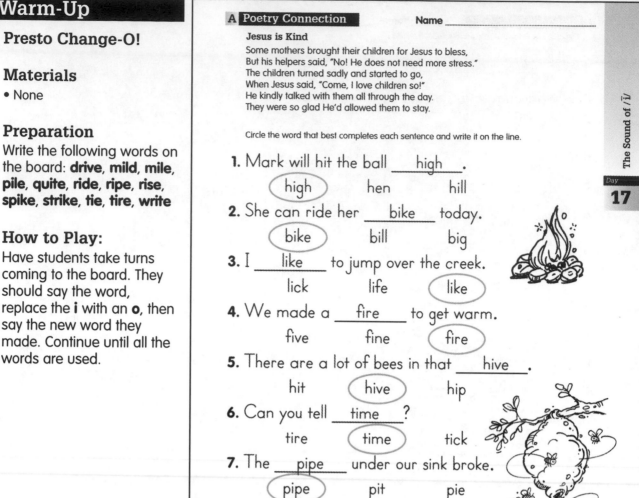

A **Poetry Connection**   Name _____

Jesus is Kind
Some mothers brought their children for Jesus to bless,
But his helpers said, "No! He does not need more stress."
The children turned sadly and started to go,
When Jesus said, "Come, I love children so!"
He kindly talked with them all through the day.
They were so glad He'd allowed them to stay.

Circle the word that best completes each sentence and write it on the line.

1. Mark will hit the ball ___high___ .
   (high)   hen   hill

2. She can ride her ___bike___ today.
   (bike)   bill   big

3. I ___like___ to jump over the creek.
   lick   life   (like)

4. We made a ___fire___ to get warm.
   five   fine   (fire)

5. There are a lot of bees in that ___hive___ .
   hit   (hive)   hip

6. Can you tell ___time___ ?
   tire   (time)   tick

7. The ___pipe___ under our sink broke.
   (pipe)   pit   pie

8. Jimmy has a big blue ___kite___ .
   kit   (kite)   kick

The Sound of /ī/

Day **17**

35

2 Poetry Connection

Have students follow along as you read the poem. Invite them to tell about a time they had looked forward to visiting someone, then been disappointed because it did not work out. (grandparents, cousins, friends) Who is someone they enjoy talking to? Remind students that Jesus loves to have us talk to Him through prayer. Discuss things we can pray about.

3 Activity Page 35

Objective:
To review the sound of /ī/

Say

Circle the word that best completes each sentence and write it on the line.

34

Name _____

Circle the word that best completes each sentence.

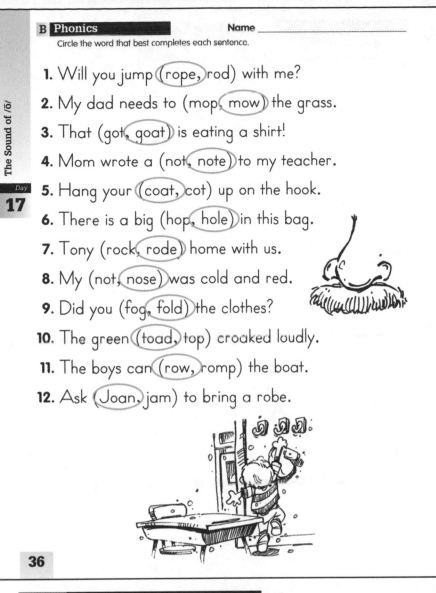

1. Will you jump (**rope**, rod) with me?

2. My dad needs to (mop, **mow**) the grass.

3. That (got, **goat**) is eating a shirt!

4. Mom wrote a (not, **note**) to my teacher.

5. Hang your (**coat**, cot) up on the hook.

6. There is a big (hop, **hole**) in this bag.

7. Tony (rock, **rode**) home with us.

8. My (not, **nose**) was cold and red.

9. Did you (fog, **fold**) the clothes?

10. The green (**toad**, top) croaked loudly.

11. The boys can (**row**, romp) the boat.

12. Ask (**Joan**, jam) to bring a robe.

36

---

4 Activity Page 36

Objective:

To review the sound of **/ō/**

(Say) Circle the word that best completes each sentence.

Warm-Up

Kingfishers and Black-birds

Materials
• Word cards for **sh** and **ck** words.

Preparation
Mix cards together in a stack and set it on the chalk tray. Divide students into two teams, the Kingfishers and the Blackbirds.

How to Play:
When the card has a word with **sh**, a player on the Kingfisher team will come to the board, say the word and keep the card for a point for their team. When the card has a word with **ck**, a player on the Blackbird team will come to the board, say the word and keep the card for a point for their team. If a player cannot say the word, no point is given. Continue until all the cards are used.

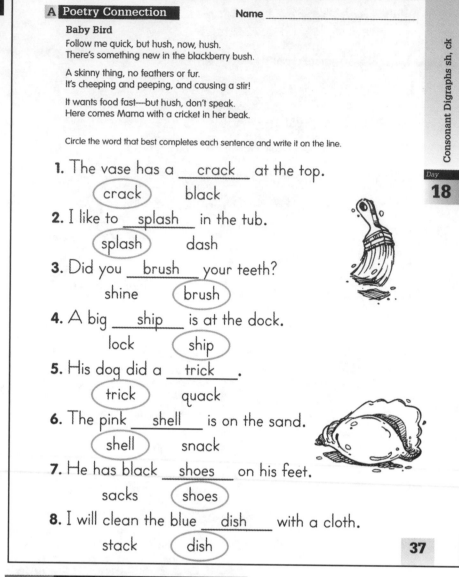

A **Poetry Connection**   Name _____

Baby Bird
Follow me quick, but hush, now, hush.
There's something new in the blackberry bush.

A skinny thing, no feathers or fur.
It's cheeping and peeping, and causing a stir!

It wants food fast—but hush, don't speak.
Here comes Mama with a cricket in her beak.

Circle the word that best completes each sentence and write it on the line.

1. The vase has a ___crack___ at the top.
   (crack)   black
2. I like to ___splash___ in the tub.
   (splash)   dash
3. Did you ___brush___ your teeth?
   shine   (brush)
4. A big ___ship___ is at the dock.
   lock   (ship)
5. His dog did a ___trick___.
   (trick)   quack
6. The pink ___shell___ is on the sand.
   (shell)   snack
7. He has black ___shoes___ on his feet.
   sacks   (shoes)
8. I will clean the blue ___dish___ with a cloth.
   stack   (dish)

37

Consonant Digraphs sh, ck   Day **18**

Poetry Connection

Have students follow along as you read the poem. Ask one of your students what the poem was describing, that was in the blackberry bush. Ask students to tell you what kind of bird they imagined it might be. You may like to explain to students that the sound of **/sh/** is usually spelled with **sh**. (hush, bush)

Activity Page 37

Objective:
To review the consonant digraphs **sh** and **ck**

 Say   Circle the word that best completes each sentence and write it on the line.

B Phonics

Name _____

Say the name of each picture. Circle the letters that stand for the consonant digraph in each name.

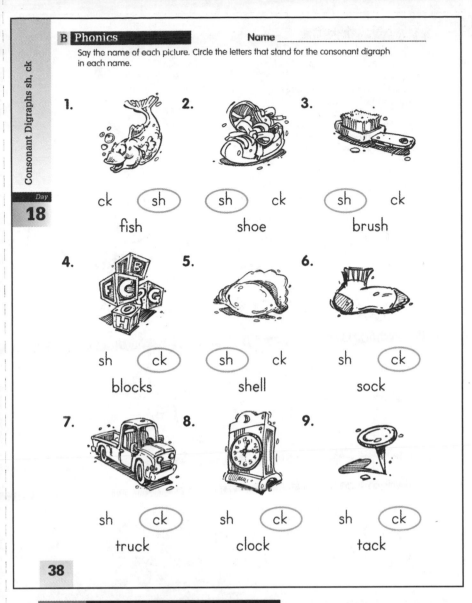

1. ck (sh) fish

2. (sh) ck shoe

3. (sh) ck brush

4. sh (ck) blocks

5. (sh) ck shell

6. sh (ck) sock

7. sh (ck) truck

8. sh (ck) clock

9. sh (ck) tack

38

Activity Page 38

Objective:
To review the consonant digraphs **sh** and **ck**

(Say) Say the name of each picture. Circle the letters that stand for the consonant digraph in each name.

1 Warm-Up

Puzzling "Y"

Materials
- Two 3"x5" cards
- Two identical 12-16 piece puzzles

Preparation
Write one of these headings on each 3"x5" card: **y = long e**; **y = long i**. Lay each card on a table with enough space to put the puzzles together. Using one of the puzzles, on the back of each piece write a word containing the letter **y** with the sound of /ē/. Using the other puzzle, on the back of each piece write a word containing the letter y with the sound of /ī/. Divide students into two teams.

How to Play:
Pass out pieces of the two puzzles so each student has at least one piece. Indicate where each puzzle will be put together. Students decide whether the y in the word on their puzzle piece has the sound of /ē/ or /ī/, then fit their piece into the correct puzzle. Continue until both puzzles are put together correctly.

A Poetry Connection

Name _____

The Little Things

The puzzling thing about puzzles,
Is all the pieces, you see.
When I first look at a pile of them,
They all look alike to me!
But I really try hard, and am happy to say,
That before I know it, I'm done.
Then feeling quite pleased, I think to myself,
"Now, I'll try a bigger one!"

Read each word. If the **y** has an /ē/ sound, color that puzzle piece blue.

1. try
2. windy
3. happy
4. my
5. puppy
6. rocky

Underline each word in which **y** has an /ī/ sound.

Tommy can <u>fry</u> an egg in this pan.
A plane can <u>fly</u> high in the <u>sky</u>.
There is a bunny <u>by</u> that tree.
<u>Why</u> did he <u>cry</u> when he saw the puppy?

39

---

2 Poetry Connection

Have students follow along as you read the poem. Invite them to describe how they put a puzzle together-starting with edges, doing sections at a time, starting in the middle, etc. Read Luke 16:10 and discuss why little things are so important in life.

---

3 Activity Page 39

Objective:
To review the vowel sounds of **y**

Read each word on the puzzle pieces. If the **y** has an /ē/ sound, color that puzzle piece blue. At the bottom, underline each word in which **y** has an /ī/ sound.

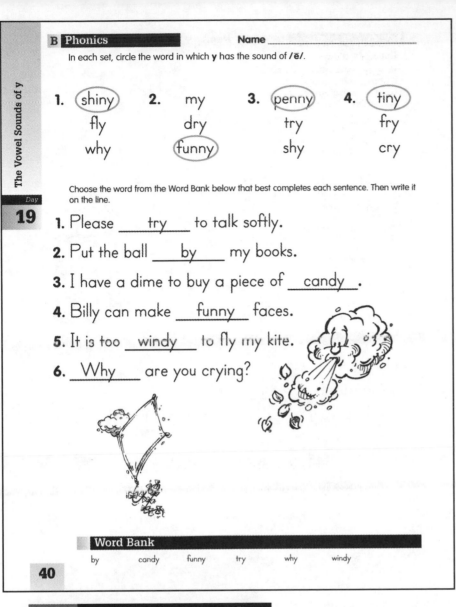

B Phonics

Name _____

In each set, circle the word in which **y** has the sound of /ē/.

1. (shiny) 2. my 3. (penny) 4. (tiny)
   fly   dry   try   fry
   why   (funny)   shy   cry

Choose the word from the Word Bank below that best completes each sentence. Then write it on the line.

1. Please ___try___ to talk softly.
2. Put the ball ___by___ my books.
3. I have a dime to buy a piece of ___candy___.
4. Billy can make ___funny___ faces.
5. It is too ___windy___ to fly my kite.
6. ___Why___ are you crying?

Word Bank
by   candy   funny   try   why   windy

40

Activity Page 40

Objective:

To review the vowel sounds of **y**

 In each set, circle the word in which **y** has the sound of /ē/. At the bottom, choose the word that best completes each sentence and write it on the line.

1 Warm-Up

When to Concentrate

Materials
• 3"x5" cards cut in half

Preparation
Prepare cards by writing one word on each card. If you have a large class, you may like to make more than one set of cards. If desired, divide students, and lay out the cards on a table or on the floor. You may like to use these words: **wren, wrench, wrong, wring, wrist, wreck, write, wrap, wheat, wheel, whistle, whale, white, while, where, when**

How to Play:
Play concentration by letting students take turns turning up 2 cards at a time. If both cards have the same consonant digraph, they may say the words and keep the cards. If the consonant digraphs are different, or they cannot say the words, they replace the cards and it is the next player's turn. Continue until all the cards are used.

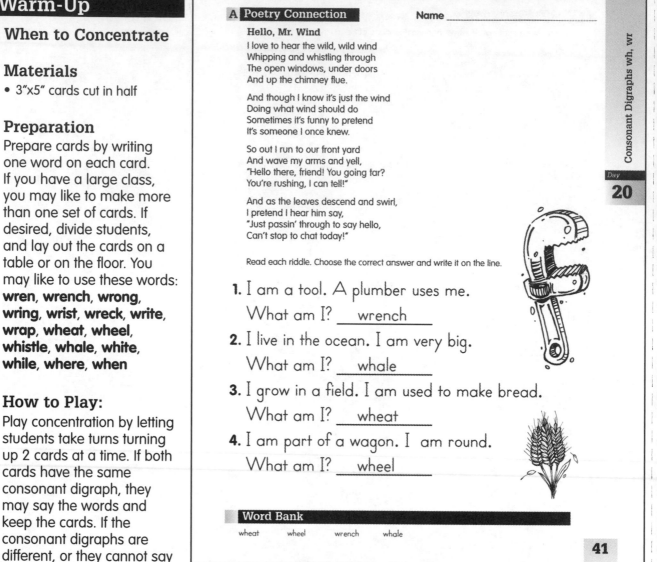

A **Poetry Connection**   Name _____

Hello, Mr. Wind
I love to hear the wild, wild wind
Whipping and whistling through
The open windows, under doors
And up the chimney flue.

And though I know it's just the wind
Doing what wind should do
Sometimes it's funny to pretend
It's someone I once knew.

So out I run to our front yard
And wave my arms and yell,
"Hello there, friend! You going far?
You're rushing, I can tell!"

And as the leaves descend and swirl,
I pretend I hear him say,
"Just passin' through to say hello,
Can't stop to chat today!"

Read each riddle. Choose the correct answer and write it on the line.

1. I am a tool. A plumber uses me. What am I? __wrench__
2. I live in the ocean. I am very big. What am I? __whale__
3. I grow in a field. I am used to make bread. What am I? __wheat__
4. I am part of a wagon. I am round. What am I? __wheel__

Word Bank
wheat   wheel   wrench   whale

41

2 Poetry Connection

Have students follow along as you read the poem. Invite them to tell you what they do or do not like about the wind. Encourage them to think of things that need and/or use the wind. (kites, sailboats, clouds with rain are moved by wind)

3 Activity Page 41

Objective:
To review the consonant digraphs **wh** and **wr**

(Say) Read each riddle. Choose the correct answer and write it on the line.

B Phonics   Name _____

Circle the word that best completes each sentence and write it on the line.

1. __Wring__ out the wet towel.

   (Wring)   What

2. Brad fell and broke his __wrist__ .

   wheat   (wrist)

3. Grandpa __wrote__ me a letter.

   wreck   (wrote)

4. __Where__ are you going?

   Wren   (Where)

5. It is __wrong__ to tell a lie.

   (wrong)   whale

6. There are __wrinkles__ in her dress.

   (wrinkles)   write

7. Can you __wrap__ this gift?

   wheel   (wrap)

8. Did you eat the __whole__ piece of cake?

   wrench   (whole)

9. We saw a __whale__ on the "Ocean" video.

   wheat   (whale)

10. Dad is going to paint the house __white__ .

    where   (white)

42

4 Activity Page 42

Objective:

To review the consonant digraphs **wh** and **wr**

(Say) Circle the word that best completes each sentence. Then write the correct word on the line in your Worktext.

Warm-Up

The Ending Has to Go

Materials

• None

Preparation

Write the following list of words on the board: **jumping, sitting, looking, swimming, wrapping, singing, blowing, raining, sleeping, mixing, camping, cooking, eating, floating, rocking, standing, talking, playing, needing, melting.** You may add words of your own to make at least one per student.

How to Play:

Have students take turns coming to the board, erasing the **-ing** ending, then saying the base word. Remind them that in words which have a double consonant, they will need to erase one of the consonant letters, also. Continue until all the words are used.

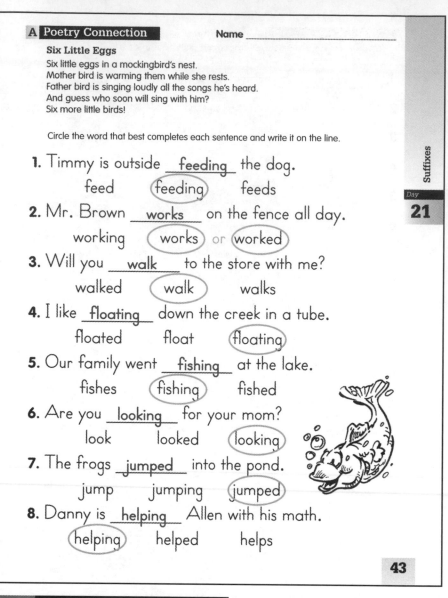

A Poetry Connection

Name _____

Six Little Eggs

Six little eggs in a mockingbird's nest.
Mother bird is warming them while she rests.
Father bird is singing loudly all the songs he's heard.
And guess who soon will sing with him?
Six more little birds!

Circle the word that best completes each sentence and write it on the line.

1. Timmy is outside __feeding__ the dog.
   feed   (feeding)   feeds

2. Mr. Brown __works__ on the fence all day.
   working   (works) or (worked)

3. Will you __walk__ to the store with me?
   walked   (walk)   walks

4. I like __floating__ down the creek in a tube.
   floated   float   (floating)

5. Our family went __fishing__ at the lake.
   fishes   (fishing)   fished

6. Are you __looking__ for your mom?
   look   looked   (looking)

7. The frogs __jumped__ into the pond.
   jump   jumping   (jumped)

8. Danny is __helping__ Allen with his math.
   (helping)   helped   helps

Suffixes

Day **21**

43

Poetry Connection

Have students follow along as you read the poem. Show them a picture of a mockingbird. Explain that a mockingbird imitates the songs of other birds. It is also the state bird of several states.

Activity Page 43

Objective:

To review suffixes

 Say Circle the word that best completes each sentence and write it on the line.

B Phonics   Name _____

Find the word that best completes each sentence and write it on the line.

1. We will be __roasting__ hot dogs at six.

2. Shelly is __hopping__ on one leg.

3. Bring your __sleeping__ bag with you.

4. Which team is __winning__ the game?

5. Adam is going __swimming__ at the pool.

6. They are __dipping__ candles to sell.

7. Mom took my sister __shopping__ for shoes.

8. Dad is __working__ at a new job today.

9. The policeman is __stopping__ the cars.

10. I should buy a tent for our __camping__ trip.

11. The children are __waiting__ for the bus.

12. Erin is __petting__ the kitten.

Word Bank					
camping	hopping	roasting	sleeping	swimming	winning
dipping	petting	shopping	stopping	waiting	working

44

Activity Page 44

Objective:

To review the suffix **-ing**

Say | Find the word that best completes each sentence and write it on the line.

1 Warm-Up

Going on a Trip

Materials
• None

Preparation
Write the following list of clusters on the board: **br, cr, dr, fl, fr, sk, sl, sp, tr**

How to Play:
Tell the students that today they are going on a trip. They may bring only things that begin with one of the consonant clusters on the board. The first student might say, "I am going on a trip and I'm going to bring a brother." The student can name anything that begins with the **br** cluster. The next student thinks of a new br word to bring on the trip. He might say, "I am going on a trip and I'm going to bring a brush." Each student will try to bring a new thing, but the word must begin with **br**. As soon as a student misses by not being able to think of another thing that begins with **br**, start bringing things that begin with **cr**. Continue until you have used each cluster and all the students have had a turn.

A **Poetry Connection**

Name _____

Hide and Seek
Our little brother likes to play
The game of hide and seek,
But every time that he is "It"
He always wants to peek.

So we explain, "You mustn't look,
Or you'll see where we run."
And every time, he nods his head
And starts again at "one."

So off we go to find a spot—
That perfect hiding place,
But sure enough, we turn around
To see that chubby face.

He'll laugh and squeal with sheer delight
And grab us by the legs,
And though he just now caught us both,
"Play more!" he'll start to beg.

We roll our eyes and shake our heads,
And say the rules again.
But I think it would really help
If he could count to ten!

Say the name of each picture. Write the cluster that stands for the sound you hear at the beginning of each word.

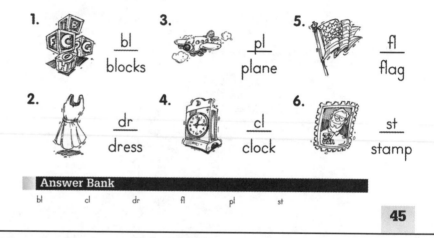

1. bl blocks
2. dr dress
3. pl plane
4. cl clock
5. fl flag
6. st stamp

Answer Bank

bl   cl   dr   fl   pl   st

45

---

2 Poetry Connection

Have students follow along as you read the poem. Ask them to raise their hands if they have a younger brother or sister that peeks when they play hide and seek. Invite them to tell you some of their favorite hiding places.

3 Activity Page 45

Objective:
To review **r**, **l**, and **s** clusters

 Say

Say the name of each picture. Write the cluster that stands for the sound you hear at the beginning of each word.

B Phonics

Name _____

Find the word that best completes each sentence and write it on the line.

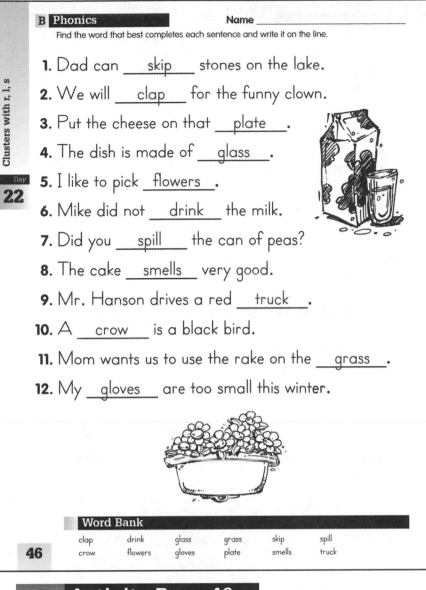

1. Dad can __skip__ stones on the lake.

2. We will __clap__ for the funny clown.

3. Put the cheese on that __plate__.

4. The dish is made of __glass__.

5. I like to pick __flowers__.

6. Mike did not __drink__ the milk.

7. Did you __spill__ the can of peas?

8. The cake __smells__ very good.

9. Mr. Hanson drives a red __truck__.

10. A __crow__ is a black bird.

11. Mom wants us to use the rake on the __grass__.

12. My __gloves__ are too small this winter.

Word Bank

clap	drink	glass	grass	skip	spill
crow	flowers	gloves	plate	smells	truck

46

Activity Page 46

4

Objective:

To review **r**, **l**, and **s** clusters

(Say) Find the word that best completes each sentence and write it on the line.

Warm-Up

Syllable Split

Materials

• None

Preparation

Write the following list of words on the board: **apple, buckle, cable, candle, castle, circle, eagle, handle, little, maple, paddle, people, pickle, puddle, rattle, saddle, single, staple, table, tattle, tickle, wiggle.** Divide students into two teams.

How to Play:

A player from **Team A** comes to the board and draws a line to divide one of the words into syllables. If correct, **Team A** gets a point. Now, a player from **Team B** comes to the board and draws a line to divide one of the words into syllables. If correct, **Team B** gets a point. Play alternates between teams until all the words are used.

A | **Poetry Connection**

Name _____

Character

School is fun, a happy place,
I'm learning lots of stuff!
But Mama says that learning math
And spelling's not enough.

Our teachers here want us to know
How children should behave.
So, when we first arrived at school,
These are the rules they gave:

"When walking down the hall, you must
March straight in single file.
And hang your coats upon the hooks,
Don't drop them in a pile."

"When time for lunch, your forks and spoons,
You really must not rattle.
Be kind to all. Please understand,
It's very rude to tattle."

My mama says that this is good,
That "character" will grow.
And though I don't know what that means,
When I have it, it will show!

Find the word that best completes each sentence and write it on the line.

1. It is fun to ___tickle___ my sister.

2. Worms ___wiggle___ in the mud after it rains.

3. The ___handle___ of the pot is hot.

4. Dad put the ___saddle___ on the horse.

5. An ___eagle___ is a huge bird.

6. Do you like to eat ___pickles___?

Word Bank

eagle   handle   pickles   saddle   tickle   wiggle

47

Poetry Connection

Have students follow along as you read the poem. Invite them to tell what they think it means to have character. You may discuss some of your school's rules and how following the rules helps to develop character. Explain to students that the sound of /l/ is often spelled with **-le**. Have the students find the two-syllable words in the poem that end in **-le**. (single, rattle, tattle)

Activity Page 47

Objective:

To review words ending in **-le**

(Say) Choose the word that best completes the sentence and write it on the line.

B Phonics

Name _____

Find the word that names each picture and write it on the line.

1. rattle

2. circle

3. apple

4. thimble

5. table

6. candle

7. buckle

8. people

9. bubbles

Word Bank

apple	buckle	circle	rattle	thimble
bubbles	candle	people	table	

48

4

Activity Page 48

Objective:

To review words ending in **-le**

Say Find the word that names each picture and write it on the line.

47

1 Warm-Up

Thumbs Up?

Materials
• None

Preparation
None

How to Play:
Tell students that you will say some words that contain the consonant digraph **ch** or **th**. If the word contains **ch**, they should point to their chin. If the word contains **th**, they should hold up their thumb. You may want to use these words:

chips, think, bath, beach, reaching, bunch, breath, chicken, through, everything, peaches, thimble, paths, cheerful, math, church.

A **Poetry Connection**   Name _____

I've Been Everywhere
I've been to lots of places in the years I've been alive.
And I've seen a million faces, 'cause my daddy likes to drive!

I've seen Ohio's rivers, and Missouri's famous zoo.
I've been in Pennsylvania, covered most of Boston, too!

We stopped in Houston, Texas, spent a day in Delaware.
Saw chickens in Rhode Island, toured the Kansas City Fair.

Stood 'neath California's redwoods, drove across Dakota's hills,
Stared amazed at Niagara Falls, and Wisconsin's mighty mills.

Touched the Great Salt Lake in Utah, then to Georgia made a trek.
Took my Grandpa to Lake Erie, after jaunting through Quebec.

When I say, "We've been everywhere!" Dad spins the globe with glee.
He spreads his arms wide, and declares, "There's a whole world yet to see!"

Circle the word that best completes each sentence.

1. Her (cheeks, peach) are red from the cold.
2. (Chin, Cheer) for your favorite baseball team.
3. Dave sat in the blue (chew, chair).
4. (The, They) went to the park to play.
5. Please hand me (that, those) blocks.
6. (Chop, Cheese) wood for the fire, please.
7. Do you (think, thing) we can go?
8. I need to give my dog a (thank, bath).

Consonant Digraphs th, ch

Day **24**

49

---

2 Poetry Connection

Have students follow along as you read the poem. Ask them to tell you some special places they have been on vacations. Point out that all the city and state names begin with capital letters.

---

3 Activity Page 49

Objective:
To review the consonant digraphs **th** and **ch**

(Say) Circle the word that best completes each sentence.

48

B Phonics _____ Name _____

Say each word. If the consonant digraph is at the beginning of the word, write it in the first column. If it is in the middle, write it in the second column. If it is at the end, write it in the third column.

Beginning	Middle	End
1. chips	6. teacher	11. bench
2. this	7. clothing	12. reach
3. think	8. neither	13. peach
4. chin	9. coaching	14. teeth
5. cheek	10. beaches	

Word Bank

beaches	cheek	chips	coaching	peach	teacher	think
bench	chin	clothing	neither	reach	teeth	this

50

Activity Page 50

Objective:

To review the consonant digraphs **th** and **ch**

(Say) Say each word. If the consonant digraph is at the beginning of the word, write it in the first column. If it is in the middle, write it in the second column. If it is at the end, write it in the third column.

1 Warm-Up

Plural Relay

Materials
• 3"x5" cards

Preparation
Write one word on each card. Draw a vertical line to divide the board into two sections. In both sections, write the headings **-s**, and **-es**. Divide students into two teams. Have the teams line up at the back of the room. Give each team a stack of word cards. You may want to use these words: **apple, box, dress, flower, fox, horse, kitten, knee, knot, ladder, match, path, star, peach, sandwich, turtle**

How to Play:
The first player on each team draws a card, races to the board and writes the plural form of the word under the correct heading. Player will run back and tag the next person, who repeats the activity. Continue until both teams have finished writing all their words.

A | Poetry Connection   Name _____

Jesus Loves Me
Jesus loves me! How do I know?
Things He created tell me so.
The pretty flowers in colors bright,
The moon and stars that shine at night,
The seasons as they come and go,
The rain and sun to help food grow,
God's Word with stories of long ago
All tell of Jesus' love, I know.

Color in the oval in front of the sentence that tells about each picture. Draw a circle around each word that begins with the digraph **kn**.

1. ○ Jeff does not (know) the answer.
   ○ Jeff turned the door (knob.)
   ● Jeff has a (knot) in his shoe lace.

2. ○ Nancy (knelt) down by her bed.
   ● Nancy (knocked) on the door.
   ○ Nancy can (knit) a scarf.

3. ○ Dad put a new (knob) on the door.
   ○ Dad hit his (knee) on the chair.
   ● Dad cut the bread with a (knife.)

Think of a word that starts with **kn** and rhymes with each word. Write it on the line.

1. snow	know	**4.** wife	knife
2. hot	knot	**5.** cob	knob
3. see	knee		

51

---

2 Poetry Connection

Have students follow along as you read the poem. Discuss the things in the poem that Jesus made for us to enjoy. Explain that these things are a silent way for God to show His love to us. Have students find and underline words in the poem that have silent consonants. (know, bright, night, grow, know)

3 Activity Page 51

Objective:
To review the consonant digraph **kn**

(Say) Color in the oval in front of the sentence that tells about each picture. Draw a circle around each word that begins with the digraph **kn**. At the bottom, think of a word that starts with **kn** and rhymes with the given word. Write it on the line.

Plural Endings -s, -es

B Phonics   Name _____

Circle the word that best completes each sentence and write it on the line.

1. Look at those shiny ___stars___ .

     star   (stars)

2. We have many __flowers__ in our yard.

     flower   (flowers)

3. The ___box___ is very heavy.

     (box)   boxes

4. We ate the bunch of __grapes__ .

     grape   (grapes)

5. There are four __seasons__ in a year.

     season   (seasons)

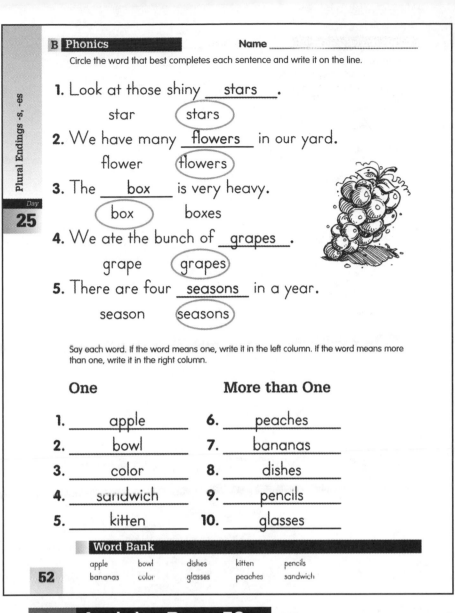

Say each word. If the word means one, write it in the left column. If the word means more than one, write it in the right column.

One   **More than One**

1. ___apple___   **6.** ___peaches___

2. ___bowl___   **7.** ___bananas___

3. ___color___   **8.** ___dishes___

4. ___sandwich___   **9.** ___pencils___

5. ___kitten___   **10.** ___glasses___

Word Bank				
apple	bowl	dishes	kitten	pencils
bananas	color	glasses	peaches	sandwich

52

Activity Page 52

Objective:

To review plurals

 (Say)

Circle the word that best completes each sentence and write it on the line. Look at the word bank. Say each word. If the word means one, write it in the left column. If the word means more than one, write it in the right column.

Warm-Up

1 Guess the Word

Materials
• 3"x5" cards

Preparation
Write words with **ar** and **or** on the cards. You may want to use these words:

bark, barn, car, corn, dark, fork, fort, garden, hard, horn, horse, jar, large, park, short, sport, star, store, storm, torn.

How to Play:
Invite a student to draw a card and give a clue to the word. If no one can guess, the student gives another clue, and so on, until someone guesses correctly. Continue until all the cards are used.

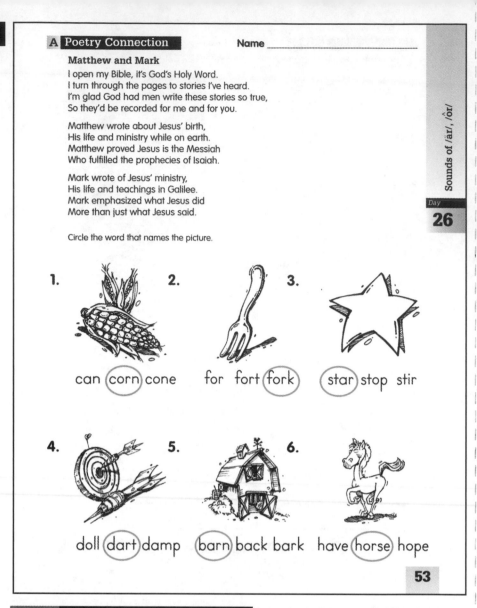

A Poetry Connection

Name _____

Matthew and Mark

I open my Bible, it's God's Holy Word.
I turn through the pages to stories I've heard.
I'm glad God had men write these stories so true,
So they'd be recorded for me and for you.

Matthew wrote about Jesus' birth,
His life and ministry while on earth.
Matthew proved Jesus is the Messiah
Who fulfilled the prophecies of Isaiah.

Mark wrote of Jesus' ministry,
His life and teachings in Galilee.
Mark emphasized what Jesus did
More than just what Jesus said.

Circle the word that names the picture.

Day **26**

1. can (corn) cone
2. for fort (fork)
3. (star) stop stir
4. doll (dart) damp
5. (barn) back bark
6. have (horse) hope

53

2 Poetry Connection

Have students follow along as you read the poem. Invite students to tell you the names of the first four books of the New Testament. Teach students that these are called the Gospels. Explain that the books were named for the men who wrote them and that each man wrote the story of Jesus' life on earth. Be sure students understand that the Bible was inspired by God. It is not just a book of stories.

3 Activity Page 53

Objective:
To review the sounds of **/är/** and **/ôr/**

 (Say) Circle the word that names the picture.

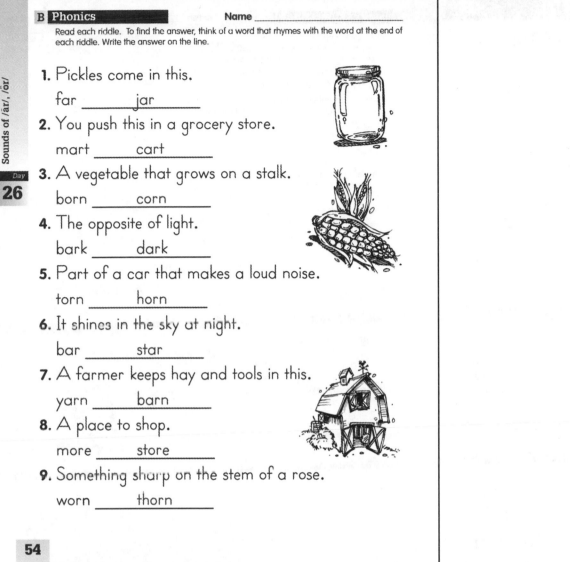

B Phonics   Name _____

Read each riddle. To find the answer, think of a word that rhymes with the word at the end of each riddle. Write the answer on the line.

Day 26

1. Pickles come in this.
   far _____ jar _____

2. You push this in a grocery store.
   mart _____ cart _____

3. A vegetable that grows on a stalk.
   born _____ corn _____

4. The opposite of light.
   bark _____ dark _____

5. Part of a car that makes a loud noise.
   torn _____ horn _____

6. It shines in the sky at night.
   bar _____ star _____

7. A farmer keeps hay and tools in this.
   yarn _____ barn _____

8. A place to shop.
   more _____ store _____

9. Something sharp on the stem of a rose.
   worn _____ thorn _____

54

Activity Page 54

4

Objective:
To review the sounds of **/är/** and **/ôr/**

 Say

Read each riddle. To find the answer, think of a word that rhymes with the word at the end of each riddle. Write the answer on the line.

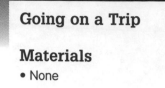

Warm-Up

Going on a Trip

Materials
• None

Preparation
Write **er**, **ir** and **ur** on the board.

How to Play:
Jesus and his disciples walked from town to town. They could take with them only what they could carry. Tell the students that today they are going on a trip. They may take only things that contain the sound of **/ûr/**. The first student might say, "I am going on a trip and I'm going to take a bird." The student can name anything that contains the sound of **/ûr/**. The next student thinks of a new **/ûr/** word to take on the trip. He might say, "I am going on a trip and I'm going to take a circle." Each student will try to take a new thing, but the word must contain the sound of **/ûr/**. Continue until all the students have had a turn.

Luke and John

I open my Bible, it's God's Holy Word.
I turn through the pages to stories I've heard.
I'm glad God had men write these stories so true,
So they'd be recorded for me and for you.

Doctor Luke wrote his gospel in such a fine style
Everyone understood it, both Jew and Gentile.
He wrote about Jesus from birth to ascension,
So we'd understand God's great salvation.

John speaks of Jesus in tones of such love
That we look to the Father in Heaven above.
John tells us Jesus, who some called the Christ,
Brings truth, and salvation, and eternal life.

Circle the word that best completes each sentence.

1. Luke wrote about the ___birth___ of Jesus.
earth (birth) burn

2. I ___turn___ the pages in my Bible carefully.
verse earn (turn)

3. Jesus died so we can have ___eternal___ life.
(eternal) evening earnest

4. It makes me happy to go to ___church___ .
crumb (church) curb

5. The ___birds___ sang all morning.
worms (birds) chirp

6. The little ___squirrel___ is eating an acorn.
(squirrel) squash short

55

Poetry Connection

Have students follow along as you read the poem. You may like to explain to students that the sound of **/ûr/** can be spelled with **ear**, **er**, **ir**, **or**, or **ur**. Write these spellings on the board and have students find a word in the poem for each spelling pattern. (Word, turn, heard, understood, birth, Father, eternal, etc.)

Activity Page 55

Objective:
To review the sound of **/ûr/**

 (Say) Circle the word that best completes each sentence. Then, Write it on the line.

B **Phonics**   Name _____

Circle each word with the same sound as the name of the picture.

| 1. | 2. | 3. |
| bird / ir | hurt / ur | herd / er |

(first)	(fur)	(germ)
(shirt)	(turtle)	(stern)
horse	(church)	short
(girl)	start	(merge)
(thirty)	(purse)	(person)

Find the name of each picture in the lists above. Write the names on the lines.

1. church   2. turtle   3. thirty

56

---

4 **Activity Page 56**

Objective:

To review the sound of **/ûr/**

(Say) Circle each word with the same sound as the name of the picture. At the bottom, find the name of each picture in the lists above. Write the names on the lines.

1 Warm-Up

Toy Joy

Materials
• A small toy

Preparation
Have students sit in a circle.

How to Play:
Show students the toy and ask them what sound they hear at the end of toy. Explain that you will pass the toy around the circle. When you clap, the student holding the toy should say a word containing the **/oi/** sound like in toy. Continue until all the students have had a turn.

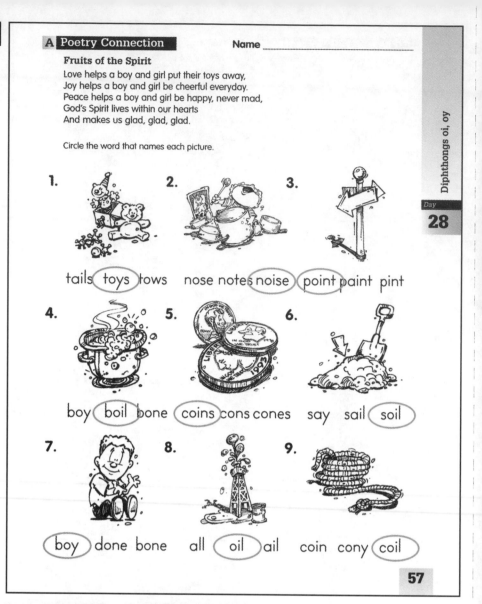

A Poetry Connection   Name _____

Fruits of the Spirit
Love helps a boy and girl put their toys away,
Joy helps a boy and girl be cheerful everyday.
Peace helps a boy and girl be happy, never mad,
God's Spirit lives within our hearts
And makes us glad, glad, glad.

Circle the word that names each picture.

1. tails (toys) tows   2. nose notes (noise)   3. (point) paint pint

4. boy (boil) bone   5. (coins) cons cones   6. say sail (soil)

7. (boy) done bone   8. all (oil) ail   9. coin cony (coil)

57

2 Poetry Connection

Have students follow along as you read the poem. Read Galatians 5:22-23 and encourage students to learn the "Fruits of the Spirit." You may like to explain to students that the sound of **/oi/** can be spelled **oi** or **oy**. Invite them to read through the poem again and circle words that contain the sound of **/oi/**. (boy, toys, Joy)

3 Activity Page 57

Objective:
To review the diphthongs **oi** and **oy**

(Say) Circle the word that names the picture.

B Phonics

Name _____

Read each sentence. Find the word in the word bank that best completes each sentence. Write it on the line.

Diphthongs oi, oy

Day
28

1. The ___boy___ won the race.

2. Some people collect stamps or ___coins___.

3. The horn makes a loud ___noise___.

4. ___Oil___ splatters are hard to clean.

5. A fruit of the spirit is ___joy___.

6. He put ___soil___ in the flower pot.

7. Sam got more ___toys___ for his birthday.

8. The ___point___ on my pencil broke.

9. The water began to ___boil___.

10. Would you like to ___join___ God's family?

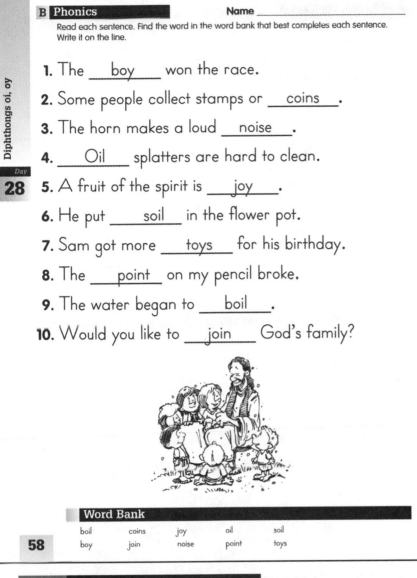

Word Bank				
boil	coins	joy	oil	soil
boy	join	noise	point	toys

58

4

Activity Page 58

Objective:

To review the diphthongs **oi** and **oy**

(Say) Read each sentence. Find the word in the word bank that best completes each sentence. Write it on the line.

1 Warm-Up

Choose a House

Materials
• None

Preparation
Draw two houses on the board. Label the first house **ou** and the second house **ow**.

How to Play:
Have students think of words containing the **/ou/** sound. If the word is spelled with **ou**, print it on the first house. If it is spelled with **ow**, print it on the second house. Continue as long as there is time or interest.

A Poetry Connection

Name _____

House on the Rock

If you hear the words of Jesus
But His voice you don't obey
Then you are like that foolish man
Who lost his house one day.

He had built upon the soft sand,
His foundations weren't dug deep.
When rain came down, and rivers flowed,
His house fell in a heap.

So please, put into practice
All the words you hear God say.
He is the Rock, so you'll be strong.
Sin can't wash you away.

Read each riddle. Choose the correct answer and write it on the line.

1. I come in many colors.
I grow in the yard. What am I? ___flowers___

2. I am a direction.
Birds fly this way in winter. What am I? ___south___

3. I hunt at night.
I live in a tree. What am I? ___owl___

4. I am something to wear.
You will wear one in heaven. What am I? ___crown___

5. A farmer uses me.
I dig up the ground. What am I? ___plow___

Word Bank

crown   flowers   owl   plow   south

59

---

2 Poetry Connection

Have students follow along as you read the poem. You may like to explain to students that the sound of **/ou/** can be spelled with **ou** or **ow**. Write these spellings on the board and have students find a word in the poem for each spelling pattern. (house, foundations, down) (Exception: flowed)

3 Activity Page 59

Objective:
To review the diphthongs **ou** and **ow**

 Read each riddle. Find the answer in the word bank and write it on the line.

B Phonics

Name _____

Read each sentence. Find the word in the word bank that best completes each sentence. Write it on the line.

1. There are pretty __flowers__ in her yard.

2. A house built on sand will fall __down__.

3. You must build your __house__ on solid rock.

4. Jesus has promised us a __crown__ in heaven.

5. An __owl__ hooted near our tent.

6. Jesus will come in a __cloud__ of angels.

7. Mother said I must go home __now__.

8. The squirrel has __brown__ fur.

9. We went to __town__ to do some shopping.

10. I learned __how__ to plant a garden.

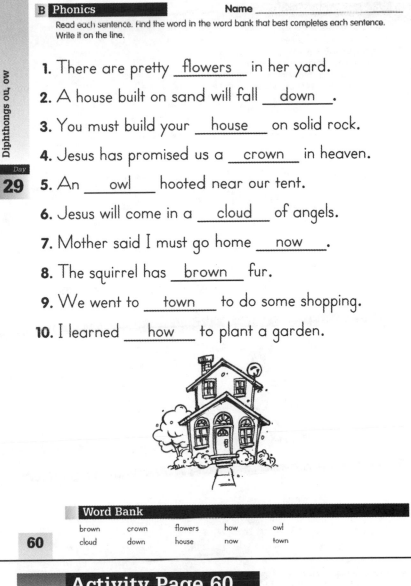

Word Bank				
brown	crown	flowers	how	owl
cloud	down	house	now	town

60

Activity Page 60

Objective:

To review the diphthongs **ou** and **ow**

(Say) Read each sentence. Find the word in the word bank that best completes each sentence. Write it on the line.

1 Warm-Up

Contraction Action

Materials
• 3"x5" cards

Preparation
Write one of the following contractions on each card: **aren't, couldn't, didn't, weren't, don't, won't, isn't, can't, he's, she's, that's, it's, you'll, we'll, they'll, she'll, I'll, he'll, you've, I've, we've, they've, you're, I'm, let's, we're**

Make as many sets as needed, so each pair of students has ten cards. Divide students into pairs.

How to Play:
Give a set of ten cards to each pair. Have one student mix the cards and lay them face down. The students should take turns turning over a card. They should read the word aloud, then name the two words it stands for. If they are successful, they get to keep the card. If they cannot think of the two words, they should lay the card back down and it becomes the other student's turn. Continue until all the cards are used.

A Poetry Connection   Name _____

Contradictions

The Pharisees and Scribes, who were teachers of the law,
Watched Jesus very closely, never liking what they saw.
They'd made a lot of extra rules for people to obey,
But Jesus showed the growing crowds that this was not His way.
God's laws were most important, and not these rules of men.
Our Father loves and heals us, and He saves us from our sin.

Write the sentences in the correct order on the lines. Use a contraction in place of the underlined words. Remember to capitalize and punctuate correctly.

1. like Jesus.   The Pharisees   <u>did not</u>

   The Pharisees **didn't** like Jesus.

2. obey God's laws.   <u>I will</u>

   I'll obey God's laws.

3. happy   help others.   <u>We are</u>   when we

   We're happy when we help others.

4. <u>is not</u>   My house   built on sand.

   My house **isn't** built on sand.

Word Bank

didn't   I'll   isn't   we're

61

Contractions   *Day* **30**

---

2 Poetry Connection

Have students follow along as you read the poem. Encourage them to think what two words **they'd** stands for. Write **they would** on the board and explain that a contraction is a shortened way to write or speak a word or words.

3 Activity Page 61

Objective:
To review contractions

 Say) Write each sentence in the correct order on the lines. Use a contraction in place of the underlined words. Be sure to punctuate your sentence correctly, and use capital letters where needed.

B Phonics   Name _____

Write the contraction that means the same as the words given.

Contractions: did not = didn't

1. did not ___didn't___   **5.** will not ___won't___

2. cannot ___can't___   **6.** is not ___isn't___

3. could not ___couldn't___   **7.** are not ___aren't___

4. do not ___don't___   **8.** were not ___weren't___

Write the word or words that mean the same as the underlined contraction.

1. Jesus <u>didn't</u> worry about the Pharisees. ___did not___

2. I <u>won't</u> tell the secret. ___will not___

3. Zacchaeus <u>couldn't</u> see over the crowd. ___could not___

4. Peter <u>isn't</u> catching any fish. ___is not___

5. Why <u>weren't</u> you doing what Mom said? ___were not___

6. The Pharisees <u>don't</u> want Jesus to heal on the

Sabbath. ___do not___

7. They <u>aren't</u> coming with us? ___are not___

8. I <u>can't</u> wait until Jesus comes again. ___cannot___

Word Bank

aren't	couldn't	don't	weren't
can't	didn't	isn't	won't

62

Contractions

Day
30

---

4 **Activity Page 62**

Objective:

To review contractions

 Say Write the contraction that means the same as the words given. At the bottom, write the word or words that mean the same as the underlined contraction.

1 Warm-Up

Going Fishing

Materials

- 18" length of 1/4" dowel stick
- 18" length of heavy string
- Magnet, Dishpan, Paper clips
- 3"x5" cards, some cut in half

Preparation

Tie one end of the piece of string to the magnet and tie the other end to the dowel stick to make a fishing rod. Write **ing** and **ed** on several cards. Put a paper clip on each card and scatter the cards in the dishpan. Make word cards with the following words on them: **look, fish, row, rain, follow, talk, cry, melt, spill, ask, wait, listen, jump, play, mix, pray, pick, bless, pass, rest.**

How to Play:

Some of Jesus' disciples were fishermen before they followed Jesus. Let students see how many "fish" they can catch. Place word cards upside down in a stack. Students use the "fishing pole" to "fish" a suffix from the dishpan. They then draw a card from the stack. They should add the suffix on their "fish" to the word they drew, and say the new word. Have them put the "fish" back in the tank after their turn. Continue until all the cards are used.

A | Poetry Connection   Name _____

Sharing With Jesus

The people loved Jesus, and Jesus loved them.
Wherever he went, crowds were following Him.
One day He was preaching and healing the sick,
The people kept coming, the crowd soon grew thick.
The disciples told Jesus, "The people can't stay,
We've nothing to feed them, they must go away."
But Jesus just asked them to wait for a while.
"My God will provide," Jesus said with a smile.
"We do have some fishes and some barley bread,
Brought here by a small lad," the good Andrew said.
And so Jesus took it, He blessed it, and then
It grew to enough to feed five thousand men!
Enough for their families, for everyone there!
Because of a young boy, so willing to share.

Read each sentence. Write the correct suffix **-ed** or **-ing** on each line.

1. A boy want_ed_ to hear Jesus' stories.
2. His mother is pack_ing_ him a lunch.
3. The people were listen_ing_ to Jesus.
4. Jesus ask_ed_ if anyone had food.
5. The people were seat_ed_ on the grass.
6. Jesus asked a bless_ing_ on the food.
7. The disciples pass_ed_ out the food.
8. Jesus began break_ing_ the bread.

Suffixes -ed, -ing

Day **31**

63

---

2 Poetry Connection

Have students follow along as you read the poem. Write the words **follow**, **preach**, **heal**, and **bless** on the board. Ask volunteers to come to the board and add **-ed** and **-ing** to each word to make other forms of the words.

3 Activity Page 63

Objective:

To review the suffixes **-ed** and **-ing**

(Say) Read each sentence. Write the correct suffix **-ed** or **-ing** on each line.

B Phonics

Name _____

Read each riddle. Circle the base word in each underlined word. Answer each riddle, using words from the word bank.

Suffixes -ed, -ing

Day **31**

Base Words: (reading)   (melted)

1. I want to listen to Jesus.
   My mother is (packing) me a lunch.
   Who am I? __small boy__

2. We were (placed) in a basket with some bread.
   There were two of us.
   What were we? ____fish____

3. We told the people to be (seated).
   We were Jesus' special friends.
   Who were we? __disciples__

4. I found a small boy with a lunch.
   I like (talking) to people.
   Who am I? __Andrew__

5. I was put in a basket.
   Jesus (blessed) and broke me.
   What was I? __bread__

Word Bank

Andrew   bread   disciples   fish   small boy

64

---

4 Activity Page 64

Objective:

To review the suffixes **-ed** and **-ing**

Read each riddle. Circle the base word in each underlined word. Answer each riddle, using words from the word bank.

Daily Lesson Plans

Letter

Provide the parent or guardian with the spelling word lists for the next unit.

Say

Show your parents or guardian this letter that tells them what your spelling words will be for the next unit. Ask them to put it in a special place where you will remember to practice them together.

Dear Parent,

We are about to begin our first spelling unit containing five weekly lessons. A set of ten words plus three challenge words will be studied each week. All the words will be reviewed in the sixth week.

Values based on the Scriptures listed below will be taught in each lesson.

Lesson 1	Lesson 2	Lesson 3	Lesson 4	Lesson 5
add	best	been	box	above
ask	ever	begin	dot	does
camp	head	digit	drop	done
fast	help	give	frog	jump
hat	left	into	gone	just
have	leg	its	lost	must
last	men	kid	lot	none
map	nest	live	odd	number
plan	next	quit	often	sum
than	set	sister	soft	what
☆ apple	☆ again	☆ because	☆ forgot	☆ bubble
☆ asked	☆ never	☆ gym	☆ job	☆ once
☆ bath	☆ sentence	☆ until	☆ tomorrow	☆ sometimes
Matt. 22:37	Luke 9:48	Matt. 5:25	Mark 9:50	Matt. 24:42

Have each student remove this letter from his or her Worktext prior to beginning Lesson 1.

The Most Important Thing

A tornado provides Tommy with plenty of excitement, as well as a chance to show his love for God.

"A tornado warning has been issued for Fulbright and Cole counties until twelve o'clock tonight. Residents of these counties are advised to take immediate precautions. Take shelter in a basement or a central room without windows such as a pantry, hallway, or bathroom. High winds and sporadic heavy rains are expected. We have just received an unconfirmed report of a funnel cloud sighting just west of Clifton. Stay tuned for up-to-the-minute information on VKJP. We repeat, a tornado warning has been issued for Fulbright and Cole counties."

Seven-year-old Tommy's wide blue eyes switched from staring at the serious looking weatherman on TV to his mother. Mrs. Rawson sat on the couch leaning slightly forward as she listened carefully to the weather report. Lisa, Tommy's big sister, lay on the carpet with an open book in front of her. She held a forgotten pencil raised midair in one hand as she watched the storm's path flash across the TV weather map again and again. The fading evening sunlight cast a strange yellow-green glow through the windows. Outdoors, the whole world seemed quiet and still, like it was waiting for something to happen.

"Okay, you two, it's bedtime." Mother turned down the volume on the TV as a commercial came on and spoke briskly to the children. "Lisa, please make sure the flashlights work well. I think some new batteries are in the drawer if we need to replace them. Tommy, please get the sleeping bags out of the hall closet and bring them downstairs to the pantry."

"But, Mom . . ." Tommy began. "It's not time for bed yet."

"You may read your new nature magazine or some books for a while, son," Mom replied firmly, "but you are going to bed in the pantry now. It is the safest place in this house."

Tommy and Lisa kept getting in each other's way as they settled into their sleeping bags on the small floor space of the kitchen pantry. "This is a perfect place for you to sleep," Lisa giggled. "You're surrounded by food!" After some poking, tickling, and bumping of heads they finally settled down. Before he drifted off to sleep, Tommy heard Dad come inside. The lull of his parents' voices as they talked quietly reassured him as the wind picked up, howling and rattling things outside.

SMACK! Tommy cracked his head soundly as he sat up the next morning. "OWWW!" he yelled. SMACK! Lisa's head cracked against the pantry shelf on her side. "OWWW!" she echoed. She glared at her little brother. "You scared me half to death! What a way to wake up!"

Tommy rubbed the sore spot on his head and smiled sheepishly. "I forgot we were sleeping with the cereal. But at least we did wake up and the pantry's still here."

Later that morning Mom turned the car radio on as she drove the children to school. Occasional branches littered the streets where the stiff winds had knocked them down. A battered stop sign flopped upside-down on its pole. Mother drove carefully through large puddles that swooshed up under the car. "A tornado demolished much of Center City as one of the worst storms in the history of Fulbright County hit shortly

before midnight last night. Details after this." The voice on the radio caught the attention of everyone in the car. They listened quietly to the report of damages the tornado made to the little town about an hour away from their own town.

The classroom was humming with talk about the tornado when Tommy entered it a few minutes later. Mrs. Morgan started class with a prayer of thanks for the safety of the children and their families. She prayed for those in Center City who had lost their homes and businesses. She prayed for those who were injured when the tornado hit, and thanked God none were killed.

"It appears that most of you have heard about the tornado that hit Center City last night," Mrs. Morgan spoke to the class. "As you may know, the tornado cut a path through the town, destroying everything in its way. I'm sure that many of you have questions or comments." She nodded at Daniel's waving hand. "Daniel?"

"We saw some pictures of it on TV this morning. It was awesome!" Daniel shook his head in amazement. "There was a car upside-down right on top of where a house used to be."

"Sometimes you couldn't even tell where a house used to be in some of those pictures," James added. "It just looked like piles of trash."

"There was a big sign with two poles, and they were twisted up like a pretzel!" Daniel continued. "One house looked fine, except that its roof was sitting in the yard instead of on top of the house."

"I heard once that a tornado can drive a straw into a telephone pole. Is that true, Mrs. Morgan?" Rosa asked.

"A tornado's incredibly strong and twisting winds can do many unusual things." Mrs. Morgan answered. "Objects can be picked up and carried long distances then set down gently with very little damage while other objects are smashed to pieces. A tornado is a fierce and unpredictable force."

"All those piles of trash used to be someone's homes

67

Lesson 1 | Day 1

where people lived and played." Sarah said quietly.

The class was quiet for a moment, then Kristin asked, "Mrs. Morgan, where will the people stay who used to live in those houses? What will happen to them? Where will they get food and clothes and beds and …everything?"

"The government and the Red Cross will help," Mrs. Morgan replied. "Many people volunteer to help as well. Churches and community buildings open shelters or places for people to stay until they can find their own place. Businesses and people from many towns in this area will raise money to help buy food and supplies needed in Center City."

Mrs. Morgan smiled as Tommy almost followed his hand up into the air when he raised it so quickly. "Tommy?"

"Couldn't we do that, too, right here at Knowlton Elementary?" Tommy was almost hopping up and down with excitement. "Couldn't we all give some money and send it to help those people in Center City?" The excitement was catching. Children across the room started nodding and waving their hands and whispering as the idea caught on.

"That's a very good idea, Tommy," Mrs. Morgan sounded pleased. "How many of you would like to help Center City recover from the tornado as a class project?" Every hand in the room was raised enthusiastically. "All right, then." Mrs. Morgan turned to the board with a big smile and wrote MRS. MORGAN'S CLASS FOR CENTER CITY!

Right beside those words she wrote Matthew 22:37. She turned and looked seriously at the boys and girls in front of her. "This is the Scripture verse we will practice this week. It says, 'Love the Lord your God with all your heart, soul, and mind.' That is exactly what you are doing this morning. Jesus said in the Scriptures that whenever we help other people, it is just like we are helping Jesus Himself. We show our love for God by being kind and unselfish in doing things for others. I am so proud of you and I know that your Heavenly Father is pleased by your choice as well."

On the way home from school, Tommy told his mother and Lisa all about the plan. "We'll each bring as much money as we can and put it all together to help the people whose houses got smashed last night in the tornado," Tommy finished.

Mom reached across the front seat and squeezed Tommy's arm. "You're growing taller and stronger every day, Tommy. Your dad and I are glad about that, but we're really glad to see you choosing to be more like Jesus each day. It shows us that you love God with everything you are, and that is the most important thing of all!"

2 Discussion Time

Check understanding of the story and development of personal values.

- Has your town ever been under a tornado warning?
- What kinds of things did your family do to get ready for the storm?
- How did you feel?
- How do you think people feel who have their home or business hit by a tornado?
- How do you think Tommy and his class felt when they shared their money?
- What are some things you can do to show you love God with all your heart, soul, and mind?

68

Name _____

1. add
2. fast
3. hat
4. plan
5. camp
6. ask
7. last
8. have
9. than
10. map

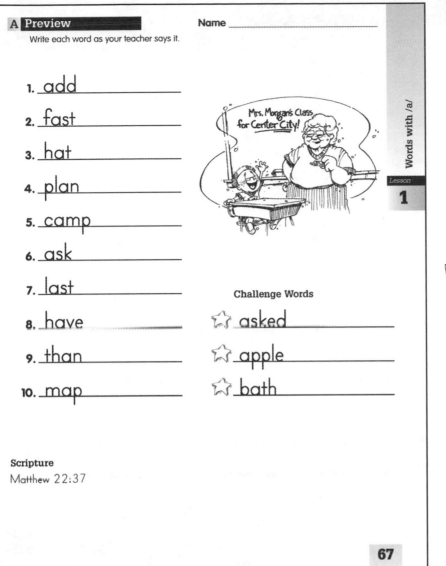

Mrs. Morgan's Class for Center City!

Challenge Words

☆ asked
☆ apple
☆ bath

Scripture
Matthew 22:37

67

Challenge

For better spellers, challenge words may be included in the weekly list. Challenge words are starred.

Correct Immediately!

 Say

Let's correct our preview. I will write each word on the board. Put a dot under each letter on your preview as I spell the word out loud. If you spelled a word wrong, rewrite it correctly.

Progress Chart

Students may record scores. (Reproducible master in Appendix B.)

Take a minute to memorize . . .

Read the memory verse twice. Have students practice it with you two more times.

Lesson 1 | Day 1

---

3 ## Preview

Test for knowledge of the correct spellings of these words. (See the instructions at the top right for challenge words.)

 Say

I will say each word once, use the word in a sentence, then say the word again. Write the word on the lines in the Worktext.

1. add — As the storm moves, the weatherman will **add** to his report.
2. fast — Mother couldn't drive **fast** because of water in the street.
3. hat — That **hat** should keep the rain off.
4. plan — The children liked Tommy's **plan** to help people in Center City.
5. camp — Many people will have to **camp** until their houses are repaired.
6. ask — You can **ask** God to help you any time and anywhere.
7. last — Tommy and Lisa went to sleep at **last**.
8. have — Do you **have** a plan of what you will do if a tornado comes?
9. than — Giving to others can make you feel happier **than** getting things.
10. map — Where is Center City on this **map**?
☆ asked — Kristin **asked**, "Where will all those people stay?"
☆ apple — The storm broke several limbs off the **apple** tree.
☆ bath — A **bath** every day helps your body stay clean and healthy.

Lesson 1 | Day 1

4 Word Shapes

Help students form a correct image of whole words.

(Say) Look at each word and think about its shape. Now, write the word in the correct word Shape Boxes. You may check off each word as you use it.

(In many words **/a/** is spelled with **a**, and it is often spelled this way when it is at the beginning or in the middle of a word.)

(Say) In the word Shape Boxes, color the letter that spells the sound of **/a/** in each word. Circle the words that begin with the sound of **/a/**.

⭐ Challenge

Draw the correctly shaped box around each letter in these words.

(Say) On a separate sheet of paper, write other words that contain one of the spelling patterns in the word list. See how many words you can write.

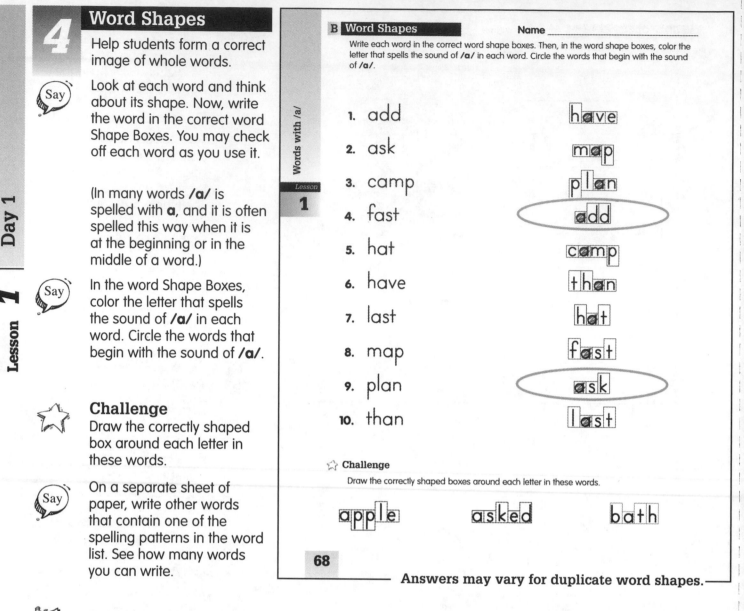

B Word Shapes

Name _____

Write each word in the correct word shape boxes. Then, in the word shape boxes, color the letter that spells the sound of /a/ in each word. Circle the words that begin with the sound of /a/.

Words with /a/ — Lesson 1

1. add
2. ask
3. camp
4. fast
5. hat
6. have
7. last
8. map
9. plan
10. than

have
map
plan
add
camp
than
hat
fast
ask
last

☆ **Challenge**

Draw the correctly shaped boxes around each letter in these words.

apple   asked   bath

68

Answers may vary for duplicate word shapes.

Be Prepared For Fun

Check these supply lists for **Fun Ways to Spell** presented **Day 2**. Purchase and/or gather these items ahead of time!

General
- Crayons
- 3 x 5 Cards cut in thirds (36 pieces per child)
- 3 x 5 Cards cut in thirds (14 more pieces for challenge words)
- Glue
- Bright Paper or Poster Board (3 pieces per child)
- Spelling List

Auditory
- Rhythm Instruments (wooden spoons, pan lids, maracas)
- Spelling List

Visual
- Sidewalk Chalk
- Spelling List

Tactile
- Cotton Balls
- Glue
- Construction Paper
- Spelling List

70

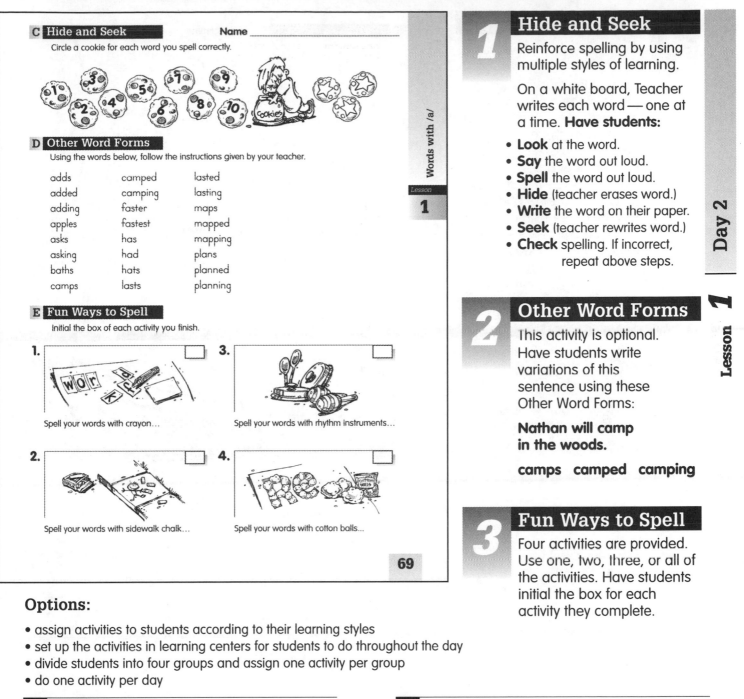

C Hide and Seek   Name _____

Circle a cookie for each word you spell correctly.

D Other Word Forms

Using the words below, follow the instructions given by your teacher.

adds	camped	lasted
added	camping	lasting
adding	faster	maps
apples	fastest	mapped
asks	has	mapping
asking	had	plans
baths	hats	planned
camps	lasts	planning

E Fun Ways to Spell

Initial the box of each activity you finish.

1. ☐

Spell your words with crayon...

2. ☐

Spell your words with sidewalk chalk...

3. ☐

Spell your words with rhythm instruments...

4. ☐

Spell your words with cotton balls...

69

1 Hide and Seek

Reinforce spelling by using multiple styles of learning.

On a white board, Teacher writes each word — one at a time. **Have students:**

- **Look** at the word.
- **Say** the word out loud.
- **Spell** the word out loud.
- **Hide** (teacher erases word.)
- **Write** the word on their paper.
- **Seek** (teacher rewrites word.)
- **Check** spelling. If incorrect, repeat above steps.

2 Other Word Forms

This activity is optional. Have students write variations of this sentence using these Other Word Forms:

Nathan will camp in the woods.

camps   camped   camping

3 Fun Ways to Spell

Four activities are provided. Use one, two, three, or all of the activities. Have students initial the box for each activity they complete.

Options:

- assign activities to students according to their learning styles
- set up the activities in learning centers for students to do throughout the day
- divide students into four groups and assign one activity per group
- do one activity per day

General

To spell your words with crayon . . .
- Write each letter of your spelling word on a card.
- Glue the cards on a sheet of paper in the right order to spell your words.
- Check your spelling.

Auditory

To spell your words with rhythm instruments . . .
- Look at a word on your spelling list.
- Close your eyes.
- Play your rhythm instruments softly while you whisper the spelling of the word.
- Open your eyes and check your spelling.

Visual

To spell your words with sidewalk chalk . . .
- Write each of your spelling words on the sidewalk (ball court or playground).
- Check your spelling.

Tactile

To spell your words with cotton balls . . .
- Choose a word from your spelling list.
- It may be a favorite word or a word you have trouble remembering how to spell.
- Write the word in tall, wide letters on a sheet of construction paper.
- Spread glue along the outline of each letter and press cotton balls into the glue.

71

1 ABC Order

Familiarize students with word meaning and usage. Remind the students that the letters of the alphabet always appear in a certain order. Invite them to say each letter of the alphabet in the proper order as you write it down. Write **fun** and **can** on the board, and ask the students which comes first in ABC order. Help them understand that the first letter of each word determines where it fits in ABC order. Next, list your students' names on the board. Ask the students to write the list on their own paper in ABC order.

(Say) Write each pair of spelling words in alphabetical order.

Words with /a/

Lesson **1**

F **ABC Order**

Write each pair of spelling words in alphabetical order.

Name _____

1. add hat   add   hat
2. plan camp   camp   plan
3. map fast   fast   map
4. than ask   ask   than
5. have last   have   last
☆ bath apple   apple   bath

A B C D E F G H I J K L M N O P Q R S T U V W X Y Z
a b c d e f g h i j k l m n o p q r s t u v w x y z

70

Take a minute to memorize...

Read the memory verse twice. Have students practice it with you two more times.

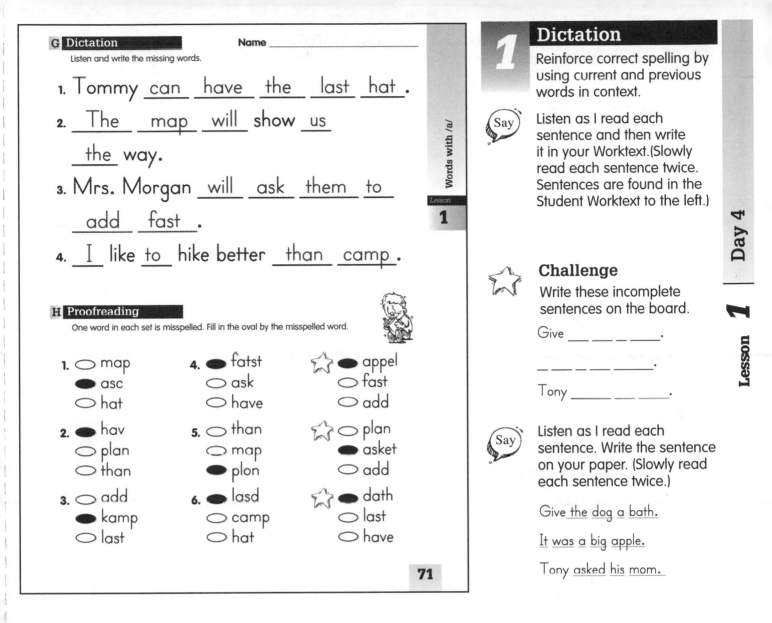

G Dictation

Listen and write the missing words.

Name _____

1. Tommy <u>can</u> <u>have</u> <u>the</u> <u>last</u> <u>hat</u>.

2. <u>The</u> <u>map</u> <u>will</u> show <u>us</u> <u>the</u> way.

3. Mrs. Morgan <u>will</u> <u>ask</u> <u>them</u> <u>to</u> <u>add</u> <u>fast</u>.

4. <u>I</u> like <u>to</u> hike better <u>than</u> <u>camp</u>.

H Proofreading

One word in each set is misspelled. Fill in the oval by the misspelled word.

1. ○ map
   ● asc
   ○ hat

2. ● hav
   ○ plan
   ○ than

3. ○ add
   ● kamp
   ○ last

4. ● fatst
   ○ ask
   ○ have

5. ○ than
   ○ map
   ● plon

6. ● lasd
   ○ camp
   ○ hat

☆ ● appel
   ○ fast
   ○ add

☆ ○ plan
   ● asket
   ○ add

☆ ● dath
   ○ last
   ○ have

71

Words with /a/

Lesson 1

Dictation — 1

Reinforce correct spelling by using current and previous words in context.

Say — Listen as I read each sentence and then write it in your Worktext.(Slowly read each sentence twice. Sentences are found in the Student Worktext to the left.)

☆ Challenge

Write these incomplete sentences on the board.

Give __ __ __ __.

__ __ __ __ __.

Tony _____ __ __.

Say — Listen as I read each sentence. Write the sentence on your paper. (Slowly read each sentence twice.)

Give <u>the</u> <u>dog</u> <u>a</u> <u>bath</u>.

<u>It</u> <u>was</u> <u>a</u> <u>big</u> <u>apple</u>.

Tony <u>asked</u> <u>his</u> <u>mom</u>.

Day 4 | Lesson 1

Proofreading — 2

Familiarize students with standardized test format and reinforce recognizing misspelled words.

Say — Look at each set of words. One word in each set is misspelled. Fill in the oval by the misspelled word. (You may wish to pronounce each set of words to help students correctly identify them.)

3 Hide and Seek

Reinforce correct spelling of current spelling words. (A reproducible master is provided in Appendix A as shown on the inset page to the right.)
Write the words one at a time on a white board.
Have students:

- **Look** at the word.
- **Say** the word out loud.
- **Spell** the word out loud.
- **Hide** (teacher erases word.)
- **Write** the word on paper.
- **Seek** (teacher rewrites word.)
- **Check** spelling. If incorrect, rewrite word correctly.

4 Suffixes

Have your students complete this activity to strengthen spelling ability and expand vocabulary.

1 Posttest

Test mastery of the spelling words. Challenge words are starred.

(Say) I will say the word once, use the word in a sentence, then say the word again. Write the word on your paper.

Hide and Seek
Check a paper for each word you spell correctly.

1 3 5 7 9
2 4 6 8 10

Suffixes
Add **s**, **ed**, and **ing** to these spelling words. Write the new words.

		+ s	+ ed	+ ing
1.	add	adds	added	adding
2.	ask	asks	asked	asking
3.	camp	camps	camped	camping
4.	last	lasts	lasted	lasting
5.	bath	baths	bathed	bathing

Double the final consonant before adding **ed** and **ing** to these spelling words. Write the new words.

6.	plan	plans	planned	planning
7.	map	maps	mapped	mapping

368

1.	ask	Mrs. Morgan allowed the class to **ask** about the tornado.
2.	last	The tornado watch will **last** until midnight.
3.	have	We **have** new batteries for the flashlights.
4.	than	A tornado is more destructive **than** most thunderstorms.
5.	map	The storm's path flashed across the weather **map** on TV.
6.	add	They decided to **add** their money together to help Center City.
7.	fast	Tornado winds are very **fast** and strong.
8.	hat	His **hat** blew away.
9.	plan	It is a good idea to **plan** what you will do if a tornado comes.
10.	camp	Let's **camp** here by the creek.
☆	apple	Do you want a red **apple** or a yellow **apple**?
☆	bath	Getting down in the **bath** tub might keep you safe in a tornado.
☆	asked	"Can a tornado put a straw into a wooden pole?" Rosa **asked**.

Progress Chart
Students may record scores. (Reproducible master in Appendix B.)

Personal Dictionary
Students may add any words they have misspelled to their personal dictionaries for reference when writing. (Cover in Appendix B.)

74

I Game

Name _____

Follow Tommy to the pantry to sleep till the tornado is past. Move one space for each word you or your team spells correctly from this week's word list.

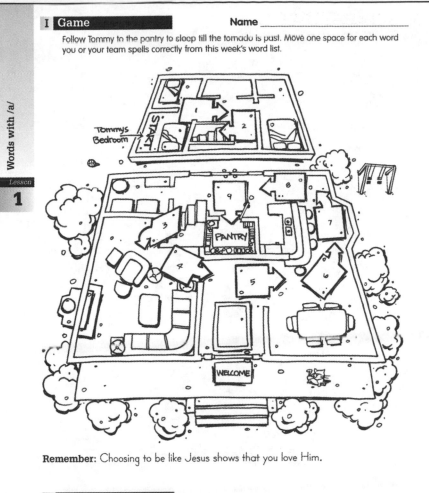

Tommy's Bedroom

START

PANTRY

WELCOME

Remember: Choosing to be like Jesus shows that you love Him.

J Journaling

Copy this sentence in your journal and finish it: **I can show I love God with all my heart, soul, and mind by. . .**

72

---

2 Game

Reinforce spelling skills and provide motivation and interest.

Materials

- game page (from student text)
- flat buttons, dry beans, pennies, or game discs (1 per child)
- game word list

Game Word List

Use of challenge words is optional.

1. **add**
2. **ask**
3. **fast**
4. **last**
5. **hat**
6. **have**
7. **plan**
8. **than**
9. **camp**
10. **map**
☆ **bath**
☆ **apple**
☆ **asked**

How to Play:

- Divide students into two teams, and decide which team will go first.
- Have each student place their game piece on Start.
- Have a student from team A go to the board.
- Read the spelling word two times slowly and clearly. (You may also wish to use the word in a sentence. Ex.: "cat — The cat climbed a tree. — cat")
- Have the student write the word on the board.
- If the word is spelled correctly, instruct all the members of team A to move their game piece forward one space on the game board. (Note: If the word is misspelled, correct the spelling immediately.)
- Alternate between teams A and B as you go down the word list.
- The team to reach the pantry first is the winner.

Non-Competitive Option: At the end of the game, say: "Class, I am proud of your efforts to spell the words correctly. If you had fun and tried your best, you are all winners!"

3 Journaling

Provide a meaningful reason for correct spelling through personal writing.

Review the story using discussion leads provided on the following page. Encourage students to apply the Scriptural value in their journaling.

 Take a minute to memorize . . .

Have the students say the memory verse with you once.

Lesson **1** | Day 5

Provide a meaningful reason for correct spelling through personal writing.

(Say)

- Sometimes storms can be frightening. Some of them do a lot of damage like the tornado that hit Center City. Many people had their homes or businesses destroyed. How did Tommy and his classmates show that they loved God? (By giving money of their own to help the people in Center City.)

- Think of some things you can do to show that you love God with all your heart, soul, and mind. (Be kind to others even when they aren't kind to you, share with others, let others go first, be polite, follow rules, etc.)

- Finish the sentence in your Worktext with something you will do to show that you love God. Write the sentence in your journal.

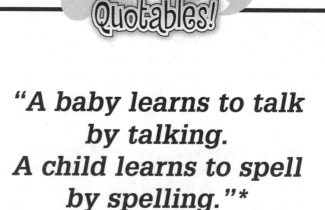

*"A baby learns to talk by talking.
A child learns to spell by spelling."**

*Wilde, Sandra. 1990. A Proposal for a New Spelling Curriculum. The Elementary School Journal, Vol. 90, No. 3, January: 275-289.

Good Deeds and Honey

Tommy and his friends help a tornado victim in an unusual way.

"**B**ut, Mom, I'm supposed to go to the Fantastic Fun Fair with Daniel and James this weekend!" Tommy sputtered. "We've been planning on going for weeks!" Tommy plunked his baseball glove onto the kitchen table and frowned at his mother's back as she washed vegetables in the sink.

"I'm aware of that, Son," Mrs. Rawson answered. "We can drop you off at the Thomason's house on our way to Center City so you can still go to the Fantastic Fun Fair. We'll pick you up late that night. I'm sure James' mother will be willing to keep an eye on you until we get back. I'll call her right after supper."

Tommy grabbed his glove and took the stairs two at a time as he headed up to his bedroom. He dropped onto his bed and stared at the ceiling. Brilliant rays of sun slashed across the bed and left warm spots where they crossed his bare arms. The early fall day was gorgeous, as if the terrible storms of last week had never happened. The news reports, however, still showed pictures of the destruction the tornado had caused when it hit Center City. Tommy held his hand up and moved it back and forth from the shadows to the bright sunlight streaming through the window.

"I've been looking forward to going to the Fantastic Fun Fair for weeks. It's going to be so much fun! Daniel said there are gobs of rides and games and shows. I want to ride the Firebird roller coaster I've heard so much about. But I guess I ought to go with Mom, Dad, and Lisa to help out in Center City. After all, it was my idea for my class at school to bring money to help the people who lost so much when the tornado hit their town." Tommy

sighed, sat up and stretched. He'd better call James and Daniel right away to tell them he wasn't going to the Fantastic Fun Fair after all.

The sun was barely peeking over the eastern edge of the world the next morning when the Rawsons headed down the highway toward Center City. Mrs. Rawson drove the car and Mr. Rawson followed in the pickup truck loaded with supplies for the people who had lost their homes. Lisa rode with her dad. Tommy rode in the car with his mom . . . AND James and Daniel.

"Wow! Look at that house!" James pointed. "The shingles are all just ripped up across the top of it."

"All those telephone poles are snapped like toothpicks," Daniel said with amazement. "And just look at that tree! Awesome!"

"Now you boys remember," Mrs. Rawson cautioned, "you must not get in the way of the clean-up workers. Mrs. Jenkins, the Red Cross worker I spoke with, said she would have some jobs just right for you boys to help with. Just remember that we're here to help and not to cause more problems."

The devastating storm had left much of Center City in shambles. A warehouse the tornado had missed was one of the places across town set up with Red Cross workers, volunteers, and supplies. James and Daniel pitched in with the Rawson family as the pickup was unloaded and the supplies were hauled to the proper places in the warehouse.

"Dog food? Why did your dad bring dog food to Center City, Tommy?" James made a funny face as

he helped carry a big bag of dog food into the warehouse. His face turned red when he realized the Red Cross worker in charge of this warehouse had heard his question.

Mrs. Jenkins, a comfortably round lady with gray hair, patted James' shoulder and smiled. "That's actually a good question. When the tornado hit, many family pets were frightened or hurt, and lost from their families. We have quite a number of dogs and cats that have been found. We keep them here and take care of them until their owners are located. That's one job you three can take care of today. Each pet needs water and food, and the dogs need to be walked outdoors. Think you can handle it?" she asked with a pretend frown.

"Yes, ma'am!" Tommy replied. The three friends spent much of the morning cleaning up cages and caring for the lost pets. Many of them had cuts and scratches, and several wore splints or casts.

Just before lunch Mrs. Jenkins herded the three boys to the food preparation and distribution area. "These three will assist you today, Mr. Culpepper," she announced to the huge man in a big white apron. Mr. Culpepper had thick black hair and a bristly mustache. He eyed the boys up and down, told them to wash their hands, and put them to work.

"You," he waved a huge fist holding a spoon toward a wide-eyed Daniel and Tommy, "you will fill those cups with water from that faucet." The spoon pointed as he spoke. "You," the spoon swung over to James, "you will help hand out those sack lunches."

The boys were amazed at the number of people who showed up for food. Grimy volunteer workers who had been cleaning up the mess left by the tornado came through line and eagerly accepted the lunches and water the boys handed out. Families that had lost everything they owned came through the line gratefully. One little boy hid behind his mother's jeans as she walked through the line.

"Hi, there." Tommy

77

Day 1

Lesson 2

smiled at the little guy. Red-rimmed eyes and a tear-streaked face peeked out, then disappeared behind his mother again.

"He's been crying all day," the mother apologized. "We can't find Honey, our dog, anywhere," she explained with a sigh.

"What does Honey look like?" Tommy questioned. "Did you look here? There are lots of lost pets here. Maybe Honey is one of them." His words tumbled out before the woman could answer. "Is Honey big or little?"

The mother gave a tired smile and her son peeked around at Tommy with hopeful eyes. "Honey is a small blond cocker spaniel with a little white spot on her left side."

"She's here!" Tommy almost shouted. "I'm sure I saw a dog like that this morning. Come see!"

In minutes Tommy was grinning from ear to ear as all traces of the boy's tears were washed away with an eager licking from a happy, wriggling, blond cocker spaniel with a little white spot on one side. The little boy's mom didn't seem quite so tired and discouraged anymore, either.

The next day at school, Daniel eagerly shared their day at Center City with the other students.

"And the little boy looked up at Tommy and said, 'Wow, you must be someone really great. Thank you for finding Honey.' As if Tommy had some kind of special power or something!" Daniel laughed.

"Maybe he was right." Mrs. Morgan got everyone's attention with that statement. "Luke 9:48 says 'Your care for others is the measure of your greatness.' Spending your day helping others and taking time to help find a little boy's lost pet showed a really great spirit, God's power, in your life."

"Well, it was a lot of fun," Daniel said after a slight pause. "And, after all, Fantastic Fun Fair will always be there later. We won't always have the chance to help out at Center City."

Tommy smiled to himself as he remembered the little boy's huge smile and words of thanks. Helping had really made him feel GREAT!

2 Discussion Time

Check understanding of the story and development of personal values.

- Why didn't Tommy want to go help in Center City?
- What jobs did the three boys do to help?
- Why was the little boy that Tommy talked to so sad?
- How was Tommy able to help him feel better?
- How do you think Tommy felt about that?
- What kinds of things can you do to help others?

A Preview

Write each word as your teacher says it.

Name _____

1. nest
2. help
3. leg
4. next
5. set
6. best
7. ever
8. left
9. men
10. head

Challenge Words

☆ again
☆ sentence
☆ never

Scripture
Luke 9:48

Words with /e/

Lesson 2

73

Challenge

For better spellers, challenge words may be included in the weekly list. Challenge words are starred.

Correct Immediately!

Say Let's correct our preview. I will write each word on the board. Put a dot under each letter on your preview as I spell the word out loud. If you spelled a word wrong, rewrite it correctly.

Progress Chart

Students may record scores. (Reproducible master in Appendix B.)

Take a minute to memorize . . .

Read the memory verse twice. Have students practice it with you two more times.

Day 1

Lesson **2**

3 Preview

Test for knowledge of the correct spellings of these words. (See the instructions at the top right for challenge words.)

Say I will say each word once, use the word in a sentence, then say the word again. Write the word on the lines in the Worktext.

1. **nest** — There was a bird's **nest** in this bush.
2. **help** — God wants us to **help** each other.
3. **leg** — Did the cat's **leg** get hurt when the tornado hit?
4. **next** — The **next** day Daniel told them about the trip to Center City.
5. **set** — Please **set** the boxes of supplies on this table.
6. **best** — Do your **best** at whatever job you have to do.
7. **ever** — Have you **ever** had to make a hard choice?
8. **left** — There wasn't much **left** of Center City where the tornado hit.
9. **men** — It took a lot of **men** to help remove the damaged buildings.
10. **head** — The boy patted Honey on the **head**.
☆ **again** — The destroyed houses and businesses all had to be built **again**.
☆ **sentence** — A **sentence** always starts with a capital letter.
☆ **never** — I hope a tornado **never** hits our town.

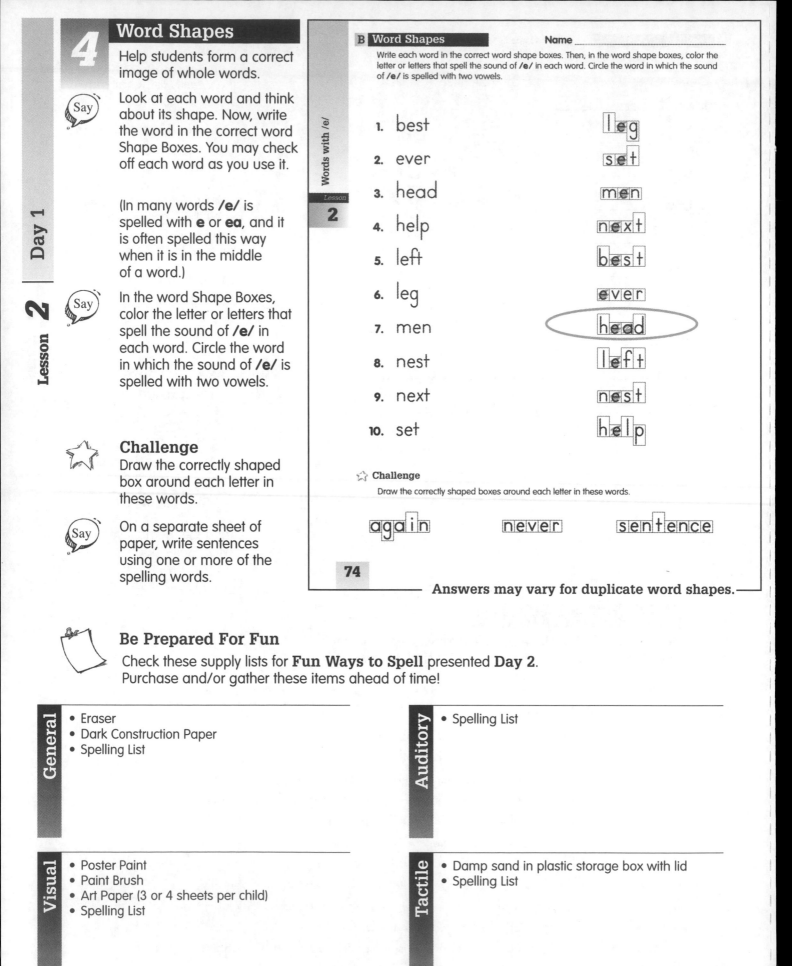

Word Shapes

Day 1   Lesson 2

4

Help students form a correct image of whole words.

Say Look at each word and think about its shape. Now, write the word in the correct word Shape Boxes. You may check off each word as you use it.

(In many words **/e/** is spelled with **e** or **ea**, and it is often spelled this way when it is in the middle of a word.)

Say In the word Shape Boxes, color the letter or letters that spell the sound of **/e/** in each word. Circle the word in which the sound of **/e/** is spelled with two vowels.

Challenge
Draw the correctly shaped box around each letter in these words.

Say On a separate sheet of paper, write sentences using one or more of the spelling words.

B Word Shapes   Name _____

Write each word in the correct word shape boxes. Then, in the word shape boxes, color the letter or letters that spell the sound of /e/ in each word. Circle the word in which the sound of /e/ is spelled with two vowels.

Words with /e/ — Lesson 2

1. best   leg
2. ever   set
3. head   men
4. help   next
5. left   best
6. leg   ever
7. men   head
8. nest   left
9. next   nest
10. set   help

☆ **Challenge**

Draw the correctly shaped boxes around each letter in these words.

again   never   sentence

74

Answers may vary for duplicate word shapes.

Be Prepared For Fun

Check these supply lists for **Fun Ways to Spell** presented **Day 2**. Purchase and/or gather these items ahead of time!

General
- Eraser
- Dark Construction Paper
- Spelling List

Auditory
- Spelling List

Visual
- Poster Paint
- Paint Brush
- Art Paper (3 or 4 sheets per child)
- Spelling List

Tactile
- Damp sand in plastic storage box with lid
- Spelling List

80

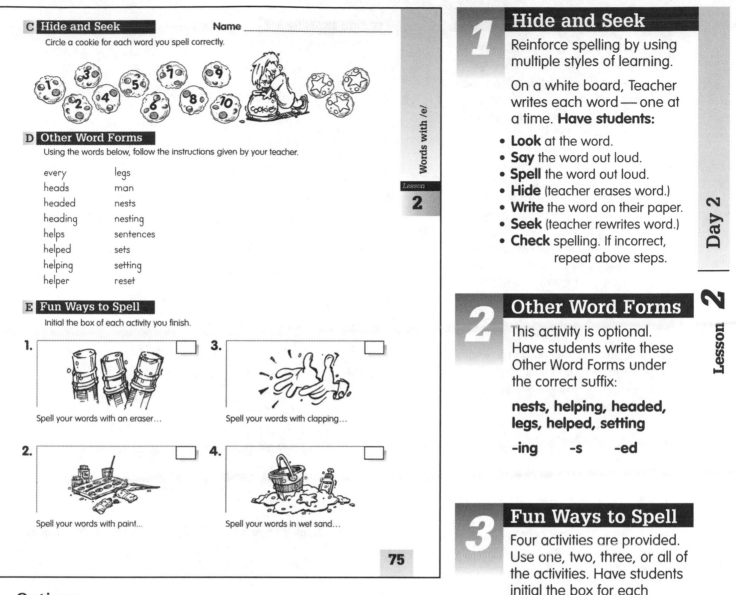

C Hide and Seek — Name _____

Circle a cookie for each word you spell correctly.

D Other Word Forms

Using the words below, follow the instructions given by your teacher.

every	legs
heads	man
headed	nests
heading	nesting
helps	sentences
helped	sets
helping	setting
helper	reset

E Fun Ways to Spell

Initial the box of each activity you finish.

1. Spell your words with an eraser...

2. Spell your words with paint...

3. Spell your words with clapping...

4. Spell your words in wet sand...

Words with /e/

Lesson 2

75

---

1 Hide and Seek

Reinforce spelling by using multiple styles of learning.

On a white board, Teacher writes each word — one at a time. **Have students:**

- **Look** at the word.
- **Say** the word out loud.
- **Spell** the word out loud.
- **Hide** (teacher erases word.)
- **Write** the word on their paper.
- **Seek** (teacher rewrites word.)
- **Check** spelling. If incorrect, repeat above steps.

Day 2

2 Other Word Forms

This activity is optional. Have students write these Other Word Forms under the correct suffix:

nests, helping, headed, legs, helped, setting

-ing   -s   -ed

Lesson 2

3 Fun Ways to Spell

Four activities are provided. Use one, two, three, or all of the activities. Have students initial the box for each activity they complete.

Options:

- assign activities to students according to their learning styles
- set up the activities in learning centers for students to do throughout the day
- divide students into four groups and assign one activity per group
- do one activity per day

General

To spell your words with an eraser . . .
- Turn your pencil upside down.
- Use the eraser to write your spelling words on a sheet of dark construction paper.
- Check your spelling.

Auditory

To spell your words with clapping . . .
- Look at a word on your spelling list.
- Close your eyes.
- Clap your hands softly while you whisper the spelling of the word.
- Open your eyes and check your spelling.

Visual

To spell your words with paint . . .
- Dip your brush in one color of paint.
- Paint a spelling word on your paper.
- Rinse your brush well in clean water and wipe it dry on a paper towel before dipping it in another color to paint another word.

Tactile

To spell your words in damp sand . . .
- Use finger to write a spelling word in damp sand.
- Check your spelling.
- Smooth the sand with your fingers and write another word.

1 Letter Change

Familiarize students with word meaning and usage. Write the word **want** on the board. Ask a volunteer to read the word. Change the **a** to **e** and ask a volunteer to read the new word. Help the students understand that the word can be changed by changing a letter or letters. You may change the word further from **went** to **west** to **test** to **nest** to **neat** and so on by changing a single letter each time.

 Say Each of the sentences in this activity contains a word with one or two underlined letters. Change the word to one of your spelling words.

F **Letter Change**

Name _____

Words with /e/ · Lesson 2

Change the underlined letter or letters and write the spelling word on the blank.

1. nest _____ Is there a baby bird in the ne<u>a</u>t?
2. ever _____ Have you eve<u>n</u> seen a tornado?
3. left _____ The tornado l<u>o</u>ft a big mess.
4. men _____ The me<u>t</u> put the trash in trucks.
5. set _____ <u>L</u>et those cups on the table.
6. next _____ The little boy was <u>t</u>ext in line.
7. head _____ He hid his hea<u>r</u> behind his mom.
8. leg _____ The dog's back l<u>o</u>g is in a cast.
9. help _____ I want to he<u>a</u>p those in need.
10. best _____ Always do your very b<u>u</u>st.
☆ never _____ I <u>l</u>ever want to be in a tornado.
☆ again _____ They will build the houses t<u>r</u>ain.
☆ sentence _____ This is the last se<u>q</u>uence.

Word Bank

best	head	left	men	next	☆ again	☆ sentence
ever	help	leg	nest	set	☆ never	

76

Take a minute to memorize...

Read the memory verse twice. Have students practice it with you two more times.

82

G Dictation

Name _____

Listen and write the missing words.

1. The bird made the best nest I've ever seen.

2. We will help the men next door.

3. Daniel hurt the left side of his head when he fell.

H Proofreading

One word in each set is misspelled. Fill in the oval by the misspelled word.

1. ● hed
   ○ left
   ○ nest

2. ○ ask
   ● nexd
   ○ camp

3. ○ hat
   ○ help
   ● mans

4. ● cet
   ○ ever
   ○ map

5. ○ last
   ● lefd
   ○ next

6. ○ have
   ○ set
   ● dest

☆ ● agen
   ○ apple
   ○ bath

☆ ○ bath
   ● nevir
   ○ asked

☆ ● sintence
   ○ apple
   ○ asked

77

---

1 Dictation

Reinforce correct spelling by using current and previous words in context.

(Say) Listen as I read each sentence and then write it in your Worktext.(Slowly read each sentence twice. Sentences are found in the Student Worktext to the left.)

☆ Challenge

Write these incomplete sentences on the board.

__ __ __ __ __ __.

Rosa __ __ __ __ __.

Try ___ write __ __.

(Say) Listen as I read each sentence. Write the sentence on your paper. (Slowly read each sentence twice.)

She will call for help again.

Rosa has never had a cat.

Try to write this sentence.

---

2 Proofreading

Familiarize students with standardized test format and reinforce recognizing misspelled words.

(Say) Look at each set of words. One word in each set is misspelled. Fill in the oval by the misspelled word. (You may wish to pronounce each set of words to help students correctly identify them.)

3 Hide and Seek

Reinforce correct spelling of current spelling words. (A reproducible master is provided in Appendix A as shown on the inset page to the right.)

Write the words one at a time on a white board.

Have students:

- **Look** at the word.
- **Say** the word out loud.
- **Spell** the word out loud.
- **Hide** (teacher erases word.)
- **Write** the word on paper.
- **Seek** (teacher rewrites word.)
- **Check** spelling. If incorrect, rewrite word correctly.

4 Making Words

Have your students complete this activity to strengthen spelling ability and expand vocabulary.

1 Posttest

Test mastery of the spelling words. Challenge words are starred.

(Say) I will say the word once, use the word in a sentence, then say the word again. Write the word on your paper.

Hide and Seek

Check a paper for each word you spell correctly.

1 3 5 7 9
2 4 6 8 10

Making Words

Add the endings to the spelling words. Write the new word in each sentence.

1. help + s — The Red Cross <u>helps</u> people.
2. set + s — Many <u>sets</u> of hands made cleaning up easier.
3. head + s — Hard hats protect their <u>heads</u>.
4. man → men — Some <u>men</u> fixed food for them.
5. help + ed — Tommy <u>helped</u> find the dog.
6. leg + s — The dog's <u>legs</u> are hurt.
7. nest + s — There were two <u>nests</u>.
8. help + ing — Tommy had fun <u>helping</u> others.
9. ever + y — God cares about <u>every</u> person.

369

---

1. **best** — Tommy made the **best** choice when he decided to help.
2. **ever** — Have you **ever** seen a place that a tornado has hit?
3. **left** — The Rawson family **left** for Center City early in the morning.
4. **men** — Many **men** helped clean up the mess the tornado left.
5. **head** — Mr. Culpepper's **head** was covered with thick black hair.
6. **nest** — This old bird's **nest** blew out of the tree.
7. **help** — Tommy and his young friends were able to **help**.
8. **leg** — This dog has a cast on his broken **leg**.
9. **next** — A lady with a little boy hiding behind her was **next** in line.
10. **set** — James **set** the dog food down in the warehouse.
☆ **never** — The little boy was afraid he would **never** find his dog.
☆ **again** — Honey, the dog, was happy to see the little boy **again**.
☆ **sentence** — What kind of mark is at the end of this **sentence**?

Progress Chart
Students may record scores. (Reproducible master in Appendix B.)

Personal Dictionary
Students may add any words they have misspelled to their personal dictionaries for reference when writing. (Cover in Appendix B.)

84

I | Game

Name _____

Tommy, Daniel, and James will carry the supplies for the families and pets of Center City into the warehouse. You lead the way by moving one space each time you or your team spells a word correctly from this week's word list.

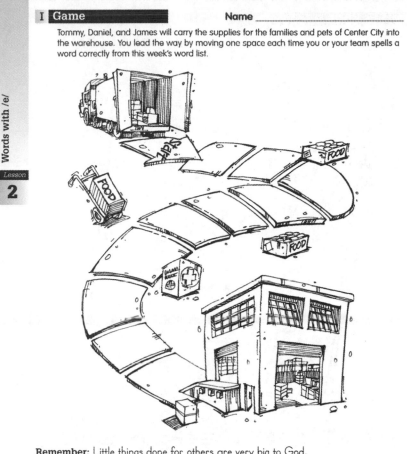

Remember: Little things done for others are very big to God.

J | Journaling

Draw a picture in your journal of something you did to help someone else that made you feel great. Label your picture.

78

Words with /e/

Lesson 2

How to Play:

- Divide students into two teams, and decide which team will go first.
- Have each student place their game piece on Start.
- Have a student from team A go to the board.
- Read the spelling word two times slowly and clearly. (You may also wish to use the word in a sentence. Ex.: "cat — The cat climbed a tree. — cat")
- Have the student write the word on the board.
- If the word is spelled correctly, instruct all the members of team A to move their game piece forward one space on the game board. (Note: If the word is misspelled, correct the spelling immediately.)
- Alternate between teams A and B as you go down the word list.
- The team to reach the warehouse first is the winner.

Non-Competitive Option: At the end of the game, say: "Class, I am proud of your efforts to spell the words correctly. If you had fun and tried your best, you are all winners!"

2 | Game

Reinforce spelling skills and provide motivation and interest.

Materials

- game page (from student text)
- flat buttons, dry beans, pennies, or game discs (1 per child)
- game word list

Game Word List

Use of challenge words is optional.

1. **best**
2. **nest**
3. **ever**
4. **help**
5. **left**
6. **leg**
7. **me**
8. **next**
9. **head**
10. **set**
☆ **again**
☆ **never**
☆ **sentence**

3 | Journaling

Provide a meaningful reason for correct spelling through personal writing.

Review the story using discussion leads provided on the following page. Encourage students to apply the Scriptural value in their journaling.

Take a minute to memorize . . .

Have the students say the memory verses from lessons 1 and 2 with you.

Day 5 | Lesson 2

85

Lesson 2 **Day 5**

Provide a meaningful reason for correct spelling through personal writing.

(Say)

- The people of Center City needed help because the tornado destroyed so much of their town. Can you think of some other times when a whole community might need help? (Floods, fire, earthquakes, hurricanes, sickness, etc.)

- Sometimes people get lost and others form groups to search for them. Why do you think the Scripture says that your care for others is the measure of your greatness?

- Tommy helped the little boy find his lost dog, Honey. Do you think what Tommy did was great? Why or why not?

- Think of a time when you did something to help someone else and felt great about it.

- In your journal, draw a picture of what you did and then label it.

> **"A major need for inventive spellers is to have someone answer their questions and correct their mistakes."***

*Lutz, Elaine. 1986. ERIC/RCS Report: Invented Spelling and Spelling Development. Language Arts, Vol. 63, No. 7, November: 742-744.

86

A Question of Quickness

*When Daniel ends up in the hospital, Beth wishes she'd
tried to solve their disagreement more quickly.*

"*L*ast one to the teeter-totters
is it!" Daniel yelled to the four children
coming out the classroom door behind
him.

Stephen, Beth, Matthew, and Tony
raced Daniel across the playground to
the three teeter-totters. Beth touched the
end of the red teeter-totter just ahead of
Tony and Stephen.

"You got a head start," Daniel
complained as he ran up behind
Matthew. "It's not fair! And I didn't
want to play tag anyway!"

"Oh, you just don't want to be it!"
Beth accused. "You're a quitter! You
quit if you don't win. You quit if you
don't get your way. You were ahead of
all of us when we walked out the door.
Now you're quitting because I won!"

"No, I just don't feel like playing
tag. We did that yesterday." Daniel
frowned as he looked around the
playground. "Let's swing, instead."

Beth and Tony followed Daniel
over to the two swings that were left.
Daniel sat down in one and grabbed the
chain of the other one. "This one's for
Tony!" Daniel yelled as he pulled the
swing out of Beth's reach.

"You can't save swings," Beth said.
She tried to pull the swing from Daniel's
hand, but Tony sat down in it before she
could yank it away.

"You're a quitter and a spoiled brat,
too!" Beth stalked off to the teeter-
totters and sat down on the yellow one
in disgust. Katelynn came over and Beth
lowered the other end of the teeter-totter
so Katelynn could climb on easily.
"Daniel is sure in a bad mood today,"
Beth said.

"Yeah, I saw him keep you from
getting the swing," Katelynn agreed.
"He can be so obnoxious." The girls

teetered back and forth a few times
without talking.

"I guess he's mad 'cause I beat him
in a race," Beth explained from her
perch on the high end of the teeter-totter.
"He sure doesn't like to lose."

"He's the one who wanted to race. I
heard him yell, 'Last one to the teeter-
totter is it,' when I came out the door,"
Katelynn said.

"Yeah," Beth looked up at Katelynn
now from the low end of the teeter-
totter. "He's been acting weird all day."

"Who's been acting weird?" Daniel
jumped from behind a tree and on to
Katelynn's end of the teeter-totter. His
weight slammed the teeter-totter into the
ground with a hard bang and almost shot
Beth off the end into the air.

"Only two on a teeter-totter!" Beth
screamed, clinging to the handle to keep
her balance. "Stop it, you little creep!"

"Make me!" Daniel mocked her.

"Okay, I will!" Beth let go of the
handle, so she could scoot down toward
Daniel.

But just as she let go, Daniel
jumped off Katelynn's end, and Beth's
end shot down towards the ground. She
bounced off the teeter-totter backwards
and bumped her head. Then suddenly,
her end flew back up into the air, and
Katelynn's end crashed down, whacking
Daniel on the way.

Beth sat up holding her head
between her hands. "Mrs. Morgan! Mrs.
Morgan!" she screamed.

Katelynn ran over and put her arm
around her friend. "Daniel is going to
get in trouble for this!" They both turned
and looked for Daniel, only to see his
crumpled form on the ground. "He's
probably faking so he won't get in so
much trouble," Katelynn said. Beth

stood up and the girls walked
around the teeter-totter to take a
closer look. "Oooh! The teeter-
totter must have hit him on the
head!" Katelynn cried. "Look,
he's bleeding!"

Mrs. Morgan hurried over to
the group of gathering children.
"What happened here?" she asked.

"I think the teeter-totter hit
him on the head," Beth explained.
"He was breaking the rules."

"Go into the office, Matthew,
and tell Mrs. Bentley to call 911,"
Mrs. Morgan instructed. "Hurry!"

It wasn't long before the loud
wail of a siren could be heard
coming closer and closer to the
school. It pulled up right onto the
playground. Two attendants
jumped out with a backboard and
carefully moved Daniel onto the
flat board and strapped him down.
Daniel never made a sound or moved a
muscle.

"Will he be okay?" Mrs. Morgan
asked.

"You never know with head
injuries," the ambulance attendant
replied. "It looks like he got knocked
pretty hard."

Mrs. Morgan led the rest of her
subdued class back into the classroom.
The afternoon seemed to drag. Everyone
was worried about Daniel. He had
looked so pale and quiet on the
backboard.

Mrs. Hill came early to pick Beth
up for her piano lesson in town. "Mom,
can we go by the hospital after piano
lessons?" Beth slid into the front seat
and buckled her seat belt.

"Why?" Mrs. Hill was curious.

"Daniel was being mean to me on
the playground today. He lied and said I
got a head start in a race I won. He kept
me from getting a swing that I got to
before Tony. Then he bounced me off the
teeter-totter that Katelynn and I were
on and made me hit my head."

"You must feel angry at him,"
Mom observed. "But what does this
have to do with the hospital?"

"Well, that's not the worst part,"
Beth continued. "When I fell
off, the teeter-totter hit

87

Daniel in the head. He never woke up. They took him to the hospital. Mrs. Morgan called the hospital a few minutes ago, but he's still not awake! He got a pretty hard bonk on the head!" Beth paused and looked down. "I wasn't very nice to him, either. I told him he was a quitter. I called him a spoiled brat and said he was a creep, too. What if he never wakes up? The last words he ever heard were 'you creep.'" Slow tears began to spill down Beth's face.

"Bethy, let's go see if your piano teacher can give you a lesson later this week, then head on over to the hospital," Mom said. "You've had a rough day, but it sounds like Daniel's having a worse one."

Beth continued to cry. "Our text this week in spelling class was 'Come to terms quickly before it is t-t-too l-l-l-late.'" Beth sobbed, "and I didn't do that quick enough." She turned a tear-stained face toward her mother, "Daniel is nice sometimes. Remember when he invited our whole class over to swim in his pool? What if he never wakes up? I'll never be able to tell him I'm sorry."

"Jesus loves you no matter what you do, Bethy. He told us to come to terms quickly because he knows how bad it can make us feel when we are angry at someone for a long time. It's always best to solve a problem as quickly as you can."

When they reached the hospital a few minutes later, a hospital volunteer directed Beth and her mom to Daniel's private room. He was propped up with pillows and was looking out the window. There was a large white bandage wrapped around his head. Beth was so surprised to see him awake, she almost forgot what she wanted to say.

"You're my first visitor. My mom and dad are on another trip." Daniel reached up to pat his bandaged head gingerly. "Guess I got what I had coming with all these stitches. I wasn't very nice to you today, Beth — I'm sorry." Daniel frowned, then laughed. "I guess I just get so

mad because you win all the time. You're so quick!"

"That's okay. I'm just so glad you woke up!" Beth sighed with relief. "You looked awful out there with blood all over your head, and when you didn't move, we were all really scared! I wasn't very nice to you, either. I called you some mean names. I'm sorry too, Daniel."

"Sounds like you two just solved a few problems," Mom smiled.

"I'm glad I had a second chance to come to terms," Beth grinned. "Next time I'll try to be quicker!"

Daniel laughed. "And I thought you were pretty quick already!"

Discussion Time

Check understanding of the story and development of personal values.

- Raise your hand if you think Daniel was being safe on the playground?
- Who have you seen get hurt at school?
- What did Daniel do that was not kind?
- What did Beth say that was not kind?
- What could Beth have said to help solve the problem quickly?
- What did Beth's mom tell her Jesus meant when He said to come to terms quickly?

Day 1

Lesson 3

88

A Preview

Write each word as your teacher says it.

Name _____

1. begin
2. quit
3. been
4. kid
5. into
6. digit
7. its
8. give
9. live
10. sister

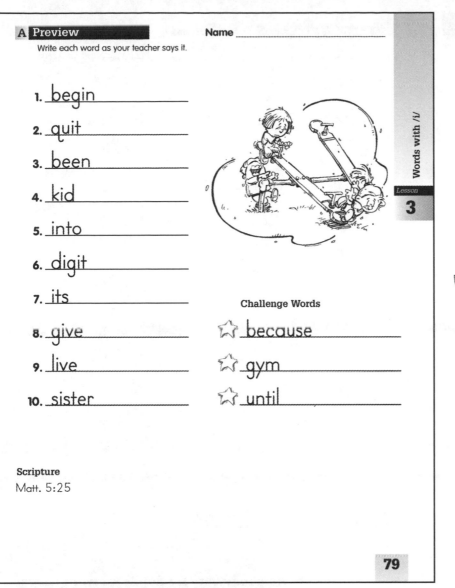

Words with /i/

Lesson 3

Challenge Words

 because

 gym

 until

Scripture
Matt. 5:25

79

 Challenge

For better spellers, challenge words may be included in the weekly list. Challenge words are starred.

Correct Immediately!

Let's correct our preview. I will write each word on the board. Put a dot under each letter on your preview as I spell the word out loud. If you spelled a word wrong, rewrite it correctly.

Progress Chart

Students may record scores. (Reproducible master in Appendix B.)

 **Take a minute to memorize . . .**

Read the memory verse twice. Have students practice it with you two more times.

---

3 Preview

Test for knowledge of the correct spellings of these words. (See the instructions at the top right for challenge words.)

 I will say each word once, use the word in a sentence, then say the word again. Write the word on the lines in the Worktext.

1.	begin	Let's **begin** by being kind to each other.
2.	quit	"You **quit** if you don't win!" accused Beth.
3.	been	"He's **been** acting weird all day." said Beth.
4.	kid	Don't bother the **kid** because he's having a bad day.
5.	into	The teeter-totter slammed **into** the ground.
6.	digit	Dial the **digit** "9" first in an emergency.
7.	its	The backboard is orange and **its** straps are black.
8.	give	Bethy, lets go see if your piano teacher can **give** you a lesson.
9.	live	It is a good idea to "**live** in peace with each other."
10.	sister	Beth does not have a **sister**.
☆	because	They took Daniel to the hospital **because** he was hurt.
☆	gym	We played on the playground, not in the **gym** today.
☆	until	Don't wait **until** it is too late.

Help students form a correct image of whole words.

(Say) Look at each word and think about its shape. Now, write the word in the correct word Shape Boxes. You may check off each word as you use it.

(In many words /i/ is spelled with **i**, and it is often spelled this way when it is at the beginning or in the middle of a word.)

(Say) In the word Shape Boxes, color the letter or letters that spell the sound of /i/ in each word. Circle the word in which the sound of /i/ is not spelled with **i**.

⭐ **Challenge**
Draw the correctly shaped box around each letter in these words.

(Say) On a separate sheet of paper, write other words that contain the spelling patterns in the word list. See how many words you can write.

📝 **Be Prepared For Fun**

Check these supply lists for **Fun Ways to Spell** presented **Day 2**. Purchase and/or gather these items ahead of time!

Day 1

Lesson 3

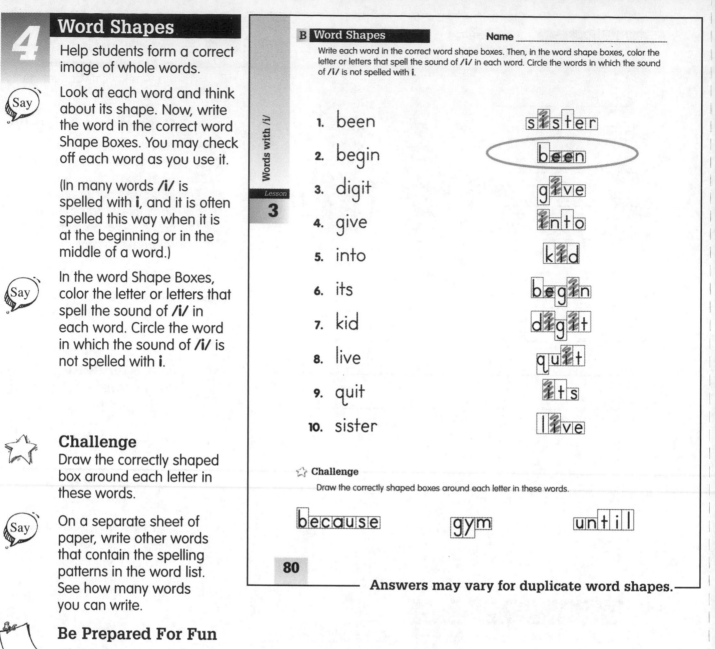

B Word Shapes

Name _____

Write each word in the correct word shape boxes. Then, in the word shape boxes, color the letter or letters that spell the sound of /i/ in each word. Circle the words in which the sound of /i/ is not spelled with i.

Words with /i/
Lesson 3

1. been
2. begin
3. digit
4. give
5. into
6. its
7. kid
8. live
9. quit
10. sister

☆ **Challenge**
Draw the correctly shaped boxes around each letter in these words.

because   gym   until

80

Answers may vary for duplicate word shapes.

General
- 3 x 5 Cards (10 per child)
- 3 x 5 Cards (3 more to spell challenge words)
- Scissors
- Spelling List

Auditory
- A Classmate
- Spelling List

Visual
- Strips of paper 2 x 11 inches (10 per student)
- Strips of paper 2 x 11 inches (3 more to spell challenge words)
- Crayons or Markers
- Tape
- Spelling List

Tactile
- Split Peas
- Glue
- Construction Paper
- Spelling List

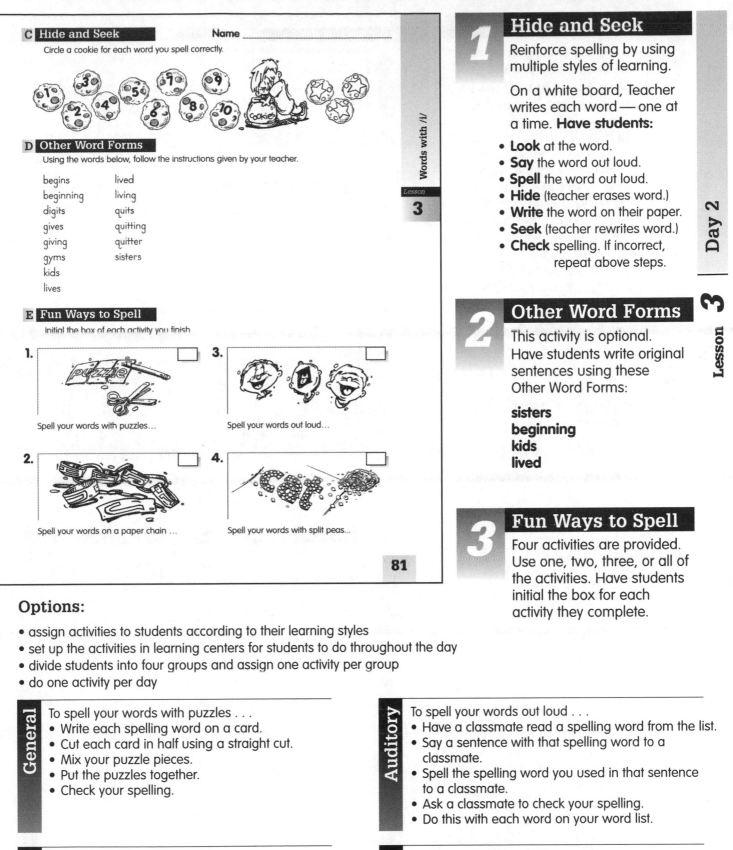

C Hide and Seek

Name _____

Circle a cookie for each word you spell correctly.

D Other Word Forms

Using the words below, follow the instructions given by your teacher.

begins	lived
beginning	living
digits	quits
gives	quitting
giving	quitter
gyms	sisters
kids	
lives	

E Fun Ways to Spell

Initial the box of each activity you finish.

1. Spell your words with puzzles…

3. Spell your words out loud…

2. Spell your words on a paper chain …

4. Spell your words with split peas…

Words with /i/

Lesson **3**

81

---

1 Hide and Seek

Reinforce spelling by using multiple styles of learning.

On a white board, Teacher writes each word — one at a time. **Have students:**

- **Look** at the word.
- **Say** the word out loud.
- **Spell** the word out loud.
- **Hide** (teacher erases word.)
- **Write** the word on their paper.
- **Seek** (teacher rewrites word.)
- **Check** spelling. If incorrect, repeat above steps.

Day 2

2 Other Word Forms

This activity is optional. Have students write original sentences using these Other Word Forms:

**sisters
beginning
kids
lived**

Lesson 3

3 Fun Ways to Spell

Four activities are provided. Use one, two, three, or all of the activities. Have students initial the box for each activity they complete.

Options:

- assign activities to students according to their learning styles
- set up the activities in learning centers for students to do throughout the day
- divide students into four groups and assign one activity per group
- do one activity per day

General

To spell your words with puzzles . . .
- Write each spelling word on a card.
- Cut each card in half using a straight cut.
- Mix your puzzle pieces.
- Put the puzzles together.
- Check your spelling.

Auditory

To spell your words out loud . . .
- Have a classmate read a spelling word from the list.
- Say a sentence with that spelling word to a classmate.
- Spell the spelling word you used in that sentence to a classmate.
- Ask a classmate to check your spelling.
- Do this with each word on your word list.

Visual

To spell your words on a paper chain . . .
- Write each spelling word on a strip of paper in big, tall letters.
- Tape the ends of one strip together to make a circle.
- Loop the next strip through the first and then tape the ends of that strip together.
- Continue in this way to form a paper chain.

Tactile

To spell your words with split peas . . .
- Choose a word from your spelling list.
- It may be a favorite word or a word you have trouble remembering how to spell.
- Write the word in tall, wide letters on a sheet of construction paper.
- Spread glue along the outline of each letter and press split peas into the glue.

91

Word Change

Familiarize students with word meaning and usage.

Write **Two boys with the same parents are in the class.** on the board. Ask the students to stand up if they can think of one word that means the same as **two boys with the same parents.** Choose a student who is standing to come up and write the word he or she is thinking of on the board. If there are different ideas, discuss which ones don't change the meaning of the sentence (brothers or twins).

Say

Replace the underlined word in each sentence with a spelling word that has the same meaning.

F Word Change   Name _____

Write spelling words in place of the underlined word or words.

Words with /i/

Lesson **3**

1. digit ____ The <u>number</u> you need to dial first is 9.
2. kid ____ Daniel is a nice <u>child</u> sometimes.
3. sister ____ Luke's <u>girl</u> <u>with</u> <u>the</u> <u>same</u> <u>parents</u> is Beth.
4. into ____ Beth went <u>inside</u> the hospital to see Daniel.
5. been ____ Have you <u>gone</u> to see Daniel?
6. its ____ Daniel has a bandage and <u>the</u> <u>bandage's</u> color is white.
7. give ____ The class will <u>hand</u> <u>over</u> a card to Daniel.
8. quit ____ <u>Stop</u> saying mean things to each other!
9. begin ____ Let's <u>start</u> by being kind to each other.
10. live ____ <u>Dwell</u> in peace with each other.
☆ until ____ They weren't nice to each other <u>before</u> Daniel got hurt.
☆ because Please glue this <u>since</u> it's broken.
☆ gym ____ The class didn't go to the <u>play</u> <u>area</u> today.

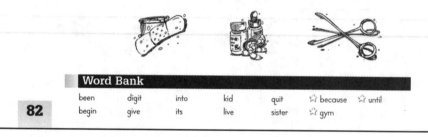

Word Bank

been	digit	into	kid	quit	☆ because	☆ until
begin	give	its	live	sister	☆ gym	

82

Take a minute to memorize...

Read the memory verse twice. Have students practice it with you two more times.

92

G Dictation

Listen and write the missing words.

Name _____

1. <u>The calf has been calling for</u>
<u>its mother.</u>

2. <u>My sister will begin</u> piano
lessons soon.

3. Stephen <u>quit</u> going <u>into the</u> room.

H Proofreading

One word in each set is misspelled. Fill in the oval by the misspelled word.

1. ● sistir
   ○ give
   ○ its

2. ○ kid
   ○ last
   ● beegin

3. ○ men
   ● kwit
   ○ best

4. ● deen
   ○ live
   ○ next

5. ○ head
   ● intoo
   ○ ever

6. ● dijit
   ○ set
   ○ help

☆ ● jym
   ○ never
   ○ apple

☆ ○ sentence
   ● untill
   ○ bath

☆ ○ again
   ○ asked
   ● beecuz

83

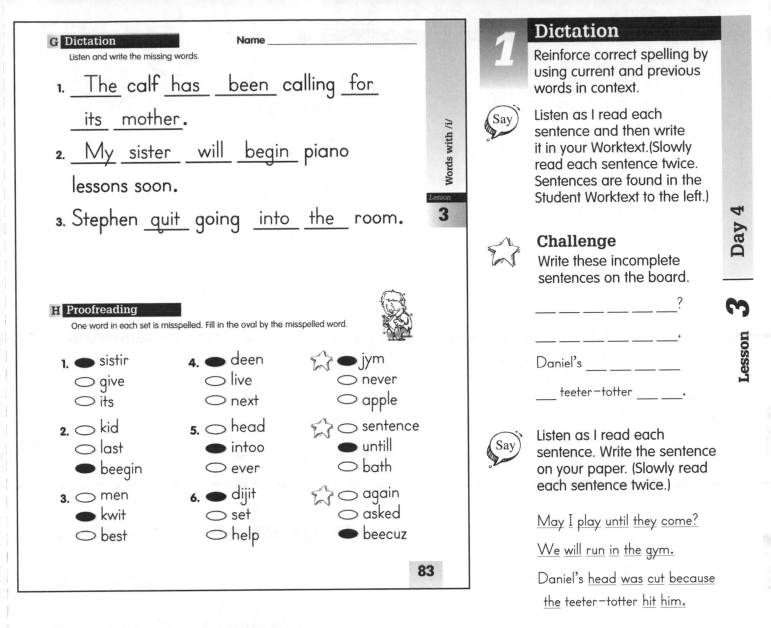

---

1 Dictation

Reinforce correct spelling by using current and previous words in context.

(Say) Listen as I read each sentence and then write it in your Worktext.(Slowly read each sentence twice. Sentences are found in the Student Worktext to the left.)

☆ **Challenge**
Write these incomplete sentences on the board.

__ __ __ __ __ __ __ ?

__ __ __ __ __ __ __ .

Daniel's __ __ __ __ __

__ teeter—totter __ __ .

(Say) Listen as I read each sentence. Write the sentence on your paper. (Slowly read each sentence twice.)

<u>May</u> <u>I</u> <u>play</u> <u>until</u> <u>they</u> <u>come</u>?

<u>We</u> <u>will</u> <u>run</u> <u>in</u> <u>the</u> <u>gym</u>.

Daniel's <u>head</u> <u>was</u> <u>cut</u> <u>because</u>
the teeter—totter <u>hit</u> <u>him</u>.

Lesson **3** | Day 4

2 Proofreading

Familiarize students with standardized test format and reinforce recognizing misspelled words.

(Say) Look at each set of words. One word in each set is misspelled. Fill in the oval by the misspelled word. (You may wish to pronounce each set of words to help students correctly identify them.)

3 Hide and Seek

Reinforce correct spelling of current spelling words. (A reproducible master is provided in Appendix A as shown on the inset page to the right.)

Write the words one at a time on a white board.

Have students:

- **Look** at the word.
- **Say** the word out loud.
- **Spell** the word out loud.
- **Hide** (teacher erases word.)
- **Write** the word on paper.
- **Seek** (teacher rewrites word.)
- **Check** spelling. If incorrect, rewrite word correctly.

4 Secret Words

Have your students complete this activity to strengthen spelling ability and expand vocabulary.

1 Posttest

Test mastery of the spelling words. Challenge words are starred.

(Say) I will say the word once, use the word in a sentence, then say the word again. Write the word on your paper.

Hide and Seek
Check a paper for each word you spell correctly.

1 3 5 7 9
2 4 6 8 10

Secret Words
Use these clues to find the words that fit in the blanks. Then use the boxed letters to discover the secret words.

1. d i g i t s
2. b e g i n n i n g
3. s i s t e r s
4. g y m s
5. k i d s

1. numbers
2. start
3. two girls with the same Mom and Dad
4. buildings for indoor play
5. children

6. choosing to share
7. gives up
8. to be alive
9. first letter of the alphabet
10. one that quits
11. starts

6. g i v i n g
7. q u i t s

8. l i v i n g
9. a
10. q u i t t e r
11. b e g i n s

Come to t e r m s quickly before it i s too l a t e.

Word Bank

beginning	digits	gyms	living	quitter
begins	giving	kids	quits	sisters

370

1. sister — Luke has a **sister** named Beth Hill.
2. kid — The **kid** could have been nicer to her classmate.
3. been — They have **been** fighting all week.
4. begin — You must **begin** to get along better.
5. its — The teeter-totter is old and **its** paint is peeling off.
6. into — You get **into** trouble when you don't follow playground rules.
7. quit — You must **quit** fighting right now.
8. digit — What **digit** do I dial first in an emergency?
9. give — The nurse had to **give** Daniel a shot for pain.
10. live — You will be happier if you **live** in peace.
☆ because — The accident happened **because** Daniel broke the rules.
☆ gym — It is nice to play in the **gym** when the playground is wet.
☆ until — Don't wait **until** someone is hurt to be kind.

Progress Chart
Students may record scores. (Reproducible master in Appendix B.)

Personal Dictionary
Students may add any words they have misspelled to their personal dictionaries for reference when writing. (Cover in Appendix B.)

94

I Game

Name _____

Help Beth take a big bunch of balloons to Daniel at the hospital. Draw one string in Beth's hand (and place a balloon at the top) each time you or your team spells a word correctly from this week's word list.

Remember: Solve your problems with others quickly.

J Journaling

Draw a picture in your journal of some playground equipment you enjoy. Write two safety rules underneath the picture.

84

How to Play:

- Divide students into two teams, and decide which team will go first.
- Have a student from team A go to the board.
- Read the spelling word two times slowly and clearly. (You may also wish to use the word in a sentence. Ex.: "cat — The cat climbed a tree. — cat")
- Have the student write the word on the board.
- If the word is spelled correctly, instruct all the members of team A to draw one balloon on a string in Beth's hand. (Note: If the word is misspelled, correct the spelling immediately.)
- Alternate between teams A and B as you go down the word list.
- The team with the most balloons when you have gone through the word list twice is the winner.

Non-Competitive Option: At the end of the game, say: "Class, I am proud of your efforts to spell the words correctly. If you had fun and tried your best, you are all winners!"

2 Game

Reinforce spelling skills and provide motivation and interest.

Materials

- game page (from student text)
- pencils (1 per child)
- game word list

Game Word List

Use of challenge words is optional.

1. **been**
2. **begin**
3. **into**
4 **digit**
5. **quit**
6. **give**
7. **live**
8. **its**
9. **kid**
10. **sister**
☆ **until**
☆ **because**
☆ **gym**

3 Journaling

Provide a meaningful reason for correct spelling through personal writing.

Review the story using discussion leads provided on the following page. Encourage students to apply the Scriptural value in their journaling.

 Take a minute to memorize . . .

Have students say the memory verses from lessons 1, 2, and 3 with you.

Provide a meaningful reason for correct spelling through personal writing.

(Say)

- What was the problem between Beth and Daniel on the playground? (Beth won the race to the teeter-totters. Daniel lost the race even though he had a head start.)

- What did Beth say that made the problem worse? (She called him a quitter if he didn't win. A quitter if he didn't get his way. A quitter because she won.)

- Daniel tried to aggravate Beth more by saving a swing for Tony so Beth couldn't use it. Did Beth finally give up and try to solve the problem quickly? (No.)

- What did she do? (She called Daniel a quitter and a spoiled brat, then went to the teeter-totters.)

- What did Daniel do a few minutes later? (He jumped on and off the teeter-totter when Beth and Katelynn were already on it.)

- Why was that not safe for Daniel to do? (He could hurt himself or others.)

- Draw a picture in your journal of some equipment at your school you like to play on. Think of two rules that keep you safe while you play on it.

My Journal

Quotables!

"When young writers are free to concentrate on what they want to say rather than mechanics, their thoughts can flow more freely." *

*Wilde, Sandra. 1990. A Proposal for a New Spelling Curriculum. The Elementary School Journal, Vol. 90, No. 3, January: 275-289.

To Live in Peace

Rachel gets a new look and a new understanding of her stepmother — all because of bubble gum!

Rachel rolled the big wad of bubble gum around in her mouth to make a ball, then carefully flattened it behind her teeth so she could blow a huge bubble. "Mmmmm! Mmmmm!" Rachel said through her nose to get her stepsister's attention. Then she kicked Vanessa's foot.

"Ouch!" Vanessa yelled. As she swung around in the back seat of the van to look at Rachel, Vanessa's elbow hit the sticky round ball and popped the enormous bubble Rachel had blown.

"Ooh. Yucky! It's on my elbow! It's all over your face! How are you ever gonna get it all off?" Vanessa moaned. "There's even some in your hair! My mom is really going to kill you!"

"Who am I going to kill?" Mrs. Jacobson asked from the front of the van.

"Rachel," Vanessa volunteered. "Her bubble gum is all over her face and my elbow."

"Rachel, are you chewing the whole pack of gum again?" Mrs. Jacobson asked. "It makes such a mess if it gets on the van, not to mention you." Rachel's new stepmother frowned. "Where do you get the stuff?"

"Daddy," Rachel said in a flat voice.

Rachel took what was left of the bubble gum out of her mouth and started to pat it across her face. "She's putting more on her face, Mom!" Vanessa yelled. "Stop the van! Rachel's gone crazy!"

Rachel looked out the window and continued to pat the sticky gum around her mouth and across her cheek toward her ear. It did an amazingly good job of taking the thin layer of the bubble off her face. Her hair was a different matter though. "Do we have any peanut butter at the house?" Rachel asked. She couldn't call it home yet. No place seemed like home without Mommy to greet her at the door.

"Yes, Rachel. I think we do. Why?" came the answer from the front.

"Because," Rachel said sullenly.

"Why does she want peanut butter?" Mrs. Jacobson asked, looking at Rachel's twelve-year-old sister, Rebecca, sitting beside her in the van.

"It helps to get gum out. My mommy was an expert at getting gum out. She liked to chew gum before she got so sick with cancer," Rebecca explained to her stepmother. "I think she liked it as much as we do."

Three hours later Rachel rushed up the stairs to the bedroom she shared with Rebecca and flopped across her striped bedspread. It felt funny when her dark hair didn't fall across her face to hide her tears. "My mommy could have gotten the gum out! Helen didn't even try very hard!" she wailed.

Helen Jacobson had used peanut butter, ice, and even mayonnaise to try to untangle the gooey mess from her stepdaughter's hair. Finally, in frustration, she'd taken Rachel to a nearby beauty salon and told them to cut her hair in a style that would get rid of the sticky mass.

"I don't like Helen! Just look at my hair!" Rachel sat up and looked in the mirror. "I look like a different person. Everyone at this new school is just beginning to recognize me with long dark hair!" Rachel flung herself back across the bed and cried into her pillow.

"Mommy used to say, 'You can talk to Jesus about any problem any time, Rache.' Dear Jesus," Rachel prayed into her pillow, "I really don't like Helen. She is not my mommy! No one can take my mommy's place. Helen is not my mommy! And she cut my hair! I can hardly remember what Mommy looked like any more. I have to look at her picture to remember what color her eyes were or how her mouth curved when she smiled at me! I miss her, Jesus."

Rebecca walked into the bedroom and plopped down beside her sobbing younger sister on the bed. "I like your hair, Rachel." She rubbed Rachel's back gently.

Rachel lifted her tear-streaked face from the pillows. "Can you remember how Mommy smiled without looking at her picture, Becka?"

"Yeah, but I was nine when she died. You were only four," Rebecca said softly. "Mommy is the one who taught you how to blow a bubble. Do you remember?"

"Yeah, right after my fourth birthday. No one could believe I could do it. Mommy was so proud of me. "

"She loved to chew gum, Rachel. Father always teased her about it. He said he had chewed enough when he was a child to last a lifetime. I really miss Mommy! But I don't think of her every day like I used to — just like the counselor told us. You need to realize that Helen is not trying to be cruel to you. She isn't really a wicked stepmother. She just isn't a gum expert like Mommy was." Rebecca reached over and tousled her younger sister's short hair. "Besides, your hair really does look cute."

The next morning Rosa Vasquez called across the parking lot at school, "Hey, Rachel, wait up." Six-year-old Rosa ran to catch up with her friend. "You got a haircut! I like it."

"Thanks," Rachel said with a smile.

A few minutes later as Rachel bent over to put her books into her desk, Mrs. Morgan walked up. "Oh, Rachel, your hair is so cute. It

97

looks great short!"

Later that morning Rosa slid into the seat beside Rachel in the school van. "What made you decide to cut your hair, Rachel?"

"Oh, it's Helen again. Vanessa bumped me and popped a huge bubble on the way home from school. Helen couldn't get it out."

"Hey, you guys!" Mrs. Morgan poked her head into the van. "Remember what we talked about. When we get to the day-care center, I want you all to line up on the sidewalk as soon as you get out of the van. Did everyone bring a favorite book to read to a child?" The students waved their books in the air to show Mrs. Morgan.

When they arrived at the day-care center, Mrs. Morgan assigned two children to each of her students.

"Come on, Benji and Adam," Rachel coaxed the four-year-old boys. "Let's go under this tree to read our book. It's about two little frogs."

"I'm not going with Adam!" Benji declared. "He's mean."

"I'm not mean!" Adam kicked at the gravel under the swings.

"It's not all gone! Why won't you share your gum with me? You have a lot left!"

"That's becau . . ."

"Boys," Rachel interrupted. "Do you know what Jesus says about the way you are acting?" The two boys stopped arguing long enough to look at Rachel and shake their heads no. "My teacher told us this morning about a text that says, 'Live in peace with each other.'"

"Does that mean Adam should give me a piece of gum?" Benji asked.

"That might be a good idea, but you need to wait to chew it until you get home. You probably aren't supposed to chew gum here at the day-care center."

"That's what I've been trying to tell him!" Adam said in exasperation. "He can have two pieces of my gum on the way home. I just don't want us to get in trouble."

"Let's be kind to each other and 'live in peace' then!" Rachel pulled the two boys down beside her on the soft grass, and gave their hands a quick squeeze. "I want to read you a story about two frogs who were not living in peace."

On the way home from school that afternoon, Mrs. Jacobson stopped at the grocery store to pick up a few things for supper. Helen unfastened little Natalie from her booster seat and smiled over at Rachel. Rachel felt a little guilty for not smiling back. "Rebecca is right. Helen is not a bad stepmother. I need to live in peace with Helen like I told those two boys this afternoon," Rachel thought.

The four girls trailed behind Helen Jacobson through the automatic doors of the grocery store. As they passed all the gum and candy machines at the entrance to the store, Mrs. Jacobson paused and dug into her purse for some coins.

"Rachel, you are special to me," Mrs. Jacobson said as she pressed some coins into the palm of her stepdaughter's hand. "Why don't you get some bubble gum?"

"Helen wants to live in peace, too," Rachel thought as she headed toward the bright red machine that sold the really big pieces of bubble gum. "She's being nice to me even when I haven't been very nice to her!"

And suddenly Rachel stopped, and turned to smile at her stepmother. "Thanks for the gum, Mom." she said.

2 Discussion Time

Check understanding of the story and development of personal values.

- How do you feel if you are at peace? (Brainstorm. Write all responses on the board.)
- Have you ever felt like you didn't want to live in peace with someone?
- Why were the feelings between Rachel and her stepmother not very peaceful?
- How do you feel when you are angry at someone?
- Do you think it is good for you to be angry for a long time?
- Why do you think Jesus told us to, "Live in peace with each other?"
- Did you know Jesus is always ready to help you live in peace?

98

A Preview

Write each word as your teacher says it.

Name _____

1. lot
2. often
3. box
4. gone
5. soft
6. odd
7. lost
8. frog
9. dot
10. drop

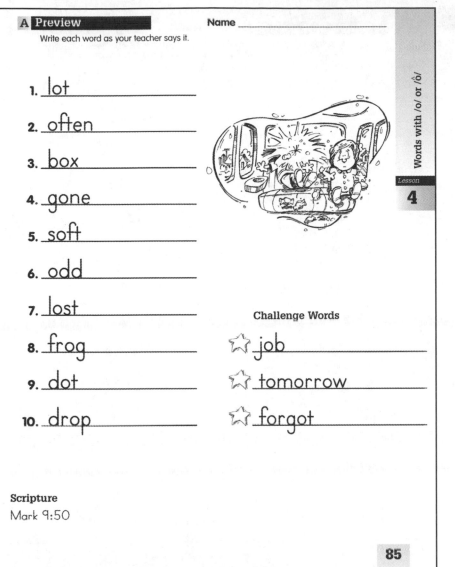

Challenge Words

☆ job
☆ tomorrow
☆ forgot

Scripture
Mark 9:50

85

Challenge

For better spellers, challenge words may be included in the weekly list. Challenge words are starred.

Correct Immediately!

Say

Let's correct our preview. I will write each word on the board. Put a dot under each letter on your preview as I spell the word out loud. If you spelled a word wrong, rewrite it correctly.

Progress Chart

Students may record scores. (Reproducible master in Appendix B.)

Take a minute to memorize . . .

Read the memory verse twice. Have students practice it with you two more times.

---

3 Preview

Test for knowledge of the correct spellings of these words. (See the instructions at the top right for challenge words.)

Say

I will say each word once, use the word in a sentence, then say the word again. Write the word on the lines in the Worktext.

1.	lot	Rachel liked to chew a **lot** of gum at once.
2.	often	How **often** do you like to chew gum?
3.	box	"Is that gum in the **box**?" asked Rachel.
4.	gone	Rachel's long hair was **gone.**
5.	soft	Rachel flung herself across the **soft** bed.
6.	odd	Does it feel **odd** to have your hair short?
7.	lost	Rachel **lost** her pack of gum.
8.	frog	In the story the **frog** was not happy.
9.	dot	That **dot** is called a period.
10.	drop	You must **drop** the money into the slot so gum will come out.
☆	job	It is Rachel's **job** to unbuckle Natalie from her car seat.
☆	tomorrow	Rosa and Rachel will still be friends **tomorrow.**
☆	forgot	Vanessa **forgot** to "live in peace" with Rachel.

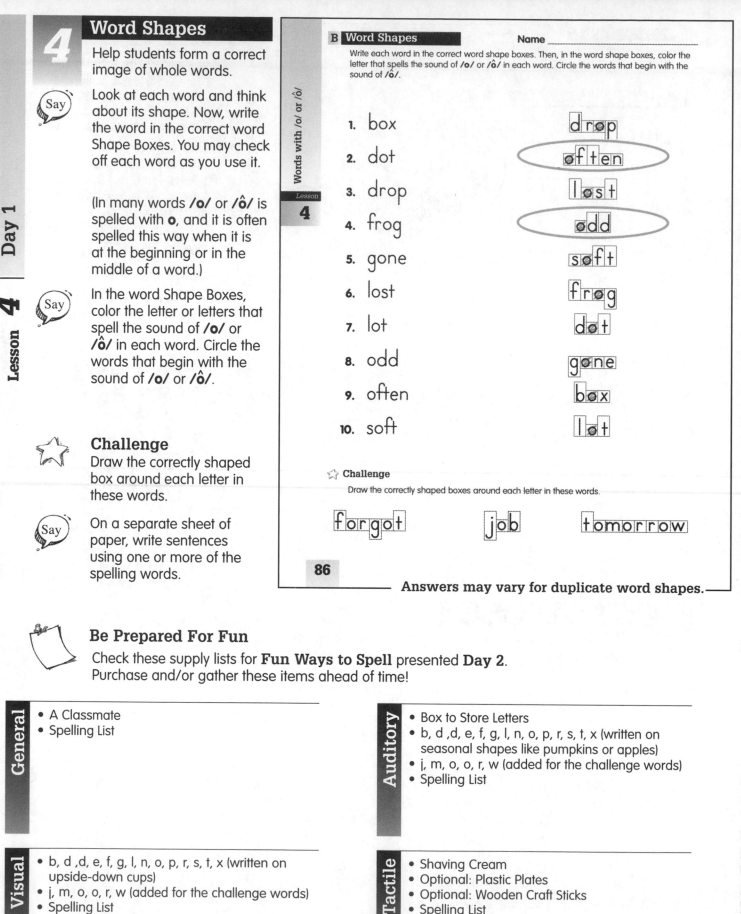

Word Shapes

4

Help students form a correct image of whole words.

Say Look at each word and think about its shape. Now, write the word in the correct word Shape Boxes. You may check off each word as you use it.

(In many words /o/ or /ô/ is spelled with **o**, and it is often spelled this way when it is at the beginning or in the middle of a word.)

Say In the word Shape Boxes, color the letter or letters that spell the sound of /o/ or /ô/ in each word. Circle the words that begin with the sound of /o/ or /ô/.

Challenge

Draw the correctly shaped box around each letter in these words.

Say On a separate sheet of paper, write sentences using one or more of the spelling words.

B Word Shapes Name _____

Write each word in the correct word shape boxes. Then, in the word shape boxes, color the letter that spells the sound of /o/ or /ô/ in each word. Circle the words that begin with the sound of /ô/.

Words with /o/ or /ô/

Lesson **4**

1. box
2. dot
3. drop
4. frog
5. gone
6. lost
7. lot
8. odd
9. often
10. soft

☆ **Challenge**
Draw the correctly shaped boxes around each letter in these words.

forgot   job   tomorrow

86

Answers may vary for duplicate word shapes.

Be Prepared For Fun

Check these supply lists for **Fun Ways to Spell** presented **Day 2**. Purchase and/or gather these items ahead of time!

General
- A Classmate
- Spelling List

Auditory
- Box to Store Letters
- b, d ,d, e, f, g, l, n, o, p, r, s, t, x (written on seasonal shapes like pumpkins or apples)
- j, m, o, o, r, w (added for the challenge words)
- Spelling List

Visual
- b, d ,d, e, f, g, l, n, o, p, r, s, t, x (written on upside-down cups)
- j, m, o, o, r, w (added for the challenge words)
- Spelling List

Tactile
- Shaving Cream
- Optional: Plastic Plates
- Optional: Wooden Craft Sticks
- Spelling List

100

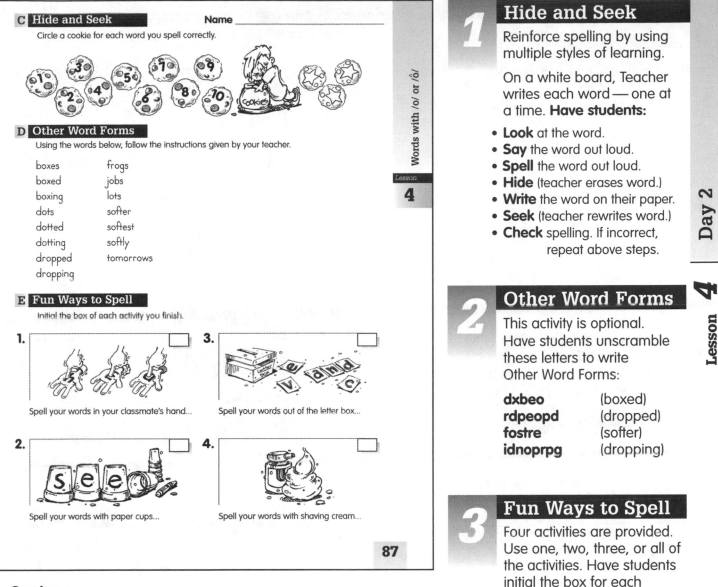

C Hide and Seek   Name _____

Circle a cookie for each word you spell correctly.

(cookies numbered 1–10)

D Other Word Forms

Using the words below, follow the instructions given by your teacher.

boxes	frogs
boxed	jobs
boxing	lots
dots	softer
dotted	softest
dotting	softly
dropped	tomorrows
dropping	

E Fun Ways to Spell

Initial the box of each activity you finish.

1. ☐

Spell your words in your classmate's hand...

3. ☐

Spell your words out of the letter box...

2. ☐

Spell your words with paper cups...

4. ☐

Spell your words with shaving cream...

87

Day 2

1 Hide and Seek

Reinforce spelling by using multiple styles of learning.

On a white board, Teacher writes each word — one at a time. **Have students:**

- **Look** at the word.
- **Say** the word out loud.
- **Spell** the word out loud.
- **Hide** (teacher erases word.)
- **Write** the word on their paper.
- **Seek** (teacher rewrites word.)
- **Check** spelling. If incorrect, repeat above steps.

Lesson 4

2 Other Word Forms

This activity is optional. Have students unscramble these letters to write Other Word Forms:

dxbeo	(boxed)
rdpeopd	(dropped)
fostre	(softer)
idnoprpg	(dropping)

3 Fun Ways to Spell

Four activities are provided. Use one, two, three, or all of the activities. Have students initial the box for each activity they complete.

Options:

- assign activities to students according to their learning styles
- set up the activities in learning centers for students to do throughout the day
- divide students into four groups and assign one activity per group
- do one activity per day

General

To spell your words in your classmate's hand . . .
- Have a classmate sit next to you and hold their palm open in front of, and facing both of you.
- Use fingertip to write a spelling word in the palm of a classmate's hand.
- Have a classmate say each letter as you write it and then say the word you spelled.
- Next, have a classmate write a word in your palm.

Auditory

To spell your words out of the letter box . . .
- Spell a word from your list by putting the letters in the right order.
- Check your spelling.
- Spell your word out loud.

Visual

To spell your words with paper cups . . .
- Spell a word from your list by putting the cups in the right order.
- Check your spelling.

Tactile

To spell your words with shaving cream . . .
- Spread a glob of shaving cream across your desk (or on a plastic plate).
- Use finger (or a wooden craft stick) to write a spelling word in the shaving cream.
- Check your spelling.
- Smear the word out with your fingers and write another.

101

1 Word Search

Familiarize students with word meaning and usage. Hide the name of your elementary school in a grid of letters on the board.

```
t       o   m       o
s   o   r   f   m   o   b
o   g   s   r   o   c
g   l   c   o   h   g   t
d   h   o   u   t   f
y   o       u       r
e   o   l   d   f   t   w
o   r   g   x       l
r
n   t
```

Write the name of your school beside the grid of letters. Explain that the words can go across or down. Ask for a volunteer to circle the name of your school hidden in the puzzle.

 Say In this activity your spelling words are hidden in the puzzle. They can go either across or down. Circle your spelling words.

F Word Search   Name _____

Using the word bank, Circle your spelling words in the puzzle. The words go across and down. Write each word in the correct blanks below.

```
t   o   m   o   r   r   o   w   z
b   o   f   r   o   g   b   l   o
o   g   l   d   f   t   d   o   d
x   o   f   o   r   g   o   t   d
e   d   d   t   x   o   f   l   x
w   r   g   x   f   n   t   o   s
s   o   f   t   p   e   e   s   o
x   p   t   t   o   r   n   t   r
d       i   j   o   b   d       w
```

Across

frog

soft

☆ tomorrow

☆ forgot

☆ job

Down

box

drop

dot

gone

often

lot

lost

odd

Word Bank

| box | drop | gone | lot | often | ☆ forgot | ☆ tomorrow |
| dot | frog | lost | odd | soft | ☆ job | |

 Take a minute to memorize...

Read the memory verse twice. Have students practice it with you two more times.

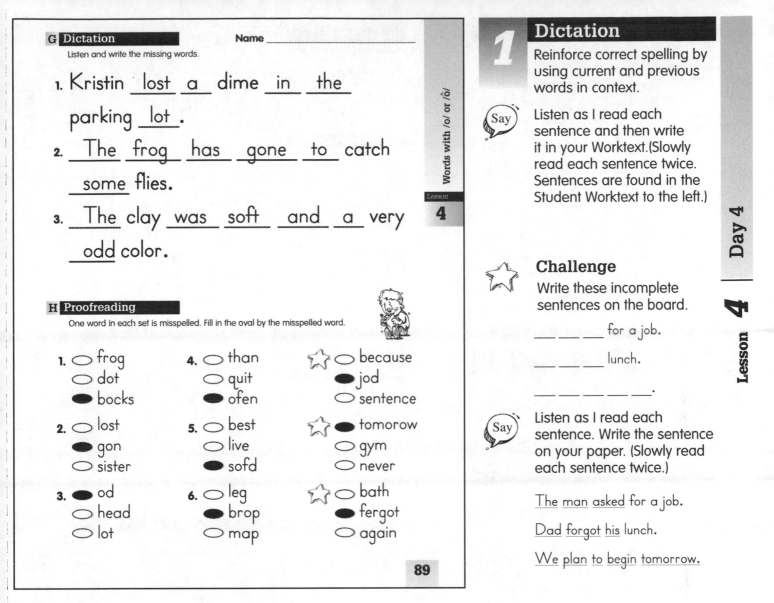

G Dictation

Listen and write the missing words.

Name _____

1. Kristin <u>lost</u> <u>a</u> dime <u>in</u> <u>the</u> parking <u>lot</u>.

2. <u>The</u> <u>frog</u> <u>has</u> <u>gone</u> <u>to</u> catch <u>some</u> flies.

3. <u>The</u> clay <u>was</u> <u>soft</u> <u>and</u> <u>a</u> very <u>odd</u> color.

Words with /o/ or /ô/

Lesson 4

H Proofreading

One word in each set is misspelled. Fill in the oval by the misspelled word.

1. ○ frog
   ○ dot
   ● bocks

2. ○ lost
   ● gon
   ○ sister

3. ● od
   ○ head
   ○ lot

4. ○ than
   ○ quit
   ● ofen

5. ○ best
   ○ live
   ● sofd

6. ○ leg
   ● brop
   ○ map

☆ ○ because
   ● jod
   ○ sentence

☆ ● tomorow
   ○ gym
   ○ never

☆ ○ bath
   ● fergot
   ○ again

89

1 Dictation

Reinforce correct spelling by using current and previous words in context.

Say) Listen as I read each sentence and then write it in your Worktext.(Slowly read each sentence twice. Sentences are found in the Student Worktext to the left.)

☆ Challenge

Write these incomplete sentences on the board.

___ ___ ___ for a job.

___ ___ lunch.

___ ___ ___ ___ ___ .

Say) Listen as I read each sentence. Write the sentence on your paper. (Slowly read each sentence twice.)

The <u>man</u> <u>asked</u> for a job.

<u>Dad</u> <u>forgot</u> <u>his</u> lunch.

<u>We</u> <u>plan</u> <u>to</u> <u>begin</u> <u>tomorrow.</u>

2 Proofreading

Familiarize students with standardized test format and reinforce recognizing misspelled words.

Say) Look at each set of words. One word in each set is misspelled. Fill in the oval by the misspelled word. (You may wish to pronounce each set of words to help students correctly identify them.)

103

3 Hide and Seek

Reinforce correct spelling of current spelling words. (A reproducible master is provided in Appendix A as shown on the inset page to the right.)
Write the words one at a time on a white board.
Have students:

- **Look** at the word.
- **Say** the word out loud.
- **Spell** the word out loud.
- **Hide** (teacher erases word.)
- **Write** the word on paper.
- **Seek** (teacher rewrites word.)
- **Check** spelling. If incorrect, rewrite word correctly.

4 Clues

Have your students complete this activity to strengthen spelling ability and expand vocabulary.

1 Posttest

Test mastery of the spelling words. Challenge words are starred.

I will say the word once, use the word in a sentence, then say the word again. Write the word on your paper.

1. gone — "Rachel's **gone** crazy!" screamed Vanessa.
2. lost — Have you ever **lost** gum out of your mouth?
3. often — It is good to ask God for help **often.**
4. odd — Rachel felt **odd** with her hair cut short.
5. lot — Rosa met Rachel in the parking **lot** the next morning.
6. soft — Rachel sat on the **soft** grass and read a story to the boys.
7. dot — The **dot** at the end of the sentence is a period.
8. drop — Do not **drop** your gum on the ground.
9. frog — Rachel read a **frog** story to Benji and Adam.
10. box — Mrs. Jacobson stopped to get a **box** of sugar at the store.
☆ forgot — Rachel **forgot** what color her Mommy's eyes were.
☆ tomorrow — Rachel and her stepmother will get along better **tomorrow.**
☆ job — It is your **job** to "live in peace with each other."

Progress Chart
Students may record scores. (Reproducible master in Appendix B.)

Personal Dictionary
Students may add any words they have misspelled to their personal dictionaries for reference when writing. (Cover in Appendix B.)

Inset page (Appendix A, Lesson 4)

Hide and Seek

Check a paper for each word you spell correctly.

Clues

Look at other forms of your spelling words in the word bank.
Use the clues to find the word that fits best in each blank.

1. cereal is packaged in these   boxes
2. little round marks   dots
3. many   lots
4. not loudly   softly
5. let go of   dropped
6. land and water animals   frogs
7. chores   jobs
8. days after today   tomorrows

Word Bank

box + es	drop + p + ed	job + s	soft + ly
dot + s	frog + s	lot + s	tomorrow + s

371

I Game

Name _____

Place a game piece over each word your teacher says and spells. If the word appears on your card more than once, place a game piece over only one of the words. When you get five game pieces in a row, raise your hand and say, "Spelling is fun!"

FREE

Remember: When you do not feel like getting along with someone, you should choose to do it anyway.

J Journaling

Write a story in your journal about not feeling peaceful. Draw a picture of the last time you were not at peace with someone.

90

How to Play:

- Fold the word cards (see **Materials**) in half, and put them in a container.
- Write each word from the **Game Word List** on the board. (Be sure to include the number in parentheses beside it.)
- Ask the students to copy these words on their game card — one word in each box. Remind them the number beside the word indicates how many times they must copy that word. (Note: Placing the words in the boxes randomly makes the game more fun!)
- Instructions for the students: "Cover the word **FREE** in the center of your card with a game piece. (pause) I will draw a word from the container, read it aloud, then spell it. Find that word on your card, and cover it with a game piece. Cover only ONE word each time, even if it's on your card twice. When you have five game pieces in a row (up-down, across, or diagonally) raise your hand and say **'Spelling is FUN!'**"
- Play as many times as you like. (As you return the word cards to the container and mix them up, remind the students to clear their game cards.)

2 Game

Reinforce spelling skills and provide motivation and interest.

Materials

- game page (from student text)
- flat buttons, dry beans, pennies, or game discs (24 per child)
- game word list
- word cards (each word from the list below written on one or more cards as indicated)

Game Word List

1. **box** (2)
2. **dot** (2)
3. **lot** (2)
4. **gone** (2)
5. **lost** (2)
6. **odd** (2)
7. **often** (2)
8. **soft** (2)
9. **drop** (2)
10. **frog** (2)
☆ **job** (2)
☆ **forgot** (1)
☆ **tomorrow** (1)

3 Journaling

Provide a meaningful reason for correct spelling through personal writing.

Review the story using discussion leads provided on the following page. Encourage students to apply the Scriptural value in their journaling.

Take a minute to memorize . . .

Have students say the memory verses from lessons 1, 2, 3, and 4 with you.

105

3 Journaling

Provide a meaningful reason for correct spelling through personal writing.

Say
- Who was not feeling very peaceful in the story? (Rachel. She was mad at her stepmother for cutting the gum out of her hair.)
- Who helped Rachel realize she should not stay angry with her stepmother? (Her sister Rebecca. Two boys at the day-care center. Her stepmother.)
- Write a story in your journal about a time when you were angry with someone. Draw a picture showing how you felt on the lines below the picture.

*"Invented spelling is not a failure to spell the conventional way but a step on the road to reaching it."**

*Wilde, Sandra. 1992. You kan red this! Portsmouth, NH: Heinemann.

Take Time to Prepare

When Tony disobeys his mother, he finds out how embarrassing it is to be unprepared.

"Tony-O, it's almost time to eat," Mama called from the front porch. "Come in and pick up your race track off the living room floor before supper!"

"Let me finish this drill," Tony said breathlessly, as he expertly guided the soccer ball through a series of bright orange plastic cones set up in his front yard.

"Okay, Tony," Mama smiled. "Just a few minutes more."

"That only took you forty-five seconds," Stephen announced, looking at the stopwatch in his hand. "You get faster every time, Tony." He handed the stopwatch to his friend. "See how long it takes me." Tony ran the stopwatch while Stephen kicked the ball through the line of cones a couple of times. "It's a good thing I'm the goalie and don't have to run up and down the field every game! I'll never be as fast as you." He flopped down beside Tony on the grass. "But I think we're ready for our game with the Stingrays!"

"We haven't lost a game yet," Tony pointed out.

"The Stingrays haven't lost any games either," Stephen reminded Tony. "Coach Larkin says we're ready. He's a great coach. He never yells, even when we mess up bad."

"And he always gives us popsicles after we win a game."

"I bet he'd give 'em to us if we lost."

"Yeah, but we never lose."

"Well, I like him. I want to be just like him," Stephen proclaimed. Tony nodded his head in agreement.

"Didn't he say he was going to come over sometime this weekend and deliver those suckers for us to sell?"

"Yeah, he brought mine over last night," Stephen said. "I told him you were at your dad's house. Too bad you weren't here. He even stayed for a while. He pretended he was the Stingray's striker and I played goalie. He's good. I was tired, even though I never left the goalie box." Stephen sat up and stretched. "Coach said he'd be back with your suckers later. He needs to talk to you about how to sell them."

"Time to eat, Tony," Mama called again. "Stephen, you may come back later, but Tony has to come in for supper now. Bring the cones with you, Tony. And don't forget to wash your hands."

The house smelled wonderful. Hot french bread was in a basket in the middle of the table. Steam rose from the bowls of pasta and Mama's special sauce. "Mmmm, my favorite!" Tony slid into his chair. "I'm starved!"

"Tony, remember to pick up your track before you . . ." The ring of the phone interrupted what Mama was saying and Tony ran to answer it. "Hello, who's calling please?" Tony said into the phone. "One moment, sir. Mama, it's Coach Larkin for you." He handed her the phone. Mama talked for a few minutes, then motioned for Tony to go ahead and eat.

Later, after a bowl of chocolate ice cream for dessert, Tony headed out for a little more soccer practice with Stephen. He remembered Mama's instructions as he stepped over a couple of sections of race track and the control box strewn across the gray carpet on the way to the front door, but decided to pick up later when it was too dark to practice soccer. Mama was busy putting the dishes away

and seemed to have forgotten the mess scattered all over the living room.

They had just gotten the cones set up for a new drill when the front door opened and Mama called in a stern voice, "Tony, I want you to come here. I think I asked you to do something before we ate supper."

Tony groaned, "Ah, Mama, can't I pick it up after it gets dark?"

"No," Mama replied firmly. Tony knew there was no more room for negotiation and trudged slowly up the front steps.

"Hey," Stephen yelled after Tony. "Can I borrow your stopwatch so I can time myself while you clean up?"

Tony dug his hand into his pocket to get the new stopwatch his dad had just gotten him the day before, but it wasn't there where he'd put it!

Worried and frustrated, he brushed past Mama without looking at her on the way to search his room.

"It won't take long to pick this up if you hurry," Mama said to his back.

He checked on his bed, then in his closet where he stored his soccer ball and cones, but it wasn't there either. He looked on top of his bookshelf and then underneath his shoes on the closet floor. "Where's my stopwatch?" he thought.

He was crawling under his bed to see if the missing stopwatch had fallen between the edge of the bed and the wall when he heard Mama calling from the living room again. "Tony, come here, please." Tony replied in an irritated voice, "I'll be there after I find my new stopwatch. What's the rush? I'm not outside having fun playing soccer. Isn't that what you want, anyway?" Tony crawled out from under the bed and stood in the middle of his room and turned around in a circle slowly. "Where is that stopwatch?" he muttered.

"Antonio Vanetti!" Mama called again.

Tony recognized the no-nonsense sound in Mama's voice, but ignored her. "The bathroom! Maybe I put the stopwatch on the counter

107

Story Continued

when I washed my hands before supper!"

"Antonio Marcus Vanetti!" Mama called.

Tony ran into the bathroom and grabbed his new stopwatch with a sigh of relief. He ran down the hall brushing past Mama. "I'll be right back. I just have to give this stopwatch to Stephen."

"Antonio!" Mama said sharply.

Tony swung around the corner and ran right into the broad chest of Coach Larkin!

"You in a hurry, Son?" Coach grinned down at him and gently put his big hands on Tony's shoulders, pushing him back a little bit so he could see into the boy's big brown eyes more clearly.

Tony saw the track mess all over the living room floor. His face got hot as he remembered how he had just talked to Mama.

"I was, sir," Tony looked sheepish, not meeting his hero's kind eyes.

"But not to obey your mama, I see," the coach observed.

Tony's face turned red. "Yes sir, I mean no, sir. I mean…"

The next morning during handwriting class, Mrs. Morgan went to the board and wrote in big bold letters: BE PREPARED, FOR YOU DON'T KNOW WHAT DAY YOUR LORD IS COMING. "Jesus said these words," Mrs. Morgan explained. "Does anyone know what He meant? Matthew?"

"We need to be ready every day because we don't know exactly when Jesus is coming back to take us to heaven," Matthew answered.

"Good, Matthew. Why would Jesus want us to make the choice to be ready, Katelynn?"

"Because He loves us and knows His way will make us happy?"

"Katelynn, what an excellent answer," Mrs. Morgan commended. "Now, give me an example of how you can be prepared, class."

Suddenly Tony understood just what Jesus

meant. He remembered the sad look on Coach Larkin's face when he realized Tony was being so disrespectful to his mama. He remembered how ashamed he felt about the mess on the living room floor they had all had to walk through and then look at while Coach explained about selling the suckers. He remembered then how Mama and Coach had helped him clean up the race track mess. When the living room was clean, Coach had put his arm around Tony and gone outside to work on the drill the boys had set up earlier in the front yard.

After it was too dark to see the soccer ball anymore, Coach had helped him pick up the orange cones and carry them inside. "Tony is a very fine player, Mrs. Vanetti," Coach said as he put the cones beside the front door Mama was standing next to. "Your son listens well at practice and goes home and does every drill I suggest. We're ready now for our game against the Stingrays. See you tomorrow at the game." He waved good-bye to them.

Tony started to raise his hand and share what he had just figured out with the class, but decided he wasn't prepared for the hot feeling he was sure to come over him when he told them about the way he had talked to Mama and not obeyed her.

So instead, Tony closed his eyes and said a quiet prayer in his mind. "I'm sorry I didn't obey Mama, Lord. Help me to listen so I'll be prepared for Coach Larkin's next visit. Help me to prepare for Your coming like I do for soccer."

2 Discussion Time

Check understanding of the story and development of personal values.

- What are some things you like to get ready for? (Brainstorm. Make a list on the board.)
- How did Stephen and Tony prepare for their games?
- Who forced them to prepare?
- How did Coach Larkin help the boys prepare for the soccer games?
- What did the boys say that tells us how they felt about Coach Larkin?
- How do you know they didn't mind doing what Coach Larkin suggested?
- Why did Tony's face get red when he realized Coach had heard the way he had talked to Mama?
- Did you know that Jesus wants to help us be prepared for His coming? All you have to do is ask Him to help you.

A Preview

Write each word as your teacher says it.

Name _____

1. must
2. done
3. number
4. jump
5. just
6. none
7. sum
8. what
9. does
10. above

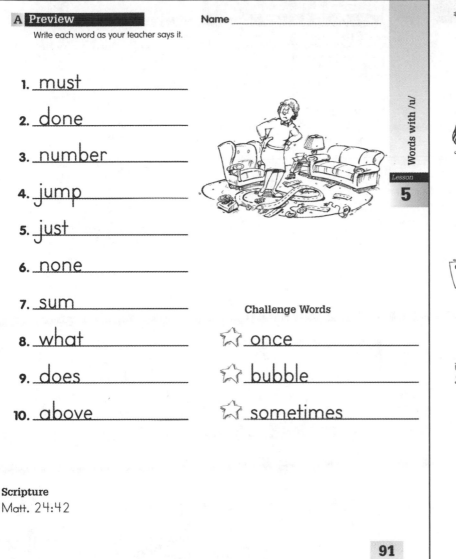

Challenge Words

☆ once
☆ bubble
☆ sometimes

Scripture
Matt. 24:42

91

Challenge

For better spellers, challenge words may be included in the weekly list. Challenge words are starred.

Correct Immediately!

Say Let's correct our preview. I will write each word on the board. Put a dot under each letter on your preview as I spell the word out loud. If you spelled a word wrong, rewrite it correctly.

Progress Chart

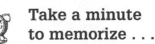

Students may record scores. (Reproducible master in Appendix B.)

Take a minute to memorize . . .

Read the memory verse twice. Have students practice it with you two more times.

---

3 Preview

Test for knowledge of the correct spellings of these words. (See the instructions at the top right for challenge words.)

Say I will say each word once, use the word in a sentence, then say the word again. Write the word on the lines in the Worktext.

1. **must** — Mama said, "You **must** come in for supper now, Tony."
2. **done** — When you are **done** picking up the track, you may play soccer.
3. **number** — The **number** of cones you pass in 30 seconds is important.
4. **jump** — The goalie can **jump** up and catch the soccer ball.
5. **just** — "I want to be **just** like Coach Larkin," Stephen said.
6. **none** — It was **none** other than Tony's coach.
7. **sum** — The **sum** of all suckers sold will become the total.
8. **what** — Be prepared, for you don't know **what** day the Lord is coming.
9. **does** — Tony **does** need to learn to obey quickly.
10. **above** — Jesus will come from **above**.
☆ **once** — Tony was sorry he had not cleaned up, **once** he saw Coach.
☆ **bubble** — Mama's yummy sauce began to boil and **bubble**.
☆ **sometimes** — It is **sometimes** best to tell only Jesus your problems.

109

4 Word Shapes

Help students form a correct image of whole words.

(Say) Look at each word and think about its shape. Now, write the word in the correct word Shape Boxes. You may check off each word as you use it.

(In many words, the sound of **/u/** is spelled with **u**, and it is often spelled this way when it is at the beginning or in the middle of a word. Some words, however, have **/u/** spelled with **o**, and a few have **/u/** spelled with **a**.)

(Say) In the word Shape Boxes, color the letter or letters that spell the sound of **/u/** in each word. Circle the words in which **/u/** is spelled with **a** or **o**.

☆ **Challenge**
Draw the correctly shaped box around each letter in these words.

(Say) On a separate sheet of paper, write other words that contain the spelling patterns in the word list. See how many words you can write.

Be Prepared For Fun

Check these supply lists for **Fun Ways to Spell** presented **Day 2**. Purchase and/or gather these items ahead of time!

B Word Shapes   Name _____

Write each word in the correct word shape boxes. Then, in the word shape boxes, color the letter or letters that spell the sound of /u/ in each word. Circle the words in which /u/ is spelled with **a** or **o**.

1. above
2. does
3. done
4. jump
5. just
6. must
7. none
8. number
9. sum
10. what

none
sum
number
must
what
above
does
jump
just
done

☆ **Challenge**

Draw the correctly shaped boxes around each letter in these words.

bubble   once   sometimes

92

Answers may vary for duplicate word shapes.

General
- Markers
- Art Paper
- Spelling List

Auditory
- Spelling List

Visual
- Letter Tiles a, b, d, e, h, j, m, n, n, o, p, r, s, s, t, u, v, w
- b, b, c, e, i, l, m (added for challenge words)
- Spelling List

Tactile
- Finger paint
- Plastic Plate or Glossy Paper
- Spelling List

110

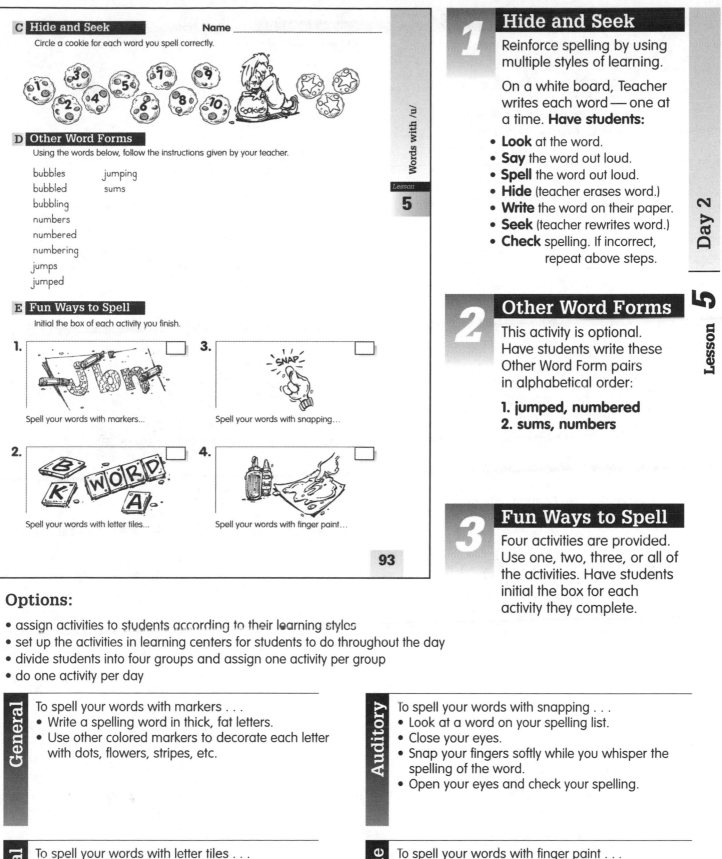

C Hide and Seek

Name _____

Circle a cookie for each word you spell correctly.

D Other Word Forms

Using the words below, follow the instructions given by your teacher.

bubbles   jumping
bubbled   sums
bubbling
numbers
numbered
numbering
jumps
jumped

E Fun Ways to Spell

Initial the box of each activity you finish.

1. ☐
Spell your words with markers...

2. ☐
Spell your words with letter tiles...

3. ☐
SNAP
Spell your words with snapping...

4. ☐
Spell your words with finger paint...

93

---

1 Hide and Seek

Reinforce spelling by using multiple styles of learning.

On a white board, Teacher writes each word — one at a time. **Have students:**

- **Look** at the word.
- **Say** the word out loud.
- **Spell** the word out loud.
- **Hide** (teacher erases word.)
- **Write** the word on their paper.
- **Seek** (teacher rewrites word.)
- **Check** spelling. If incorrect, repeat above steps.

2 Other Word Forms

This activity is optional. Have students write these Other Word Form pairs in alphabetical order:

1. **jumped, numbered**
2. **sums, numbers**

3 Fun Ways to Spell

Four activities are provided. Use one, two, three, or all of the activities. Have students initial the box for each activity they complete.

Options:

- assign activities to students according to their learning styles
- set up the activities in learning centers for students to do throughout the day
- divide students into four groups and assign one activity per group
- do one activity per day

General

To spell your words with markers . . .
- Write a spelling word in thick, fat letters.
- Use other colored markers to decorate each letter with dots, flowers, stripes, etc.

Auditory

To spell your words with snapping . . .
- Look at a word on your spelling list.
- Close your eyes.
- Snap your fingers softly while you whisper the spelling of the word.
- Open your eyes and check your spelling.

Visual

To spell your words with letter tiles . . .
- Spell a word from your list by putting the tiles in the right order.
- Check your spelling.

Tactile

To spell your words with finger paint . . .
- Smear paint across your plate.
- Use finger to write a spelling word in paint.
- Check your spelling.
- Smear the word out with your fingers and write another word.

1 Sentence Order

Familiarize students with word meaning and usage. Tape the word **Tony** (written on a piece of paper) to a playground ball (basketball, soccer ball, or foursquare ball). Tape the word **loves** to a second ball. Tape the word **soccer** to the third ball. Place two cones (or chairs) at the front of the room about three feet apart. Invite three students to stand in the front of the room. Direct one student to stand between the cones. Place one student to the left of the two cones and the last student to the right of the cones. Making sure the words are not in order, hand each student a ball. Time the three students to see how long it takes them to get the sentence in the correct order. You may want to do this activity with other sentences and other students.

 Say Put each set of word groups in order to write a sentence. After you have written the sentence, circle the spelling words in each sentence.

Take a minute to memorize...

Read the memory verse twice. Have students practice it with you two more times.

Put each set of word groups in order to write a sentence. Circle the spelling words.

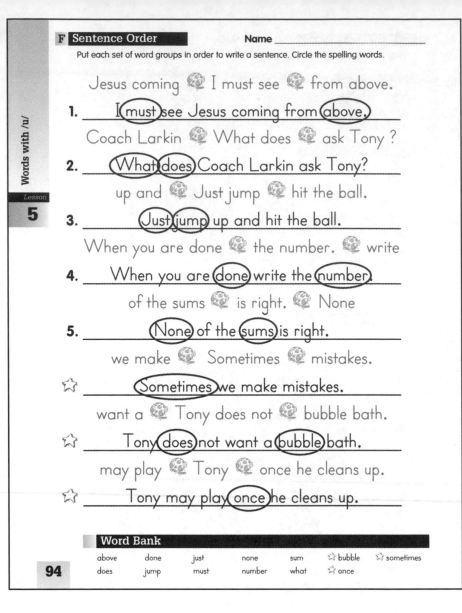

Words with /u/ — Lesson 5

Jesus coming 🌐 I must see 🌐 from above.
1. I(must)see Jesus coming from(above.)
Coach Larkin 🌐 What does 🌐 ask Tony?
2. (What)(does)Coach Larkin ask Tony?
up and 🌐 Just jump 🌐 hit the ball.
3. (Just)(jump)up and hit the ball.
When you are done 🌐 the number. 🌐 write
4. When you are(done)write the(number)
of the sums 🌐 is right. 🌐 None
5. (None)of the(sums)is right.
we make 🌐 Sometimes 🌐 mistakes.
☆ (Sometimes)we make mistakes.
want a 🌐 Tony does not 🌐 bubble bath.
☆ Tony(does)not want a(bubble)bath.
may play 🌐 Tony 🌐 once he cleans up.
☆ Tony may play(once)he cleans up.

Word Bank

| above | done | just | none | sum | ☆ bubble | ☆ sometimes |
| does | jump | must | number | what | ☆ once | |

94

112

G Dictation

Listen and write the missing words.

Name _____

1. __Just__ __jump__ over this rope.

2. __What__ __was__ __the__ __first__ __digit__ __of__ __the__ __number__ ?

3. Christopher __has__ __done__ __none__ __of__ __his__ chores yet.

4. __You__ __must__ __add__ __to__ __find__ __the__ __sum__ .

H Proofreading

One word in each set is misspelled. Fill in the oval by the misspelled word.

1. ○ none
   ● whot
   ○ jump

2. ● duz
   ○ number
   ○ soft

3. ● dun
   ○ number
   ○ just

4. ○ drop
   ● nust
   ○ camp

5. ○ nest
   ● abuv
   ○ set

6. ● som
   ○ often
   ○ frog

☆ ● buble
   ○ tomorrow
   ○ until

☆ ○ again
   ○ apple
   ● sumtimes

☆ ● wunce
   ○ because
   ○ never

95

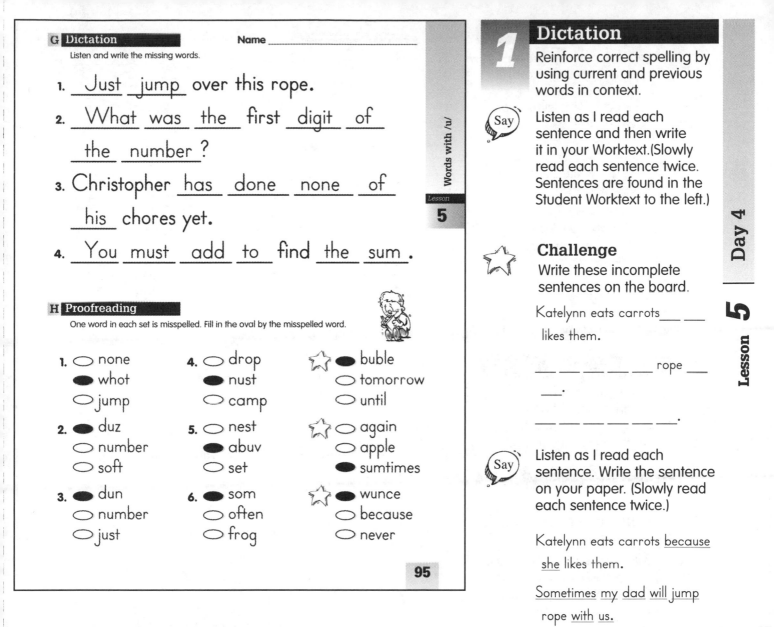

1 Dictation

Reinforce correct spelling by using current and previous words in context.

Say Listen as I read each sentence and then write it in your Worktext.(Slowly read each sentence twice. Sentences are found in the Student Worktext to the left.)

☆ Challenge

Write these incomplete sentences on the board.

Katelynn eats carrots____ ___ likes them.

__ __ __ __ __ rope __ __.

__ __ __ __ __ __.

Say Listen as I read each sentence. Write the sentence on your paper. (Slowly read each sentence twice.)

Katelynn eats carrots <u>because</u> <u>she</u> likes them.

<u>Sometimes</u> <u>my</u> <u>dad</u> <u>will</u> <u>jump</u> rope <u>with</u> <u>us</u>.

<u>He</u> <u>has</u> <u>been</u> <u>to</u> <u>camp</u> <u>once</u>.

2 Proofreading

Familiarize students with standardized test format and reinforce recognizing misspelled words.

Say Look at each set of words. One word in each set is misspelled. Fill in the oval by the misspelled word. (You may wish to pronounce each set of words to help students correctly identify them.)

113

3 Hide and Seek

Reinforce correct spelling of current spelling words. (A reproducible master is provided in Appendix A as shown on the inset page to the right.)

Write the words one at a time on a white board.

Have students:

- **Look** at the word.
- **Say** the word out loud.
- **Spell** the word out loud.
- **Hide** (teacher erases word.)
- **Write** the word on paper.
- **Seek** (teacher rewrites word.)
- **Check** spelling. If incorrect, rewrite word correctly.

4 Code

Have your students complete this activity to strengthen spelling ability and expand vocabulary.

1 Posttest

Test mastery of the spelling words. Challenge words are starred.

(Say) I will say the word once, use the word in a sentence, then say the word again. Write the word on your paper.

1. done — "Tony, please clean up the mess when you are **done**."
2. number — The **number** of goals you make depends on how well you play.
3. sum — He added up Tony's scores and found the **sum** was 200.
4. jump — You may **jump** high and hit the soccer ball with your head.
5. just — It **just** depends on how well you do this drill.
6. what — Tony learned **what** the Scripture meant.
7. does — Coach still **does** want to help Tony.
8. none — The suckers were gone. There were **none** left.
9. above — Our God, in heaven **above**, loves every one of us.
10. must — We **must** always be ready for Jesus to come.
☆ once — You may play **once** you eat and clean up your mess.
☆ sometimes — Do you like to clean up **sometimes**?
☆ bubble — Tony checked his time through the clear **bubble** stopwatch face.

Progress Chart
Students may record scores. (Reproducible master in Appendix B.)

Personal Dictionary
Students may add any words they have misspelled to their personal dictionaries for reference when writing. (Cover in Appendix B.)

Appendix A — Lesson 5

Hide and Seek
Check a paper for each word you spell correctly.

1 3 5 7 9
2 4 6 8 10

Code

Mrs. Morgan's class likes to wear Knowlton Elementary's blue soccer jerseys when they play team games. Mrs. Morgan kept track of who used them on her clipboard last week. While she supervised recess one day, she made a spelling code with the names on her clipboard. Count over the number of letters indicated by the student's jersey numbers before their names and circle the letter. Write the letters you circled, in order, on the lines below each day to discover some other word forms of your spelling words.

Monday
13 Stephen Wilson
5 Setsuko Noma
4 Tommy Rawson
11 Rachel Jacobson
2 Beth Hill
3 Sarah
16 Katelynn Hatasaki
13 Stephen Wilson
15 Christopher Wright

Tuesday
13 Stephen Wilson
9 Rosa Vasquez
4 Tommy Rawson
11 Rachel Jacobson
2 Beth Hill
3 Sarah
6 Matthew Schilling
7 Daniel DeVore

Wednesday
1 James Thompson
9 Rosa Vasquez
3 Tommy Rawson
8 Christopher Wright
2 Beth Hill
7 Daniel DeVore

n u m b e r + i n g   n u m b e r + e d   j u m p + e d

Thursday
1 James Thompson
9 Rosa Vasquez
4 Kristin Wright
10 Tony Vanetti
12 Matthew Schilling
6 Katelynn Hatasaki

Friday
4 Kristin Wright
9 Rosa Vasquez
3 Tommy Rawson
1 Setsuko Noma

j u s t + l y   s u m + s

372

I | Game

Name _____

Run a drill through the cones with Tony or Stephen. Color one space for each word you or your team spells correctly from this week's word list.

Remember: Live as though Jesus were coming today.

J | Journaling

Write a story in your journal about getting ready for Jesus to come.

96

2 | Game

Reinforce spelling skills and provide motivation and interest.

Materials

- game page (from student text)
- crayons or colored pencils (1 per child)
- game word list

Game Word List

Use of challenge words is optional.

1. **above**
2. **does**
3. **done**
4. **none**
5. **number**
6. **jump**
7. **just**
8. **must**
9. **sum**
10. **what**
☆ **bubble**
☆ **sometimes**
☆ **once**

3 | Journaling

Provide a meaningful reason for correct spelling through personal writing.

Review the story using discussion leads provided on the following page. Encourage students to apply the Scriptural value in their journaling.

Take a minute to memorize . . .

Have students say the memory verses from lessons 1, 2, 3, 4, and 5 with you.

How to Play:

- Dribbling is a skill used in basketball as well as soccer.
- Divide students into two teams, and decide which team will go first. Have one team "run" the drill with Tony and one team with Stephen.
- Optional: If you have an even number of students, you may wish to pair students from opposing teams and have them share a game page, each coloring the spaces for their own team on that page.
- Have a student from team A go to the board.
- Read the spelling word two times slowly and clearly. (You may also wish to use the word in a sentence. Ex.: "cat — The cat climbed a tree. — cat")
- Have the student write the word on the board.
- If the word is spelled correctly, instruct all the members of team A to color one space, beginning at Start, on the game board. (Note: If the word is misspelled, correct the spelling immediately.)
- Alternate between teams A and B as you go down the word list.
- The team to reach the end of the drill first is the winner.

Non-Competitive Option: At the end of the game, say: "Class, I am proud of your efforts to spell the words correctly. If you had fun and tried your best, you are all winners!"

3 Journaling

Provide a meaningful reason for correct spelling through personal writing.

(Say)

- What were Tony and Stephen preparing for? (Soccer games.)

- How did they feel about Coach Larkin? (They wanted to be just like him.)

- Was Tony expecting Coach Larkin to come to his house? (Yes, but he wasn't sure when.)

- Who has promised to come back and take us to heaven? (Jesus.)

- Think about how you feel about seeing Jesus. What are some things we can do to prepare for Jesus' coming? (Ask Jesus to help you make good choices every day. Spend time in prayer and study. Help others. Ask Jesus to help you follow God's rules.)

- In your journal, write about what you can do to prepare for Jesus' coming.

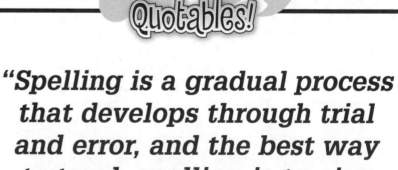

"Spelling is a gradual process that develops through trial and error, and the best way to teach spelling is to give students freedom to take risks in their writing."*

*Scott, Jill E. 1994. Spelling for Readers and Writers. The Reading Teacher, Vol. 48, No. 2, October: 188-190.

Lollipops and Love

Rosa's actions show everyone that she loves God — even strangers can see it.

"Happy birthday to you, happy birthday to you, happy birthday, dear Rosa! Happy birthday to you!" Mrs. Morgan's students sang with great spirit. The light brown skin on seven-year-old Rosa's smiling face blushed rosy pink. "Happy birthday! Happy birthday, Rosa!" her classmates called out.

"Okay, everyone," Mrs. Morgan held up one hand and the clapping and birthday wishes quieted. "We have a special surprise for Rosa's seventh birthday. But first, let's clean up our mess." Mrs. Morgan smiled and looked pointedly around the room. Colorful streamers, balloons, cupcake wrappers, and pointed paper party hats were scattered around the classroom mixed with the regular lunch time clutter of paper bags, juice boxes, and wrappers. When the trash was cleared away and the party things were picked up neatly, Mrs. Morgan asked the children to line up at the door.

"Did Mrs. Morgan forget the surprise?" James wondered aloud. "Why are we going out to recess without the surprise?"

"Maybe the surprise is for later," Beth guessed. "Do you know, Rosa?" she asked the birthday girl who walked in front of her as they left the school building. Rosa shrugged and smiled.

"Hey, look at that!" came the excited squeal from the first student to burst out the door onto the playground. "What is it?" someone else asked. "It's a piñata, of course," another child said. "Haven't you ever seen one before?"

The enthusiastic class crowded around the swing set. The swings had been removed and a rope thrown over the top of the empty swing set. A cute, donkey-shaped piñata hung from one end of the rope. Its pink and white paper "hair" ruffled in the breeze as the piñata swung gently back and forth.

Mr. Vasquez, Rosa's father, held the other end of the rope in his hands and winked at Rosa. A whole stream of questions poured from the excited group of children. "What are we going to do with the piñata?" "Has it got anything in it?" "Who's going first?" "Where did you get it?" "Did you make it yourself?" "I've heard people wear blindfolds to do this. Are we going to wear blindfolds, too?"

Mrs. Morgan raised one hand and waited as each child who noticed her raised hand stopped talking and raised his or her hand, too. When the noise died down, all eyes turned toward the teacher. "In Mexico it is the custom to celebrate birthdays with a piñata. Rosa is sharing her special birthday piñata with us." Mrs. Morgan rested a hand on Rosa's shoulder. "Now, there is a little piece of paper in this box for each of you with your name on it. Rosa will draw a name and that person will get to put on the blindfold and try to break the piñata with this stick first."

The children had a tremendous time watching each other take wild swings at the piñata. They laughed till they could hardly stand. Mr. Vasquez made it more difficult when he raised or lowered the piñata by pulling on his end of the rope. Finally, Tommy hit a solid whack that broke the piñata and sent the candy flying! Everyone scrambled after it.

After supper that evening Rosa got to open her presents. She sat in the middle of the floor between her twelve-year-old brother, Carlos, and nine-year-old sister Maria. Grandpa Joe and Grandma Ruth Anderson, the family's good friends and adopted grandparents who lived down the road, watched from the couch. Rosa's dad took pictures as she ripped into her brightly-colored packages. She discovered new leather boots just like she wanted; a cute shirt in red, her favorite color; a heart-shaped wooden box to keep her special things in; a beautiful purse; a version of the Scriptures that was written in words she could read herself; and a craft set with lots of paints, markers, papers, stencils, and a variety of paintbrushes. She almost missed her last birthday gift in the pile of gifts and wrapping paper and ribbons. A small white envelope with a card inside said, "To our special Rosita. Use this to get something you really want. Grandpa Joe and Grandma Ruth." Rosa pulled a crisp ten dollar bill out of the envelope and looked up with shining eyes.

"Oh, thank you, Grandpa Joe and Grandma Ruth! Thank you so much!" Rosa gave everyone big hugs and thank-yous. "This has been a lovely birthday!"

After school the next day Dad swung the blue jeep into the crowded parking lot of a store. "Okay, troop, let's move. We've got to pick up a few things that we need." Dad locked the jeep after they all piled out. Rosa grabbed his hand as they headed for the store. With a cart load of soap, toothpaste and other household supplies, the Vasquez family waited in a checkout line. Magazines, gum, and candy lined the racks on either side of them. One display had huge round lollipops of all colors sticking out like limbs on a tree.

"M-m-m-m, look at these, Dad." Carlos picked up a shiny red one. "'Cinnamon Sensation.' I bet it tastes terrific."

"I'm sure it does, Son," Dad commented absently as he began to place the items from the cart on the checkout counter.

"And look at this one." Maria was examining the lollipop display as well. "I just love

117

Day 1

Review 6

apple-flavored candy!" she pointed at a bright green lollipop.

"Very nice." Dad glanced at the lollipops and turned back to put the last items on the checkout counter.

"Dad," Rosa tapped his arm, "may I buy a lollipop with my birthday money?"

Dad turned and really looked at the lollipops and then at Rosa. "Sure, Rosita, if that's what you're sure you want." He smiled and tucked a strand of her black hair behind one ear before turning back to pay the cashier. When Dad was done, Rosa stepped up to make her purchase. She carefully laid three lollipops on the counter and handed over her ten dollar bill. The cashier gave her some change, which she put in her new purse.

Rosa handed a shiny red lollipop with a label that read "Cinnamon Sensation" to her big brother. "This one's for you." Then she held out a bright green "Absolutely Apple" lollipop to Maria. "And this one's for you." Then, picking up the last lollipop, she said, "And this 'Cherry Delight' is mine."

"Thank you, sis!" Carlos and Maria said at the same time. Dad gave Rosa his special wink as the Vasquez family headed towards the door.

"Just a minute, sir." A nicely dressed woman spoke to Mr. Vasquez just before he reached the door. "Could I have a word with you, please?"

"Certainly," the children's surprised father responded. "Troop, you head on out to the jeep and put the bags in the back." He tossed his keys to Maria and Carlos, who pushed the shopping cart filled with bags out the door while Rosa held on to the side. The children were buckled into their seats and waiting several minutes before Mr. Vasquez crossed the parking lot to the jeep.

"What did she want, Dad?" Carlos asked the question they were all wondering about as their father started the car. "Is something wrong?"

"No, nothing's wrong," Dad answered. "I think I'll tell you all about it later. How about a quick stop at Taco Time for supper tonight?" He headed the blue jeep that way when the three Vasquez children unanimously agreed it was a great idea.

That evening a pajama-clad Rosa climbed into Dad's lap, as Maria leaned against his shoulder and Carlos sat on the carpet nearby. "The lady at the store today just wanted to tell me what wonderful children I have." Dad's smile warmed them all. "She was right behind us in the checkout line and was impressed that you two," he nodded toward Maria and Carlos, "didn't argue or fuss when I didn't buy the lollipops you wanted. She was amazed that Rosa spent her own birthday money to buy them for you. That lady said she just had to know what made you children so different from many other children who are selfish and unkind. I was able to tell her that it is your love for Jesus that helps you love each other like you do."

As Rosa snuggled into her bed, Dad came in quietly and sat beside her. "Little Rosita, did you know there's a verse in the Scripture that talks about you?" Rosa's sleepy eyes opened a little wider. Dad smiled and continued, "It's found in John 13 and it says, 'Your strong love for each other will prove to the world that you are my disciples.' You've been proving that very clearly the last few days. You shared the special birthday piñata that your Uncle Mario sent all the way from New Mexico with your classmates. You shared your new paints and craft supplies with your brother and sister. And today you used some of your birthday money to buy something special for them. There are always people watching what we do, whether we know it or not, like the lady at the store. I'm so glad your actions prove that you are Jesus' disciple. I love you."

"I love you, Daddy," Rosa returned. After a goodnight kiss, Dad left quietly. Rosa shut her eyes and whispered, "And I love You, too, Jesus."

Discussion Time

Check understanding of the story and development of personal values.

- What gifts did Rosa get for her birthday?
- Why did the lady at the store want to talk to Rosa's father?
- What things did Rosa do that showed everyone she was Jesus' disciple?
- How do you think Rosa felt?
- What can you do to show the world that you are Jesus' disciple?

118

Test-Challenge Words

On a separate sheet of paper, challenge words may be tested using the sentences below.

4 Test-Sentences

Reinforce recognizing misspelled words.

(Say) Read each sentence carefully. The underlined words in each sentence are misspelled. Write the sentences on the lines in your Worktext, spelling each underlined word correctly.

Take a minute to memorize...

Read the memory verse twice. Have students practice it with you two more times.

A Test-Words   Name _____

Write each spelling word on the line as your teacher says it.

1. gone   6. lot
2. hat   7. box
3. above   8. last
4. head   9. sister
5. just   10. give

Review
Lesson 6

B Test-Sentences

The two underlined words in each of the sentences are misspelled. Write the sentences on the lines below, spelling each underlined word correctly.

Show <u>Gawd's</u> love by the way you <u>liv</u>.

1. Show God's love by the way you live.

Jesus was <u>gled</u> Rosa had <u>ben</u> kind.

2. Jesus was glad Rosa had been kind.

It is <u>tim</u> to <u>kwit</u>.

3. It is time to quit.

☆ **Test-Challenge Words**
On a sheet of paper, write each challenge word as your teacher says it.

97

---

3 Test-Words

Test for knowledge of the correct spellings of these words. (See the instructions at the top right for challenge words.)

(Say) I will say each word once, use the word in a sentence, then say the word again. Write the word on the lines in your Worktext.

1.	gone	The cake and ice cream are all **gone**.
2.	hat	This pointed party **hat** is Kristin's.
3.	above	Rosa's piñata swung **above** the children's heads.
4.	head	The blindfold was tied around Tommy's **head**.
5.	just	Tommy swung at the piñata at **just** the right instant.
6.	lot	A **lot** of candy scattered across the ground.
7.	box	Rosa opened the **box** wrapped with red ribbons.
8.	last	The **last** gift Rosa opened held a ten dollar bill.
9.	sister	Rosa bought an "Absolutely Apple" lollipop for her **sister**.
10.	give	What kind of lollipop did Rosa **give** to Carlos?
☆	apple	Maria's favorite candy was **apple**-flavored.
☆	asked	The lady at the store **asked** why the children acted so well.
☆	because	Dad told her it was **because** they loved Jesus.

119

1 Test-Dictation

Reinforce correct spelling by using current and previous words in context.

(Say) Listen as I read each sentence. Then write the missing words in your Worktext. (Slowly read each sentence twice. Sentences are found in the student text to the right. The words **does**, **must**, and **drop** are found in this unit.)

2 Test-Proofreading

Familiarize students with standardized test format and reinforce recognizing misspelled words.

(Say) Look at each set of words. One word in each set is misspelled. Fill in the oval by the misspelled word.

Test-Challenge Words

On a separate sheet of paper, challenge words may be tested using the sentences below.

(Say) I will say the word once, use the word in a sentence, then say the word again. Write the word on your paper.

☆ tomorrow   **Tomorrow** is Rosa's seventh birthday.
☆ forgot   I **forgot** to put a ribbon on the package.
☆ bubble   That piece of candy looks like a red **bubble.**
☆ sentence   The **sentence** said, "Use this to get something you really want."

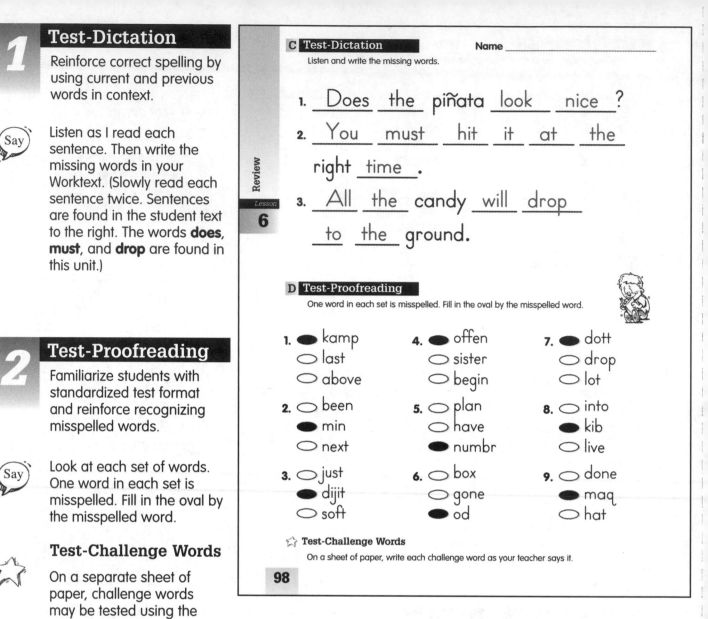

C Test-Dictation

Review Lesson 6

Listen and write the missing words.

Name _____

1. Does the piñata look nice ?
2. You must hit it at the right time .
3. All the candy will drop to the ground.

D Test-Proofreading

One word in each set is misspelled. Fill in the oval by the misspelled word.

1. ● kamp
   ○ last
   ○ above

2. ○ been
   ● min
   ○ next

3. ○ just
   ● dijit
   ○ soft

4. ● offen
   ○ sister
   ○ begin

5. ○ plan
   ○ have
   ● numbr

6. ○ box
   ○ gone
   ● od

7. ● dott
   ○ drop
   ○ lot

8. ○ into
   ● kib
   ○ live

9. ○ done
   ● maq
   ○ hat

☆ Test-Challenge Words

On a sheet of paper, write each challenge word as your teacher says it.

98

120

E Test-Shapes   Name _____

Color each piece of candy on which the word is spelled incorrectly.

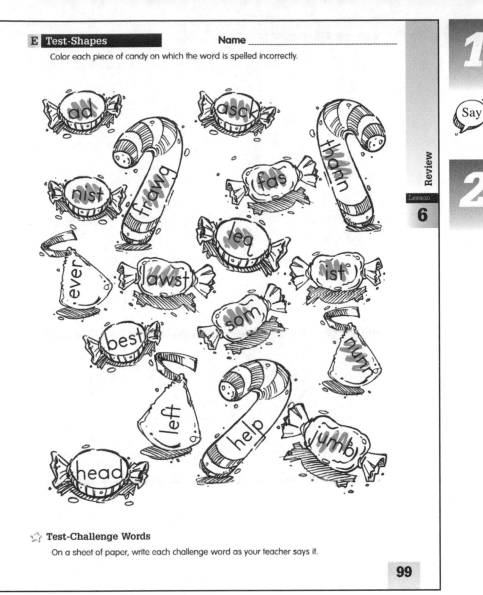

⭐ **Test-Challenge Words**

On a sheet of paper, write each challenge word as your teacher says it.

99

---

1 — Test-Shapes

Test mastery of words in this unit.

(Say) Look at each piece of candy. If the word is misspelled, color the piece of candy.

2 — Action Game

Reinforce spelling skills and provide motivation and interest.

Materials

- one 12-cup muffin tin with a number 1, 2, or 3 in the bottom of each cup
- a quarter
- masking tape

How to Play:

With masking tape, make a toe-line on the floor. Place the muffin tin approximately 3 feet away. Have the students line up behind the toe-line. Have the first student in line put his toes just behind the mark and toss the quarter into the muffin tin. (Allow him to try till he successfully gets the quarter in the tin.) If the quarter lands in a cup marked 1, give him a word to spell tested on Day 1; if in a cup marked 2, a word tested on Day 2; and, if in a cup marked 3, a word tested on Day 3. If he spells the word correctly, have him return to his desk; if not, have him go to the end of the line. Continue the game until every student has spelled a word correctly.

Test-Challenge Words

On a separate sheet of paper, challenge words may be tested using the sentences below.

I will say the word once, use the word in a sentence, then say the word again. Write the word on your paper.

☆	**gym**	We will play in the **gym** since it's raining.
☆	**never**	It seems like the rain will **never** stop.
☆	**bath**	The muddy dog needs a **bath.**
☆	**again**	He will probably get dirty **again.**
☆	**job**	Giving the dog a bath is a big **job.**

121

1 Game

Materials
- game page (from student text)
- stickers (13 per child)
- markers (1 per child)
- game word list

Game Word List
Check off each word lightly in pencil as it is used.

The Cinnamon Sensations
1. gone
2. hat
3. above
4. head
5. just
6. lot
7. box
8. last
9. sister
10. give
11. live
12. been
13. quit

The Absolutely Apples
1. does
2. must
3. drop
4. camp
5. men
6. digit
7. often
8. number
9. odd
10. dot
11. kid
12. map
13. does

The Cherry Delights
1. add
2. ask
3. fast
4. than
5. nest
6. leg
7. its
8. lost
9. frog
10. none
11. jump
12. sum
13. add

F Game   Name _____

Rosa showed Jesus' love when she unselfishly bought her brother and sister lollipops at the grocery store. The kinds of lollipops they chose will be your team names for this game. Place a sticker each time you or your team spells a review word correctly.

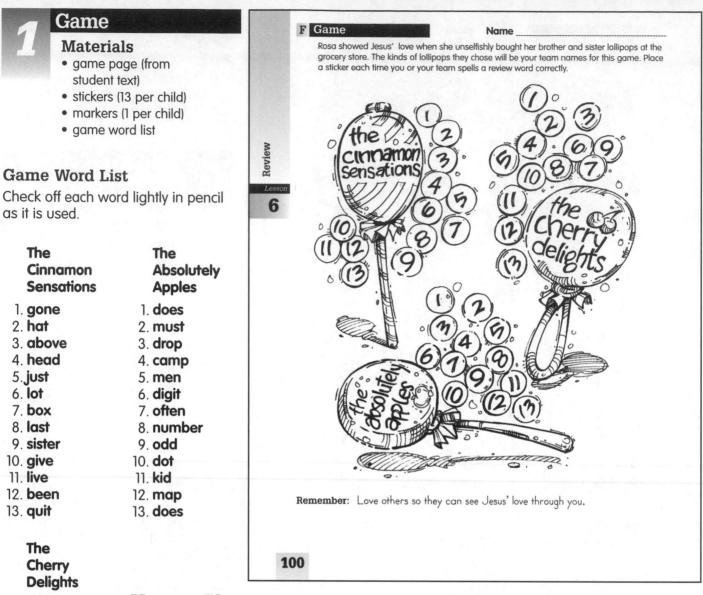

Remember: Love others so they can see Jesus' love through you.

100

How to Play:

- Divide students into three teams. Name one team **The Cinnamon Sensations**, one **The Absolutely Apples**, and one **The Cherry Delights**. (Option: You may wish to seat students in groups of three, each child from a different team. They should share one game page.) Decide which team goes first, second, and third.
- Read the instructions from the student game page aloud.
- Have a student from the first team choose a number from 1 to 13.
- Say the word that matches that number (from the team's word list) aloud twice. (You may also use the word in a sentence. Ex.: "cat — The cat climbed a tree. — cat")
- Have the student who chose the number write the word on the board.
- If the word is spelled correctly, have all the members of that team put a sticker on that number by their team name. If the word is misspelled, have them put an "X" through that number. They may not choose that number again. (Note: If the word is misspelled, correct the spelling immediately.)
- Repeat this process with the second team and then the third. (Be sure to use a different student from each team for each round.)
- When the words from all three lists have been used, the team with the most stickers is the winner.

Non-Competitive Option: At the end of the game, say: "Class, I'm proud of your efforts to spell the words correctly. If you had fun and tried your best, you are all winners!"

Test-Challenge Words

On a separate sheet of paper, challenge words may be tested using the sentences below.

2 Test-Sentences

Reinforce recognizing misspelled words.

(Say) Read each sentence carefully. The underlined words in each sentence are misspelled. Write the sentences on the lines in your Worktext, spelling each underlined word correctly.

G Test-Words   Name _____

Write each spelling word on the line as your teacher says it.

1. have
2. plan
3. what
4. done
5. left
6. help
7. into
8. begin
9. ever
10. next

H Test-Sentences

The two underlined words in each of the sentences are misspelled. Write the sentences on the lines below, spelling each underlined word correctly.

Rosa got a <u>nise</u> craft <u>cet</u>.

1. Rosa got a nice craft set.

Rosa's new <u>reb</u> shirt was very <u>souft</u>.

2. Rosa's new red shirt was very soft.

Which <u>wun</u> do you like the <u>dest</u>?

3. Which one do you like the best?

☆ **Test-Challenge Words**

On a sheet of paper, write each challenge word as your teacher says it.

101

---

1 Test-Words

Test for knowledge of the correct spellings of these words. (See the instructions at the top right for challenge words.)

(Say) I will say each word once, use the word in a sentence, then say the word again. Write the word on the lines in your Worktext.

1.	have	Do you **have** a birthday this month?
2.	plan	We will **plan** a special birthday party for Rosa.
3.	what	Do you know **what** you want for your birthday?
4.	done	Is everyone **done** with their cake and ice cream?
5.	left	There isn't any cake **left**.
6.	help	Let's all **help** clean up the room.
7.	into	Throw the paper plates **into** the trash can.
8.	begin	It's time to **begin** trying to hit the piñata.
9.	ever	Will someone **ever** manage to hit it?
10.	next	Tommy's turn is **next**.
☆	once	James almost hit the piñata **once**.
☆	sometimes	She raises or lowers the piñata **sometimes**.
☆	until	Keep trying **until** someone breaks the piñata.

3 Writing Assessment

Assess student's spelling, grammar, and composition skills through personal writing.

Say
- In Mexico, a piñata is a special way to celebrate. Have you ever tried to hit a piñata?

- What are some of the special birthday celebrations you enjoy? (Cake and ice cream, pin-the-tail-on-the-donkey, or other games, blowing out candles, etc.)

- Do you think opening her birthday presents or sharing them made Rosa feel better? Should we do kind things even if we don't really feel like it?

- Remember, whether we know it or not, there are always people watching what we do. Write a paragraph in your journal telling how everyone will be able to see that you are Jesus' disciple by your actions.

I Writing Assessment

Review Lesson **6**

Write a paragraph telling how everyone will be able to see that you are Jesus' disciple by your actions. Write at least four sentences.

Name _____

_____

_____

_____

_____

_____

_____

Scripture
John 13:35

102

A rubric for scoring is provided in Appendix B.

---

4 Action Game

Reinforce spelling skills and provide motivation and interest.

Materials

- any kind of book (one less than the number of children in the class)
- one **A Reason For Spelling®** Worktext
- audio player with music
- small prizes (erasers, pencils, stickers)

How to Play:

Place the books and the **A Reason For Spelling®** Worktext in a circle around a table. Play music as the students march around the table. When you stop the music, each student must touch the book beside him. Have the student touching the **A Reason For Spelling®** Worktext spell a word from today's test. If he spells it incorrectly, have him march again; if he spells it correctly, give him a prize and have him return to his desk.

Remove one book each time a student drops out and continue the game until every student has spelled a word correctly.

Spelling Is Fun!

ABC's

This certificate is awarded to

_____

for practicing the following words, by doing terrific
spelling activities and playing great spelling games!

Date _____

add	best	been	box	above
ask	ever	begin	dot	does
camp	head	digit	drop	done
fast	help	give	frog	jump
hat	left	into	gone	just
have	leg	its	lost	must
last	men	kid	lot	none
map	nest	live	odd	number
plan	next	quit	often	sum
than	set	sister	soft	what
☆ apple	☆ again	☆ because	☆ forgot	☆ bubble
☆ asked	☆ never	☆ gym	☆ job	☆ once
☆ bath	☆ sentence	☆ until	☆ tomorrow	☆ sometimes

5 Certificate

Provide an opportunity
for parents or guardians
to encourage and assess
their child's progress.

Say
- Write your name on the first line.
- Now I will write the date on the board for you to copy on the next line.
- Follow along as I read the certificate out loud.
- Be sure to show your parents or guardian all the words you've practiced spelling.

Take a minute to memorize...

Have students say the
memory verse from
lessons 1, 2, 3, 4, 5, and
6 with you.

125

6 Letter

Provide the parent or guardian with the spelling word lists for the next unit.

Say Show your parents or guardian this letter that tells them what your spelling words will be for the next unit. Ask them to put it in a special place where you will remember to practice them together.

Dear Parent,

We are about to begin a new spelling unit containing five weekly lessons. A set of ten words plus three challenge words will be studied each week. All the words will be reviewed in the sixth week.

Values based on the Scriptures listed below will be taught in each lesson.

Lesson 7	Lesson 8	Lesson 9	Lesson 10	Lesson 11
bake	be	buy	boat	blow
cake	clean	cry	cold	grow
came	east	dry	hold	know
game	even	fly	home	low
gate	he's	I'm	hope	own
gave	keep	light	most	row
grade	people	might	old	slow
late	read	night	road	snow
name	tree	right	roll	throw
page	we'll	tie	told	tow
☆ break	☆ between	☆ Bible	☆ don't	☆ below
☆ great	☆ Jesus	☆ child	☆ over	☆ mowing
☆ obey	☆ sleep	☆ high	☆ wrote	☆ snowman
Mark 5:19	Luke 11:36	Luke 1:46, 47	Matthew 22:39	Luke 21:33

Quotables!

"Inventive spelling refers to young children's attempts to use their best judgment about spelling."*

*Lutz, Elaine. 1986. ERIC/RCS Report: Invented Spelling and Spelling Development. Language Arts, Vol. 63, No. 7, November: 742-744.

Lost and Found

After an eventful day at the Fantastic Fun Fair, Beth has a real-life "lost and found" story to share with her classmates.

"**I** can't believe we get to spend all day at the Fantastic Fun Fair!" Katelynn's eyes flashed as she climbed into the Hill's car.

"Whadya want to ride first?" Beth asked her best friend.

"Tommy said the new Firebird roller coaster is the best! He rode it thirteen times!" Katelynn said excitedly. "But I'm not sure I want to, because it turns upside down!"

"Really? That would be fun! But when did Tommy ride it? I thought Daniel, James, and Tommy helped clean up after the tornado instead of going to the Fantastic Fun Fair with Daniel's family."

"They did, but Mr. DeVore surprised everyone and took them last weekend. I heard my mom talking to Daniel's mom. She said Daniel's dad was so proud of the boys' choice to help the people in Center City after the tornado instead of going to Fantastic Fun Fair that he skipped a meeting so he could take them all to the fair last weekend. Mrs. DeVore said her husband has never skipped a business meeting before!"

"So are you going to go with me on the Firebird roller coaster, or do I have to get my four-year-old brother to go with me?" teased Beth.

"I'll have to see it first," smiled Katelynn. "Maybe I'll go and maybe I won't."

"I'll go. I'll go." offered Luke from his seat beside Beth.

"I don't think so," said Mom turning around. "You aren't tall enough. The straps on the roller coaster have to fit snuggly to keep you from falling out."

"Awe, Mom," complained Luke. "I won't fall out."

The three children continued to talk excitedly about all the rides they wanted to go on and everything they wanted to see as they drove to the Fantastic Fun Fair. About an hour down the road Luke decided it was time to arrive and started asking every few minutes, "How much farther, Mom? How long will that take?" After Luke repeated his questions four or five times, Mrs. Hill put a story tape in the cassette deck and passed out coloring books and crayons to keep everyone distracted and occupied for the remainder of the two-hour trip. Finally they arrived at the huge Fantastic Fun Fair complex. Mr. Hill was guided to a parking place by attendants dressed up as animals.

"Why does that red bird want us to park so far away?" asked Luke. "It will take too long to walk."

"There's a tram that will come pick us up, Son," explained Mr. Hill.

When the girls climbed out of the car Katelynn looked up. "I don't think I want to go on that roller coaster!" She gazed at the tracks of the Firebird soaring above Fantastic Fun Fair.

The parking attendant overheard their conversation. "You'd love it!" he said.

"Agggg! You scared me!" Katelynn jumped. "Hey! Birds can't talk!"

Luke ran up beside the two bigger girls. "Why is your picture on the sign by our car?" he asked the big red bird.

"So you can help your daddy remember where he parked the car," answered the bird.

"Oh!" Luke said, his eyes wide, then ran to catch up with his parents.

After the tram ride to the entrance, the Hill family and Katelynn got their tickets scanned by a hippo and went in to explore the Fantastic Fun Fair. It was near the end of the day before Katelynn got up enough nerve to ride the Firebird roller coaster. She was surprised how much fun it was! After two rides they met Mr. and Mrs. Hill with Luke at the exit to the ride.

"Let's go one more time!" Katelynn suggested.

"I want to go!" begged Luke.

"No, Luke," Dad answered. "The tiger at the Firebird entrance said you weren't big enough yet. Maybe next year. We need to head toward the car soon. We still have a two-hour drive home. This will have to be your last ride, girls."

The two girls ran ahead to the entrance of the ride. Dad went to buy everyone some popcorn from a nearby stand and Mom plopped down on a bench to rest her weary feet.

"Can I go over to the fence and watch them ride?" Luke asked his mom.

"Sure," Mom said leaning back on the bench. A few minutes later Mr. Hill came back with five boxes of popcorn and sat down on the bench beside his wife. "Where's Luke?" he asked.

"Right over there trying to spot the girls on the roller coaster," Mrs. Hill turned to look, then froze. "He was there just a second ago! Luke! Luke come here!" Both parents crossed the paved path so they could see down the fence more clearly.

"Lucas!" Dad called. "This is not a game! Come here now!"

Mom ran one way and Dad ran the other. They both returned to the spot in the fence across from the bench — without four-year-old Luke.

"I'm going to go meet the girls at the exit of the Firebird so that we don't lose Beth and Katelynn too," said Mom.

"I'm going to talk to security and see if anyone has found him. Of course he may not even know he's lost yet!" said Dad.

"What if someone took him, Ken?" Mom said frantically

Dad tried to push down his own panic. "Go meet the girls . . . and pray," he said.

When Mom returned

127

with the girls a few minutes later, Dad was talking to an elephant. "Do you have a picture of Luke in your purse, Janette? He wants to take it to the entrance and show it to staff so that more people can start looking for him." Dad paused. "Did Luke have on his red shirt today with jeans?"

"Yes, he did," Mom answered, digging in her purse.

"One of you should wait here since this is where you saw him last. He might come back here looking for you," instructed the elephant. The other one needs to come with me.

Mom sat between the two frightened girls on the bench. No one wanted to eat the popcorn anymore. Beth started to cry. Soon Katelynn was in tears too. "What will happen to Luke? Do you think someone took him? Where could he have gone?" questioned Beth.

"Bethy, I don't know the answer to any of those questions," said Mom. "Our Heavenly Father does though. While Jesus was here on earth He told some stories about people who lost something. A shepherd lost one lamb from his flock of 100 sheep. He wanted to find the lamb and looked long and hard until he discovered him caught in some thorny bushes. He was so excited about finding the lost sheep that as soon as he got back home with the little lamb he told all of his friends and asked them over to celebrate."

"That's kinda like the little boy who lost his dog Honey during the tornado. Tommy took care of Honey at the warehouse where we helped after the tornado but Honey's master didn't know about that," said Beth.

"Tommy said that the dog's master was not going to give up looking for his dog," added Katelynn. "He told us that after the little boy found Honey he carried her around and told everyone about how he'd lost her, but now she was found."

"Good thinking girls!" Mom noticed that they'd quit crying, "The next story Jesus

told was about how a woman lost one of her ten valuable coins. She lit a candle and swept every inch of her house searching for the coin. When she finally found it she was so excited she couldn't help but go tell all her friends. She announced to anyone who would listen, 'Remember the valuable coin I lost? Well, I found it!'"

"I know how that feels," said Beth. "Remember when I couldn't find the video we rented? We had looked everywhere. I thought I was going to have to use my allowance for a year to pay for that video. But we found it in Luke's bed," explained Beth. "He liked the big dog in the movie and wanted to sleep with him."

"I know, silly, because you brought the movie and told us all about it at school. You were so excited you couldn't wait until 'show and tell' to tell. Remember?"

"Oh, where can that little guy be?" Beth's eyes began to fill with tears again. "I'd buy him that movie to sleep with if I could just have him back."

"Let's pray," suggested Katelynn. "Jesus knows where Luke is."

The three bowed their heads and Mom asked the Lord to look after Luke and help them find him before it got dark and the park closed.

As they opened their eyes Dad rushed up, but Luke was not with him.

"They found him at the car!" Dad almost shouted. "He made it by himself all the way to the car. He must have remembered that we parked by the red bird. I haven't talked to him yet. I wanted to come tell you so you wouldn't be worried." Dad ran a hand across his face. "The bird attendant we saw this morning in the parking lot radioed the office to tell them that Luke was waiting at the car for us!"

"Thank You, Lord." Beth prayed as they all hurried toward the car. "Thank You for taking care of my little brother. And thank You for those lost and found stories. I can hardly wait to tell my class at school tomorrow about Your newest one!"

2 Discussion Time

Check understanding of the story and development of personal values.

- What are some things you have lost? (Brainstorm. Make a list on the board.)
- How did you feel while you were looking?
- Tell about a time you found something you'd been trying to find for a long time.
- How did you feel when it was finally found?
- Who did you tell when you finally found what you'd lost?
- Remember God is delighted when you tell others the wonderful things He does for you!

A Preview

Name _____

Write each word as your teacher says it.

1. grade
2. page
3. bake
4. cake
5. came
6. game
7. gate
8. name
9. late
10. gave

Challenge Words

☆ break
☆ obey
☆ great

Words with /ā/

Lesson 7

Scripture
Mark 5:19

105

Challenge

For better spellers, challenge words may be included in the weekly list. Challenge words are starred.

Correct Immediately!

 Say

Let's correct our preview. I will write each word on the board. Put a dot under each letter on your preview as I spell the word out loud. If you spelled a word wrong, rewrite it correctly.

Progress Chart

Students may record scores. (Reproducible master in Appendix B.)

Take a minute to memorize . . .

Read the memory verse twice. Have students practice it with you two more times.

---

3 Preview

Test for knowledge of the correct spellings of these words. (See the instructions at the top right for challenge words.)

Say

I will say each word once, use the word in a sentence, then say the word again. Write the word on the lines in the Worktext.

1. grade — You will get a good **grade** on this test if you studied.
2. page — What **page** are you on in spelling?
3. bake — Did you **bake** the cake for Rosa's party last week?
4. cake — Did you have a **cake** on your birthday?
5. came — Mr. Hill **came** back with five boxes of popcorn.
6. game — "This is not a **game**!" called Dad.
7. gate — Dad ran to the entrance **gate** to talk to the security people.
8. name — "What's your son's **name**?" asked the elephant.
9. late — It was getting **late** and Luke was still lost.
10. gave — Mom **gave** Beth a hug and suggested they pray.
☆ break — It will **break** their hearts if they don't find Luke.
☆ obey — Always **obey** your parents and always stay where you can see them.
☆ great — What a **great** God we have!

Help students form a correct image of whole words.

Say Look at each word and think about its shape. Now, write the word in the correct word Shape Boxes. You may check off each word as you use it.

(In many words, the sound of /ā/ is spelled with **a-consonant-e**. A consonant cluster is two or more consonant sounds said together and spelled with more than one letter.)

Say In the word Shape Boxes, color the letters that spell the sound of /ā/ in each word. Circle the word that begins with the consonant cluster **gr**.

☆ Challenge

Draw the correctly shaped box around each letter in these words.

Say On a separate sheet of paper, write sentences using one or more of the spelling words.

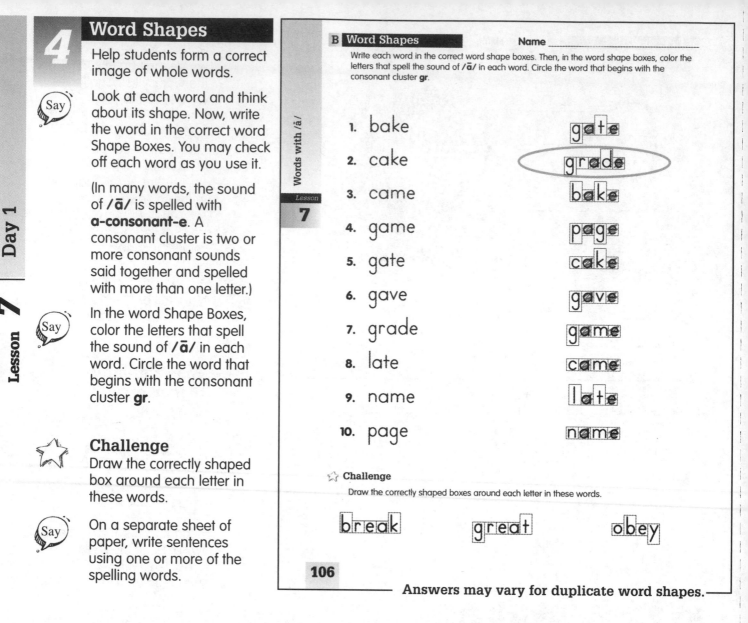

B Word Shapes   Name _____

Write each word in the correct word shape boxes. Then, in the word shape boxes, color the letters that spell the sound of /ā/ in each word. Circle the word that begins with the consonant cluster **gr**.

1. bake   gate
2. cake   grade
3. came   bake
4. game   page
5. gate   cake
6. gave   gave
7. grade   game
8. late   came
9. name   late
10. page   name

☆ **Challenge**

Draw the correctly shaped boxes around each letter in these words.

break   great   obey

106

Answers may vary for duplicate word shapes.

Be Prepared For Fun

Check these supply lists for **Fun Ways to Spell** presented **Day 2**. Purchase and/or gather these items ahead of time!

General
- Crayons
- 3 x 5 Cards cut in thirds (41 pieces per child)
- 3 x 5 Cards cut in thirds (14 more pieces to spell challenge words)
- Glue
- Bright Paper or Poster Board (about 3 pieces per child)
- Spelling List

Auditory
- Rhythm instruments (two wooden spoons, two pan lids, maracas)
- Spelling List

Visual
- Sidewalk Chalk
- Spelling List

Tactile
- Cotton Balls
- Glue
- Construction Paper
- Spelling List

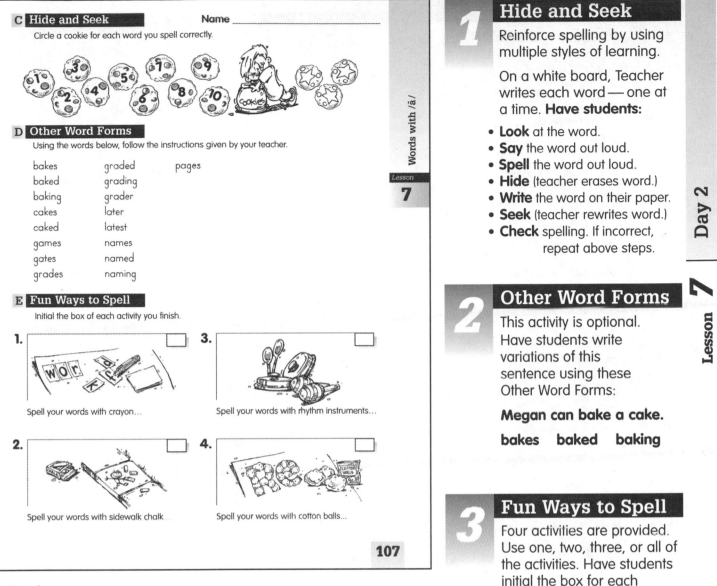

C Hide and Seek — Name _____

Circle a cookie for each word you spell correctly.

D Other Word Forms

Using the words below, follow the instructions given by your teacher.

bakes	graded	pages
baked	grading	
baking	grader	
cakes	later	
caked	latest	
games	names	
gates	named	
grades	naming	

E Fun Ways to Spell

Initial the box of each activity you finish.

1. Spell your words with crayon...

2. Spell your words with sidewalk chalk...

3. Spell your words with rhythm instruments...

4. Spell your words with cotton balls...

107

1 Hide and Seek

Reinforce spelling by using multiple styles of learning.

On a white board, Teacher writes each word — one at a time. **Have students:**

- **Look** at the word.
- **Say** the word out loud.
- **Spell** the word out loud.
- **Hide** (teacher erases word.)
- **Write** the word on their paper.
- **Seek** (teacher rewrites word.)
- **Check** spelling. If incorrect, repeat above steps.

2 Other Word Forms

This activity is optional. Have students write variations of this sentence using these Other Word Forms:

Megan can bake a cake.

bakes   baked   baking

3 Fun Ways to Spell

Four activities are provided. Use one, two, three, or all of the activities. Have students initial the box for each activity they complete.

Options:

- assign activities to students according to their learning styles
- set up the activities in learning centers for students to do throughout the day
- divide students into four groups and assign one activity per group
- do one activity per day

General

To spell your words with crayon . . .
- Write each letter of your spelling word on a card.
- Glue the cards on a sheet of paper in the right order to spell your words.
- Check your spelling.

Auditory

To spell your words with rhythm instruments . . .
- Look at a word on your spelling list.
- Close your eyes.
- Play your rhythm instruments softly while you whisper the spelling of the word.
- Open your eyes and check your spelling.

Visual

To spell your words with sidewalk chalk . . .
- Write each of your spelling words on the sidewalk (ball court or playground).
- Check your spelling.

Tactile

To spell your words with cotton balls . . .
- Choose a word from your spelling list.
- It may be a favorite word or a word you have trouble remembering how to spell.
- Write the word in tall, wide letters on a sheet of construction paper.
- Spread glue along the outline of each letter and press cotton balls into the glue.

131

1 ABC Order

Familiarize students with word meaning and usage. Write the alphabet on the board. Remind the students that when alphabetizing the letters always appear in this order. Write your name on the board. Ask for a volunteer to write their name on the board. Invite them to stand on your right if their name comes before yours in the alphabet and on your left if it comes after your name. Ask another child to join you. After writing their name on the board, help the second student to stand in correct ABC order with you. You may challenge your class by inviting more than two students up at once.

(Say) Write each set of spelling words in alphabetical order.

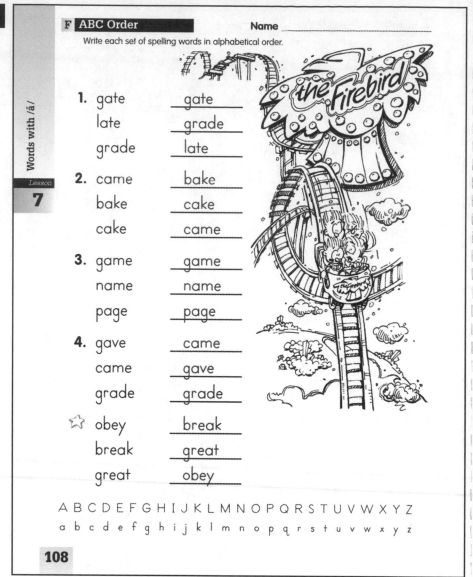

F ABC Order   Name _____

Write each set of spelling words in alphabetical order.

Words with /ā/

Lesson **7**

1. gate   gate
   late   grade
   grade   late

2. came   bake
   bake   cake
   cake   came

3. game   game
   name   name
   page   page

4. gave   came
   came   gave
   grade   grade

☆ obey   break
   break   great
   great   obey

A B C D E F G H I J K L M N O P Q R S T U V W X Y Z
a b c d e f g h i j k l m n o p q r s t u v w x y z

108

**Take a minute
to memorize.... .**

Read the memory verse twice. Have students practice it with you two more times.

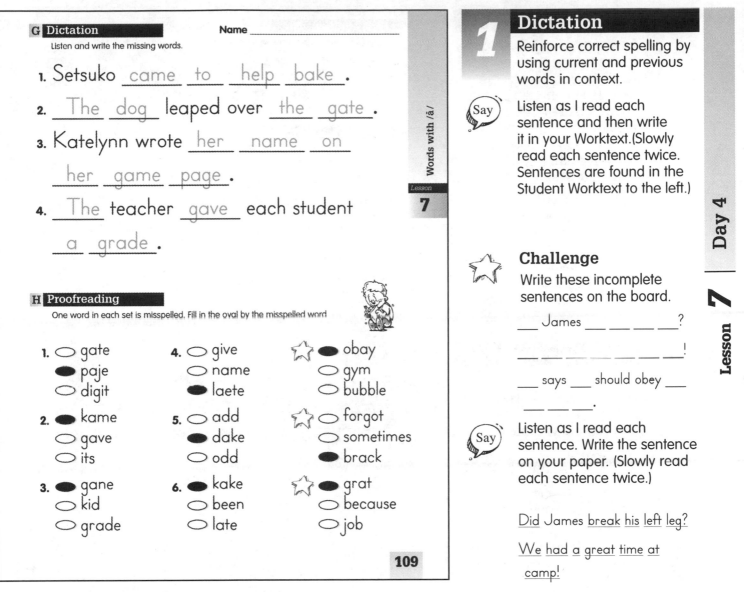

G Dictation

Listen and write the missing words.

1. Setsuko <u>came to help bake</u> .

2. <u>The dog</u> leaped over <u>the gate</u> .

3. Katelynn wrote <u>her name on her game page</u> .

4. <u>The</u> teacher <u>gave</u> each student <u>a grade</u> .

H Proofreading

One word in each set is misspelled. Fill in the oval by the misspelled word

1. ○ gate
   ● paje
   ○ digit

2. ● kame
   ○ gave
   ○ its

3. ● gane
   ○ kid
   ○ grade

4. ○ give
   ○ name
   ● laete

5. ○ add
   ● dake
   ○ odd

6. ● kake
   ○ been
   ○ late

☆ ● obay
   ○ gym
   ○ bubble

☆ ○ forgot
   ○ sometimes
   ● brack

☆ ● grat
   ○ because
   ○ job

Words with /ā/

Lesson 7

109

Day 4 · Lesson 7

1 Dictation

Reinforce correct spelling by using current and previous words in context.

(Say) Listen as I read each sentence and then write it in your Worktext.(Slowly read each sentence twice. Sentences are found in the Student Worktext to the left.)

☆ Challenge

Write these incomplete sentences on the board.

___ James ___ ___ ___ ___?

___ ___ ___ ___ ___ ___ ___!

___ says ___ should obey ___

___ ___ ___ .

(Say) Listen as I read each sentence. Write the sentence on your paper. (Slowly read each sentence twice.)

<u>Did James break his left leg?</u>

<u>We had a great time at camp!</u>

<u>God says I should obey my mom and dad.</u>

2 Proofreading

Familiarize students with standardized test format and reinforce recognizing misspelled words.

 (Say) Look at each set of words. One word in each set is misspelled. Fill in the oval by the misspelled word. (You may wish to pronounce each set of words to help students correctly identify them.)

133

3 Hide and Seek

Reinforce correct spelling of current spelling words. (A reproducible master is provided in Appendix A as shown on the inset page to the right.)

Write the words one at a time on a white board.

Have students:

- **Look** at the word.
- **Say** the word out loud.
- **Spell** the word out loud.
- **Hide** (teacher erases word.)
- **Write** the word on paper.
- **Seek** (teacher rewrites word.)
- **Check** spelling. If incorrect, rewrite word correctly.

4 Suffixes

Have your students complete this activity to strengthen spelling ability and expand vocabulary.

1 Posttest

Test mastery of the spelling words. Challenge words are starred.

(Say) I will say the word once, use the word in a sentence, then say the word again. Write the word on your paper.

Hide and Seek

Check a paper for each word you spell correctly.

1 3 5 7 9
2 4 6 8 10

Suffixes

Add **s**, **ed**, or **ing** to make new words from your spelling words.

+ s

1. bake + s   bakes
2. cake + s   cakes
3. game + s   games
4. name + s   names
5. gate + s   gates
6. grade + s   grades
7. page + s   pages
8. break + s   breaks
9. obey + s   obeys

+ ed

1. bake – e + ed   baked
2. name – e + ed   named
3. grade – e + ed   graded
4. page – e + ed   paged
5. obey + ed   obeyed

+ ing

1. bake – e + ing   baking
2. name – e + ing   naming
3. grade – e + ing   grading
4. break + ing   breaking
5. obey + ing   obeying

373

---

1. grade   You are in the second **grade.**
2. page   Do this **page** neatly.
3. bake   Did Grandma Anderson **bake** Rosa a cake?
4. cake   Did your grandma ever bake a **cake** for you?
5. gave   They all **gave** the hippo their tickets to scan at the entrance.
6. name   The **name** of the roller coaster was the Firebird.
7. late   It was **late** in the day when Katelynn rode in the Firebird.
8. gate   Luke went through the entrance **gate** and back to the car.
9. game   Luke was not playing a **game** with his parents.
10. came   Dad **came** back and said that Luke was found at the car.
☆ obey   It is a good idea to **obey** God's rules.
☆ break   It will **break** God's heart if you choose not to love Him.
☆ great   God is **great**!

Progress Chart

Students may record scores. (Reproducible master in Appendix B.)

Personal Dictionary

Students may add any words they have misspelled to their personal dictionaries for reference when writing. (Cover in Appendix B.)

I Game

Name _____

Get in line to ride the Firebird Roller Coaster. Move up in line one space for each word you or your team spells correctly from this week's word list.

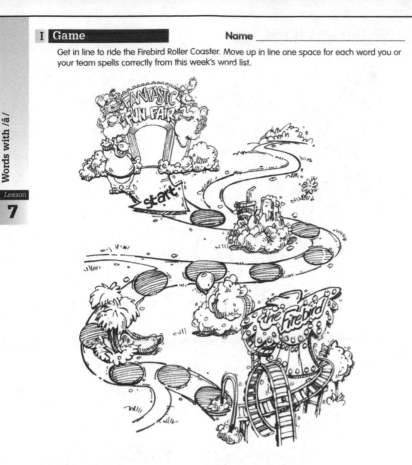

Remember: Praise God for each special thing He does for you.

J Journaling

Write three sentences in your journal about what wonderful things God has done for you.

110

How to Play:

- Divide students into two teams, and decide which team will go first. Have one team race to the roller coaster with Katelynn, and one team with Beth.
- Optional: If you have an even number of students, you may wish to pair students from opposing teams and have them share a game page, each moving spaces for their own team on that page.
- Have each student place their game piece on Start.
- Have a student from team A go to the board.
- Read each spelling word two times slowly and clearly. (You may also wish to use the word in a sentence. Ex.: "cat — The cat climbed a tree. — cat")
- Have the student write the word on the board.
- If the word is spelled correctly, instruct all the members of team A to move their game piece forward one space on the game board. (Note: If the word is misspelled, correct the spelling immediately.)
- Alternate between teams A and B as you go down the word list.
- The team to reach the Firebird roller coaster first is the winner.

Non-Competitive Option: At the end of the game, say: "Class, I am proud of your efforts to spell the words correctly. If you had fun and tried your best, you are all winners!"

2 Game

Reinforce spelling skills and provide motivation and interest.

Materials

- game page (from student text)
- flat buttons, dry beans, pennies, or game discs (1 per child)
- game word list

Game Word List

Check off each word lightly in pencil as it is used.

1. **bake**
2. **cake**
3. **came**
4. **game**
5. **name**
6. **gate**
7. **late**
8. **gave**
9. **grade**
10. **page**
☆ **break**
☆ **great**
☆ **obey**

3 Journaling

Provide a meaningful reason for correct spelling through personal writing.

Review the story using discussion leads provided on the following page. Encourage students to apply the Scriptural value in their journaling.

 **Take a minute to memorize . . .**

Have students say the memory verse with you once.

3 Journaling

Provide a meaningful reason for correct spelling through personal writing.

- The morning after she went to the Fantastic Fun Fair, what did Beth want to tell her classmates about? (How Luke had been lost and found at the Fantastic Fun Fair.)
- What are some wonderful things God has done for you? (Help the students make a list on the board.)
- Write at least three things in your journal that God has done for you.

Quotables!

"When students invent spellings, they are thinking and learning about words."*

*Scott, Jill E. 1994. Spelling for Readers and Writers. The Reading Teacher, Vol. 48, No. 2, October: 188-190.

A Light Inside

Christopher learns that letting God's light shine through you makes even the worst circumstances more bearable.

In the empty lot next door, seven-year-old Christopher Wright placed his left foot on a firm branch and reached for the next handhold in the familiar old climbing tree. His mind wasn't really on his hands and feet as he headed up to his favorite thinking spot. A nicely curved limb about halfway up the old tree made a perfect place to relax and think . . . and to get away from his sisters when he wanted to. He was almost there when his right hand slipped. Grabbing wildly for a handhold with his left hand, Christopher lost his balance and fell.

"Mom! Mom!" Kristin shrieked as she slammed through the back door. "Mom! Christopher fell! MOM! Come quick!" Mrs. Wright dropped the towel she'd been folding and rushed out the door behind Christopher's frantic twin.

Later, at the hospital, the doctor put the finishing touches on a clean white cast covering Christopher's left arm. "It's not a really bad break, so we should be able to take the cast off in a few weeks," the doctor told Mrs. Wright as he worked. "During the day he'll need to keep the broken arm in this sling. He does have several bumps and bruises, so he'll be sore for a few days." The doctor smiled at Christopher. "Well, at least it's your left arm that broke. You'll still be able to do most things for yourself. Won't you, young man?" Christopher glanced up at his mother who stood close by.

"Actually, he's left-handed." Mom smiled at the surprised look on the doctor's face.

"Well, I guess you'll be learning how to do lots of new things with your right hand." The doctor chuckled. "Just try to get more food inside you than all over you with that right hand. Your body is going to need lots of good food to help it mend this broken bone."

At supper that evening Christopher found out just what the doctor meant. Try as he might, the soup in his spoon just didn't seem to make it into his mouth very often. He was tired and frustrated and his arm hurt. "Would you like for me to help you, Son?" Mom asked. Christopher nodded and blinked the tears back. Mom spooned the soup into his mouth like she used to for his baby brother Cory, but Christopher was too worn out to care if he looked silly. After supper Dad got Cory ready for bed while Mom helped Christopher. She combed his brown hair, washed his face and hands with a wash cloth, changed him into pajamas and even brushed his teeth.

When Christopher awoke the next morning something seemed different. He looked groggily around the room. The book on Air Force jets that he'd been looking at yesterday lay open on his desk. His precious red Cloud Runner remote control airplane was hanging in the corner right where it was supposed to be. But the sun seemed awfully bright and the house seemed awfully quiet. Christopher started to hop out of bed to investigate when the sore spots all along his left side made him wince. The cast on his arm reminded him of yesterday's events. "Mom!" Christopher called.

"How are you feeling this morning, Son?" Mom asked as she entered the room. She sat gently on the edge of Christopher's bed and ran her fingers through his tousled brown hair.

"I hurt," Christopher whimpered.

"I'll get one of the pills the doctor said you should have for pain." Mom stood and started out of the room. "What would you like for breakfast?"

"Uh, bread with peanut butter and honey, I guess," Christopher responded. "What time is it? Where're the girls?"

Mom checked her watch. "It's nine-fifteen. Your dad went in to work later than usual so he could take Kristin and Cathy to school this morning. I'll be right back." She disappeared out the door just as Christopher's little brother Cory came in dragging his yellow blanket. He stopped at the edge of Christopher's bed and stared seriously at Christopher's cast.

"Kisterfer got bad owee," he stated solemnly. "Kisterfer hurt bad?" he asked, using his own name for his big brother.

"It doesn't feel very good." Christopher sighed as he tried to find a comfortable position.

Christopher spent the day taking it easy. He watched videos with his little brother and slept quite a bit. Mom fed him his meals, combed his hair, straightened his bed and brought him drinks. She wrapped his cast in plastic and gave him a bath. She read to him and brought him books and magazines to look at.

Over the next few days Christopher found lots of things the cast on his arm made more difficult. Even though he did get better at doing things with his right hand he still couldn't draw or color. He couldn't work on his model planes. He couldn't play ball or ride his bike. He couldn't comb his hair, brush his teeth or feed himself. He couldn't button his shirt or tie his shoes.

At school, the other children all wanted to write on his cast. Soon it was covered with colorful drawings and words as each of his classmates added to the artwork. And Christopher found more things that he couldn't do. When the other students

137

cut things out, Christopher couldn't. He couldn't write, either. He couldn't even write his own name well. "Mrs. Morgan," James said to their teacher, "it looks like a bird made tracks all over Christopher's paper." It seemed to Christopher that everyone laughed.

One evening Christopher was lying across the plaid bedspread in his room staring at the ceiling when Mom called, "Christopher, time to set the table, Son." Christopher jumped up and stormed down the hall into the kitchen.

"Why do I have to do this?" he griped as he flung place mats around the table. "I can only use one hand. Why can't Kristin or Cathy do this? They both have two perfectly good arms. It's not fair. It's so hard for me to do things! I shouldn't have to do any of this! And my arm hurts. And itches! Why should I . . ." Christopher's angry words stopped mid-sentence when he felt Dad's hand drop onto his shoulder.

"Finish setting the table, Son." Dad's voice was quiet, but firm. "Right now." Dad looked into Christopher's stormy green eyes, and squeezed his shoulder lightly. Christopher did as he was told.

"Another delicious meal, Maggy." Dad winked across the table at Mom as the Wright family finished up the last of the baked potatoes, salad, and rolls on their plates. "I need to run into the store for the parts to fix that leaky faucet." Dad waved his hand at the kitchen sink that steadily dripped. "Want to come along, Christopher?" Dad's question took Christopher by surprise.

"Yeah, sure," Christopher replied. Going to the store with his dad made him feel important. This was a job for the men of the family. In just a few minutes Mr. Wright and Christopher arrived at the store and headed toward the faucets and plumbing supplies. As Dad chose the items he needed, Christopher noticed a

man come around the corner. He was moving slowly in a specially designed wheelchair. One hand lay limply in his lap while the other hand operated the controls on the chair. His legs looked small and shrunken. Christopher stared and then turned red when the man looked up at him and smiled.

"Hello, young man." The man's voice was kind and his eyes twinkled. "I bet you're a big help to your dad."

"Uh, um, uh . . ." Christopher replied. Dad turned and spoke with the man in the wheelchair for a few moments before placing the part that the man needed in the special wire basket attached to the back of the chair.

On the way home Christopher asked, "Dad, what was wrong with that man?"

"I don't know, Son. He didn't say," Dad replied. "Maybe he was born that way or perhaps he was in an accident of some kind that paralyzed his legs and one arm."

After a short silence Christopher said, "He was sure nice, wasn't he, Dad?"

"Yes, son. Whatever happened to ruin part of his body, he hasn't let it ruin his life. He did tell me that knowing God helped him make it day by day." Dad paused and added, "When bad things happen to us we can either get angry and lash out at others, or we can ask God to help us be patient and kind. When we ask God for help it's like a light inside that others can see even when bad things happen to us." After another pause Dad said thoughtfully, "I think it's Luke 11:36 that says 'If you are filled with light . . . then your face will be radiant too.' Just like that man at the store."

When Christopher and his dad entered the house, the other Wright children were already in bed. Christopher started down the hall to his room, but stopped short when he noticed his mother. She sat on the couch with her head leaning back and her eyes closed. "She looks so tired," Christopher thought with a jolt. "She's done so much for me since my arm got

broken — practically everything!" he suddenly realized. "And I said such awful things when she asked me to set the table, instead of thanking her for all the stuff she does for me."

"Dear Jesus," Christopher prayed as he headed for his room, "please help me. Put your love inside me so everyone can see it like a light on my face."

After Dad helped him get ready for bed and tucked him in, Christopher's mom came in to say goodnight. There was just enough light filtering in the door that Christopher could see her smile as he whispered, "I'm sorry for what I said before supper. Thank you for always taking care of me. You're the best mom in the world, and I love you."

Discussion Time

2 Check understanding of the story and development of personal values.

- What happened to Christopher?
- Why was it hard for Christopher to do many things?
- Can you name some things he found difficult to do?
- How did Christopher react when his arm hurt and itched and he couldn't do the things he wanted to do?
- What was different about the man Christopher and his dad saw at the store?
- What lesson did Christopher learn from that man?

Name _____

1. tree
2. be
3. he's
4. keep
5. clean
6. even
7. east
8. read
9. we'll
10. people

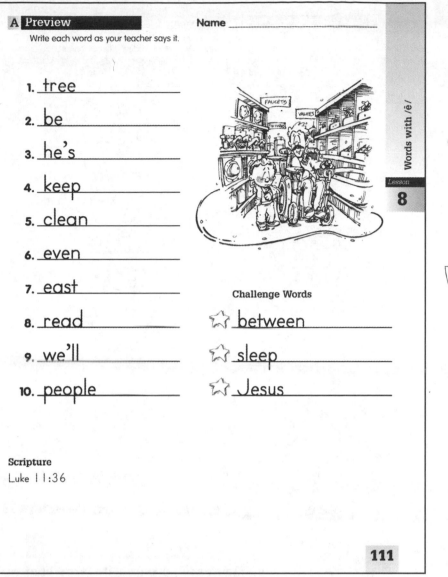

Challenge Words

☆ between
☆ sleep
☆ Jesus

Scripture
Luke 11:36

Words with /ē/

Lesson **8**

111

Challenge

For better spellers, challenge words may be included in the weekly list. Challenge words are starred.

Correct Immediately!

Let's correct our preview. I will write each word on the board. Put a dot under each letter on your preview as I spell the word out loud. If you spelled a word wrong, rewrite it correctly.

Progress Chart

Students may record scores. (Reproducible master in Appendix B.)

Take a minute to memorize . . .

Read the memory verse twice. Have students practice it with you two more times.

Lesson **8** | **Day 1**

---

3 Preview

Test for knowledge of the correct spellings of these words. (See the instructions at the top right for challenge words.)

Say I will say the word once, use the word in a sentence, then say the word again. Write the word on the lines in the Worktext.

1. **tree**   Christopher fell out of the **tree**.
2. **be**   Do you think he'll **be** all right?
3. **he's**   Now **he's** got a broken arm.
4. **keep**   He will have to **keep** the cast on his arm for a few weeks.
5. **clean**   Mom had to help Christopher **clean** up.
6. **even**   Christopher can't **even** comb his own hair very well.
7. **east**   It is hard for him to write the word "**east**."
8. **read**   His mom will **read** a book to him.
9. **we'll**   Then **we'll** sign our names on Christopher's cast.
10. **people**   Doctors take care of **people** who get hurt.
☆ **between**   The bone is broken **between** his wrist and his elbow.
☆ **sleep**   Mom let Christopher **sleep** late the next morning.
☆ **Jesus**   **Jesus** cares about each one of us.

139

4 Word Shapes

Help students form a correct image of whole words.

Say Look at each word and think about its shape. Now, write the word in the correct word Shape Boxes. You may check off each word as you use it.

(In many words, the sound of /ē/ is spelled with **e**, **ee**, or **ea**. A contraction is a short form of two words. An apostrophe takes the place of letters that are left out.)

Say In the word Shape Boxes, color the letter or letters that spell the sound of /ē/ in each word. Circle the words that are contractions. Draw a line under the words that begin with the consonant clusters **cl** or **tr**.

Challenge

Draw the correctly shaped box around each letter in these words.

Say On a separate sheet of paper, write other words that contain the spelling patterns in the word list. See how many words you can write.

Be Prepared For Fun

Check these supply lists for **Fun Ways to Spell** presented **Day 2**. Purchase and/or gather these items ahead of time!

B Word Shapes   Name _____

Write each word in the correct word shape boxes. Then, in the word shape boxes, color the letter or letters that spell the sound of /ē/ in each word. Circle the words that are contractions. Draw a line under the words that begin with the consonant clusters **cl** or **tr**.

Words with /ē/

Lesson
8

1. be
2. clean
3. east
4. even
5. he's
6. keep
7. people
8. read
9. tree
10. we'll

east
he's
read
we'll
clean
tree
keep
even
be
people

☆ **Challenge**

Draw the correctly shaped boxes around each letter in these words.

between   Jesus   sleep

112

Answers may vary for duplicate word shapes.

General
- Eraser
- Dark Construction Paper
- Spelling List

Auditory
- Spelling List

Visual
- Poster Paint
- Paint Brush
- Art Paper (3 or 4 sheets per child)
- Spelling List

Tactile
- Damp sand in plastic storage box with lid
- Spelling List

140

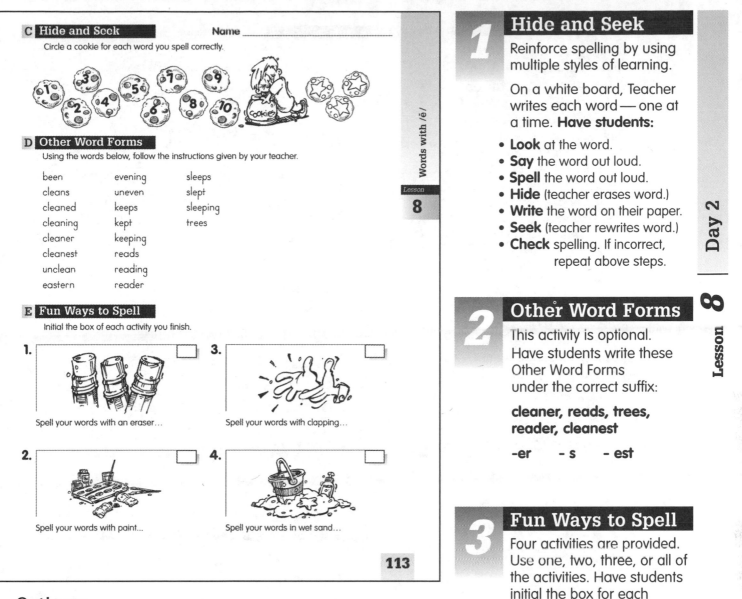

C Hide and Seek   Name _____

Circle a cookie for each word you spell correctly.

D Other Word Forms

Using the words below, follow the instructions given by your teacher.

been	evening	sleeps
cleans	uneven	slept
cleaned	keeps	sleeping
cleaning	kept	trees
cleaner	keeping	
cleanest	reads	
unclean	reading	
eastern	reader	

E Fun Ways to Spell

Initial the box of each activity you finish.

1. ☐

Spell your words with an eraser...

3. ☐

Spell your words with clapping...

2. ☐

Spell your words with paint...

4. ☐

Spell your words in wet sand...

113

Hide and Seek

1

Reinforce spelling by using multiple styles of learning.

On a white board, Teacher writes each word — one at a time. **Have students:**

- **Look** at the word.
- **Say** the word out loud.
- **Spell** the word out loud.
- **Hide** (teacher erases word.)
- **Write** the word on their paper.
- **Seek** (teacher rewrites word.)
- **Check** spelling. If incorrect, repeat above steps.

Day 2

Other Word Forms

2

This activity is optional. Have students write these Other Word Forms under the correct suffix:

cleaner, reads, trees, reader, cleanest

-er   - s   - est

Lesson 8

Fun Ways to Spell

3

Four activities are provided. Use one, two, three, or all of the activities. Have students initial the box for each activity they complete.

Options:

- assign activities to students according to their learning styles
- set up the activities in learning centers for students to do throughout the day
- divide students into four groups and assign one activity per group
- do one activity per day

General

To spell your words with an eraser . . .
- Turn your pencil upside down.
- Use the eraser to write your spelling words on a sheet of dark construction paper.
- Check your spelling.

Auditory

To spell your words with clapping . . .
- Look at a word on your spelling list.
- Close your eyes.
- Clap your hands softly while you whisper the spelling of the word.
- Open your eyes and check your spelling.

Visual

To spell your words with paint . . .
- Dip your brush in one color of poster paint.
- Paint a spelling word on your paper.
- Rinse your brush well in clean water and wipe it dry on a paper towel before dipping it in another color to paint another word.

Tactile

To spell your words in damp sand . . .
- Use finger to write a spelling word in damp sand.
- Check your spelling.
- Smooth the sand with your fingers and write another word.

141

1 Clues

Familiarize students with word meaning and usage. Write the words **not tall** on the board. Explain to the students that these are clue words. Ask the students what word these clue words make them think of. Ask a volunteer to write the answer, **short**, on the board. Write **house** on the board. Invite students to suggest clue words of their own for **house** and other words.

(Say) In this activity a clue is given for each of your spelling words. Find the spelling word that matches each clue.

F Clues

Use the clues to write the spelling words.

Name _____

1. <u>he's</u>   he is
2. <u>we'll</u>   we will
3. <u>even</u>   not odd
4. <u>clean</u>   not dirty
5. <u>people</u>   human beings
6. <u>keep</u>   fulfill, like a promise
7. <u>be</u>   exist or to take place
8. <u>tree</u>   a tall plant with a trunk
9. <u>east</u>   face this way to see the sun rise
10. <u>read</u>   know what written words mean
☆ <u>between</u> in the middle of
☆ <u>sleep</u>   to take a nap
☆ <u>Jesus</u>   the Son of God

Word Bank

| be | east | he's | people | tree | ☆ between | ☆ sleep |
| clean | even | keep | read | we'll | ☆ Jesus | |

114

Take a minute to memorize . . .

Have students say the memory verses from lessons 1 and 2 with you. Read the memory verse twice. Have students practice it with you two more times.

142

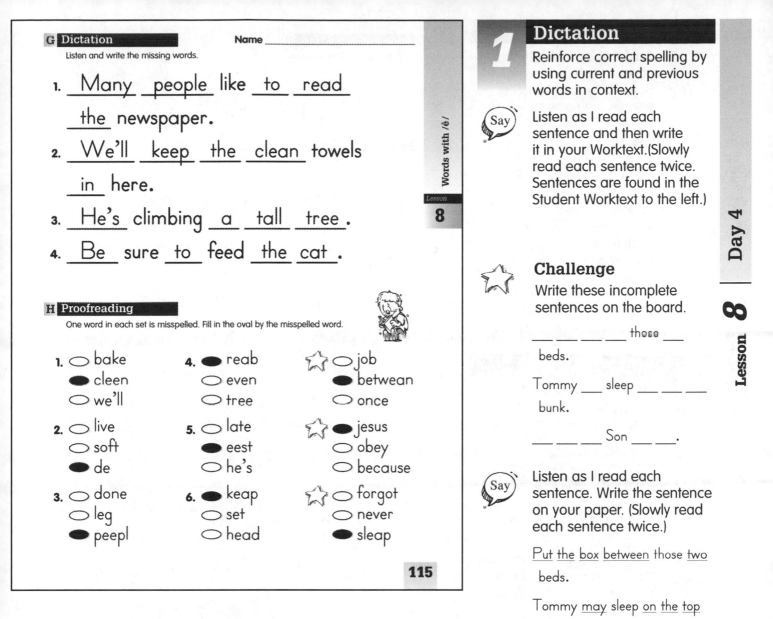

G Dictation

Listen and write the missing words.

1. Many people like to read the newspaper.

2. We'll keep the clean towels in here.

3. He's climbing a tall tree.

4. Be sure to feed the cat.

H Proofreading

One word in each set is misspelled. Fill in the oval by the misspelled word.

1. ○ bake
   ● cleen
   ○ we'll

2. ○ live
   ○ soft
   ● de

3. ○ done
   ○ leg
   ● peepl

4. ● reab
   ○ even
   ○ tree

5. ○ late
   ● eest
   ○ he's

6. ● keap
   ○ set
   ○ head

☆ ○ job
   ● betwean
   ○ once

☆ ● jesus
   ○ obey
   ○ because

☆ ○ forgot
   ○ never
   ● sleap

115

---

1 Dictation

Reinforce correct spelling by using current and previous words in context.

(Say) Listen as I read each sentence and then write it in your Worktext.(Slowly read each sentence twice. Sentences are found in the Student Worktext to the left.)

☆ Challenge

Write these incomplete sentences on the board.

___ ___ ___ ___ those ___ beds.

Tommy ___ sleep ___ ___ ___ bunk.

___ ___ ___ Son ___ ___.

(Say) Listen as I read each sentence. Write the sentence on your paper. (Slowly read each sentence twice.)

P̲u̲t̲ the̲ b̲o̲x̲ b̲e̲t̲w̲e̲e̲n̲ those t̲w̲o̲ beds.

Tommy m̲a̲y̲ sleep o̲n̲ the̲ t̲o̲p̲ bunk.

J̲e̲s̲u̲s̲ i̲s̲ the̲ Son o̲f̲ G̲o̲d̲.

---

2 Proofreading

Familiarize students with standardized test format and reinforce recognizing misspelled words.

(Say) Look at each set of words. One word in each set is misspelled. Fill in the oval by the misspelled word. (You may wish to pronounce each set of words to help students correctly identify them.)

3 Hide and Seek

Reinforce correct spelling of current spelling words. (A reproducible master is provided in Appendix A as shown on the inset page to the right.)

Write the words one at a time on a white board.

Have students:

- **Look** at the word.
- **Say** the word out loud.
- **Spell** the word out loud.
- **Hide** (teacher erases word.)
- **Write** the word on paper.
- **Seek** (teacher rewrites word.)
- **Check** spelling. If incorrect, rewrite word correctly.

4 Sentence Fun

Have your students complete this activity to strengthen spelling ability and expand vocabulary.

1 Posttest

Test mastery of the spelling words. Challenge words are starred.

(Say) I will say the word once, use the word in a sentence, then say the word again. Write the word on your paper.

1.	clean	The doctor put a **clean** cast on Christopher's broken arm.
2.	read	Can you **read** the label on this bottle of pills?
3.	east	The big tree is on the **east** side of the house.
4.	tree	Christopher won't be able to climb his favorite **tree** for a while.
5.	keep	Mom put plastic over the cast to **keep** it dry in the bathtub.
6.	even	The man in the wheelchair is happy **even** though he can't walk.
7.	he's	Because he has God's light inside, **he's** nice to be around.
8.	people	Sometimes **people** get mad when things don't go well for them.
9.	be	Which kind of person do you want to **be**?
10.	we'll	Today **we'll** ask God to shine His light through us all the time.
☆	sleep	It was hard for Christopher to go to **sleep**.
☆	between	The man guided his wheelchair **between** the store aisles.
☆	Jesus	Ask **Jesus** for help whenever you're tempted to be unkind.

Progress Chart
Students may record scores. (Reproducible master in Appendix B.)

Personal Dictionary
Students may add any words they have misspelled to their personal dictionaries for reference when writing. (Cover in Appendix B.)

Appendix A — Lesson 8

Hide and Seek
Check a paper for each word you spell correctly.

1 3 5 7 9
2 4 6 8 10

Sentence Fun
Read each sentence. Write the missing words in the sentence.

1. Christopher was __being__ selfish and unkind when __he__ argued about setting the table.
2. Christopher __slept__ late the morning after he had __been__ hurt.
3. Mom __kept__ him busy by __reading__ to him.
4. That __evening__ Mom __cleaned__ his face and combed his hair.
5. Christopher __kept__ making funny lines when he tried to write __eastern__.
6. __We__ can be fun to be around by __keeping__ Jesus in our hearts.

Word Bank					
being	cleaned	evening	keeping	kept	reading
been	eastern	he	kept	slept	we

374

I Game

Name _____

Retrace Christopher's path the day he broke his arm. Move one space each time you or your team spells a word correctly from this week's word list.

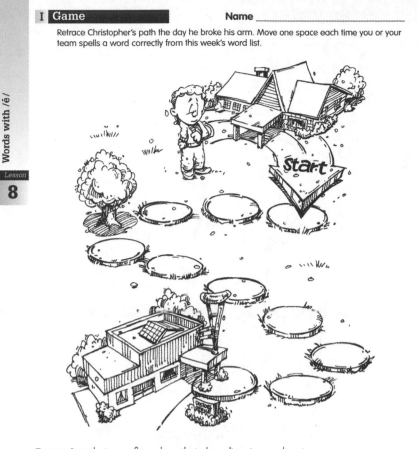

Remember: Let your face show that Jesus lives in your heart.

J Journaling

Write your own prayer in your journal asking God to fill you with His love so everyone can see it like a light on your face.

116

How to Play:

- Divide students into two teams, and decide which team will go first.
- Have each student place their game piece on Start.
- Have a student from team A go to the board.
- Read the spelling word two times slowly and clearly. (You may also wish to use the word in a sentence. Ex.: "cat — The cat climbed a tree. — cat")
- Have the student write the word on the board.
- If the word is spelled correctly, instruct all the members of team A to move their game piece forward one space on the game board. (Note: If the word is misspelled, correct the spelling immediately.)
- Alternate between teams A and B as you go down the word list.
- The team to reach the hospital first is the winner.

Non-Competitive Option: At the end of the game, say: "Class, I am proud of your efforts to spell the words correctly. If you had fun and tried your best, you are all winners!"

2 Game

Reinforce spelling skills and provide motivation and interest.

Materials

- game page (from student text)
- flat buttons, dry beans, pennies, or game discs (1 per child)
- game word list

Game Word List

Use of challenge words is optional.

1. **be**
2. **clean**
3. **east**
4. **even**
5. **he's**
6. **keep**
7. **people**
8. **read**
9. **tree**
10. **we'll**
☆ **between**
☆ **sleep**
☆ **Jesus**

3 Journaling

Provide a meaningful reason for correct spelling through personal writing.

Review the story using discussion leads provided on the following page. Encourage students to apply the Scriptural value in their journaling.

Take a minute to memorize . . .

Have students say the memory verses from lessons 7 and 8 with you.

145

3 Journaling

Provide a meaningful reason for correct spelling through personal writing.

Say

- Christopher was very frustrated when he broke his arm. What did he say when his mother asked him to set the table? ("Why do I have to do this? Why can't Kristin or Cathy do this? I shouldn't have to do any of this? My arm hurts. And itches!")

- The man in the wheelchair at the store couldn't walk at all or use one arm. Did he act angry and frustrated like Christopher did? (No). What did he say helped him to make it day by day? (Knowing God.)

- How do you think knowing God helped him? (When he felt frustrated, angry, or upset he could talk to God and ask Him for help. God would help him be patient and kind.)

- Christopher asked God to put His love inside so everyone could see it like a light on his face. In your journal, write your own prayer asking God to fill you with His love.

"*Spelling is more than rote memorization and drill.*"*

*Read, Charles, and Richard Hodges. 1982. "Spelling." In Encyclopedia of Educational Research, edited by H. Mitzel. 5th ed. New York: Macmillan.

A Bad Choice

When Tommy makes a big mistake, his dad helps him understand what God is like.

"*L*ook at this, Tommy." Daniel brought out another new toy. "It's a super-duper high power water gun. It can shoot twenty feet easy." Daniel held the water gun up to his shoulder and pretended to aim at different things in the room. "Pow, Pow, pu-pu-pu-pu-PUM!" He blasted imaginary enemies. "Do you want to go outside and really see it in action?"

"Nah. Let's go play on the computer," Tommy suggested. "I like that new game you have that you can earn money to help the town build a playground and park. You wanna?"

"I guess, but just for a little while. It gets boring," Daniel replied and led the way back to his bedroom from the large playroom where the boys had spent a lot of their time that afternoon. The computer sat on a desk along one wall of Daniel's bedroom. Tommy soon was caught up in trying to earn enough money to plant grass in the park. Daniel lost interest in a few minutes. "Come on, Tommy, let's go play with my racetrack set!"

"In a minute," Tommy replied. "I just have to get a little more money and I can put swings in the playground."

Daniel tried again. "I have a foosball table. I bet you'd be really good at that. You know, where you turn the handles and it makes the little plastic men on the field kick the ball around till it goes in the goal and earns points."

"Okay. Just a minute," Tommy replied absently.

Daniel wandered through the door into the playroom but was soon back. "Look at this, Tommy." He held out something.

When Tommy glanced up, he saw a brand-new black baseball glove with a shiny white ball resting inside. "I thought your glove was brown," Tommy said.

"I decided I wanted a black one, so my mom got this one for me." Daniel grinned. "Let's try it out."

Tommy glanced out the large window in Daniel's room and frowned. The clouds that had threatened to spill over all morning were now dropping their load of moisture. "It's raining, so we can't go outside." Tommy started to turn back to the computer when Daniel tossed the ball to him and Tommy grabbed it by instinct. "Watch out, Daniel! We can't throw that in here!" Tommy handed the ball back. "It'll break something."

"So we won't throw it in here," Daniel replied. "We'll go in the playroom. There's nothing in there that would break if we're really careful. Come on, let's play catch! You can even use my new black glove and I'll use my old one. It'll be a lot of fun, Tommy. Nothing can happen if we're careful," Daniel argued.

"Well," Tommy said hesitantly, "I don't know . . ."

"Come on, Tommy. My mom won't mind," Daniel added.

Within minutes the boys were playing catch in the large playroom. The new black glove fit Tommy perfectly. "Watch this throw." Tommy pretended to wind up like a major league pitcher and then let the ball roll gently across the floor toward Daniel instead of pitching it. Both boys were clowning around and giggling. "Now, this is a curve ball," Tommy announced as he threw the ball in a high arc to Daniel. Daniel returned a "knuckle ball." "Okay, here comes a fast one." Tommy turned as Daniel pretended to be a fielder and ran across the room. The ball sailed toward Daniel, right past his glove, through the door and straight into the computer monitor sitting on the desk in Daniel's bedroom.

The boys were still standing there staring at the mess when Daniel's mother arrived upstairs.

At home that evening a miserable Tommy sat across the table from his parents. Lisa was in her room doing homework. Dad shook his head and started to say something, then stopped and shook his head again.

"Tommy, I know you knew better than to play catch indoors. What I'd like to know is why you decided to do it anyway?" Mom asked in a serious voice.

"Well," Tommy began quietly. "Daniel said it was okay and that his mom wouldn't mind. But she minded. A lot."

"Did you really think it was okay to play catch, son?" Mom looked right into his eyes and Tommy ducked his head.

"No, I guess not. I just really wanted to, so I did," Tommy whispered. "It was a bad choice."

"I'm glad that you realize that, Son," Mom continued in a quiet tone. "And I'm glad that you apologized to Mrs. DeVore. But there are always consequences for our wrong actions, even when we are sorry. The computer monitor that was broken cost $450. Of course, you don't have any way to get that much money, so your Dad gave $450 to Mrs. DeVore to replace what you broke. He had been saving that money to buy a computer for our family. We know that you and Lisa enjoy playing computer games and many of the games are good for you because they teach you new things. A computer would be a big help to your Dad in keeping records and doing other things as well. But now it will be a while longer before we

147

Day 1

Lesson 9

have one. Do you understand, Son?" Mom finished in the same quiet voice.

Tommy nodded miserably as the tears spilled out of his tightly shut eyes. "I, I'm s-s-s-sorry," he choked out. He heard his dad get up and felt his mother's hand stroke his arm. Then his father wrapped him in a warm hug, chair and all.

"We forgive you, Son," his dad said. "We love you." Tommy buried his head in his dad's chest, wrapped his arms tightly around his dad's neck and hung on.

As Tommy started to turn his covers down on his bed that night, he had to move a stack of papers that he had brought home from school that day. The handwriting border sheet on the very top of the stack caught his attention. "Oh, how I praise the Lord. How I rejoice in God my Savior!" he had written as neatly as he could on the sheet.

"So, that's what God is like," Tommy thought. "Even when I make mistakes, God saves me — just like Dad saved me from the bad mistake I made today." Then Tommy bowed his head. "Thank you, God, for saving me." he prayed. "And thank you for my dad who loves me, too!"

2

Discussion Time

Check understanding of the story and development of personal values.

- Where were Daniel and Tommy playing?
- What did Tommy want to do?
- What bad choice did the boys make?
- What happened because they did something they shouldn't have done?
- Who helped Tommy pay for the broken monitor?
- Why wouldn't Tommy's family be able to get a computer very soon?
- How was what Tommy's dad did like what God does for us?

148

A Preview

Name _____

Write each word as your teacher says it.

1. light _____
2. dry _____
3. right _____
4. fly _____
5. buy _____
6. cry _____
7. I'm _____
8. might _____
9. tie _____
10. night _____

Challenge Words

☆ Bible _____
☆ child _____
☆ high _____

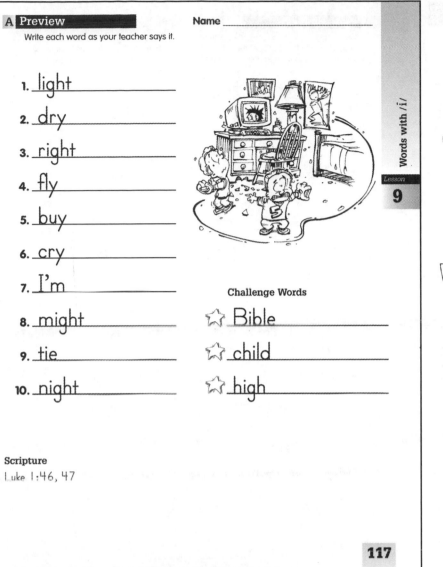

Words with /ī/

Lesson
9

Scripture
Luke 1:46, 47

117

Challenge

For better spellers, challenge words may be included in the weekly list. Challenge words are starred.

Correct Immediately!

 Let's correct our preview. I will write each word on the board. Put a dot under each letter on your preview as I spell the word out loud. If you spelled a word wrong, rewrite it correctly.

Progress Chart

 Students may record scores. (Reproducible master in Appendix B.)

Take a minute to memorize . . .

Read the memory verse twice. Have students practice it with you two more times.

---

3 Preview

Test for knowledge of the correct spellings of these words. (See the instructions at the top right for challenge words.)

Say I will say the word once, use the word in a sentence, then say the word again. Write the word on the lines in the Worktext.

1. light — The **light** from the window was dim since it was raining.
2. dry — It wasn't **dry** enough to play outside.
3. right — It wasn't **right** for Tommy and Daniel to play catch indoors.
4. fly — The ball could **fly** right through the open doorway.
5. buy — It would take $450 to **buy** a new computer monitor.
6. cry — Did Tommy want to **cry** when he broke the monitor?
7. I'm — **I'm** sure Tommy felt very bad.
8. might — Tommy's family **might** not get a computer for a long time.
9. tie — Do you know how to **tie** a square knot?
10. night — That **night** Tommy thanked God for saving him.
☆ Bible — The **Bible** says that God is our Savior.
☆ child — Which **child** broke the monitor?
☆ high — Tommy threw the ball in a **high** arc.

149

Word Shapes

4

Help students form a correct image of whole words.

(Say) Look at each word and think about its shape. Now, write the word in the correct word Shape Boxes. You may check off each word as you use it.

(In many words, the sound of /ī/ is spelled with **ie**, **igh**, or **y**. The word **I** and contractions with the word **I** are always capitalized.)

(Say) In the word Shape Boxes, color the letter or letters that spell the sound of /ī/ in each word. Circle the word that has a contraction. Draw a line under the silent letters **gh**.

Challenge

Draw the correctly shaped box around each letter in these words.

(Say) On a separate sheet of paper, write sentences using one or more of the spelling words.

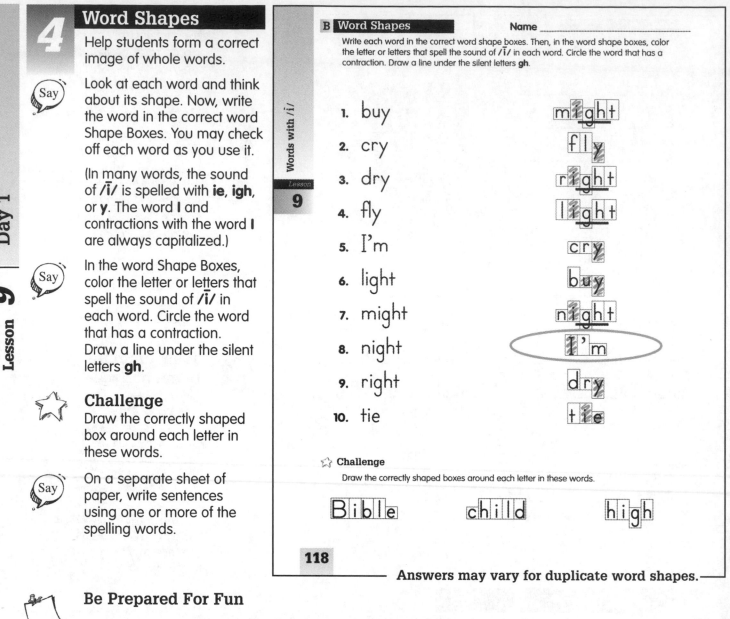

B Word Shapes   Name _____

Write each word in the correct word shape boxes. Then, in the word shape boxes, color the letter or letters that spell the sound of /ī/ in each word. Circle the word that has a contraction. Draw a line under the silent letters **gh**.

Words with /ī/
Lesson **9**

1. buy
2. cry
3. dry
4. fly
5. I'm
6. light
7. might
8. night
9. right
10. tie

might
fly
right
light
cry
buy
night
I'm
dry
tie

☆ Challenge

Draw the correctly shaped boxes around each letter in these words.

Bible   child   high

118

Answers may vary for duplicate word shapes.

Be Prepared For Fun

Check these supply lists for **Fun Ways to Spell** presented **Day 2**. Purchase and/or gather these items ahead of time!

General
- 3 x 5 Cards (10 per child)
- 3 x 5 Cards (3 more to spell challenge words)
- Scissors
- Spelling List

Auditory
- A Classmate
- Spelling List

Visual
- Strips of paper 2 x 11 inches (10 per student)
- Strips of paper 2 x 11 inches (3 more to spell challenge words)
- Crayons or Markers
- Tape
- Spelling List

Tactile
- Split Peas
- Glue
- Construction Paper
- Spelling List

150

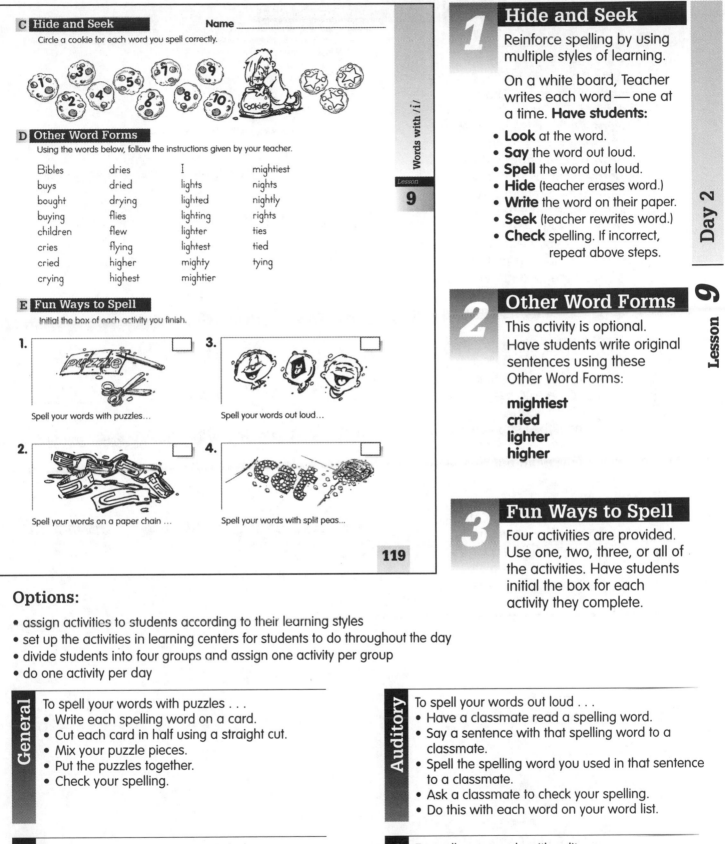

C Hide and Seek

Name _____

Circle a cookie for each word you spell correctly.

D Other Word Forms

Using the words below, follow the instructions given by your teacher.

Bibles	dries	I	mightiest
buys	dried	lights	nights
bought	drying	lighted	nightly
buying	flies	lighting	rights
children	flew	lighter	ties
cries	flying	lightest	tied
cried	higher	mighty	tying
crying	highest	mightier	

E Fun Ways to Spell

Initial the box of each activity you finish.

1. Spell your words with puzzles...

3. Spell your words out loud...

2. Spell your words on a paper chain ...

4. Spell your words with split peas...

Words with /ī/

Lesson **9**

119

---

1 Hide and Seek

Reinforce spelling by using multiple styles of learning.

On a white board, Teacher writes each word — one at a time. **Have students:**

- **Look** at the word.
- **Say** the word out loud.
- **Spell** the word out loud.
- **Hide** (teacher erases word.)
- **Write** the word on their paper.
- **Seek** (teacher rewrites word.)
- **Check** spelling. If incorrect, repeat above steps.

2 Other Word Forms

This activity is optional. Have students write original sentences using these Other Word Forms:

mightiest
cried
lighter
higher

3 Fun Ways to Spell

Four activities are provided. Use one, two, three, or all of the activities. Have students initial the box for each activity they complete.

Options:

- assign activities to students according to their learning styles
- set up the activities in learning centers for students to do throughout the day
- divide students into four groups and assign one activity per group
- do one activity per day

General

To spell your words with puzzles . . .
- Write each spelling word on a card.
- Cut each card in half using a straight cut.
- Mix your puzzle pieces.
- Put the puzzles together.
- Check your spelling.

Auditory

To spell your words out loud . . .
- Have a classmate read a spelling word.
- Say a sentence with that spelling word to a classmate.
- Spell the spelling word you used in that sentence to a classmate.
- Ask a classmate to check your spelling.
- Do this with each word on your word list.

Visual

To spell your words on a paper chain . . .
- Write each spelling word on a strip of paper in big, tall letters.
- Tape the ends of one strip together to make a circle.
- Loop the next strip through the first and then tape the ends of that strip together.
- Continue in this way to form a paper chain.

Tactile

To spell your words with split peas . . .
- Choose a word from your spelling list.
- It may be a favorite word or a word you have trouble remembering how to spell.
- Write the word in tall, wide letters on a sheet of construction paper.
- Spread glue along the outline of each letter and press split peas into the glue.

1 Words in Sentences

Familiarize students with word meaning and usage. Write the words **ask** and **add** on the board. Draw a triangle in front of each word. Write the words **nest** and **men** on the board. Draw a star in front of these words. Next, draw another triangle on the board. After this triangle write the sentence, **Can you _____ five and two?** Help the students understand that since a triangle appears before this sentence, they will choose a word from the triangle word bank to write in the blank. Explain that the word bank words in their worktexts have baseballs, computers, and gloves in front of them. In this assignment they should choose words from the appropriate word bank.

Say) A shape appears in each sentence in this activity. Use the group of words with the matching shape to find the spelling word to complete the sentences.

F Words in Sentences   Name _____

Use the shapes to find the words in the word bank that best completes each sentence. Write it in the blank.

1. It __might__ start to rain soon.

2. Turn the playroom __light__ on.

3. Always make the __right__ choice.

4. It may rain all __night__.

5. You __cry__ when you feel sad.

6. This ball can really __fly__.

7. You need to __tie__ your shoe.

8. The umbrella keeps you __dry__.

9. They will __buy__ a new monitor.

10. __I'm__ glad God saves me!

Word Bank

dry	night	buy	light	cry	right
might	fly	tie	I'm		

120

Take a minute to memorize . . .

Read the memory verse twice. Have students practice it with you two more times.

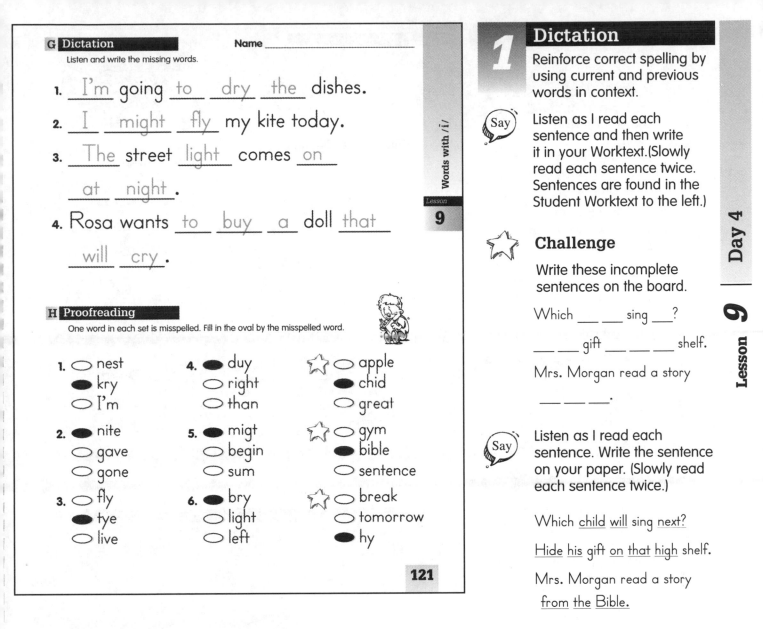

G Dictation

Name _____

Listen and write the missing words.

1. __I'm__ going __to__ __dry__ __the__ dishes.
2. __I__ __might__ __fly__ my kite today.
3. __The__ street __light__ comes __on__ __at__ __night__.
4. Rosa wants __to__ __buy__ __a__ doll __that__ __will__ __cry__.

H Proofreading

One word in each set is misspelled. Fill in the oval by the misspelled word.

1. ○ nest
   ● kry
   ○ I'm

2. ● nite
   ○ gave
   ○ gone

3. ○ fly
   ● tye
   ○ live

4. ● duy
   ○ right
   ○ than

5. ● migt
   ○ begin
   ○ sum

6. ● bry
   ○ light
   ○ left

☆ ○ apple
   ● chid
   ○ great

☆ ○ gym
   ● bible
   ○ sentence

☆ ○ break
   ○ tomorrow
   ● hy

121

---

1 Dictation

Reinforce correct spelling by using current and previous words in context.

Say Listen as I read each sentence and then write it in your Worktext.(Slowly read each sentence twice. Sentences are found in the Student Worktext to the left.)

☆ Challenge

Write these incomplete sentences on the board.

Which ___ ___ sing ___?

___ ___ gift ___ ___ ___ shelf.

Mrs. Morgan read a story

___ ___ ___.

Say Listen as I read each sentence. Write the sentence on your paper. (Slowly read each sentence twice.)

Which <u>child</u> <u>will</u> sing <u>next</u>?

<u>Hide</u> <u>his</u> gift <u>on</u> <u>that</u> <u>high</u> shelf.

Mrs. Morgan read a story <u>from</u> <u>the</u> <u>Bible.</u>

2 Proofreading

Familiarize students with standardized test format and reinforce recognizing misspelled words.

Say Look at each set of words. One word in each set is misspelled. Fill in the oval by the misspelled word. (You may wish to pronounce each set of words to help students correctly identify them.)

153

3 Hide and Seek

Reinforce correct spelling of current spelling words. (A reproducible master is provided in Appendix A as shown on the inset page to the right.)

Write the words one at a time on a white board.

Have students:

- **Look** at the word.
- **Say** the word out loud.
- **Spell** the word out loud.
- **Hide** (teacher erases word.)
- **Write** the word on paper.
- **Seek** (teacher rewrites word.)
- **Check** spelling. If incorrect, rewrite word correctly.

4 Hidden Words

Have your students complete this activity to strengthen spelling ability and expand vocabulary.

1 Posttest

Test mastery of the spelling words. Challenge words are starred.

(Say) I will say the word once, use the word in a sentence, then say the word again. Write the word on your paper.

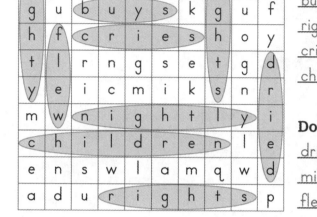

Hide and Seek

Check a paper for each word you spell correctly.

1 3 5 7 9 2 4 6 8 10

Hidden Words

Using the word bank below, find the words in the puzzle. Circle and write each word.

m	k	i	r	I	a	p	l	s	t
i	g	b	c	s	p	h	i	p	a
g	u	b	u	y	s	k	g	u	f
h	f	c	r	i	e	s	h	o	y
t	l	r	n	g	s	e	t	g	d
y	e	i	c	m	i	k	s	n	r
m	w	n	i	g	h	t	l	y	i
c	h	i	l	d	r	e	n	l	e
e	n	s	w	l	a	m	q	w	d
a	d	u	r	i	g	h	t	s	p

Across

nightly
buys
rights
cries
children

Down

dried
mighty
flew
lights

Word Bank

buys	cries	flew	mighty	rights
children	dried	lights	nightly	

375

1. buy — Daniel's parents **buy** him any toy he wants.
2. might — The boys **might** have played lots of other things.
3. I'm — **I'm** sure they made the wrong choice.
4. fly — Tommy let the ball **fly** out of his hand.
5. right — The ball flew **right** at the computer monitor.
6. light — A bright **light** flashed as the ball shattered the screen.
7. tie — The game might end in a **tie**.
8. night — Tommy's mom and dad talked to him that **night**.
9. cry — Tommy wanted to **cry** because Dad had paid $450.
10. dry — He needed a tissue to **dry** his tears.
☆ high — Put the ball and glove on a **high** shelf.
☆ child — Mr. Rawson paid for the mistake his **child** made.
☆ Bible — The **Bible** says God pays for our mistakes if we ask Him to.

Progress Chart

Students may record scores. (Reproducible master in Appendix B.)

Personal Dictionary

Students may add any words they have misspelled to their personal dictionaries for reference when writing. (Cover in Appendix B.)

154

I | Game

Name _____

Daniel and Tommy made a poor choice to throw the ball inside the house. Follow the path of the baseball toward the computer monitor. Color one space for each word you or your team spells correctly from this week's word list.

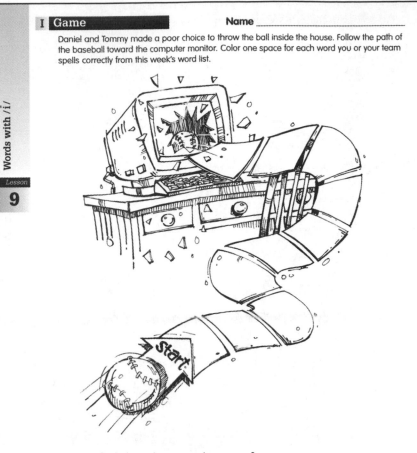

Remember: God always loves us and wants to forgive us.

J | Journaling

Write at least four sentences in your journal about a time when you were in trouble and needed help.

122

2 | Game

Reinforce spelling skills and provide motivation and interest.

Materials

- game page (from student text)
- crayons or colored pencils (1 per child)
- game word list

Game Word List

Use of challenge words is optional.

1. **buy**
2. **cry**
3. **dry**
4. **fly**
5. **tie**
6. **I'm**
7. **light**
8. **might**
9. **night**
10. **right**
☆ **child**
☆ **high**
☆ **Bible**

3 | Journaling

Provide a meaningful reason for correct spelling through personal writing.

Review the story using discussion leads provided on the following page. Encourage students to apply the Scriptural value in their journaling.

 Take a minute to memorize . . .

Have students say the memory verses from lessons 7, 8, and 9 with you.

How to Play:

- Divide students into two teams, and decide which team will go first.
- Have a student from team A go to the board.
- Read the spelling word two times slowly and clearly. (You may also wish to use the word in a sentence. Ex.: "cat — The cat climbed a tree. — cat")
- Have the student write the word on the board.
- If the word is spelled correctly, instruct all the members of team A to color one space, beginning at Start, on the game board. (Note: If the word is misspelled, correct the spelling immediately.)
- Alternate between teams A and B as you go down the word list.
- The team to reach the broken computer monitor first is the winner.

Non-Competitive Option: At the end of the game, say: "Class, I am proud of your efforts to spell the words correctly. If you had fun and tried your best, you are all winners!"

3 Journaling

Provide a meaningful reason for correct spelling through personal writing.

Say

- Did Tommy really think it was O.K. to play catch in the house? (No. He just wanted to very much so he chose to do it even though he really knew it wasn't all right.)

- Could Tommy have paid for the computer monitor he broke without his dad's help? (Since it cost $450, it probably would have taken him years.)

- Do you think it was good that Tommy would have to wait for a while to get a computer at his house? (It was very good for Tommy to realize how serious his mistake was. He needed to see that his mistake affected the rest of his family, too.)

- Have you ever made a bad mistake like Tommy did? Aren't you glad that God can save you if you ask Him to?

- In your journal write about a time when you were in trouble and needed help. (For example: Got lost, around a mean dog, got hurt, did something wrong, very sick, etc.)

"The kinds of errors that achieving children make change systematically, and each new stage reflects a logical step toward mastery of our complex spelling system."

*Henderson, Edmund, 1985. Teaching Spelling. Boston Houghton Mifflin Company.

What Our Actions Show

When Kristin's class does charades, she learns how important actions really are.

Kristin's breath puffed out little white clouds in the freezing air as she and her twin brother, Christopher, hurried from the car. When they opened the school door, the warmth welcomed them inside. The cheery lights in the classroom were doing a better job than the sun on this bitterly cold morning.

"Good morning, everyone," Mrs. Morgan greeted her thawing students with a warm smile and a twinkle in her eyes. "This morning we're going to do something a little different to start our day. Can anyone tell me what 'charades' are?" She nodded toward Katelynn's waving hand. "Katelynn, thank you for raising your hand. What do you think charades are?"

"When you act out a story or something, but don't say any words."

"Exactly." Mrs. Morgan nodded her head in approval. "I will divide you into groups of four and give each group a story from the Bible. I want you to meet with your group and plan how you'll act out the story so the rest of us can guess what it is." Soon the children were scattered around the room in whispered planning sessions.

Noah and the Ark was pretty easy to guess, especially when Tommy and James repeatedly entered the "Ark" that Beth and Tony had built of chairs. First, they came in flapping their wings like birds; then they left the Ark and re-entered as different animals. They acted like elephants, swinging their trunks. Then they pretended to be frogs, hopping. The part that took the longest was when they came in slithering along the floor like snakes.

Naaman and his cure from leprosy was next. Kristin had it all figured out as soon as Matthew dipped down

behind the blue beanbag seven times, then jumped up and down with a big grin on his face. She waved her hand along with everyone else who wanted to guess. Daniel, who had played the part of Elisha, pointed to her and said, "Kristin, you can guess first."

"You guys acted out the story of A-A-A-ACHOO Naaman." Kristin grabbed for a tissue.

"'ACHOO Naaman!'" Daniel mimicked Kristin in a silly voice that made everyone giggle. "No, that's not it. Rosa, you can guess."

"Matthew was Naaman and you were Elisha," Rosa answered through her giggles. "Setsuko [pronounced set-sool-koh] was the little maid, and Christopher was one of Naaman's soldiers!"

"Now that's right." Daniel nodded and pretended to be relieved.

Kristin's group went next. They acted out the story of the man and woman of Shunem, who built a special room on the top of their house just for Elisha to stay in when he passed by on his travels. It was very quiet as everyone watched the charade carefully, trying to guess what the story was. That is, it was quiet until Kristin, who was showing the new room to Elisha, gave a great big sneeze. Elisha, who was actually Rachel with a cloth thrown around her shoulders, jumped and dropped the yardstick in her hand that was serving as the prophet's staff. Even Mrs. Morgan laughed.

"Okay, I guess we're done," Rachel rearranged her costume and turned to her laughing classmates. "Tony, you can guess."

"That's easy!" Tony declared. "Your charade was the story of the man

and woman of Shunem building a room for ACHOO Elisha!" Tony's pretend sneeze started everyone laughing again.

"You all did very well with the charades this morning in spite of a few unexpected events," Mrs. Morgan chuckled. "The story of Noah building the Ark and Naaman and his cure from leprosy both show us that we should obey and do what God tells us to do. The story of the man and woman of Shunem has a very important lesson for us as well. What can we learn from that story, James?"

"To, uh, be nice to people?" James turned his answer into a question.

"That's right, James," Mrs. Morgan nodded. "The man and woman of Shunem used their time and possessions to do something very nice and unselfish for the prophet Elisha." Mrs. Morgan noticed Sarah's half-raised hand. "Sarah, did you have something to add?"

"Well, it's kind of like the Scripture we practiced for handwriting yesterday, isn't it?" Sarah asked timidly. "You know, 'Love your neighbor as much as you love yourself.' They did that, didn't they?"

Mrs. Morgan's eyes sparkled. "Very good thinking, Sarah. Their act of kindness surely shows that they had that kind of love. I wonder, do our actions show that we love our neighbors as much as we love ourselves?"

After school, Kristin and Christopher bundled into their matching red and blue coats before leaving the warm building. The cold wind tugged at their hair and tried to blow them away as they headed for the Wright family's green station wagon. Christopher hopped in the back while Kristin pulled open the front passenger door only to find her little sister already in the seat. "Cathy!" she yelled. "It's my turn to sit in the front seat! A-A-A-ACHOO!"

Even as Kristin heard her own angry demand, she remembered what Mrs. Morgan had said: "Do our actions show that we love our neighbors as much as we love

157

ourselves?" "Never mind," Kristin said in a much calmer voice. "I'll sit in the back this time." She closed the front door and crawled in the back by three-year-old Cory's car seat.

Cathy looked over the back of the seat with wide, surprised eyes. "Uh, thank you, Kristin. You can sit up here when it's my turn tomorrow."

The phone was ringing when the Wright children and their mother got home. "Hello," Mrs. Wright grabbed the phone as she lowered Cory to the floor and set her purse and keys on the counter. "Oh, okay, just a moment, please." She placed her hand over the receiver and turned to Kristin. "Honey, this call may take a few minutes. Would you help Cory take off his coat and hang it up. Also, the clothes in the washing machine need to be put in the dryer. Would you do that for me?"

"I just got home," was Kristin's first thought. *"Christopher and Cathy are off doing whatever they want to do already. Mom could put those clothes in the dryer after she finishes talking on the phone."* The thoughts flashed through her mind quickly, but then another one followed. *"'Do our actions show that we love our neighbors as much as we love ourselves?'"*

"Sure, Mom," Kristin flashed her mother a smile, and left to find Cory.

Later that evening Dad called the Wright children to the living room for their bedtime story. Before she headed to the living room, Kristin chose a story called "What Happened to Debbie?" that looked really interesting. Christopher, Cathy, and Cory — all in pajamas, with their teeth freshly-scrubbed — were piled around Dad on the couch. Kristin started to hand the book to Dad, but Dad already had a book in his hand! "Dad," Kristin objected. "It's my day to A-A-A-CHOO choose the bedtime story!" Mom handed Kristin a tissue.

"I wanted to hear this story tonight."

"Oh, that's right, sweetie," Dad opened her book and set the other one down as Kristin found a spot on the couch.

"But, Kristin," Christopher argued, "we didn't get to read the story I picked out last night 'cause it got too late, and we didn't have time for a story. Couldn't we read it tonight instead? Please?"

Kristin looked across at her twin. *"Do our actions show that we love our neighbors as much as we love ourselves?"* Mrs. Morgan's question flew through her mind. "Okay, we can read your story tonight, Christoph . . . A-A-A-A-CHOO!"

"All right! Thanks, Sis!" Christopher grinned. "It's a good stor . . . A-A-A-A-CHOOO!" Christopher blinked in surprise as Mom brought him a tissue.

"Kristin!" Cathy exclaimed. "I really like the way you've been so nice to everybody today and shared your turns and stuff — but you don't have to share your cold, too!"

And everyone laughed, as Kristin answered, "A-A-A-A-A-CHOOO!"

2 Discussion Time

Check understanding of the story and development of personal values.

- What are charades?
- What charades did the second graders act out?
- What does the story of the man and woman of Shunem help us learn?
- How did Kristin's actions show that she loved her neighbor as much as herself?
- What did Kristin share that the others didn't really want?
- Is it easy to treat others like we want to be treated? Why or why not?

A Preview

Write each word as your teacher says it.

Name _____

1. cold
2. boat
3. road
4. hold
5. old
6. roll
7. most
8. home
9. hope
10. told

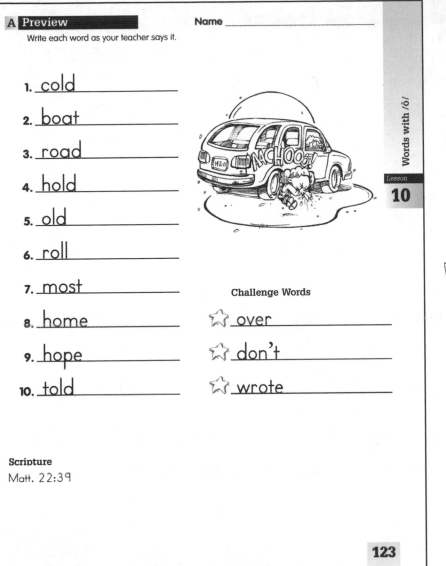

Challenge Words

☆ over
☆ don't
☆ wrote

Scripture
Matt. 22:39

123

 Challenge

For better spellers, challenge words may be included in the weekly list. Challenge words are starred.

 Correct Immediately!

Let's correct our preview. I will write each word on the board. Put a dot under each letter on your preview as I spell the word out loud. If you spelled a word wrong, rewrite it correctly.

 **Progress Chart**

Students may record scores. (Reproducible master in Appendix B.)

 **Take a minute to memorize . . .**

Read the memory verse twice. Have students practice it with you two more times.

3 Preview

Test for knowledge of the correct spellings of these words. (See the instructions at the top right for challenge words.)

Say: I will say the word once, use the word in a sentence, then say the word again. Write the word on the lines in the Worktext.

1. cold — Kristin had a bad **cold**.
2. boat — Noah built a big **boat** called the ark.
3. road — Elisha traveled on the **road** past the man and woman's house.
4. hold — Rachel will **hold** the stick and pretend it's the prophet's staff.
5. old — This **old** cloth makes a good costume.
6. roll — We can **roll** the teacher's chair to the front of the room.
7. most — Not all, but **most** of the charades were easy to guess.
8. home — At **home**, Mom asked Kristin to put the clothes in the dryer.
9. hope — I **hope** we all love our neighbors as much as we love ourselves.
10. told — Kristin **told** Cathy she could ride in the front seat.
☆ over — Cathy looked at Kristin **over** the back of the seat.
☆ don't — Cathy said, "Kristin, you **don't** have to share your cold, too!"
☆ wrote — She **wrote**, "Love your neighbor as much as you love yourself."

159

Word Shapes

4

Help students form a correct image of whole words.

(Say) Look at each word and think about its shape. Now, write the word in the correct word Shape Boxes. You may check off each word as you use it.

(In many words, the sound of /ō/ is spelled with o, oa, or o-e.)

(Say) In the word Shape Boxes, color the letter or letters that spell the sound of /ō/ in each word. Circle the words in which /ō/ is spelled with o-e. Draw a line under the words in which /ō/ is spelled with oa.

Challenge

Draw the correctly shaped box around each letter in these words.

(Say) On a separate sheet of paper, write the two words that the contraction stands for, then use them in a sentence.

Day 1

Lesson 10

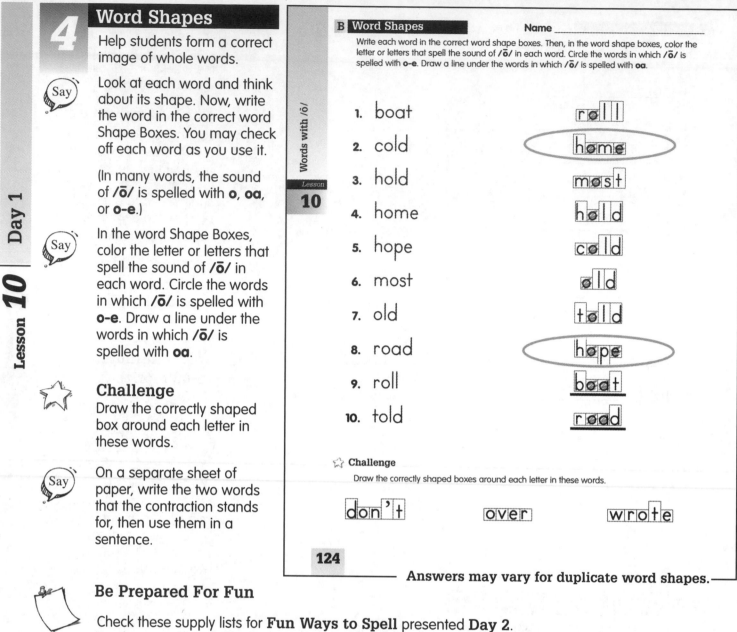

Answers may vary for duplicate word shapes.

Be Prepared For Fun

Check these supply lists for **Fun Ways to Spell** presented **Day 2**. Purchase and/or gather these items ahead of time!

General
- A Classmate
- Spelling List

Auditory
- Box to Store Letters
- a, b, c, d, e, h, l, l, m, o, p, r, s, t (written on seasonal shapes like snowflakes or snowmen)
- n, v, w (added for challenge words)
- Spelling List

Visual
- a, b, c, d, e, h, l, l, m, o, p, r, s, t, (written on upside down cups)
- n, v, w (added for challenge words)
- Spelling List

Tactile
- Shaving Cream
- Optional: Plastic Plates
- Optional: Wooden Craft Sticks
- Spelling List

160

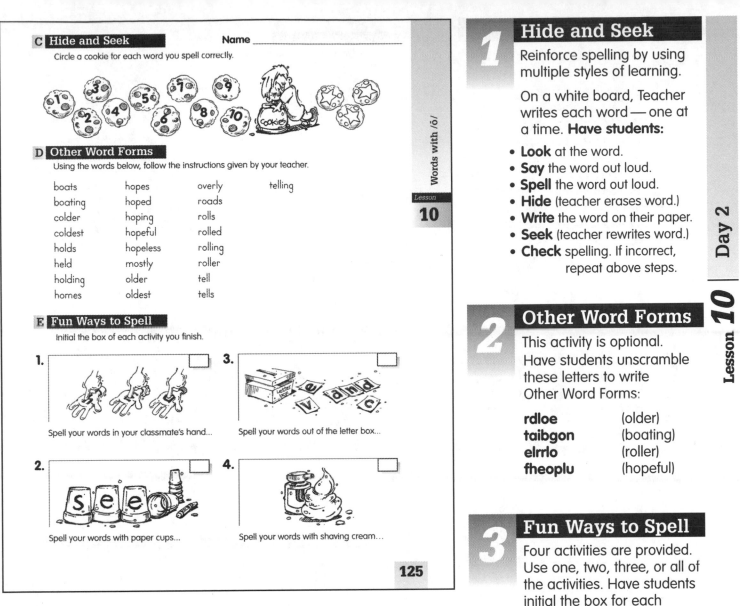

C **Hide and Seek**

Name _____

Circle a cookie for each word you spell correctly.

D **Other Word Forms**

Using the words below, follow the instructions given by your teacher.

boats	hopes	overly	telling
boating	hoped	roads	
colder	hoping	rolls	
coldest	hopeful	rolled	
holds	hopeless	rolling	
held	mostly	roller	
holding	older	tell	
homes	oldest	tells	

E **Fun Ways to Spell**

Initial the box of each activity you finish.

1. [ ]

Spell your words in your classmate's hand...

3. [ ]

Spell your words out of the letter box...

2. [ ]

Spell your words with paper cups...

4. [ ]

Spell your words with shaving cream...

125

---

1 Hide and Seek

Reinforce spelling by using multiple styles of learning.

On a white board, Teacher writes each word — one at a time. **Have students:**

- **Look** at the word.
- **Say** the word out loud.
- **Spell** the word out loud.
- **Hide** (teacher erases word.)
- **Write** the word on their paper.
- **Seek** (teacher rewrites word.)
- **Check** spelling. If incorrect, repeat above steps.

Day 2

Lesson 10

2 Other Word Forms

This activity is optional. Have students unscramble these letters to write Other Word Forms:

rdloe	(older)
taibgon	(boating)
elrrlo	(roller)
fheoplu	(hopeful)

3 Fun Ways to Spell

Four activities are provided. Use one, two, three, or all of the activities. Have students initial the box for each activity they complete.

Options:

- assign activities to students according to their learning styles
- set up the activities in learning centers for students to do throughout the day
- divide students into four groups and assign one activity per group
- do one activity per day

General

To spell your words in your classmate's hand . . .
- Have a classmate sit next to you and hold their palm open in front of, and facing both of you.
- Use fingertip to write a spelling word in the palm of a classmate's hand.
- Have a classmate say each letter as you write it and then say the word you spelled.
- Next, have a classmate write a word in your palm.

Auditory

To spell your words out of the letter box . . .
- Spell a word from your list by putting the letters in the right order.
- Check your spelling.
- Spell your word out loud.

Visual

To spell your words with paper cups . . .
- Spell a word from your list by putting the cups in the right order.
- Check your spelling.

Tactile

To spell your words with shaving cream . . .
- Spread a glob of shaving cream across your desk (or on a plastic plate).
- Use finger (or a wooden craft stick) to write a spelling word in the shaving cream.
- Check your spelling.
- Smear the word out with your fingers and write another.

161

Crossword

1

Familiarize students with word meaning and usage.

Draw five connecting (crossword type) boxes on the board. Ask the students what comes out of a faucet. Write **water** in the boxes. Draw two boxes above the **t** in **water**. Ask the students what they do at lunch time. Write **ea** in the boxes to form the word **eat**. Explain to the students that we call this a crossword because the words are written across each other and share some letters.

Say) Write your spelling words in the crossword puzzle. Use the clues to decide which word to write in each space.

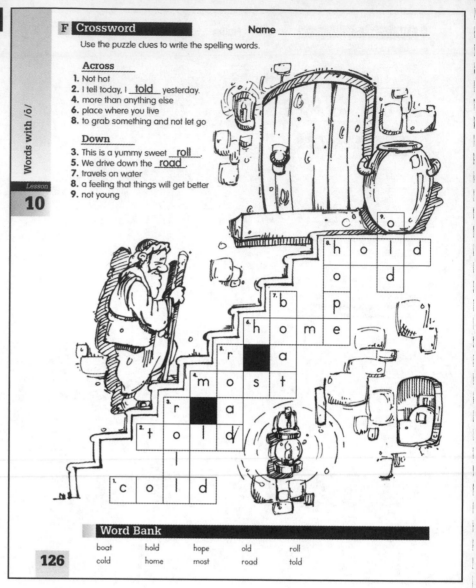

F Crossword

Name _____

Use the puzzle clues to write the spelling words.

Across
1. Not hot
2. I tell today, I __told__ yesterday.
4. more than anything else
6. place where you live
8. to grab something and not let go

Down
3. This is a yummy sweet __roll__.
5. We drive down the __road__.
7. travels on water
8. a feeling that things will get better
9. not young

Words with /ō/

Lesson **10**

Word Bank

| boat | hold | hope | old | roll |
| cold | home | most | road | told |

126

Take a minute to memorize . . .

Read the memory verse twice. Have students practice it with you two more times.

162

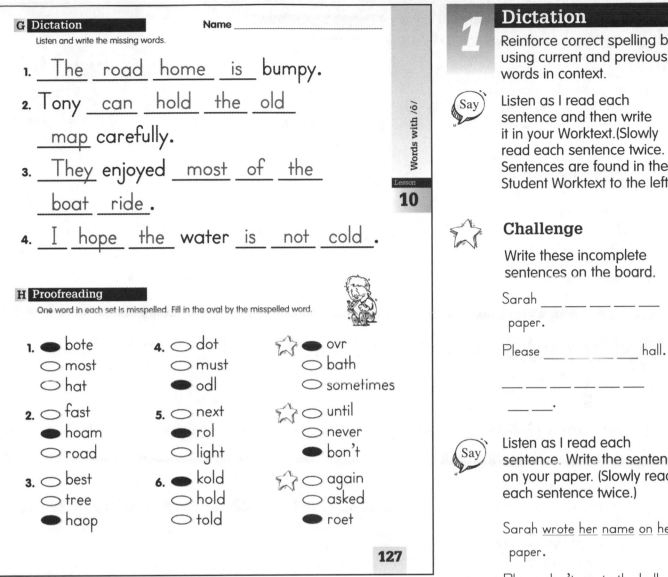

G Dictation

Listen and write the missing words.

Name _____

1. The road home is bumpy.

2. Tony can hold the old map carefully.

3. They enjoyed most of the boat ride.

4. I hope the water is not cold.

H Proofreading

One word in each set is misspelled. Fill in the oval by the misspelled word.

1. ● bote
   ○ most
   ○ hat

2. ○ fast
   ● hoam
   ○ road

3. ○ best
   ○ tree
   ● haop

4. ○ dot
   ○ must
   ● odl

5. ○ next
   ● rol
   ○ light

6. ● kold
   ○ hold
   ○ told

☆ ● ovr
   ○ bath
   ○ sometimes

☆ ○ until
   ○ never
   ● bon't

☆ ○ again
   ○ asked
   ● roet

127

1 Dictation

Reinforce correct spelling by using current and previous words in context.

Say Listen as I read each sentence and then write it in your Worktext.(Slowly read each sentence twice. Sentences are found in the Student Worktext to the left.)

☆ **Challenge**

Write these incomplete sentences on the board.

Sarah __ __ __ __ paper.

Please __ __ __ __ hall.

__ __ __ __ __ __ __ __.

Say Listen as I read each sentence. Write the sentence on your paper. (Slowly read each sentence twice.)

Sarah wrote her name on her paper.

Please don't run in the hall.

The big dog can jump over that gate.

2 Proofreading

Familiarize students with standardized test format and reinforce recognizing misspelled words.

Say Look at each set of words. One word in each set is misspelled. Fill in the oval by the misspelled word. (You may wish to pronounce each set of words to help students correctly identify them.)

3 Hide and Seek

Reinforce correct spelling of current spelling words. (A reproducible master is provided in Appendix A as shown on the inset page to the right.)

Write the words one at a time on a white board.

Have students:

- **Look** at the word.
- **Say** the word out loud.
- **Spell** the word out loud.
- **Hide** (teacher erases word.)
- **Write** the word on paper.
- **Seek** (teacher rewrites word.)
- **Check** spelling. If incorrect, rewrite word correctly.

4 Secret Word

Have your students complete this activity to strengthen spelling ability and expand vocabulary.

1 Posttest

Test mastery of the spelling words. Challenge words are starred.

I will say the word once, use the word in a sentence, then say the word again. Write the word on your paper.

Hide and Seek
Check a paper for each word you spell correctly.

1 2 3 4 5 6 7 8 9 10

Secret Word
Use these clues to find the word that fits in each blank. Then use the boxed letters to discover the secret word.

1. colder than anything else
2. houses that people live in
3. smooth paths to drive on
4. a ball or wheel does this
5. things you can sail or ride in on the water
6. not as young
7. to say
8. almost all

1. c o l d e s t
2. h o m e s
3. r o a d s
4. r o l l s
5. b o a t s
6. o l d e r
7. t e l l
8. m o s t l y

Kristin's class liked c h a r a d e s.

Word Bank

boats	homes	older	rolls
coldest	mostly	roads	tell

376

1. **cold** — It was a very **cold** winter day.
2. **most** — The twins' warm coats kept **most** of the cold air out.
3. **told** — Mrs. Morgan **told** the class they were going to do charades.
4. **boat** — Beth and Tony made a **boat** out of chairs for the ark.
5. **road** — Matthew pretended to walk down the **road** to the river.
6. **roll** — We can **roll** up this mat to use for a bed for Elisha.
7. **hope** — I **hope** you can guess what this charade is about.
8. **home** — The phone was ringing when the Wrights got **home**.
9. **old** — Kristin found a good story in the **old** book.
10. **hold** — Dad will **hold** Cory while he reads the story.
☆ **over** — Kristin will get **over** her cold soon.
☆ **don't** — I **don't** think it's fun being sick.
☆ **wrote** — The children **wrote** the Scripture text for handwriting.

Progress Chart
Students may record scores. (Reproducible master in Appendix B.)

Personal Dictionary
Students may add any words they have misspelled to their personal dictionaries for reference when writing. (Cover in Appendix B.)

I Game

Name _____

Place a game piece over each word your teacher says and spells. If the word appears on your card more than once, place a game piece over only one of the words each time it is said. When you get five game pieces in a row, raise your hand and say, "Spelling is fun!"

Remember: Do kind things for others as often as you do them for yourself.

J Journaling

Make a list of ways your actions can show you love your neighbor as much as you love yourself.

128

How to Play:

- Fold the word cards (see **Materials**) in half, and put them in a container.
- Write each word from the **Game Word List** on the board. (Be sure to include the number in parentheses beside it.)
- Ask the students to copy these words on their game card — one word in each box. Remind them the number beside the word indicates how many times they must copy that word. (Note: Placing the words in the boxes randomly makes the game more fun!)
- Instructions for the students: "Cover the word **FREE** in the center of your card with a game piece. (pause) I will draw a word from the container, read it aloud, then spell it. Find that word on your card, and cover it with a game piece. Cover only ONE word each time, even if it's on your card twice. When you have five game pieces in a row (up-down, across, or diagonally) raise your hand and say 'Spelling is FUN!'"
- Play as many times as you like. (As you return the word cards to the container and mix them up, remind the students to clear their game cards.)

2 Game

Reinforce spelling skills and provide motivation and interest.

Materials

- game page (from student text)
- flat buttons, dry beans, pennies, or game discs (24 per child)
- game word list
- word cards (each word from the list below written on one or more cards as indicated)

Game Word List

1. **cold** (2)
2. **hold** (2)
3. **old** (2)
4. **told** (2)
5. **roll** (2)
6. **boat** (2)
7. **most** (2)
8. **road** (2)
9. **home** (2)
10. **hope** (2)
☆ **wrote** (2)
☆ **don't** (1)
☆ **over** (1)

3 Journaling

Provide a meaningful reason for correct spelling through personal writing.

Review the story using discussion leads provided on the following page. Encourage students to apply the Scriptural value in their journaling.

 Take a minute to memorize . . .

Have students say the memory verses from lessons 7, 8, 9, and 10 with you.

165

3 Journaling

Provide a meaningful reason for correct spelling through personal writing.

(Say)

- Mrs. Morgan's class had a lot of fun doing charades. What story from Scripture were Tommy and James acting out when they slithered along the floor like snakes? (The story of Noah and the Ark.)

- What story did Kristin's group act out? (The man and woman of Shunem who built a special room on the top of their house for Elisha to stay in when he passed by.)

- Mrs. Morgan helped the class see that their kind of love for others is what Scripture says we should have. What question did she ask? (Do our actions show that we love our neighbors as much as we love ourselves?)

- Kristin remembered that question all day and changed the way she acted toward others.

- In your journal make a list of ways your actions can show that you love your neighbor as much as you love yourself.
(For example: Let others go first, pick up something someone dropped, listen when someone is talking to you, etc.)

"You may choose not to correct spelling errors if the child is not considered ready to learn a spelling pattern or concept."*

*Lutz, Elaine. 1986. ERIC/RCS Report: Invented Spelling and Spelling Development. Language Arts, Vol. 63, No. 7, November: 742-744.

166

Beth Says Goodbye

When her grandfather's health fails, Beth clings to God's promise to wipe away all our tears, knowing that God's words are always true.

"**B**eth! Help Luke with his shoes, grab your coats, then run and get in the car." Mom called urgently from the bottom of the stairs. "Grandma just called and said she's taking Grandpa to the hospital. We need to go meet them there. He's having chest pains again! Hurry!"

"Okay," Beth answered. She quickly helped her brother get his shoes on and grabbed her CD player and CDs as she rushed out of her room to get their jackets. "Hurry, Luke," she said, taking his hand. "Grandpa may be really sick again."

Beth scrambled up into the old pickup after Luke and helped him buckle his seat belt. A cloud of gray dust flew up behind them as Mom drove rapidly down the long driveway. Beth looked out the window and thought about her grandpa. She watched the dust blow across their pasture, turning the grass a deeper shade of gray. He'd had a heart attack last year, right after school started. Grandma said he'd almost died. They'd flown him in a helicopter to the big hospital in Fayetteville where it seemed like they kept him forever! "I was so glad when he got home!" Beth thought to herself.

Things were never quite the same again after Grandpa's trip to the hospital. He had hired a girl named Suzi to do a lot of the things he'd always liked to do. He paid her to take care of his flower beds, wash the cars, mow the lawn, and feed the horses. He took little white pills at every meal and long naps in the afternoon. One thing had not changed — Grandpa Ellis always had time for his grandchildren. He still took time to go on walks, help Beth and Luke ride the horses, or play catch. Grandpa and she

were almost finished with a bed for her "Just Like Me" doll in Grandpa's woodshop. "How long will he be sick this time?" Beth wondered.

When they arrived at the hospital, Mom parked the pickup, grabbed her childrens' hands and hurried them across the parking lot towards the emergency entrance of the hospital. "Has Mr. Ellis been admitted yet?" Mom asked in an anxious voice.

"He just came in," the kind nurse said. "His wife is filling out some forms around the cor . . ."

Mrs. Hill didn't wait for the nurse to finish, but hurried to where her mother sat. "How is he, Mom?"

Tears spilled out of the corners of Grandma Ellis's eyes. Beth felt her stomach twist into a tight knot as Mom's hand tightened around hers. Her frightened eyes met Luke's wide blue ones as they leaned forward to look at each other around the front of Mom's khaki slacks and olive green blouse. "I don't know yet. They took him in there," Grandma Ellis said, pointing to two swinging doors.

Mrs. Hill sat down beside her aging mother and pulled her close. "Jesus said that when He comes again He will wipe away all our tears," Mom comforted.

"I don't know the text yet, but in school today Mrs. Morgan taught us something else Jesus said," Beth added. "Mrs. Morgan told us that it means no matter what happens, no matter how bad things are, Jesus will keep His promises."

Luke sat down on the other side of his grandma and snuggled up against her. "Jesus might not come 'til tomorrow, Grandma. I'll go get a tissue." He popped up and trotted over to the

tissue box he saw sitting on a nearby table.

"Thank you, Lucas. I'm glad you're here." Grandma said, smiling through her tears. "I'm so scared. I'll miss that old man so much if he dies."

A doctor came out of the examining room a few minutes later and told them they were taking Grandpa up to the Intensive Care Unit. He was stable, but not out of danger yet. Katelynn's mom came for Beth and Luke. In the confusion no one was sure how she even knew to come pick them up. Mom stayed at the hospital with Grandma and Grandpa.

Just as she was drifting off to sleep in her own bed that night, Beth heard the phone ring. "Oh, Janette," Daddy said. "I am so sorry. I'll call Mrs. Rawson to see if she can come over and stay with the kids. I'll be there as soon as I can. I know. I love you. Bye."

Beth padded down the hall and sat down beside her daddy on the bed. He was looking at the phone in his hand and tears were running down his cheeks. Beth felt her stomach twist into a tight knot again. Daddy grabbed her hand and pulled her close. "Grandpa's heart just couldn't do its work anymore. He just passed away, Bethy."

"'Though all heaven and earth shall pass away' . . . What was that text?" Beth thought to herself as she stumbled down the hall back to her room.

Daddy sat on the edge of her bed after he tucked the blanket back up under her chin. "I'm going to go be with Grandma and Mom. We will all miss Grandpa, Bethy, but Grandma will need extra love and attention because she is used to having him around all the time. They will both cry a lot because they are sad. It will hurt when we want to talk to him and he isn't here," Daddy said, giving her a kiss. After he left, Beth lay staring at the ceiling, thinking about Grandpa for a long time.

Mrs. Rawson took Beth and Luke with her to

167

Lesson 11 Day 1

Grandma and Grandpa's house the next morning. Beth helped her dust the living room and watched her put food in the refrigerator and freezer as it was delivered by thoughtful friends and neighbors. After awhile she wandered out into the yard and looked at the flower beds that Grandpa had planted. There were still a few things blooming even this late in the year. She walked across the neat yard and opened the door to the woodshop. She saw the little bed sitting on the workbench where she and Grandpa had left it freshly painted yesterday afternoon. Beth rubbed her hand across the smooth paint. It was dry now.

She felt the knot tighten in her stomach again. "Who will help me finish it now?" she thought.

Grandma came back home late in the morning with Mr. and Mrs. Hill. The funeral was scheduled for the next day. Beth didn't really want to go, but Daddy said it would help her be able to say "good-bye" to Grandpa and show Grandma that she cared.

Beth sat under a blue tent in the cemetery with her family the next afternoon. Mom's sister Ellen was there with her husband. Their son Daniel was sitting between them. Grandma was sitting between her two daughters. A young girl played soft music on a violin. The lid to Grandpa's casket was open. It looked like he was taking one of his long afternoon naps. A gray-haired man in a freshly pressed but out-of-style black suit stood up beside Grandpa's casket and began to talk about all the memories he had about Grandpa. Beth recognized him as one of Grandpa's friends, but she couldn't remember his name. The violinist continued to play softly. The man talked about Grandpa's love for God, flowers, horses, and people. He reminded everyone about when Grandpa was a city councilman and then mayor. He told how Grandpa loved to read the Scriptures and was always ready to help someone in need.

"Jesus says that he is coming back to take us to live with Him in heaven," the man said in conclusion. "He promises to wipe away all our tears. Luke 21:33 says, 'Though all heaven and earth shall pass away, yet My words remain forever true.'"

"Luke 21:33!" Beth thought. *"That's the text we learned in school the day Grandpa died. Was that only three days ago? It seems like forever! Mom, Aunt Ellen, and Grandma cry when they aren't busy. Daddy tries to be brave for them and not cry at all. Luke is tired and cries all the time. I'm the only one not crying! I just want this to all go away."*

Beth looked back at the silver casket. "We are going to miss Harry Ellis," the man in the old black suit said. "We feel awful right now, but we can count on Jesus to keep His word and wipe away our tears." The man sat down.

"'My words remain forever true.'" Beth whispered to herself. "Jesus, please hurry and come back to get us. There are a lot of tears to wipe away down here." And as the music began to play once more, a tear slipped slowly down Beth's cheek.

2 Discussion Time

Check understanding of the story and development of personal values.

- Raise your hand if someone in your family has died.
- How did you feel when you couldn't be with them or talk to them anymore?
- How do you act when you are sad?
- Do you cry like Luke, or do you keep your feelings inside like Beth?
- Did you know that Jesus promised to wipe away all your tears?
- No matter what happens, no matter how bad things are (even if heaven and earth pass away) Jesus keeps promises!

168

A Preview

Write each word as your teacher says it.

Name _____

1. low
2. throw
3. blow
4. slow
5. grow
6. snow
7. tow
8. row
9. own
10. know

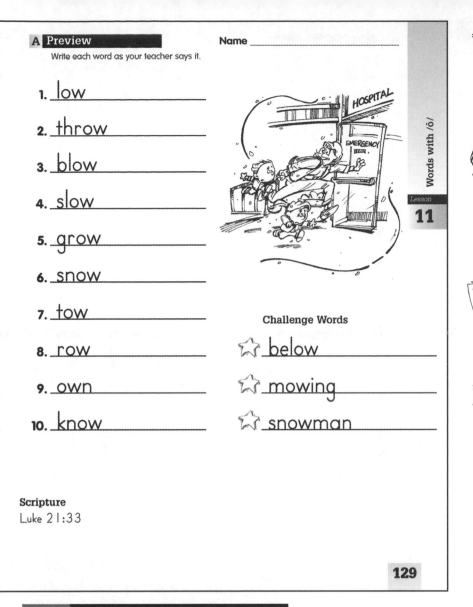

HOSPITAL
EMERGENCY

Words with /ō/

Lesson **11**

Challenge Words

 ☆ below
☆ mowing
☆ snowman

Scripture
Luke 21:33

129

Challenge

For better spellers, challenge words may be included in the weekly list. Challenge words are starred.

Correct Immediately!

Say — Let's correct our preview. I will write each word on the board. Put a dot under each letter on your preview as I spell the word out loud. If you spelled a word wrong, rewrite it correctly.

Progress Chart

Students may record scores. (Reproducible master in Appendix B.)

Take a minute to memorize . . .

Read the memory verse twice. Have students practice it with you two more times.

Lesson **11** | Day 1

---

3 Preview

Test for knowledge of the correct spellings of these words. (See the instructions at the top right for challenge words.)

Say — I will say the word once, use the word in a sentence, then say the word again. Write the word on the lines in the Worktext.

1.	low	The pickup is not **low** to the ground.
2.	throw	The pickup wheels **throw** up a cloud of dust.
3.	blow	Watch the dust **blow** across the pasture.
4.	slow	It was not a **slow** trip to the hospital.
5.	grow	As you **grow** up, sad things will happen.
6.	snow	There was no **snow** when Grandpa died.
7.	tow	They will **tow** the old pickup back to the house.
8.	row	Beth was sitting on the front **row** at the funeral.
9.	own	Jesus can be your very **own** friend.
10.	know	Did you **know** Jesus promises to wipe away all tears.
☆	below	The food they brought is in the freezer **below** the corn.
☆	mowing	Grandpa used to pay a girl to do the **mowing.**
☆	snowman	There wasn't any snow to make a **snowman** yet.

169

Word Shapes

4

Help students form a correct image of whole words.

Say Look at each word and think about its shape. Now, write the word in the correct word Shape Boxes. You may check off each word as you use it.

(In many words, the sound of /ō/ is spelled with **ow**.)

Say In the word Shape Boxes, color the letters that spell the sound of /ō/ in each word. Circle the words that begin with a consonant cluster.

Challenge
Draw the correctly shaped box around each letter in these words.

Say On a separate sheet of paper, write sentences using one or more of the spelling words.

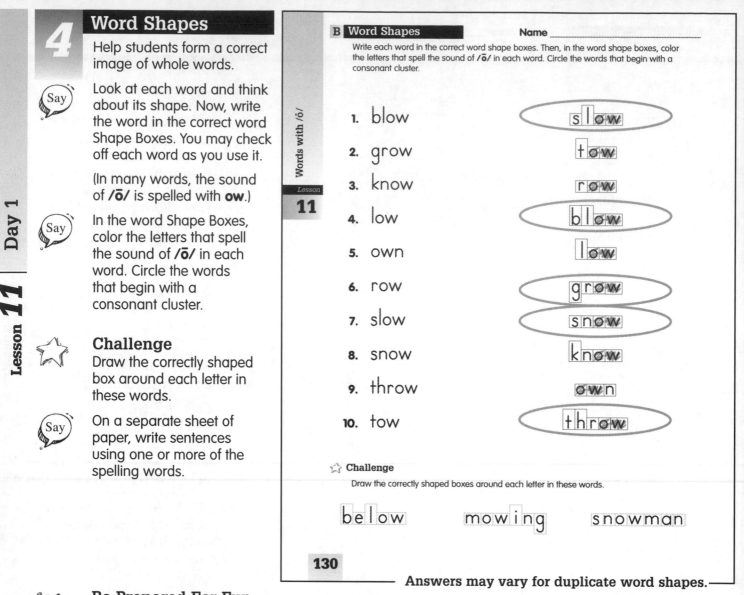

B Word Shapes Name _____

Write each word in the correct word shape boxes. Then, in the word shape boxes, color the letters that spell the sound of /ō/ in each word. Circle the words that begin with a consonant cluster.

Words with /ō/ Lesson 11

1. blow   s l o w
2. grow   t o w
3. know   r o w
4. low   b l o w
5. own   l o w
6. row   g r o w
7. slow   s n o w
8. snow   k n o w
9. throw   o w n
10. tow   t h r o w

☆ **Challenge**
Draw the correctly shaped boxes around each letter in these words.

below   mowing   snowman

130

Answers may vary for duplicate word shapes.

Be Prepared For Fun

Check these supply lists for **Fun Ways to Spell** presented **Day 2**. Purchase and/or gather these items ahead of time!

General
• Markers
• Art Paper
• Spelling List

Auditory
• Spelling List

Visual
• Letter Tiles b, g, h, k, l, n, o, r, s, t, w
• a, e, i, m, n (added for challenge words)
• Spelling List

Tactile
• Finger Paint
• Plastic Plate or Glossy Paper
• Spelling List

170

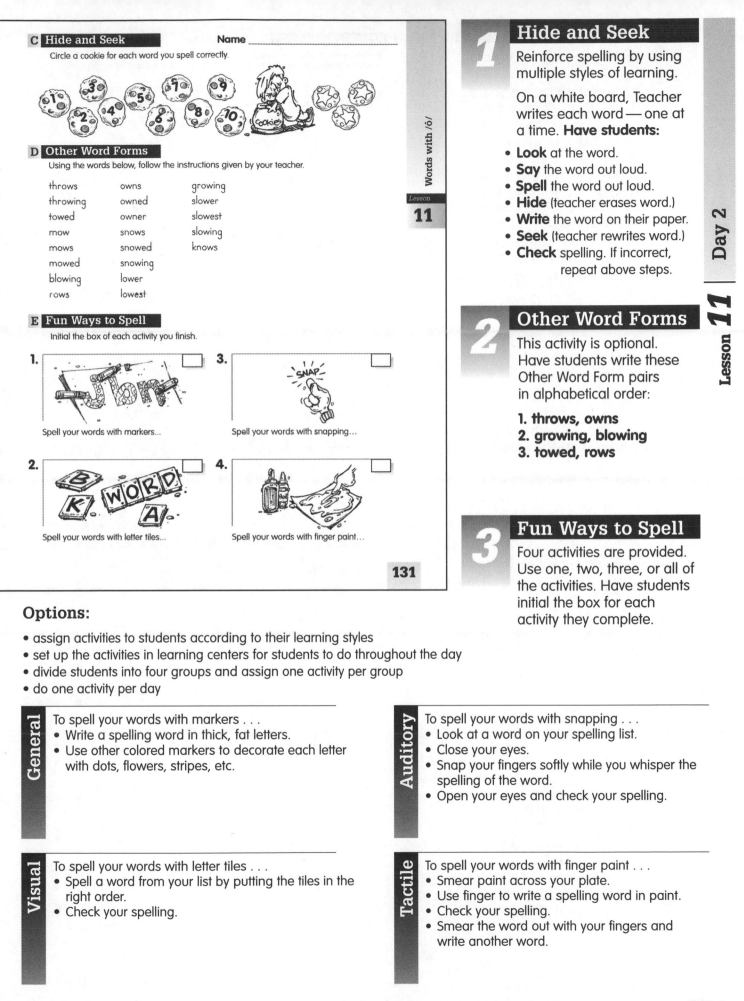

C Hide and Seek

Name _____

Circle a cookie for each word you spell correctly.

D Other Word Forms

Using the words below, follow the instructions given by your teacher.

throws	owns	growing
throwing	owned	slower
towed	owner	slowest
mow	snows	slowing
mows	snowed	knows
mowed	snowing	
blowing	lower	
rows	lowest	

E Fun Ways to Spell

Initial the box of each activity you finish.

1.
Spell your words with markers...

2.
Spell your words with letter tiles...

3.
SNAP
Spell your words with snapping...

4.
Spell your words with finger paint...

Words with /ō/

Lesson 11

131

---

1 Hide and Seek

Reinforce spelling by using multiple styles of learning.

On a white board, Teacher writes each word — one at a time. **Have students:**

- **Look** at the word.
- **Say** the word out loud.
- **Spell** the word out loud.
- **Hide** (teacher erases word.)
- **Write** the word on their paper.
- **Seek** (teacher rewrites word.)
- **Check** spelling. If incorrect, repeat above steps.

Day 2

2 Other Word Forms

This activity is optional. Have students write these Other Word Form pairs in alphabetical order:

1. **throws, owns**
2. **growing, blowing**
3. **towed, rows**

Lesson 11

3 Fun Ways to Spell

Four activities are provided. Use one, two, three, or all of the activities. Have students initial the box for each activity they complete.

Options:

- assign activities to students according to their learning styles
- set up the activities in learning centers for students to do throughout the day
- divide students into four groups and assign one activity per group
- do one activity per day

General

To spell your words with markers . . .
- Write a spelling word in thick, fat letters.
- Use other colored markers to decorate each letter with dots, flowers, stripes, etc.

Auditory

To spell your words with snapping . . .
- Look at a word on your spelling list.
- Close your eyes.
- Snap your fingers softly while you whisper the spelling of the word.
- Open your eyes and check your spelling.

Visual

To spell your words with letter tiles . . .
- Spell a word from your list by putting the tiles in the right order.
- Check your spelling.

Tactile

To spell your words with finger paint . . .
- Smear paint across your plate.
- Use finger to write a spelling word in paint.
- Check your spelling.
- Smear the word out with your fingers and write another word.

1 Unscramble Words

Familiarize students with word meaning and usage. Write **eloswfr** on the board. Ask students to raise their hands if they recognize the word. Explain that putting letters in the correct order makes it easier for others to understand what you are trying to say. Write **Grandpa likes to grow _____.** on the board. Explain that the scrambled letters make a word that will fit in the blank. Suggest that the words in this sentence are a clue to help them think of the word the scrambled letters make.

(Say) In this activity change the scrambled letters to write your spelling words in the blanks. Then find the scrambled spelling words and follow them through Grandpa's flower garden.

F Unscramble Words Name _____

Change the scrambled letters to write your spelling words in the blanks. Trace Beth's path through Grandpa's flower garden by following your scrambled spelling words.

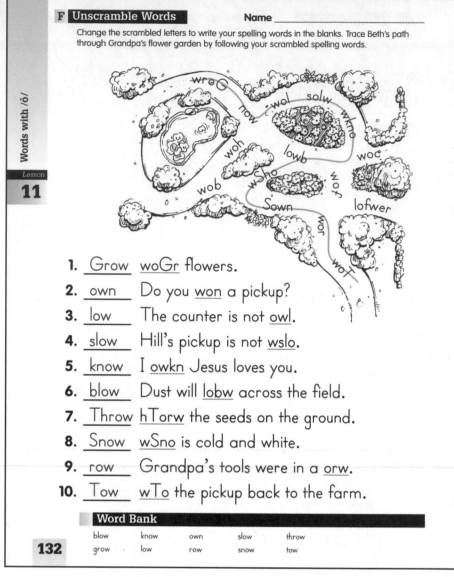

1. __Grow__ woGr flowers.
2. __own__ Do you won a pickup?
3. __low__ The counter is not owl.
4. __slow__ Hill's pickup is not wslo.
5. __know__ I owkn Jesus loves you.
6. __blow__ Dust will lobw across the field.
7. __Throw__ hTorw the seeds on the ground.
8. __Snow__ wSno is cold and white.
9. __row__ Grandpa's tools were in a orw.
10. __Tow__ wTo the pickup back to the farm.

Word Bank

blow	know	own	slow	throw
grow	low	row	snow	tow

132

Take a minute to memorize . . .

Read the memory verse twice. Have students practice it with you two more times.

G Dictation

Name _____

Listen and write the missing words.

1. Show _us_ _how_ _to_ _row_ _the_ _boat_.

2. _Do_ _you_ _know_ _if_ _this_ plant _will_ _grow_?

3. Tommy _will_ _blow_ _a_ bubble _of_ _his_ _own_.

4. _Dad_ _can_ shovel _this_ _soft_ _snow_.

H Proofreading

One word in each set is misspelled. Fill in the oval by the misspelled word.

1. ○ best
   ● thro
   ○ blow

2. ○ slow
   ○ row
   ● jrow

3. ○ cry
   ● kno
   ○ road

4. ○ digit
   ○ kid
   ● sno

5. ● oan
   ○ number
   ○ tow

6. ○ men
   ● loe
   ○ light

☆ ○ sleep
   ○ child
   ● beelo

☆ ○ Bible
   ● mowig
   ○ job

☆ ○ wrote
   ○ gym
   ● snoman

133

---

1 Dictation

Reinforce correct spelling by using current and previous words in context.

(Say) Listen as I read each sentence and then write it in your Worktext.(Slowly read each sentence twice. Sentences are found in the Student Worktext to the left.)

☆ Challenge

Write these incomplete sentences on the board.

Stephen ___ ___ ___ grass.

Write ___ address ___ ___ ___.

___ built ___ ___ ___.

(Say) Listen as I read each sentence. Write the sentence on your paper. (Slowly read each sentence twice.)

Stephen is mowing the grass.

Write your address below your name.

They built a tall snowman.

2 Proofreading

Familiarize students with standardized test format and reinforce recognizing misspelled words.

(Say) Look at each set of words. One word in each set is misspelled. Fill in the oval by the misspelled word. (You may wish to pronounce each set of words to help students correctly identify them.)

3 Hide and Seek

Reinforce correct spelling of current spelling words. (A reproducible master is provided in Appendix A as shown on the inset page to the right.)
Write the words one at a time on a white board.
Have students:

- **Look** at the word.
- **Say** the word out loud.
- **Spell** the word out loud.
- **Hide** (teacher erases word.)
- **Write** the word on paper.
- **Seek** (teacher rewrites word.)
- **Check** spelling. If incorrect, rewrite word correctly.

4 Sentence Fun

Have your students complete this activity to strengthen spelling ability and expand vocabulary.

1 Posttest

Test mastery of the spelling words. Challenge words are starred.

(Say) I will say the word once, use the word in a sentence, then say the word again. Write the word on your paper.

Hide and Seek

Check a paper for each word you spell correctly.

3 5 7
1   9
2 4 6 8 10

Sentence Fun

Look at other forms of your spelling words in the word bank.
Use the clues to find the word that fits best in each blank.

1. Flowers are __growing__ in Grandpa's garden.
2. Jesus __knows__ when you are sad.
3. The wind is __blowing__ the dust.
4. Grandpa __owned__ horses.
5. The __rows__ are crooked.
6. Beth is __throwing__ the trash away.
7. Mom wasn't __slowing__ down for the curve.
8. It hasn't __snowed__ yet.
9. The big truck __towed__ the pickup back home.
10. It __snows__ in the winter.

Word Bank

blow + ing	know + s	row + s	snow + ed	throw + ing
grow + ing	own + ed	slow + ing	snow + s	tow + ed

377

---

1. blow — The wind will **blow** the truck's dust across the field.
2. grow — I hope your love for God will continue to **grow**.
3. know — I **know** that Jesus loves each one of you.
4. low — Luke is too **low** to see over the counter.
5. own — Does your family **own** a pickup?
6. row — The drill bits were in a neat **row** on the workbench.
7. throw — You can't **throw** Grandpa's Bible away.
8. slow — The Hill's old pickup was not **slow**.
9. snow — It will **snow** on Beth's sledding hill sometime this winter.
10. tow — Dad will pay the man to **tow** the pickup back to the farm.
☆ mowing — Grandpa liked **mowing** his yard.
☆ below — The nails are stored **below** the workbench.
☆ snowman — There wasn't any snow to build a **snowman** in Beth's yard.

Progress Chart
Students may record scores. (Reproducible master in Appendix B.)

Personal Dictionary
Students may add any words they have misspelled to their personal dictionaries for reference when writing. (Cover in Appendix B.)

174

I Game

Name _____

Take a walk with Beth as she enjoys memories of times shared with her grandpa. Move one space for each word you or your team spells correctly from this week's word list.

Remember: No matter what happens, God never changes.

J Journaling

Write in your journal about a time you felt very sad.

134

---

2 Game

Reinforce spelling skills and provide motivation and interest.

Materials

- game page (from student text)
- flat buttons, dry beans, pennies, or game discs (1 per child)
- game word list

Game Word List

Use of challenge words is optional.

1. **blow**
2. **grow**
3. **know**
4. **low**
5. **own**
6. **row**
7. **throw**
8. **slow**
9. **snow**
10. **tow**
☆ **mowing**
☆ **below**
☆ **snowman**

3 Journaling

Provide a meaningful reason for correct spelling through personal writing.

Review the story using discussion leads provided on the following page. Encourage students to apply the Scriptural value in their journaling.

  Take a minute to memorize . . .

Read the memory verse twice. Have students practice it with you two more times.

How to Play:

- Divide students into two teams, and decide which team will go first.
- Have each student place their game piece on Start.
- Have a student from team A go to the board.
- Read the spelling word two times slowly and clearly. (You may also wish to use the word in a sentence. Ex.: "cat — The cat climbed a tree. — cat")
- Have the student write the word on the board.
- If the word is spelled correctly, instruct all the members of team A to move their game piece forward one space on the game board. (Note: If the word is misspelled, correct the spelling immediately.)
- Alternate between teams A and B as you go down the word list.
- The team to return to Grandpa's woodshop first is the winner.

Non-Competitive Option: At the end of the game, say: "Class, I am proud of your efforts to spell the words correctly. If you had fun and tried your best, you are all winners!"

3 Journaling

Provide a meaningful reason for correct spelling through personal writing.

Say

- Who was sad in the story this week? (Beth and her family because Grandpa died.)

- Did everyone in Beth's family act the same way when they were sad? (No.)

- How did Beth and Luke act? (Luke cried. Beth kept her feeling inside.)

- Do you think Luke was sadder because he cried? (No, he just let everyone know how he felt inside.)

- What are some ways you have seen people show their sadness? (Brainstorm. You may want to write the students' responses on the board.)

- Because of sin many things in this world are sad. In your journal, write about something that makes you feel sad.

Invented spelling may be encouraged in journal writing and when writing first drafts. Spelling can be edited for finished work.

Chores & Changes

Matthew and Alex learn how choosing to use the things God created in a harmful way (like using alcohol) can be destructive.

"When will they get here? When will they get here?" Alex Shilling could barely contain his excitement.

Mom stopped scrubbing the tub to look at her eager five-year-old. "Sometime this afternoon, Son. It depends when they left the motel. Why don't you go put the blocks away in the playroom so it will look nice when they get here."

"Okay!" Alex ran off down the hall.

When his mom came into the playroom a little while later, Alex jumped. "Are they here?" he asked eagerly.

"Not yet," Mom answered. She was happily surprised to see the blocks stacked neatly in the bright red cubicle where they belonged. Alex had convinced his older brother Matthew to help him do the job in record time.

"Andrew and Richard haven't seen our train, have they?" Alex flipped the switch and made the steam engine start creeping along the track.

"We just got it," Matthew reasoned. "We haven't seen our cousins for a long time!"

"Do you think Victoria will like our train?" Alex wondered.

"Victoria isn't like Rachel's big sister, Rebecca. Victoria likes to play with us," Matthew reminded his little brother. "Remember when she helped us build a dam in the creek last time?"

"And she took you four boys to the pool every day during your sister Emily's naps," Mom said.

"Yeah, and she made the fort with us from real logs," Alex added. "I think she'll like playing with our train, and building a western town around Fort Bravo."

"You boys are blessed to have such delightful cousins!" Mother smiled. "Now, go wait on the front porch while I finish cleaning the bathroom. The other Schillings should be here soon."

Mom was just hanging fresh towels in the bathroom when Alex shouted from his perch on the front porch railing. "They're here! Andrew, Richard, and Victoria are here!"

Mom looked in the bathroom mirror and tucked a few stray hairs back in the clasp that held her long dark hair. She smiled in anticipation. "It will be good to see Caroline and Theodore again," Elizabeth thought as she hurried down to greet her in-laws.

The car pulled to a stop in front of the house just as Mom opened the front door. Matthew and Alex were already waiting beside the driveway. Victoria's door popped opened first. Mom was surprised at the clothes she was wearing. "They certainly don't look like the tastefully coordinated outfits Victoria wore last year," she thought. "Maybe Caroline is letting her buy her own clothes now."

Mom's thoughts were interrupted by Victoria's loud voice. "I'm going to use the bathroom before I haul any of this junk in!" she shouted, slamming the car door. "It'll just have to wait!"

Alex and Matthew stepped back as their cousin brushed by without even glancing in their direction.

Aunt Caroline and Uncle Theodore looked embarrassed as they got out of the car, but greeted Mom and the boys with a smile, then came over to hug them all. Andrew and Richard followed behind their parents. They looked like they had been crying and didn't say anything at first. But after a few awkward comments the cousins were all talking at once. The adults started to gather things up to take inside and the four boys ran in to look at the new train.

As the three adults were walking up the sidewalk with the last load from the car, Victoria flung open the front door. "Your suitcase and backpack are still in the trunk, Victoria," Uncle Theodore said. "And please clean up the trash in the back seat."

Victoria glared at her father, slammed the door behind her, and stomped down the steps without a word.

Mom looked at Aunt Caroline and raised her eyebrows. "What's going on?" she asked.

"It's a long story," Caroline sighed. "I'll tell you about it later."

Alex opened the door for Victoria as she came up the walk with her suitcase and backpack a few minutes later. "Want to see our train?" he asked.

"No way," Victoria said in disgust. "There's something I want to see on TV."

"It's broken right now," Matthew replied, as he walked up to stand next to his brother. "But Dad said it would be ready to pick up Monday."

"That's just great!" The boys were surprised by the angry look on her face. "No TV all weekend! I just can't believe this!"

"Don't you want to see our train?" Alex asked softly. But Victoria only stomped off.

"She doesn't want to do much of anything anymore except listen to her CDs and watch TV," Andrew explained. "She's not really mad at you — she's mad at the whole world!"

The next evening, the two Schilling families gathered in the living room for worship. Three-year-old Emily sat happily on the floor in the middle of the four boys. Victoria sat in a big blue overstuffed chair, her legs tucked underneath her. She looked bored.

First the group sang some favorite praise songs, then Dad opened his Bible. "He created everything there is — nothing exists

177

that He didn't make," Dad read. "What do you think that text means? Does anyone have an idea?"

"Well, God made our dog Sambo," Andrew said.

"God made apples and peanuts for us to eat!" Richard grinned.

"God made the trees that made our house," Matthew added.

"God cweated me," Emily said, pointing to herself.

"That's right!" Dad smiled gently. "What do you think, Alex?"

"I'm glad God made Victoria!" Alex looked at his cousin with bright, admiring eyes.

Victoria gave Alex a startled look, then grabbed her CD player and ran from the room. "What did I say?" Alex asked, close to tears.

"It's not your fault, Alex. You made her feel special, and that embarrassed her." Dad put his arm around his small son. "Let's all kneel for prayer." As everyone knelt, Dad asked the God of the universe to watch over them all.

Later that evening Dad paused on the edge of Matthew's bed after tucking him in. He brushed the brown curly hair away from his son's eyes. "Dad," Matthew asked, "What's wrong with Victoria? Why isn't she nice to us anymore?"

Dad's forehead wrinkled in thought. "Well, Alex, Victoria made some bad choices since she was last here. First, she decided she wanted to be friends with some 'popular' kids at school. They always seemed to be having a good time. They told her they all drank alcohol, so Victoria started drinking, too, so she could impress them. The alcohol made her feel comfortable around her new 'friends', so she started to drink more often. Pretty soon she felt like she needed to drink all the time — but it made her really sick."

"But why would Victoria drink something

that would make her sick?" Alex asked.

"Some people think it tastes good," Dad said, "but Victoria did it mostly to be popular with these kids at school. When the alcohol went out of her system, Victoria felt even sicker, and she also remembered what she used to be like. That made her feel awkward, so she drank even more alcohol to make the feeling go away. But the alcohol filled her up so she wasn't hungry for healthy food anymore. It killed some of her brain cells, and even began to destroy other organs in her body."

Dad shook his head sadly, then continued. "Aunt Caroline and Uncle Theodore took her to a special hospital, but she's still having a difficult time. She isn't drinking anymore, but her body has gotten used to alcohol. Now a counselor is working with her so she can feel comfortable around people without using alcohol. She wasn't drinking when she had fun here last time, so her counselor thought it would be good to try that again."

The room was quiet for a few minutes. Then Alex asked from his bed, "Did God make alcohol too?"

Matthew sat up suddenly. "That's a silly question," he huffed.

"Wait a minute, Matthew," Dad said. "Actually that's a good question. Our text tonight said, 'God made everything — nothing exists that He didn't make.' And that's true. God made corn, and grain, and grapes for us to eat. But sometimes people make them into juices, and store them until they're old to make alcohol. God created lots of wonderful things in this world for us to enjoy, but sometimes people choose to change those things into something harmful."

"I never thought of it that way before." Matthew frowned thoughtfully.

"Can I pray for Victoria?" Alex asked.

"Good idea," Dad smiled at his son. Then the three of them knelt beside Matthew's bed. "Dear God," Alex prayed, "help us to make good choices. And help us to love Victoria even when she isn't nice. And help Victoria not to kill any more brain cells. Amen."

"Dad, can I have a drink?" Matthew

asked, as he crawled back into bed.

"Only if it's water," Dad teased.

"Water would be great, Dad!" Matthew looked up at his father with a smile. "After seeing how it's hurt Victoria, I wouldn't even want to taste alcohol!"

2 Discussion Time

Check understanding of the story and development of personal values.

- What are some things God made. (Brainstorm. Make a list on the board.)
- Is drinking alcohol a good way to feel better or forget your problems for a while?
- Do people keep feeling good for a long time after they drink alcohol?
- Are the problems still there when the alcohol is gone from a person's system?
- Who can you go to for help if you have a problem? (Make a list. You may want to suggest a school counselor, parent, grandparent, teacher, God.)
- Drinking alcohol is not a good choice. If you know someone who has a problem with alcohol talk to an adult you trust and get some help for the person.

A · Test-Words

Name _____

Write each spelling word on the line as your teacher says it.

1. be
2. buy
3. cold
4. blow
5. cake

6. cry
7. dry
8. hold
9. came
10. even

Review
Lesson
12

B · Test-Sentences

The two underlined words in each of the sentences are misspelled. Write the sentences on the lines below, spelling each underlined word correctly.

I <u>wil</u> help <u>cleen</u> out the garage.

1. I <u>will</u> help <u>clean</u> out the garage.

There are <u>mor</u> cookies to <u>baek</u>.

2. There are <u>more</u> cookies to <u>bake</u>.

Did <u>yu</u> <u>gro</u> an inch this year?

3. Did <u>you</u> <u>grow</u> an inch this year?

☆ **Test-Challenge Words**

On a sheet of paper, write each challenge word as your teacher says it.

135

Test-Challenge Words

On a separate piece of paper, challenge words may be tested using the sentences below.

4 · Test-Sentences

Reinforce recognizing misspelled words.

 (Say)
Read each sentence carefully. The underlined words in each sentence are misspelled. Write the sentences on the lines in your Worktext, spelling each underlined word correctly.

Take a minute to memorize . . .

Have students say the memory verses from lessons 1, 2, 3, 4, 5, and 6 with you.

---

3 · Test-Words

Test for knowledge of the correct spellings of these words. (See the instructions at the top right for challenge words.)

(Say)
I will say the word once, use the word in a sentence, then say the word again. Write the word on the lines in your Worktext.

1. be — Our cousins will **be** here soon.
2. buy — Mom let us **buy** special snacks for their visit.
3. cold — Will it be **cold** while they're here?
4. blow — The wind may **blow** a little.
5. cake — Alex helped make a **cake** for dessert.
6. cry — Did Andrew and Richard **cry** in the car?
7. dry — Give the boys tissues to **dry** their eyes.
8. hold — Matthew can **hold** the door open for them.
9. came — They **came** to visit over a year ago.
10. even — Victoria didn't **even** say hello.
☆ wrote — Mrs. Schilling **wrote** her sister-in-law a letter.
☆ great — The families hoped to have a **great** time visiting together.
☆ child — Mom's **child** Alex was eager for his cousins to arrive.

179

Review 12 | Day 2

1 Test-Dictation

Reinforce correct spelling by using current and previous words in context.

(Say) Listen as I read each sentence. Then write the missing words in your Worktext. (Slowly read each sentence twice. Sentences are found in the student text to the right. The words **he's**, **keep**, and **know** are found in this unit.)

2 Test-Proofreading

Familiarize students with standardized test format and reinforce recognizing misspelled words.

(Say) Look at each set of words. One word in each set is misspelled. Fill in the oval by the misspelled word.

Test-Challenge Words

On a separate piece of paper, challenge words may be tested using the sentences below.

(Say) I will say the word once, use the word in a sentence, then say the word again. Write the word on your paper.

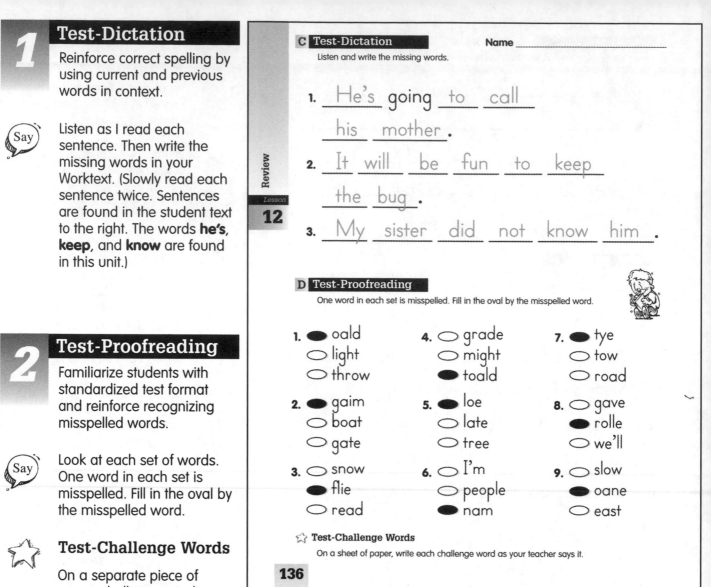

C Test-Dictation
Listen and write the missing words.

1. He's going to call his mother.
2. It will be fun to keep the bug.
3. My sister did not know him.

D Test-Proofreading
One word in each set is misspelled. Fill in the oval by the misspelled word.

1. ● oald
   ○ light
   ○ throw
2. ● gaim
   ○ boat
   ○ gate
3. ○ snow
   ● flie
   ○ read
4. ○ grade
   ○ might
   ● toald
5. ● loe
   ○ late
   ○ tree
6. ○ I'm
   ○ people
   ● nam
7. ● tye
   ○ tow
   ○ road
8. ○ gave
   ● rolle
   ○ we'll
9. ○ slow
   ● oane
   ○ east

Test-Challenge Words
On a sheet of paper, write each challenge word as your teacher says it.

136

☆ mowing — Is Dad **mowing** the grass before they get here?
☆ below — Mrs. Schilling put the cleaner **below** the sink.
☆ break — Matthew and Alex are careful not to **break** their train.
☆ between — They stacked the red blocks **between** the blue and green ones.

180

Copyright ©2012 by The Concerned Group, Inc. All rights reserved.

E Test-Shapes

Name _____

Color each train car on which the word is spelled incorrectly.

even · 2½ · i'm · gaet · bote

cake · raed · liht · mots

thro · gaev · trea · lot · dry

cold · buy · peepel · ro

☆ **Test-Challenge Words**

On a sheet of paper, write each challenge word as your teacher says it.

Review

Lesson **12**

137

1 Test-Shapes

Test mastery of words in this unit.

(Say) Look at each train car. If the word is misspelled, color the train car.

2 Action Game

Reinforce spelling skills and provide motivation and interest.

Materials
- 5 large squares of paper marked O
- 5 large squares of paper marked X
- 9 chairs

How to Play:

Divide students into two teams: **X**'s and **O**'s. Place nine chairs in the front of the room in three rows of three. The chairs will form a tic-tac-toe grid. Alternate between the two teams, giving spelling words tested on days 1, 2, and 3. If a student spells a word correctly, give him an **X** or **O** square to hold depending on which team he represents. Continue playing until all the words tested on days 1, 2, and 3 have been reviewed and/or the tic-tac-toe game in progress has been completed.

Test-Challenge Words

On a separate piece of paper, challenge words may be tested using the sentences below.

(Say) I will say the word once, use the word in a sentence, then say the word again. Write the word on your paper.

☆	high	Alex and Matthew can build a **high** wall with the toy logs.
☆	don't	They **don't** know why Victoria is so grumpy and rude.
☆	sleep	Victoria wanted to **sleep** a lot.
☆	over	Victoria put the headphones **over** her ears.
☆	snowman	They will not build a **snowman** together.

1 Game

Materials

- game page (from student text)
- stickers (13 per child)
- markers (1 per child)
- game word list

Game Word List

Use of challenge words is optional.

The Corn Flakes

1. be
2. buy
3. cold
4. blow
5. cake
6. cry
7. dry
8. hold
9. came
10. even
11. clean
12. bake
13. grow

The Raisins

1. he's
2. keep
3. know
4. old
5. game
6. fly
7. told
8. low
9. name
10. tie
11. roll
12. own
13. he's

The Corn Chips

1. gate
2. people
3. I'm
4. boat
5. row
6. late
7. read
8. light
9. most
10. throw
11. gave
12. tree
13. gate

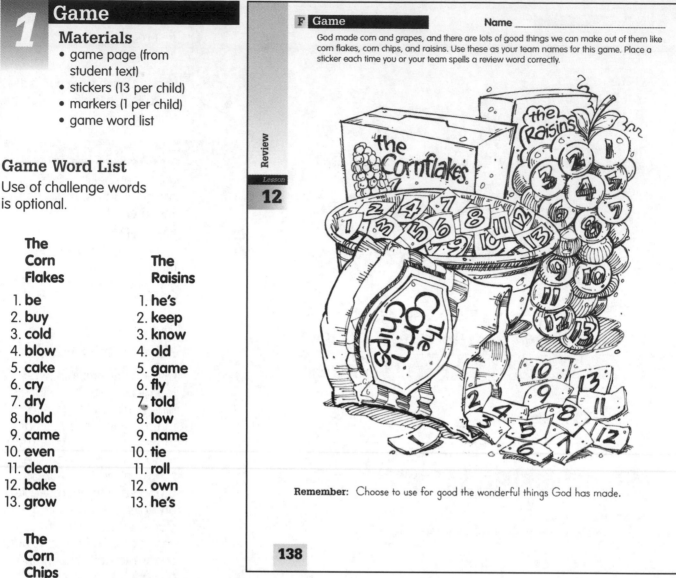

F Game   Name _____

God made corn and grapes, and there are lots of good things we can make out of them like corn flakes, corn chips, and raisins. Use these as your team names for this game. Place a sticker each time you or your team spells a review word correctly.

Review Lesson **12**

Remember: Choose to use for good the wonderful things God has made.

138

How to Play:

- Divide students into three teams. Name one team **The Corn Flakes**, one **The Corn Chips**, and one **The Raisins**. (Option: You may wish to seat students in groups of three, each child from a different team. They should share one game page.) Decide which team goes first, second, and third.
- Read the instructions from the student game page aloud.
- Have a student from the first team choose a number from 1 to 13.
- Say the word that matches that number (from the team's word list) aloud twice. (You may also wish to use the word in a sentence.)
  Ex.: "cat — The cat climbed a tree. — cat")
- Have the student who chose the number write the word on the board.
- If the word is spelled correctly, have all the members of that team put a sticker on that number by their team name. If the word is misspelled, have them put an "X" through that number. They may not choose that number again. (Note: If the word is misspelled, correct the spelling immediately.)
- Repeat this process with the second team and then the third. (Be sure to use a different student from each team for each round.)
- When the words from all three lists have been used, the team with the most stickers is the winner.

Non-Competitive Option: When the game ends, say: "Class, I'm proud of your efforts to spell the words correctly. If you had fun and tried your best, you are all winners!"

G Test-Words

Name _____

Write each spelling word on the line as your teacher says it.

1. might
2. slow
3. grade
4. we'll
5. page

6. snow
7. east
8. right
9. hope
10. tow

Review Lesson 12

H Test-Sentences

The two underlined words in each of the sentences are misspelled. Write the sentences on the lines below, spelling each underlined word correctly.

I can ried my bike on this raod.

1. I can ride my bike on this road.

The sky was a deep bloo last nite.

2. The sky was a deep blue last night.

You may take the bal hoam.

3. You may take the ball home.

☆ **Test-Challenge Words**

On a sheet of paper, write each challenge word as your teacher says it.

139

☆ **Test-Challenge Words**

On a separate piece of paper, challenge words may be tested using the sentences below.

2 Test-Sentences

Reinforce recognizing misspelled words.

(Say) Read each sentence carefully. The underlined words in each sentence are misspelled. Write the sentences on the lines in your Worktext, spelling each underlined word correctly.

---

1 Test-Words

Test for knowledge of the correct spellings of these words. (See the instructions at the top right for challenge words.)

(Say) I will say the word once, use the word in a sentence, then say the word again. Write the word on the lines in your Worktext.

1. might — Victoria **might** play with us.
2. slow — Their car will **slow** down before it stops here.
3. grade — What **grade** is Victoria in at school?
4. we'll — Tonight **we'll** read from God's Word before bed.
5. page — Dad turned a **page** in his Bible.
6. snow — It won't **snow** during their visit.
7. east — Victoria's family lives **east** of the Mississippi River.
8. right — Victoria knew she was not doing **right**.
9. hope — We **hope** she chooses to obey God.
10. tow — The boys toy train can **tow** many rail cars.
☆ Bible — Alex and Matthew's dad read from the **Bible**.
☆ obey — Does Victoria want to **obey** God and her parents?
☆ Jesus — **Jesus** will help us do right even when it's not easy.

183

3 Writing Assessment

Assess student's spelling, grammar, and composition skills through personal writing.

Say
- What did Victoria do that changed the way she acted? (Became addicted to alcohol.)
- What were some of the things she did differently? (She dressed differently. She wasn't respectful to her parents. She wanted to watch a lot of TV. She didn't want to play with her cousins. She was rude to Matthew and Alex.)
- Write in your Worktext about why it is important for you not to drink alcohol.

I Writing Assessment

Write five sentences about why it is important for you not to drink alcohol.

Name _____

Review
Lesson
12

_____

_____

_____

_____

_____

_____

_____

_____

Scripture
John 1:3

140

A rubric for scoring is provided in Appendix B.

---

4 Action Game

Reinforce spelling skills and provide motivation and interest.

Materials

- one **A Reason For Spelling®** Worktext
- a bell (optional)
- small prizes (erasers, pencils, stickers)

How to Play:

Seat the children in a circle. Give one student the **A Reason For Spelling®** Worktext. Have the students pass the book around the circle. When the teacher rings the bell (or says "stop"), have the child holding the book spell a word from today's test. If he spells it incorrectly, he remains in the circle; if he spells it correctly, he receives a prize and drops out of the game. Continue the game until every student has spelled a word correctly.

Spelling Is Fun!

A B C's

This certificate is awarded to

_____

for practicing the following words, by doing terrific
spelling activities and playing great spelling games!

Date _____

bake	be	buy	boat	blow
cake	clean	cry	cold	grow
came	east	dry	hold	know
game	even	fly	home	low
gate	he's	I'm	hope	own
gave	keep	light	most	row
grade	people	might	old	slow
late	read	night	road	snow
name	tree	right	roll	throw
page	we'll	tie	told	tow
☆ break	☆ between	☆ Bible	☆ don't	☆ below
☆ great	☆ Jesus	☆ child	☆ over	☆ mowing
☆ obey	☆ sleep	☆ high	☆ wrote	☆ snowman

---

5 Certificate

Provide an opportunity
for parents or guardians
to encourage and assess
their child's progress.

Say
- Write your name on the first line.
- Now I will write the date on the board for you to copy on the next line.
- Follow along as I read the certificate out loud.
- Be sure to show your parents or guardian all the words you've practiced spelling.

Take a minute to memorize...

Read the memory verse
twice. Have students
practice it with you two
more times.

Review **12** | Day 5

185

6 Letter

Provide the parent or guardian with the spelling word lists for the next unit.

Say) Show your parents or guardian this letter that tells them what your spelling words will be for the next unit. Ask them to put it in a special place where you will remember to practice them together.

Dear Parent,

We are about to begin a new spelling unit containing five weekly lessons. A set of ten words plus three challenge words will be studied each week. All the words will be reviewed in the sixth week.

Values based on the Scriptures listed below will be taught in each lesson.

Lesson 13	Lesson 14	Lesson 15	Lesson 16	Lesson 17
paint	arm	air	bird	any
pay	barn	bear	circle	baby
plays	car	eye	color	every
pray	card	fine	first	family
rain	dark	fire	purple	holy
say	far	like	under	only
stay	farm	line	water	penny
today	hard	their	were	ready
train	part	where	word	story
way	yard	write	work	very
☆ birthday	☆ heart	☆ beside	☆ heard	☆ city
☆ praise	☆ large	☆ care	☆ third	☆ easy
☆ stayed	☆ party	☆ while	☆ world	☆ study
Matt. 16:24	Luke 6:37	John 18:37	Luke 4:8	Luke 1:68

Quotables!

You may let parents and others know you are aware of children's invented spelling by stamping papers with "Unedited," "First Draft," "Sloppy Copy," or "Work in Progress."

A New Challenge

Tommy's grandma develops severe Alzheimer's. The Rawson family makes a choice knowing that following God isn't always easy.

"**C**ome and get it before I throw it out!" Tommy and Lisa came quickly when they heard Dad's call. Both of them arrived in the kitchen at the same time, but stopped short when they spotted their six-foot, one-inch dad standing over the stove. He was wearing Mom's pink gingham apron, which covered only a little bit of him, while he stirred something steaming in a pan.

"Hey, Dad!" Lisa pointed to the three places set at the table. "Where's Mom? I thought she was supposed to be home by supper time."

"Yeah," Tommy washed his hands in the kitchen sink and dried them on the dish towel. "Wasn't she just going to take Grandma a few groceries or something?"

"Your mother called about an hour ago to let us know she'd be later than planned." Dad set the steaming pan on a hot pad in the center of the round table. "You like my new outfit?" He twirled in a clumsy imitation of a ballerina, and then curtsied holding the edges of the little pink apron.

"It's just lovely." Lisa giggled, playing along. "That shade of pink goes well with your plaid flannel shirt and boots!"

"Yeah, right," Tommy muttered as he slid into his chair. "Don't let Daniel see you in Mom's apron or I'll never hear the end of it! Let's eat." He paused and looked at the pan. "Uh . . . what exactly are we eating?"

"You two are in luck tonight!" Dad picked up a bowl and started filling it. "This is my famous homemade stew. You'll love it!" He placed the full bowl on Tommy's placemat.

Tommy poked his spoon around the bowl suspiciously. "If it's so famous, how come we've never eaten it before?"

"Oh, I promise it won't be too bad," Dad chuckled, as he settled into his chair. He bowed his head, and Tommy and Lisa joined him. "Our heavenly Father, we want to thank You tonight for this food. Please help us to use the strength that it gives us to follow You in every part of our lives. Amen."

Tommy was almost asleep when he finally heard his mother come in. "I wonder what took Mom so long tonight." He sighed, and snuggled deeper into his warm bed. "I guess everything's okay now. That stew of Dad's was pretty good after all, but it's still nice to have Mom home."

School was almost over the next day when Mrs. Bentley came into the classroom. She spoke briefly to Tommy's teacher, then walked over to his desk by the window. "Tommy," the gray-haired school secretary leaned over his desk. "You're supposed to go home with James Thomason today. Your mother called and said she wouldn't be able to pick you up after school."

"What happened?" Tommy forgot to whisper. "What about Lisa? Is she going to James' house, too? Is Mom okay?" The questions came thick and fast, but Mrs. Bentley didn't have any answers.

"She sounded all right, Tommy," Mrs. Bentley shrugged with a smile. "But she didn't tell me what happened. I'm sure everything is fine."

"What's going on?" Tommy's thoughts spun. *"Mom always comes to get us when school is out. I wonder if she's sick. Or maybe she had a wreck. Or maybe something happened to Dad. Maybe the house caught on fire. Maybe the car just won't start. I wonder . . ."*

By 5:30, when his mother's familiar red sedan pulled up in front of James' house, Tommy had thought of even more possibilities. He tore out the front door and crossed the Thomason's yard without a coat. "Mom, where have you be . . ." his voice trailed away as his dad got out of the car instead of Mom.

"Everything's going to be fine, Son." Dad grabbed his shoulder and squeezed it reassuringly. "I'll tell you all about it at home. First, let's thank James' parents, and collect Lisa."

That evening the Rawson family gathered in the living room. Mom sat in her favorite wing-back chair by the window, her face drawn with tired lines. Lisa sprawled across the carpet on her tummy just like she always did. Tommy leaned his back against the arm of the couch in his regular spot. But something was different. Dad smiled gently at Mom and then rubbed his hand over his rough face.

"Grandma isn't doing very well," he began. Lisa and Tommy sat up straight to listen. "Yesterday, when your mother took the groceries over, she found a huge mess. Grandma forgot what kind of soap to put in the dishwasher. She put laundry detergent in. You can imagine the mess that Mom cleaned up last night and why it took so long. When your mother went by to check on Grandma after lunch today, she found the door hanging open and Grandma gone. She finally found her several blocks away. Grandma couldn't remember why she left the house or where she was going. She was lost."

"Is that why she doesn't always know who we are when we go to see her?" Tommy glanced from Mom to Dad. "Does she forget who we are, like she forgot those things?"

"That's right, Son," Dad held Tommy's gaze. "It's not that she quit loving us or caring about us. It's just that something is

187

wrong in her brain that makes her forget us sometimes, as well as a lot of other important things."

"Can't she take medicine or something and get well?" Lisa stared at the thick carpet and rubbed her finger back and forth across it.

Dad shook his head. "No one knows how to help someone with this kind of problem get well. There just isn't any cure right now." Silence hung heavy for a moment, then Dad asked quietly, "Would you two be willing to have Grandma move in with us for a while? Taking care of Grandma will be a lot of work. Would you be willing to help your mother and me by doing extra jobs that you don't do now?"

"What would happen if she didn't come here?" Lisa's finger rubbed faster across the carpet.

"There are nursing homes and other places that care for people with problems like Grandma's."

Lisa jumped up, and flung herself into Mom's arms. "I'll help! I'll help you a lot! Even if she doesn't remember us, Grandma still needs to be with people who love her!"

"How about you, Son?" Dad tilted Tommy's chin up with one hand.

"I can do a lot to help. I want Grandma here with us, too." Tommy jumped up. "Let's get the guest room ready for her right now!"

"Whoa, Son!" Dad scooped Tommy back up on the couch beside him with one arm. "We'll fix the study for Grandma to live in since it's downstairs. But we'll do it tomorrow." Dad stood up and left the room without explanation, but was back in an instant with the handwriting page Tommy had brought home from school that afternoon. "I think this is a good motto for our whole family," he said. "'If anyone wants to be a follower of Mine, let him take up his cross and follow Me.' Let's ask for help to follow God closely, even if it's hard to do in the days to come."

The next day Grandma moved into the Rawson home. And a pretty wooden frame appeared on the wall in the kitchen. Inside was Tommy's handwriting sheet — now the Rawson family motto.

2 Discussion Time

Check understanding of the story and development of personal values.

- Why did Dad fix supper for Tommy and Lisa?
- What did Tommy think might have happened when Mom didn't come to pick him up after school?
- What was wrong with Tommy's grandmother?
- Do you know someone like Tommy's grandma who can't always remember things?
- Do you think it would be easy for Tommy's family to have Grandma live with them?
- How were Tommy and Lisa followers of God?

A Preview

Write each word as your teacher says it.

Name _____

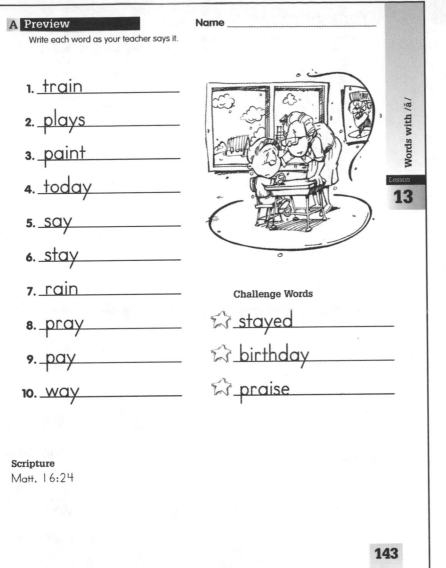

Words with /ā/

Lesson **13**

1. train
2. plays
3. paint
4. today
5. say
6. stay
7. rain
8. pray
9. pay
10. way

Challenge Words

 stayed

 birthday

 praise

Scripture
Matt. 16:24

143

Challenge

For better spellers, challenge words may be included in the weekly list. Challenge words are starred.

Correct Immediately!

Say) Let's correct our preview. I will write each word on the board. Put a dot under each letter on your preview as I spell the word out loud. If you spelled a word wrong, rewrite it correctly.

Progress Chart

Students may record scores. (Reproducible master in Appendix B.)

Take a minute to memorize . . .

Read the memory verse twice. Have students practice it with you two more times.

---

3 Preview

Test for knowledge of the correct spellings of these words. (See the instructions at the top right for challenge words.)

Say) I will say the word once, use the word in a sentence, then say the word again. Write the word on the lines in the Worktext.

1. train — Tommy has a toy **train** set.
2. plays — Tommy **plays** baseball very well.
3. paint — The **paint** on Mrs. Rawson's car was red.
4. today — Tommy's dad made supper **today**.
5. say — Dad will **say** the blessing.
6. stay — Grandma needed to **stay** with someone to take care of her.
7. rain — Grandma might go out in the **rain**.
8. pray — We will **pray** that Grandma will be all right.
9. pay — They could **pay** someone else to take care of Grandma.
10. way — Tommy and Lisa chose God's **way**, even though it wasn't easy.
☆ stayed — Mom **stayed** to help clean up the mess at Grandma's house.
☆ birthday — Tommy will be eight on his next **birthday**.
☆ praise — We can **praise** God for all the wonderful things He's done.

189

Word Shapes

4 Help students form a correct image of whole words.

Say Look at each word and think about its shape. Now, write the word in the correct word Shape Boxes. You may check off each word as you use it.

(In many words, the sound of /ā/ is spelled with **ai** or **ay**.)

Say In the word Shape Boxes, color the letters that spell the sound of /ā/ in each word. Circle the words that begin with a consonant cluster.

Challenge
Draw the correctly shaped box around each letter in these words.

Say On a separate sheet of paper, write other words that contain the spelling patterns in the word list. See how many words you can write.

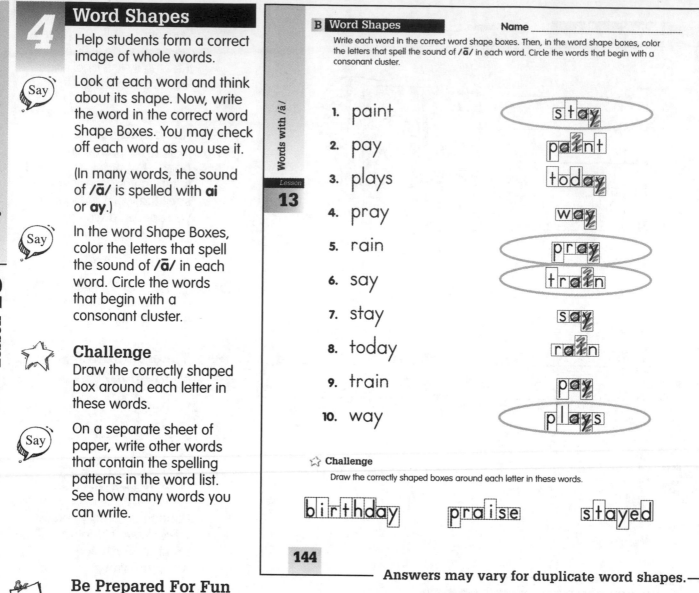

B Word Shapes

Name _____

Write each word in the correct word shape boxes. Then, in the word shape boxes, color the letters that spell the sound of /ā/ in each word. Circle the words that begin with a consonant cluster.

1. paint
2. pay
3. plays
4. pray
5. rain
6. say
7. stay
8. today
9. train
10. way

☆ **Challenge**
Draw the correctly shaped boxes around each letter in these words.

birthday   praise   stayed

144

Answers may vary for duplicate word shapes.

Be Prepared For Fun

Check these supply lists for **Fun Ways to Spell** presented **Day 2**. Purchase and/or gather these items ahead of time!

General
- Crayons
- 3 x 5 Cards cut in thirds (41 pieces per child)
- 3 x 5 Cards cut in thirds (20 more to spell challenge words)
- Glue
- Bright Paper or Poster Board (about 3 pieces per child)
- Spelling List

Auditory
- Rhythm instruments (two wooden spoons, two pan lids, maracas)
- Spelling List

Visual
- Letter Stencils
- Colored Pencils
- Paper (2 sheets per child)
- Spelling List

Tactile
- Cotton Balls
- Glue
- Construction Paper
- Spelling List

190

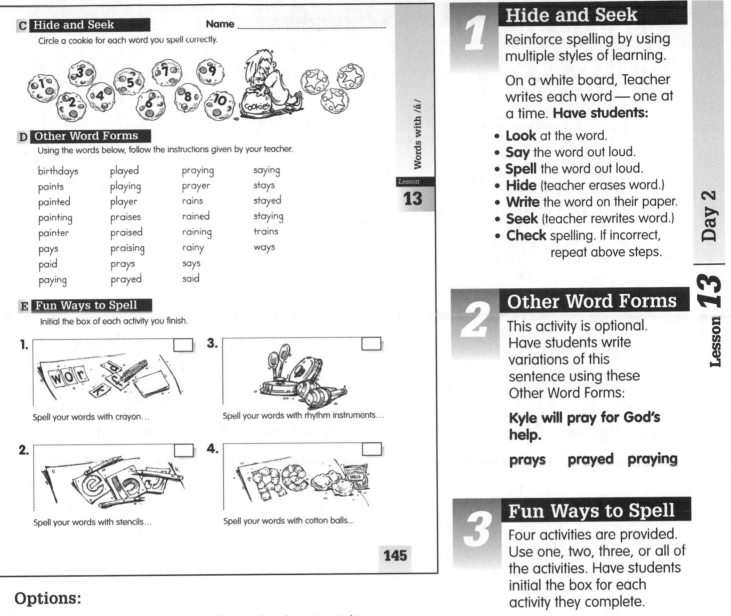

C Hide and Seek

Name _____

Circle a cookie for each word you spell correctly.

D Other Word Forms

Using the words below, follow the instructions given by your teacher.

birthdays	played	praying	saying
paints	playing	prayer	stays
painted	player	rains	stayed
painting	praises	rained	staying
painter	praised	raining	trains
pays	praising	rainy	ways
paid	prays	says	
paying	prayed	said	

E Fun Ways to Spell

Initial the box of each activity you finish.

1. Spell your words with crayon...

2. Spell your words with stencils...

3. Spell your words with rhythm instruments...

4. Spell your words with cotton balls...

Words with /ā/

Lesson **13**

145

1 Hide and Seek

Reinforce spelling by using multiple styles of learning.

On a white board, Teacher writes each word — one at a time. **Have students:**

- **Look** at the word.
- **Say** the word out loud.
- **Spell** the word out loud.
- **Hide** (teacher erases word.)
- **Write** the word on their paper.
- **Seek** (teacher rewrites word.)
- **Check** spelling. If incorrect, repeat above steps.

2 Other Word Forms

This activity is optional. Have students write variations of this sentence using these Other Word Forms:

Kyle will pray for God's help.

prays   prayed   praying

3 Fun Ways to Spell

Four activities are provided. Use one, two, three, or all of the activities. Have students initial the box for each activity they complete.

Options:

- assign activities to students according to their learning styles
- set up the activities in learning centers for students to do throughout the day
- divide students into four groups and assign one activity per group
- do one activity per day

General

To spell your words with crayon . . .
- Write each letter of your spelling word on a card.
- Glue the cards on a sheet of paper in the right order to spell your words.
- Check your spelling.

Auditory

To spell your words with rhythm instruments . . .
- Look at a word on your spelling list.
- Close your eyes.
- Play your rhythm instruments softly while you whisper the spelling of the word.
- Open your eyes and check your spelling.

Visual

To spell your words with stencils . . .
- Trace the outline of each letter of the spelling word.
- Color in the letters.

Tactile

To spell your words with cotton balls . . .
- Choose a word from your spelling list.
- It may be a favorite word or a word you have trouble remembering how to spell.
- Write the word in tall, wide letters on a sheet of construction paper.
- Spread glue along the outline of each letter and press cotton balls into the glue.

191

1 ABC Order

Familiarize students with word meaning and usage. Write the names of three students (that begin with different letters) on the board. Ask the students which of the three would be first in ABC order. Ask which name would be next. Write the three names in correct ABC order. Invite the students to look about the room and name three objects they see. Make sure they understand how to write them in ABC order.

(Say) Write each set of spelling words in alphabetical order.

F ABC Order   Name _____

Write each set of spelling words in alphabetical order.

1. plays, say, rain   plays   rain   say
2. way, train, pray   pray   train   way
3. stay, pay, today   pay   stay   today
4. rain, paint, way   paint   rain   way
5. train, stay, plays   plays   stay   train
6. way, today, pray   pray   today   way
7. paint, say, rain   paint   rain   say
8. way, train, pay   pay   train   way
9. say, plays, today   plays   say   today
10. rain, paint, stay   paint   rain   stay

A B C D E F G H I J K L M N O P Q R S T U V W X Y Z
a b c d e f g h i j k l m n o p q r s t u v w x y z

146

Take a minute to memorize . . .

Read the memory verse twice. Have students practice it with you two more times.

192

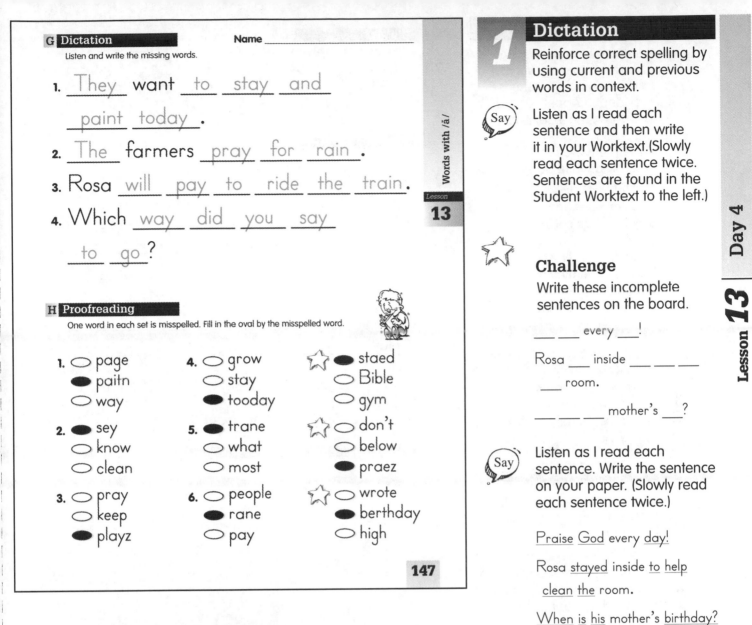

G Dictation

Listen and write the missing words.

Name _____

1. They want to stay and paint today.

2. The farmers pray for rain.

3. Rosa will pay to ride the train.

4. Which way did you say to go?

Words with /ā/

Lesson 13

H Proofreading

One word in each set is misspelled. Fill in the oval by the misspelled word.

1. ○ page
   ● paitn
   ○ way

2. ● sey
   ○ know
   ○ clean

3. ○ pray
   ○ keep
   ● playz

4. ○ grow
   ○ stay
   ● tooday

5. ● trane
   ○ what
   ○ most

6. ○ people
   ● rane
   ○ pay

☆ ● staed
   ○ Bible
   ○ gym

☆ ○ don't
   ○ below
   ● praez

☆ ○ wrote
   ● berthday
   ○ high

147

1 Dictation

Reinforce correct spelling by using current and previous words in context.

Say Listen as I read each sentence and then write it in your Worktext.(Slowly read each sentence twice. Sentences are found in the Student Worktext to the left.)

☆ Challenge

Write these incomplete sentences on the board.

___ ___ every ___!

Rosa ___ inside ___ ___ ___ ___ room.

___ ___ ___ mother's ___?

Say Listen as I read each sentence. Write the sentence on your paper. (Slowly read each sentence twice.)

Praise God every day!

Rosa stayed inside to help clean the room.

When is his mother's birthday?

Day 4

Lesson 13

2 Proofreading

Familiarize students with standardized test format and reinforce recognizing misspelled words.

Say Look at each set of words. One word in each set is misspelled. Fill in the oval by the misspelled word. (You may wish to pronounce each set of words to help students correctly identify them.)

3 Hide and Seek

Reinforce correct spelling of current spelling words. (A reproducible master is provided in Appendix A as shown on the inset page to the right.)

Write the words one at a time on a white board.

Have students:

- **Look** at the word.
- **Say** the word out loud.
- **Spell** the word out loud.
- **Hide** (teacher erases word.)
- **Write** the word on paper.
- **Seek** (teacher rewrites word.)
- **Check** spelling. If incorrect, rewrite word correctly.

4 Suffixes

Have your students complete this activity to strengthen spelling ability and expand vocabulary.

1 Posttest

Test mastery of the spelling words. Challenge words are starred.

(Say) I will say the word once, use the word in a sentence, then say the word again. Write the word on your paper.

Lesson 13 | Appendix A

Hide and Seek

Check a paper for each word you spell correctly.

1 3 5 7 9 2 4 6 8 10

Suffixes

Add **s**, **ed**, and **ing** to these spelling words. Write the new words.

	+ s	+ ed	+ ing
1. pray	prays	prayed	praying
2. stay	stays	stayed	staying
3. paint	paints	painted	painting
4. rain	rains	rained	raining
5. train	trains	trained	training
6. play	plays	played	playing

	+ s	+ ing
7. say	says	sayind
8. pay	pays	paying

378

1.	say	Mrs. Bentley didn't **say** why she couldn't pick him up.
2.	today	Tommy will go to James' house after school **today**.
3.	train	They will play with James' **train**.
4.	rain	They can play outside if it doesn't **rain**.
5.	plays	Tommy **plays** on James swing set.
6.	paint	The blue **paint** on the swing set is peeling off in places.
7.	stay	Tommy will **stay** until his parents come to get him.
8.	pay	Mrs. Rawson will **pay** for the groceries.
9.	way	Grandma went outside and lost her **way** back.
10.	pray	God always listens when we **pray**.
☆	stayed	Tommy **stayed** at James' house all afternoon.
☆	birthday	Grandma doesn't remember Tommy's **birthday**.
☆	praise	We can **praise** God even when things aren't easy.

Progress Chart

Students may record scores. (Reproducible master in Appendix B.)

Personal Dictionary

Students may add any words they have misspelled to their personal dictionaries for reference when writing. (Cover in Appendix B.)

194

I Game

Name _____

Tommy and Lisa's dad made stew for supper while their mom was away helping their grandmother. Be the first to the dinner table by moving one space each time you or your team spells a word correctly from this week's word list.

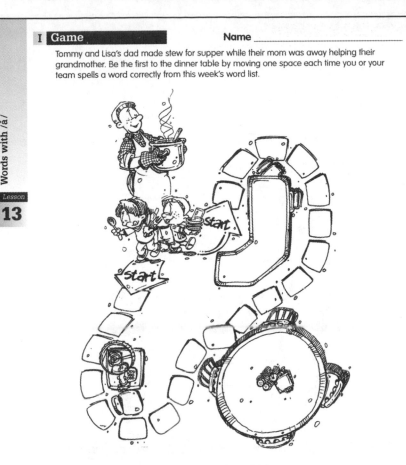

Remember: Follow Jesus by doing what He would do.

J Journaling

Write a promise to God in your journal that you will be His follower even when it's not easy to do.

148

How to Play:

- Divide students into two teams, and decide which team will go first. Have one team race to the dinner table with Tommy and one team with Lisa.
- Optional: If you have an even number of students, you may wish to pair students from opposing teams and have them share a game page, each coloring the spaces for their own team on that page.
- Have a student from team A go to the board.
- Read the spelling word two times slowly and clearly. (You may also wish to use the word in a sentence. Ex.: "cat — The cat climbed a tree. — cat")
- Have the student write the word on the board.
- If the word is spelled correctly, instruct all the members of team A to color one space, beginning at Start, on the game board. (Note: If the word is misspelled, correct the spelling immediately.)
- Alternate between teams A and B as you go down the word list.
- The team to reach the dinner table first is the winner.

Non-Competitive Option: At the end of the game, say: "Class, I am proud of your efforts to spell the words correctly. If you had fun and tried your best, you are all winners!"

2 Game

Reinforce spelling skills and provide motivation and interest.

Materials

- game page (from student text)
- flat buttons, dry beans, pennies, or game discs (1 per child)
- game word list

Game Word List

Check off each word lightly in pencil as It is used.

1. **plays**
2. **pray**
3. **say**
4. **stay**
5. **today**
6. **way**
7. **pay**
8. **paint**
9. **rain**
10. **train**
☆ **praise**
☆ **stayed**
☆ **birthday**

3 Journaling

Provide a meaningful reason for correct spelling through personal writing.

Review the story using discussion leads provided on the following page. Encourage students to apply the Scriptural value in their journaling.

Take a minute to memorize . . .

Have students say the memory verse with you once.

Provide a meaningful reason for correct spelling through personal writing.

Say
- Tommy was frightened when his mom didn't come home as usual and didn't pick him up after school. Why was she late? (One day she had to clean up the big mess at Grandma's house because Grandma put the wrong soap in the dishwasher. The next day she was trying to find Grandma who had left her house and gotten lost.)

- Why couldn't Tommy's grandmother live alone anymore? (Something was wrong in her brain and she couldn't remember things. She might get hurt or lost on her own.)

- Tommy and Lisa wanted their grandma to live with them even though it would be a lot more work for all of them. How was this taking up their cross to follow Jesus? (They were willing to do the extra work because they wanted to help their grandma.)

- Following God isn't always easy. Write your promise to be God's follower in your journal. Draw a picture of yourself underneath the promise.

Quotables!

Reading children's writing and letting them know what you think helps them learn how words are spelled.

Unkind Words

Kristin wishes she'd never spoken a critical word when she finds out how it feels to be criticized.

Kristin twirled in front of the full-length mirror in her mother's bedroom. She smiled and her reflection smiled back. She looked good! This new outfit was the latest style—the kind of clothes all the girls were wearing. Kristin tossed her head, and her ponytail of rich brown wavy hair flipped over one shoulder. Her green eyes sparkled. YES!

As Mrs. Wright drove the children to school, Kristin hummed a little to herself and gazed out the window at the gray morning around them. Smoke rose from the chimneys of homes along the way, drifting and curling in the still, cold air. The lights from the windows looked cozy and warm. Even though they were almost late, Kristin still felt great as she and Christopher rushed into their classroom.

Quickly hanging up her red winter coat, Kristin hurried across the room to her desk. She slipped into her seat just as Mrs. Morgan called for everyone's attention to begin the day. Kristin glanced across the room at her friend Rosa.

"I love your new outfit." Rosa mouthed the words silently across the room as Mrs. Morgan wrote in her record book.

Kristin batted her eyes and smiled as she mouthed back, "Thank you."

At recess, Katelynn caught up with Kristin as she headed for a good spot to jump rope. "Hey, Kristin." Katelynn was bouncing a red four-square ball. "You want to play four square with Beth and me?"

"Okay." Kristin changed directions, and the girls gathered with a few others to start the game. The ball bounced back and forth, high and low, fast and slow between the players. A fast-twisting bounce into Kristin's square caught her off guard. She was out, and joined the waiting line as Sarah took her place. Kristin glanced up and noticed Setsuko flying down the slide. Her red corduroy pants didn't match the blue and yellow flowered sweater, or pink coat she wore.

Katelynn got out next, and came to stand by Kristin. "Your new clothes are great, Kristin. Where did you get them? At the mall?"

"No." Kristin smoothed a hand down her sleeve. "Mom got them for me at that new store next to the post office. It has lots of really neat clothes for kids. I got a new dress, too." Without really thinking about it, Kristin added, "It sure wouldn't hurt Setsuko to get some new clothes. She always looks so awful. None of her clothes ever really go together."

Just then Beth got out, and it was Kristin's turn to step back into the four-square game. She never even noticed that Setsuko wasn't at the slide anymore. She had been standing right there, just a few feet away. But Mrs. Morgan saw, and followed as Setsuko hurried away.

As the children started back to their classroom after recess, they met an older class coming down the hall. Kristin spotted Carol Hughes, a sixth-grade girl who lived just a couple of blocks down Appleby Road. Carol's dad worked for the same company as Kristin's dad. Since Carol's mom and Kristin's mom had been friends for a long time, the girls often saw each other. "Hi, Carol!" Kristin paused as she passed Carol. "Like my new outfit?"

"Yeah, sure." Carol moved on down the hall.

Kristin walked backwards a step or two and called cheerfully, "Bye! Have a good recess!" Just as she started through the classroom door, Kristin remembered the jump rope she had taken out to recess and never used. Quickly she spun around and hurried back down the hall. The class rule was clear: if you took something out to play with at recess, it was your job to make sure you brought it back inside. Kristin shoved on the heavy door leading to the playground. As it began to open, she heard something that stopped her in her tracks.

An unseen girl's voice made it clear she was making fun of someone. "So, Carol, who's the funny little kid with the 'new clothes?'" Kristin froze. That was her. She was the "little kid with the new clothes" who had spoken to Carol. Kristin's breath seemed to stop. What would Carol say? Carol was her friend. Of course, Carol would tell that awful girl that Kristin was a friend, that they did things together sometimes, and that their families were friends. Carol had just been at the Wright house last week for supper and games. They'd had a great time. So naturally Carol would tell that other girl that Kristin was her friend. Kristin's stiff hold on the door relaxed a bit. Then Carol's voice answered.

"Oh, that kid." Kristin heard Carol laugh. "She's just someone who lives in our neighborhood. She won't ever leave me alone. Honestly, I guess she doesn't have any friends her own age 'cause she's always hanging around me!" The voices and laughter faded as the older girls walked out onto the playground. Kristin sagged against the cold door and closed her burning eyes. How could Carol say such mean things?

She jumped when she felt a hand on her shoulder. Opening her eyes, she blinked up into the kind face of her teacher. As Kristin's tears began to gather, Mrs. Morgan smiled sympathetically and squeezed her shoulder. "I

197

heard enough of that to know how unkind it was. Did you leave something outside, Kristin?"

Kristin nodded. "A jump rope." She sniffed and swiped a hand across her eyes.

"I'm sure one of the boys would be happy to go get the jump rope this time." Mrs. Morgan gently urged Kristin down the hall, past the classroom, to the office. "Mrs. Bentley, Kristin isn't feeling very well right now. May she rest here for a little while?" Kristin's tears spilled over. "She can come back to the classroom when she's feeling better."

"Of course. The poor dear." Mrs. Bentley jumped up and rushed over to open the door to the little room where students who got sick could lie down until they went home.

A little while later Kristin slipped quietly back into her classroom. Her classmates were all busy, and hardly noticed her arrival.

As Mrs. Wright drove the children home that afternoon, Kristin gazed quietly out the window at the gray skies. The bare trees looked cold and miserable, frozen in place along the road. The houses looked lonely, staring out at the cold world with dark, blank window eyes.

"How was your day?" Mom asked cheerfully, listening to Christopher and Cathy's replies. Kristin didn't answer. Later that night, cuddled in Mom's lap in the rocking chair, she told all about her day — how Carol had hurt her feelings; how Mrs. Morgan had found time to talk quietly with her before school was over; how Mrs. Morgan helped her understand that Carol probably didn't really feel that way, but probably just wasn't strong enough to stand up to some of her classmates; and how Mrs. Morgan had let Kristin know that her own unkind words had hurt Setsuko in much the same way.

"Oh, Mom," Kristin snuggled closer in her mother's arms. "I just feel so bad that I made Setsuko feel as awful as Carol made me feel. I asked Setsuko to forgive me and she did," Kristin sniffed. "I never want to hurt anyone like that again! Never!" She shook her head fiercely.

Mom hugged Kristin and planted a kiss on the top of her head. "Well, sweetheart, it sounds like you learned a whole lot more at school today than how to read, write, and do arithmetic."

Kristin smiled weakly. "Yeah. I even memorized the handwriting text already. It's 'Never criticize or condemn — or it will all come back on you.' And that's one Scripture I'm never going to forget!!"

Discussion Time

Check understanding of the story and development of personal values.

- Why was Kristin feeling really good as the day began?
- What did Kristin do that made Setsuko feel bad?
- How would you feel if you were in Setsuko's place?
- What happened to help Kristin understand how unkind she'd been to Setsuko?
- Have you said something that made someone else feel badly?
- How can you be careful not to hurt someone's feelings?

A Preview

Write each word as your teacher says it.

Name _____

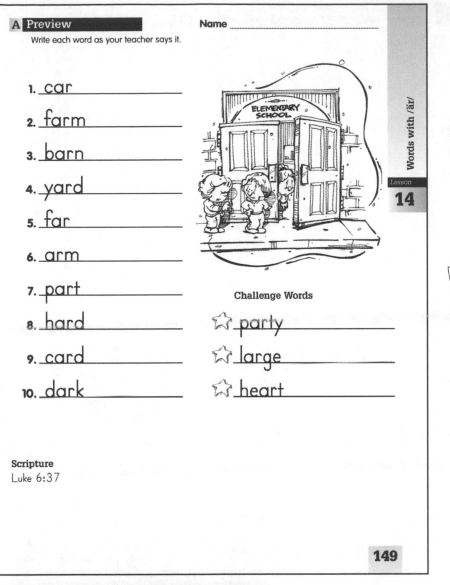

1. car
2. farm
3. barn
4. yard
5. far
6. arm
7. part
8. hard
9. card
10. dark

Challenge Words

☆ party
☆ large
☆ heart

Scripture
Luke 6:37

149

Challenge

For better spellers, challenge words may be included in the weekly list. Challenge words are starred.

Correct Immediately!

 Say

Let's correct our preview. I will write each word on the board. Put a dot under each letter on your preview as I spell the word out loud. If you spelled a word wrong, rewrite it correctly.

Progress Chart

Students may record scores. (Reproducible master in Appendix B.)

Take a minute to memorize . . .

Read the memory verse twice. Have students practice it with you two more times.

---

3 Preview

Test for knowledge of the correct spellings of these words. (See the instructions at the top right for challenge words.)

Say

I will say the word once, use the word in a sentence, then say the word again. Write the word on the lines in the Worktext.

1. car — Kristin gazed out the window of the **car** on the way to school.
2. farm — The road went past a **farm**.
3. barn — There was a large red **barn** behind the house.
4. yard — A picket fence surrounded the **yard**.
5. far — It wasn't very **far** from the school.
6. arm — Kristin carried the jump rope over her **arm**.
7. part — The girls played four square on **part** of the paved area.
8. hard — Beth bounced the ball **hard**.
9. card — Do you think Kristin should make a **card** for Setsuko?
10. dark — It gets **dark** early in the winter.
☆ party — Carol had come to a **party** at Kristin's house.
☆ large — A **large** tear slipped down Kristin's cheek.
☆ heart — Kristin had a change of **heart**.

Word Shapes

Help students form a correct image of whole words.

(Say) Look at each word and think about its shape. Now, write the word in the correct word Shape Boxes. You may check off each word as you use it.

(In most words, the sound of /är/ is spelled with **ar**.)

(Say) In the word Shape Boxes, color the letters that spell the sound of /är/ in each word.

☆ **Challenge**

Draw the correctly shaped box around each letter in these words.

(Say) On a separate sheet of paper, write sentences using one or more of the spelling words.

Lesson 14 | Day 1

Words with /är/

Lesson **14**

B Word Shapes   Name _____

Write each word in the correct word shape boxes. Then, in the word shape boxes, color the letters that spell the sound of /är/ in each word.

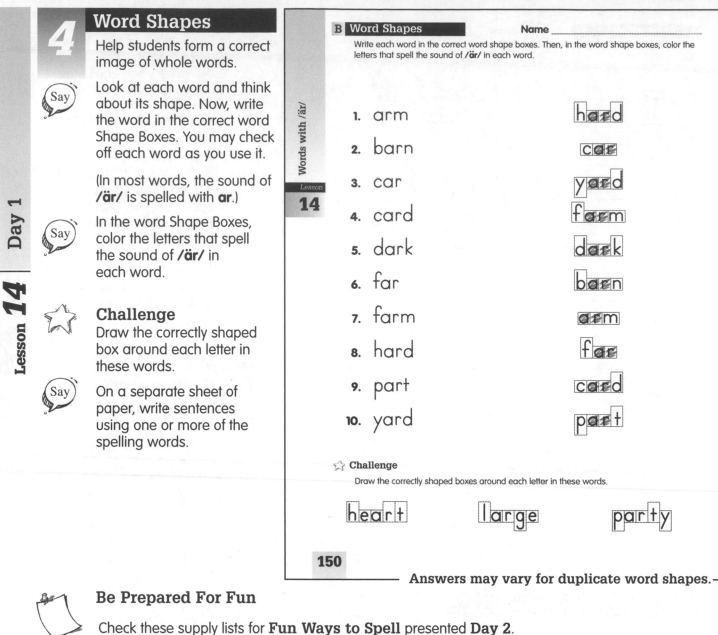

1. arm — hard
2. barn — car
3. car — yard
4. card — farm
5. dark — dark
6. far — barn
7. farm — arm
8. hard — far
9. part — card
10. yard — part

☆ **Challenge**

Draw the correctly shaped boxes around each letter in these words.

heart   large   party

150

Answers may vary for duplicate word shapes.

Be Prepared For Fun

Check these supply lists for **Fun Ways to Spell** presented **Day 2**. Purchase and/or gather these items ahead of time!

General
- Eraser
- Dark Construction Paper
- Spelling List

Auditory
- Spelling List

Visual
- Poster Paint
- Paint Brush
- Art Paper (3 or 4 sheets per child)
- Spelling List

Tactile
- Damp sand in plastic storage box with lid
- Spelling List

200

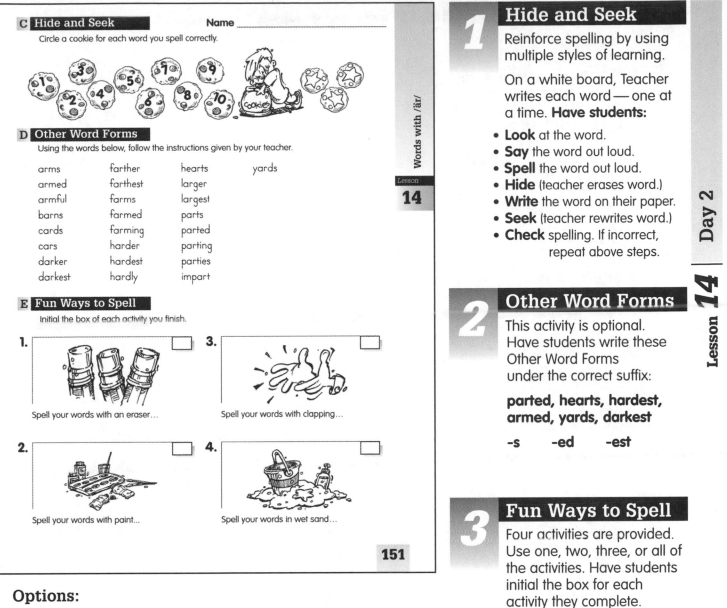

C Hide and Seek

Name _____

Circle a cookie for each word you spell correctly.

D Other Word Forms

Using the words below, follow the instructions given by your teacher.

arms	farther	hearts	yards
armed	farthest	larger	
armful	farms	largest	
barns	farmed	parts	
cards	farming	parted	
cars	harder	parting	
darker	hardest	parties	
darkest	hardly	impart	

E Fun Ways to Spell

Initial the box of each activity you finish.

1. ☐
Spell your words with an eraser...

2. ☐
Spell your words with paint...

3. ☐
Spell your words with clapping...

4. ☐
Spell your words in wet sand...

Words with /är/

Lesson **14**

151

---

1 Hide and Seek

Reinforce spelling by using multiple styles of learning.

On a white board, Teacher writes each word — one at a time. **Have students:**

- **Look** at the word.
- **Say** the word out loud.
- **Spell** the word out loud.
- **Hide** (teacher erases word.)
- **Write** the word on their paper.
- **Seek** (teacher rewrites word.)
- **Check** spelling. If incorrect, repeat above steps.

Day 2

Lesson 14

2 Other Word Forms

This activity is optional. Have students write these Other Word Forms under the correct suffix:

parted, hearts, hardest, armed, yards, darkest

-s   -ed   -est

3 Fun Ways to Spell

Four activities are provided. Use one, two, three, or all of the activities. Have students initial the box for each activity they complete.

Options:

- assign activities to students according to their learning styles
- set up the activities in learning centers for students to do throughout the day
- divide students into four groups and assign one activity per group
- do one activity per day

General

To spell your words with an eraser . . .
- Turn your pencil upside down.
- Use the eraser to write your spelling words on a sheet of dark construction paper.
- Check your spelling.

Auditory

To spell your words with clapping . . .
- Look at a word on your spelling list.
- Close your eyes.
- Clap your hands softly while you whisper the spelling of the word.
- Open your eyes and check your spelling.

Visual

To spell your words with paint . . .
- Dip your brush in one color of poster paint.
- Paint a spelling word on your paper.
- Rinse your brush well in clean water and wipe it dry on a paper towel before dipping it in another color to paint another word.

Tactile

To spell your words in damp sand . . .
- Use finger to write a spelling word in damp sand.
- Check your spelling.
- Smooth the sand with your fingers and write another word.

1 Rhyme Time

Familiarize students with word meaning and usage. Write **Do you think the cat likes to wear the hat?** on the board. Ask the students to name two words in the sentence that end the same. Explain that the words **cat** and **hat** rhyme. Ask the students to name more words that rhyme with **cat**. Invite the students to think of other rhyming word pairs.

(Say) Under each group of words, write the spelling words that rhyme with them.

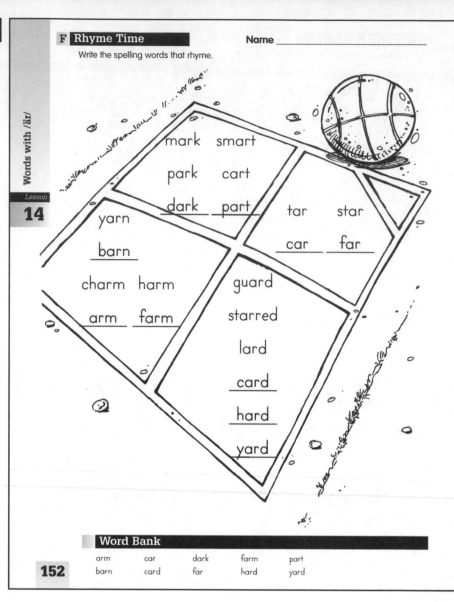

F Rhyme Time

Write the spelling words that rhyme.

Name _____

Words with /är/

Lesson **14**

mark smart
park cart
dark part
yarn
barn
charm harm
arm farm

tar star
car far

guard
starred
lard
card
hard
yard

Word Bank

152

| arm | car | dark | farm | part |
| barn | card | far | hard | yard |

Take a minute to memorize . . .

Read the memory verse twice. Have students practice it with you two more times.

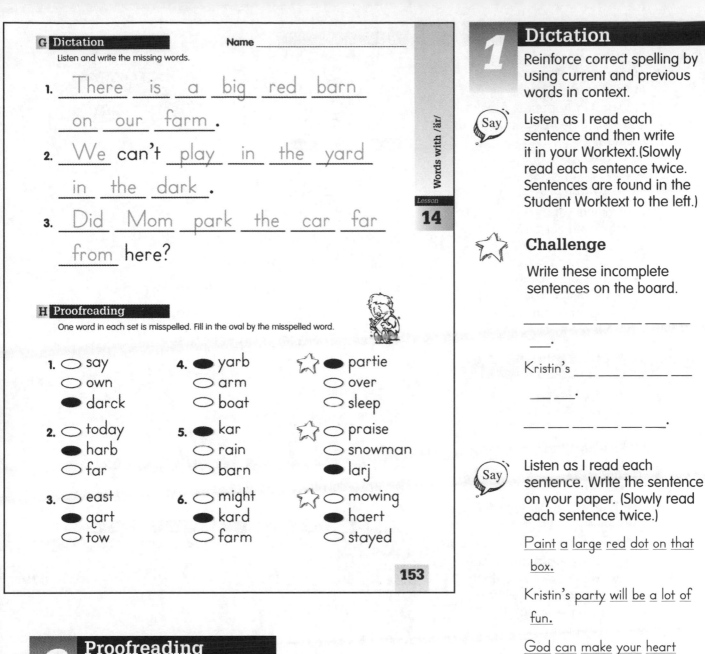

G Dictation

Listen and write the missing words.

Name _____

1. There is a big red barn on our farm.

2. We can't play in the yard in the dark.

3. Did Mom park the car far from here?

H Proofreading

One word in each set is misspelled. Fill in the oval by the misspelled word.

1. ○ say
   ○ own
   ● darck

2. ○ today
   ● harb
   ○ far

3. ○ east
   ● qart
   ○ tow

4. ● yarb
   ○ arm
   ○ boat

5. ● kar
   ○ rain
   ○ barn

6. ○ might
   ● kard
   ○ farm

☆ ● partie
  ○ over
  ○ sleep

☆ ○ praise
  ○ snowman
  ● larj

☆ ○ mowing
  ● haert
  ○ stayed

153

---

1 Dictation

Reinforce correct spelling by using current and previous words in context.

 Say Listen as I read each sentence and then write it in your Worktext.(Slowly read each sentence twice. Sentences are found in the Student Worktext to the left.)

☆ Challenge

Write these incomplete sentences on the board.

_ _ _ _ _ _ _ _ _ _.

Kristin's _ _ _ _ _ _ _ _.

_ _ _ _ _ _ _ _ _.

Say Listen as I read each sentence. Write the sentence on your paper. (Slowly read each sentence twice.)

Paint a large red dot on that box.

Kristin's party will be a lot of fun.

God can make your heart clean.

2 Proofreading

Familiarize students with standardized test format and reinforce recognizing misspelled words.

Say Look at each set of words. One word in each set is misspelled. Fill in the oval by the misspelled word. (You may wish to pronounce each set of words to help students correctly identify them.)

203

3 Hide and Seek

Reinforce correct spelling of current spelling words. (A reproducible master is provided in Appendix A as shown on the inset page to the right.)

Write the words one at a time on a white board.

Have students:

- **Look** at the word.
- **Say** the word out loud.
- **Spell** the word out loud.
- **Hide** (teacher erases word.)
- **Write** the word on paper.
- **Seek** (teacher rewrites word.)
- **Check** spelling. If incorrect, rewrite word correctly.

4 Sentence Fun

Have your students complete this activity to strengthen spelling ability and expand vocabulary.

1 Posttest

Test mastery of the spelling words. Challenge words are starred.

(Say) I will say the word once, use the word in a sentence, then say the word again. Write the word on your paper.

Hide and Seek
Check a paper for each word you spell correctly.

1 3 5 7 9
2 4 6 8 10

Sentence Fun
Read each sentence. Write the missing word in the sentence.

1. The __darkest__ color on these post-cards __cards__ is black.
2. There are different types of __barns__ on different __farms__.
3. All __cars__ need headlights turned on as it gets __darker__ in the evening.
4. Your __arms__ will get very tired if you mow several __yards__ with a push mower.
5. It is __hardest__ to mow the __parts__ that are not level.
6. If you throw the ball __harder__ it will fly through the air __farther__.

Word Bank

arms	cards	darker	farms	harder	parts
barns	cars	darkest	farther	hardest	yards

379

---

1. **arm**   Kristin shoved on the door to the playground with one **arm**.
2. **hard**   It was **hard** for Kristin to know why Carol said unkind things.
3. **far**   Carol didn't live **far** from Kristin's house.
4. **car**   Mom drove the children home in their green **car**.
5. **dark**   The windows of the houses looked **dark** and lonely.
6. **farm**   There is a black horse at that **farm**.
7. **barn**   It may be in the **barn** today.
8. **yard**   A large dog is lying in the **yard**.
9. **card**   It looks like the collie on that **card**.
10. **part**   Kristin didn't take **part** in the talk on the way home.
☆ **large**   Kristin made a **large** mistake.
☆ **heart**   God can forgive our mistakes and give us a pure **heart**.
☆ **party**   Do you think Kristin will invite Carol to her **party**?

Progress Chart
Students may record scores. (Reproducible master in Appendix B.)

Personal Dictionary
Students may add any words they have misspelled to their personal dictionaries for reference when writing. (Cover in Appendix B.)

204

I Game

Name _____

Kristin wants to apologize to Setsuko for her unkind words. Lead the way by moving one space each time you or your team spells a word correctly from this week's word list.

Remember: Before you say something unkind about someone, think how you would feel if the unkind words were about you.

J Journaling

What do you think Kristin should do about hurting Setsuko's feelings? Write your ideas down in your journal.

154

How to Play:

- Divide students into two teams, and decide which team will go first.
- Have a student from team A go to the board.
- Read the spelling word two times slowly and clearly. (You may also wish to use the word in a sentence. Ex.: "cat — The cat climbed a tree. — cat")
- Have the student write the word on the board.
- If the word is spelled correctly, instruct all the members of team A to move their game piece forward one space on the game board. (Note: If the word is misspelled, correct the spelling immediately.)
- Alternate between teams A and B as you go down the word list.
- The team to reach Setsuko first is the winner.

Non-Competitive Option: At the end of the game, say: "Class, I am proud of your efforts to spell the words correctly. If you had fun and tried your best, you are all winners!"

2 Game

Reinforce spelling skills and provide motivation and interest.

Materials

- game page (from student text)
- flat buttons, dry beans, pennies, or game discs (1 per child)
- game word list

Game Word List

Use of challenge words is optional.

1. **arm**
2. **barn**
3. **car**
4. **dark**
5. **far**
6. **farm**
7. **card**
8. **hard**
9. **part**
10. **yard**
☆ **large**
☆ **party**
☆ **heart**

3 Journaling

Provide a meaningful reason for correct spelling through personal writing.

Review the story using discussion leads provided on the following page. Encourage students to apply the Scriptural value in their journaling.

 Take a minute to memorize . . .

Have students say the memory verses from lessons 13 and 14 with you.

205

3 Journaling

Provide a meaningful reason for correct spelling through personal writing.

(Say)

- Kristin felt good in her new outfit. Did she mean to be unkind to Setsuko? (Not really. She didn't realize Setsuko would hear her, but what she said was unkind.)

- Is it O.K. to say things that might hurt someone's feelings if they're not around? (No. We should always think about what we say before we say it and make sure it doesn't put anyone else down, whether they're there or not.)

- How did Kristin feel when she heard the things Carol said about her? (Very hurt. Betrayed by her friend.)

- Kristin learned how it felt to have someone say unkind things about you. She was very sorry for hurting Setsuko's feelings. In your journal, write down what you think Kristin should do about the situation. (For example: Apologize to Setsuko, ask Setsuko to play with her at recess, write a nice note to Setsuko, ask God to forgive her, etc.)

"Students will learn how to spell and will learn the value of correct spelling, if they write often for authentic purposes."*

*Scott, Jill E. 1994. Spelling for Readers and Writers. The Reading Teacher, Vol. 48, No. 2, October: 188-190.

Learning to Love the Truth

Tony finds out that being truthful is really the better way.

"*I* am not out!" Tony screamed. "Yes, you are!" Daniel yelled back.

"Am not! Am not! Am not!" Tony shouted in Daniel's face.

"Mrs. Morgan, Tony says he's not out and I hit him with the ball!" Daniel complained, running up to his teacher.

"I didn't feel it!" Tony defended himself.

"Don't lie! It hit the hood of your coat! You had to feel it!" Daniel argued.

"Well, it hit my coat, not me." Tony looked at the grass.

"Go back to the game, Daniel. I need to talk to Tony for a minute." After Daniel was out of earshot, Mrs. Morgan knelt down in front of Tony and gently lifted his chin so she could see into his eyes. "If it hit your coat, Tony, then you are 'out' in dodge ball," she quietly explained. "When you get hit by the ball, you ought to get out of the circle without being told. If you choose to play you should play by the rules and tell the truth."

"Okay," Tony mumbled, an embarrassed look on his face.

A few minutes later Mrs. Morgan blew her whistle to call the children in from morning recess. Everyone lined up outside the door of their classroom. "Who brought those jump ropes out?" she asked. No one said anything.

"They don't have legs," Mrs. Morgan smiled. "Whose legs carried them out of our classroom?" More silence.

"I saw Tony and Stephen playing with them," Beth finally said.

"But Rachel and Rosa used them after we were finished," Stephen said. "They said they would bring them in if we let them have a turn."

Mrs. Morgan told the class to go on inside and get out their spelling books. She called Tony and Stephen over to her and put an arm around each boy. "What is our class rule about playground equipment, Stephen?"

Stephen looked at Tony, but avoided Mrs. Morgan's kind eyes. "Whoever brings it out brings it in," he said quietly.

"That's correct. I'm disappointed in your choices, boys. It was sad when you didn't follow the rules, but it was doubly sad for you not to speak up when I asked who brought the jump ropes out." She turned to go back into the room. "You may not use the jump ropes for the rest of the week. It is important to tell the truth. It is one way others can tell you are friends with Jesus."

Tony and Stephen walked out of the classroom after they were dismissed that afternoon. "Can you come over to play at my house today?" Stephen asked.

"I have to finish my math," Tony said. "I didn't get it all done in class today and you know Grandma Miller's rule about getting homework done before I play."

"Just don't tell her," Stephen suggested. "She doesn't know whether you got your math done or not. Do it after your mom comes home. Then we can play while it's still light out."

"Wouldn't that be lying?" Tony asked as he opened the door to Grandma Miller's car. He watched Stephen shrug his shoulders and shake his head as climbed into the car.

"How was your day, Tony-O? Did you learn a new verse this week in spelling?" Grandma asked.

"Yep, it says, 'I came to bring truth to the world. All who love the truth are My followers.'"

"That's a good one. I hope you never forget it. It's hard to find people who love the truth — even adults. Do you have any homework?"

"So much for not telling her," Tony thought. *"Oh! I don't want to tell the truth about my math. I want to play with Stephen!"* Then the words of Jesus popped back into Tony's thoughts. *"All who love the truth are My followers. All who love the truth are My followers."*

"Yeah . . . I still have some math to finish," Tony said.

Tony was gulping down the last of his milk at lunch the next day when Mrs. Morgan said it was time for noon recess. He ate his candy bar as he walked toward the trash can with his carrots and the rest of his sandwich hidden inside his lunch sack. Just as he dropped the remains of his lunch into the trash can, he remembered the class rule about lunches. "Always take what is left of your lunch home so your lunch maker will know if they are giving you too much food."

"Grandma Miller won't like it when she sees that I ate my candy bar, but not my carrots," Tony thought. Then he remembered what Mrs. Morgan had told him so kindly the day before. "It is important to tell the truth. It is one way others can tell you are friends with Jesus."

"Are you coming, Tony?" Mrs. Morgan called from the doorway.

"Yeah, I just need to get something."

Tony got his coat on and grabbed a four-square ball. He really didn't want Mrs. Morgan to see him digging in the trash. He glanced over at his teacher and saw her talking to the twins and made a dash for the trash can to retrieve the remains of his lunch.

"Tony," he jumped at the sound of his teacher's voice. "Did you lose something in the trash?"

"No, it's right here," he said, picking up his lunch sack.

Mrs. Morgan was puzzled for a minute until

207

she saw the bulge in the wadded up lunch sack. "I'm proud of you, Tony," she said, giving the boy a squeeze with one arm. "You made a good choice. I can see you are starting to love the truth."

2 Discussion Time

Check understanding of the story and development of personal values.

- Raise your hand if someone has ever told you a lie.
- How did you feel?
- If Grandma Miller hadn't asked, would it have been okay for Tony not to tell her about his math homework? Why?
- Why is it important to be truthful about little things?
- Why would you like to be known as someone who loves the truth?

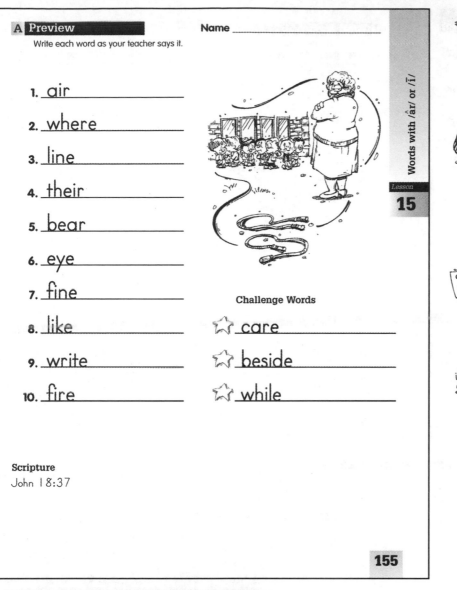

A Preview

Write each word as your teacher says it.

Name _____

Words with /âr/ or /ī/

Lesson **15**

1. air _____
2. where _____
3. line _____
4. their _____
5. bear _____
6. eye _____
7. fine _____
8. like _____
9. write _____
10. fire _____

Challenge Words

☆ care _____
☆ beside _____
☆ while _____

Scripture
John 18:37

155

Challenge

For better spellers, challenge words may be included in the weekly list. Challenge words are starred.

Correct Immediately!

Say

Let's correct our preview. I will write each word on the board. Put a dot under each letter on your preview as I spell the word out loud. If you spelled a word wrong, rewrite it correctly.

Progress Chart

Students may record scores. (Reproducible master in Appendix B.)

Take a minute to memorize . . .

Read the memory verse twice. Have students practice it with you two more times.

Lesson **15** | Day 1

Preview

Test for knowledge of the correct spellings of these words. (See the instructions at the top right for challenge words.)

Say

I will say the word once, use the word in a sentence, then say the word again. Write the word on the lines in the Worktext.

1.	air	The ball flew through the **air** and hit Tony.
2.	where	Do you know **where** should you go after being hit in dodge ball?
3.	line	The children were standing in a **line.**
4.	their	All of **their** jump ropes were lying on the ground.
5.	bear	The commandment says, "Thou shall not **bear** false witness."
6.	eye	Tony did not want to look Mrs. Morgan in the **eye.**
7.	fine	It will be **fine** if you tell the truth.
8.	like	Grandma Miller won't **like** it if Tony throws away his carrots.
9.	write	Please **write** this word neatly.
10.	fire	If you tell the truth, your boss may not **fire** you.
☆	care	It is important to **care** about the truth.
☆	beside	Write the number 12 **beside** this word.
☆	while	"We can play **while** it is still light out," Stephen suggested.

Help students form a correct image of whole words.

Say Look at each word and think about its shape. Now, write the word in the correct word Shape Boxes. You may check off each word as you use it.

(In many words, the sound of /âr/ is spelled with **air**, **ear**, **eir**, or **ere**. The sound of /ī/ is often spelled with **i**-consonant-**e**. A digraph is a single sound spelled by two letters.)

Say In the word Shape Boxes, color the letters that spell the sound of /âr/ or /ī/ in each word. Circle the words that begin with the digraph **th** or **wh**.

☆ Challenge

Draw the correctly shaped box around each letter in these words.

Say On a separate sheet of paper, write other words that contain the spelling patterns in the word list. See how many words you can write.

Lesson 15 | **Day 1**

B Word Shapes   Name _____

Write each word in the correct word shape boxes. Then, in the word shape boxes, color the letters that spell the sound of /âr/ or /ī/ in each word. Circle the words that begin with the digraph **th** or **wh**.

Words with /âr/ or /ī/

Lesson **15**

1. air   eye
2. bear   write
3. eye   where
4. fine   line
5. fire   air
6. like   like
7. line   bear
8. their   their
9. where   fine
10. write   fire

☆ Challenge

Draw the correctly shaped boxes around each letter in these words.

beside   care   while

156

Answers may vary for duplicate word shapes.

Be Prepared For Fun

Check these supply lists for **Fun Ways to Spell** presented **Day 2**. Purchase and/or gather these items ahead of time!

General
- 3 x 5 Cards (10 per child)
- 3 x 5 Cards (3 more to spell challenge words)
- Scissors
- Spelling List

Auditory
- A Classmate
- Spelling List

Visual
- Strips of paper 2 x 11 inches (10 per student)
- Strips of paper 2 x 11 inches (3 more to spell challenge words)
- Crayons or Markers
- Tape
- Spelling List

Tactile
- Split Peas
- Glue
- Construction Paper
- Spelling List

210

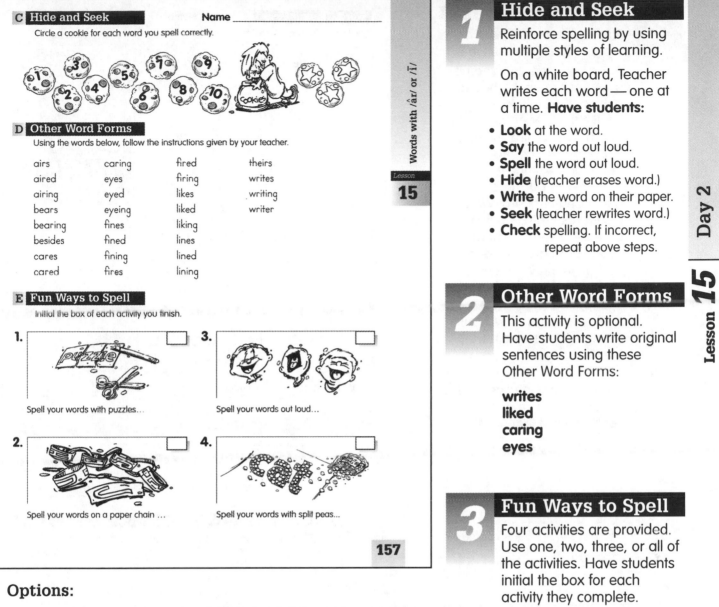

C Hide and Seek

Name _____

Circle a cookie for each word you spell correctly.

D Other Word Forms

Using the words below, follow the instructions given by your teacher.

airs	caring	fired	theirs
aired	eyes	firing	writes
airing	eyed	likes	writing
bears	eyeing	liked	writer
bearing	fines	liking	
besides	fined	lines	
cares	fining	lined	
cared	fires	lining	

E Fun Ways to Spell

Initial the box of each activity you finish.

1. ☐
   Spell your words with puzzles...

2. ☐
   Spell your words on a paper chain ...

3. ☐
   Spell your words out loud...

4. ☐
   Spell your words with split peas...

157

1 Hide and Seek

Reinforce spelling by using multiple styles of learning.

On a white board, Teacher writes each word — one at a time. **Have students:**

- **Look** at the word.
- **Say** the word out loud.
- **Spell** the word out loud.
- **Hide** (teacher erases word.)
- **Write** the word on their paper.
- **Seek** (teacher rewrites word.)
- **Check** spelling. If incorrect, repeat above steps.

2 Other Word Forms

This activity is optional. Have students write original sentences using these Other Word Forms:

writes
liked
caring
eyes

3 Fun Ways to Spell

Four activities are provided. Use one, two, three, or all of the activities. Have students initial the box for each activity they complete.

Options:

- assign activities to students according to their learning styles
- set up the activities in learning centers for students to do throughout the day
- divide students into four groups and assign one activity per group
- do one activity per day

General

To spell your words with puzzles . . .
- Write each spelling word on a card.
- Cut each card in half using a straight cut.
- Mix your puzzle pieces.
- Put the puzzles together.
- Check your spelling.

Auditory

To spell your words out loud . . .
- Have a classmate read a spelling word.
- Say a sentence with that spelling word to a classmate.
- Spell the spelling word you used in that sentence to a classmate.
- Ask a classmate to check your spelling.
- Do this with each word on your word list.

Visual

To spell your words on a paper chain . . .
- Write each spelling word on a strip of paper in big, tall letters.
- Tape the ends of one strip together to make a circle.
- Loop the next strip through the first and then tape the ends of that strip together.
- Continue in this way to form a paper chain.

Tactile

To spell your words with split peas . . .
- Choose a word from your spelling list.
- It may be a favorite word or a word you have trouble remembering how to spell.
- Write the word in tall, wide letters on a sheet of construction paper.
- Spread glue along the outline of each letter and press split peas into the glue.

211

1 Word Change

Familiarize students with word meaning and usage. Ask a volunteer to **write** his or her name on the board. Ask another volunteer to **spell** his or her name on the board. Ask a third volunteer to **print** his or her name on the board. Ask the last volunteer to **put** his or her name on the board. Write the words **write**, **spell**, **print**, and **put** before the phrase **your name on the board**. Underline the word **write**. Explain that you could change the word **write** to **spell**, **print**, or **put** without changing the meaning of the sentence.

Say Replace the underlined word in each sentence with a spelling word that has the same meaning.

F Word Change — Name _____

Write a spelling word in place of the underlined word or words.

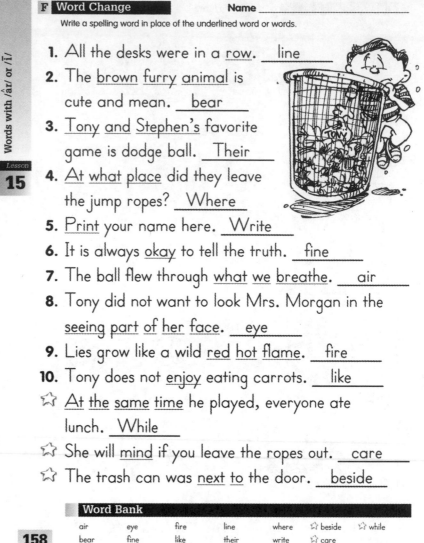

1. All the desks were in a row. __line__
2. The brown furry animal is cute and mean. __bear__
3. Tony and Stephen's favorite game is dodge ball. __Their__
4. At what place did they leave the jump ropes? __Where__
5. Print your name here. __Write__
6. It is always okay to tell the truth. __fine__
7. The ball flew through what we breathe. __air__
8. Tony did not want to look Mrs. Morgan in the seeing part of her face. __eye__
9. Lies grow like a wild red hot flame. __fire__
10. Tony does not enjoy eating carrots. __like__
☆ At the same time he played, everyone ate lunch. __While__
☆ She will mind if you leave the ropes out. __care__
☆ The trash can was next to the door. __beside__

Word Bank

| air | eye | fire | line | where | ☆ beside | ☆ while |
| bear | fine | like | their | write | ☆ care | |

158

Take a minute to memorize . . .

Read the memory verse twice. Have students practice it with you two more times.

212

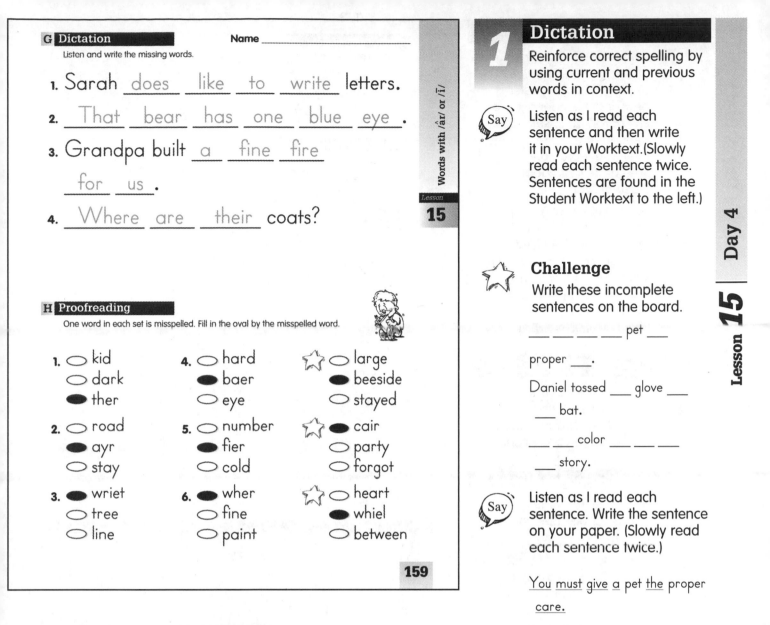

G Dictation

Name _____

Listen and write the missing words.

1. Sarah _does_ _like_ _to_ _write_ letters.

2. _That_ _bear_ _has_ _one_ _blue_ _eye_ .

3. Grandpa built _a_ _fine_ _fire_
   for _us_ .

4. _Where_ _are_ _their_ coats?

Words with /âr/ or /ī/

Lesson
15

H Proofreading

One word in each set is misspelled. Fill in the oval by the misspelled word.

1. ○ kid   4. ○ hard   ☆ ○ large
   ○ dark   ● baer   ● beeside
   ● ther   ○ eye   ○ stayed

2. ○ road   5. ○ number   ☆ ● cair
   ● ayr   ● fier   ○ party
   ○ stay   ○ cold   ○ forgot

3. ● wriet   6. ● wher   ☆ ○ heart
   ○ tree   ○ fine   ● whiel
   ○ line   ○ paint   ○ between

159

Dictation

Reinforce correct spelling by using current and previous words in context.

Say Listen as I read each sentence and then write it in your Worktext.(Slowly read each sentence twice. Sentences are found in the Student Worktext to the left.)

Challenge

Write these incomplete sentences on the board.

__ __ __ __ pet __

proper __ .

Daniel tossed __ glove __
   __ bat.

__ __ color __ __ __
   __ story.

Say Listen as I read each sentence. Write the sentence on your paper. (Slowly read each sentence twice.)

You must give a pet the proper
care.

Daniel tossed his glove beside
his bat.

You may color while I read
this story.

Proofreading

Familiarize students with standardized test format and reinforce recognizing misspelled words.

Say Look at each set of words. One word in each set is misspelled. Fill in the oval by the misspelled word. (You may wish to pronounce each set of words to help students correctly identify them.)

213

3 Hide and Seek

Reinforce correct spelling of current spelling words. (A reproducible master is provided in Appendix A as shown on the inset page to the right.)

Write the words one at a time on a white board.

Have students:

- **Look** at the word.
- **Say** the word out loud.
- **Spell** the word out loud.
- **Hide** (teacher erases word.)
- **Write** the word on paper.
- **Seek** (teacher rewrites word.)
- **Check** spelling. If incorrect, rewrite word correctly.

4 Secret Words

Have your students complete this activity to strengthen spelling ability and expand vocabulary.

1 Posttest

Test mastery of the spelling words. Challenge words are starred.

 Say

I will say the word once, use the word in a sentence, then say the word again. Write the word on your paper.

Hide and Seek

Check a paper for each word you spell correctly.

1 3 5 7 9
2 4 6 8 10

Secret Words

Use these clues to write the words that fit in the blanks. Then use the boxed letters to discover the secret word.

1. are started with matches
2. cute but wild animals
3. overdue books will get you these
4. what the class does for Handwriting
5. Grandma did this to blankets on clothesline
6. there are lots of these on notebook paper
7. what you are doing in the blanks
8. how the class feels about recess
9. Jesus does this for you

```
1. f i r e s
2. b e a r s
3. f i n e s
4. w r i t e s
5. a i r e d
6. l i n e s
7. w r i t i n g
8. l i k e s
9. c a r e s
```

Being honest is a f a n t a s t i c idea.

Word Bank

| aired | cares | fires | lines | writing |
| bears | fines | likes | writes | |

380

---

1. **line** — Everyone **line** up at the door to go out for recess.
2. **their** — It seems **their** favorite game is dodge ball.
3. **air** — The **air** was cold when they went out for recess.
4. **where** — The boys didn't remember where they left their jump ropes.
5. **bear** — "Thou shalt not **bear** false witness," means do not lie.
6. **eye** — When you tell the truth, you can look me in the **eye**.
7. **fine** — It is always **fine** to tell the truth.
8. **fire** — There is not a **fire** in the trash can.
9. **like** — Grandma Miller would **like** Tony to eat his carrots.
10. **write** — Try to **write** this word carefully.
☆ **care** — Jesus will always **care** for you.
☆ **beside** — The jump ropes were left **beside** the sidewalk.
☆ **while** — It is no fun to eat lunch **while** everyone else plays.

Progress Chart
Students may record scores. (Reproducible master in Appendix B.)

Personal Dictionary
Students may add any words they have misspelled to their personal dictionaries for reference when writing. (Cover in Appendix B.)

I Game

Name _____

Tony wants to obey the class rule and take home the part of his lunch he did not eat. Help Tony get his uneaten lunch out of the trash can. Move one space for each word you or your team spells correctly.

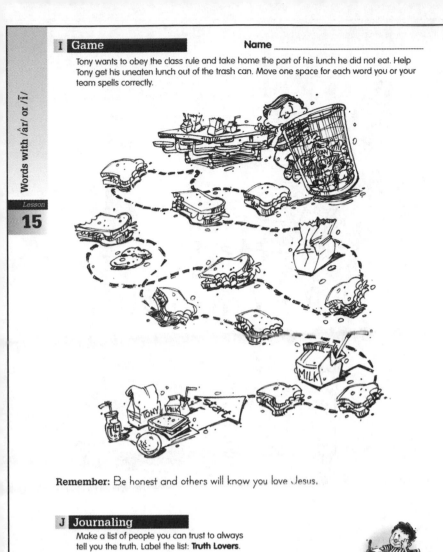

Remember: Be honest and others will know you love Jesus.

J Journaling

Make a list of people you can trust to always tell you the truth. Label the list: **Truth Lovers**.

160

---

2 Game

Reinforce spelling skills and provide motivation and interest.

Materials

- game page (from student text)
- flat buttons, dry beans, pennies, or game discs (1 per child)
- game word list

Game Word List

Use of challenge words is optional.

1. **air**
2. **their**
3. **where**
4. **bear**
5. **eye**
6. **fire**
7. **fine**
8. **line**
9. **like**
10. **write**
☆ **care**
☆ **beside**
☆ **while**

3 Journaling

Provide a meaningful reason for correct spelling through personal writing.

Review the story using discussion leads provided on the following page. Encourage students to apply the Scriptural value in their journaling.

 Take a minute to memorize . . .

Have students say the memory verses from lessons 13, 14, and 15 with you.

215

How to Play:

- Divide students into two teams, and decide which team will go first.
- Have each student place their game piece on Start.
- Have a student from team A go to the board.
- Read the spelling word two times slowly and clearly. (You may also wish to use the word in a sentence. Ex.: "cat — The cat climbed a tree. — cat")
- Have the student write the word on the board.
- If the word is spelled correctly, instruct all the members of team A to move their game piece forward one space on the game board. (Note: If the word is misspelled, correct the spelling immediately.)
- Alternate between teams A and B as you go down the word list.
- The team to reach the trash can first is the winner.

Non-Competitive Option: At the end of the game, say: "Class, I am proud of your efforts to spell the words correctly. If you had fun and tried your best, you are all winners!"

Provide a meaningful reason for correct spelling through personal writing.

Say

- Jesus says that everyone who loves the truth are His followers. Who learned to love the truth in the story this week? (Tony.)

- How do you think Tony feels when he tells the truth? (Content, happy, peaceful.)

- Why do you think it is important to tell the truth? (You can be trusted.)

- Make a list in your journal of people you know you can trust. Your list may include adults and children.

Lesson 15 | Day 5

*"Reading may be the backbone of informal spelling instruction but writing is the lifeblood."**

*Scott, Jill E. 1994. Spelling for Readers and Writers. The Reading Teacher, Vol. 48, No. 2, October: 188-190.

216

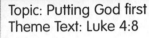
Putting God First

Katelynn realizes she's gotten things in the wrong order when she spends her time thinking about her doll.

"I like this English riding outfit!" Rachel pointed to a picture in the catalog spread out on Katelynn's desk.

Katelynn turned the page. "I like this camping stuff better! Look! You can even get hiking boots and a real tent for the dolls to sleep in!"

Beth walked up to the group gathered around Katelynn's desk. "When did you get this new catalog, Katelynn?"

"It came yesterday with the stuff I ordered. I got the in-line skate things with my birthday money. There is a helmet for my doll that really fits her. It even came with knee pads and wrist guards. Do you want to see?" All the girls gathered around Katelynn's desk to admire the beautiful doll dressed to go roller blading. The doll was 18 inches tall and had black hair and eyes just like Katelynn's.

"How neat!" Rosa said. "Do you have any other clothes?"

"Yes, I have a Chinese New Year outfit my Uncle Sam sent for my birthday, plus the jeans, T-shirt, and baseball cap that came with Katie."

"Who's Katie?" Sarah asked, joining the group.

"She's my doll," Katelynn explained with a smile.

Sarah reached out to gently touch the doll's shiny dark hair. "She looks just like you, Katelynn."

"Come look at all the stuff you can get to go with her, Sarah." Rachel said, moving so Sarah could see the catalog.

"Oh, I like that outfit! I wonder if the black children in Malawi dress like that all the time or just on holidays. Look at the head wrap! Isn't it . . ." Sarah was interrupted by the shrill sound of the morning bell.

"Everyone to your own seats," Mrs. Morgan said from the back of the classroom.

Katelynn continued to flip through the pages of the catalog, admiring the different dolls and all the clothes, furniture, and accessories that went with them. She was trying to figure out how many allowances it would take to buy the soccer gear while Mrs. Morgan took roll and collected money for the class mission project in Malawi, Africa.

When she was finished, Mrs. Morgan walked over and stood by a big cardboard box on the table. "I got an e-mail message on my computer yesterday from my friend who works at the orphanage in Blantyre, Malawi. She said that when the weather starts getting cold, they won't have enough warm clothes for all the orphan children. Malawi has winter when we have summer, so we could send them a box of clothes before it gets cold over there. What do you think?" The room buzzed with excited voices as the children decided that they liked their teacher's latest idea.

After the discussion Mrs. Morgan asked everyone to stand for the pledge of allegiance to the flag. Katelynn put her hand over her heart, but continued to look at the catalog still open on her desk.

"Would you please have prayer for us this morning, Daniel?" Mrs. Morgan asked after the pledge.

Daniel nodded. "Please bow your heads. Dear Jesus, Thank you for . . ."

Katelynn bowed her head, looking at the catalog again. "I will only need one more allowance before I can order these pajamas with glow-in-the-dark stars all over them." She peeked at the price. "No, I think I have enough already. Maybe I should get myself this cap to match Katie's. It would be fun to dress like my doll."

". . . and be with the orphans at the mission in Malawi. Help them to stay warm this winter, amen," Daniel concluded.

Katelynn turned to the front of the catalog to a page she had marked. "Grandma said she was going to pay me for reading books. Hmmm, I could put that money with the rest of the money I got for my birthday and maybe I'll have enough for the brass bed. Let's see. How much was . . ."

"Katelynn."

Katelynn jumped at the sound of her teacher's voice and looked up. Her face turned red as she realized she was the only one in the class still standing.

"What do you think this text means, Katelynn?"

Katelynn looked at the board where Mrs. Morgan had written the words, "We must worship God, and Him alone. So it is written in the Scriptures." Luke 4:8 "I don't know," she mumbled, quickly sliding the doll catalog into her desk.

"What did we decide yesterday in our discussion, Matthew? Mrs. Morgan looked at him and smiled.

"Jesus says that we should only worship God. Nothing should be more important than our friendship with God."

"Great, you summed that up well, Matthew." Mrs. Morgan turned to write on the board. "Beth, what . . ."

Katelynn's mind began to wander again. "I wonder how much money Aunt Jenny will send me? She hasn't sent me anything for my birthday and I usually get money from her. I don't think I want the . . . it would be more fun to have . . . maybe I should make a list of . . ."

". . . so on your journaling page in your Worktext," Mrs. Morgan continued, "I would like you to make a list of things that you like to spend time doing. When you are finished, put a number one by the thing you like to do most." Mrs. Morgan started passing out the spelling Worktexts from the shelf beside her desk. "Put a two by what you like to do second best. Keep numbering until all the things you like to do have a number by them."

Later during the morning recess, all the girls gathered around Katelynn to admire her doll.

"Can I hold Katie?" Sarah asked, her eyes wide with anticipation.

Katelynn noticed the dirt under Sarah's fingernails and her rumpled dress. "I don't think so," she answered, not noticing Sarah's disappointed look.

Some of the girls looked at the catalog and discussed what they liked best. "Here, let's put her in the Chinese outfit," Beth offered, taking the doll. No one saw Sarah turn away and leave.

Beth hooked the black oriental clasps on the tunic and put the gong in Katie's hand. "You should see the bed I have for my doll. Grandpa's friend came over and helped me put the lacquer on it, so it's all finished. It looks exactly like my real bed!"

After recess, Katelynn pulled out her Worktext to finish the journaling assignment. She labeled the list "Things I Like To Do," then neatly printed "four square," "going to the Fantastic Fun Fair," and "ordering things for my doll" on her list. She stuck the end of her pencil in her mouth. "If I use all of my allowance this week instead of saving some, borrow the money I was saving for our class mission project, and use the book money from Grandma and the birthday money Aunt Jenny will send, then I should have enough to get the pajamas, soccer gear, and baseball cap." She took the pencil out of her mouth and wrote the number one by "ordering things for my doll" in her journal. She heard a sniffle like someone was crying and turned around to see Sarah staring longingly at Katie, now dressed in the red Chinese tunic embroidered with dancing golden dragons. Sarah wiped her eyes, but her eyelashes were still wet from crying.

"Oh, Sarah must feel awful!" Katelynn suddenly realized. "Her family doesn't even have money to buy her nice clothes, and I'm sure she'll never get a doll to dress in beautiful clothes." Katelynn looked at the board where Mrs. Morgan had written, "Nothing should be more important than our friendship with God," then back at her beautiful doll.

"And I wouldn't even let her touch Katie." Katelynn frowned to herself. "All I've thought about today is me and my doll." She sat very still for a moment, thinking hard.

"P-s-s-s-t, Sarah," she whispered suddenly, leaning back in her chair. "Would you like to take Katie home with you for a sleepover tonight?" The look of astonished joy on Sarah's face quickly told Katelynn the answer to her question.

"Dear Jesus," Katelynn prayed as she turned to face the front of the classroom again. "Help me not to be selfish again. And help me to always make my friendship with You the most important thing."

2 Discussion Time

Check understanding of the story and development of personal values.

- What is your favorite thing to do? (Brainstorm. Make a list on the board.)
- What were some of the things Katelynn liked to do?
- What did Katelynn do that showed you her doll was the most important thing to her.
- Why is it important to show respect to our country, adults, and God?
- What did Katelynn do that didn't show respect for her country? Her teacher? God?
- What did Katelynn do to show Sarah and God she was sorry for the choices she'd made?

A Preview

Write each word as your teacher says it.

Name _____

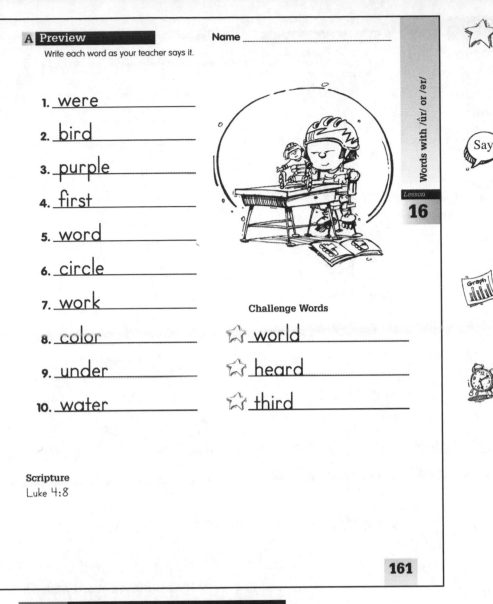

1. were
2. bird
3. purple
4. first
5. word
6. circle
7. work
8. color
9. under
10. water

Challenge Words

☆ world
☆ heard
☆ third

Scripture
Luke 4:8

161

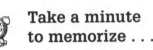

Challenge

For better spellers, challenge words may be included in the weekly list. Challenge words are starred.

Correct Immediately!

(Say) Let's correct our preview. I will write each word on the board. Put a dot under each letter on your preview as I spell the word out loud. If you spelled a word wrong, rewrite it correctly.

Progress Chart

Students may record scores. (Reproducible master in Appendix B.)

Take a minute to memorize . . .

Read the memory verse twice. Have students practice it with you two more times.

---

3 Preview

Test for knowledge of the correct spellings of these words. (See the instructions at the top right for challenge words.)

(Say) I will say the word once, use the word in a sentence, then say the word again. Write the word on the lines in the Worktext.

1. were — The girls **were** gathered around Katelynn's desk.
2. bird — The **bird** sang outside the window.
3. purple — Katelynn's doll does not have **purple** clothes.
4. first — Katelynn's doll was the most important thing to her at **first**.
5. word — Katelynn looked at the **word** on the board.
6. circle — Mrs. Morgan put a **circle** around the word.
7. work — Kind people **work** at the orphanage.
8. color — The **color** of your skin is not important.
9. under — Sarah has dirt **under** her fingernails.
10. water — They washed their hands with soap and **water.**
☆ world — God should be the most important thing in the **world** to you.
☆ heard — Katelynn **heard** a sniffle like someone crying.
☆ third — This is the **third** challenge word.

(Say) Look at each word and think about its shape. Now, write the word in the correct word Shape Boxes. You may check off each word as you use it.

(In many words, the sound of /ûr/ or /ər/ is spelled with **ir**, **er**, **ur**, or **or**.)

(Say) In the word Shape Boxes, color the letters that spell the sound of /ûr/ or /ər/ in each word. Circle the words which have two syllables.

☆ **Challenge**
Draw the correctly shaped box around each letter in these words.

(Say) On a separate sheet of paper, write sentences using one or more of the spelling words.

Words with /ûr/ or /ər/

Lesson **16**

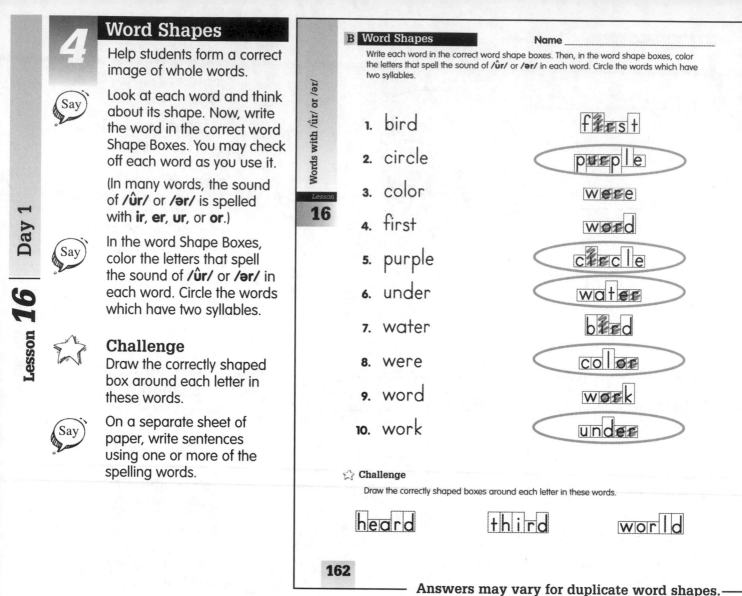

B Word Shapes

Name _____

Write each word in the correct word shape boxes. Then, in the word shape boxes, color the letters that spell the sound of /ûr/ or /ər/ in each word. Circle the words which have two syllables.

1. bird
2. circle
3. color
4. first
5. purple
6. under
7. water
8. were
9. word
10. work

☆ **Challenge**
Draw the correctly shaped boxes around each letter in these words.

heard   third   world

162

— Answers may vary for duplicate word shapes. —

Be Prepared For Fun

Check these supply lists for **Fun Ways to Spell** presented **Day 2**.
Purchase and/or gather these items ahead of time!

General
• A Classmate
• Spelling List

Auditory
• Box to Store Letters
• a, b, c, c, d, e, e, f, i, k, l, n, o, o, p, p, r, s, t, u, w (written on seasonal shapes like hearts or stovepipe hats)
• h (added for challenge words)
• Spelling List

Visual
• a, b, c, c, d, e, e, f, i, k, l, n, o, o, p, p, r, s, t, u, w (written on upside-down cups)
• h (added for challenge words)
• Spelling List

Tactile
• Shaving Cream
• Optional: Plastic Plates
• Optional: Wooden Craft Sticks
• Spelling List

220

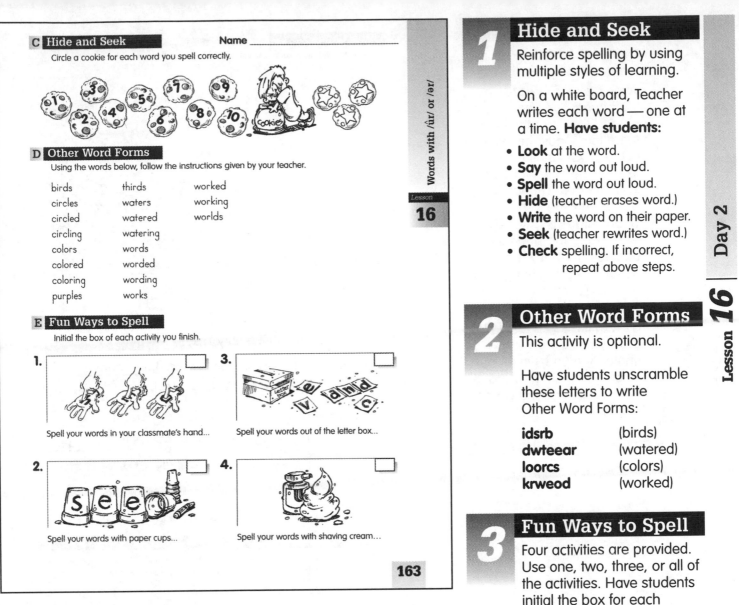

C Hide and Seek

Name _____

Circle a cookie for each word you spell correctly.

D Other Word Forms

Using the words below, follow the instructions given by your teacher.

birds	thirds	worked
circles	waters	working
circled	watered	worlds
circling	watering	
colors	words	
colored	worded	
coloring	wording	
purples	works	

E Fun Ways to Spell

Initial the box of each activity you finish.

1. Spell your words in your classmate's hand...

3. Spell your words out of the letter box...

2. Spell your words with paper cups...

4. Spell your words with shaving cream...

163

---

1 Hide and Seek

Reinforce spelling by using multiple styles of learning.

On a white board, Teacher writes each word — one at a time. **Have students:**

- **Look** at the word.
- **Say** the word out loud.
- **Spell** the word out loud.
- **Hide** (teacher erases word.)
- **Write** the word on their paper.
- **Seek** (teacher rewrites word.)
- **Check** spelling. If incorrect, repeat above steps.

Day 2

Lesson 16

2 Other Word Forms

This activity is optional.

Have students unscramble these letters to write Other Word Forms:

idsrb	(birds)
dwteear	(watered)
loorcs	(colors)
krweod	(worked)

3 Fun Ways to Spell

Four activities are provided. Use one, two, three, or all of the activities. Have students initial the box for each activity they complete.

Options:

- assign activities to students according to their learning styles
- set up the activities in learning centers for students to do throughout the day
- divide students into four groups and assign one activity per group
- do one activity per day

General

To spell your words in your classmate's hand . . .
- Have a classmate sit next to you and hold their palm open in front of, and facing both of you.
- Use fingertip to write a spelling word in the palm of a classmate's hand.
- Have a classmate say each letter as you write it and then say the word you spelled.
- Next, have a classmate write a word in your palm.

Auditory

To spell your words out of the letter box . . .
- Spell a word from your list by putting the letters in the right order.
- Check your spelling.
- Spell your word out loud.

Visual

To spell your words with paper cups . . .
- Spell a word from your list by putting the cups in the right order.
- Check your spelling.

Tactile

To spell your words with shaving cream . . .
- Spread a glob of shaving cream across your desk (or on a plastic plate).
- Use finger (or a wooden craft stick) to write a spelling word in the shaving cream.
- Check your spelling.
- Smear the word out with your fingers and write another.

221

1 Letter Change

Familiarize students with word meaning and usage. Write the word **sword** on the board. Ask a volunteer to read the word then invite them to change the letters **sw** to **L**. Ask another student to read the new word then invite them to change the **L** to **w**. Ask the last volunteer to say the new word. Help the students understand that words can be changed by changing a letter or letters.

 Say Each of the sentences in this activity contain a word with one or two underlined letters. Change the word to one of your spelling words.

F Letter Change

Name _____

Change the underlined letter or letters, and write the spelling word in the blank.

Words with /ûr/ or /ər/

Lesson **16**

1. Sarah's eyes <u>th</u>ere wet. ___were___
2. The girls were in a circ<u>us</u>
   around Katelynn's desk. ___circle___
3. The Bible is God's <u>c</u>ord. ___word___
4. The <u>th</u>ird is in its cage. ___bird___
5. Keep God <u>th</u>irst in your life. ___first___
6. Drink lots of <u>l</u>ater every day. ___water___
7. The co<u>v</u>er of Katie's hair is black. ___color___
8. They will <u>f</u>ork for the kids in Malawi. ___work___
9. The dancing dragon tunic is not pu<u>dd</u>le. ___purple___
10. Sarah had dirt <u>wo</u>nder her fingernails. ___under___
☆ Girls all over the work<u>s</u> love dolls. ___world___
☆ Katelynn is thir<u>st</u>. ___third___
☆ She <u>b</u>eard Katelynn liked dolls. ___heard___

Word Bank

164

bird	color	purple	water	word	☆ heard	☆ world
circle	first	under	were	work	☆ third	

 Take a minute to memorize . . .

Have students say the memory verses from lessons 7, 8, 9, 10, and 11 with you.

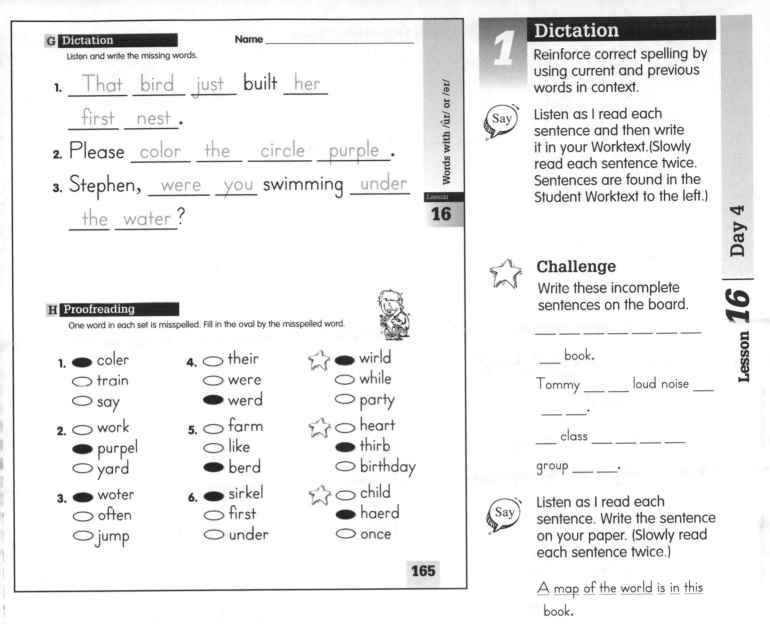

G Dictation

Listen and write the missing words.

1. That bird just built her first nest.

2. Please color the circle purple.

3. Stephen, were you swimming under the water?

H Proofreading

One word in each set is misspelled. Fill in the oval by the misspelled word.

1. ● coler
   ○ train
   ○ say

2. ○ work
   ● purpel
   ○ yard

3. ● woter
   ○ often
   ○ jump

4. ○ their
   ○ were
   ● werd

5. ○ farm
   ○ like
   ● berd

6. ● sirkel
   ○ first
   ○ under

☆ ● wirld
   ○ while
   ○ party

☆ ○ heart
   ● thirb
   ○ birthday

☆ ○ child
   ● haerd
   ○ once

165

Day 4 — Lesson 16

1 Dictation

Reinforce correct spelling by using current and previous words in context.

Say) Listen as I read each sentence and then write it in your Worktext.(Slowly read each sentence twice. Sentences are found in the Student Worktext to the left.)

☆ Challenge

Write these incomplete sentences on the board.

__ __ __ __ __ __ __

___ book.

Tommy ___ ___ loud noise ___

___ ___.

___ class __ __ __ __ ___

group ___ ___.

Say) Listen as I read each sentence. Write the sentence on your paper. (Slowly read each sentence twice.)

A map of the world is in this book.

Tommy heard a loud noise in the yard.

Our class will be the third group to play.

---

2 Proofreading

Familiarize students with standardized test format and reinforce recognizing misspelled words.

Say) Look at each set of words. One word in each set is misspelled. Fill in the oval by the misspelled word. (You may wish to pronounce each set of words to help students correctly identify them.)

223

3 Hide and Seek

Reinforce correct spelling of current spelling words. (A reproducible master is provided in Appendix A as shown on the inset page to the right.)
Write the words one at a time on a white board.
Have students:

- **Look** at the word.
- **Say** the word out loud.
- **Spell** the word out loud.
- **Hide** (teacher erases word.)
- **Write** the word on paper.
- **Seek** (teacher rewrites word.)
- **Check** spelling. If incorrect, rewrite word correctly.

4 Clues

Have your students complete this activity to strengthen spelling ability and expand vocabulary.

1 Posttest

Test mastery of the spelling words. Challenge words are starred.

(Say) I will say the word once, use the word in a sentence, then say the word again. Write the word on your paper.

Hide and Seek

Check a paper for each word you spell correctly.

1 3 5 7 9
2 4 6 8 10

Clues

Look at the endings added to the spelling words in the word bank. Use the clues to write one of the new words in each sentence.

1. made up of letters __words__
2. it does okay __works__
3. animals that fly __birds__
4. shapes with no corners __circles__
5. what you did with crayons __colored__
6. what you are doing on this page __working__
7. what you did to plants __watered__
8. can divide something this way __thirds__
9. a name for far away planets __worlds__
10. more than one shade of purple __purples__

Word Bank

bird + s	color + ed	third + s	word + s	work + ing
circle + s	purple + s	water + ed	work + s	world + s

381

1.	circle	The girls were in a **circle** around Katelynn's desk.
2.	purple	The doll's dancing dragon tunic is not **purple**.
3.	bird	You can buy a pretend **bird** for your doll.
4.	color	The **color** of Katie's hair is black.
5.	first	Keep God **first** in your life.
6.	word	God's **word** says we should worship God and Him alone.
7.	work	Mrs. Morgan's friend will **work** at the orphanage in Malawi.
8.	under	Katelynn noticed the dirt **under** Sarah's fingernails.
9.	water	Wash you hands with warm **water** and soap.
10.	were	Sarah's eyes **were** wet from crying.
☆	third	You will be in the **third** grade soon.
☆	world	It is good to care for others in the **world**.
☆	heard	Have you **heard** about the orphans in Malawi?

Progress Chart
Students may record scores. (Reproducible master in Appendix B.)

Personal Dictionary
Students may add any words they have misspelled to their personal dictionaries for reference when writing. (Cover in Appendix B.)

224

I Game

Name _____

Place a game piece over each word your teacher says and spells. If the word appears on your card more than once, place a game piece over only one of the words. When you get five game pieces in a row, raise your hand and say, "Spelling is fun!"

Remember: Love and obey God. Nothing is more important.

J Journaling

Make a list just like Mrs. Morgan's class did in the story. Label the list: **Things I Like To Do.**

166

---

2 Game

Reinforce spelling skills and provide motivation and interest.

Materials

- game page (from student text)
- flat buttons, dry beans, pennies, or game discs (24 per child)
- game word list
- word cards (each word from the list below written on one or more cards as indicated)

Game Word List

1. **bird** (2)
2. **circle** (2)
3. **first** (2)
4. **color** (2)
5. **word** (2)
6. **work** (2)
7. **purple** (2)
8. **under** (2)
9. **water** (2)
10. **were** (2)
☆ **world** (2)
☆ **heard** (1)
☆ **third** (1)

3 Journaling

Provide a meaningful reason for correct spelling through personal writing.

Review the story using discussion leads provided on the following page. Encourage students to apply the Scriptural value in their journaling.

 Take a minute to memorize . . .

Have students say the memory verses from lessons 13, 14, 15, and 16 with you.

How to Play:

- Fold the word cards (see **Materials**) in half, and put them in a container.
- Write each word from the **Game Word List** on the board. (Be sure to include the number in parentheses beside it.)
- Ask the students to copy these words on their game card — one word in each box. Remind them the number beside the word indicates how many times they must copy that word. (Note: Placing the words in the boxes randomly makes the game more fun!)
- Instructions for the students: "Cover the word **FREE** in the center of your card with a game piece. (pause) I will draw a word from the container, read it aloud, then spell it. Find that word on your card, and cover it with a game piece. Cover only ONE word each time, even if it's on your card twice. When you have five game pieces in a row (up-down, across, or diagonally) raise your hand and say **'Spelling is FUN!'**"
- Play as many times as you like. (As you return the word cards to the container and mix them up, remind the students to clear their game cards.)

3 Journaling

Provide a meaningful reason for correct spelling through personal writing.

(Say)

- What did the girls in Mrs. Morgan's class like to do? (Play with their dolls.)

- Is there anything wrong with liking to play dolls? (No, not if you keep it in balance.)

- Why was playing with dolls a problem for Katelynn? (It was the most important thing for her.)

- Make a list in your journal of things you like to do. Remember to keep God #1 in your life.

Quotables!

"**The reason children learn to spell is to be able to write. The reason children learn to write is to provide themselves and others with things to read. The reason children learn to read is to be able to read what they and others have written. They all go together.**"*

*Harp, Bill. 1988. When the Principal Asks, "Why Are Your Kids Giving Each Other Spelling Tests?" Reading Teacher, Vol. 41, No. 7, March: 702-704.

Little Lost Dog

When her dog, Chimi, is lost, Setsuko understands God's redemption better and wants to praise Him more.

*A*lmost before the silver minivan came to a stop in the carport, Setsuko was out the door and skipping up the two steps into the duplex. "Don't forget your . . ." Setsuko's mother never finished her sentence. With a resigned smile, Mrs. Noma gathered up Setsuko's small violin in its black case and the music books that had scattered across the floor of the minivan. By the time she entered the kitchen Setsuko had changed into warm playclothes, and was pulling on her coat to go back outside.

"Okasan, may I take a treat to Chimi? I want to teach her to sit and lie down." Setsuko's fingers were busy buttoning her coat.

"You may give her five or six of her little doggy bones." Mother laid the violin and music on the small kitchen table. "But don't forget that you must come in to practice before supper time, Setsuko-chan." Setsuko grabbed the box of dog biscuits off the shelf in the utility room before rushing outside.

"Chimi! Here Chimi!" Setsuko called as she bounced into the fenced backyard. "Come on, chiisai (small) Chimi-chan. Where are you?" Setsuko looked in the doghouse, neatly painted in brown and white to match the duplex, but the doghouse was empty. Next, Setsuko checked the spot behind the evergreen bush. The vent in the wall there blew out warm air from the clothes dryer. The little dip in the ground right under the vent was one of Chimi's favorite spots in the winter. She would curl into a ball and soak up the warmth. But that spot was empty, too. "CHIMI!" Setsuko was getting worried. She looked everywhere for the little white terrier.

Mrs. Noma was ironing a shirt when a frantic Setsuko burst through the door.

"Okasan! I can't find Chimi anywhere! She's gone!" Mother put her coat on quickly, and she and Setsuko walked through the neighborhood calling, looking, and asking neighbors if they had seen a small West Highland Terrier.

"She has a red collar with a heart-shaped name tag attached to it." Setsuko held her mother's hand tightly as Mrs. Noma spoke with still another neighbor.

"We'll keep our eyes open for her." The very heavy-set woman standing in the doorway bobbed her head up and down. "We surely will. It's just too bad for a little girl to lose her dog."

They gave up the search as darkness fell. While mother fixed supper, Setsuko struggled to concentrate on practicing her new violin pieces. She kept messing up when her mind wandered away from the notes in front of her to wondering where Chimi could be.

At six o'clock Mr. Noma walked in to the mouth-watering smells of supper and an extremely upset daughter. "Otosan!" Setsuko flung herself into his arms. He smelled like the hospital where he worked as an X-ray technician. She buried her face in his shoulder as mother explained about the missing Chimi.

"Genki o dashi-nasai (cheer up)!" Father squeezed Setsuko, then held her away from him. He looked into her eyes. "She has to be around somewhere. We'll find her, Suzy-Q. Now, your mother has made your favorite meal for supper. Let's eat and then we'll make some posters to put up around the neighborhood so everyone will know to call us if they spot Chimi, okay?"

Setsuko nodded and went to wash her hands. The yaki-soba (roasted buckwheat noodles with vegetables) was absolutely delicious, but somehow it didn't taste as good as it usually did to Setsuko. Mother had even gotten out the hashi (chopsticks). Setsuko loved the intricately-colored chopsticks, and usually had great fun using them. Except for special occasions, the Noma family used forks and spoons like everyone else. But tonight she just poked at the pile of noodles on her plate as her father and mother talked.

When Mother woke her up the next morning, Setsuko felt like she had just gone to bed. She was tired. Her sleep had been interrupted with upsetting dreams of Chimi. She would see Chimi, her little five-inch tail wagging furiously, and run to her. Just as she started to reach for her, the dream would change and the small West Highland Terrier would just disappear. Before she even got dressed, Setsuko flung on her coat and checked the backyard for Chimi. Just in case, she looked in the front yard, too. No Chimi.

"Have you seen Chimi?" Setsuko called to Andrea Summers when she came out to check the mailbox. The young woman and her husband lived in the other half of the duplex. They were college students and were gone late to classes each evening.

"No, I haven't, Setsuko." Andrea flipped her long, straight brown hair back over her shoulder. "Is she missing?" When Setsuko nodded, Andrea frowned. "Oh, I'm so sorry. Rick and I will watch for her. Surely she'll show up somewhere." She patted Setsuko's head reassuringly.

But Chimi did not show up. Not that day or the next. Setsuko and her father placed posters all around the community. No one called. She and her mother drove slowly up and down the streets calling and looking. No little white terrier came running. Setsuko straightened the shelf in the utility room where Chimi's things were. The brush, doggy biscuits, bright red leash, dog food, and favorite tennis ball sat neatly in order. But

Lesson 17 | Day 1

Chimi wasn't there to use them.

Thursday night, Father pushed his chair back from the supper table and said, "If Chimi hasn't shown up by tomorrow afternoon, we'll go check the animal shelter." He looked down at Setsuko. "Maybe she got picked up by the animal control officer. Perhaps something happened to her identification tag, and they don't know who she belongs to. It's worth checking, anyway."

"Oh, can't we go tonight?" Setsuko jumped up from the table.

Father chuckled. "Sit down, Suzy-Q. The animal shelter is already closed today. I'll pick you up tomorrow right after school, and if Chimi's not back, we'll go."

True to his word, Mr. Noma was waiting in the parking area for Setsuko when she rushed out of Knowlton Elementary School Friday afternoon. She jumped into his small red pickup, plopped her books and papers down beside her, and snapped the seat belt in place. "Let's go, Otosan!" Setsuko bounced a little on the seat.

"I want to make sure you understand that we're just checking, Setsuko." Father said in a serious voice. "Chimi might not be there." He turned the key and started the pickup.

"She's got to be!" Setsuko crossed her fingers. "She's just got to be."

The lady at the animal shelter listened to Mr. Noma explain how Chimi had disappeared a few days before. "I really can't tell if your dog is here, sir." The lady walked around the edge of the counter, to a door on the far wall. "But if you'll come this way, you may walk through the kennels and check for yourself." Huge dogs and tiny dogs and all colors of dogs all seemed to be barking. Setsuko felt so sorry for all of them locked up here with no one to care about them. She blinked and kept looking for Chimi. In the last cage at the end of the

long hall a little West Highland White Terrier spotted Setsuko, and began to bark and yap as loud as it could.

"CHIMI!" Setsuko knelt by the cage and stuck her fingers through the wire. Chimi wriggled all over and licked Setsuko's fingers eagerly. It took just a few minutes to get Chimi out of the animal shelter. Somehow she'd lost her collar, so Setsuko picked her up and carried her to the car. Chimi licked her face and squirmed so much she was hard to hold. When Setsuko dumped her in the pickup, she practically turned wrong side out wagging her stump of a tail so hard.

"Hey, Chimi!" Father pushed her back and rescued Setsuko's school books and papers from the middle of the seat before the joyful dog destroyed them. He smoothed the wrinkles out of the handwriting border sheet on the top of the stack with one hand.

"Listen to this, Suzy-Q." Father glanced at the happy girl and her dog. "'Praise the Lord, for He has come to visit His people and has redeemed them,'" he read. "Finding Chimi and paying to get her out of the animal shelter to take her home again is a great example of what your handwriting Scripture is talking about this week." He turned the little red pickup toward home.

"You mean that God loves me like I love Chimi?" Setsuko cuddled her precious pet close. "That God redeems me like you paid to get Chimi out, so we could take her home?"

Father nodded. "Yes, Setsuko. And God loves you even more!"

"Wow, Chimi," Setsuko whispered into her fuzzy, pointed ear. "I guess that means God cares about me a whole lot!"

2 Discussion Time

Check understanding of the story and development of personal values.

- What did Setsuko want to do as soon as she got home from school?
- Why couldn't Setsuko concentrate on practicing her violin that evening?
- How do you think you'd feel if you lost your own very special pet?
- Where did they finally find Chimi?
- How was paying to get Chimi out of the animal shelter like the Scripture Setsuko had practiced writing that week?

228

A Preview

Write each word as your teacher says it.

Name _____

1. family
2. baby
3. every
4. only
5. very
6. penny
7. ready
8. holy
9. any
10. story

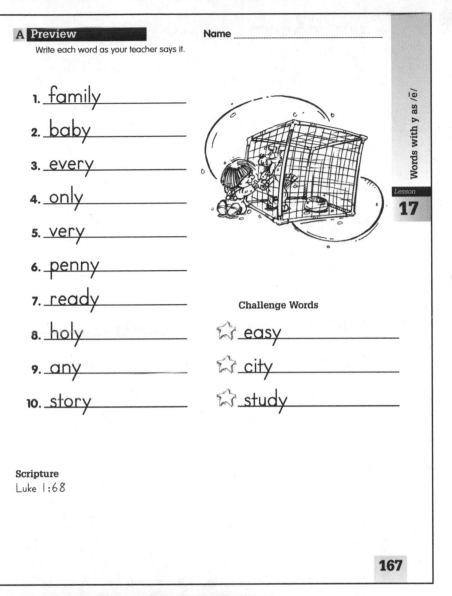

Challenge Words

☆ easy
☆ city
☆ study

Scripture
Luke 1:68

167

Challenge

For better spellers, challenge words may be included in the weekly list. Challenge words are starred.

Correct Immediately!

Say Let's correct our preview. I will write each word on the board. Put a dot under each letter on your preview as I spell the word out loud. If you spelled a word wrong, rewrite it correctly.

Progress Chart

Students may record scores. (Reproducible master in Appendix B.)

Take a minute to memorize . . .

Read the memory verse twice. Have students practice it with you two more times.

---

3 Preview

Test for knowledge of the correct spellings of these words.
(See the instructions at the top right for challenge words.)

Say I will say the word once, use the word in a sentence, then say the word again. Write the word on the lines in the Worktext.

1. **family**   The Noma **family** lived in a brown and white duplex.
2. **baby**   Setsuko got Chimi when the terrier was just a **baby.**
3. **every**   She played with the puppy **every** day.
4. **only**   Chimi was Setsuko's **only** pet.
5. **very**   Setsuko was **very** upset that Chimi was lost.
6. **penny**   It cost more than a **penny** to get Chimi out of the shelter.
7. **ready**   Chimi was **ready** to go home.
8. **holy**   Some people worship idols, which are not **holy.**
9. **any**   There aren't **any** homes for many of the pets at the shelter.
10. **story**   Have you heard the **story** of the lost sheep?
☆ **easy**   It isn't **easy** finding a lost animal.
☆ **city**   There were many dogs in the **city** animal shelter.
☆ **study**   It was hard for Setsuko to **study** while Chimi was missing.

229

Help students form a correct image of whole words.

(Say) Look at each word and think about its shape. Now, write the word in the correct word Shape Boxes. You may check off each word as you use it.

(In many words with two or more syllables, the sound of /ē/ is spelled with **y**.)

(Say) In the word Shape Boxes, color the letter or letters that spell the sound of /ē/ in each word. Circle the words which have two syllables. Draw a line under the word which has three syllables.

Challenge

Draw the correctly shaped box around each letter in these words.

(Say) On a separate sheet of paper, write other words that contain the spelling patterns in the word list. See how many words you can write.

B Word Shapes   Name _____

Write each word in the correct word shape boxes. Then, in the word shape boxes, color the letter that spells the sound of /ē/ in each word. Circle the words which have two syllables. Draw a line under the word which has three syllables.

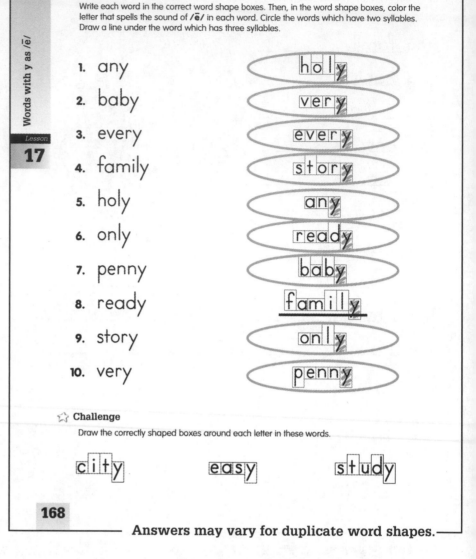

1. any
2. baby
3. every
4. family
5. holy
6. only
7. penny
8. ready
9. story
10. very

☆ **Challenge**

Draw the correctly shaped boxes around each letter in these words.

c i t y   e a s y   s t u d y

168

Answers may vary for duplicate word shapes.

Be Prepared For Fun

Check these supply lists for **Fun Ways to Spell** presented **Day 2**. Purchase and/or gather these items ahead of time!

General
- Markers
- Art Paper
- Spelling List

Auditory
- Spelling List

Visual
- Letter Tiles a, b, b, d, e, e, f, h, i, l, m, n, n, o, p, r, s, t, v, y
- c, u (added for challenge words)
- Spelling List

Tactile
- Finger Paint
- Plastic Plate or Glossy Paper
- Spelling List

230

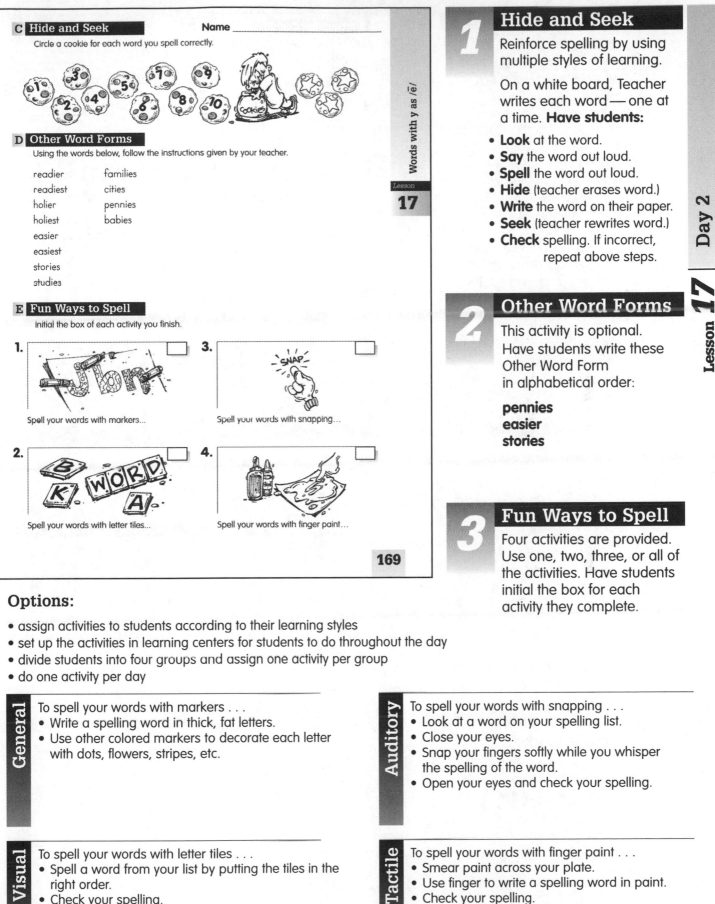

C Hide and Seek

Name _____

Circle a cookie for each word you spell correctly.

D Other Word Forms

Using the words below, follow the instructions given by your teacher.

readier   families
readiest   cities
holier   pennies
holiest   babies
easier
easiest
stories
studies

E Fun Ways to Spell

Initial the box of each activity you finish.

1. Spell your words with markers...

3. SNAP
Spell your words with snapping...

2. Spell your words with letter tiles...

4. Spell your words with finger paint...

169

---

1 Hide and Seek

Reinforce spelling by using multiple styles of learning.

On a white board, Teacher writes each word — one at a time. **Have students:**

- **Look** at the word.
- **Say** the word out loud.
- **Spell** the word out loud.
- **Hide** (teacher erases word.)
- **Write** the word on their paper.
- **Seek** (teacher rewrites word.)
- **Check** spelling. If incorrect, repeat above steps.

2 Other Word Forms

This activity is optional. Have students write these Other Word Form in alphabetical order:

pennies
easier
stories

3 Fun Ways to Spell

Four activities are provided. Use one, two, three, or all of the activities. Have students initial the box for each activity they complete.

Options:

- assign activities to students according to their learning styles
- set up the activities in learning centers for students to do throughout the day
- divide students into four groups and assign one activity per group
- do one activity per day

General

To spell your words with markers . . .
- Write a spelling word in thick, fat letters.
- Use other colored markers to decorate each letter with dots, flowers, stripes, etc.

Auditory

To spell your words with snapping . . .
- Look at a word on your spelling list.
- Close your eyes.
- Snap your fingers softly while you whisper the spelling of the word.
- Open your eyes and check your spelling.

Visual

To spell your words with letter tiles . . .
- Spell a word from your list by putting the tiles in the right order.
- Check your spelling.

Tactile

To spell your words with finger paint . . .
- Smear paint across your plate.
- Use finger to write a spelling word in paint.
- Check your spelling.
- Smear the word out with your fingers and write another word.

1 **Sentence Order**

Familiarize students with word meaning and usage. Write **to eat time It is**. on the board. Ask for a volunteer to read the sentence. Ask the students why the sentence doesn't make sense. Invite the students to put the words into the correct order to form a sentence.

Say Put each set of word groups in order to write a sentence. After you have written the sentences, circle the spelling words in each sentence.

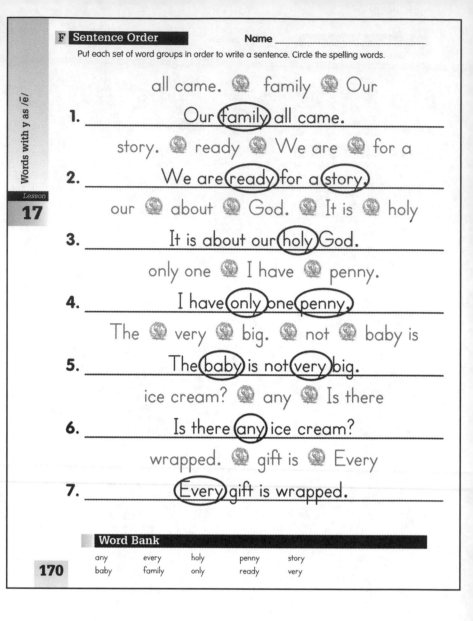

F **Sentence Order**

Name _____

Put each set of word groups in order to write a sentence. Circle the spelling words.

Words with y as /ē/

Lesson **17**

all came. 🌐 family 🌐 Our

1. _____ Our (family) all came. _____

story. 🌐 ready 🌐 We are 🌐 for a

2. _____ We are (ready) for a (story.) _____

our 🌐 about 🌐 God. 🌐 It is 🌐 holy

3. _____ It is about our (holy) God. _____

only one 🌐 I have 🌐 penny.

4. _____ I have (only) one (penny.) _____

The 🌐 very 🌐 big. 🌐 not 🌐 baby is

5. _____ The (baby) is not (very) big. _____

ice cream? 🌐 any 🌐 Is there

6. _____ Is there (any) ice cream? _____

wrapped. 🌐 gift is 🌐 Every

7. _____ (Every) gift is wrapped. _____

Word Bank

170

any	every	holy	penny	story
baby	family	only	ready	very

⏰ **Take a minute to memorize . . .**

Read the memory verse twice. Have students practice it with you two more times.

232

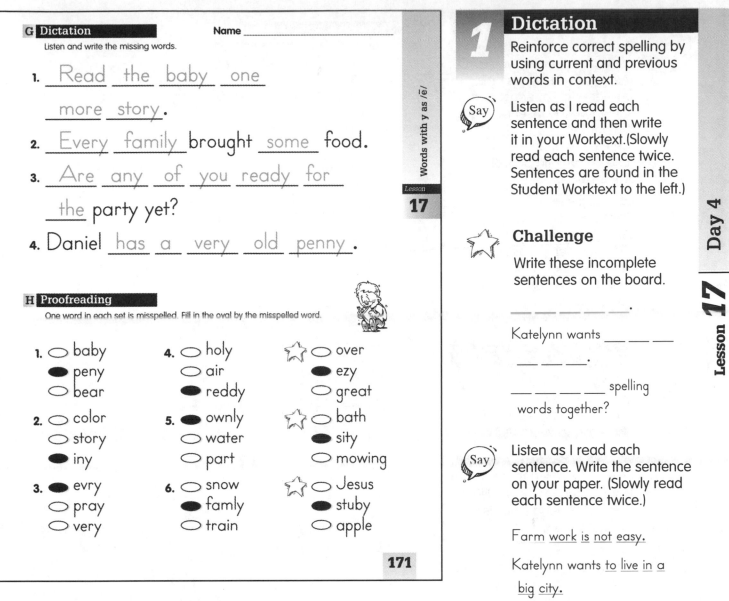

G Dictation

Name _____

Listen and write the missing words.

1. Read the baby one more story.

2. Every family brought some food.

3. Are any of you ready for the party yet?

4. Daniel has a very old penny.

H Proofreading

One word in each set is misspelled. Fill in the oval by the misspelled word.

1. ○ baby
   ● peny
   ○ bear

2. ○ color
   ○ story
   ● iny

3. ● evry
   ○ pray
   ○ very

4. ○ holy
   ○ air
   ● reddy

5. ● ownly
   ○ water
   ○ part

6. ○ snow
   ● famly
   ○ train

☆ ○ over
   ● ezy
   ○ great

☆ ○ bath
   ● sity
   ○ mowing

☆ ○ Jesus
   ● stuby
   ○ apple

171

---

1 Dictation

Reinforce correct spelling by using current and previous words in context.

(Say) Listen as I read each sentence and then write it in your Worktext.(Slowly read each sentence twice. Sentences are found in the Student Worktext to the left.)

☆ Challenge

Write these incomplete sentences on the board.

___ ___ ___ ___ .

Katelynn wants ___ ___ ___ ___ ___ ___ .

___ ___ ___ ___ spelling words together?

(Say) Listen as I read each sentence. Write the sentence on your paper. (Slowly read each sentence twice.)

Farm <u>work</u> <u>is</u> <u>not</u> <u>easy.</u>

Katelynn wants <u>to</u> <u>live</u> <u>in</u> <u>a</u> big <u>city.</u>

<u>Can</u> <u>we</u> <u>study</u> <u>our</u> spelling words together?

---

2 Proofreading

Familiarize students with standardized test format and reinforce recognizing misspelled words.

(Say) Look at each set of words. One word in each set is misspelled. Fill in the oval by the misspelled word. (You may wish to pronounce each set of words to help students correctly identify them.)

233

3 Hide and Seek

Reinforce correct spelling of current spelling words. (A reproducible master is provided in Appendix A as shown on the inset page to the right.)

Write the words one at a time on a white board. **Have students:**

- **Look** at the word.
- **Say** the word out loud.
- **Spell** the word out loud.
- **Hide** (teacher erases word.)
- **Write** the word on paper.
- **Seek** (teacher rewrites word.)
- **Check** spelling. If incorrect, rewrite word correctly.

4 Code

Have your students complete this activity to strengthen spelling ability and expand vocabulary.

1 Posttest

Test mastery of the spelling words. Challenge words are starred.

Say

I will say the word once, use the word in a sentence, then say the word again. Write the word on your paper.

1.	family	The Noma **family** looked for Chimi everywhere.
2.	penny	The neighbors have a dog named **Penny**.
3.	baby	Setsuko looked at **baby** pictures of Chimi.
4.	holy	God is **holy**, meaning perfect and awesome.
5.	any	There wasn't **any** sign of the little terrier.
6.	ready	Setsuko was **ready** to go to the shelter right then.
7.	only	Chimi wasn't the **only** animal at the shelter.
8.	very	Setsuko was **very** happy to see Chimi.
9.	story	Setsuko told her mother the **story** of how they found Chimi.
10.	every	God has redeemed **every** one of us.
☆	city	Is there an animal shelter in your **city**?
☆	study	Do you **study** a musical instrument like Setsuko does?
☆	easy	Learning to play the violin is not **easy**.

Progress Chart
Students may record scores. (Reproducible master in Appendix B.)

Personal Dictionary
Students may add any words they have misspelled to their personal dictionaries for reference when writing. (Cover in Appendix B.)

234

Inset page (Appendix A):

Hide and Seek
Check a paper for each word you spell correctly.

1 3 5 7 9
2 4 6 8 10

Code
Use the code to write the spelling words.

a b c d e f g h i j k l m

n o p q r s t u v w x y z

1. b a b i e s
2. f a m i l i e s
3. p e n n i e s
4. s t o r i e s
5. s t u d i e s
6. c i t i e s

382

I Game

Name _____

Help Setsuko find Chimi. Color one space for each word you or your team spells correctly from this week's word list.

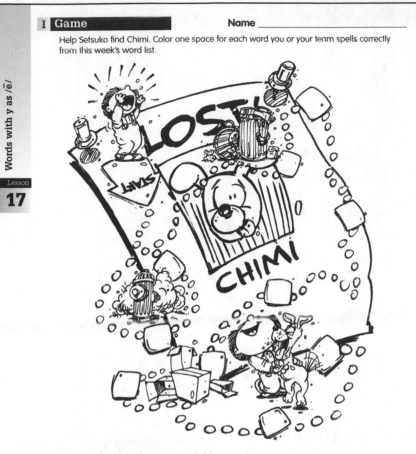

Remember: God loved you so much He sent Jesus to save you.

J Journaling

Finish this message to God in your journal: **Thank You for. . . I praise You because. . . When I feel lost I will. . . I know You love me because. . .**

172

2 Game

Reinforce spelling skills and provide motivation and interest.

Materials

• game page (from student text)
• crayons or colored pencils (1 per child)
• game word list (provided below)

Game Word List

Use of challenge words is optional.

1. **any**
2. **baby**
3. **every**
4. **family**
5. **only**
6. **holy**
7. **penny**
8. **ready**
9. **story**
10. **very**
☆ **easy**
☆ **city**
☆ **study**

How to Play:

• Divide students into two teams, and decide which team will go first.
• Have a student from team A go to the board.
• Read the spelling word two times slowly and clearly. (You may also wish to use the word in a sentence. Ex.: "cat — The cat climbed a tree. — cat")
• Have the student write the word on the board.
• If the word is spelled correctly, instruct all the members of team A to color one space, beginning at Start, on the game board. (Note: If the word is misspelled, correct the spelling immediately.)
• Alternate between teams A and B as you go down the word list.
• The team to reach Chimi first is the winner.

Non-Competitive Option: At the end of the game, say: "Class, I am proud of your efforts to spell the words correctly. If you had fun and tried your best, you are all winners!"

3 Journaling

Provide a meaningful reason for correct spelling through personal writing.

Review the story using discussion leads provided on the following page. Encourage students to apply the Scriptural value in their journaling.

Take a minute to memorize . . .

Read the memory verse twice. Have students practice it with you two more times.

235

Provide a meaningful reason for correct spelling through personal writing.

Say
- Do you have, or have you ever had, a special pet like Chimi?
- What kind of things do you like to do with your pet?
- Setsuko was very upset when they couldn't find Chimi. What did the Noma family do to try to find her? (Put posters up around the neighborhood, went door to door asking if anyone had seen Chimi, and drove up and down the streets calling and looking.)
- Why didn't the animal control officer call to tell them that Chimi had been picked up? (She had lost her collar somehow that had her name and the Noma's telephone number on it.)
- Like Mr. Noma paid to get Chimi out of the shelter, God has paid the price to redeem us. He loves us a whole lot. Write a message to God in your journal by finishing the four sentences in your Worktext.

My Journal

Quotables!

"Purposeful writing experiences are the key to cognitive growth in spelling."*

*Lutz, Elaine. 1986. ERIC/RCS Report: Invented Spelling and Spelling Development. Language Arts, Vol. 63, No. 7, November: 742-744.

To the End of the World

Tony learns that God is always with each of us, when his friend, Stephen, is hit by a car.

Errrrrrrrk! Tires screamed as the bright red sports car skidded on the warm pavement and slammed into the blue bicycle in the middle of the road. Tony watched in horror as Stephen flew through the air and landed with a sickening thud in the ditch several feet away. He scrambled off his own bike and dropped it with a loud clank on the sidewalk. "Help! Somebody help!" he screamed, running toward his friend. "Stephen got hit! Help!"

The driver of the sports car flung open his door and leaped onto the road. "Don't touch him, kid!" he yelled as he dialed 911 on his cell phone.

The front door of the nearest duplex burst open and Mr. Wilson bolted across the street toward his son's crumpled form lying on the grass. "Don't touch him!" the driver warned again. "If anything's broken, it could hurt him more." The driver talked rapidly into his phone giving the location of the accident to the dispatcher. A small group was gathering around Stephen. The driver took off his big down jacket and draped it lightly over the unconscious boy. His voice shook with emotion, "Everyone step back. Give him room to breathe. Don't touch him. We need to keep him warm until the ambulance gets here." He shook his head. "The boy rode right out in front of me."

Mr. Wilson's chin began to quiver and he wiped his eyes with his shirt sleeve. "I know . . . I saw it all happen from the big window. He knows to look both ways. I should have gone with him. I should have . . . oh my boy, my boy!"

"His helmet is cracked!" Tony moaned. Everyone looked at Stephen's black helmet with blue and yellow lightning bolts zigzagging down the side and saw a huge crack. Blood oozed from a big gash on his chin, and his right leg looked funny. The siren of the ambulance grew louder as it came closer to the terrified group.

"How come he doesn't move, or at least cry?" Tony asked, tears in his voice. "Is he dead?"

The driver gently touched Stephen's neck. "His heart's pumping strong! The paramedics will be here any second. The impact to his head probably knocked him out, and by the looks of those legs I'm sure he'll cry when he wakes up."

Tony saw Rachel and her stepsister Vanessa come running across Mason Springs Park and join the crowd of people gathering quietly on the sidewalk. "Oh no, Vanessa!" he heard Rachel cry. "It's Stephen from my class at school! Tony," she yelled, "Tony, is Stephen going to . . ." The wailing siren drowned out her voice as the orange and white ambulance jerked to a stop beside Stephen's motionless body.

Tony went over to stand near Rachel. His chest was tight with worry and tension. It was hard for him to breathe. The paramedics expertly maneuvered a backboard under Stephen and strapped him securely to a stretcher. They wheeled him around to the big doors of the ambulance and carefully lifted him inside. The two children watched Mr. Wilson climb in beside his son before the paramedic closed the big doors and latched them.

Tony and Rachel stared at the back of the ambulance as it pulled away with their friend inside. Tears were running down Tony's cheeks and his whole body shook. "Rachel, what if he dies? We were just going to the park to ride on the bike trail. Stephen got a new bike for his birthday. Now look at it, all twisted and ruined." Rachel followed Tony over to the battered and bent bike and ran her hand over the twisted blue frame. "He was so excited he forgot to look. We never have many cars on our road. Do you think he'll wake up like Daniel did?"

Rachel didn't know what to say. She knew what good friends Tony and Stephen were. She wanted to comfort Tony, but what could she say? Suddenly she remembered the border sheets they'd made that morning in handwriting. "Remember what Jesus said, Tony?" she asked. "He said 'I am with you always, even to the end of the world.' We can pray for Stephen right now!" Tony nodded and the two children bowed their heads by Stephen's smashed bike and asked the God of heaven and earth to be with the bike's owner and help him ride again.

Grandma Miller came up just as Rachel finished praying. "Tony-O, am I glad to see you! I thought they might have taken you away in that ambulance! Who is this young lady? And where's Stephen?" Grandma stopped chattering suddenly as she noticed the crumpled bike at Tony's feet. When Tony lifted his tear-stained face, Grandma knew instantly who was inside the ambulance. "Oh, Tony-O, come with me. We'll go to the hospital and find out how Stephen is." Grandma Miller gathered her grandson in her arms and gave him a warm hug. "We will ask Jesus to be with him," she added in his ear.

Grandma and Tony prayed all the way to the hospital. Tony was beginning to feel better by the time they entered the emergency room and walked up to the tall desk. "Hello, Marie. How is the little Wilson boy doing?" Grandma asked the nurse.

A piercing scream came from behind a nearby door. The nurse raised her eyebrows. "Well, Mrs. Miller, I think that's a sign he's awake now. He's probably just beginning to feel those fractured tibia and fibula bones poking into places they shouldn't be." The nurse smiled. "At

237

least he made one good choice today. That helmet saved his brain. The doctor said he'll need casts on his right leg and left foot, along with some stitches in his chin — but now that he's awake, he'll probably pull through this thing just fine."

"Yes!" Tony grinned, waving a fist in the air. As he unclenched his fists he felt the tension slowly leave his taut muscles for the first time since the accident. He closed his eyes and looked heavenward for a brief second. "Thanks for being with him, God." Then he put his feet together and hopped over to his grandma. "Gram! Can I call Rachel and tell her about Stephen?"

"Yes, but don't you want to thank someone else first, Tony-O?"

"Sure, Gram — but that's already done," Tony grinned.

Grandma reached over and brushed a smudge of dirt from Tony's face, then cupped his chin in her hand. "Jesus wasn't just with Stephen today, Tony. I think He was with you, too." Grandma turned to looked at Marie. "Is there a phone we can use to spread some good news about a God that's with us always?"

Marie nodded and pointed to the office phone.

"Even to the end of the world!" Tony said as he hopped toward the phone.

2 Discussion Time

Check understanding of the story and development of personal values.

- What are some accidents you have seen?
- Who have you known that was involved in an accident?
- How did you feel?
- Tell about an accident you had while riding your bike.
- Do you always wear your helmet when you ride your bike?
- What other rules keep you safe when you ride?
- It is a good idea to ask Jesus to be with you — always.

A Test-Words

Name _____

Write each spelling word on the line as your teacher says it.

1. car _____
2. air _____
3. arm _____
4. say _____
5. bird _____

6. any _____
7. pray _____
8. where _____
9. baby _____
10. barn _____

Review
Lesson **18**

B Test-Sentences

The two underlined words in each of the sentences are misspelled. Write the sentences on the lines below, spelling each underlined word correctly.

Each <u>dey</u> she <u>plaez</u> with me.

1. Each **day** she **plays** with me.

Put <u>som</u> sand in <u>thier</u> bucket.

2. Put **some** sand in **their** bucket.

Let's all <u>sitt</u> in a <u>sirkle</u>.

3. Let's all **sit** in a **circle**.

☆ **Test-Challenge Words**

On a sheet of paper, write each challenge word as your teacher says it.

173

Test-Challenge Words

On a separate piece of paper, challenge words may be tested using the sentences below.

4 Test-Sentences

Reinforce recognizing misspelled words.

Say) Read each sentence carefully. The underlined words in each sentence are misspelled. Write the sentences on the lines in your Worktext, spelling each underlined word correctly.

Take a minute to memorize . . .

Have students say the memory verses from lessons 7, 8, 9, 10, 11, and 12 with you.

---

3 Test-Words

Test for knowledge of the correct spellings of these words. (See the instructions at the top right for challenge words.)

Say) I will say the word once, use the word in a sentence, then say the word again. Write the word on the lines in your Worktext.

1. car   The man drove a red sports **car**.
2. air   Stephen and his bike flew through the **air**.
3. arm   Tony waved his **arm** for help.
4. say   Tony was too stunned to **say** anything.
5. bird   A **bird** watched from a nearby tree.
6. any   They do not know if he has **any** broken bones.
7. pray   Tony, Rachel, and Vanessa will **pray** for Stephen.
8. where   Grandma Miller asked **where** Stephen was.
9. baby   A **baby** cannot ride a bike.
10. barn   No one on that street has a **barn**.
☆ birthday   Did Stephen get the bike for his **birthday**?
☆ large   There was a **large** crack in Stephen's helmet.
☆ heart   "His **heart** is pumping strong," said the sports car driver.

1 Test-Dictation

Reinforce correct spelling by using current and previous words in context.

(Say) Listen as I read each sentence. Then write the missing words in your Worktext. (Slowly read each sentence twice. Sentences are found in the student text to the right. The words **bear**, **family**, and **today** are found in this unit.)

2 Test-Proofreading

Familiarize students with standardized test format and reinforce recognizing misspelled words.

(Say) Look at each set of words. One word in each set is misspelled. Fill in the oval by the misspelled word.

☆ Test-Challenge Words

On a separate piece of paper, challenge words may be tested using the sentences below.

(Say) I will say the word once, use the word in a sentence, then say the word again. Write the word on your paper.

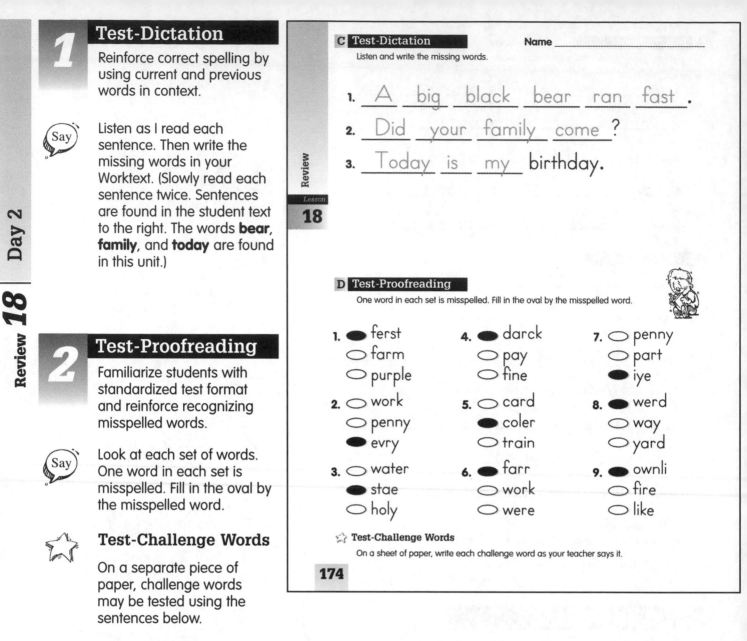

C Test-Dictation
Listen and write the missing words.

Name _____

Review
Lesson
18

1. A big black bear ran fast .
2. Did your family come ?
3. Today is my birthday.

D Test-Proofreading
One word in each set is misspelled. Fill in the oval by the misspelled word.

1. ● ferst
   ○ farm
   ○ purple

2. ○ work
   ○ penny
   ● evry

3. ○ water
   ● stae
   ○ holy

4. ● darck
   ○ pay
   ○ fine

5. ○ card
   ● coler
   ○ train

6. ● farr
   ○ work
   ○ were

7. ○ penny
   ○ part
   ● iye

8. ● werd
   ○ way
   ○ yard

9. ● ownli
   ○ fire
   ○ like

☆ **Test-Challenge Words**
On a sheet of paper, write each challenge word as your teacher says it.

174

☆ **beside**   Mr. Wilson knelt **beside** his son on the grass.
☆ **while**   They kept Stephen covered **while** they waited for the ambulance.
☆ **third**   Mr. Wilson was the **third** person to get into the ambulance.
☆ **stayed**   Stephen's dad **stayed** with him at the emergency room.

E Test-Shapes

Name _____

Color each bike helmet on which the word is spelled incorrectly.

☆ **Test-Challenge Words**

On a sheet of paper, write each challenge word as your teacher says it.

175

Test-Shapes

1 Test mastery of words in this unit.

Say — Look at each bike helmet. If the word is misspelled, color the bike helmet.

Action Game

2 Reinforce spelling skills and provide motivation and interest.

Materials
- 5 pails or buckets with a number 1, 2, or 3 in the bottom
- a bean bag

How to Play:

With masking tape, make a toe-line on the floor. Place the pails or buckets in a cluster approximately 3 feet away. Have the students line up behind the toe-line. Have the first student in line put his toes just behind the mark and toss the bean bag into a bucket. (Allow him to try until he successfully gets the bean bag into a bucket.) If the bean bag lands in a bucket marked 1, have him spell a word tested on Day 1; if in a bucket marked 2, a word tested on Day 2; and, if in a bucket marked 3, a word tested on Day 3. If he spells the word correctly, have him return to his desk; if not, have him go to the end of the line. Continue the game until each student has spelled a word correctly.

 ## Test-Challenge Words

On a separate piece of paper, challenge words may be tested using the sentences below.

Say — I will say the word once, use the word in a sentence, then say the word again. Write the word on your paper.

☆	easy	It was **easy** for Tony to cry when he knew his friend was hurt.
☆	heard	Tony's grandmother **heard** the ambulance siren.
☆	city	There is a nice hospital in their **city**.
☆	care	Stephen received good **care** at the hospital
☆	party	Stephen's friends can have a welcome–home **party** for him.

241

Materials
- game page (from student text)
- stickers (13 per child)
- markers (1 per child)
- game word list

Game Word List

Use of challenge words is optional.

The Ambulance Drivers

1. car
2. air
3. arm
4. say
5. bird
6. any
7. pray
8. where
9. baby
10. barn
11. plays
12. their
13. circle

The Paramedics

1. bear
2. family
3. today
4. first
5. every
6. stay
7. dark
8. color
9. far
10. eye
11. word
12. only
13. rain

The Emergency Room Doctors

1. way
2. farm
3. fire
4. work
5. holy
6. pay
7. card
8. fine
9. purple
10. penny
11. paint
12. hard
13. yard

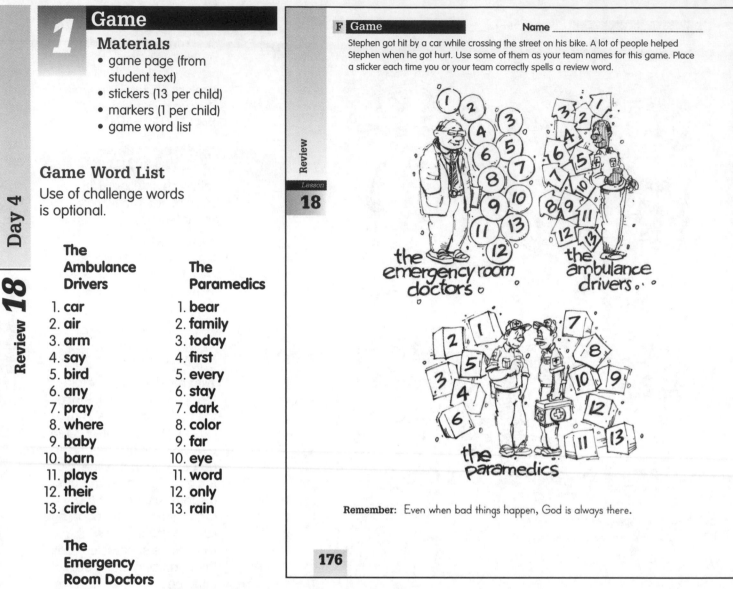

F Game   Name _____

Stephen got hit by a car while crossing the street on his bike. A lot of people helped Stephen when he got hurt. Use some of them as your team names for this game. Place a sticker each time you or your team correctly spells a review word.

Review

Lesson **18**

the emergency room doctors

the ambulance drivers

the paramedics

Remember: Even when bad things happen, God is always there.

176

How to Play:

- Divide students into three teams. Name one team **The Ambulance Drivers**, one **The Paramedics**, and one **The Emergency-Room Doctors**. (Option: You may wish to seat students in groups of three, each child from a different team. They should share one game page.) Decide which team goes first, second, and third.
- Read the instructions from the student game page aloud.
- Have a student from the first team choose a number from 1 to 13.
- Say the word that matches that number (from the team's word list) aloud twice. (You may also wish to use the word in a sentence. Ex.: "cat — The cat climbed a tree. — cat")
- Have the student who chose the number write the word on the board.
- If the word is spelled correctly, have all the members of that team put a sticker on that number by their team name. If the word is misspelled, have them put an "X" through that number. They may not choose that number again. (Note: If the word is misspelled, correct the spelling immediately.)
- Repeat this process with the second team and then the third. (Be sure to use a different student from each team for each round.)
- When the words from all three lists have been used, the team with the most stickers is the winner.

Non-Competitive Option: When the game ends, say: "Class, I'm proud of your efforts to spell the words correctly. If you had fun and tried your best, you are all winners!"

Test-Challenge Words

On a separate piece of paper, challenge words may be tested using the sentences below.

G Test-Words   Name _____

Write each spelling word on the line as your teacher says it.

1. yard   6. part
2. under   7. like
3. train   8. water
4. rain   9. write
5. line   10. were

Review

Lesson
18

H Test-Sentences

The two underlined words in each of the sentences are misspelled. Write the sentences on the lines below, spelling each underlined word correctly.

Dad was <u>hapie</u> to read the <u>stori</u>.

1. Dad was **happy** to read the **story**.

<u>muthir</u> has dinner <u>redy</u> for us.

2. **Mother** has dinner **ready** for us.

The <u>broun</u> leaf is <u>veri</u> brittle.

3. The **brown** leaf is **very** brittle.

☆ Test-Challenge Words

On a sheet of paper, write each challenge word as your teacher says it.

177

---

2 ## Test-Sentences

Reinforce recognizing misspelled words.

Say

Read each sentence carefully. The underlined words in each sentence are misspelled. Write the sentences on the lines in your Worktext, spelling each underlined word correctly.

Review **18** | Day 5

---

1 ## Test-Words

Test for knowledge of the correct spellings of these words.
(See the instructions at the top right for challenge words.)

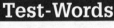
Say

I will say the word once, use the word in a sentence, then say the word again. Write the word on the lines in your Worktext.

1. yard   Mr. Wilson ran across the **yard** towards Stephen.
2. under   The paramedics slid a backboard **under** Stephen.
3. train   They could hear a **train** whistle in the distance.
4. rain   It did not **rain** that day.
5. line   The **line** of cars stopped to let the ambulance pass.
6. part   Which **part** of Stephen's helmet was cracked?
7. like   His bike was twisted **like** a pretzel.
8. water   The nurse gave Stephen a drink of **water**.
9. write   The girls will **write** a get-well letter to Stephen
10. were   They **were** thankful that God was with them.
☆ study   Stephen needs to **study** at home for a few days.
☆ world   Jesus is with us even to the end of the **world**.
☆ praise   They will **praise** God for being with them.

243

3 Writing Assessment

Assess student's spelling, grammar, and composition skills through personal writing.

Say

- Bad things sometimes happen to people. What happened to Stephen in the story? (He got hit by a car while he was riding his bike.)

- What bicycle safety rule did Stephen obey that saved his life? (He was wearing his helmet.)

- Draw a picture of a bicycle accident that you saw happen or one that you were in.

- In your Worktext write as many bicycle rules as you can remember and will fit on the page.

- Don't forget that Jesus is with you even when bad things happen.

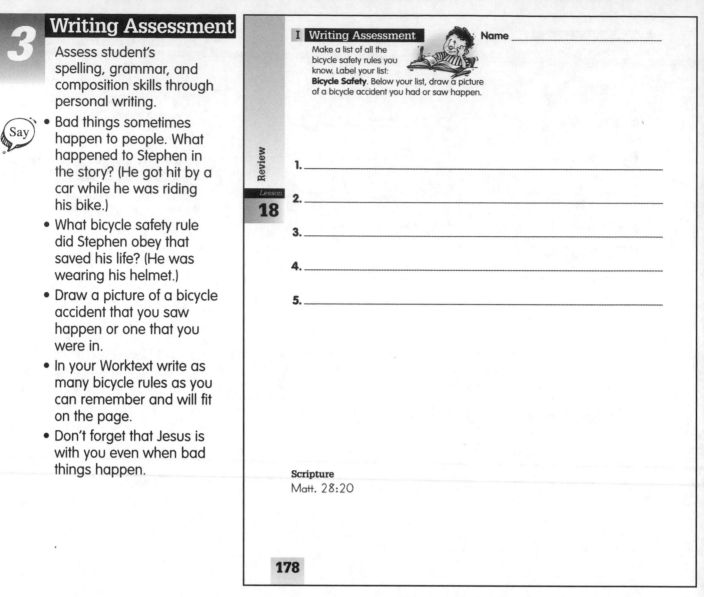

I **Writing Assessment**

Make a list of all the bicycle safety rules you know. Label your list: **Bicycle Safety**. Below your list, draw a picture of a bicycle accident you had or saw happen.

Name _____

Review

Lesson
18

1. _____

2. _____

3. _____

4. _____

5. _____

Scripture
Matt. 28:20

178

A rubric for scoring is provided in Appendix B.

4 Action Game

Reinforce spelling skills and provide motivation and interest.

Materials

- construction paper (7 sheets of same color)
- marker
- scissors

How to Play:

Cut each piece of construction paper in half lengthwise. Print a spelling word tested today on each half; then, cut each half crosswise into two pieces dividing the spelling word approximately in half and creating two puzzle pieces.

Give each student a puzzle piece, face down. At your signal, have each student turn over his puzzle piece and move about to find the player whose puzzle piece fits with his to form a word. Instruct the students to run to you when they think they have a correct match. If they have a match, have them write the word neatly on the board and return to their seats; if they do not, have them return to the group to continue the hunt for their match.

Continue the game until all the word puzzles are completed.

Spelling Is Fun!

This certificate is awarded to

_____

for practicing the following words, by doing terrific spelling activities and playing great spelling games!

Date _____

paint	arm	air	bird	any
pay	barn	bear	circle	baby
plays	car	eye	color	every
pray	card	fine	first	family
rain	dark	fire	purple	holy
say	far	like	under	only
stay	farm	line	water	penny
today	hard	their	were	ready
train	part	where	word	story
way	yard	write	work	very
☆ birthday	☆ heart	☆ beside	☆ heard	☆ city
☆ praise	☆ large	☆ care	☆ third	☆ easy
☆ stayed	☆ party	☆ while	☆ world	☆ study

5 Certificate

Provide an opportunity for parents or guardians to encourage and assess their child's progress.

Say
- Write your name on the first line.
- Now I will write the date on the board for you to copy on the next line.
- Follow along as I read the certificate out loud.
- Be sure to show your parents or guardian all the words you've practiced spelling.

Take a minute to memorize . . .

Read the memory verse twice. Have students practice it with you two more times.

245

6 Letter

Provide the parent or guardian with the spelling word lists for the next unit.

(Say) Show your parents or guardian this letter that tells them what your spelling words will be for the next unit. Ask them to put it in a special place where you will remember to practice them together.

Dear Parent,

We are about to begin a new spelling unit containing five weekly lessons. A set of ten words plus three challenge words will be studied each week. All the words will be reviewed in the sixth week.

Values based on the Scriptures listed below will be taught in each lesson.

Lesson 19	Lesson 20	Lesson 21	Lesson 22	Lesson 23
books	food	around	boys	also
could	new	bow	door	always
dear	noon	count	enjoy	children
ear	room	cow	form	draw
full	soon	found	horse	each
hear	too	house	Lord	small
here	tooth	round	noise	such
took	use	sound	orange	walk
wood	who	south	store	want
would	zoo	vowel	toy	which
☆ looked	☆ balloon	☆ cloud	☆ before	☆ called
☆ stood	☆ knew	☆ crown	☆ important	☆ lunch
☆ year	☆ through	☆ flower	☆ voice	☆ wanted
Matthew 6:34	Luke 15:10	Mark 4:23,24	Luke 11:13	Luke 11:28

Quotables!

"Learning to write involves using real language in meaningful and developmentally appropriate ways."*

*Hoffman, Stevie and Nancy Knipping. 1988. Spelling Revisited: The Child's Way. Childhood Education, June: 284-287.

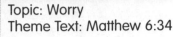
A Worrisome Day

After Stephen's bicycle accident, Rachel finds herself worrying about riding her bike.

"**O**uch! Watch out for my leg!" Stephen grabbed the big wheels of his wheelchair and gave a hard push, jerking his mom's hands free. "I can wheel this thing myself without hitting my leg on stuff!"

Mrs. Wilson stepped back. *"This is going to be a long three months,"* she thought as she followed her son down the hall toward his classroom.

Stephen turned the next corner much too fast. A stack of homework slid from his lap towards the floor, crashing into his other leg on the way. "Oh, my foot! Ouch! Ouch!" Stephen gripped the wheels of his chair tightly, his face twisted in pain.

Mrs. Wilson quickly moved the big math Worktext resting against the toes sticking out of Stephen's light blue cast. "I'm sorry you're getting banged around this morning." Mom adjusted the soft pillow Stephen was sitting on. "Is that better?"

Stephen leaned over to pick up his papers, but the two casts on his broken legs made it impossible.

"Let me help you, Son." Mrs. Wilson squatted down and began gathering the books strewn across the hallway. "I think this is going to be harder for Stephen than for me!" she thought. "He's always liked to do things for himself."

Stephen avoided his mother's eyes. "I guess I could use a little help if you're . . ."

"Stephen! You're back!" Tony knelt beside Mrs. Wilson and helped her pick up Stephen's school books. "How long do you get to ride in that fancy chair?"

"The Doc says I'll be out of the casts before summer vacation, but not the chair." Stephen rubbed his fingers along the shiny, chrome edge of the wheels. "No T-ball for me this spring!"

"Well, I'm glad it was your legs that got broken and not your head. I couldn't believe the big crack in your bike helmet! You didn't throw it away did you?"

"Nope, I brought it to show everyone. It's right here." Stephen turned to get the helmet he'd looped over the handle of his chair — but it wasn't there. "Guess I left it in the car. I'll run and get it." Stephen stopped and looked down at his two casts, then up at his mom with a groan. "I guess I won't be running anywhere for a while, huh?"

"This is going to take some getting used to, Stephen." Mom squeezed his shoulder. "I'll get the helmet. You go on to class. I'll be back in a minute."

"I'll push you the rest of the way, Stephen." Tony grabbed the handles of the wheelchair. "You hold on to the books. Mrs. Morgan's room coming right up!"

Tony started through the door, then jerked the chair to a stop as Stephen's outstretched leg slammed into Katelynn. "Hey, Tony! Who taught you how to drive?" Katelynn rubbed her leg. "You're dangerous!" Neither of them noticed Stephen's eyes squeezed shut from the throbbing ache in his leg.

"I was the first to get rammed by your cast, so I get to sign it before any one else!" Katelynn joked as she turned toward her desk. "Let me get my purple marker."

"I have one, Katelynn." Stephen looked up. "You have to use a permanent marker so it won't wear off."

"I don't think she heard you. Here, let me sign your cast!" Tony whipped the chair around, crashing Stephen's foot against the wall.

"Ouch! Go help someone else!" Stephen banged his fist on the arm of the chair. "No one is going to sign my cast anyway! My leg hurts too much."

Katelynn was coming back from her desk, but stopped at the sound of Stephen's angry words. She noticed the frustrated tears in his eyes, and saw Tony looking like he'd lost his best friend — which was close to the truth. She turned to Rachel who was standing near. "What's wrong with Stephen?"

"Well, how would you feel if you couldn't play the sports you love because your left leg was sticking straight out in front of you in a cast from your toes to your hip, and your right leg was in a walking cast up to your knee." Rachel took a deep breath. "And maybe you'd like having twenty stitches in your face, and your head bonked so hard it broke your helmet. Not me!" Rachel put her hands on her hips. "I bet his leg hurts a whole lot more than yours, where his cast hit you!" And with that, she stalked off.

Mrs. Morgan walked into the classroom with a stack of papers just in time to hear the end of Rachel's angry speech. It was quiet enough to hear an eraser drop. Mrs. Morgan stooped down in front of Stephen and patted the knee that wasn't encased. "I'm glad you're back today, Stephen. I met your mom in the hall and she said you're all caught up with your school work. You've really been working hard."

Stephen smiled through his tears. "I brought a special pen. Would you like to sign my cast Mrs. Morgan?"

"I'd be honored," smiled his teacher.

Later that day after school, Rachel sat on the front steps of her house with her chin in her hands, and gazed across the street at Mason Springs Park. "I told Mom I was going to the park to ride bikes with Tony. I guess I better go meet him like we planned," she thought.

Reluctantly she picked up her bike, then slowly wheeled it across the street — after checking for cars in both directions four times!

247

Story Continued

She looked up to see Tony pedaling wildly down the bike trail.

"Where have you been?" He skidded to a stop in front of her. "I've been around this trail three times already!"

"I don't really feel like riding bikes today . . . and maybe never again."

"Why?" Tony's forehead wrinkled with concern. "I thought you liked to ride bikes."

"I did." Rachel kicked at a clump of grass with the toe of her shoe.

"Well, then why don't you anymore?" Tony asked.

"What if I fall and need stitches in my face like Stephen?"

"A car hit him. There aren't any cars on the bike trail." Tony hopped off his bike.

"Yeah, but what if I fall and hit my head or break my legs?"

"Rachel, Stephen didn't just fall off his bike. He flew thirty feet through the air after the car hit him! That's what broke his legs and helmet."

"I know, but I'm just worried about getting hurt. I don't think riding a bike is safe even with a helmet. It only protects your head. It doesn't help the rest of your body. I want to play T-ball and be on the swim team this summer, not ride around in a wheelchair with stitches all over my body and casts on my legs!"

Tony looked thoughtful for a second, then smiled. "So that's why you got so mad at us this morning. You were worried that what happened to Stephen could happen to you." He paused. "Stephen didn't look before he rode his new bike across the street. That's why he got rammed by a car. Bicycle safety rules are important! But not riding your bike ever again is silly, Rachel!" Tony swung back onto his bike. "Remember what we wrote in handwriting class today: 'God will take care of your tomorrow. Live one day at a time.' You almost drowned last year in Daniel's pool, but you still go swimming! What if you get hurt playing T-ball? Are you just going to sit in your room the rest of your life so you'll be safe?"

Rachel looked down and kicked at the clump of grass again, thinking about Tony's words. "I guess God is big enough to take care of tomorrow . . . and today, too." She smiled. "Hey, I still have half an hour before supper. Wanta race to the bridge?"

"Sure," Tony grinned as he stepped hard on the petals. "But aren't you worried I'll win?"

2 Discussion Time

Check understanding of the story and development of personal values.

- What was Rachel worried about?
- How did she act when she was worried?
- What do you worry about?
- How do you feel when you worry about what's going to happen?
- Did you know Jesus said God would take care of your tomorrow? You need to live just one day at a time.

248

Name _____

1. hear

2. could

3. dear

4. took

5. books

6. here

7. would

8. ear

9. full

10. wood

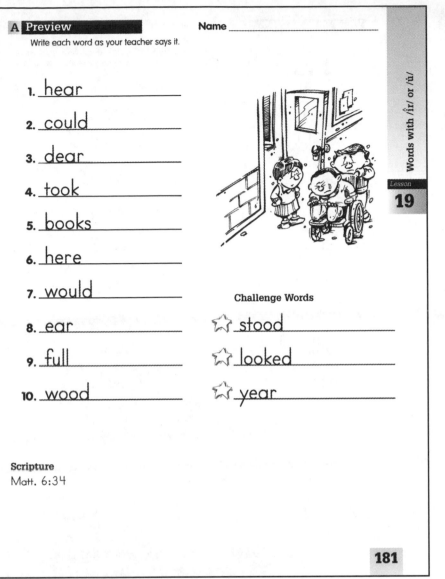

Challenge Words

☆ stood

☆ looked

☆ year

Scripture
Matt. 6:34

181

Challenge

 For better spellers, challenge words may be included in the weekly list. Challenge words are starred.

Correct Immediately!

 Let's correct our preview. I will write each word on the board. Put a dot under each letter on your preview as I spell the word out loud. If you spelled a word wrong, rewrite it correctly.

Progress Chart

 Students may record scores. (Reproducible master in Appendix B.)

Take a minute to memorize . . .

Read the memory verse twice. Have students practice it with you two more times.

---

3 Preview

Test for knowledge of the correct spellings of these words. (See the instructions at the top right for challenge words.)

(Say) I will say the word once, use the word in a sentence, then say the word again. Write the word on the lines in the Worktext.

1.	hear	Did you **hear** what happened to Stephen?
2.	could	He **could** have been hurt worse.
3.	dear	Oh **dear**, how can Stephen play baseball now?
4.	took	Tony **took** Stephen's homework to him.
5.	books	Tony will return Stephen's library **books** for him.
6.	here	"Stephen will be **here** in school tomorrow," Mrs. Morgan said.
7.	would	It **would** be nice not to stare at Stephen.
8.	ear	Stephen didn't hurt his **ear**.
9.	full	Stephen's lap was **full** of books.
10.	wood	The **wood** had been cut weeks before Stephen's accident.
☆	stood	Rachel **stood** by her desk and stared at Stephen.
☆	looked	Rachel **looked** at Stephen's cast and the stitches in his face.
☆	year	This is Stephen's second **year** at Knowlton Elementary School.

249

4 Word Shapes

Help students form a correct image of whole words.

Say Look at each word and think about its shape. Now, write the word in the correct word Shape Boxes. You may check off each word as you use it.

(In many words, the sound of /îr/ is spelled with **ear** or **ere**. The sound of /u̇/ can be spelled **oo**, **ou**, or **u**.)

Say In the word Shape Boxes, color the letters that spell the sound of /îr/ or /u̇/ in each word. Circle the words in which /u̇/ is spelled with **ou**.

☆ Challenge

Draw the correctly shaped box around each letter in these words.

Say On a separate sheet of paper, write sentences using one or more of the spelling words.

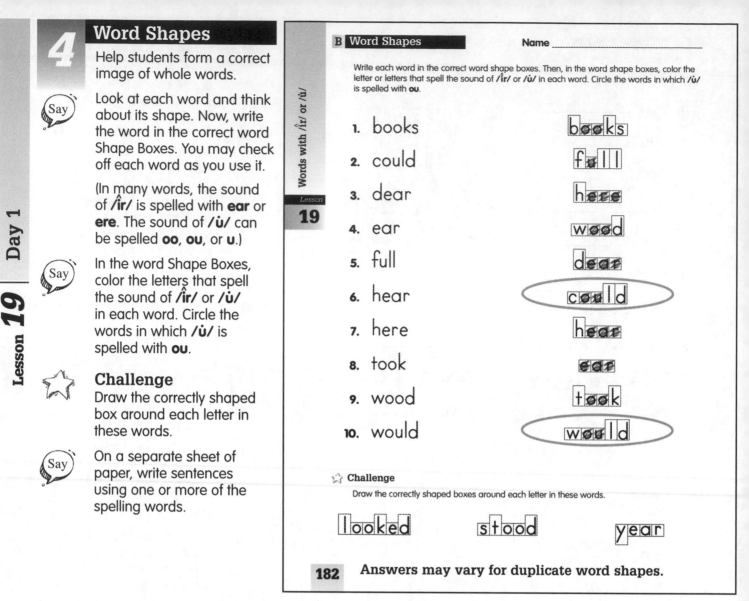

B Word Shapes   Name _____

Words with /îr/ or /u̇/   Lesson 19

Write each word in the correct word shape boxes. Then, in the word shape boxes, color the letter or letters that spell the sound of /îr/ or /u̇/ in each word. Circle the words in which /u̇/ is spelled with **ou**.

1. books   b**oo**ks
2. could   f**u**ll
3. dear   h**ere**
4. ear   w**oo**d
5. full   d**ear**
6. hear   (c**ou**ld)
7. here   h**ear**
8. took   **ear**
9. wood   t**oo**k
10. would   (w**ou**ld)

☆ **Challenge**
Draw the correctly shaped boxes around each letter in these words.

looked   stood   year

182   **Answers may vary for duplicate word shapes.**

Be Prepared For Fun

Check these supply lists for **Fun Ways to Spell** presented **Day 2**. Purchase and/or gather these items ahead of time!

General
- Crayons
- 3 x 5 Cards cut in thirds (42 pieces per child)
- 3 x 5 Cards cut in thirds (15 more to spell challenge words)
- Glue
- Bright Paper or Poster Board (about 3 pieces per child)
- Spelling List

Auditory
- Rhythm instruments (two wooden spoons, two pan lids, maracas)
- Spelling List

Visual
- Letter Stencils
- Colored Pencils
- Paper (2 sheets per child)
- Spelling List

Tactile
- Cotton Balls
- Glue
- Construction Paper
- Spelling List

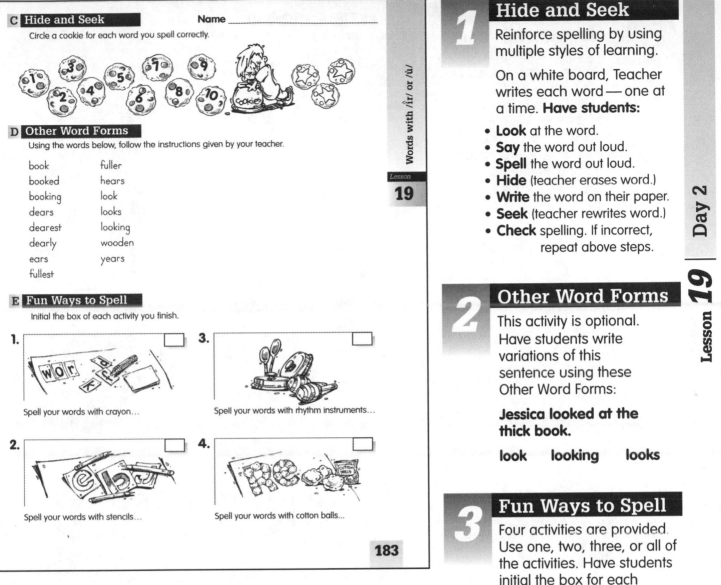

C | Hide and Seek

Name _____

Circle a cookie for each word you spell correctly.

D | Other Word Forms

Using the words below, follow the instructions given by your teacher.

book	fuller
booked	hears
booking	look
dears	looks
dearest	looking
dearly	wooden
ears	years
fullest	

E | Fun Ways to Spell

Initial the box of each activity you finish.

1.

Spell your words with crayon…

3.

Spell your words with rhythm instruments…

2.

Spell your words with stencils…

4.

Spell your words with cotton balls…

183

---

1 Hide and Seek

Reinforce spelling by using multiple styles of learning.

On a white board, Teacher writes each word — one at a time. **Have students:**

- **Look** at the word.
- **Say** the word out loud.
- **Spell** the word out loud.
- **Hide** (teacher erases word.)
- **Write** the word on their paper.
- **Seek** (teacher rewrites word.)
- **Check** spelling. If incorrect, repeat above steps.

2 Other Word Forms

This activity is optional. Have students write variations of this sentence using these Other Word Forms:

Jessica looked at the thick book.

look   looking   looks

3 Fun Ways to Spell

Four activities are provided. Use one, two, three, or all of the activities. Have students initial the box for each activity they complete.

Options:

- assign activities to students according to their learning styles
- set up the activities in learning centers for students to do throughout the day
- divide students into four groups and assign one activity per group
- do one activity per day

General

To spell your words with crayon . . .
- Write each letter of your spelling word on a card.
- Glue the cards on a sheet of paper in the right order to spell your words.
- Check your spelling.

Auditory

To spell your words with rhythm instruments . . .
- Look at a word on your spelling list.
- Close your eyes.
- Play your rhythm instruments softly while you whisper the spelling of the word.
- Open your eyes and check your spelling.

Visual

To spell your words with stencils . . .
- Trace the outline of each letter of the spelling word.
- Color in the letters.

Tactile

To spell your words with cotton balls . . .
- Choose a word from your spelling list.
- It may be a favorite word or a word you have trouble remembering how to spell.
- Write the word in tall, wide letters on a sheet of construction paper.
- Spread glue along the outline of each letter and press cotton balls into the glue.

1 ABC Order

Familiarize students with word meaning and usage. Write the words **when**, **cent**, **ten**, and **hen** on the board. Explain to the students that alphabetizing means to put the words in ABC order. Guide the students in putting the four words in ABC order.

(Say) Look at each set of words in this activity. Write them in ABC order on the lines.

F ABC Order

Name _____

Write each set of spelling words in alphabetical order.

1. would   ear
   full   full
   ear   took
   took   would

2. dear   books
   books   could
   could   dear
   here   here

3. took   dear
   wood   hear
   hear   took
   dear   wood

   ☆ stood   lamp
   year   looked
   looked   stood
   lamp   year

A B C D E F G H I J K L M N O P Q R S T U V W X Y Z
a b c d e f g h i j k l m n o p q r s t u v w x y z

184

Take a minute to memorize . . .

Read the memory verse twice. Have students practice it with you two more times.

252

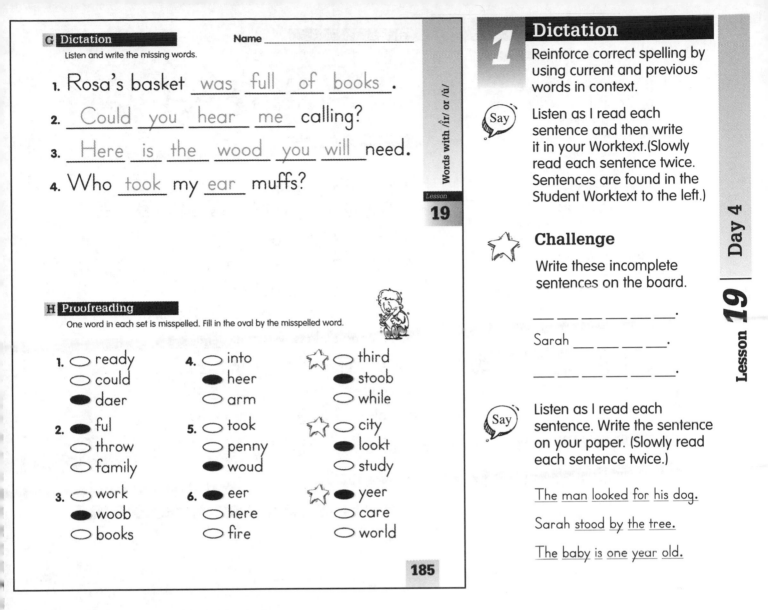

G Dictation

Name _____

Listen and write the missing words.

1. Rosa's basket _was_ _full_ _of_ _books_ .

2. _Could_ _you_ _hear_ _me_ calling?

3. _Here_ _is_ _the_ _wood_ _you_ _will_ need.

4. Who _took_ my _ear_ muffs?

H Proofreading

One word in each set is misspelled. Fill in the oval by the misspelled word.

1. ○ ready
   ○ could
   ● daer

2. ● ful
   ○ throw
   ○ family

3. ○ work
   ● woob
   ○ books

4. ○ into
   ● heer
   ○ arm

5. ○ took
   ○ penny
   ● woud

6. ● eer
   ○ here
   ○ fire

☆ ○ third
   ● stoob
   ○ while

☆ ○ city
   ● lookt
   ○ study

☆ ● yeer
   ○ care
   ○ world

185

---

1 Dictation

Reinforce correct spelling by using current and previous words in context.

(Say) Listen as I read each sentence and then write it in your Worktext.(Slowly read each sentence twice. Sentences are found in the Student Worktext to the left.)

☆ Challenge

Write these incomplete sentences on the board.

__ __ __ __ __ .

Sarah __ __ __ __ .

__ __ __ __ __ .

(Say) Listen as I read each sentence. Write the sentence on your paper. (Slowly read each sentence twice.)

The man looked for his dog.

Sarah stood by the tree.

The baby is one year old.

---

2 Proofreading

Familiarize students with standardized test format and reinforce recognizing misspelled words.

(Say) Look at each set of words. One word in each set is misspelled. Fill in the oval by the misspelled word. (You may wish to pronounce each set of words to help students correctly identify them.)

3 Hide and Seek

Reinforce correct spelling of current spelling words. (A reproducible master is provided in Appendix A as shown on the inset page to the right.)

Write the words one at a time on a white board.

Have students:

- **Look** at the word.
- **Say** the word out loud.
- **Spell** the word out loud.
- **Hide** (teacher erases word.)
- **Write** the word on paper.
- **Seek** (teacher rewrites word.)
- **Check** spelling. If incorrect, rewrite word correctly.

4 Sentence Fun

Have your students complete this activity to strengthen spelling ability and expand vocabulary.

1 Posttest

Test mastery of the spelling words. Challenge words are starred.

(Say) I will say the word once, use the word in a sentence, then say the word again. Write the word on your paper.

1.	dear	"The poor **dear**," Grandma Miller said.
2.	hear	"I **hear** Stephen is back today," said Rosa.
3.	here	Stephen was not **here** for school yesterday.
4.	ear	"Did he hurt his **ear**?"
5.	books	"I will take Stephen's **books** to him," Tony said.
6.	took	Tony **took** Stephen his homework.
7.	would	It **would** be a good idea not to worry about tomorrow.
8.	could	You **could** ask God to take care of your tomorrow.
9.	full	His glass is **full** of water.
10.	wood	Stack the **wood** beside the garage.
☆	looked	Rachel **looked** four times before she crossed the street.
☆	stood	Rachel **stood** on the sidewalk and kicked at the clump of grass.
☆	year	This is your second **year** of elementary school.

Progress Chart

Students may record scores. (Reproducible master in Appendix B.)

Personal Dictionary

Students may add any words they have misspelled to their personal dictionaries for reference when writing. (Cover in Appendix B.)

Inset page (Appendix A)

Hide and Seek

Check a paper for each word you spell correctly.

1 3 5 7 9
2 4 6 8 10

Sentence Fun

Add the endings to the spelling words. Write one of the new words in each sentence.

1. You are my __dearest__ friend.
2. The __dearly__ loved dog sleeps on her bed.
3. Jesus always __hears__ you.
4. If you have __ears__, listen!
5. The __books__ crashed to the floor.
6. The __wooden__ stool was by the sink.
7. Stephen's glass was the __fullest__.
8. The trail led through the __woods__.
9. Stephen is seven __years__ old.
10. This jar is __fuller__ than that one.
11. That loud noise hurts my __ears__.
12. I like __hearing__ the birds sing.

Word Bank

book + s	dear + ly	ear + s	full + est	hear + ing	wood + en
dear + est	ear + s	full + er	hear + s	wood + s	year + s

383

254

I Game

Name _____

Sign Stephen's cast. Each time a person on your team spells a word correctly from this week's word list, write their name on Stephen's cast.

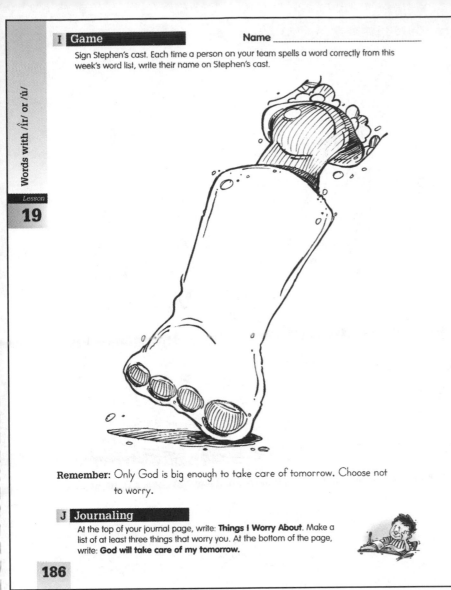

Remember: Only God is big enough to take care of tomorrow. Choose not to worry.

J Journaling

At the top of your journal page, write: **Things I Worry About**. Make a list of at least three things that worry you. At the bottom of the page, write: **God will take care of my tomorrow.**

186

How to Play:

- Divide students into two teams, and decide which team will go first.
- Have a student from team A go to the board.
- Read the spelling word two times slowly and clearly. (You may also wish to use the word in a sentence. Ex.: "cat — The cat climbed a tree. — cat")
- Have the student write the word on the board.
- If the word is spelled correctly, instruct all the members of team A to write that team member's name on Stephen's cast. (Note: If the word is misspelled, correct the spelling immediately.)
- Alternate between teams A and B as you go down the word list.
- The team with the most names on Stephen's cast when you have gone through the word list twice is the winner.

Non-Competitive Option: At the end of the game, say: "Class, I am proud of your efforts to spell the words correctly. If you had fun and tried your best, you are all winners!"

2 Game

Reinforce spelling skills and provide motivation and interest.

Materials

- game page (from student text)
- colored pencils or markers (2 or 3 per child)
- game word list

Game Word List

Check off each word lightly in pencil as it is used.

1. **dear**
2. **hear**
3. **here**
4. **ear**
5. **books**
6. **took**
7. **wood**
8. **would**
9. **could**
10. **full**
☆ **stood**
☆ **looked**
☆ **year**

3 Journaling

Provide a meaningful reason for correct spelling through personal writing.

Review the story using discussion leads provided on the following page. Encourage students to apply the Scriptural value in their journaling.

Take a minute to memorize . . .

Have students say the memory verse with you once.

255

3 Journaling

Provide a meaningful reason for correct spelling through personal writing.

Say • In our story this week Rachel was worried about something. Do you remember what it was? (She was worried about hurting herself on her bike like Stephen had.)

• God is big enough to take care of all our worries.

• Make a list of things that worry you in your journal. As you write "God will take care of my tomorrow" at the bottom of your page, ask Jesus to take care of your worries.

Encourage children to write and communicate their ideas.

256

Twenty Dollar Temptation

Christopher finds a twenty-dollar bill. Will he keep it?

The school day was almost over, and Mrs. Morgan's students were busy cleaning up and getting ready to go home. It was Christopher's week to carry the trash from the classroom to the big dumpster outside. Quickly he gathered up the scattered pieces of paper that had missed the trash can, tossed them inside, and tied the bag closed. Hefting it over his shoulder, he hurried down the hall to the exit at the far end of the building, and across the corner of the parking lot to the dumpster.

"One, two . . ." Christopher counted out loud as he swung the trash bag with both hands. "THREE!" He gave a mighty heave, and the bag sailed up and over the edge of the huge steel box. Whump! Thunk! The bag hit the side, then rolled to the bottom.

Christopher dashed back into the school, rubbing his hands together against the cold. "Hey, what's that on the floor over there? Did I drop a piece of trash on the way out?" He slowed to a walk. "Looks like some kind of paper," he thought as he squatted down and picked it up. "Money! I bet it's a dollar bill all wrinkled up!"

Christopher straightened the bill across the knee of his jeans, then stared in disbelief. "Twenty dollars! Wow, this is a twenty dollar bill!" He glanced down the hall in both directions, but didn't see anyone. Then he stuck the bill in his pocket, and started slowly back to his classroom.

The last moments of school passed in a blur. Before he knew it, he and his sisters were loaded in the green station wagon and on their way home. Cathy started singing and Kristin joined in. *"I've got the joy, joy, joy, joy, down in my heart, down in my heart, down in my heart . . ."*

Christopher stared out the window. He could almost feel that twenty dollar bill in his pocket. "The money wasn't near the office or the door to a classroom, so it would be really hard to find out who dropped it. If I turned it in, someone might claim it even though it wasn't theirs." Thoughts flashed through Christopher's mind as rapidly as the telephone poles flashing by the car windows. "I sure could use twenty dollars myself. I could get that space shuttle I saw at the mall. It even has doors that open like the real space shuttle does. Or I could get . . ." And he began thinking of all the ways he could spend twenty dollars.

"I have the peace that passes understanding down in my heart, down in my heart, down in my heart. I have the peace that passes understanding down in my heart, down in my heart to stay."

The girls finished the song with a flourish and burst into laughter as three-year-old Cory finished a beat or two behind and a little off key. "It's my money now, anyway." Christopher frowned to himself. "Finders keepers!"

After supper Christopher decided to make a list of all the things he could get with the twenty dollar bill. Then he could look them over and choose the one he wanted the most. He rummaged through the drawers of his desk to find his pad. He looked on the floor under the desk and in his closet. "Mom!" Christopher found his mother in Cory's room putting away laundry. "I can't find my big pad of paper anywhere. Have you seen it?"

Mrs. Wright pushed a wavy lock of hair behind her ear. "No, Son," she smiled. "Have you checked with the girls?"

Christopher turned without answering, and followed the sound of his sisters' voices to their room. "Have you seen my big pad of paper?"

"Nope." Cathy made Madeline's head shake back and forth. Madeline was her two-foot-tall doll with light brown hair and green eyes just like Cathy's.

"Uh-uh." Kristin shrugged and went on combing her doll's hair.

Christopher scowled and went to check in the living room. "Cory! That's my pad of paper!" Christopher snatched it away from his surprised little brother. "Look at this! You used four sheets of my paper without even asking! That's stealing, Cory!"

Cory looked up with large eyes. "I'm sorry, Kisterfer." He picked up one of the brightly-colored drawings and held it up. "I made pikters. This one's yours." Christopher grabbed it and started to leave the living room. "I dinnut know it was your paper, Kisterfer. It was on the floor. I'm really sorry." Cory's sad little voice stopped Christopher in his tracks. He looked at the picture his little brother had made just for him . . . a plane with lopsided wings.

"It's okay, Cory." Christopher turned back with a smile. "Use my paper whenever you want. This is a great picture."

Cory's face lit up. "It's a Cloudrunner, just like yours!" he told Christopher proudly.

Back in his room, Christopher settled down at his desk. The blank pad of paper lay in front of him, but his thoughts were far away. The twenty dollar bill seemed to burn in his pocket. He had yelled, "That's stealing!" at Cory. If it wasn't right for Cory to use the paper he found lying on the floor, was it right for Christopher to use the money he'd found lying on the floor? The answer

Lesson 20 Day 1

seemed pretty clear.

The next morning before school started, Christopher made a quick trip to the school office. "Uh, Mrs. Bentley?" He cleared his throat and held out the twenty dollar bill. "I, uh . . . I found this in the hall . . . yesterday afternoon."

"Thank you, Christopher." Mrs. Bentley's smile made Christopher feel good all over. "It would be easy to steal something like this. I'm glad you chose to be honest instead."

At spelling time, Mrs. Morgan asked if anyone could remember the spelling Scripture for the week — Luke 15:10. When Sarah repeated, "There is joy in the presence of the angels of God when one sinner repents," Christopher grinned. He could imagine the angels celebrating over him, even singing with joy!

And so, when Christopher lugged the trash out to the dumpster at the end of the day, he sang with them.

"*I've got the joy, joy, joy, joy, down in my heart, down in my heart, down in my heart . . .*"

A big two-handed swing sent the trash bag flying over the edge of the dumpster. Whump! Thunk! And Christopher sang even louder. "Down in my heart to stay!"

2 Discussion Time

Check understanding of the story and development of personal values.

- Have you ever found something that didn't belong to you?
- How would you feel if you found a twenty-dollar bill like Christopher did?
- Why wasn't it okay for Christopher to keep the money for himself?
- How would you feel if someone found something of yours and kept it without trying to find out who it belonged to?
- How did Christopher feel after he gave the money to Mrs. Bentley?
- How do you feel when you make something right that you have done wrong?
- Why do you think the angels are happy when we are sorry for doing something wrong?

258

A Preview

Write each word as your teacher says it.

Name _____

1. room
2. noon
3. tooth
4. who
5. use
6. food
7. soon
8. too
9. zoo
10. new

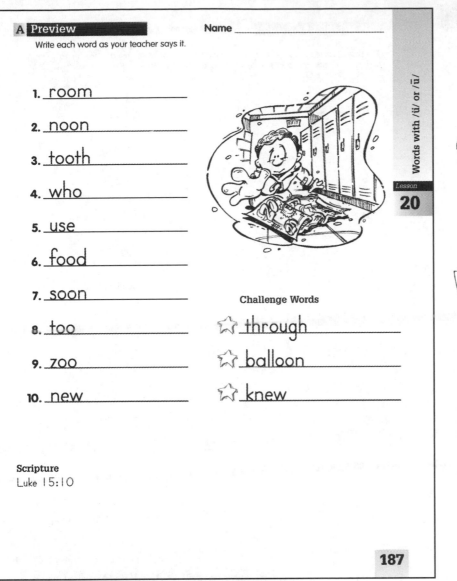

Challenge Words

☆ through
☆ balloon
☆ knew

Scripture
Luke 15:10

187

Challenge

For better spellers, challenge words may be included in the weekly list. Challenge words are starred.

Correct Immediately!

Say Let's correct our preview. I will write each word on the board. Put a dot under each letter on your preview as I spell the word out loud. If you spelled a word wrong, rewrite it correctly.

Progress Chart

Students may record scores. (Reproducible master in Appendix B.)

Take a minute to memorize . . .

Read the memory verse twice. Have students practice it with you two more times.

---

3 Preview

Test for knowledge of the correct spellings of these words. (See the instructions at the top right for challenge words.)

Say I will say the word once, use the word in a sentence, then say the word again. Write the word on the lines in the Worktext.

1. room — There was lots of **room** for trash in the dumpster.
2. noon — The children ate their lunches at **noon.**
3. tooth — Does Cory have a loose **tooth**?
4. who — Christopher didn't know **who** lost the twenty-dollar bill.
5. use — We shouldn't **use** things that don't belong to us without asking.
6. food — What kind of **food** is your favorite?
7. soon — It will **soon** be time to take out the trash.
8. too — When his sisters sang a song, Cory sang, **too.**
9. zoo — I found a quarter when we went to the **zoo.**
10. new — Christopher's pad of paper was almost **new.**
☆ through — Christopher carried the trash **through** the hall.
☆ balloon — Do you know whose blue **balloon** this is?
☆ knew — God **knew** that Christopher planned to keep the twenty dollars.

Lesson 20 | **Day 1**

Help students form a correct image of whole words.

(Say) Look at each word and think about its shape. Now, write the word in the correct word Shape Boxes. You may check off each word as you use it.

(In many words, the sound of /ü/ or /ū/ is spelled with **o**, **oo**, **ew**, **u**, or **ou**.)

(Say) In the word Shape Boxes, color the letters that spell the sound of /ü/ or /ū/ in each word. Circle the word which has the sound of /ū/.

⭐ **Challenge**
Draw the correctly shaped box around each letter in these words.

(Say) On a separate sheet of paper, write other words that contain the spelling patterns in the word list. See how many words you can write.

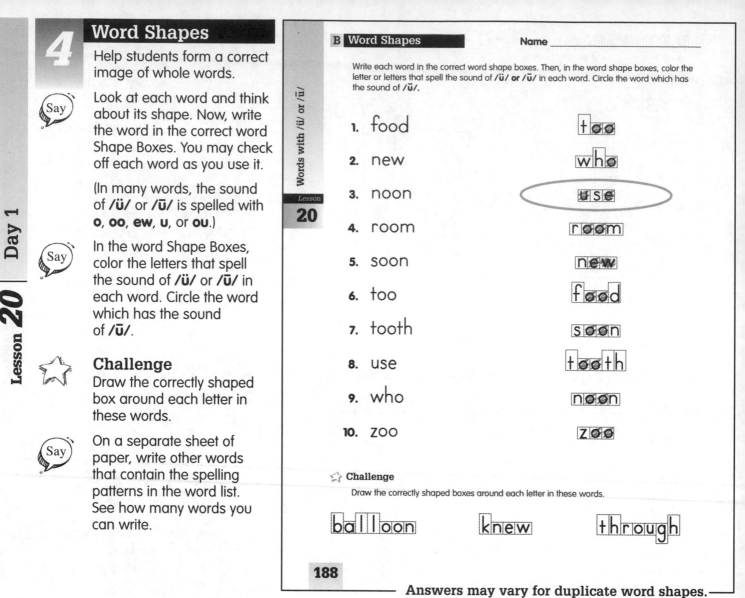

B Word Shapes   Name _____

Write each word in the correct word shape boxes. Then, in the word shape boxes, color the letter or letters that spell the sound of /ü/ or /ū/ in each word. Circle the word which has the sound of /ū/.

Words with /ü/ or /ū/ — Lesson 20

1. food   too
2. new   who
3. noon   use
4. room   room
5. soon   new
6. too   food
7. tooth   soon
8. use   tooth
9. who   noon
10. zoo   zoo

☆ **Challenge**
Draw the correctly shaped boxes around each letter in these words.

balloon   knew   through

188

Answers may vary for duplicate word shapes.

Be Prepared For Fun

Check these supply lists for **Fun Ways to Spell** presented **Day 2**. Purchase and/or gather these items ahead of time!

General
• Eraser
• Dark Construction Paper
• Spelling List

Auditory
• Spelling List

Visual
• Poster Paint
• Paint Brush
• Art Paper (3 or 4 sheets per child)
• Spelling List

Tactile
• Damp Sand in plastic storage box with lid
• Spelling List

260

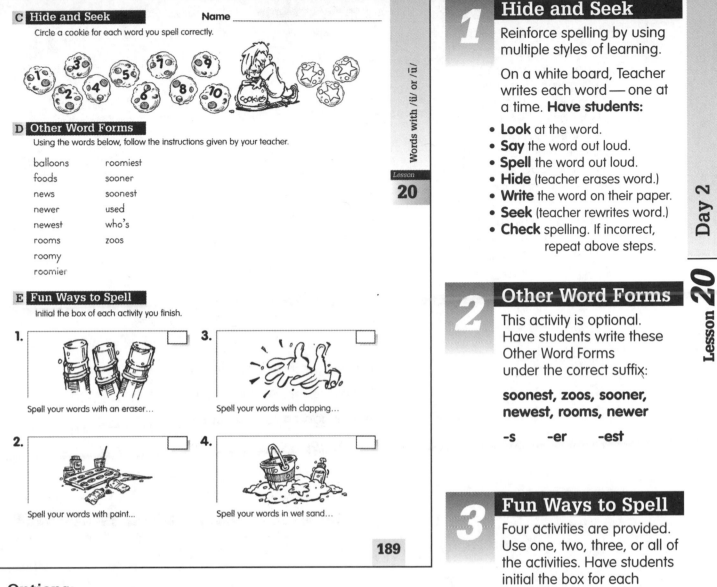

C Hide and Seek

Name _____

Circle a cookie for each word you spell correctly.

D Other Word Forms

Using the words below, follow the instructions given by your teacher.

balloons   roomiest
foods   sooner
news   soonest
newer   used
newest   who's
rooms   zoos
roomy
roomier

E Fun Ways to Spell

Initial the box of each activity you finish.

1. ☐ Spell your words with an eraser...

3. ☐ Spell your words with clapping...

2. ☐ Spell your words with paint...

4. ☐ Spell your words in wet sand...

189

Hide and Seek

1

Reinforce spelling by using multiple styles of learning.

On a white board, Teacher writes each word — one at a time. **Have students:**

- **Look** at the word.
- **Say** the word out loud.
- **Spell** the word out loud.
- **Hide** (teacher erases word.)
- **Write** the word on their paper.
- **Seek** (teacher rewrites word.)
- **Check** spelling. If incorrect, repeat above steps.

Day 2

Lesson 20

Other Word Forms

2

This activity is optional. Have students write these Other Word Forms under the correct suffix:

soonest, zoos, sooner, newest, rooms, newer

-s   -er   -est

Fun Ways to Spell

3

Four activities are provided. Use one, two, three, or all of the activities. Have students initial the box for each activity they complete.

Options:

- assign activities to students according to their learning styles
- set up the activities in learning centers for students to do throughout the day
- divide students into four groups and assign one activity per group
- do one activity per day

General

To spell your words with an eraser . . .
- Turn your pencil upside down.
- Use the eraser to write your spelling words on a sheet of dark construction paper.
- Check your spelling.

Auditory

To spell your words with clapping . . .
- Look at a word on your spelling list.
- Close your eyes.
- Clap your hands softly while you whisper the spelling of the word.
- Open your eyes and check your spelling.

Visual

To spell your words with paint . . .
- Dip your brush in one color of poster paint.
- Paint a spelling word on your paper.
- Rinse your brush well in clean water and wipe it dry on a paper towel before dipping it in another color to paint another word.

Tactile

To spell your words in damp sand . . .
- Use finger to write a spelling word in damp sand.
- Check your spelling.
- Smooth the sand with your fingers and write another word.

1 Clues

Familiarize students with word meaning and usage.

Ask the students to raise their hands if they enjoy solving riddles. Explain how riddles have clues that help you find the answer. (Example: What is black and white and "read" all over? Answer: A newspaper.)

Say Read each clue below. Find the spelling word that fits the clue. Write the word in the blank.

F Clues

Use the clues to write the spelling words.

Name _____

Words with /ü/ or /ū/

Lesson 20

1. Place animals live: ___zoo___
2. Something to eat: ___food___
3. Middle of the day: ___noon___
4. ___Who___ lost twenty dollars?
5. Not a long time: ___soon___
6. I have a ___new___ pad of paper.
7. You may not ___use___ my pad of paper!
8. He stared out the window of his ___room___.
9. Your front one may have fallen out: ___tooth___
10. You can choose to repent, ___too___.
☆ Christopher ___knew___ he should not yell at Cori.
☆ Something you can pop: ___balloon___
☆ Christopher was ___through___ with his job at school.

Word Bank						
food	noon	soon	tooth	who	☆ balloon	☆ through
new	room	too	use	zoo	☆ knew	

190

Take a minute to memorize . . .

Read the memory verse twice. Have students practice it with you two more times.

262

G Dictation
Listen and write the missing words.

Name _____

1. There is room for the food in here.

2. Our family will go to the zoo at noon.

3. Who can use the new camera?

4. Did you lose a tooth, too?

H Proofreading
One word in each set is misspelled. Fill in the oval by the misspelled word.

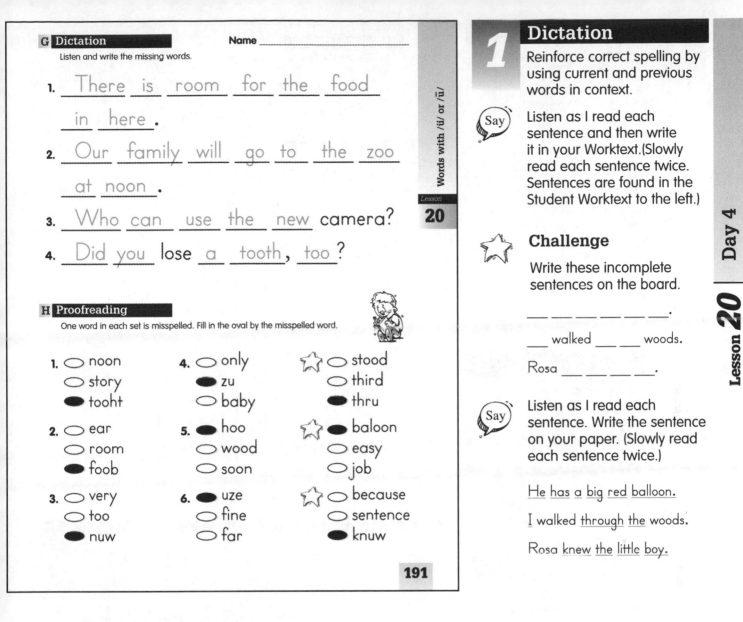

1. ○ noon
   ○ story
   ● tooht

2. ○ ear
   ○ room
   ● foob

3. ○ very
   ○ too
   ● nuw

4. ○ only
   ● zu
   ○ baby

5. ● hoo
   ○ wood
   ○ soon

6. ● uze
   ○ fine
   ○ far

☆ ● stood
   ○ third
   ● thru

☆ ● baloon
   ○ easy
   ○ job

☆ ○ because
   ○ sentence
   ● knuw

191

Dictation

1

Reinforce correct spelling by using current and previous words in context.

Say
Listen as I read each sentence and then write it in your Worktext.(Slowly read each sentence twice. Sentences are found in the Student Worktext to the left.)

☆ Challenge

Write these incomplete sentences on the board.

__ __ __ __ __ __.

__ walked __ __ woods.

Rosa __ __ __ __.

Say
Listen as I read each sentence. Write the sentence on your paper. (Slowly read each sentence twice.)

He has a big red balloon.

I walked through the woods.

Rosa knew the little boy.

Proofreading

2

Familiarize students with standardized test format and reinforce recognizing misspelled words.

Say
Look at each set of words. One word in each set is misspelled. Fill in the oval by the misspelled word. (You may wish to pronounce each set of words to help students correctly identify them.)

3 Hide and Seek

Reinforce correct spelling of current spelling words. (A reproducible master is provided in Appendix A as shown on the inset page to the right.)

Write the words one at a time on a white board.

Have students:

- **Look** at the word.
- **Say** the word out loud.
- **Spell** the word out loud.
- **Hide** (teacher erases word.)
- **Write** the word on paper.
- **Seek** (teacher rewrites word.)
- **Check** spelling. If incorrect, rewrite word correctly.

4 Secret Words

Have your students complete this activity to strengthen spelling ability and expand vocabulary.

1 Posttest

Test mastery of the spelling words. Challenge words are starred.

(Say) I will say the word once, use the word in a sentence, then say the word again. Write the word on your paper.

1. noon — We will clean up our classroom at **noon**.
2. use — He had to **use** both hands to throw the trash into the dumpster.
3. new — This dollar bill is crisp and **new**.
4. who — The list shows **who** will take out the trash this week.
5. zoo — The trash cans at the **zoo** have pictures of monkeys on them.
6. tooth — You visit the dentist if you have a sore **tooth**.
7. too — Make sure you pick up the trash off the floor, **too**.
8. soon — We will **soon** finish cleaning up the classroom.
9. room — The **room** looks very nice now.
10. food — Eating good **food** helps your body grow strong and healthy.
☆ knew — Christopher **knew** the twenty–dollar bill wasn't really his.
☆ balloon — The bright red **balloon** rose slowly into the air.
☆ through — Christopher looked **through** the house for his pad.

Progress Chart

Students may record scores. (Reproducible master in Appendix B.)

Personal Dictionary

Students may add any words they have misspelled to their personal dictionaries for reference when writing. (Cover in Appendix B.)

Appendix A — Lesson 20

Hide and Seek

Check a paper for each word you spell correctly.

1 3 5 7 9
2 4 6 8 10

Secret Words

Use these clues to write the words that fit in the blanks. Then use the boxed letters to discover the secret words.

1. We have these in our house
2. The newspaper reports this
3. The letter after o
4. Is not new
5. Is opposite of later
6. My two front ones are missing from my mouth
7. People visit animals in them

1. r o o m s
2. n e w s
3. p
4. u s e d
5. s o o n e r
6. t e e t h
7. z o o s

There is joy when one sinner r e p e n t s!

Word Bank

news	sooner	used
rooms	teeth	zoos

384

I | Game

Name _____

Christopher wants to return the money he found. Lead the way to the school office by moving one space each time you or your team spells a word correctly from this week's word list.

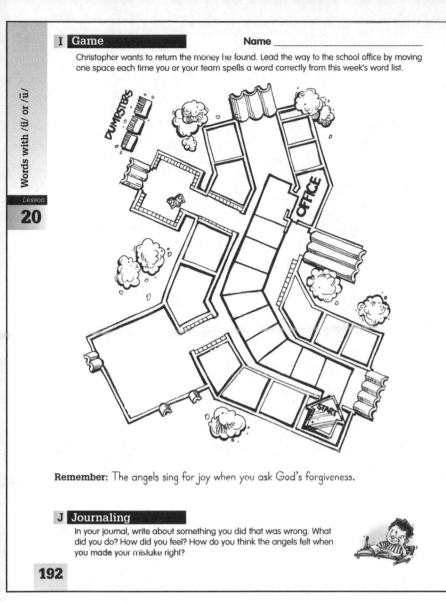

Remember: The angels sing for joy when you ask God's forgiveness.

J | Journaling

In your journal, write about something you did that was wrong. What did you do? How did you feel? How do you think the angels felt when you made your mistake right?

192

How to Play:

- Divide students into two teams, and decide which team will go first.
- Have each student place their game piece on Start.
- Have a student from team A go to the board.
- Read the spelling word two times slowly and clearly. (You may also wish to use the word in a sentence. Ex.: "cat — The cat climbed a tree. — cat")
- Have the student write the word on the board.
- If the word is spelled correctly, instruct all the members of team A to move their game piece forward one space on the game board. (Note: If the word is misspelled, correct the spelling immediately.)
- Alternate between teams A and B as you go down the word list.
- The team to reach the school office first is the winner.

Non-Competitive Option: At the end of the game, say: "Class, I am proud of your efforts to spell the words correctly. If you had fun and tried your best, you are all winners!"

2 | Game

Reinforce spelling skills and provide motivation and interest.

Materials

- game page (from student text)
- flat buttons, dry beans, pennies, or game discs (1 per child)
- game word list

Game Word List

Use of challenge words is optional.

1. **food**
2. **room**
3. **soon**
4. **noon**
5. **too**
6. **tooth**
7. **zoo**
8. **who**
9. **new**
10. **use**
☆ **balloon**
☆ **through**
☆ **knew**

3 | Journaling

Provide a meaningful reason for correct spelling through personal writing.

Review the story using discussion leads provided on the following page. Encourage students to apply the Scriptural value in their journaling.

 Take a minute to memorize . . .

Have students say the memory verses from lessons 19 and 20 with you.

265

3 Journaling

Provide a meaningful reason for correct spelling through personal writing.

(Say)

- Finding something, especially money, is exciting! But Christopher didn't feel so good inside when he decided to keep the money he found instead of trying to find out who it belonged to.

- What happened to Christopher that helped him understand that it wasn't right to use the money he'd found without trying to find it's owner? (Cory found Christopher's pad of paper and used several sheets of it without asking Christopher if he could.)

- Who was happy when Christopher gave the money to Mrs. Bentley? (God, the angels, and Christopher!)

- Think about a time when you were sorry for something you did wrong. Write sentences in your journal to answer the questions in your Worktext.

Children learn more about writing every time they write independently.

Ears That Hear

Matthew and Alex find out that not following directions can lead to all kinds of trouble.

"Where's my uniform, Mom?" Matthew called from his room. "Didn't you wash it?"

"Not if you didn't put it in the dirty clothes hamper like I asked you to," Mom said as she climbed the stairs. "I don't remember seeing it. I guess you'll just have to wear it dirty."

"But it is all wrinkled and we have a scrimmage game tonight."

"I love for you to look nice, Matthew, but even if I wanted to there's not enough time for me to wash and dry that uniform before the game. Now get your stuff together. We need to leave or we'll be late."

"Don't forget your bats, boys," Mom said a few minutes later as she snapped the buckle on Emily's car seat. "And it would be a good idea to bring your jackets, too. The evenings are still cool." Matthew and Alex groaned, but turned around and headed back into the house.

"I need to grab your jacket, too, little Lady." Mom touched the tip of Emily's nose with her finger and smiled at the curly-headed three-year-old. "Here, hold this soft ball. I'll be right back."

"What's the name of your team again, Alex?" Matthew climbed up into the Suburban and tossed his new glove onto the back seat.

"The Cardinals!" Alex proudly adjusted his new red baseball cap.

"So when do you red birds practice next?"

"I think . . . Tuesday. When's my practice, Mom?"

"Not until Wednesday, Champ." Mom started the car, then checked to make sure both boys were buckled in before pulling out of the driveway.

"My team has practice tonight and Wednesday. How can we both practice on Wednesday, Mom?" Matthew picked the practice schedule off the floor of the Suburban where he'd left it the night before. "My practice is at 6:30. When does Alex's start?"

"I'm not sure, Matthew, but if they're at the same time Dad can go with one of you." Mom turned the corner and headed toward the baseball fields in Mason Springs Park.

"May I go to the batting cages while Matthew is in practice?" Alex pleaded.

"You don't need practice being pitched to, Alex," Mom answered. "You're in T-Ball this year, remember?"

"I know but I like to practice hitting the ball without the Tee."

"We'll see, Alex. I don't know if I brought any cash with me." Mom pulled up in front of the baseball diamonds and stopped. "Okay, Matthew, here we are. See your team?" Matthew nodded. "Jump out, and run so your team won't have to wait!" Mom watched as Matthew ran slowly and a little clumsily across the field toward the group of boys around Coach Morgan. "Just do your best, Matthew," Mom called. She noticed the droop of his shoulders as he slipped quietly in behind everyone else. She parked the Suburban then walked around to unbuckle Emily from her car seat.

"Get your bat, Alex. I found a dollar in my purse, so I guess you can practice with the pitching machine in the batting cages for a while."

"I wanna bat!" Emily threw the ball on the floor.

Alex picked up the ball and handed it back to his little sister. "No, you're too small. You have to hit the ball off your little blue Tee at home, Em." Alex reached under the seat to get his bat. "Oh no, I forgot my bat! And they don't have one here little enough for me. Can we go back home and get it, Mom?"

"Didn't you go back in the house to get it before we left?" Mom asked.

"I got my jacket, but I forgot my bat." Alex checked under the seat again. "It wasn't in my closet. I think maybe it's in the garage. I grabbed my jacket off the hook, then forgot all about my bat. Can't we go get it? It isn't far. Please?"

"I'd like to take you home to get your bat, Alex, but I can't leave Matthew here alone." Mother's forehead wrinkled. "He doesn't know anyone on his team yet, and Emily won't like getting back into her car seat." Mom knelt down in front of Alex so she could see his eyes. "And you need to learn a lesson about listening. Maybe this will help you remember to listen next time Mommy asks you to do something." She gave Alex a pat on the back. "Come on, let's go watch Matthew practice."

"Can't I just use one of the bats here?" Alex pleaded again.

"No, I'm afraid not. It wouldn't be good practice for you if their bat is too heavy and you can't make a level swing."

Alex shut the door of the Suburban and walked over behind the backstop. He tossed his ball up in the air and caught it. Then he tossed it up again. And again. And again. "I can't believe I left my bat at home in the garage," he thought, throwing the ball up into the air again.

Matthew ran up to where Emily and Mom were rolling the ball back and forth on the sidewalk. "Mom, where's my jacket? It's getting cold."

"Wherever you put it, Matthew." Mom rolled the ball back to Emily and stood up. "Is it still in the Suburban?"

"I guess so," shrugged Matthew.

"Go back to practice and I'll get it for you." Mom jogged over to the Suburban and looked in the front seat, then the back seat, then under the seats. There was no jacket to be seen. She walked over to the backstop. "It's not there, Matthew. Is it in the dugout?" They turned at the same time to stare at the empty bench in the dugout.

"I must have left it on the floor when I picked up my bat. I'm cold. Can't we go home now?"

"No, son. You're part of a team, and if you don't learn to work together you won't play well this season. I reminded you to get a jacket. You need to listen when I tell you to do things. Maybe this will help you remember next time." Matthew turned on his heel and trudged slowly back to right field.

"Okay kids! Let's go get some tacos for supper," Mom suggested as they all climbed back into the Suburban. "Dad has a long meeting tonight and won't be home for dinner."

"Yea!" Matthew and Alex yelled together.

Matthew put his glove under his seat, and bucked up. "I want a burrito."

"I want a Kid's Meal!" Alex called from the back of the Suburban.

"Kid Meal! Kid Meal!" chimed Emily from her car seat.

Later that evening Mom sat on Matthew's bed and watched the boys finish straightening their room.

Alex set his ball on the shelf beside Matthew's stuff. "Hey, where's my glove, Mom?"

"I don't know, Champ. You had it at Matthew's practice because I remember you playing catch with yourself behind the backstop." Mom raised an eyebrow. "You didn't take it into the taco place did you?"

Alex hung his head and looked back at the shelf where his glove went. "I probably left it on the chair after I showed Luke. He hadn't seen it yet."

Alex's lower lip began to quiver. "Now I'll probably never see it again!"

Mom got up off the bed and went over to Alex. "I'll go call the taco place. They may have it. You did ask Dad to put your name in it didn't you?"

"I can't remember." Alex began to cry.

Mom returned to the boys' room a few minutes later, and sat back down on the bed. "Come here, guys." She patted the bed beside her. "While I was making that phone call, I read the handwriting border sheet you brought home this week. It's on the bulletin board in the kitchen. Do you remember the Scripture verse you wrote, Matthew?"

"It was something about if you have ears listen! And be sure to do what you hear!"

"That's pretty close. While I was waiting for the people at the taco place to check for your glove, I started thinking about everything that happened today." Mom gave Alex's knee a squeeze. "You forgot your bat after I told you to go get it. And Matthew," Mom reached out and pulled one of Matthew's curls out straight. "You, young man, wore a dirty uniform because you forgot to put it in the hamper after your last practice, and you froze because you forgot and left your jacket at home."

Mom turned to look at Alex again. "And Alex, you didn't ask Dad to write your name in your glove like I suggested, and you took it into the taco place to show Luke after I warned you about how easy it would be to leave it there." Mom paused. "I think you both need to understand that listening means more than hearing what someone tells you. It also includes doing what you hear. That's what your text this week is all about, Matthew."

"Mom," Alex said quietly. "Did they find my glove?"

"Yes, they found it." Mom smiled. "And we can go back to the taco place and get it tomorrow."

"Can I get a Kid's Meal?" Emily called from her bed in the next room.

"I don't think so," Mom laughed.

"Go to sleep, Em." Mom put an arm around each boy and gave them a squeeze. "I can't believe she's still awake! She sure has ears that are listening well." Mom smiled and picked up her Bible.

"And if she's learned to do what she hears," Matthew grinned, "she'll go right to sleep."

Discussion Time

Check understanding of the story and development of personal values.

- Raise your hand if you think Alex remembered his bat the next time Mom reminded him?
- Will Matthew put his uniform in the dirty clothes hamper? Why? What about remembering to take a jacket to T-Ball practice?
- Do you think Mom was trying to make her kids miserable by telling them to do so many things? Why or why not?
- When was the last time you didn't listen to what someone in charge suggested?
- What kinds of problems did it cause?
- Why is it important to do what you hear?

Write each word as your teacher says it.

1. house
2. south
3. cow
4. bow
5. around
6. round
7. sound
8. found
9. vowel
10. count

Challenge Words

 cloud

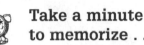 crown

 flower

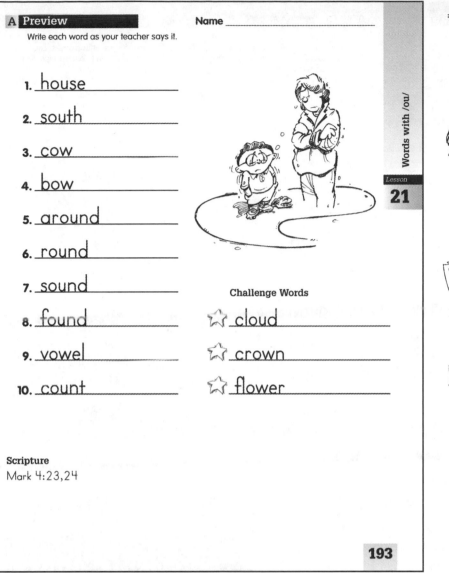

Scripture
Mark 4:23,24

193

Challenge

For better spellers, challenge words may be included in the weekly list. Challenge words are starred.

Correct Immediately!

Say Let's correct our preview. I will write each word on the board. Put a dot under each letter on your preview as I spell the word out loud. If you spelled a word wrong, rewrite it correctly.

Progress Chart

Students may record scores. (Reproducible master in Appendix B.)

Take a minute to memorize . . .

Read the memory verse twice. Have students practice it with you two more times.

3 Preview

Test for knowledge of the correct spellings of these words. (See the instructions at the top right for challenge words.)

Say I will say the word once, use the word in a sentence, then say the word again. Write the word on the lines in the Worktext.

1. **house**   Mom told them to get some things before they left the **house.**
2. **south**   Mom drove **south** to Mason Springs Park.
3. **cow**   A **cow** cannot play T-Ball.
4. **bow**   Take a **bow** after that fine catch.
5. **around**   Matthew joined the group of boys **around** Coach Morgan.
6. **round**   The softball is **round.**
7. **sound**   If you have ears, listen to the **sound** of God's voice.
8. **found**   They **found** Alex's glove at the taco place.
9. **vowel**   The **vowel** "o" with "w" makes the /ou/ sound in the word "cow."
10. **count**   Now **count** the number of words you got right.
   ☆ **cloud**   It was cold when the huge **cloud** covered the sun.
   ☆ **crown**   When you go to heaven, you will wear a **crown.**
   ☆ **flower**   The **flower** seeds have not sprouted in Mason Springs Park.

269

4 Word Shapes

Help students form a correct image of whole words.

(Say) Look at each word and think about its shape. Now, write the word in the correct word Shape Boxes. You may check off each word as you use it.

(In many words, the sound of **/ou/** is spelled with **ou** or **ow**. A diphthong is two vowel sounds that are sounded together in the same syllable.)

(Say) In the word Shape Boxes, color the letters that spell **/ou/** in each word. Circle the words in which **/ou/** is spelled with **ow**.

⭐ Challenge

Draw the correctly shaped box around each letter in these words.

(Say) On a separate sheet of paper, write other words that contain the spelling patterns in the word list. See how many words you can write.

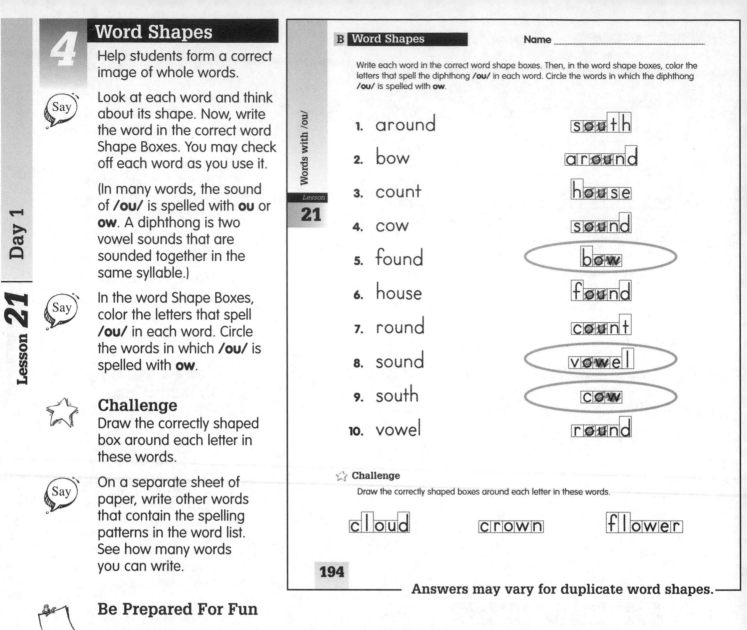

B Word Shapes

Name _____

Write each word in the correct word shape boxes. Then, in the word shape boxes, color the letters that spell the diphthong **/ou/** in each word. Circle the words in which the diphthong **/ou/** is spelled with **ow**.

1. around — south
2. bow — around
3. count — house
4. cow — sound
5. found — bow
6. house — found
7. round — count
8. sound — vowel
9. south — cow
10. vowel — round

☆ **Challenge**

Draw the correctly shaped boxes around each letter in these words.

cloud   crown   flower

194

Answers may vary for duplicate word shapes.

Be Prepared For Fun

Check these supply lists for **Fun Ways to Spell** presented **Day 2**. Purchase and/or gather these items ahead of time!

General
- 3 x 5 Cards (10 per child)
- 3 x 5 Cards (3 more to spell challenge words)
- Scissors
- Spelling List

Auditory
- A Classmate
- Spelling List

Visual
- Strips of paper 2 x 11 inches (10 per student)
- Strips of paper 2 x 11 inches (3 more to spell challenge words)
- Crayons or Markers
- Tape
- Spelling List

Tactile
- Split Peas
- Glue
- Construction Paper
- Spelling List

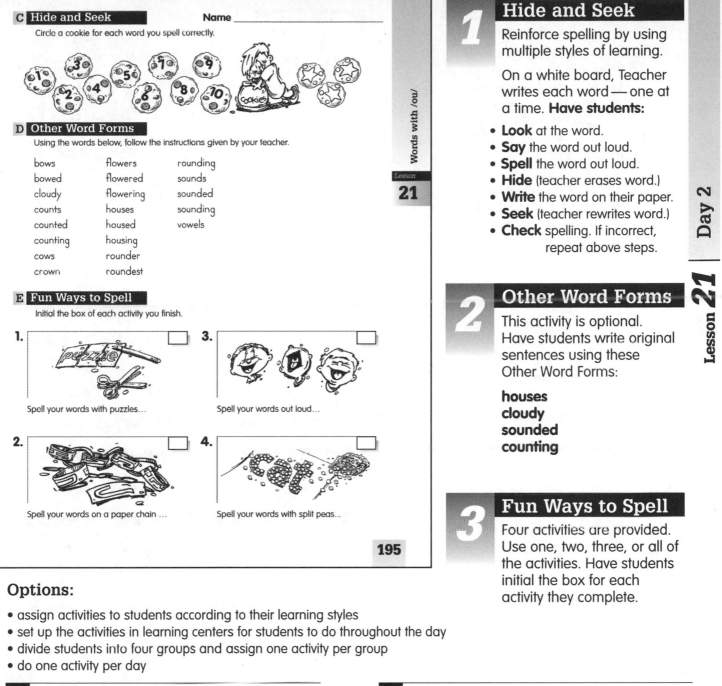

C Hide and Seek

Name _____

Circle a cookie for each word you spell correctly.

D Other Word Forms

Using the words below, follow the instructions given by your teacher.

bows	flowers	rounding
bowed	flowered	sounds
cloudy	flowering	sounded
counts	houses	sounding
counted	housed	vowels
counting	housing	
cows	rounder	
crown	roundest	

E Fun Ways to Spell

Initial the box of each activity you finish.

1. ☐ Spell your words with puzzles...

2. ☐ Spell your words on a paper chain...

3. ☐ Spell your words out loud...

4. ☐ Spell your words with split peas...

Words with /ou/

Lesson **21**

Day 2

Lesson **21**

1 **Hide and Seek**

Reinforce spelling by using multiple styles of learning.

On a white board, Teacher writes each word — one at a time. **Have students:**

- **Look** at the word.
- **Say** the word out loud.
- **Spell** the word out loud.
- **Hide** (teacher erases word.)
- **Write** the word on their paper.
- **Seek** (teacher rewrites word.)
- **Check** spelling. If incorrect, repeat above steps.

2 **Other Word Forms**

This activity is optional. Have students write original sentences using these Other Word Forms:

houses
cloudy
sounded
counting

3 **Fun Ways to Spell**

Four activities are provided. Use one, two, three, or all of the activities. Have students initial the box for each activity they complete.

Options:

- assign activities to students according to their learning styles
- set up the activities in learning centers for students to do throughout the day
- divide students into four groups and assign one activity per group
- do one activity per day

General

To spell your words with puzzles . . .
- Write each spelling word on a card.
- Cut each card in half using a straight cut.
- Mix your puzzle pieces.
- Put the puzzles together.
- Check your spelling.

Auditory

To spell your words out loud . . .
- Have a classmate read a spelling word.
- Say a sentence with that spelling word to a classmate.
- Spell the spelling word you used in that sentence to a classmate.
- Ask a classmate to check your spelling.
- Do this with each word on your word list.

Visual

To spell your words on a paper chain . . .
- Write each spelling word on a strip of paper in big, tall letters.
- Tape the ends of one strip together to make a circle.
- Loop the next strip through the first and then tape the ends of that strip together.
- Continue in this way to form a paper chain.

Tactile

To spell your words with split peas . . .
- Choose a word from your spelling list.
- It may be a favorite word or a word you have trouble remembering how to spell.
- Write the word in tall, wide letters on a sheet of construction paper.
- Spread glue along the outline of each letter and press split peas into the glue.

1 Words In Sentences

Familiarize students with word meaning and usage. Write this incomplete sentence on the board: **The five _____ in the alphabet are a, e, i, o u.** Have a volunteer complete the sentence.

Say

Choose the spelling word that best completes each sentence, and write it in the blank.

F Words In Sentences

Words with /ou/

Lesson

21

Write the spelling word to complete each sentence.

Name _____

1. The softball is __round__.
2. It is warmer in the __south__.
3. We learned what the __vowel__ "o" says with "w."
4. There was a pleading __sound__ in Matthew's voice.
5. Alex __found__ his glove at the taco place.
6. Go back in the __house__ and get your jacket.
7. Don't __count__ on winning every T-Ball game.
8. The boys stood __around__ their coach.
9. The __cow__ stood in the field and ate grass.
10. Take a __bow__ after that fine catch.
☆ The __cloud__ covered the sun.
☆ You will have stars in your __crown__.
☆ One __flower__ was blooming in the garden.

Word Bank						
around	count	found	round	south	☆ cloud	☆ flower
bow	cow	house	sound	vowel	☆ crown	

196

Take a minute to memorize . . .

Read the memory verse twice. Have students practice it with you two more times.

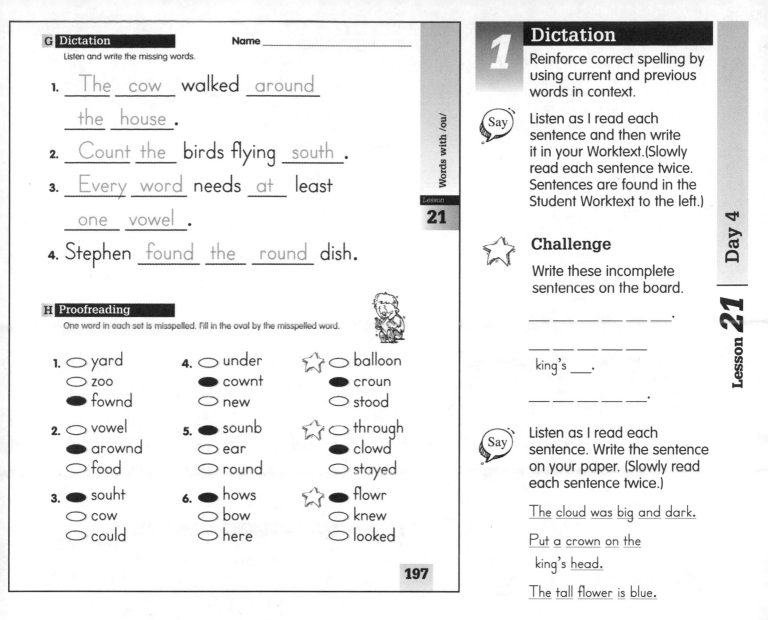

G Dictation

Name _____

Listen and write the missing words.

1. The cow walked around the house .

2. Count the birds flying south .

3. Every word needs at least one vowel .

4. Stephen found the round dish.

H Proofreading

One word in each set is misspelled. Fill in the oval by the misspelled word.

1. ○ yard
   ○ zoo
   ● fownd

2. ○ vowel
   ● arownd
   ○ food

3. ● souht
   ○ cow
   ○ could

4. ○ under
   ● cownt
   ○ new

5. ● sounb
   ○ ear
   ○ round

6. ● hows
   ○ bow
   ○ here

☆ ○ balloon
   ● croun
   ○ stood

☆ ○ through
   ● clowd
   ○ stayed

☆ ● flowr
   ○ knew
   ○ looked

197

1 Dictation

Reinforce correct spelling by using current and previous words in context.

(Say) Listen as I read each sentence and then write it in your Worktext.(Slowly read each sentence twice. Sentences are found in the Student Worktext to the left.)

☆ **Challenge**

Write these incomplete sentences on the board.

___ ___ ___ ___ ___ .

___ ___ ___ ___ ___

  king's ___ .

___ ___ ___ ___ ___ .

(Say) Listen as I read each sentence. Write the sentence on your paper. (Slowly read each sentence twice.)

The cloud was big and dark.

Put a crown on the king's head.

The tall flower is blue.

Lesson 21   **Day 4**

2 Proofreading

Familiarize students with standardized test format and reinforce recognizing misspelled words.

(Say) Look at each set of words. One word in each set is misspelled. Fill in the oval by the misspelled word. (You may wish to pronounce each set of words to help students correctly identify them.)

3 Hide and Seek

Reinforce correct spelling of current spelling words. (A reproducible master is provided in Appendix A as shown on the inset page to the right.)

Write the words one at a time on a white board.

Have students:

- **Look** at the word.
- **Say** the word out loud.
- **Spell** the word out loud.
- **Hide** (teacher erases word.)
- **Write** the word on paper.
- **Seek** (teacher rewrites word.)
- **Check** spelling. If incorrect, rewrite word correctly.

4 Word Sort Suffixes

Have your students complete this activity to strengthen spelling ability and expand vocabulary.

1 Posttest

Test mastery of the spelling words. Challenge words are starred.

(Say) I will say the word once, use the word in a sentence, then say the word again. Write the word on your paper.

1.	count	Can you **count** the kids in the Schilling family?
2.	house	Mom asked them to go back in the **house** and get their jackets.
3.	around	Matthew turned **around** and headed back into the house.
4.	round	Emily held the **round** ball tightly in her hands.
5.	sound	Mom didn't give in to the pleading **sound** in Alex's voice.
6.	found	Matthew **found** his jacket on the floor where he had left it.
7.	south	It is warmer in the **south**.
8.	bow	You should **bow** to your mother's wishes.
9.	cow	The **cow** was eating grass on the baseball diamond.
10.	vowel	Put the **vowel** "o" with "u" or "w" in this week's words.
☆	cloud	The **cloud** cover made the day seem dreary.
☆	crown	You will have stars in your **crown**.
☆	flower	One **flower** was poking up in the garden.

Progress Chart
Students may record scores. (Reproducible master in Appendix B.)

Personal Dictionary
Students may add any words they have misspelled to their personal dictionaries for reference when writing. (Cover in Appendix B.)

Inset page (Appendix A — Lesson 21)

Hide and Seek
Check a paper for each word you spell correctly.

1 3 5 7 9
2 4 6 8 10

Word Sort Suffixes
Write the spelling words with **ow**.
Write the spelling words with **ou**.

ow	ou	
1. cow	1. count	6. house
2. bow	2. around	7. south
3. vowel	3. found	8. cloud
4. crown	4. round	
5. flower	5. sound	

Add **s**, **ed**, or **ing** to make new words from your spelling words.

		+ s	+ ed	+ ing
1.	count	counts	counted	counting
2.	bow	bows	bowed	bowing
3.	round	rounds	rounded	rounding
4.	sound	sounds	sounded	sounding

Word Bank

around	cloud	cow	flower	house	sound	vowel
bow	count	crown	found	round	south	

385

I Game

Name _____

Matthew and Alex each forgot something. Run home to find what they left behind. Color one space each time you or your team spells a word correctly from this week's word list.

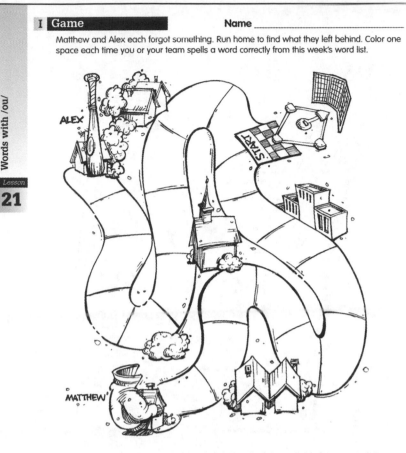

ALEX

START

MATTHEW

Remember: Listen carefully to what you are told to do and then do it carefully.

J Journaling

Design a sign in your journal telling kids to listen and do what they are told.

198

How to Play:

- Divide students into two teams, and decide which team will go first. Have one team run home for Matthew and one team for Alex. (Optional: If you have an even number of students, you may wish to pair students from opposing teams and have them share a game page, each coloring the spaces for their own team on that page.)
- Have a student from team A go to the board.
- Read the spelling word two times slowly and clearly. (You may also wish to use the word in a sentence. Ex.: "cat — The cat climbed a tree. — cat")
- Have the student write the word on the board.
- If the word is spelled correctly, instruct all the members of team A to color one space, beginning at Start, on the game board. (Note: If the word is misspelled, correct the spelling immediately.)
- Alternate between teams A and B as you go down the word list.
- The team to reach home first is the winner.

Non-Competitive Option: At the end of the game, say: "Class, I am proud of your efforts to spell the words correctly. If you had fun and tried your best, you are all winners!"

Game

Reinforce spelling skills and provide motivation and interest.

Materials

- game page (from student text)
- crayons or colored pencils (1 per child)
- game word list

Game Word List

Use of challenge words is optional.

1. **count**
2. **cow**
3. **bow**
4. **around**
5. **found**
6. **round**
7. **sound**
8. **house**
9. **south**
10. **vowel**
☆ **cloud**
☆ **crown**
☆ **flower**

3 Journaling

Provide a meaningful reason for correct spelling through personal writing.

Review the story using discussion leads provided on the following page. Encourage students to apply the Scriptural value in their journaling.

  Take a minute to memorize . . .

Have students say the memory verses from lessons 19, 20, and 21 with you.

3 Journaling

Provide a meaningful reason for correct spelling through personal writing.

(Say)

- In our story this week, what did Matthew and Alex keep forgetting to do? (They didn't listen carefully and do what Mom asked them to.)

- What happened when Matthew and Alex didn't listen? (Matthew wore a dirty uniform because he hadn't put it in the dirty clothes to be washed. Alex didn't get to go to the batting cage because he forgot his bat. Matthew was cold because he didn't bring his jacket to practice. Alex left his glove at the taco place.)

- Create a sign in your journal to help kids remember to listen carefully!

Quotables!

"Children grow into competent writers, not when they are taught to copy someone else's writing, but when they are encouraged to write their own ideas in their own known ways."*

*Hoffman, Stevie and Nancy Knipping. 1988. Spelling Revisited: The Child's Way. Childhood Education, June: 284-287.

An Answered Prayer

When faced with a difficult choice, Christopher learns there is a source of help and wisdom even when no one else is around.

Christopher flopped on the living room couch like a rag doll. It was raining again! What was there to do on a rainy day with no school? His eyes wandered around the room, barely noticing the way the lamps glowed warmly in contrast to the dark, dreary day outside.

Leaning over, he swung his arm off the couch, and bumped a magazine off the coffee table. As he leaned over to pick it up, he spotted a row of photo albums neatly stacked on the shelf underneath. He sat up with his legs crossed Indian-style, and pulled one of the albums into his lap.

"Hey, that's me!" There in the photo was a much younger Christopher sitting in a high chair, with chocolate icing smeared across his face. He was poking his finger into a birthday cake with a single large candle on top. There was also a picture showing one-year-old Kristin staring intently at one candle on the cake in front of her. "That must have been our first birthday!" Christopher thought. Across the page was a picture of Gramps holding both twins. Gramps was laughing as Christopher reached up a baby hand to grab his chin. Kristin was nestled in Gramps' other arm, staring straight at the camera. Fascinated, Christopher turned one page . . . then another . . . then another.

"Well, Son, I wondered where you were." Mom sank down onto the couch beside him. "Your sisters and Cory have been underfoot all afternoon but I haven't heard a word from you!" Mrs. Wright reached over and tousled Christopher's brown hair.

"Who's this, Mom?" Christopher tilted the photo album and pointed at one of the pictures.

"Why, that's my cousin, Judy." Mom scooted closer and leaned in to see the picture better. "You probably don't remember her very well, but she came to visit us just after Cory was born. She was my very best friend when I was a little girl." Mom smiled remembering the good times they'd had. "And that's Cory when he was just born." Mrs. Wright pointed out another photo. "He was a much bigger baby than you twins and Cathy were. And look at this picture . . ."

"I remember this trip!" Christopher exclaimed a few pages further in the album. "We went camping at that place with the big cave and all the huge rocks to climb on. Remember, we roasted marshmallows and Cory got marshmallow goo all in his hair?"

"How could I forget!" Mom chuckled. "Cleaning him up was a major job. He hadn't learned to walk yet, but he surely could crawl fast!"

"That's for sure!" Christopher grumped good-naturedly. "I was always having to go after him and haul him back where he was supposed to be. And we had to watch all the time to make sure he didn't stick something in his mouth." Christopher pointed to a picture of himself lugging an unhappy Cory through the campsite. "Mom, why did he always want to taste everything he could get his hands on?"

"It's not just Cory, Son. All babies try to put things in their mouths. You did, too!" Mom tickled Christopher's ribs. "It's just a baby's way of learning about the things around him. Babies don't know what things are harmful — or that they could swallow something small and choke. It's our job to watch them and keep them safe. And it's our job to teach them what's dangerous, too."

"We had to teach Cory lots of stuff 'cause he was so little and didn't know anything. Right?" Christopher turned to the next page in the album.

"Yes, we had to teach him many things, and he's still learning — but then, so are we." Mom put her arm around Christopher's shoulders. "There are many times we don't know what to do."

"Even grown ups?" Christopher looked surprised.

"Even grown ups," Mom nodded. "We need someone to help us know what to do just like Cory needs us to help him. Our Father in Heaven has promised to send the Holy Spirit if we will ask. Then, the Holy Spirit helps us know what to do. We just have to be quiet inside and listen for His 'still, small voice' to show us what is right."

"Well, Maggy, my dear." Dad walked into the living room. "Have you decided to make me go to this company dinner all by myself?" Dad stopped in front of the couch, his hands on hips, and a pretend frown on his face.

"Oh, no!" Mom jumped up and glanced at her watch. "I didn't realize it was getting so late! Christopher and I were having such a good time looking at family photos that the time just flew!" Her voice faded as she rushed out of the room. "I'll be ready in a few minutes."

A short while later Mr. and Mrs. Wright gave last minute instructions as they started out the door. "Stephanie, our cell phone number is on the pad by the phone where it usually is. You can make sandwiches and . . . well, you know where everything is and what to do since you babysit for us all the time. We'll be back around 10:30 or 11:00." Mom aimed the last few words over her shoulder as Dad ushered her out the door.

Stephanie McDougal was lots of fun. She had been the Wright's baby sitter long enough that everyone knew what to expect and things went smoothly. While she

277

fixed a simple supper the children picked up their toys. "Well, that didn't take long." Christopher thought, glancing around his room again just to be sure. "Toys all put away. Books straight on the shelf. Bedspread neat. Clothes hung up and closet door closed. I guess I'll go see if Cory needs any help picking up. After all, he's still really little."

Christopher walked quickly down the hall toward his little brother's room, but stopped short as he passed the open bathroom door. He clapped his hand over his mouth so he wouldn't laugh out loud and startle Cory. What a sight! Cory stood on his stool in front of the bathroom mirror. He had Dad's shaving cream all over his face and he was carefully "shaving" with his toothbrush.

"What a great picture for the photo album. Mom and Dad would love it!" Christopher hurried quietly to the study, opened the cupboard door, and reached for the camera. Then dropped his hand back to his side. "Uh, oh," he thought. "Dad said not to touch the camera when he wasn't around to help us. He said it was expensive and we couldn't use it until we were older. But Cory's so cute, and there won't be another chance to get this picture! Mom and Dad won't even get to see this if I don't use the camera by myself."

Christopher started to reach for the camera again, then stopped. "I just don't know what to do!" He leaned his forehead against the cabinet. Then he remembered what Mom had said about asking God for help. He squeezed his eyes shut and prayed. "Dear Father in Heaven, I need help. Please send your Holy Spirit to help me. I'll be real quiet now and listen for His voice."

A few minutes later Christopher poked his head around the bathroom door. Stephanie stepped into the doorway behind him. FLASH! Cory dropped his toothbrush "razor" in surprise as Stephanie took his picture in a bright flash of light.

"Gotcha, young man!" she

grinned, holding up the camera.

While Stephanie cleaned up Cory, Christopher put away the shaving cream and cleaned up the mess in the sink. "I didn't disobey Dad, and we still got a great picture of Cory for the album," he thought. "Thank you, God. I'm glad I'm here to help little Cory, and I'm glad Your Holy Spirit's always there to help me, too!"

2 Discussion Time

Check understanding of the story and development of personal values.

- What do you like to do when it's raining outside?
- Do you have pictures of some special things your family has done together? Share some.
- What family pictures are your favorites?
- Have there ever been times when you weren't sure what you should do?
- How do you feel when you're not sure what to do?
- What happens when you ask God for help? Isn't it nice to know that He will ALWAYS send His Holy Spirit to help you know exactly what to do?

278

A Preview

Write each word as your teacher says it.

Name _____

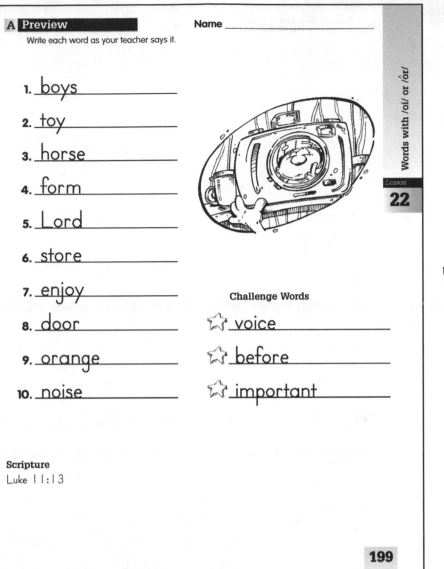

1. boys
2. toy
3. horse
4. form
5. Lord
6. store
7. enjoy
8. door
9. orange
10. noise

Challenge Words

☆ voice
☆ before
☆ important

Scripture
Luke 11:13

199

Challenge

For better spellers, challenge words may be included in the weekly list. Challenge words are starred.

Correct Immediately!

Say) Let's correct our preview. I will write each word on the board. Put a dot under each letter on your preview as I spell the word out loud. If you spelled a word wrong, rewrite it correctly.

Progress Chart

Students may record scores. (Reproducible master in Appendix B.)

Take a minute to memorize . . .

Read the memory verse twice. Have students practice it with you two more times.

---

3 Preview

Test for knowledge of the correct spellings of these words. (See the instructions at the top right for challenge words.)

Say) I will say the word once, use the word in a sentence, then say the word again. Write the word on the lines in the Worktext.

1.	boys	There are two **boys** in the Wright family.
2.	toy	Christopher put each **toy** where it belonged.
3.	horse	This toy **horse** won't fit in the stable with the others.
4.	form	You can **form** lots of things with clay.
5.	Lord	You can always ask the **Lord** to help you know what to do.
6.	store	We will get the pictures developed at the **store** next week.
7.	enjoy	We all **enjoy** seeing pictures of our families.
8.	door	Through the open **door**, Christopher saw Cory pretending to shave.
9.	orange	Cory was "shaving" with his **orange** toothbrush.
10.	noise	He didn't want to make any **noise** that might startle Cory.
☆	voice	We can pray and then listen for the **voice** of the Holy Spirit.
☆	before	They picked up their toys **before** supper.
☆	important	It is **important** to obey God.

4 Word Shapes

Help students form a correct image of whole words.

Say Look at each word and think about its shape. Now, write the word in the correct word Shape Boxes. You may check off each word as you use it.

(In many words, the sound of **/ôr/** is spelled **or** or **ore**. The sound of **/oi/** is spelled with **oi** or **oy**.)

Say In the word Shape Boxes, color the letters that spell the sound of **/ôr/** or the diphthong **/oi/** in each word. Circle the word in which **/ôr/** is spelled with **oor**.

☆ **Challenge**
Draw the correctly shaped box around each letter in these words.

Say On a separate sheet of paper, write other words that contain the spelling patterns in the word list. See how many words you can write.

B Word Shapes

Name _____

Write each word in the correct word shape boxes. Then, in the word shape boxes, color the letters that spell the sound of **/ôr/** or the diphthong **/oi/** in each word. Circle the word in which **/ôr/** is spelled with **oor**.

1. boys — s t o r e
2. door — (d o o r)
3. enjoy — L o r d
4. form — t o y
5. horse — n o i s e
6. Lord — o r a n g e
7. noise — b o y s
8. orange — e n j o y
9. store — f o r m
10. toy — h o r s e

☆ **Challenge**
Draw the correctly shaped boxes around each letter in these words.

b e f o r e   i m p o r t a n t   v o i c e

200

Answers may vary for duplicate word shapes.

Be Prepared For Fun

Check these supply lists for **Fun Ways to Spell** presented **Day 2**.
Purchase and/or gather these items ahead of time!

General
- A Classmate
- Spelling List

Auditory
- Box to Store Letters
- a, b, d, e, f, g, h, i, j, L, m, n, o, o, r, s, t, y (written on seasonal shapes like clouds or umbrellas)
- c, e, p, t, v (added for challenge words)
- Spelling List

Visual
- Paper or Polystyrene Cups
- a, b, d, e, f, g, h, i, j, L, m, n, o, o, r, s, t, y written on upside down cups
- c, e, p, t, v (added for challenge words)
- Spelling List

Tactile
- Shaving Cream
- Optional: Plastic Plates
- Optional: Wooden Craft Sticks
- Spelling List

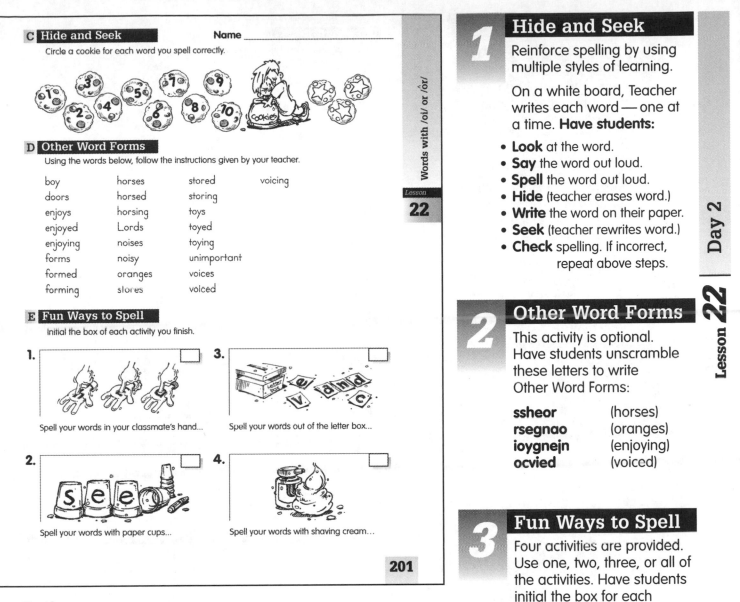

C Hide and Seek   Name _____

Circle a cookie for each word you spell correctly.

D Other Word Forms

Using the words below, follow the instructions given by your teacher.

boy	horses	stored	voicing
doors	horsed	storing	
enjoys	horsing	toys	
enjoyed	Lords	toyed	
enjoying	noises	toying	
forms	noisy	unimportant	
formed	oranges	voices	
forming	stores	voiced	

E Fun Ways to Spell

Initial the box of each activity you finish.

1. ☐ Spell your words in your classmate's hand...

2. ☐ Spell your words with paper cups...

3. ☐ Spell your words out of the letter box...

4. ☐ Spell your words with shaving cream...

201

Words with /oi/ or /ôr/

Lesson **22**

Day 2

Lesson 22

1 Hide and Seek

Reinforce spelling by using multiple styles of learning.

On a white board, Teacher writes each word — one at a time. **Have students:**

- **Look** at the word.
- **Say** the word out loud.
- **Spell** the word out loud.
- **Hide** (teacher erases word.)
- **Write** the word on their paper.
- **Seek** (teacher rewrites word.)
- **Check** spelling. If incorrect, repeat above steps.

2 Other Word Forms

This activity is optional. Have students unscramble these letters to write Other Word Forms:

ssheor	(horses)
rsegnao	(oranges)
ioygnejn	(enjoying)
ocvied	(voiced)

3 Fun Ways to Spell

Four activities are provided. Use one, two, three, or all of the activities. Have students initial the box for each activity they complete.

Options:

- assign activities to students according to their learning styles
- set up the activities in learning centers for students to do throughout the day
- divide students into four groups and assign one activity per group
- do one activity per day

General

To spell your words in your classmate's hand . . .
- Have a classmate sit next to you and hold their palm open in front of, and facing both of you.
- Use fingertip to write a spelling word in the palm of a classmate's hand.
- Have a classmate say each letter as you write it and then say the word you spelled.
- Next, have a classmate write a word in your palm.

Auditory

To spell your words out of the letter box . . .
- Spell a word from your list by putting the letters in the right order.
- Check your spelling.
- Spell your word out loud.

Visual

To spell your words with paper cups . . .
- Spell a word from your list by putting the cups in the right order.
- Check your spelling.

Tactile

To spell your words with shaving cream . . .
- Spread a glob of shaving cream across your desk (or on a plastic plate).
- Use finger (or a wooden craft stick) to write a spelling word in the shaving cream.
- Check your spelling.
- Smear the word out with your fingers and write another.

Crossword

1

Familiarize students with word meaning and usage. Draw four connecting boxes on the board with a number one in the first box. Explain that a crossword is a puzzle in which words are put into numbered squares using clues. Ask the students the name of Christopher's little brother. Write **C-o-r-y** in the four boxes on the board.

Say) In this activity you will write your spelling words in the crossword puzzle. Use the clues to decide which word to write in each space.

Words with /oi/ or /ôr/

Lesson
22

F Crossword
Use the puzzle clues to write the spelling words.

Name _____

Across
3. open the _____
5. color
8. something to play with
9. to like
10. a place to buy things

Down
1. to shape
2. animal
4. God
6. loud sound
7. not girls but _____

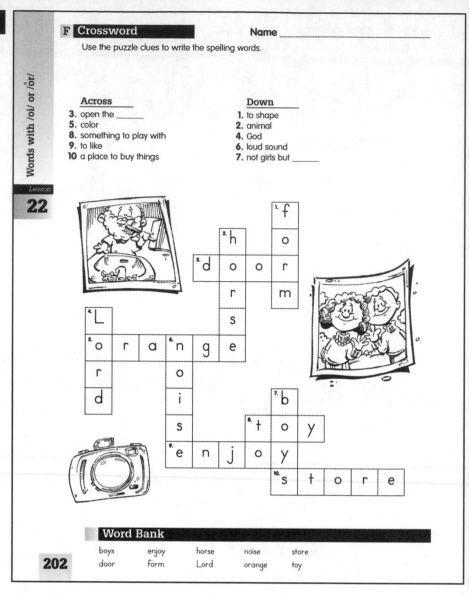

Word Bank

| boys | enjoy | horse | noise | store |
| door | form | Lord | orange | toy |

202

Take a minute to memorize . . .

Have students say the memory verses from lessons 13, 14, 15, 16, and 17 with you.

282

G Dictation

Name _____

Listen and write the missing words.

1. __The boys enjoy the toy__ airplane.

2. Daniel led __the horse__ through __the barn door__.

3. __I can buy an orange at the store__.

4. __The Lord__ loves __each of us__.

Words with /oi/ or /ôr/

Lesson
22

H Proofreading

One word in each set is misspelled. Fill in the oval by the misspelled word.

1. ○ Lord
   ○ dear
   ● engoy

2. ● hors
   ○ took
   ○ toy

3. ○ first
   ● boyz
   ○ where

4. ○ noon
   ○ store
   ● dor

5. ○ circle
   ○ line
   ● noiz

6. ● ornge
   ○ baby
   ○ form

☆ ○ flower
   ● importnt
   ○ stood

☆ ○ crown
   ● befour
   ○ through

☆ ○ easy
   ● vois
   ○ year

203

---

1 **Dictation**

Reinforce correct spelling by using current and previous words in context.

Say Listen as I read each sentence and then write it in your Worktext.(Slowly read each sentence twice. Sentences are found in the Student Worktext to the left.)

☆ **Challenge**

Write these incomplete sentences on the board.

___ ___ ___ ___ ___ message.

___ ___ bath ___ ___ ___
___ ___ .

Setsuko ___ ___ ___ ___ .

Say Listen as I read each sentence. Write the sentence on your paper. (Slowly read each sentence twice.)

I have an important message.

Take a bath before you go to bed.

Setsuko has a soft voice.

Day 4

Lesson **22**

---

2 **Proofreading**

Familiarize students with standardized test format and reinforce recognizing misspelled words.

Say Look at each set of words. One word in each set is misspelled. Fill in the oval by the misspelled word. (You may wish to pronounce each set of words to help students correctly identify them.)

Copyright © 2012 by The Concerned Group, Inc. All rights reserved.

283

3 Hide and Seek

Reinforce correct spelling of current spelling words. (A reproducible master is provided in Appendix A as shown on the inset page to the right.)

Write the words one at a time on a white board.

Have students:

- **Look** at the word.
- **Say** the word out loud.
- **Spell** the word out loud.
- **Hide** (teacher erases word.)
- **Write** the word on paper.
- **Seek** (teacher rewrites word.)
- **Check** spelling. If incorrect, rewrite word correctly.

4 Suffixes

Have your students complete this activity to strengthen spelling ability and expand vocabulary.

1 Posttest

Test mastery of the spelling words. Challenge words are starred.

(Say) I will say the word once, use the word in a sentence, then say the word again. Write the word on your paper.

Appendix A — Lesson 22

Hide and Seek

Check a paper for each word you spell correctly.

1 3 5 7 9
2 4 6 8 10

Suffixes

Add **s**, **ed**, or **ing** to make new words from your spelling words.

+ s			+ ed	
1. door	doors		1. form	formed
2. enjoy	enjoys		2. enjoy	enjoyed
3. form	forms		3. toy	toyed
4. horse	horses		4. horse – e	horsed
5. noise	noises		5. store – e	stored
6. orange	oranges			
7. store	stores		**+ ing**	
8. toy	toys		1. enjoy	enjoying
9. voice	voices		2. form	forming
			3. horse – e	horsing
			4. store – e	storing
			5. toy	toying

386

---

1. **store** — Don't forget to buy film when you go to the **store**.
2. **orange** — Christopher put the **orange** ball in the toy box.
3. **Lord** — The **Lord** sends His Holy Spirit to help us know what to do.
4. **horse** — There was a picture in the album of the twins riding a **horse**.
5. **form** — Rocks that **form** from the roof of caves are called stalactites.
6. **door** — Mom gave instructions as she went out the **door** with Dad.
7. **toy** — The children like to play with **toy** horses.
8. **enjoy** — Mom and Dad will **enjoy** the company dinner.
9. **boys** — The **boys** and girls shouldn't touch the camera without Dad.
10. **noise** — The rain made a gentle pattering **noise** as it fell on the roof.
☆ **voice** — The Holy Spirit speaks to us in a "still, small **voice**."
☆ **important** — It is **important** to ask God for help in everything we do.
☆ **before** — The children ate supper **before** Stephanie arrived.

Progress Chart

Students may record scores. (Reproducible master in Appendix B.)

Personal Dictionary

Students may add any words they have misspelled to their personal dictionaries for reference when writing. (Cover in Appendix B.)

I Game

Place a game piece over each word your teacher says and spells. If the word appears on your card more than once, place a game piece over only one of the words. When you get five game pieces in a row, raise your hand and say, "Spelling is fun!"

Remember: God gives us the Holy Spirit to guide us, but we may choose to listen.

J Journaling

In your journal, write about a time that you didn't know the right thing to do. Finish this sentence in your journal: **When I don't know what I should do, I will. . .**

204

Words with /oi/ or /ȯr/

Lesson **22**

How to Play:

- Fold the word cards (see **Materials**) in half, and put them in a container.
- Write each word from the **Game Word List** on the board. (Be sure to include the number in parentheses beside it.)
- Ask the students to copy these words on their game card — one word in each box. Remind them the number beside the word indicates how many times they must copy that word. (Note: Placing the words in the boxes randomly makes the game more fun!)
- Instructions for the students: "Cover the word **FREE** in the center of your card with a game piece. (pause) I will draw a word from the container, read it aloud, then spell it. Find that word on your card, and cover it with a game piece. Cover only ONE word each time, even if it's on your card twice. When you have five game pieces in a row (up-down, across, or diagonally) raise your hand and say '**Spelling is FUN!**'"
- Play as many times as you like. (As you return the word cards to the container and mix them up, remind the students to clear their game cards.)

---

2 Game

Reinforce spelling skills and provide motivation and interest.

Materials

- game page (from student text)
- flat buttons, dry beans, pennies, or game discs (24 per child)
- game word list
- word cards (each word from the list below written on one or more cards as indicated)

Game Word List

1. **noise** (2)
2. **boys** (2)
3. **enjoy** (2)
4. **toy** (2)
5. **door** (2)
6. **form** (2)
7. **horse** (2)
8. **Lord** (2)
9. **orange** (2)
10. **store** (2)
☆ **important** (2)
☆ **before** (1)
☆ **voice** (1)

Day 5

Lesson **22**

3 Journaling

Provide a meaningful reason for correct spelling through personal writing.

Review the story using discussion leads provided on the following page. Encourage students to apply the Scriptural value in their journaling.

 Take a minute to memorize . . .

Have students say the memory verses from lessons 19, 20, 21, and 22 with you.

285

Provide a meaningful reason for correct spelling through personal writing.

(Say)

- Pictures can help us remember the special, fun times in our lives like birthdays or vacations. In the story this week Christopher wanted to get a funny picture of his little brother to put in the family photo album. Why was he not sure he should take the picture? (His dad had told the children that they mustn't touch the camera when he wasn't there to help them because it was expensive.)

- What had Christopher's mom told him that helped him? (That whenever he didn't know what he should do he could ask the Heavenly Father to send His Holy Spirit to help him know.)

- How did Christopher obey his dad and still get a picture of Cory? (He asked the baby sitter, Stephanie, to take the picture.) In your journal, write about a time when you didn't know the right thing to do.

- Copy the sentence in your Worktext into your journal and finish it. Always remember to ask your Heavenly Father for help when you need it!

Quotables!

*"Reading is not deciphering; writing is not copying."**

*Ferreiro, E., and Teberosky, A. 1979. Los sistemas de escritura en el desarrollo del niño. Mexico: Siglo Veintiuno Editores, (English translation, Literacy before schooling. Exeter, NH: Heinemann, 1982.)

Gifts From the Heart

Setsuko's example helps Katelynn see the value in gladly doing things for others.

"What are we gonna do with this?" Katelynn turned the top piece of paper over on the colorful stack in the center of the table. "What kind of paper is it? It's only colored on one side."

"We're going to make bunnies today." Mrs. Hill held up two bunnies shaped from folded paper, and hopped them across the table toward Katelynn. "This paper is called 'origami' [pronounced or-ah-gah¹-mee] paper, and origami is the Japanese word for . . ." She stopped, and looked at the dark-haired girl sitting beside her. "You tell them Setsuko."

Setsuko looked down and rubbed a piece of the colorful paper between her fingers. "Paper folding," she said softly. "It is an old art form of the Japanese people."

"How do you do this, Setsuko?" Mrs. Hill handed a bunny and a piece of white paper to her. Setsuko examined Mrs. Hill's bunny carefully for a minute, then quickly and expertly folded her paper into another bunny! "What a beautiful job!" said Mrs. Hill. "Will you help me show everyone how to do this, Setsuko? I'm just learning myself." She smiled at Setsuko again. Setsuko glanced up just long enough to notice the looks of admiration on the faces of her classmates. The corners of her mouth turned up a tiny bit as she just barely nodded her head.

"What does this have to do with going to Pleasant Valley Retirement Center?" Katelynn looked at Beth and raised her eyebrows. She reached out and picked up the two sample bunnies and compared them. "Are we going to hop with these bunnies to Pleasant Valley tomorrow?"

"No, I think we'll just go in vans," Mrs. Hill teased. "Your teacher thought it would be nice to give the people in the retirement center something you made. Many of them are lonely and the gifts of your smile and time will help them feel special. And when they see the bunny it will remind them that you cared enough to visit. Jesus once said, 'Anything you did for one of the least important of these brothers and sisters of mine, you did for me.'"

Beth took one of the bunnies Katelynn held and made it stand up. "This bunny wants to meet your bunny." Beth hopped the paper bunny over to Setsuko's white one. The girls made the two bunnies touch noses, then laughed.

Mrs. Hill handed out white sheets of paper to the four girls sitting around her table. "Don't we get to use the colored paper?" Rachel held up a piece of rich brown paper in one hand and a piece of hot pink in the other. "I wanted to make a brown one with a pink jacket — like your bunny."

"You can, Rachel. But we are going to practice with the scrap paper first." Mrs Hill demonstrated as she talked. "The first step is to fold the paper in half and then open it back up. Like this."

"Is everyone making bunnies?" Beth folded her paper in half the wrong way, then refolded it like Setsuko showed her.

"No, I think each group is doing something different. You go to Mrs. Schilling's table next." Mrs. Hill explained the next step as she folded both top corners to the middle fold line. "It looks like the roof of a house now doesn't it, girls?"

"I don't want to give my bunny away to somebody I don't even know," Katelynn whispered loud enough for the other three girls to hear. "I want to keep him."

"Me, too." Beth made her piece of paper look like a roof. "I want to make mine gray."

"Do we have to give them away?" Katelynn folded the roof in half like Setsuko showed her. "I want to keep mine."

"Once you learn I think you can make some bunnies to take home, too." Mrs. Hill looked at the clock. "The ones we make today are for the people in the retirement center. There are lots of people who live there, so I'm sure we'll need every bunny we can make."

Katelynn continued to work on the bunny . . . slowly. Setsuko helped her finish three before it was time to go to Mrs. Schilling's table. Katelynn left two on the table, but slipped the third bunny she'd made into the big pocket of her jumper. "I made two bunnies for the retired people, so I'll just keep one," Katelynn thought as she walked over to join her friends.

"We're going to make footprint bookmarks today, girls." Mrs. Schilling pointed to pieces of posterboard on the table in the shape of bunny tracks. "And these are bunny track patterns."

"Oh, how cute!" Beth reached for a pattern and some gray construction paper.

"Setsuko," Rachel picked up a pencil and a pair of scissors, "Will you hand me some brown construction paper, please?"

"You are going to trace around the pattern five times on a piece of construction paper and cut out four paw prints." Mrs. Schilling picked up a piece of paper, and began showing them how it was done.

Katelynn finished quickly. "Are these for the people at Pleasant Valley too?" She wrinkled her forehead.

"Why, yes," Mrs. Schilling smiled. "When you are done cutting I want you to write this verse on your marker." Mrs. Schilling held up a card that had "Lead Us Not Into Temptation" printed on it neatly.

"Why are we writing that?" Rachel picked up a

Lesson **23**

Day 1

blue marker. "How are the people at Pleasant Valley going to lead us into temptation?"

"When you give this gift to the people at Pleasant Valley, you can tell them how Jesus taught us to pray, 'Lead us not into temptation', like your bookmark says. God gives us strength to stay away from trouble if we ask. And reading the Bible helps us know what to do when we are tempted to do wrong. You can suggest that they use your Paw Print Bookmark in their Bibles. It will remind them that God leads them away from trouble, when they pray for help. Now glue paws onto the bookmark like this." Mrs. Schilling held up a sample.

The group of four worked hard on making as many markers as they could for the retirees. They laughed and talked until it was time to go to the next table.

"Your text today is written on the board, ladies." Mrs. Wilson pointed to the board as the girls scooted their chairs up to her table. "It says, 'Blessed are all who hear the Word of God and put it into practice.' Color the bunny on your border sheet, then write the text in your best handwriting. There are some extra ones here. We need to make more than one each because there are a lot of people at Pleasant Valley."

The girls reached for markers and started to color neatly. "What do you think this text means?" Mrs. Wilson looked at Katelynn.

"We should do what God tells us to in the Scriptures." Katelynn colored the window above the bunny on the border sheet.

"Like ask Him for help when we are tempted to do wrong," Beth added, thinking about the bookmarks she had just made.

"Or be kind to people because He says it is like being kind to Him," Rachel suggested.

Katelynn squirmed in her chair as she listened to her friends. She thought about the bunny she had slipped out of her pocket

and into her desk. "I'll just take the bunny home tonight so I can make one to keep for myself. I need a pattern," she thought.

The next morning, Katelynn walked up to her desk, then squealed with delight. There on her desk sat a whole family of origami bunnies. There was a brown daddy bunny, a mommy, and three tiny little baby bunnies with fluffy cotton tails. Katelynn looked across at Beth's desk and saw a gray family of bunnies arranged in a circle. Rachel had a family on her desk, too. The bunnies were made much better than Katelynn could have done. The little ones were delicate and tiny. Only an expert could have done such a nice job. Katelynn looked around the room for Setsuko and saw her hanging up her bright pink coat. "Setsuko, did you make these bunnies?" Setsuko nodded. "Oh, They're so cute! Will you show me how to make the babies?" Setsuko nodded again.

Katelynn frowned as she thought about the bunny still hidden inside her desk. She hadn't even remembered to take him home last night. "I bet the Pleasant Valley people will like these bunnies as much as I do," she thought. "I sure hope we have enough for everyone that lives there." She took the bunny she'd made the day before out of her desk. "I've been thinking just about me!" she prayed. "Please keep me out of trouble today, Lord, and help me to think of others before myself." Then she walked over to the origami table and added her bunny to the big stack in the center.

"That was a nice surprise to find bunnies on my desk this morning, Setsuko." Katelynn walked over to Setsuko's desk. "How did you ever have time to make so many? Will you help me make more for the people at Pleasant Valley before school starts?"

"Sure." Setsuko smiled shyly. "That would be fun!"

2 Discussion Time

Check understanding of the story and development of personal values.

- Who do you know that lives in a retirement center or long term health care facility?
- Tell about a time you visited a retirement center or long-term health care facility?
- How did you like being there?
- How do you think God feels when we take time to share our talents and smiles with lonely people?
- What does He say about that in the Scriptures?
- Why is it important to put God's word into practice?

288

A Preview

Write each word as your teacher says it.

Name _____

1. children
2. each
3. walk
4. want
5. which
6. draw
7. small
8. such
9. always
10. also

Challenge Words

☆ called
☆ wanted
☆ lunch

Scripture
Luke 11:28

205

Challenge

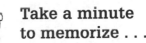

For better spellers, challenge words may be included in the weekly list. Challenge words are starred.

Correct Immediately!

Say Let's correct our preview. I will write each word on the board. Put a dot under each letter on your preview as I spell the word out loud. If you spelled a word wrong, rewrite it correctly.

Progress Chart

Students may record scores. (Reproducible master in Appendix B.)

Take a minute to memorize . . .

Read the memory verse twice. Have students practice it with you two more times.

---

3 Preview

Test for knowledge of the correct spellings of these words.
(See the instructions at the top right for challenge words.)

Say I will say the word once, use the word in a sentence, then say the word again. Write the word on the lines in the Worktext.

1.	children	The **children** were making things for the people at the center.
2.	each	Mrs. Morgan planned to have a bunny for **each** person.
3.	walk	Katelynn wanted to hop instead of **walk**.
4.	want	"I **want** a bunny for myself," thought Katelynn.
5.	which	To **which** retirement center were the students going?
6.	draw	Mrs. Schilling said, "Please **draw** around the paw patterns."
7.	small	Katelynn loved the **small** bunnies Setsuko made for her.
8.	such	Sometimes **such** small things bring people happiness.
9.	always	It is **always** good to put God's word into practice.
10.	also	It is **also** important to ask God to help you make good choices.
☆	called	Mrs. Hill **called** the paper folding "origami."
☆	wanted	Beth **wanted** to keep her origami bunny.
☆	lunch	The class finished their projects before it was time for **lunch**.

289

4 Word Shapes

Help students form a correct image of whole words.

(Say) Look at each word and think about its shape. Now, write the word in the correct word Shape Boxes. You may check off each word as you use it.

(In many words, the sound of /ȯ/ is spelled with **a** or **aw**.

(Say) In the word Shape Boxes, color the letters that spell the sound of /ȯ/ or /ch/ in each word. Circle the word which has two digraphs.

☆ Challenge
Draw the correctly shaped box around each letter in these words.

(Say) On a separate sheet of paper, write sentences using one or more of the spelling words.

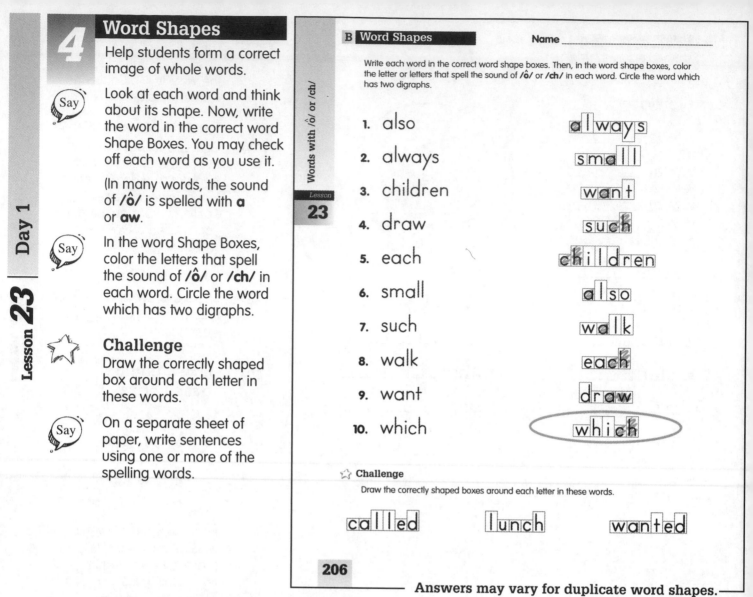

B Word Shapes

Name _____

Write each word in the correct word shape boxes. Then, in the word shape boxes, color the letter or letters that spell the sound of /ȯ/ or /ch/ in each word. Circle the word which has two digraphs.

Words with /ȯ/ or /ch/
Lesson 23

1. also
2. always
3. children
4. draw
5. each
6. small
7. such
8. walk
9. want
10. which

always
small
want
such
children
also
walk
each
draw
which

☆ **Challenge**
Draw the correctly shaped boxes around each letter in these words.

called   lunch   wanted

206

Be Prepared For Fun

Check these supply lists for **Fun Ways to Spell** presented **Day 2**. Purchase and/or gather these items ahead of time!

General
- Markers
- Art Paper
- Spelling List

Auditory
- Spelling List

Visual
- Letter Tiles a, a, c, d, e, h, h, i, k, l, l, m, n, o, r, s, t, u, w, y
- Challenge words may be spelled out of the letter tiles listed above.
- Spelling List

Tactile
- Finger Paint
- Plastic Plate or Glossy Paper
- Spelling List

290

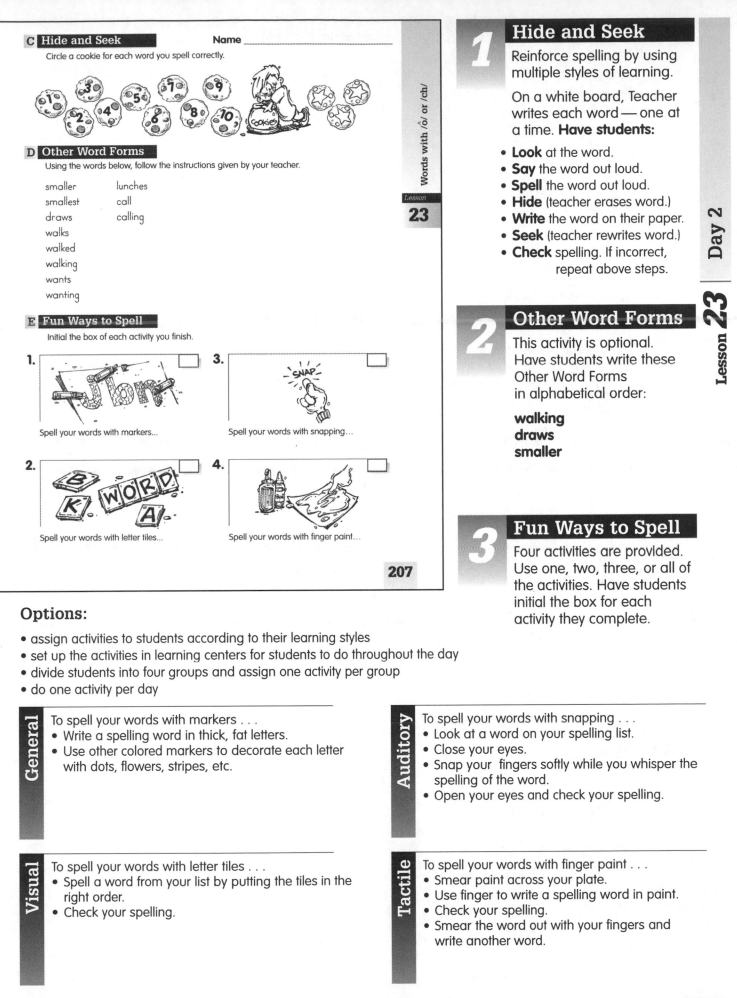

C Hide and Seek

Name _____

Circle a cookie for each word you spell correctly.

D Other Word Forms

Using the words below, follow the instructions given by your teacher.

smaller   lunches
smallest   call
draws   calling
walks
walked
walking
wants
wanting

E Fun Ways to Spell

Initial the box of each activity you finish.

1. Spell your words with markers...

2. Spell your words with letter tiles...

3. SNAP! Spell your words with snapping...

4. Spell your words with finger paint...

Words with /ȯ/ or /ch/

Lesson 23

207

1 Hide and Seek

Reinforce spelling by using multiple styles of learning.

On a white board, Teacher writes each word — one at a time. **Have students:**

- **Look** at the word.
- **Say** the word out loud.
- **Spell** the word out loud.
- **Hide** (teacher erases word.)
- **Write** the word on their paper.
- **Seek** (teacher rewrites word.)
- **Check** spelling. If incorrect, repeat above steps.

2 Other Word Forms

This activity is optional. Have students write these Other Word Forms in alphabetical order:

walking
draws
smaller

3 Fun Ways to Spell

Four activities are provided. Use one, two, three, or all of the activities. Have students initial the box for each activity they complete.

Options:

- assign activities to students according to their learning styles
- set up the activities in learning centers for students to do throughout the day
- divide students into four groups and assign one activity per group
- do one activity per day

General

To spell your words with markers . . .
- Write a spelling word in thick, fat letters.
- Use other colored markers to decorate each letter with dots, flowers, stripes, etc.

Auditory

To spell your words with snapping . . .
- Look at a word on your spelling list.
- Close your eyes.
- Snap your fingers softly while you whisper the spelling of the word.
- Open your eyes and check your spelling.

Visual

To spell your words with letter tiles . . .
- Spell a word from your list by putting the tiles in the right order.
- Check your spelling.

Tactile

To spell your words with finger paint . . .
- Smear paint across your plate.
- Use finger to write a spelling word in paint.
- Check your spelling.
- Smear the word out with your fingers and write another word.

291

Unscramble Words

1

Unscramble Words

Familiarize students with word meaning and usage. Write the letters **saol** on the board. Help the students understand that the scrambled letters **saol** spell one of their spelling words when they are arranged correctly. Guide the students in ordering the letters to spell **also**.

(Say) Each of the sentences contains one scrambled word from this lesson. Write the word on the line by writing the letters from the underlined word in the correct order.

F Unscramble Words   **Name** _____

Use the underlined letters to write a spelling word.

1. children ___ The <u>lirdench</u> made origami bunnies.
2. each ___ They made <u>hace</u> one by folding paper.
3. also ___ Setsuko <u>laso</u> made some baby bunnies.
4. small ___ The baby bunnies were very <u>mlasl</u>.
5. draw ___ Can you <u>wrad</u> a picture of a bunny?
6. want ___ We <u>tanw</u> to be kind to others.
7. walk ___ Some older people find it hard to <u>lakw</u>.
8. such ___ Visiting them is <u>hsuc</u> a nice thing to do.
9. always ___ Helping others is <u>slawya</u> a good choice.
10. which ___ <u>Wchih</u> bunny do you like the best?

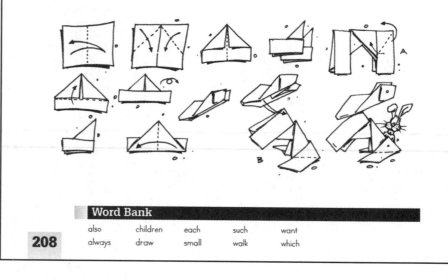

Word Bank

also	children	each	such	want
always	draw	small	walk	which

208

Take a minute to memorize . . .

Read the memory verse twice. Have students practice it with you two more times.

292

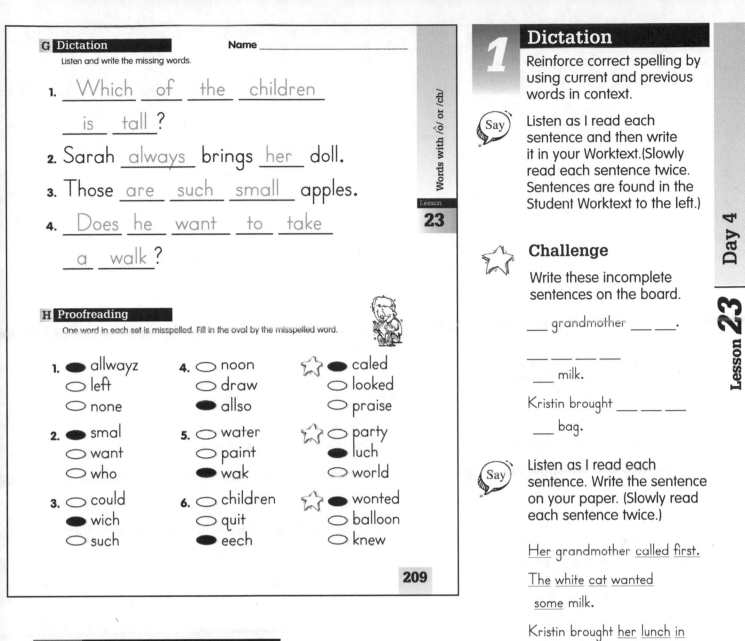

G Dictation

Name _____

Listen and write the missing words.

1. __Which__ __of__ __the__ __children__ __is__ __tall__ ?

2. Sarah __always__ brings __her__ doll.

3. Those __are__ __such__ __small__ apples.

4. __Does__ __he__ __want__ __to__ __take__ __a__ __walk__ ?

H Proofreading

One word in each set is misspelled. Fill in the oval by the misspelled word.

1. ● allwayz
   ○ left
   ○ none

2. ● smal
   ○ want
   ○ who

3. ○ could
   ● wich
   ○ such

4. ○ noon
   ○ draw
   ● allso

5. ○ water
   ○ paint
   ● wak

6. ○ children
   ○ quit
   ● eech

☆ ● caled
   ○ looked
   ○ praise

☆ ○ party
   ● luch
   ○ world

☆ ● wonted
   ○ balloon
   ○ knew

209

---

1 Dictation

Reinforce correct spelling by using current and previous words in context.

(Say) Listen as I read each sentence and then write it in your Worktext.(Slowly read each sentence twice. Sentences are found in the Student Worktext to the left.)

☆ **Challenge**

Write these incomplete sentences on the board.

___ grandmother ___ ___.

___ ___ ___ ___ ___ milk.

Kristin brought ___ ___ ___ ___ bag.

(Say) Listen as I read each sentence. Write the sentence on your paper. (Slowly read each sentence twice.)

Her grandmother called first.

The white cat wanted some milk.

Kristin brought her lunch in a bag.

2 Proofreading

Familiarize students with standardized test format and reinforce recognizing misspelled words.

(Say) Look at each set of words. One word in each set is misspelled. Fill in the oval by the misspelled word. (You may wish to pronounce each set of words to help students correctly identify them.)

293

3 Hide and Seek

Reinforce correct spelling of current spelling words. (A reproducible master is provided in Appendix A as shown on the inset page to the right.)

Write the words one at a time on a white board.

Have students:

- **Look** at the word.
- **Say** the word out loud.
- **Spell** the word out loud.
- **Hide** (teacher erases word.)
- **Write** the word on paper.
- **Seek** (teacher rewrites word.)
- **Check** spelling. If incorrect, rewrite word correctly.

4 Secret Words

Have your students complete this activity to strengthen spelling ability and expand vocabulary.

1 Posttest

Test mastery of the spelling words. Challenge words are starred.

(Say) I will say the word once, use the word in a sentence, then say the word again. Write the word on your paper.

1. draw — I'll **draw** around the pattern.
2. walk — It is too far to **walk** to the retirement center.
3. small — The bunnies were delicate and **small**.
4. want — Katelynn did not **want** to give away her bunnies.
5. always — It is **always** good to ask God for help.
6. also — It is **also** good to put God's word into practice.
7. children — All **children** are special.
8. such — Jesus said, "The kingdom of heaven belongs to **such** as these."
9. each — In the end, **each** girl made a good choice.
10. which — Decide **which** girl you want to be like.
☆ called — Setsuko **called** paper folding "origami."
☆ wanted — Setsuko **wanted** to make bunnies for her friends.
☆ lunch — The class ate **lunch** and went out to recess.

Progress Chart
Students may record scores. (Reproducible master in Appendix B.)

Personal Dictionary
Students may add any words they have misspelled to their personal dictionaries for reference when writing. (Cover in Appendix B.)

Hide and Seek
Check a paper for each word you spell correctly.

1 3 5 7 9
2 4 6 8 10

Secret Word
Use these clues to find the word that fits in each blank. Then use the boxed letters to discover the secret word.

1. not as big
2. Run, runs. Walk,_____.
3. a person who is not yet grown up
4. a picture done with a pencil
5. moving slower than running
6. littlest
7. meals in a bag or box
8. would like to have

1. s m a l l e r
2. w a l k s
3. c h i l d
4. d r a w i n g
5. w a l k i n g
6. s m a l l e s t
7. l u n c h e s
8. w a n t s

It is fun to play on a s w i n g s e t.

Word Bank
child	lunches	smallest	walks
drawing	smaller	walking	wants

387

I Game

Name _____

Follow the rabbit tracks to Pleasant Valley Retirement Center. Move one space each time you or your team spells a word correctly from this week's word list.

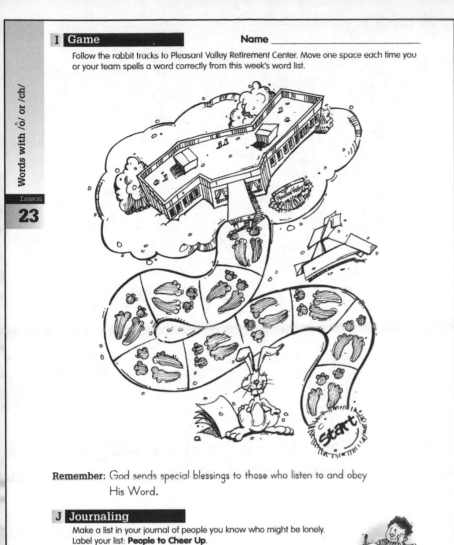

Remember: God sends special blessings to those who listen to and obey His Word.

J Journaling

Make a list in your journal of people you know who might be lonely. Label your list: **People to Cheer Up.**

210

Reinforce spelling skills and provide motivation and interest.

Materials

- game page (from student text)
- flat buttons, dry beans, pennies, or game discs (1 per child)
- game word list

Game Word List

Use of challenge words is optional.

1. **also**
2. **always**
3. **draw**
4. **small**
5. **walk**
6. **want**
7. **which**
8. **children**
9. **such**
10. **each**
☆ **called**
☆ **wanted**
☆ **lunch**

How to Play:

- Divide students into two teams, and decide which team will go first.
- Have each student place their game piece on Start.
- Have a student from team A go to the board.
- Read the spelling word two times slowly and clearly. (You may also wish to use the word in a sentence. Ex.: "cat — The cat climbed a tree. — cat")
- Have the student write the word on the board.
- If the word is spelled correctly, instruct all the members of team A to move their game piece forward one space on the game board. (Note: If the word is misspelled, correct the spelling immediately.)
- Alternate between teams A and B as you go down the word list.
- The team to reach Pleasant Valley Retirement Center first is the winner.

Non-Competitive Option: At the end of the game, say: "Class, I am proud of your efforts to spell the words correctly. If you had fun and tried your best, you are all winners!"

3 Journaling

Provide a meaningful reason for correct spelling through personal writing.

Review the story using discussion leads provided on the following page. Encourage students to apply the Scriptural value in their journaling.

Take a minute to memorize . . .

Read the memory verse twice. Have students practice it with you two more times.

295

3 Journaling

Provide a meaningful reason for correct spelling through personal writing.

(Say)

- Katelynn liked making origami bunnies in this week's story. How did she feel about giving them away to the people in the retirement center at the beginning of the story? (She didn't want to give any away.)

- What did Mrs. Hill teach the girls about being kind to the retirees? ("Jesus said, 'Anything you did for one of the least important of these brothers and sisters of mine, you did for me.'")

- What did Katelynn find on her desk the next morning? (A little family of bunnies that Setsuko had made for her.)

- What did Katelynn decide about sharing the bunnies and putting into practice what she'd heard from the Word of God? (She asked Setsuko to help her make extra bunnies for the retirees.)

- Make a list in your journal of people you know who might be lonely.

Quotables!

"When children read and write, they grow as spellers."*

*Wilde, Sandra. 1990. A Proposal for a New Spelling Curriculum. The Elementary School Journal, Vol. 90, No. 3, January: 275-289.

Do Unto Others

Kristin learns about the Golden Rule when the Rawsons stop to help an elderly couple with a flat tire.

"You kids need to get ready for bed just as soon as we get home." Mom looked over her shoulder into the back seat. "It's getting late and tomorrow is a school day."

"I think we already lost this one, Maggy." Dad laughed and tipped his head toward the middle of the front seat. Cathy was slumped over with her head resting against his side. In the back seat the twins, Christopher and Kristin, talked quietly over three-year-old Cory's head as he sat in his car seat and played with a small fire engine.

The green station wagon hummed down the highway toward home. The family had spent the evening shopping, then Dad had treated them to dinner at a nice family restaurant. It was "Kids' Night," and a man and lady dressed in clown costumes made funny animals and other things out of long, skinny balloons. Christopher's black balloon sword rested across his lap. Kristin held her white poodle and Cathy's pink bunny. Cory had already popped his Indian headdress.

Suddenly, the car slowed quickly and Dad pulled to the side of the road. "What is it, Charles?" Mom's head jerked up from the back of the seat where it had been resting.

"It's okay." Dad turned to check the oncoming traffic, then backed the car carefully along the shoulder. "There's a car stopped back there. Looks like an elderly man trying to change a tire. I'm just going to give him a hand." Dad stopped just in front of the disabled car. He flipped on the hazard switch that made the taillights blink so that cars coming down the highway could see them more easily.

"May we unbuckle our seat belts so we can see better, Mom?" Kristin twisted her neck around trying to see out the back window.

"Yes, you may." Mom peered out the back window herself. "But you must stay in the car."

Kristin helped Cory get unbuckled, then she knelt in her seat and rested her elbows on the back. She watched Dad approach a stooped, elderly man standing by a flat tire on the other car. The man's head was almost bald, but what little hair he had left was silvery gray.

"There's an older lady in the car, too." Christopher peered out his side of the rear window. The blinking lights illuminated the scene as Mr. Wright quickly jacked up the car and changed the tire while the elderly man stood by.

"He's trying to give Dad some money." Kristin exclaimed as the man pulled out his wallet. "Oh, Dad won't take it. They're sure talking and smiling a lot." Kristin wished she could get out and hear what they were saying. She watched Dad lean over and say something to the woman in the car. Then he reached out and shook the trembling, gnarled hand of the elderly man before returning to the station wagon.

"Who are they, Dad? What did they say? Why didn't you take the money? Where are they going?" The children asked a string of questions as Dad settled back into the driver's seat.

"All right, all right!" Dad chuckled. He took the tissue Mom handed him and wiped his hands. "Their names are Ed and Birdie Johnson. They're on their way to visit their son and his family. Mr. Johnson has severe arthritis in his hands, so it's difficult for him to do some things like changing that flat." Dad started the car, the children buckled up, and the

family all waved at the Johnsons as Dad drove back on to the highway. Kristin thought she saw Mrs. Johnson dab at her eyes with a white handkerchief as they pulled away.

"I didn't take the money they offered because I just wanted to help them," Dad said. "After all, the Scriptures say 'do for others what you want them to do for you.' If I were in trouble I'd want someone to lend me a hand." Suddenly Dad noticed the dashboard clock. "Whew! Now it's really late! You children are going to be very tired tomorrow."

"Not Cathy." Christopher pointed out. "She slept through the whole thing."

"She'll be upset she missed all the excitement." Kristin settled back for the rest of the ride.

Mom smiled across the front seat at Dad. "I'm glad you saw them and stopped, Charles."

"So am I." Christopher added.

"Me, too." Kristin leaned her head back.

"I glad too." Cory nodded.

The next day at school Kristin yawned for what seemed the millionth time, and tried to concentrate on what Mrs. Morgan was saying.

"So we see that there are many different geometric shapes right here in our own classroom." Mrs. Morgan began passing a piece of paper out to each student. "The picture that I'm giving you has lots of geometric shapes in it. Please use your markers or crayons to color each shape according to the directions at the top of the page. What color will all the squares be, Tony?"

"The squares are supposed to be blue," Tony answered. "But what if there's something inside the square — like the door to this birdhouse?" Tony held up his picture. "The birdhouse is square, but the door is on it and it's round. Do we color the circle red and the rest of the square blue?"

"That's right, Tony. That's exactly the way to do it." Mrs. Morgan smiled. "If any of you have time when you've finished this

297

Day 1

Review 24

picture, try drawing your own picture using different geometric shapes."

Kristin reached into her desk and got out her brand-new markers. Mom had bought them for her last night when they were shopping. The box held sixteen different colored markers that were scented. She pulled the cap off a pretty red one and sniffed it. Ummmm. Strawberry. She started coloring the little circle on the front of the birdhouse. Out of the corner of her eye she saw Katelynn still looking in her desk.

"What's wrong?" Kristin whispered across the aisle between their desks.

"My markers are at home." Katelynn frowned. "I took them home to use last weekend and forgot to bring them back. I don't have anything to color with."

Kristin turned back to her picture. "It's not my fault Katelynn forgot her markers," she thought. "Mrs. Morgan could probably give her some to use. Or someone else. Mine are brand new! If I share them with anyone they'll be gone a whole lot sooner."

Kristin finished the circle on the birdhouse, and started on the next circle in the picture. It was a car tire — like the tire on the Johnson's car on the highway last night — like the tire that Dad had stopped to change because the Scriptures say "do for others what you want them to do for you."

Suddenly Kristin leaned across the aisle. "Here, Katelynn." She held out the brand-new box of scented markers. "You can use some of my markers."

"Thank you!" Katelynn grinned.

And with a big smile, Kristin went back to coloring her circles again.

Discussion Time

2

Check understanding of the story and development of personal values.

- Have you ever been stuck by the side of the road with a flat tire or car trouble?
- Are there other times that you have needed help and someone helped you?
- How did you feel when they helped you?
- Have you ever helped someone who needed your help? Tell about it.
- How did helping them make you feel?
- Should we just help our friends or those who can do something for us in return?
- Can you think of some things that you can do to help others?

A Test-Words Name ______________________

Write each spelling word on the line as your teacher says it.

1. books	6. use
2. food	7. found
3. also	8. each
4. full	9. too
5. dear	10. vowel

Review Lesson 24

B Test-Sentences

The two underlined words in each of the sentences are misspelled. Write the sentences on the lines below, spelling each underlined word correctly.

The gerl will cownt the money.

1. The girl will count the money.

The blak dog made a lot of noiz.

2. The black dog made a lot of noise.

In touwn there is a bigger stor.

3. In town there is a bigger store.

☆ **Test-Challenge Words**

On a sheet of paper, write each challenge word as your teacher says it.

211

3 Test-Words

Test for knowledge of the correct spellings of these words. (See the instructions at the top right for challenge words.)

Say: I will say the word once, use the word in a sentence, then say the word again. Write the word on the lines in your Worktext.

1.	books	The children looked at **books** on the way to the mall.
2.	food	The **food** at the restaurant was very good.
3.	also	Cathy got a balloon **also**.
4.	full	Everyone felt **full** when they left.
5.	dear	"Those people need help, **Dear**," said Christopher's dad.
6.	use	The elderly man could not **use** the jack.
7.	found	He **found** a lug wrench in his trunk.
8.	each	Kristin's dad tightened **each** lug nut on the spare tire.
9.	too	The woman in the car said "thank-you," **too**.
10.	vowel	Do you know your long and short **vowel** sounds?
☆	wanted	Dad **wanted** to take the family out to eat.
☆	stood	The two clowns **stood** by the restaurant door.
☆	year	The clowns come to the restaurant several times a **year**.

☆ Test-Challenge Words

On a separate piece of paper, challenge words may be tested using the sentences below.

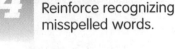

4 Test-Sentences

Reinforce recognizing misspelled words.

Say: Read each sentence carefully. The underlined words in each sentence are misspelled. Write the sentences on the lines in your Worktext, spelling each underlined word correctly.

Take a minute to memorize . . .

Have students say the memory verses from lessons 13, 14, 15, 16, 17, and 18 with you.

1 Test-Dictation

Reinforce correct spelling by using current and previous words in context.

(Say) Listen as I read each sentence. Then write the missing words in your Worktext. (Slowly read each sentence twice. Sentences are found in the student text to the right. The words **always**, **orange**, and **hear** are found in this unit.)

2 Test-Proofreading

Familiarize students with standardized test format and reinforce recognizing misspelled words.

(Say) Look at each set of words. One word in each set is misspelled. Fill in the oval by the misspelled word.

⭐ **Test-Challenge Words**

On a separate piece of paper, challenge words may be tested using the sentences below.

(Say) I will say the word once, use the word in a sentence, then say the word again. Write the word on your paper.

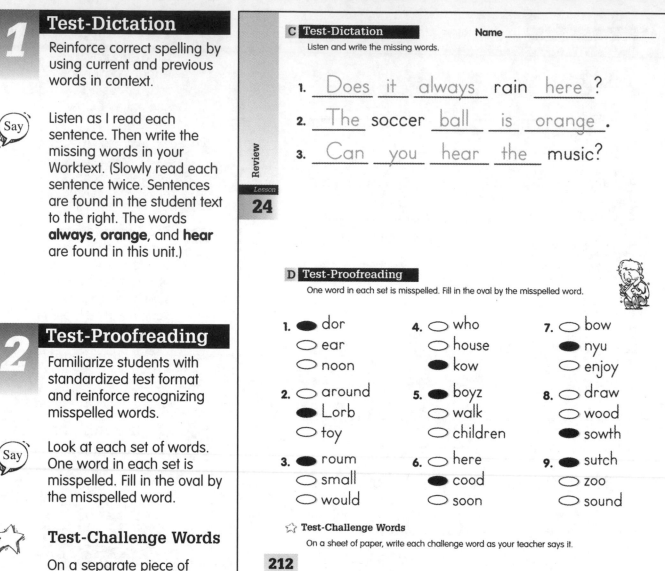

C Test-Dictation

Listen and write the missing words.

Name _____

1. __Does__ __it__ __always__ rain __here__ ?
2. __The__ soccer __ball__ __is__ __orange__ .
3. __Can__ __you__ __hear__ __the__ music?

D Test-Proofreading

One word in each set is misspelled. Fill in the oval by the misspelled word.

1. ● dor
   ○ ear
   ○ noon

2. ○ around
   ● Lorb
   ○ toy

3. ● roum
   ○ small
   ○ would

4. ○ who
   ○ house
   ● kow

5. ● boyz
   ○ walk
   ○ children

6. ○ here
   ● cood
   ○ soon

7. ○ bow
   ● nyu
   ○ enjoy

8. ○ draw
   ○ wood
   ● sowth

9. ● sutch
   ○ zoo
   ○ sound

☆ **Test-Challenge Words**

On a sheet of paper, write each challenge word as your teacher says it.

212

☆	cloud	The white balloon looked like a **cloud**.
☆	balloon	Cathy's **balloon** was in the shape of a bunny.
☆	crown	The clown had a funny **crown** on his head.
☆	before	The children washed their hands **before** they ate dinner.

300

E Test-Shapes

Name _____

Color each marker on which the word is spelled incorrectly.

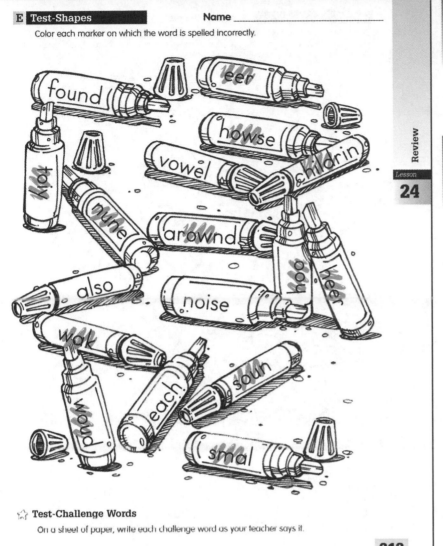

⭐ **Test-Challenge Words**

On a sheet of paper, write each challenge word as your teacher says it.

213

 Test-Challenge Words

On a separate piece of paper, challenge words may be tested using the sentences below.

(Say) I will say the word once, use the word in a sentence, then say the word again. Write the word on your paper.

⭐	through	The family is **through** with their meal.
⭐	important	Kristin's dad felt it was **important** to stop and help the man.
⭐	looked	The elderly man **looked** relieved that someone stopped to help.
⭐	called	If they needed help, Dad could have **called** on the cell phone.
⭐	lunch	After **lunch** they learned the names of many geometric shapes.

---

1 Test-Shapes

Test mastery of words in this unit.

(Say) Look at each marker. If the word is misspelled, color the piece of marker.

2 Action Game

Reinforce spelling skills and provide motivation and interest.

Materials
- container with nine folded cards (3 marked 1, 3 marked 2, 3 marked 3)
- small prizes (erasers, pencils, stickers)

How to Play:

Have the students form a line. Have the first student in line choose a card from the container. If the card reads 1, give him a word to spell tested on Day 1; if the card reads 2, give him a word tested on Day 2, and, if the card reads 3, a word tested on day 3. If he spells it correctly, give him a prize and have him return to his desk; if he spells it incorrectly, have him go to the end of the line. (Each time the container is emptied, return all the cards to the container and continue down the line.) Continue playing until every student has spelled a word correctly.

Game

Materials

- game page (from student text)
- stickers (13 per child)
- markers (1 per child)
- game word list

Game Word List

Use of challenge words is optional.

The Octagons

1. books
2. food
3. also
4. full
5. dear
6. use
7. found
8. each
9. too
10. vowel
11. count
12. noise
13. store

The Triangles

1. always
2. orange
3. hear
4. door
5. Lord
6. room
7. cow
8. boys
9. could
10. new
11. south
12. such
13. zoo

The Rectangles

1. ear
2. noon
3. around
4. toy
5. small
6. would
7. who
8. house
9. walk
10. children
11. here
12. soon
13. tooth

F Game

Name _____

Kristin shared her markers with Katelynn when their class was completing a worksheet on geometric shapes. Use shapes as your team names for this game. Place a sticker each time you or your team spells a review word correctly.

Remember: Treat others the way you want to be treated.

214

How to Play:

- Divide students into three teams. Name one team **The Octagons**, one **The Triangles**, and one **The Rectangles**. (Option: You may wish to seat students in groups of three, each child from a different team. They should share one game page.) Decide which team goes first, second, and third.
- Read the instructions from the student game page aloud.
- Have a student from the first team choose a number from 1 to 13.
- Say the word that matches that number (from the team's word list) aloud twice. (You may also use the word in a sentence. Ex.: "cat — The cat climbed a tree. — cat")
- Have the student who chose the number write the word on the board.
- If the word is spelled correctly, have all the members of that team put a sticker on that number by their team name. If the word is misspelled, have them put an "X" through that number. They may not choose that number again. (Note: If the word is misspelled, correct the spelling immediately.)
- Repeat this process with the second team and then the third. (Be sure to use a different student from each team for each round.)
- When the words from all three lists have been used, the team with the most stickers is the winner.

Non-Competitive Option: At the end of the game, say: "Class, I'm proud of your efforts to spell the words correctly. If you had fun and tried your best, you are all winners!"

G Test-Words

Name _____

Write each spelling word on the line as your teacher says it.

1. bow
2. enjoy
3. wood
4. zoo
5. sound

6. which
7. took
8. draw
9. form
10. want

Review

Lesson
24

H Test-Sentences

The two underlined words in each of the sentences are misspelled. Write the sentences on the lines below, spelling each underlined word correctly.

My <u>muther</u> said we could ride the <u>hors</u>.

1. My **mother** said we could ride the **horse**.

<u>may</u> I keep this <u>touth</u> I pulled ?

2. **May** I keep this **tooth** I pulled ?

All the <u>litle</u> beads are <u>rownd</u>.

3. All the **little** beads are **round**.

☆ **Test-Challenge Words**

On a sheet of paper, write each challenge word as your teacher says it.

215

Test-Challenge Words

On a separate piece of paper, challenge words may be tested using the sentences below.

2 Test-Sentences

Reinforce recognizing misspelled words.

Day 5

Review **24**

Say

Read each sentence carefully. The underlined words in each sentence are misspelled. Write the sentences on the lines in your Worktext, spelling each underlined word correctly.

1 Test-Words

Test for knowledge of the correct spellings of these words. (See the instructions at the top right for challenge words.)

Say

I will say the word once, use the word in a sentence, then say the word again. Write the word on the lines in your Worktext.

1. bow — They will **bow** their heads to pray before the meal.
2. enjoy — The clowns know children **enjoy** balloons.
3. wood — The restaurant tables were made of **wood**.
4. zoo — Kristin used her new markers to color **zoo** animals.
5. sound — She tried not to make a **sound** when she yawned.
6. which — She told them **which** shape was an octagon.
7. took — Kristin **took** her markers out of her desk.
8. draw — Mrs. Morgan said they may **draw** pictures.
9. form — Geometric shapes can **form** pretty patterns.
10. want — Kristin thought, "I **want** to live by God's Word."
☆ flower — Kristin colored the **flower** with her red marker.
☆ knew — Kristin **knew** that Jesus wanted her to share.
☆ voice — "Use my markers," said Kristin with a kind **voice**.

3 Writing Assessment

Assess student's spelling, grammar, and composition skills through personal writing.

(Say) • In our story this week the Wright family had gone shopping and then out to eat at a restaurant. What happened on their way home? (They saw an elderly couple by the side of the road who needed help changing a flat tire. They stopped and Mr. Wright changed the tire.)

• The children asked their dad why he hadn't taken the money the elderly couple tried to give him for changing the tire. What did he tell them? (That he just wanted to help and that the Scriptures say "do for others what you want them to do for you.")

• At school the next day Kristin remembered that Scripture. What did she do to help someone? (She shared her markers.)

• Write in your journal about a time you helped someone.

I Writing Assessment
Write at least four sentences about a time when you helped someone.

Name _____

Review

Lesson
24

1. _____
   _____

2. _____
   _____

3. _____
   _____

4. _____
   _____

Scripture
Matt. 7:12

216

A rubric for scoring is provided in Appendix B.

---

4 Action Game

Reinforce spelling skills and provide motivation and interest.

Materials

• None

How to Play:
Choose two students to hold up their hands to form a bridge. Have all other students line up to march under the bridge. Have the students march and sing (to the tune of London Bridge):
Someone needs to spell a word, spell a word, spell a word. Someone needs to spell a word. It is you! Instruct the students forming the bridge that they are to lower the bridge over a student at the end of the song. Have the student caught by the bridge spell a word tested on today's test. If he misspells the word, have him continue marching; if he spells the word correctly, have him take the place of one of the students forming the bridge. Have the student he replaced march if he has not spelled a word correctly; have him return to his desk if he has.
Continue playing until every student has spelled a word correctly.

Spelling Is Fun!

This certificate is awarded to

_____

for practicing the following words, by doing terrific spelling activities and playing great spelling games!

Date _____

books	food	around	boys	also
could	new	bow	door	always
dear	noon	count	enjoy	children
ear	room	cow	form	draw
full	soon	found	horse	each
hear	too	house	Lord	small
here	tooth	round	noise	such
took	use	sound	orange	walk
wood	who	south	store	want
would	zoo	vowel	toy	which
☆ looked	☆ balloon	☆ cloud	☆ before	☆ called
☆ stood	☆ knew	☆ crown	☆ important	☆ lunch
☆ year	☆ through	☆ flower	☆ voice	☆ wanted

5 Certificate

Provide an opportunity for parents or guardians to encourage and assess their child's progress.

Say
- Write your name on the first line.
- Now I will write the date on the board for you to copy on the next line.
- Follow along as I read the certificate out loud.
- Be sure to show your parents or guardian all the words you've practiced spelling.

Take a minute to memorize...

Read the memory verse twice. Have students practice it with you two more times.

6 Letter

Provide the parent or guardian with the spelling word lists for the next unit.

(Say) Show your parents or guardian this letter that tells them what your spelling words will be for the next unit. Ask them to put it in a special place where you will remember to practice them together.

Dear Parent,

We are about to begin a new spelling unit containing five weekly lessons. A set of ten words plus three challenge words will be studied each week. All the words will be reviewed in the sixth week.

Values based on the Scriptures listed below will be taught in each lesson.

Lesson 25	Lesson 26	Lesson 27	Lesson 28	Lesson 29
dish	band	back	another	bell
finish	bend	bring	both	better
fish	blind	clock	other	dress
shoe	candy	duck	thank	funny
shop	end	hang	these	grass
should	find	milk	thick	guess
show	grand	sick	thin	mitten
shut	Indian	sing	think	pull
wash	kind	talk	those	rabbit
wish	pond	truck	thought	still
☆ shelf	☆ friend	☆ along	☆ brother	☆ different
☆ shoes	☆ index	☆ block	☆ father	☆ dinner
☆ short	☆ second	☆ something	☆ together	☆ letter
Luke 4:19	John 8:32	Matt. 5:47	Matt. 4:17	Luke 12:37

Quotables!

Command of oral language is the foundation for success in reading and writing.

First Base Blessing

Stephen finds it hard to see God's blessings when he can't play at recess.

"Run, Tony! Go home! Go! Go!" Stephen kicked aside the foot rest on his wheelchair and leaned forward to grab the backstop with his hands. "Run!" Stephen stood and balanced on his left foot wrapped in the hard, blue cast. His other leg was still in a cast up past his knee. It was nearly impossible to stand without holding on to something.

"Hey, Stephen. Want to play catch with me?" Matthew threw the blue and white T-Ball up and caught it in his glove. "I brought your glove." He took it out from under his arm and tossed it on the seat of the wheelchair as he walked up.

"Sure, I'll play. I'm not doing much good here." Stephen reached for his glove, but lost his balance and sat right on top of it. "Playing catch would at least keep my arms in shape, I guess." He leaned over the side of his wheelchair and pulled his glove out of the seat, his right leg sticking out awkwardly in front of him. He kicked the foot rest back down with his other foot, shoved his hand in the glove, and maneuvered the wheelchair so he faced Matthew.

"Here it comes!" Matthew tossed the ball high in the air. Stephen stretched but couldn't reach the ball as it went sailing over his head.

"A little lower next time, Matthew." Stephen wheeled over, picked up the ball, and threw it back to his friend. Matthew's next throw bounced about four feet in front of the wheelchair, glanced off Stephen's cast, and rolled out of Stephen's reach. Stephen watched Matthew run to retrieve it. "Right here, Matthew." Stephen hit the inside of his glove with his fist. "Line drive."

Instead Matthew rolled the ball on the ground toward Stephen's wheelchair. "Get this one, Stephen." Stephen leaned over and tried to nab the ball as it rolled by, but missed. "I'll get it," Matthew yelled, racing after the ball again.

Stephen threw off his glove in defeat. "I never used to miss a ball. Now I can't even catch one rolled to me!" Stephen spun his chair around. "Matthew, I'm going to go get a drink." He wheeled across the grass toward the school's back door with little bursts of speed. He was out of breath when he reached the door. Then he realized he couldn't open it by himself. "I know it's a blessing I broke my legs rather than my head when I rode my bike in front of that car," he thought, "but I'm really tired of this wheelchair! Recess is no fun when I can't play T-Ball." He wiped his eyes with the back of his hand as tears of frustration formed in his eyes.

Matthew came running up huffing and puffing and pulled open the heavy door. "I'm not very good at T-Ball stuff, but I'll play you a game of UNO®. I brought mine from home. Mrs. Morgan said I could go get it out of my desk." Matthew ran down the hall toward the classroom.

"Who says I want to play UNO®," Stephen asked the empty hall.

After losing three hands in a row Stephen slouched over in his chair. "I'm not any better at this than playing catch, Matthew! I think I'll go out and watch the T-Ball game again. At least I understand that game."

Matthew shrugged and started picking up the cards. "Wonder what's bugging Stephen?" he thought to himself. "I guess he's just tired of being in that wheelchair."

At noon recess, Matthew tried again. "Want to listen to these new story CDs, Stephen? They're really good. They came with some neat pictures to color, and word searches and stuff. You can choose the CD and page to work on." Matthew held out the book of CDs. "The first CD is a story about soccer."

Stephen perked up as Matthew mentioned soccer. "I should be back to normal by soccer season. Maybe I can get some ideas from the CD. Does it teach anything about soccer?"

"I don't know. I haven't heard any of these yet. We just got 'em last night."

The two boys moved to a picnic table and Matthew started the CD player. Suddenly a four-square ball bounced across the table, scattering the markers. "Sorry," Katelynn said as she ran past after the ball.

Stephen watched Matthew scurry after the markers and put them back on the table. "Okay! Let's try this again." Just as Stephen clicked on the CD, a gust of wind caught their papers and blew them away. Matthew hurried after them. Stephen watched as he jumped over benches and crawled under tables collecting the scattered sheets.

Wanting to help, he awkwardly maneuvered his wheelchair around the nearest table, kicked the foot rest aside, and reached over to pick up a word search sheet. Just as he was about to grab the elusive paper, another puff of wind blew it a few feet away. Stephen kicked his wheelchair in frustration, then looked up. "Lord, I could use another blessing today," he prayed to himself. "Nothing is going right!" Matthew grabbed the last paper, then came back to the table.

Suddenly, Matthew's little brother skidded to a stop in front of them. "Hey, guess what! Miss Grant said I could be the first baseman today, Matthew! You guys wanna come watch our game?"

"Nah!" Stephen wrinkled his forehead and frowned. "We're going to listen to a CD."

"Oh, come on Stephen. It might be fun." Matthew

307

scooped everything off the table and back in the bag. "We haven't had much luck with this CD, anyway." Hanging the bag on the handle, he began to push Stephen's wheelchair toward the T-Ball field. "I really thought it would be fun to listen to that CD," he thought as the chair bumped over a clump of grass. "I've tried everything I can think of to help Stephen have a good recess. I know how he hates this chair."

He pushed Stephen right up beside first base. Miss Grant was giving directions from behind home plate. "Cindy, I think you were out, sweetheart," Miss Grant called. "Come back behind the backstop."

"I got there before Alex caught the ball, Miss Grant. Why am I out?"

"Did you see that play, Stephen?" Miss Grant walked toward first base.

"Yes, ma'am. She looked safe to me."

"Okay, Cindy. Stephen says you're safe. Go back to first." Cindy turned around and ran back to first base. Miss Grant put the ball on the Tee for the next batter who hit a pop fly to the short stop. The short stop caught it, and even remembered to throw it toward first. Cindy was halfway to second before she heard her team screaming at her to go back. Alex expertly caught the ball and touched the base just before Cindy got back.

"Tie goes to the runner." Cindy looked at Miss Grant to make the call.

"Was it a tie, Stephen?"

"No, I'm afraid she was out this time, Miss Grant," Stephen laughed.

Matthew watched his friend serve as first base umpire for the whole recess. Stephen was really good. He knew a lot about T-Ball. The first graders thought it was neat that an older student was interested in their game. Miss Grant liked having someone help her make the hard calls. Matthew was just glad to see Stephen smiling again.

"I didn't think there was anything I could do at recess that would be fun," Stephen said as the bell rang and Matthew began pushing the wheelchair toward the school. "I asked God to help me find something fun to do, and I got to be an umpire!"

"I didn't think there was anything that would help you forget about your wheelchair! I sure tried everything." Matthew smiled.

As they came back into the classroom, both boys saw the text written on the board at the same time. "God is ready to give blessings to all who come to Him," Matthew read out loud.

"You can say that again!" Stephen grinned. "But you had to push me over to first base so I could see it!"

2 Discussion Time

Check understanding of the story and development of personal values.

- How did Stephen feel about recess?
- Raise your hand if you would feel like Stephen if you were in a wheelchair.
- Was Matthew being a good friend?
- What did he do to help Stephen enjoy recess?
- When was the last time you felt like everything was going wrong?
- How did you feel?
- Did God use Matthew to help Stephen?
- Can God use people to bring His blessings to you?

A Preview

Write each word as your teacher says it.

Name _____

1. should
2. shop
3. wish
4. show
5. finish
6. fish
7. shoe
8. shut
9. dish
10. wash

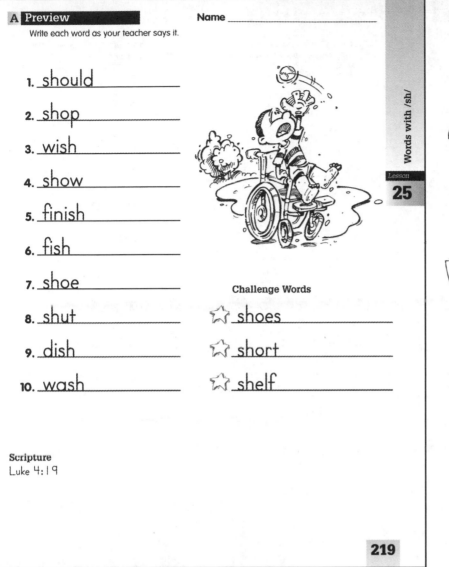

Challenge Words

☆ shoes
☆ short
☆ shelf

Scripture
Luke 4:19

219

Challenge

For better spellers, challenge words may be included in the weekly list. Challenge words are starred.

Correct Immediately!

Let's correct our preview. I will write each word on the board. Put a dot under each letter on your preview as I spell the word out loud. If you spelled a word wrong, rewrite it correctly.

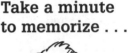

Progress Chart

Students may record scores. (Reproducible master in Appendix B.)

Take a minute to memorize . . .

Read the memory verse twice. Have students practice it with you two more times.

---

3 ## Preview

Test for knowledge of the correct spellings of these words. (See the instructions at the top right for challenge words.)

Say

I will say the word once, use the word in a sentence, then say the word again. Write the word on the lines in the Worktext.

1.	should	You **should** have fun at recess.
2.	shop	Stephen didn't need to **shop** for new baseball stuff this year.
3.	wish	"I **wish** I could play baseball," Stephen said.
4.	show	"You'll have to **show** me how to play the game," Stephen said.
5.	finish	"Don't you want to **finish** the game, Stephen?" Matthew asked.
6.	fish	Stephen could **fish** from his wheelchair.
7.	shoe	Stephen's **shoe** would not fit over his cast.
8.	shut	The door was **shut** and Stephen couldn't open it.
9.	dish	The **dish** was out of Stephen's reach.
10.	wash	It is good to **wash** your hands before you eat.
☆	shoes	Stephen didn't need to wear **shoes**.
☆	short	Stephen's arm was too **short** to reach the ball.
☆	shelf	The **shelf** was over Stephen's head.

4 Word Shapes

Help students form a correct image of whole words.

(Say) Look at each word and think about its shape. Now, write the word in the correct word Shape Boxes. You may check off each word as you use it.

(Say) In the word Shape Boxes, color the letters that spell the sound of /sh/ in each word. Circle the words that end with the digraph **sh**.

⭐ Challenge

Draw the correctly shaped box around each letter in these words.

(Say) On a separate sheet of paper, write other words that contain the spelling patterns in the word list. See how many words you can write.

B Word Shapes   Name _____

Write each word in the correct word shape boxes. Then, in the word shape boxes, color the letters that spell the sound of /sh/ in each word. Circle the words that end with the digraph **sh**.

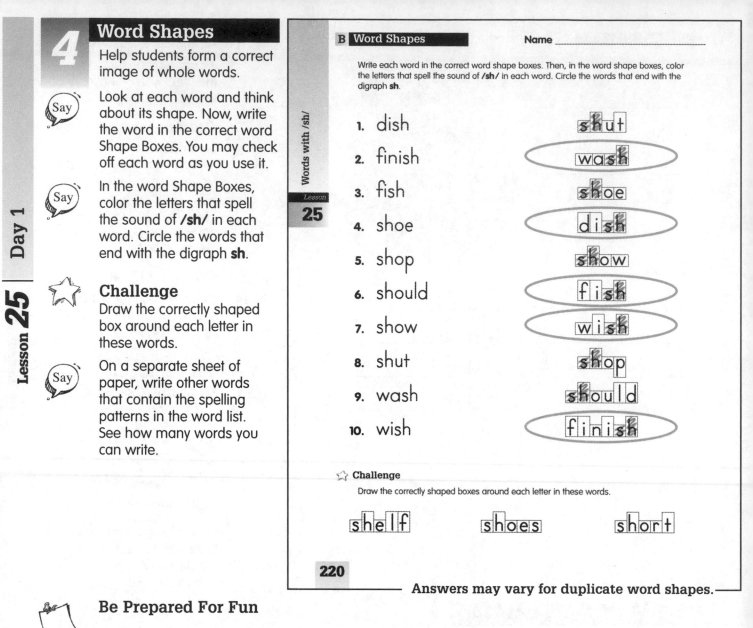

1. dish
2. finish
3. fish
4. shoe
5. shop
6. should
7. show
8. shut
9. wash
10. wish

Word shape boxes (answers):
shut, wash, shoe, dish, show, fish, wish, shop, should, finish

☆ Challenge

Draw the correctly shaped boxes around each letter in these words.

shelf   shoes   short

220

Be Prepared For Fun

Check these supply lists for **Fun Ways to Spell** presented **Day 2**. Purchase and/or gather these items ahead of time!

General
- Crayons
- 3 x 5 Cards cut in thirds (44 pieces per child)
- 3 x 5 Cards cut in thirds (15 more pieces to spell challenge words)
- Glue
- Bright Paper or Poster Board (about 3 pieces per child)
- Spelling List

Auditory
- Rhythm instruments (two wooden spoons, two pan lids, maracas)
- Spelling List

Visual
- Sidewalk Chalk
- Spelling List

Tactile
- Cotton Balls
- Glue
- Construction Paper
- Spelling List

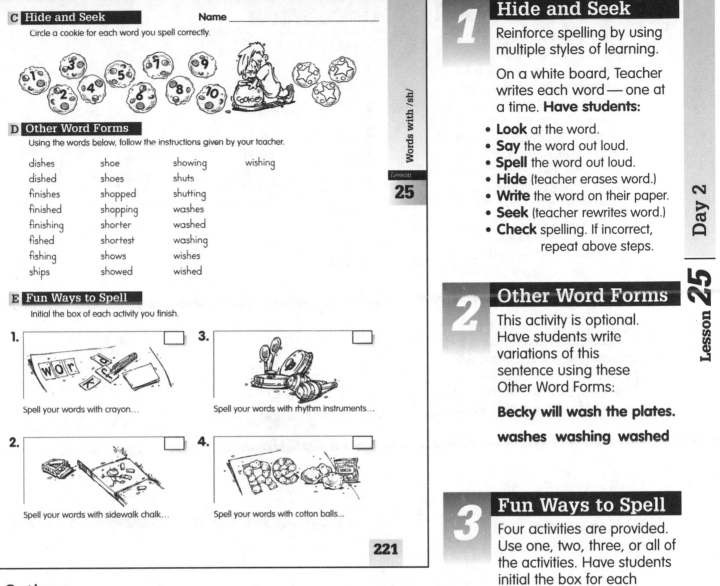

C Hide and Seek

Name _____

Circle a cookie for each word you spell correctly.

D Other Word Forms

Using the words below, follow the instructions given by your teacher.

dishes	shoe	showing	wishing
dished	shoes	shuts	
finishes	shopped	shutting	
finished	shopping	washes	
finishing	shorter	washed	
fished	shortest	washing	
fishing	shows	wishes	
ships	showed	wished	

E Fun Ways to Spell

Initial the box of each activity you finish.

1. ☐
Spell your words with crayon...

2. ☐
Spell your words with sidewalk chalk...

3. ☐
Spell your words with rhythm instruments...

4. ☐
Spell your words with cotton balls...

221

---

1 Hide and Seek

Reinforce spelling by using multiple styles of learning.

On a white board, Teacher writes each word — one at a time. **Have students:**

- **Look** at the word.
- **Say** the word out loud.
- **Spell** the word out loud.
- **Hide** (teacher erases word.)
- **Write** the word on their paper.
- **Seek** (teacher rewrites word.)
- **Check** spelling. If incorrect, repeat above steps.

2 Other Word Forms

This activity is optional. Have students write variations of this sentence using these Other Word Forms:

Becky will wash the plates.

washes washing washed

3 Fun Ways to Spell

Four activities are provided. Use one, two, three, or all of the activities. Have students initial the box for each activity they complete.

Options:

- assign activities to students according to their learning styles
- set up the activities in learning centers for students to do throughout the day
- divide students into four groups and assign one activity per group
- do one activity per day

General

To spell your words with crayon . . .
- Write each letter of your spelling word on a card.
- Glue the cards on a sheet of paper in the right order to spell your words.
- Check your spelling.

Auditory

To spell your words with rhythm instruments . . .
Look at a word on your spelling list.
- Close your eyes.
- Play your rhythm instruments softly while you whisper the spelling of the word.
- Open your eyes and check your spelling.

Visual

To spell your words with sidewalk chalk . . .
- Write each of your spelling words on the sidewalk (ball court or playground).
- Check your spelling.

Tactile

To spell your words with cotton balls . . .
- Choose a word from your spelling list.
- It may be a favorite word or a word you have trouble remembering how to spell.
- Write the word in tall, wide letters on a sheet of construction paper.
- Spread glue along the outline of each letter and press cotton balls into the glue.

311

Lesson **25**

1 Letter Change

Familiarize students with word meaning and usage.

Write **The man wore a hit on his head.** on the board. Ask the students to read the sentence silently and to raise their hands when they know which word doesn't fit in the sentence. Help them to see that by changing just one letter the whole word may be changed to one that does make sense in the sentence. Have a volunteer change the word from **hit** to **hat** in the sentence on the board.

(Say) Each of the sentences in this activity contain a word with one or two underlined letters. Change the word to one of your spelling words.

Words with /sh/

Lesson **25**

F Letter Change   Name _____

Help Stephen with his homework. Change the underlined letter or letters and write the spelling word on the blank.

1. dish _____ The d<u>a</u>sh was full of potatoes.
2. fish _____ The gold fis<u>t</u> swam to the top.
3. wish _____ I w<u>a</u>sh I could play T-ball.
4. shoe _____ Your sho<u>d</u> string is untied.
5. shop _____ This shi<u>p</u> sells tapes and books.
6. should _____ We <u>w</u>ould thank God.
7. show _____ Matthew will <u>s</u>low me how.
8. shut _____ The back door is sh<u>o</u>t.
9. wash _____ We w<u>i</u>sh our hands.
10. finish _____ Let's f<u>a</u>mish the game now.

Word Bank

dish	fish	shop	show	wash
finish	shoe	should	shut	wish

222

Take a minute to memorize . . .

Read the memory verse twice. Have students practice it with you two more times.

312

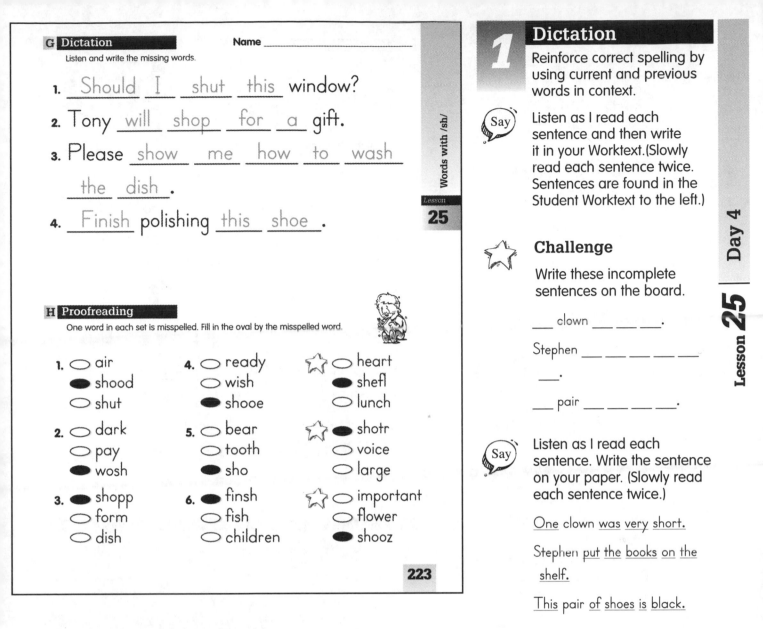

313

3 Hide and Seek

Reinforce correct spelling of current spelling words. (A reproducible master is provided in Appendix A as shown on the inset page to the right.)

Write the words one at a time on a white board.

Have students:

- **Look** at the word.
- **Say** the word out loud.
- **Spell** the word out loud.
- **Hide** (teacher erases word.)
- **Write** the word on paper.
- **Seek** (teacher rewrites word.)
- **Check** spelling. If incorrect, rewrite word correctly.

4 Making Words

Have your students complete this activity to strengthen spelling ability and expand vocabulary.

1 Posttest

Test mastery of the spelling words. Challenge words are starred.

I will say the word once, use the word in a sentence, then say the word again. Write the word on your paper.

Hide and Seek

Check a paper for each word you spell correctly.

Making Words

Look at other forms of your spelling words in the word bank.
Use the clues to find the word that fits best in each blank.

1. The man ___fishes___ from the boat.
2. When he ___finishes___ eating we'll go.
3. The ___shops___ were all closed.
4. Stephen ___wishes___ he could play.
5. He couldn't carry the ___dishes___.
6. Matthew ___shows___ Stephen how to play.
7. Stephen couldn't tie his ___shoes___.
8. Mother ___shuts___ the windows.
9. The rain ___washes___ the earth.

Word Bank

dish + es	fish + es	shop + s	shut + s	wish + es
finish + es	shoe + s	show + s	wash + es	

388

1.	dish	"Can you reach that **dish** from your wheelchair, Stephen?"
2.	shut	The door **shut** in Stephen's face before anyone noticed.
3.	show	Matthew will **show** Stephen how to use the CD player.
4.	fish	Stephen sat in his chair and watched the **fish** swim by.
5.	wash	Mrs. Wilson didn't need to **wash** Stephen's baseball uniform.
6.	wish	"I **wish** I could get these casts off," thought Stephen.
7.	should	Matthew thought Stephen **should** have fun at recess.
8.	finish	The first graders will **finish** the game with Stephen as the umpire.
9.	shoe	Stephen does not need a **shoe** for either foot yet.
10.	shop	Stephen needed to **shop** for shorts that would fit over his casts.
☆	short	The ball fell **short** of Stephen's chair.
☆	shelf	The gloves go on that **shelf**.
☆	shoes	Those can't be Stephen's **shoes** because they wouldn't fit.

Progress Chart

Students may record scores. (Reproducible master in Appendix B.)

Personal Dictionary

Students may add any words they have misspelled to their personal dictionaries for reference when writing. (Cover in Appendix B.)

314

I Game

Name _____

Run the bases in a game of T-ball while Stephen umpires. Move one space each time you or your team spells a word correctly from this week's word list.

Remember: Call out to God and ask Him for His blessing.

J Journaling

Write a thank-you letter in your journal to someone who has been a blessing to you.

224

How to Play:

- Divide students into two teams, and decide which team will go first.
- Have each student place their game piece on Start.
- Have a student from team A go to the board.
- Read the spelling word two times slowly and clearly. (You may also wish to use the word in a sentence. Ex.: "cat — The cat climbed a tree. — cat")
- Have the student write the word on the board.
- If the word is spelled correctly, instruct all the members of team A to move their game piece forward one space on the game board. (Note: If the word is misspelled, correct the spelling immediately.)
- Alternate between teams A and B as you go down the word list.
- The team to reach home plate first is the winner.

Non-Competitive Option: At the end of the game, say: "Class, I am proud of your efforts to spell the words correctly. If you had fun and tried your best, you are all winners!"

---

2 Game

Reinforce spelling skills and provide motivation and interest.

Materials

- game page (from student text)
- flat buttons, dry beans, pennies, or game discs (1 per child)
- game word list

Game Word List

Check off each word lightly in pencil as it is used.

1. **dish**
2. **fish**
3. **wish**
4. **finish**
5. **shoe**
6. **shop**
7. **should**
8. **show**
9. **shut**
10. **wash**
☆ **short**
☆ **shelf**
☆ **shoes**

3 Journaling

Provide a meaningful reason for correct spelling through personal writing.

Review the story using discussion leads provided on the following page. Encourage students to apply the Scriptural value in their journaling.

 Take a minute to memorize . . .

Have students say the memory verse with you once.

315

3 Journaling

Provide a meaningful reason for correct spelling through personal writing.

(Say)
- What were some of the ways Matthew tried to help Stephen have a good time during recess? (Played catch with him. Played UNO® with him. Brought tapes for him to listen to.)
- What did Matthew finally help Stephen discover he could do during recess? (Stephen could be the umpire for the first graders T-Ball game.)
- How does God use people to bring blessings to others? (Brainstorm. You may want to write the responses on the board.)
- Write a letter in your journal to someone who has been a blessing to you.

Children will write like the authors they read.

316

Freedom To Love

Tony realizes that there are things he doesn't need to worry about since the truth is that God loves him and is taking care of him.

Tony walked slowly out the front door with his black leather baseball glove under his arm and checked up and down the street again for Papa's red sports car. He looked down at his watch. Six o'clock! He kicked his backpack aside and slumped down on the top step. "One, two, three, four, five, six . . . that makes twelve little holes for the shoe string to go through in this shoe . . . twelve more in the other one . . . let's see, that's twenty-four . . . twenty-four little holes in my shoes." He reached down and tied his right shoelace in a double knot, then checked the time again. "Where is Papa?" Tony wondered to himself.

Tony unzipped his backpack, took out his new baseball, threw it hard into his glove, grabbed it out, then slammed it into his glove again. "Papa is never on time for his visits!" thought Tony. "He should have been here half an hour ago. Where can he be?" Tony made little squiggly lines in the dust with the toe of his shoe. He heard the phone ring inside the duplex, and Grandma Miller's voice as she answered it.

"Tony-O, your papa is on the phone. He wants to talk to you." Grandma held the door open and watched Tony run through the living room to the phone.

"Hello, Papa! When will you be here? . . . Oh, but you said . . . I guess . . . But, Marilee could come too . . . Wait! Wait! I have a baseball game tomorrow. Can you come? . . . Okay. Bye Papa."

Tony dropped the phone back into its place and went to get his backpack off the front porch.

As he walked by, Grandma Miller scooped him into her arms. "I'm sorry, Tony-O. I know you're disappointed. Maybe your papa will have more time

next week. Things will slow down at his company once school is out." She tousled Tony's dark hair. "Come on, let's build something with your blocks. Then I'll fix supper."

"Where's Mama? Isn't she coming home for supper?"

"Your mama went by the Parks and Recreation office to register you for soccer camp this summer and to help Coach Larkin. She called when she got off work and said she probably wouldn't make it in time for supper. She thought you'd be out with your papa until nine." Grandma gave Tony a squeeze. "Now where are those blocks?"

Tony pulled away. "I don't really feel like playing blocks. I'm hungry. Let's just eat, Grandma."

As Grandma began to get the meal ready, Tony walked out onto the porch and sat down on the top step again. "It's always Marilee this and Marilee that," he thought. "All Papa seems to care about anymore is his new wife." Tony sighed. "I only get to see him one night a week and one weekend a month — but he doesn't even come when he says he will. And even when he does, he's late." Tony stomped his foot on the dusty cement step. "Grandma Miller is nice, but I wish Mama was home."

The next afternoon Tony looked anxiously from the bench in the dugout toward the bleachers. "I wonder if Papa will make it? He said he would." Tony adjusted his red cap. Mama was sitting beside Grandma Miller on the front row. Stephen watched from his wheelchair at the end of the bleachers. Tony saw Mama's face brighten as she looked his way and waved. Maybe Papa was here!

"Hi, Tony!" Coach Larkin's deep

voice startled Tony and he jumped. "Oops! I didn't mean to scare you, buddy. What position are you playing tonight?"

"First base, sir."

"Well, I'll be cheering for you!" Coach Larkin walked over toward Mama. Tony saw him smile and say something to Stephen, then rap on his friend's cast with his knuckles. Stephen laughed. As Coach Larkin sat down beside Mama, he leaned over to whisper something to her, too. Mama smiled and tucked her hair behind her ear.

"Why is my soccer coach coming to my baseball game?" Tony wondered. "And where will Papa sit when he gets here?" He didn't have any more time to think about it because the game started and his team had the field.

Tony's team worked well together. Tony did his part by hitting a triple deep into right field in the third inning with the bases loaded. He even caught a pop fly, and made a double play when he tagged the runner trying to make it back to first. He checked the bleachers all through the game to see if Papa was in the crowd. But he only saw Mama and Coach Larkin cheering him on.

After the game, Coach Larkin pushed Stephen's wheelchair through the gravel to the dugout. Mama and Grandma Miller followed. "Good game, Tony. I was really impressed with that triple you hit." Coach Larkin smiled at Mama. "You've got quite a little athlete here, Maria."

"That double play was cool!" Stephen's eyes flashed. "I can hardly wait to get these casts off so I can get my legs back in shape. I want to be ready for soccer this fall."

"When do those casts come off, Stephen?" Coach Larkin put his hand on Stephen's shoulder.

"Well, I have an appointment tomorrow." He looked up. "The doctor said he might take them off then. That way I can get rid of the wheelchair and use crutches while I build up the strength in this leg." Stephen tapped the yellow cast that went all the way above his right knee.

"Well, you two guys are my key players, and I need you both this fall." He paused. "I think you should keep up your strength with some ice cream tonight, and celebrate a game well played. What do you think, Maria?"

"Oh, you don't have to do that Eddie!" Maria Vanetti smiled, then looked down at her son. "You did great out there tonight, Tony. All your hard practice has paid off." She pulled his cap down over his eyes. "Gather your stuff. And don't forget your bat!"

Tony came out of the dugout a few minutes later with his bat and glove. Mama, Coach Larkin, Grandma Miller, and Stephen were gathered around Coach's pickup. *"YES!"* he thought excitedly. *"Mama must have decided we could get ice cream after all."* Tony took off running.

Suddenly a big hand reached out and halted his progress. Tony spun around to see who had grabbed his arm. "Papa! What are you doing here?"

"How'd your game go?" Papa knelt down beside Tony. "I just got here."

"We did great, but you missed it all," Tony said. "I've got to go now, Papa. Coach Larkin is taking us all out for ice cream."

"Coach Larkin?" Papa raised his eyebrows.

"Yeah, he watched my game tonight with Mama. See ya later." Tony ran off as Mr. Vanetti turned and walked back to his car.

Grandma Miller said she'd had enough excitement for one day, and decided to head home. Coach Larkin walked her over to her car, then came back and put Stephen's chair in the back of his pickup. Stephen needed to sit on the passenger side because of his leg, so Tony and Mama got in from Coach's side of the pickup. Tony jumped in first and Mama had to sit beside Coach Larkin. It was pretty crowded, but Coach didn't seem to mind at all.

When they got home, Mama sent Tony on into the house to get his pajamas on. He peeked out his bedroom window to see what was taking Mama so long to come inside. She was standing on the porch looking out across Mason Springs Park, and talking softly to Coach Larkin. He saw Coach Larkin smile at Mama, and Mama smile back. "Coach Larkin seems to like us," Tony told the bear sitting on his bed. He let the curtain fall, then scampered into the bathroom to brush his teeth.

A few minutes later, Mama came in and sat on the edge of his bed. "So, Tony-O. What was your favorite part of the day?"

"Oh, I liked my triple, my double play — and the ice cream!"

Mama tucked the covers up under his chin. "You had quite an exciting evening, didn't you."

Tony nodded, then wrinkled his forehead thoughtfully. "Mama, can I ask you something?"

"Sure, Tony." Mama reached down and brushed the hair out of Tony's eyes.

"Is Coach Larkin going to come to our house and take Papa's place?"

Mama was quiet as she thought about her answer. "Eddie and I are becoming good friends, Tony," she said after a long pause. "But no one will ever take your papa's place. He will always be your papa, no matter how I feel about Mr. Larkin. Your papa made some choices that you and I didn't want, but we can't change that. It's been over two years now since he left, and I do enjoy Eddie's company, but it's way too soon to tell if he would ever choose to become a part of our family."

"Did Papa leave because of me? Was I too much trouble?" Tony snuggled closer to Mama. "Papa never seems to have much time for kids."

"No, Tony," Mama assured him. "Papa's leaving had nothing to do with you."

"Will Coach Larkin get tired of me, like Papa and Marilee, and quit spending time with our family, too?"

"That's something Mr. Larkin will have to decide." Mama smoothed Tony's hair. "But there's one thing you can count on, Tony. You are my son, and I will always love you and take care of you as long as you need me." Mama leaned over and kissed Tony on the forehead. "

If God wants Coach Larkin in our family, then God will work it out." She paused. "Does that answer your questions?"

"Yes. Good night, Mama."

"I guess this is a grown-up problem," Tony thought, as Mama walked back down the hall. *"Mama says it's not my fault. And Mama won't ever leave me."* He sighed, feeling much better. Then he remembered the Scripture verse they'd learned that morning in school. "You will know the truth, and the truth will set you free." *"Jesus loves me and so does Mama,"* thought Tony. *"No matter what Coach decides, or whether Papa spends more time with me or not, the truth is that Jesus and Mama both love me, and always will!"*

And Tony felt light and free as he quickly drifted off to sleep. "It's good to know the truth."

2 Discussion Time

Check understanding of the story and development of personal values.

- How does Tony feel about Coach Larkin?
- How does Coach Larkin show he cares about Tony and his mama?
- Is it all right for Tony to enjoy being with Coach Larkin?
- Does Tony love his papa?
- Is Tony disappointed his papa doesn't choose to spend a lot of time with him?
- Is it okay to love someone who doesn't always make good choices?
- If you remember that Jesus always loves you, it sets you free to love others even when they choose to do things that make you feel sad.

A Preview

Write each word as your teacher says it.

Name _____

1. bend
2. candy
3. grand
4. kind
5. end
6. blind
7. band
8. find
9. pond
10. Indian

Challenge Words

☆ friend
☆ index
☆ second

Scripture
John 8:32

225

Challenge

For better spellers, challenge words may be included in the weekly list. Challenge words are starred.

 Say

Correct Immediately!

Let's correct our preview. I will write each word on the board. Put a dot under each letter on your preview as I spell the word out loud. If you spelled a word wrong, rewrite it correctly.

Progress Chart

Students may record scores. (Reproducible master in Appendix B.)

Take a minute to memorize . . .

Read the memory verse twice. Have students practice it with you two more times.

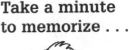

Lesson **26** | **Day 1**

---

3 ## Preview

Test for knowledge of the correct spellings of these words. (See the instructions at the top right for challenge words.)

Say

I will say the word once, use the word in a sentence, then say the word again. Write the word on the lines in the Worktext.

1.	bend	Soon Stephen will be able to **bend** both knees.
2.	candy	Mama and Coach Larkin ate some **candy** at the game.
3.	grand	Tony felt **grand** when the crowd cheered as he ran the bases.
4.	kind	Coach Larkin is **kind** to Mama and Tony.
5.	end	Mama talked to Tony at the **end** of the day.
6.	blind	Tony is not **blind** to Papa's faults.
7.	band	Tony and Mama are bound by a strong **band** of love.
8.	find	You will never **find** a better friend than Jesus.
9.	pond	Tony likes to catch the frogs in the **pond** near his house.
10.	Indian	There is not an **Indian** on the team.
☆	friend	Coach Larkin is a **friend** of Tony and his mama.
☆	index	Look up the word "love" in the **index**.
☆	second	Tony got the runner out on **second** base too.

319

Word Shapes

4

Word Shapes

Help students form a correct image of whole words.

(Say) Look at each word and think about its shape. Now, write the word in the correct word Shape Boxes. You may check off each word as you use it.

(The letters **nd** can be in the middle or at the end of a word.)

(Say) In the word Shape Boxes, color the letters **nd** in each word. Circle the words in which **nd** comes in the middle of the word.

Challenge

Draw the correctly shaped box around each letter in these words.

(Say) On a separate sheet of paper, write sentences using one or more of the spelling words.

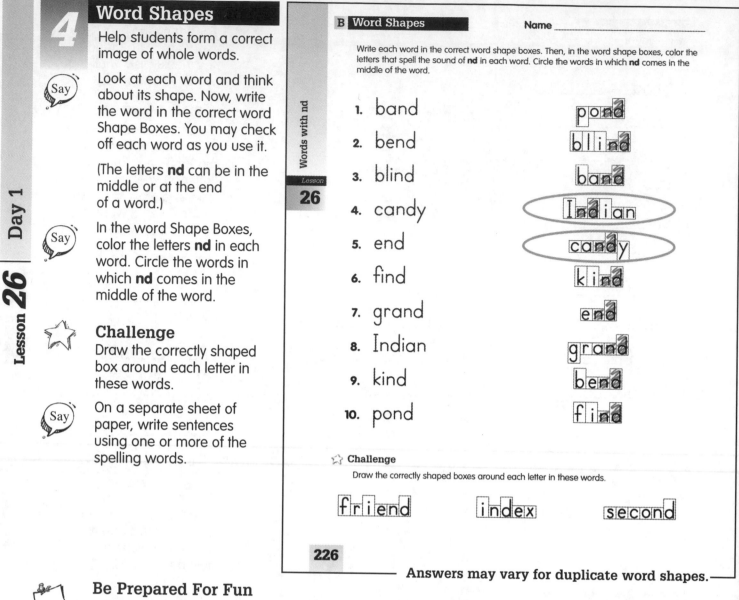

B Word Shapes

Name _____

Write each word in the correct word shape boxes. Then, in the word shape boxes, color the letters that spell the sound of **nd** in each word. Circle the words in which **nd** comes in the middle of the word.

Words with nd

Lesson **26**

1. band   pond
2. bend   blind
3. blind   band
4. candy   ⟨Indian⟩
5. end   ⟨candy⟩
6. find   kind
7. grand   end
8. Indian   grand
9. kind   bend
10. pond   find

☆ **Challenge**

Draw the correctly shaped boxes around each letter in these words.

friend   index   second

226

Answers may vary for duplicate word shapes.

Be Prepared For Fun

Check these supply lists for **Fun Ways to Spell** presented **Day 2**. Purchase and/or gather these items ahead of time!

General
- Eraser
- Dark Construction Paper
- Spelling List

Auditory
- Spelling List

Visual
- Poster Paint
- Paint Brush
- Art Paper (3 or 4 sheets per child)
- Spelling List

Tactile
- Damp Sand in plastic storage box with lid
- Spelling List

320

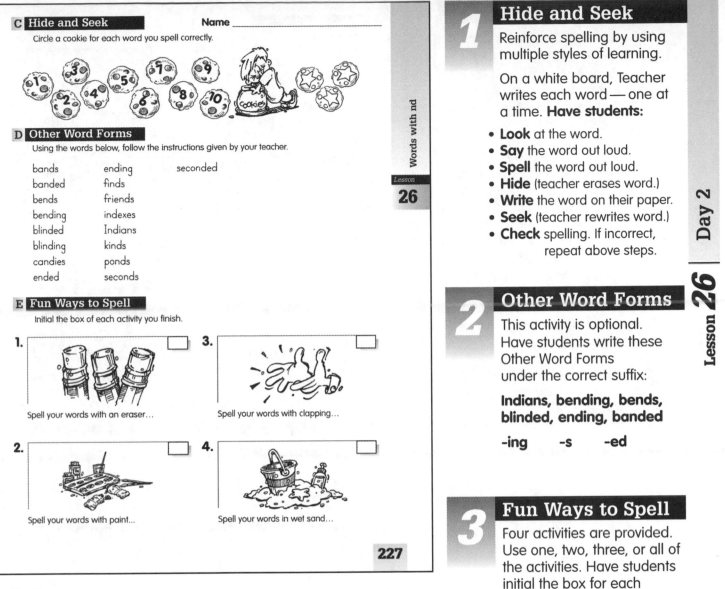

C Hide and Seek

Name _____

Circle a cookie for each word you spell correctly.

D Other Word Forms

Using the words below, follow the instructions given by your teacher.

bands	ending	seconded
banded	finds	
bends	friends	
bending	indexes	
blinded	Indians	
blinding	kinds	
candies	ponds	
ended	seconds	

E Fun Ways to Spell

Initial the box of each activity you finish.

1.
Spell your words with an eraser…

3.
Spell your words with clapping…

2.
Spell your words with paint…

4.
Spell your words in wet sand…

227

---

1 Hide and Seek

Reinforce spelling by using multiple styles of learning.

On a white board, Teacher writes each word — one at a time. **Have students:**

- **Look** at the word.
- **Say** the word out loud.
- **Spell** the word out loud.
- **Hide** (teacher erases word.)
- **Write** the word on their paper.
- **Seek** (teacher rewrites word.)
- **Check** spelling. If incorrect, repeat above steps.

2 Other Word Forms

This activity is optional. Have students write these Other Word Forms under the correct suffix:

Indians, bending, bends, blinded, ending, banded

-ing   -s   -ed

3 Fun Ways to Spell

Four activities are provided. Use one, two, three, or all of the activities. Have students initial the box for each activity they complete.

Options:

- assign activities to students according to their learning styles
- set up the activities in learning centers for students to do throughout the day
- divide students into four groups and assign one activity per group
- do one activity per day

General

To spell your words with an eraser . . .
- Turn your pencil upside down.
- Use the eraser to write your spelling words on a sheet of dark construction paper.
- Check your spelling.

Auditory

To spell your words with clapping . . .
- Look at a word on your spelling list.
- Close your eyes.
- Clap your hands softly while you whisper the spelling of the word.
- Open your eyes and check your spelling.

Visual

To spell your words with paint . . .
- Dip your brush in one color of poster paint.
- Paint a spelling word on your paper.
- Rinse your brush well in clean water and wipe it dry on a paper towel before dipping it in another color to paint another word.

Tactile

To spell your words in damp sand . . .
- Use finger to write a spelling word in damp sand.
- Check your spelling.
- Smooth the sand with your fingers and write another word.

321

1 Guide Words

Familiarize students with word meaning and usage. Write **him - jam** and **fast - hat** on the board. Explain that word pairs like these are guide words that appear in a dictionary so that words can be easily located. Now write **girl** on the board. Help the students determine which pair of guide words the word **girl** would be found between. Write **bag - bug** on the board. Help the students learn to look at the second letter when the beginning letters of two words are the same.

Say) Write your spelling words beneath the correct pair of guide words.

F Guide Words   Name _____

These word pairs are guide words like those that appear in a dictionary. Write your spelling words on the lines below the set of guide words for the page on which each spelling word would appear. Use words from the Word Bank below.

ball – big
band
bend
black – dog
blind
candy
far – green
find
grand

ear – every
end
ice cream – itch
Indian

keep – know
kind
pick – race
pond

Word Bank

band	blind	end	grand	kind
bend	candy	find	Indian	pond

228

Take a minute to memorize . . .

Read the memory verse twice. Have students practice it with you two more times.

322

G Dictation

Name _____

Listen and write the missing words.

1. It is grand to watch a marching band .
2. Taffy is candy that will bend .
3. There is a pond at the end of this road .
4. The Indian was kind .

Words with nd

Lesson 26

H Proofreading

One word in each set is misspelled. Fill in the oval by the misspelled word.

1. ○ been
   ● candi
   ○ grand

2. ● podn
   ○ soft
   ○ find

3. ● dand
   ○ show
   ○ plan

4. ○ end
   ○ sister
   ● blinde

5. ○ wash
   ● biend
   ○ kind

6. ○ must
   ● indian
   ○ shoe

☆ ● frend
   ○ through
   ○ shoes

☆ ○ crown
   ○ shelf
   ● endex

☆ ● secund
   ○ beside
   ○ short

229

---

1 Dictation

Reinforce correct spelling by using current and previous words in context.

Say Listen as I read each sentence and then write it in your Worktext.(Slowly read each sentence twice. Sentences are found in the Student Worktext to the left.)

☆ **Challenge**

Write these incomplete sentences on the board.

Tony's __ __ __ __ __.

__ __ __ __ __ back __ __ book.

__ __ __ __ __ .

Say Listen as I read each sentence. Write the sentence on your paper. (Slowly read each sentence twice.)

Tony's <u>friend</u> came to <u>his</u> <u>game.</u>

The <u>index</u> <u>is</u> <u>at</u> the back <u>of</u> <u>the</u> book.

<u>One</u> <u>second</u> <u>goes</u> <u>by</u> <u>fast.</u>

2 Proofreading

Familiarize students with standardized test format and reinforce recognizing misspelled words.

Say Look at each set of words. One word in each set is misspelled. Fill in the oval by the misspelled word. (You may wish to pronounce each set of words to help students correctly identify them.)

3 Hide and Seek

Reinforce correct spelling of current spelling words. (A reproducible master is provided in Appendix A as shown on the inset page to the right.)

Write the words one at a time on a white board.

Have students:

- **Look** at the word.
- **Say** the word out loud.
- **Spell** the word out loud.
- **Hide** (teacher erases word.)
- **Write** the word on paper.
- **Seek** (teacher rewrites word.)
- **Check** spelling. If incorrect, rewrite word correctly.

4 Suffixes

Have your students complete this activity to strengthen spelling ability and expand vocabulary.

1 Posttest

Test mastery of the spelling words. Challenge words are starred.

(Say) I will say the word once, use the word in a sentence, then say the word again. Write the word on your paper.

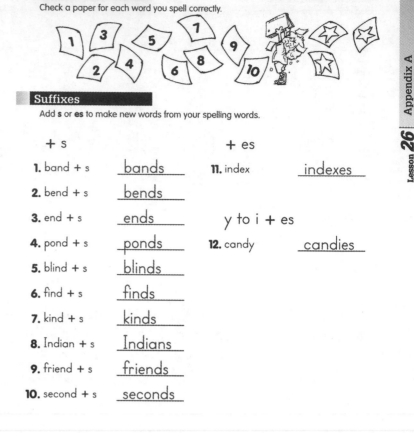

Hide and Seek
Check a paper for each word you spell correctly.

Suffixes
Add **s** or **es** to make new words from your spelling words.

+ s

1. band + s   bands
2. bend + s   bends
3. end + s   ends
4. pond + s   ponds
5. blind + s   blinds
6. find + s   finds
7. kind + s   kinds
8. Indian + s   Indians
9. friend + s   friends
10. second + s   seconds

+ es

11. index   indexes

y to i + es

12. candy   candies

389

1. **band** — There was not a **band** at Tony's ball game.
2. **grand** — Tony did not hit a **grand** slam.
3. **candy** — Grandma Miller shared her **candy** with Stephen at the game.
4. **bend** — Stephen cannot **bend** both knees.
5. **blind** — Tony is not **blind** to the kindness of Coach Larkin.
6. **end** — Papa came at the **end** of the game.
7. **kind** — Coach Larkin is **kind** to the Vanetti family.
8. **find** — You will **find** Jesus to be an excellent friend.
9. **Indian** — The **Indian** lives in India.
10. **pond** — Tony has a **pond** by his house.
☆ **friend** — Stephen is Tony's **friend**.
☆ **index** — Look up "truth" in the **index**.
☆ **second** — Tony did not make it to **second** base on that hit.

Progress Chart
Students may record scores. (Reproducible master in Appendix B.)

Personal Dictionary
Students may add any words they have misspelled to their personal dictionaries for reference when writing. (Cover in Appendix B.)

I Game

Name _____

Tony is getting treated to ice cream after his baseball game. Lead the way to the ice cream shop by moving one space each time you or your team spells a word correctly from this week's word list.

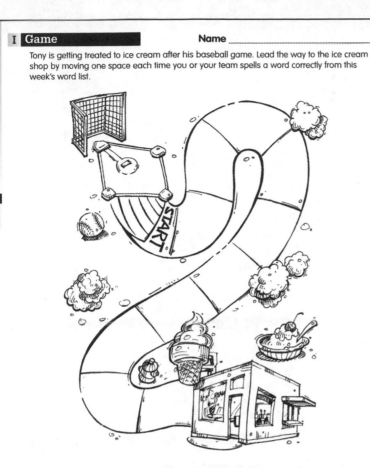

Remember: God does not want you to feel guilty for the sins of others.

J Journaling

In your journal, make a list of people whom you love.
Label the list: **People I Love**.

230

---

2 Game

Reinforce spelling skills and provide motivation and interest.

Materials

- game page (from student text)
- flat buttons, dry beans, pennies, or game discs (1 per child)
- game word list

Game Word List

Use of challenge words is optional.

1. **band**
2. **grand**
3. **candy**
4. **end**
5. **bend**
6. **pond**
7. **blind**
8. **find**
9. **kind**
10. **Indian**
☆ **friend**
☆ **index**
☆ **second**

3 Journaling

Provide a meaningful reason for correct spelling through personal writing.

Review the story using discussion leads provided on the following page. Encourage students to apply the Scriptural value in their journaling.

  Take a minute to memorize . . .

Have students say the memory verses from lessons 25 and 26 with you.

How to Play:

- Divide students into two teams, and decide which team will go first.
- Have each student place their game piece on Start.
- Have a student from team A go to the board.
- Read the spelling word two times slowly and clearly. (You may also wish to use the word in a sentence. Ex.: "cat — The cat climbed a tree. — cat")
- Have the student write the word on the board.
- If the word is spelled correctly, instruct all the members of team A to move their game piece forward one space on the game board. (Note: If the word is misspelled, correct the spelling immediately.)
- Alternate between teams A and B as you go down the word list.
- The team to reach the ice cream shop first is the winner.

Non-Competitive Option: At the end of the game, say: "Class, I am proud of your efforts to spell the words correctly. If you had fun and tried your best, you are all winners!"

325

Journaling

Provide a meaningful reason for correct spelling through personal writing.

(Say)

- Why was Tony feeling sad at the beginning of the story? (Papa didn't come to pick him up for their evening together. Papa didn't make it to Tony's game the next evening, either.)
- What did Tony, Mama, and Coach do together? (They went to Tony's game and ate ice cream afterward.)
- After Tony talked to his mom, he realized that Jesus loved him no matter what. It set him free to love his papa, mama, and Coach Larkin.
- Think of people who you know. Make a list in your journal of the ones who you love.

"*Anytime a child pays close attention to what's written, spelling awareness increases.*"*

*Scott, Jill E. 1994. Spelling for Readers and Writers. The Reading Teacher, Vol. 48, No. 2, October: 188-190.

The Angry Lady

A shopping trip turns into a lesson on prejudice for Setsuko.

Setsuko gazed through the glass display case at the lovely watches inside. They came in all different sizes and shapes. Many were silver and gold with intricate details. Some had diamonds around the watch face or in place of the numbers. A watch with a huge round case stood out from the others. Setsuko held her arm up near the glass. That watch would be bigger than her wrist! A whole row of watches had action figures on them meant to appeal to kids. A nice-looking watch with a leather band had a place on the face of it where a little moon went across.

Setsuko didn't really mind waiting here with her mother while the lady behind the counter rummaged around in the cabinet below the cash register. After all, they were looking for the perfect watch for Setsuko's father. It hadn't taken them long to agree on a beautiful simple watch with a black leather band, but it was taking the sales lady a long time to find the case and paper work that went with it. "Oh well, there are plenty of neat watches to look at while we wait." Setsuko moved a couple of feet down the counter to look at another group of watches. That one was really cute. There were hearts all around the band and . . .

"It's such a shame they let so many foreigners into our country." A loud voice broke into Setsuko's thoughts. "Why, they don't belong here at all! They've got their own countries to live in. I say let them stay there and leave us alone." A woman waiting for the clerk to help her stood a few feet away along the counter and spoke loudly to the friend with her. "Coming here and taking jobs away from honest Americans, they ought to be ashamed. Especially those Japanese! They won't settle for just any job, no. They go after our best jobs, don't you know? And they take over our good American businesses, too. Why, there are more Japanese-made cars out in this parking lot than solid American cars! It's a disgrace, I tell you! An absolute shame! And something ought to be done about it!"

The tirade seemed to go on and on. Setsuko glanced nervously up at her mother. Mrs. Noma looked paler than usual, but she stood calmly at the counter and didn't so much as glance at the angry woman nearby. The sales clerk behind the counter had finally located the case and necessary papers. Her face was red with embarrassment as she quickly rang up the purchase and made change.

"That took long enough! Now, I want . . ." The angry voice seemed to follow them, and everyone in the store seemed to be looking their way as Setsuko and her mother moved away from the jewelry counter. Mrs. Noma held her head high and pushed the shopping cart to the pet supplies aisle of the department store.

"Okasan, why was that lady so angry?" Setsuko fingered a pretty blue collar that would just about fit Chimi. "We didn't do anything to her. And what did she mean about foreigners? We're Americans just like she is." Setsuko's forehead wrinkled and her troubled gaze rested on dozens of dog toys without seeing any of them.

"Some people don't feel comfortable around anyone who is different from them in any way," Mrs. Noma answered slowly. "They don't trust or appreciate people who look or act differently from what they are used to. It's called prejudice, Setsuko-chan, and it can cause all kinds of bad feelings." Mother placed a bag of dog food in the shopping cart and moved the small bag containing the watch they'd just purchased so it wouldn't get smashed.

"People are a little bit like all those watches we looked at a few minutes ago, Setsuko. They all look different on the outside, but inside they are all watches. They are all made to keep time on the inside, but look very different on the outside. People are the same. You don't look like your friend Rosa and Rosa doesn't look like Beth, but inside you are all kids. We are all made to be children of our Heavenly Father, but look very different from each other."

Setsuko thought about that as they continued their shopping. Mother turned the cart down another aisle. She stopped to select a box of tissues. Suddenly, another shopping cart wheeled around the corner and almost hit a cart with a little boy in it. At the last minute the newcomer swerved her cart and it crashed into the stacks of paper towels instead of the little boy's cart. Rolls went flying all over the place. What a mess! Setsuko looked at the shopper who had caused it all by not watching where she was going. It was the angry woman from the jewelry counter who didn't like people who were different from her!

Setsuko turned to leave, but was amazed when her mother calmly walked over and began to pick up and restack the rolls of paper towels. The young mother, after checking to make sure her little boy was okay, bent to help Mrs. Noma. Setsuko almost laughed at the look on the angry woman's face! She looked so surprised! Setsuko picked up a roll of paper towels decorated with tulips and placed it on the shelf. She bit her lip to keep from giggling when the woman who didn't like people who were different stooped beside Mrs. Noma to pick up the last of the mess.

"Well, that takes care of that," the young mother said with a smile at Mrs. Noma as she pushed her cart away.

327

Lesson 27 Day 1

"I, uh, um . . ." The shopper from the jewelry counter couldn't seem to get any words out and she didn't look right at Setsuko's mother.

"Have a lovely afternoon." Mother smiled warmly at the woman and turned to go.

Setsuko climbed in the silver van and buckled her seat belt. When Mother climbed into the driver's seat, Setsuko burst into laughter. "Oh, Okasan, did you see the look on that woman's face when you started to help her?"

Mrs. Noma looked out the rear window as she backed the van carefully out of the parking space. "She was a bit surprised, wasn't she?" Mother chuckled.

"When I saw that it was her, I just wanted to leave and let her clean up her own mess. She was so mean and said such horrible things!" Setsuko shook her head. "But it was worth picking it up just to see her face!"

"Well, it is much easier to help a friend or someone who's been kind to us." Mother checked the traffic and pulled out onto the road from the store parking lot. "But our heavenly Father asks us to be kind to EVERYONE. The Scriptures say that if we are friendly only to our friends, then there really isn't any difference between us and those who don't love God. We show God's love in us by being kind even to those who are rude to us." Mrs. Noma slowed to a stop at a red light.

Setsuko looked across at her mother. "Or to those who are prejudiced against us," she added softly.

Later that evening while Mother fixed supper, Setsuko wrapped the birthday watch at the kitchen table. "This really is a nice-looking watch. Father's going to love it. It's going to be such fun surprising him with a birthday party! Andrea and Rick Summers will come over from next door. Aunt Miyako [pronounced mee-yahl-kew] and Uncle Taku [pronounced tahl-kew] will come and bring my cousins. The Piersons are coming. I just can't wait! It's so much fun doing nice things for people you love." Setsuko remembered the scene at the store as she taped the wrapping paper and placed the big red bow. "Dear heavenly Father, please help me to also do nice things for those who aren't nice to me, and to be friendly to those who aren't my friends."

2 Discussion Time

Check understanding of the story and development of personal values.

- Why were Setsuko and her mother at the jewelry counter?
- What things did they hear a woman say very loudly to the person with her?
- How do you think that made Setsuko and her mother feel?
- Why did the woman who said the unkind things knock the paper towels down?
- Who helped pick them all up again?
- How do you think that woman felt about them helping her?
- How did Setsuko and her mother show that they were different from people who don't love God?

A Preview

Write each word as your teacher says it.

Name _____

1. clock
2. duck
3. talk
4. sick
5. back
6. truck
7. hang
8. bring
9. sing
10. milk

Challenge Words

☆ block
☆ something
☆ along

Scripture
Matt. 5:47

231

Challenge

For better spellers, challenge words may be included in the weekly list. Challenge words are starred.

Correct Immediately!

Say

Let's correct our preview. I will write each word on the board. Put a dot under each letter on your preview as I spell the word out loud. If you spelled a word wrong, rewrite it correctly.

Progress Chart

Students may record scores. (Reproducible master in Appendix B.)

Take a minute to memorize . . .

Read the memory verse twice. Have students practice it with you two more times.

---

3 Preview

Test for knowledge of the correct spellings of these words. (See the instructions at the top right for challenge words.)

Say

I will say the word once, use the word in a sentence, then say the word again. Write the word on the lines in the Worktext.

1. **clock**   That large watch is almost as big as a **clock**.
2. **duck**   Mother didn't **duck** her head when the lady said mean things.
3. **talk**   We should never **talk** in an unkind way.
4. **sick**   Prejudice is a **sick** way of thinking.
5. **back**   Setsuko helped stack the paper towels **back** on the shelf.
6. **truck**   Setsuko's dad drives a small red pickup **truck**.
7. **hang**   Setsuko will **hang** streamers for Father's birthday party.
8. **bring**   Aunt Miyako and Uncle Taku will **bring** Setsuko's cousins.
9. **sing**   They will **sing**, "Happy Birthday to You."
10. **milk**   Will they have **milk** with the birthday cake?
☆ **block**   Setsuko's house is the third on this **block**.
☆ **something**   It was fun choosing **something** for a gift for Father.
☆ **along**   The dog food is further **along** the next aisle.

4 Word Shapes

Help students form a correct image of whole words.

(Say) Look at each word and think about its shape. Now, write the word in the correct word Shape Boxes. You may check off each word as you use it.

(In many words, the sound of **/k/** is spelled with **ck** or **k**.)

(Say) In the word Shape Boxes, color the letters that spell the sound of **/ng/** or **/k/** in each word. Circle the word which has a silent **l**.

Challenge

Draw the correctly shaped box around each letter in these words.

(Say) On a separate sheet of paper, write other words that contain the spelling patterns in the word list. See how many words you can write.

B Word Shapes   Name _____

Write each word in the correct word shape boxes. Then, in the word shape boxes, color the letter or letters that spell the sound of **/ng/** or **/k/** in each word. Circle the word which has a silent **l**.

1. back   c l o c k

2. bring   (t a l k)

3. clock   d u c k

4. duck   s i n g

5. hang   m i l k

6. milk   h a n g

7. sick   b a c k

8. sing   b r i n g

9. talk   s i c k

10. truck   t r u c k

☆ **Challenge**

Draw the correctly shaped boxes around each letter in these words.

a l o n g   b l o c k   s o m e t h i n g

232

Be Prepared For Fun

Check these supply lists for **Fun Ways to Spell** presented **Day 2**. Purchase and/or gather these items ahead of time!

General
- 3 x 5 Cards (10 per child)
- 3 x 5 Cards (3 more to spell challenge words)
- Scissors
- Spelling List

Auditory
- A Classmate
- Spelling List

Visual
- Strips of paper 2 x 11 inches (10 per student)
- Strips of paper 2 x 11 inches (3 more to spell challenge words)
- Crayons or Markers
- Tape
- Spelling List

Tactile
- Split Peas
- Glue
- Construction Paper
- Spelling List

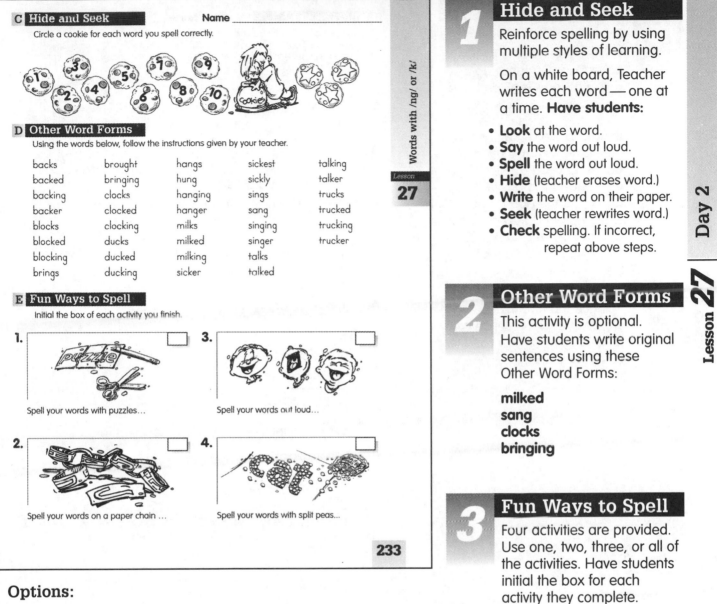

C Hide and Seek

Name _____

Circle a cookie for each word you spell correctly.

D Other Word Forms

Using the words below, follow the instructions given by your teacher.

backs	brought	hangs	sickest	talking
backed	bringing	hung	sickly	talker
backing	clocks	hanging	sings	trucks
backer	clocked	hanger	sang	trucked
blocks	clocking	milks	singing	trucking
blocked	ducks	milked	singer	trucker
blocking	ducked	milking	talks	
brings	ducking	sicker	talked	

E Fun Ways to Spell

Initial the box of each activity you finish.

1. Spell your words with puzzles…

2. Spell your words on a paper chain …

3. Spell your words out loud…

4. Spell your words with split peas…

233

1 Hide and Seek

Reinforce spelling by using multiple styles of learning.

On a white board, Teacher writes each word — one at a time. **Have students:**

- **Look** at the word.
- **Say** the word out loud.
- **Spell** the word out loud.
- **Hide** (teacher erases word.)
- **Write** the word on their paper.
- **Seek** (teacher rewrites word.)
- **Check** spelling. If incorrect, repeat above steps.

Day 2

Lesson 27

2 Other Word Forms

This activity is optional. Have students write original sentences using these Other Word Forms:

milked
sang
clocks
bringing

3 Fun Ways to Spell

Four activities are provided. Use one, two, three, or all of the activities. Have students initial the box for each activity they complete.

Options:

- assign activities to students according to their learning styles
- set up the activities in learning centers for students to do throughout the day
- divide students into four groups and assign one activity per group
- do one activity per day

General

To spell your words with puzzles . . .
- Write each spelling word on a card.
- Cut each card in half using a straight cut.
- Mix your puzzle pieces.
- Put the puzzles together.
- Check your spelling.

Auditory

To spell your words out loud . . .
- Have a classmate read a spelling word.
- Say a sentence with that spelling word to a classmate.
- Spell the spelling word you used in that sentence to a classmate.
- Ask a classmate to check your spelling.
- Do this with each word on your word list.

Visual

To spell your words on a paper chain . . .
- Write each spelling word on a strip of paper in big, tall letters.
- Tape the ends of one strip together to make a circle.
- Loop the next strip through the first and then tape the ends of that strip together.
- Continue in this way to form a paper chain.

Tactile

To spell your words with split peas . . .
- Choose a word from your spelling list.
- It may be a favorite word or a word you have trouble remembering how to spell.
- Write the word in tall, wide letters on a sheet of construction paper.
- Spread glue along the outline of each letter and press split peas into the glue.

1 Word Change

Familiarize students with word meaning and usage.

Write **Can you jump up and down on one leg?** on the board. Ask the students to raise their hands if they can think of a word that means the same as **jump up and down**. Choose a student who knows the answer to hop up to the board and write the word **hop** in place of **jump up and down**. The student may hop back to his/her desk.

Say Replace the underlined words in each sentence with a spelling word that has the same meaning.

F Word Change   Name _____

Write spelling words in place of the underlined words.

1. Setsuko likes to <u>say words</u> to her cousins. __talk__
2. They will <u>fasten</u> a banner on the wall. __hang__
3. Everyone will <u>carry in</u> birthday presents. __bring__
4. Father will come through the <u>not in front</u> door. __back__
5. The <u>thing that tells time</u> just struck six o'clock. __clock__
6. I think I hear his <u>bigger than a car</u> coming now. __truck__
7. <u>Bend down</u> behind the couch to surprise him! __duck__
8. We'll <u>make music with voices</u> "Happy Birthday to You." __sing__
9. Do you want a glass of <u>white drink</u> with your cake? __milk__

Word Bank				
back	clock	hang	sick	talk
bring	duck	milk	sing	truck

234

Take a minute to memorize . . .

Read the memory verse twice. Have students practice it with you two more times.

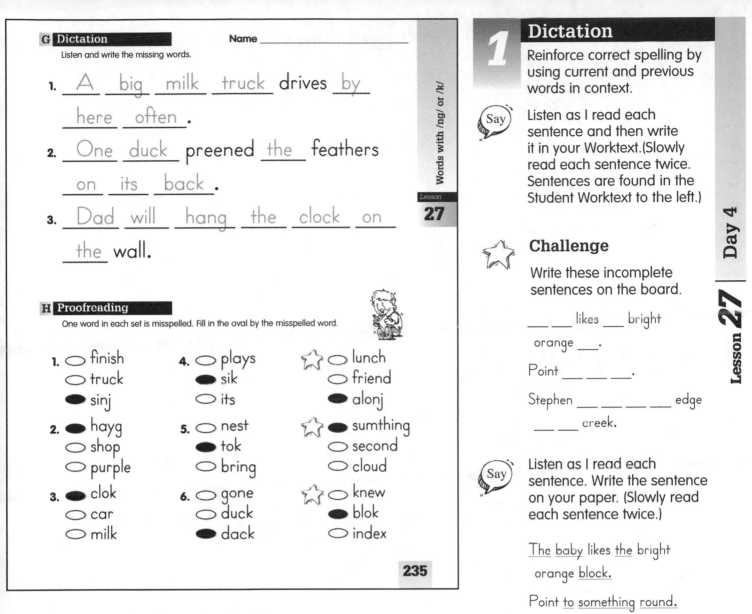

G Dictation

Listen and write the missing words.

1. A big milk truck drives by here often.

2. One duck preened the feathers on its back.

3. Dad will hang the clock on the wall.

H Proofreading

One word in each set is misspelled. Fill in the oval by the misspelled word.

1. ○ finish
   ○ truck
   ● sinj

2. ● hayg
   ○ shop
   ○ purple

3. ● clok
   ○ car
   ○ milk

4. ○ plays
   ● sik
   ○ its

5. ○ nest
   ● tok
   ○ bring

6. ○ gone
   ○ duck
   ● dack

☆ ○ lunch
   ○ friend
   ● alonj

☆ ● sumthing
   ○ second
   ○ cloud

☆ ○ knew
   ● blok
   ○ index

235

---

1 Dictation

Reinforce correct spelling by using current and previous words in context.

Say Listen as I read each sentence and then write it in your Worktext.(Slowly read each sentence twice. Sentences are found in the Student Worktext to the left.)

☆ Challenge

Write these incomplete sentences on the board.

__ __ likes __ bright orange __.

Point __ __ __.

Stephen __ __ __ __ edge __ __ creek.

Say Listen as I read each sentence. Write the sentence on your paper. (Slowly read each sentence twice.)

The baby likes the bright orange block.

Point to something round.

Stephen will run along the edge of the creek.

2 Proofreading

Familiarize students with standardized test format and reinforce recognizing misspelled words.

Say Look at each set of words. One word in each set is misspelled. Fill in the oval by the misspelled word. (You may wish to pronounce each set of words to help students correctly identify them.)

333

3 Hide and Seek

Reinforce correct spelling of current spelling words. (A reproducible master is provided in Appendix A as shown on the inset page to the right.)

Write the words one at a time on a white board.

Have students:

- **Look** at the word.
- **Say** the word out loud.
- **Spell** the word out loud.
- **Hide** (teacher erases word.)
- **Write** the word on paper.
- **Seek** (teacher rewrites word.)
- **Check** spelling. If incorrect, rewrite word correctly.

4 Hidden Words

Have your students complete this activity to strengthen spelling ability and expand vocabulary.

1 Posttest

Test mastery of the spelling words. Challenge words are starred.

(Say) I will say the word once, use the word in a sentence, then say the word again. Write the word on your paper.

1. **clock** — That **clock** looks like a plate.
2. **truck** — Another clock has a picture of a **truck** on it.
3. **hang** — A boy might want to **hang** that clock in his room.
4. **duck** — That funny clock has a **duck** that pecks at corn.
5. **talk** — The lady at the store wouldn't **talk** like that if she loved God.
6. **back** — Mother looked behind her so she could **back** up safely.
7. **bring** — Aunt Miyako will **bring** a gift for Setsuko's father.
8. **sing** — Will they **sing** "Happy Birthday" in Japanese or English?
9. **milk** — There are **milk** and berries to make home made ice cream.
10. **sick** — Eating too much cake might make you **sick**.
☆ **block** — There are four houses on this **block**.
☆ **along** — Setsuko walked **along** beside the cart.
☆ **something** — There is **something** wrong with Father's old watch.

Progress Chart
Students may record scores. (Reproducible master in Appendix B.)

Personal Dictionary
Students may add any words they have misspelled to their personal dictionaries for reference when writing. (Cover in Appendix B.)

Inset page (Appendix A, Lesson 27)

Hide and Seek
Check a paper for each word you spell correctly.

1 3 5 7 9
2 4 6 8 10

Hidden Words
Find these words in the puzzle. Circle and write each word.

s	o	t	b	r	o	u	g	h	t
r	x	s	i	n	g	s	t	u	z
e	t	i	l	p	m	r	g	n	d
b	a	c	k	s	a	o	e	g	u
k	l	k	d	r	k	y	z	e	c
c	k	e	h	p	e	m	q	d	k
a	i	s	g	c	l	o	c	k	s
d	n	t	r	u	c	k	e	r	h
m	g	n	q	e	m	a	y	q	p
m	i	l	k	i	n	g	d	g	e

Across
trucker
sings
brought
milking
backs
clocks

Down
ducks
sickest
hung
talking

Word Bank
backs   clocks   hung   sickest   talking
brought   ducks   milking   sings   trucker

390

334

I | Game

Name _____

Setsuko and her mother picked up the rolls of paper towels for the woman who said unkind things about them. You help too by coloring one roll each time you or your team spells a word correctly from this week's word list.

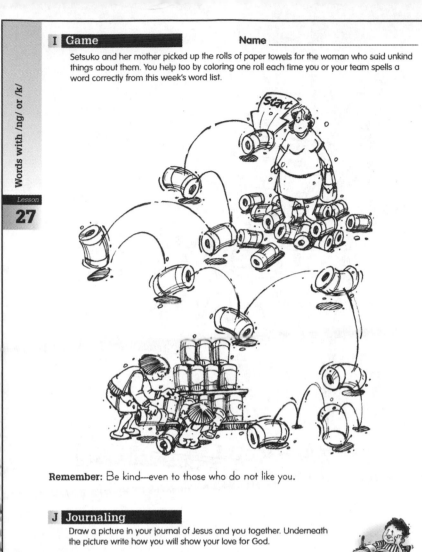

Start

Remember: Be kind—even to those who do not like you.

J | Journaling

Draw a picture in your journal of Jesus and you together. Underneath the picture write how you will show your love for God.

236

---

2 | Game

Reinforce spelling skills and provide motivation and interest.

Materials

• game page (from student text)
• crayons or colored pencils (1 per child)
• game word list

Game Word List

Use of challenge words is optional.

1. **hang**
2. **bring**
3. **sing**
4. **back**
5. **clock**
6. **duck**
7. **sick**
8. **truck**
9. **talk**
10. **milk**
☆ **block**
☆ **something**
☆ **along**

How to Play:

• Divide students into two teams, and decide which team will go first.
• Have a student from team A go to the board.
• Read the spelling word two times slowly and clearly. (You may also wish to use the word in a sentence. Ex.: "cat — The cat climbed a tree. — cat")
• Have the student write the word on the board.
• If the word is spelled correctly, instruct all the members of team A to color one space, beginning at Start, on the game board. (Note: If the word is misspelled, correct the spelling immediately.)
• Alternate between teams A and B as you go down the word list.
• The team to reach the shelf of paper towels first is the winner.

Non-Competitive Option: At the end of the game, say: "Class, I am proud of your efforts to spell the words correctly. If you had fun and tried your best, you are all winners!"

---

3 | Journaling

Provide a meaningful reason for correct spelling through personal writing.

Review the story using discussion leads provided on the following page. Encourage students to apply the Scriptural value in their journaling.

 Take a minute to memorize . . .

Have students say the memory verses from lessons 25, 26, and 27 with you.

335

3 Journaling

Provide a meaningful reason for correct spelling through personal writing.

(Say)

- Was it fun for Setsuko to help pick out a gift and wrap it for her father? (Yes.)

- Can you tell about something special you've done to surprise someone in your family, or a good friend?

- Is it fun to do kind things for those who are mean to us or prejudiced against us? Why or why not?

- Why should we do kind things for these unkind people? (Because we love God and He says that we are not different from those who don't love Him if we are friendly only to our friends.)

- Draw a picture in your journal of Jesus and you together. Remember how Setsuko and her mother showed their love for God while they were at the store. Underneath the picture write how you will show your love for God. (By being friendly to everyone, even those who are not nice.)

Quotables!

> ## "Standard spelling is the result of writing and reading — not the way to it."*

*Scott, Jill E. 1994. Spelling for Readers and Writers. The Reading Teacher, Vol. 48, No. 2, October: 188-190.

Rachel's Turn

Rachel finds it hard to deal with the anger she feels inside until she turns to God for help.

"Mom told us both to pick up our doll stuff!" Vanessa glared at Rachel.

"I'm just going to finish putting Samantha's nightgown on." Rachel lifted her new doll's long dark hair and buttoned the tiny buttons down the back of the white nightgown. "She can't go to bed in her clothes!"

Nine-year-old Vanessa folded her doll's patchwork quilt and put it neatly inside the wooden hand-painted trunk beside the pillow. "Mom said we need to hurry and eat so we can go to Tony's ballgame."

"Vanessa, leave me alone! You are not my mom!" Rachel put the yellow crocheted slippers on her doll, then reached for the kimono hanging in Samantha's black steamer trunk. "This'll take just a minute."

"Come on, Rachel. Mom is just trying to do something you said you wanted to do." Rachel's oldest stepsister put the last dress in her doll's trunk and shut the lid. "Now clean up your doll mess or I'm going to tell my mom."

"Just go ahead and tell your mom! I'm sure she'll listen to you because you're her real daughter." Rachel's eyes were angry narrow slits as she picked up three dresses and threw them toward the black trunk.

"Well, my mom is the one who just got you that doll you love so much! Your mom never did that!" Vanessa put her hands on her hips and glared down into Rachel's seething eyes.

Without thinking, Rachel reached over and slapped her stepsister's face, grabbed her blond hair and gave it a hard yank, then shoved her to the floor. "Don't talk about my mommy like that! She was never your mommy, and you'll never be my sister! I was just four when Mommy died and she was sick before that. I hate you and Father's new wife, Helen!" Rachel stomped out of the living room, grabbing Samantha and scooping the rest of her doll's clothes into the trunk as she went.

"Mom!" Vanessa screamed. "Rachel hit me!"

Mrs. Jacobson walked into the living room and listened quietly to Vanessa's side of the story before following her stepdaughter up the stairs. "Rachel, Rachel. How am I going to help you deal with all the anger inside," she whispered to herself as she knocked softly on Rachel and Rebecca's door.

When the bell rang the next morning, Mrs. Morgan stood before her class. "Daniel's mother sent a note this morning inviting us all to a pool party at their house this Sunday afternoon at three o'clock. She will have supper for us at five-thirty." Mrs. Morgan smiled at Daniel. "This sounds like fun, Daniel. Thank you for inviting us. Now," Mrs. Morgan continued, "take out your spelling Worktexts and turn to the journaling page."

Rachel put her spelling book on her desk and looked at the cover. "We'd just moved here when Daniel asked us all over last year. I almost drowned in a race with him. I hope no one remembers that!" Rachel turned to the correct page in her spelling book and listened as Mrs. Morgan explained the assignment.

"It says in Matthew 4:17, 'Turn from sin, and turn to God, for the kingdom of heaven is near.' Today on your journal page, you're going to make a list of some things you should turn from or quit doing. At the bottom of your list write . . ."

"I know what I will put at the top of my list." Rachel thought about Vanessa's tear-streaked face and how sad her stepmom had looked the night before when she'd sat on her bed and explained how hitting other people was not the way to solve problems. Helen hadn't even yelled at her. "I'm sure she heard me say how I hate her and Vanessa." Rachel frowned, then picked up her pencil and wrote "hitting" on the first line in her Worktext and "being mean to Helen" on the second line.

At recess time everyone gathered behind the backstop to pick teams for a softball game. "Want to go swing, Rache?" Rosa sat down beside Rachel on the bleachers.

"I want to practice softball. We never played in Dallas. I think it's fun, don't you?" Rachel picked up her glove and shoved it onto her left hand.

"Hey, Rachel." Tony tossed a softball to Rachel. "Where were you last night? I thought you were going to come to my ball game."

Rachel reached out and caught the ball easily. *I don't really want to tell Tony I couldn't come because I hit Vanessa,* Rachel thought. "I was, but Helen changed her mind and wouldn't let me go. She made me do some work instead," she lied. *Well, part of that is true,* Rachel thought to herself. *Helen wouldn't let me go to the game and made me clean up the doll mess.*

"Well, maybe Monday." Tony put his glove on and walked toward Stephen who was leaning against the backstop. "We have another game at six-thirty."

Suddenly Rachel didn't feel like playing ball anymore. "Let's go swing," she suggested to Rosa. "I don't really want to play baseball today, do you?" Rosa's eyebrows shot up in surprise, but she just shrugged her shoulders and followed her friend toward the swings.

Daniel looked up and saw Rosa and Rachel walking away. "I thought you wanted to play baseball, Rachel," he taunted. "But I guess I wouldn't want to play either

337

if I couldn't even hit off the Tee like you."

Rachel felt her face get warm.

"Didn't they ever play baseball in Dallas, city girl?"

Rachel turned and walked back toward Daniel. "No, we didn't, goat-roper! There wasn't room for a field at our school. But I wouldn't need much practice to be better than you."

"Well, I hope you've been practicing your swimming. I'd hate for you to drown in our pool again this year," Daniel bellowed so everyone on the playground could hear.

Rachel clenched her fist and hit Daniel in the stomach with all her strength. The punch knocked all the air out of him. Daniel's eyes got big as he tried to suck in a breath, but couldn't.

"Rachel!" Rachel jerked her hand back and looked down at Daniel, then up into eyes of the teacher supervising the playground.

"Miss Grant, I . . . Daniel, he . . ."

"I saw what you did, Rachel. Go back to your classroom. I'll talk to you later," Miss Grant knelt down beside Daniel to survey the damage.

Rachel hung her head as pools of tears formed in her eyes. By the time she got to the classroom, big sobs shook her whole body.

"What happened, Rachel?" Mrs. Morgan put her blue pen down beside the spelling Worktexts she was grading. "Do you want to talk about it?"

"I slapped Vanessa . . . I lied about Helen to Tony . . . and I punched Daniel," she choked out, ". . . and He won't let me go to the Kingdom," she wailed. "Miss Grant sent me."

"Miss Grant sent you to what kingdom?" Mrs. Morgan wrapped her arms around the sobbing girl. "Who won't let you go where?"

"You know . . ." she sobbed. "The Kingdom of heaven like . . . like in our memory verse this week. Jesus won't want me in Heaven because I hit everyone and . . .

and . . . and I'll burn for my sin!" Rachel choked out.

"I think our memory verse says, 'Turn from sin, and turn to God for the Kingdom of heaven is near', sweetheart." Mrs. Morgan thumbed through the stack of Worktexts and pulled out Rachel's. "I was just reading what you wrote on your journal page this morning. You want to quit hitting and being mean to Helen. That is the first step in making a change — admitting that you need to and wanting to do it."

"But I can't change. I wrote that this morning and then went right out and punched Daniel in the stomach when he made fun of how I almost drowned in his pool last year."

"That is the second step, Rachel: admitting that you can't change by yourself. You need help. See this line at the bottom of the list?" Mrs. Morgan pointed to the bottom of the journaling page. "You didn't write the prayer asking Jesus to help you make better choices. That's the next step — giving your problems to Jesus."

"That's what Helen said . . . that it's not bad to feel angry, but it's not a good choice to hit other people because I'm angry. She says I should give God time to change the other person's heart and ask God to change mine instead of trying to take care of it all myself."

"She sounds like a wise woman."

"That's what my father thinks. I just wish my real mommy hadn't died. I miss her so much."

"I'm sure you do, Rachel, but being angry and hitting other people is not going to bring her back to you."

"I know." Rachel sighed.

"Would you like to finish this page while we wait for the others to come back in for math?"

Rachel wiped her face with the back of her hand and nodded her head. She could hear her classmates coming in from recess. "Dear God . . ." she wrote on the bottom line.

Tony stopped by Rachel's desk on the way to the drinking fountain. "So, Rache, do you think that mean old stepmother of yours will let me come over tonight so we can practice batting? We'll show Daniel how fast a city girl can learn," he whispered.

"I think Helen will let me play. She wouldn't let me come to your game last night because I slapped Vanessa. I was being punished." Rachel looked down at her spelling book. "Helen didn't make me work last night. The only work I did yesterday was picking up all the new doll clothes she got for my doll."

Tony raised his eyebrows for a moment. "Well, I'll come over after I eat supper then," he said with a grin, "if you promise not to beat me up."

A sudden smile spread across Rachel's face as she picked up her pencil. "I haven't even finished writing this prayer," she thought, "and Jesus is already helping me make better choices."

"Okay!" she told Tony, then smiled even more as she finished her prayer.

2 Discussion Time

Check understanding of the story and development of personal values.

- How does Rachel feel about her stepsister Vanessa?
- What did she do to her classmate Daniel?
- Why do you think Rachel gets so angry?
- Do you think it is okay for Rachel to feel that way?
- Why does Rachel want to quit hitting people when she is angry?
- Can she do it by herself? Why?
- Who did she turn to for help?
- Did you know that Jesus will help you turn from the sin in your life like our memory verse says?

A Preview

Write each word as your teacher says it.

Name _____

1. another
2. both
3. other
4. those
5. thought
6. think
7. thank
8. these
9. thin
10. thick

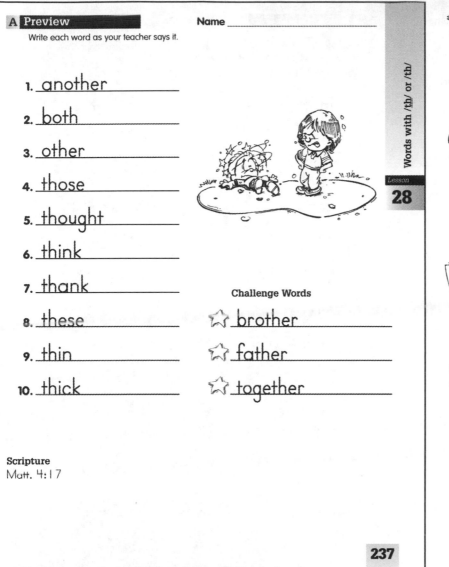

Challenge Words

 brother

 father

☆ together

Scripture
Matt. 4:17

237

Challenge

For better spellers, challenge words may be included in the weekly list. Challenge words are starred.

Correct Immediately!

Say

Let's correct our preview. I will write each word on the board. Put a dot under each letter on your preview as I spell the word out loud. If you spelled a word wrong, rewrite it correctly.

Progress Chart

Students may record scores. (Reproducible master in Appendix B.)

Take a minute to memorize . . .

Read the memory verse twice. Have students practice it with you two more times.

---

3 Preview

Test for knowledge of the correct spellings of these words. (See the instructions at the top right for challenge words.)

Say

I will say the word once, use the word in a sentence, then say the word again. Write the word on the lines in the Worktext.

1.	another	We should love one **another**.
2.	both	Rachel and Daniel were **both** wrong.
3.	other	Be kind to each **other**.
4.	those	**Those** unkind words can't be taken back.
5.	thought	Rachel **thought** she could change herself.
6.	think	**Think** about some changes you should make.
7.	thank	**Thank** God for helping you.
8.	these	"Remember **these** steps," Mrs. Morgan said.
9.	thin	That book is **thin**.
10.	thick	This book is **thick**.
☆	brother	Rachel doesn't have a **brother**.
☆	father	Rachel's **father** is a lawyer.
☆	together	Get along **together** and be happy.

Word Shapes

4

Help students form a correct image of whole words.

(Say) Look at each word and think about its shape. Now, write the word in the correct word Shape Boxes. You may check off each word as you use it.

(The letters **th** have the sound of /**th**/ or /**th**/.)

(Say) In the word Shape Boxes, color the letters that spell the sound of /**th**/ or /**th**/ in each word.

⭐ **Challenge**
Draw the correctly shaped box around each letter in these words.

(Say) On a separate sheet of paper, write sentences using one or more of the spelling words.

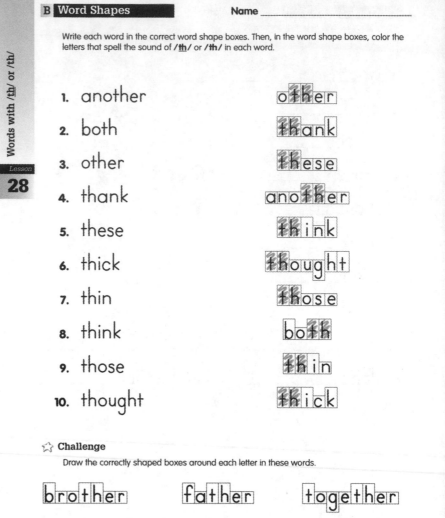

Words with /th/ or /th/

Lesson 28

B Word Shapes   Name _____

Write each word in the correct word shape boxes. Then, in the word shape boxes, color the letters that spell the sound of /th/ or /th/ in each word.

1. another — other
2. both — thank
3. other — these
4. thank — another
5. these — think
6. thick — thought
7. thin — those
8. think — both
9. those — thin
10. thought — thick

⭐ **Challenge**
Draw the correctly shaped boxes around each letter in these words.

brother   father   together

238

Answers may vary for duplicate word shapes.

Be Prepared For Fun

Check these supply lists for **Fun Ways to Spell** presented **Day 2**. Purchase and/or gather these items ahead of time!

General
- A Classmate
- Spelling List

Auditory
- Box to Store Letters
- a, b, c, e, e, g, h, h, i, k, n, o, r, s, t, t, u (written on seasonal shapes like baseball mitts or watermelon slices)
- f, r (added for challenge words)
- Spelling List

Visual
- Paper or Polystyrene Cups
- a, b, c, e, e, g, h, h, i, k, n, o, r, s, t, t, u written on upside down cups
- f, r (added for challenge words)
- Spelling List

Tactile
- Shaving Cream
- Optional: Plastic Plates
- Optional: Wooden Craft Sticks
- Spelling List

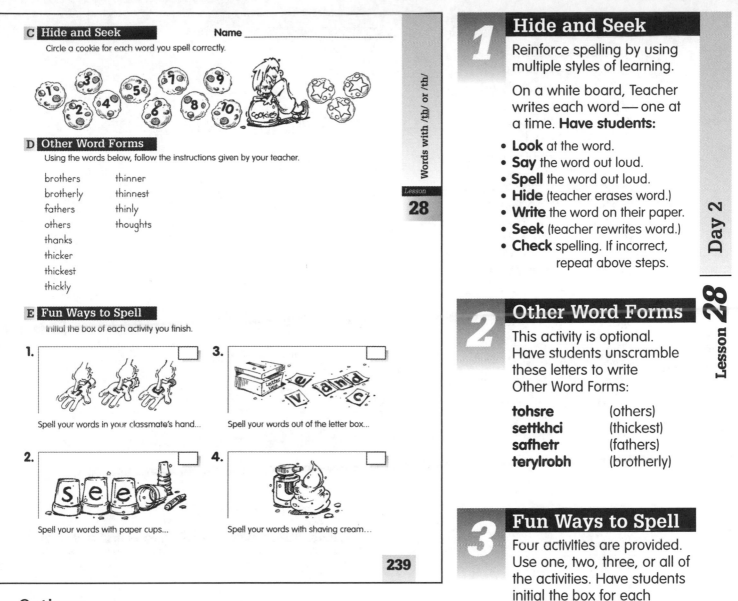

C Hide and Seek Name _____

Circle a cookie for each word you spell correctly.

1 2 3 4 5 6 7 8 9 10 cookies

D Other Word Forms

Using the words below, follow the instructions given by your teacher.

brothers   thinner
brotherly   thinnest
fathers   thinly
others   thoughts
thanks
thicker
thickest
thickly

E Fun Ways to Spell

Initial the box of each activity you finish.

1. Spell your words in your classmate's hand...

3. Spell your words out of the letter box...

2. Spell your words with paper cups...

4. Spell your words with shaving cream...

239

Words with /th/ or /th/

Lesson 28

Day 2

Lesson 28

1 Hide and Seek

Reinforce spelling by using multiple styles of learning.

On a white board, Teacher writes each word — one at a time. **Have students:**

- **Look** at the word.
- **Say** the word out loud.
- **Spell** the word out loud.
- **Hide** (teacher erases word.)
- **Write** the word on their paper.
- **Seek** (teacher rewrites word.)
- **Check** spelling. If incorrect, repeat above steps.

2 Other Word Forms

This activity is optional. Have students unscramble these letters to write Other Word Forms:

tohsre   (others)
settkhci   (thickest)
safhetr   (fathers)
terylrobh   (brotherly)

3 Fun Ways to Spell

Four activities are provided. Use one, two, three, or all of the activities. Have students initial the box for each activity they complete.

Options:

- assign activities to students according to their learning styles
- set up the activities in learning centers for students to do throughout the day
- divide students into four groups and assign one activity per group
- do one activity per day

General
To spell your words in your classmate's hand . . .
- Have a classmate sit next to you and hold their palm open in front of, and facing both of you.
- Use fingertip to write a spelling word in the palm of a classmate's hand.
- Have a classmate say each letter as you write it and then say the word you spelled.
- Next, have a classmate write a word in your palm.

Auditory
To spell your words out of the letter box . . .
- Spell a word from your list by putting the letters in the right order.
- Check your spelling.
- Spell your word out loud.

Visual
To spell your words with paper cups . . .
- Spell a word from your list by putting the cups in the right order.
- Check your spelling.

Tactile
To spell your words with shaving cream . . .
- Spread a glob of shaving cream across your desk (or on a plastic plate).
- Use finger (or a wooden craft stick) to write a spelling word in the shaving cream.
- Check your spelling.
- Smear the word out with finger and write another.

1 Rhyme Time

Familiarize students with word meaning and usage. Write the words **doll** and **ball** on the board. Ask a volunteer if the words end the same. Invite the students to raise their hands if they think the words rhyme. Help the students to see that the words **doll** and **ball** rhyme even though the ending sound is spelled with different letters. Invite the students to name more rhyming words whose ending sounds are not spelled the same way.

(Say) Beside each word, write the spelling word or words that rhyme with it.

F Rhyme Time   Name _____

Write the spelling words that rhyme with the words in the list.

Words with /th/ or /th/

Lesson **28**

1. win, _____thin_____

2. mother, _____other_____ _____another_____
   ☆ _____brother_____

3. hose, _____those_____

4. bank, _____thank_____

5. stick, _____thick_____

6. fought, _____thought_____

7. sink, _____think_____

8. growth, _____both_____

9. cheese, _____these_____

☆ bother, _____father_____

☆ weather, _____together_____

240

Word Bank						
another	other	these	thin	those	☆ brother	☆ together
both	thank	thick	think	thought	☆ father	

Take a minute to memorize . . .

Have students say the memory verses from lessons 19, 20, 21, 22, and 23 with you.

G Dictation

Listen and write the missing words.

Name _____

1. Thank him for these thick blankets.

2. Setsuko thought both dresses were pretty.

3. Have another thin cookie.

4. I think the other game is fun.

H Proofreading

One word in each set is misspelled. Fill in the oval by the misspelled word.

1. ○ candy
   ● theez
   ○ clock

2. ● anuther
   ○ Indian
   ○ thank

3. ○ sick
   ○ fish
   ● thoze

4. ○ thick
   ● thout
   ○ blind

5. ○ back
   ● uther
   ○ thin

6. ● bothe
   ○ should
   ○ think

☆ ○ something
   ● bruther
   ○ block

☆ ● fother
   ○ obey
   ○ along

☆ ○ don't
   ● togethr
   ○ second

241

---

1 Dictation

Reinforce correct spelling by using current and previous words in context.

Say) Listen as I read each sentence and then write it in your Worktext.(Slowly read each sentence twice. Sentences are found in the Student Worktext to the left.)

☆ Challenge

Write these incomplete sentences on the board.

Setsuko's ___ ___ ___

___ ___.

___ ___ ___ ___ ___ watch.

___ ___ lunch ___.

Say) Listen as I read each sentence. Write the sentence on your paper. (Slowly read each sentence twice.)

Setsuko's brother has a

toy train.

My father lost his new watch.

We'll eat lunch together.

---

2 Proofreading

Familiarize students with standardized test format and reinforce recognizing misspelled words.

Say) Look at each set of words. One word in each set is misspelled. Fill in the oval by the misspelled word. (You may wish to pronounce each set of words to help students correctly identify them.)

343

3 Hide and Seek

Reinforce correct spelling of current spelling words. (A reproducible master is provided in Appendix A as shown on the inset page to the right.)

Write the words one at a time on a white board.

Have students:

- **Look** at the word.
- **Say** the word out loud.
- **Spell** the word out loud.
- **Hide** (teacher erases word.)
- **Write** the word on paper.
- **Seek** (teacher rewrites word.)
- **Check** spelling. If incorrect, rewrite word correctly.

4 Clues

Have your students complete this activity to strengthen spelling ability and expand vocabulary.

1 Posttest

Test mastery of the spelling words. Challenge words are starred.

(Say) I will say the word once, use the word in a sentence, then say the word again. Write the word on your paper.

Hide and Seek

Check a paper for each word you spell correctly.

Clues

Look at other forms of your spelling words in the word bank.
Use the clues to find the word that fits best in each blank.

1. what you tell someone who has done something nice _____ thanks
2. two boys with the same mother _____ brothers
3. men who have children _____ fathers
4. how you spread something you like _____ thickly
5. someone who is more thin _____ thinner
6. the person who is the most thin _____ thinnest
7. a sandwich that is more thick _____ thicker
8. the sandwich that has the most in it _____ thickest

Word Bank

| brother + s | thank + s | thick + est | thin + n + er |
| father + s | thick + er | thick + ly | thin + n + est |

391

---

1. **both**   Mom told them **both** to pick up their doll stuff.
2. **think**   Rachel didn't **think** before she slapped Vanessa.
3. **another**   Rachel hit **another** person.
4. **other**   Hitting each **other** is not the way to solve problems.
5. **thought**   Mrs. Morgan **thought** Rachel needed to ask Jesus for help.
6. **thank**   Remember to **thank** Daniel for inviting us to swim.
7. **thick**   This is a **thick** Worktext to grade.
8. **those**   All of **those** Worktexts are already graded.
9. **these**   Are **these** journaling pages done well?
10. **thin**   That is a **thin** book to read.
☆ **brother**   Tony is not Rachel's **brother.**
☆ **father**   Rachel's **father** loves Helen.
☆ **together** Rachel and Vanessa live **together** in a blended family.

Progress Chart

Students may record scores. (Reproducible master in Appendix B.)

Personal Dictionary

Students may add any words they have misspelled to their personal dictionaries for reference when writing. (Cover in Appendix B.)

344

I Game

Name _____

Place a game piece over each word your teacher says and spells. If the word appears on your card more than once, place a game piece over only one of the words. When you get five game pieces in a row, raise your hand and say, "Spelling is fun!"

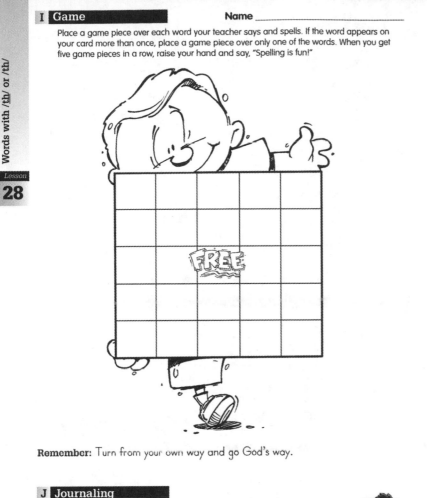

Remember: Turn from your own way and go God's way.

J Journaling

Make a list in your journal of things you should "turn from" or quit doing. At the bottom of your list, write a note to Jesus asking Him to help you.

242

---

2 Game

Reinforce spelling skills and provide motivation and interest.

Materials

- game page (from student text)
- flat buttons, dry beans, pennies, or game discs (24 per child)
- game word list
- word cards (each word from the list below written on one or more cards as indicated)

Game Word List

1. **another** (2)
2. **both** (2)
3. **other** (2)
4. **thin** (2)
5. **thick** (2)
6. **those** (2)
7. **thought** (2)
8. **these** (2)
9. **thank** (2)
10. **think** (2)
☆ **brother** (2)
☆ **father** (1)
☆ **together** (1)

3 Journaling

Provide a meaningful reason for correct spelling through personal writing.

Review the story using discussion leads provided on the following page. Encourage students to apply the Scriptural value in their journaling.

Take a minute to memorize . . .

Have students say the memory verses from lessons 25, 26, 27, and 28 with you.

How to Play:

- Fold the word cards (see **Materials**) in half, and put them in a container.
- Write each word from the **Game Word List** on the board. (Be sure to include the number in parentheses beside it.)
- Ask the students to copy these words on their game card — one word in each box. Remind them the number beside the word indicates how many times they must copy that word. (Note; Placing the words in the boxes randomly makes the game more fun!)
- Instructions for the students: "Cover the word **FREE** in the center of your card with a game piece. (pause) I will draw a word from the container, read it aloud, then spell it. Find that word on your card, and cover it with a game piece. Cover only ONE word each time, even if it's on your card twice. When you have five game pieces in a row (up-down, across, or diagonally) raise your hand and say **'Spelling is FUN!'"**
- Play as many times as you like. (As you return the word cards to the container and mix them up, remind the students to clear their game cards.)

Provide a meaningful reason for correct spelling through personal writing.

Say
- Rachel was feeling angry at her stepmother in the story this week. What did she do that showed she was angry? (She said mean things about her stepmother. She pulled Vanessa's hair and yelled at her. She hit Daniel at school the next day.)

- Was she happy with the way she was feeling and acting? (No. She wanted to change, but she didn't know how.)

- In your journal make a list of things you should "turn from" or quit doing.

- Can you quit doing the things on your list all by yourself? (No.)

- Who can help you? (God.)

- At the bottom of your list write a note to Jesus asking Him to help you.

My Journal

Quotables!

"Teaching a child to be a good speller involves both mental and verbal processes and needs to include the active participation of the child."*

*Downing, John, Robert M. Coughlin and Gene Rich. 1986. Children's Invented Spellings in the Classroom. The Elementary School Journal, Vol. 86: No. 3, January: 295-303.

Ready to Go

Rosa gets an unexpected reward when she is ready and waiting ahead of time for her trip to her aunt and uncle's ranch.

"**D**ad! Dad!" Rosa's call was somewhat muffled because she was digging around in the storage closet at the end of the hall. "Dad! Whu mff stukeses? Iss gobbee eer summer." Knocking and scraping sounds came from the closet as Mr. Vasquez walked through the hall carrying a pile of clean laundry.

"Maybe we should get a cat after all." Dad pushed open the closet door a bit more with the toe of his shoe. "We seem to have really big mice in the house."

"Dad, it's me!" Rosa turned to the door and shoved the black hair out of her face to peer up at her father.

"Really big mice!" Dad grinned over the folded yellow towel topping the stack of laundry in his arms.

"D-a-a-d!" Rosa blew out a puff of breath through her bottom lip that flipped her bangs into the air.

"So, what are you looking for, Miss Mouse?" Mr. Vasquez leaned his shoulder against the door frame.

"My suitcase." Rosa waved a hand vaguely at the shelves around her. Each shelf was stacked with things like games, tennis rackets, long rolls of wrapping paper, and all sorts of other stuff. "I know I had it when we went on that trip last fall. Remember, Dad? And Carlos' and Maria's suitcases are right here where they're supposed to be." Rosa pointed to the suitcases sitting neatly in their space under the bottom shelf at the back of the closet. "I just can't find mine anywhere."

Dad gazed thoughtfully around the small storage space, then straightened quickly. "Hold these for a minute." Passing the stack of sweet-smelling laundry to Rosa, he squeezed past her into the closet. After moving a couple of boxes on the top shelf he lowered a blue suitcase to the floor in front of Rosa. "Ta da! Sir Vasquez at your service, fair maiden." Dad bowed low, but his royal bow was somewhat spoiled when he bumped his elbow on a box of gift bows, which tipped and showered him in rainbow colors of ribbon.

"All right, all right, show's over." Dad chuckled. He picked up a red gift bow and stuck it on his laughing daughter's head. "What did you want your suitcase for, anyway, Miss Mouse?" Dad squatted down to pick up the ribbons and return them to their box.

Rosa tried to control her giggles long enough to reply. "I'm packing to go to Uncle Mario's ranch."

"But, Rosita, Uncle Mario isn't coming to get you until school is out." Dad replaced the ribbon box on the shelf and took the stack of laundry out of Rosa's arms. "You've got the rest of this week and all of next week before he gets here."

"I know, Dad." Rosa picked up her suitcase and headed for her room. "I just want to be sure I'm ready to go. Thank you for finding my suitcase for me, Sir Vasquez." She dropped a quick curtsy and ducked around the corner into her room, listening to her dad's chuckle fade down the hall.

Rosa placed the suitcase on her bed and opened it. "Now, what do I need to take? I know I'll need jeans for riding horses, and my old swimsuit for playing in the swimming hole." Rosa stacked jeans and swimsuit on the bed and turned back to the closet. Each summer, Rosa and her brother and sister spent a month at Sunrise Vista Ranch, their

Uncle Mario and Aunt Mimi's place in New Mexico. Along with the horses to ride and the cool clear swimming hole, there was a huge barn to explore, calves to bottle-feed, and Pedro, an ancient donkey who thought he was a dog. There were always an assortment of babies to enjoy, foals, kittens, puppies, chicks, even a baby coyote one summer. And then there were the cousins. Even though Alisha was only five and Willie was almost three, the Vasquez children had a wonderful time with their little cousins.

"I'd better take my jacket. It can get pretty cool in the evenings, and we might get to sleep out again." Rosa was rummaging in the back of her closet for the jacket when Maria came in.

"Hey, Rosa," Maria adjusted the chin strap on the bicycle helmet in her hands. "Let's go for a bike ride. Carlos wants to and we can take the dogs if we stay on the country roads. Come on! Rosa?"

Rosa spotted the jacket and pulled it out of the closet. "You guys go ahead. I want to get finished packing this afternoon." She tossed the jacket across the growing pile on her bed and pulled open a dresser drawer.

"But, Rosa!" Maria stared at her little sister. "You've been working on that all day. We don't leave for the ranch for a couple of weeks. Uncle Mario won't even get here until after next week. You've got plenty of time to pack and it's a beautiful day. Come on and go for a ride with us."

"Have you seen my flashlight, Maria?" Rosa poked around in the drawer. "I must've left it on the back porch."

"I don't know where your old flashlight is!" Maria clapped the helmet on her head. "You can just look for it yourself! I'm going to have fun this afternoon!"

A few minutes later Rosa heard Carlos whistle for the dogs. Barkley and Digby barked gleefully as they led the bike riders off down the narrow country road. Rosa

347

sighed and added a tube of sunscreen to the collection of things on her bed before going to look for the missing flashlight.

"Okay, troop, time to eat!" Dad called from the kitchen. "Wash up and come to the table."

"Wow, Dad!" Carlos exclaimed after the blessing. "We saw a deer down in the meadow by Smith's old barn. He was awesome!"

"He was beautiful." Maria paused with her fork halfway to her mouth. "He had these huge antlers and he just stood there staring at us till the dogs spotted him."

"I've never seen anything move so fast!" Carlos picked up the story. "He was there one minute and the next he was gone! Poof! He just jumped and disappeared."

"Too bad you didn't go with us, Rosa." Maria picked up her glass of juice and took a drink. "Do you still think packing a whole week early was such a good idea?"

"I'm sure the buck was magnificent," Dad intervened with a warning look at Maria. "But being prepared for things ahead of time is a good habit to develop." Dad poured some more juice into his glass and changed the subject. "Don't you all have a piano recital next week?"

"Yes. It's on Tuesday night. Mrs. Winston said to be sure to come a little early." Maria picked up her napkin and wiped the corners of her mouth.

"She said we're going to have cookies and punch afterwards, Dad." Rosa rubbed her finger through the moisture on the side of her glass. "We're supposed to bring two dozen cookies."

"Hmmm," Mr. Vasquez tapped his fingers on the table. "I think we can handle that."

"Let's make. . ." DING DONG! The unexpected sound of the doorbell interrupted Carlos' sentence.

"I'll be right back, troop." Dad headed for the front door. He was back in moments

with someone right behind him. "Surprise!" Dad stepped aside and Uncle Mario came into the kitchen.

"Surprise! We thought we'd come a few days early!" Uncle Mario grinned and opened his arms wide as the three Vasquez children launched themselves at him. Aunt Mimi came in next with Alisha dancing beside her and a wriggling little Willie in her arms.

The two Vasquez families sat around the kitchen table for quite a while that evening catching up and having a good visit. "You can go to our piano recital and our school picnic with us next week." Maria bounced Willie on her lap. "We can make cookies for the recital and go for a bike ride down by the Smith's meadow and show you our fort and you can meet Grandma Ruth and Grandpa Joe and . . ."

"Whoa, sweetheart." Dad stood and began clearing the table. "We can all do some of those things, but don't forget that you'll have to spend some time packing your things to take to the ranch."

"Oh." Maria sat still and looked across at Rosa. "I forgot all about that. I guess you're smarter than I thought you were, Rosa. You'll have a lot more time to play with Alisha and Willie and do things with Aunt Mimi and Uncle Mario than I will."

After the flurry of bringing in luggage and making beds ready for everyone, the two families gathered in the living room for worship. Dad picked up his open Bible off the side table. A smile spread across his face as he glanced at the scripture that Rosa had been practicing earlier for handwriting. He read from Luke 12:37, "'There will be great joy for those who are ready and waiting for His return.' It seems that our little Rosita has been a good example for all of us. Let's each be ready and waiting for our heavenly Father, just as Rosa was ready and waiting for her uncle to arrive."

Rosa looked around the room at her family. She thought of the blue suitcase in her room, packed and ready to go. She was going to have so much fun with her cousins, aunt and uncle during the next

week. It was so good to be together. "Dear heavenly Father, help me to be ready and waiting for You. It is so good to be together."

2 Discussion Time

Check understanding of the story and development of personal values.

- What was Rosa looking for in the storage closet?
- Why did she want her suitcase?
- Why did Maria and Carlos think she shouldn't pack yet?
- How do you think Rosa felt when she missed seeing the buck on the bike ride?
- How do you think she felt when her uncle and aunt came a week early?
- Do you think Maria and Carlos wished they had already packed?
- Think about it. Are you ready and waiting for your heavenly Father?

A Preview

Write each word as your teacher says it.

Name _____

1. pull

2. funny

3. still

4. mitten

5. dress

6. bell

7. guess

8. grass

9. rabbit

10. better

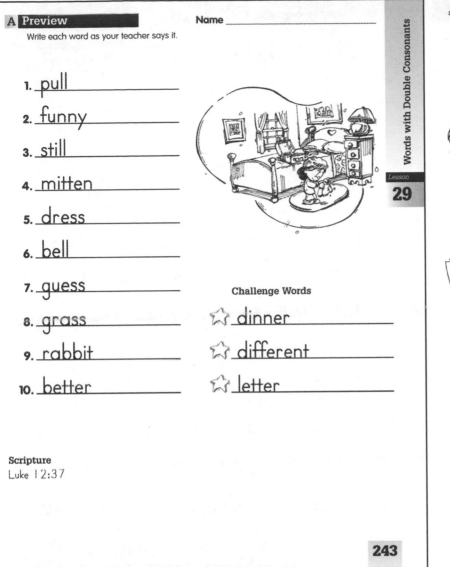

Challenge Words

☆ dinner

☆ different

☆ letter

Scripture
Luke 12:37

243

Challenge

For better spellers, challenge words may be included in the weekly list. Challenge words are starred.

Correct Immediately!

 Let's correct our preview. I will write each word on the board. Put a dot under each letter on your preview as I spell the word out loud. If you spelled a word wrong, rewrite it correctly.

Progress Chart

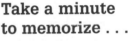 Students may record scores. (Reproducible master in Appendix B.)

Take a minute to memorize . . .

 Read the memory verse twice. Have students practice it with you two more times.

---

3 Preview

Test for knowledge of the correct spellings of these words. (See the instructions at the top right for challenge words.)

Say I will say the word once, use the word in a sentence, then say the word again. Write the word on the lines in the Worktext.

1. pull — Dad reached up to **pull** the suitcase off the shelf.
2. funny — Dad looked **funny** in ribbons and bows.
3. still — It is **still** a week before Uncle Mario comes.
4. mitten — Rosa found a single **mitten** in the back of her closet.
5. dress — Rosa will take one **dress** to the ranch.
6. bell — Maria's bike has a **bell** on the handlebars.
7. guess — Can you **guess** what Carlos and Maria saw on their bike ride?
8. grass — The buck was eating the tall **grass**.
9. rabbit — The **rabbit** dashed across the road in front of the bikes.
10. better — It is **better** to be ready ahead of time than to rush at the end.
☆ dinner — Dad called the children to **dinner**.
☆ different — There are lots of **different** things to do at the ranch.
☆ letter — Aunt Mimi's **letter** said they would come after school was out.

349

Word Shapes

4

Help students form a correct image of whole words.

(Say) Look at each word and think about its shape. Now, write the word in the correct word Shape Boxes. You may check off each word as you use it.

(A double consonant can be in the middle or at the end of a word.)

(Say) In the word Shape Boxes, color the double consonants in each word. Circle the words that have two syllables.

☆ **Challenge**
Draw the correctly shaped box around each letter in these words.

(Say) On a separate sheet of paper, write sentences using one or more of the spelling words.

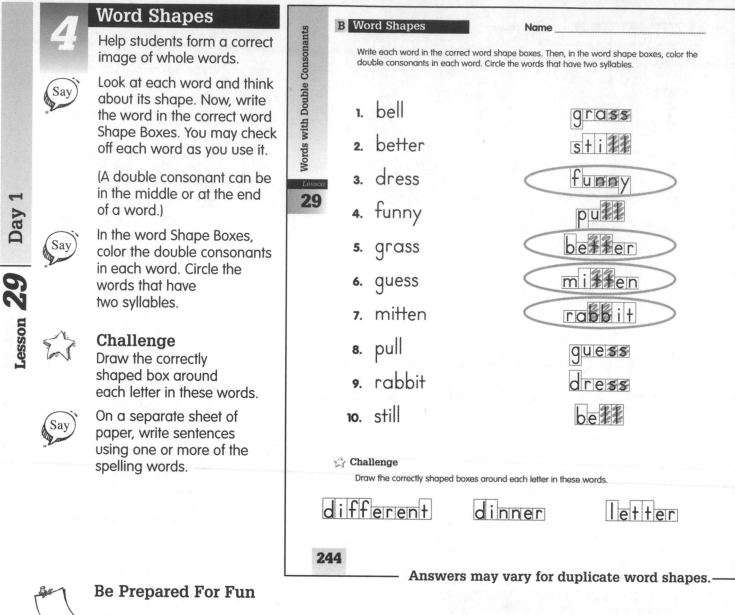

B Word Shapes

Name _____

Words with Double Consonants
Lesson **29**

Write each word in the correct word shape boxes. Then, in the word shape boxes, color the double consonants in each word. Circle the words that have two syllables.

1. bell
2. better
3. dress
4. funny
5. grass
6. guess
7. mitten
8. pull
9. rabbit
10. still

grass
still
funny
pull
better
mitten
rabbit
guess
dress
bell

☆ **Challenge**
Draw the correctly shaped boxes around each letter in these words.

different   dinner   letter

244

Answers may vary for duplicate word shapes.

Be Prepared For Fun

Check these supply lists for **Fun Ways to Spell** presented **Day 2**. Purchase and/or gather these items ahead of time!

General
- Markers
- Art Paper
- Spelling List

Auditory
- Spelling List

Visual
- Letter Tiles a, b, b, d, d, e, e, f, g, i, l, l, m, n, n, o, p, r, s, s, t, t, u, y
- f (added for challenge words)
- Spelling List

Tactile
- Finger paint
- Plastic Plate or Glossy Paper
- Spelling List

350

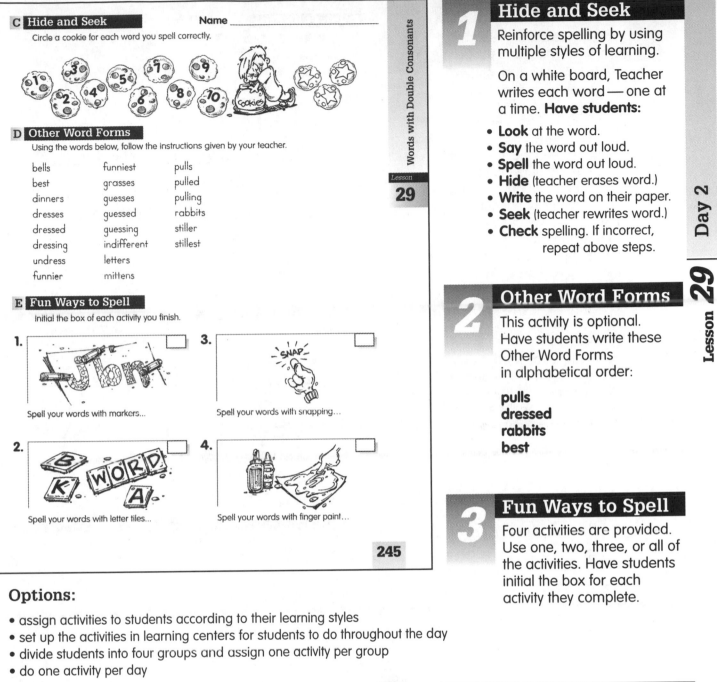

C Hide and Seek

Name _____

Circle a cookie for each word you spell correctly.

D Other Word Forms

Using the words below, follow the instructions given by your teacher.

bells	funniest	pulls
best	grasses	pulled
dinners	guesses	pulling
dresses	guessed	rabbits
dressed	guessing	stiller
dressing	indifferent	stillest
undress	letters	
funnier	mittens	

E Fun Ways to Spell

Initial the box of each activity you finish.

1. ☐

Spell your words with markers...

3. SNAP ☐

Spell your words with snapping...

2. ☐

Spell your words with letter tiles...

4. ☐

Spell your words with finger paint...

245

1 Hide and Seek

Reinforce spelling by using multiple styles of learning.

On a white board, Teacher writes each word—one at a time. **Have students:**

- **Look** at the word.
- **Say** the word out loud.
- **Spell** the word out loud.
- **Hide** (teacher erases word.)
- **Write** the word on their paper.
- **Seek** (teacher rewrites word.)
- **Check** spelling. If incorrect, repeat above steps.

2 Other Word Forms

This activity is optional. Have students write these Other Word Forms in alphabetical order:

pulls
dressed
rabbits
best

3 Fun Ways to Spell

Four activities are provided. Use one, two, three, or all of the activities. Have students initial the box for each activity they complete.

Options:

- assign activities to students according to their learning styles
- set up the activities in learning centers for students to do throughout the day
- divide students into four groups and assign one activity per group
- do one activity per day

General
To spell your words with markers . . .
- Write a spelling word in thick, fat letters.
- Use other colored markers to decorate each letter with dots, flowers, stripes, etc.

Auditory
To spell your words with snapping . . .
- Look at a word on your spelling list.
- Close your eyes.
- Snap your fingers softly while you whisper the spelling of the word.
- Open your eyes and check your spelling.

Visual
To spell your words with letter tiles . . .
- Spell a word from your list by putting the tiles in the right order.
- Check your spelling.

Tactile
To spell your words with finger paint . . .
- Smear paint across your plate.
- Use finger to write a spelling word in paint.
- Check your spelling.
- Smear the word out with your fingers and write another word.

1 Sentence Order

Familiarize students with word meaning and usage. Write **It is** on a blank sheet of paper. Write **fun to** on another sheet, **play** on another, and **games** on the fourth sheet. Invite four students to stand in the front of the room. Making sure the papers are not in order, hand each student one of them. Time the four students to see how long it takes them to get the sentence in the correct order. You may wish to do this activity with other sentences and other students.

(Say) Put each set of word groups in order to write a sentence. After you have written the sentences, circle the spelling words in each sentence.

Words with Double Consonants

Lesson **29**

F **Sentence Order**   **Name** _____

Put each set of word groups in order to write a sentence. Circle the spelling words.

looked 🔔 Dad 🔔 in ribbons. 🔔 funny

1. _____ Dad looked (funny) in ribbons.

rope to 🔔 the bell. 🔔 ring 🔔 Pull the

2. _____ (Pull) the rope to ring the (bell.)

the mitten 🔔 I guess 🔔 is lost.

3. _____ I (guess) the (mitten) is lost.

grass. 🔔 eats 🔔 The rabbit 🔔 fresh

4. _____ The (rabbit) eats fresh (grass.)

had better 🔔 this dress. 🔔 Rosa 🔔 wear

5. _____ Rosa had (better) wear this (dress.)

and proud. 🔔 stood still 🔔 The buck

6. _____ The buck stood (still) and proud.

Word Bank				
bell	dress	grass	mitten	rabbit
better	funny	guess	pull	still

246

Take a minute to memorize . . .

Read the memory verse twice. Have students practice it with you two more times.

352

G Dictation

Name _____

Listen and write the missing words.

1. The funny rabbit ate the grass .
2. I guess he can still pull the wagon.
3. The odd dress is still here .
4. One purple mitten is in the box .

H Proofreading

One word in each set is misspelled. Fill in the oval by the misspelled word.

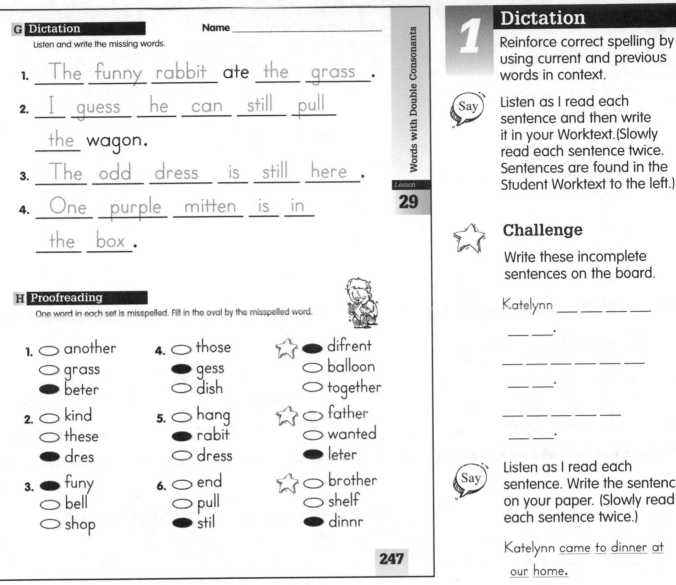

1. ○ another
   ○ grass
   ● beter

2. ○ kind
   ○ these
   ● dres

3. ● funy
   ○ bell
   ○ shop

4. ○ those
   ● gess
   ○ dish

5. ○ hang
   ● rabit
   ○ dress

6. ○ end
   ○ pull
   ● stil

☆ ● difrent
  ○ balloon
  ○ together

☆ ○ father
  ○ wanted
  ● leter

☆ ○ brother
  ○ shelf
  ● dinnr

247

---

1 Dictation

Reinforce correct spelling by using current and previous words in context.

(Say) Listen as I read each sentence and then write it in your Worktext.(Slowly read each sentence twice. Sentences are found in the Student Worktext to the left.)

☆ Challenge

Write these incomplete sentences on the board.

Katelynn __ __ __ __

__ __.

__ __ __ __ __

__ __.

__ __ __ __ __

__ __.

(Say) Listen as I read each sentence. Write the sentence on your paper. (Slowly read each sentence twice.)

Katelynn came to dinner at our home.

She will paint her room a different color.

The letter was very old and brown.

2 Proofreading

Familiarize students with standardized test format and reinforce recognizing misspelled words.

(Say) Look at each set of words. One word in each set is misspelled. Fill in the oval by the misspelled word. (You may wish to pronounce each set of words to help students correctly identify them.)

3 Hide and Seek

Reinforce correct spelling of current spelling words. (A reproducible master is provided in Appendix A as shown on the inset page to the right.)

Write the words one at a time on a white board.

Have students:

- **Look** at the word.
- **Say** the word out loud.
- **Spell** the word out loud.
- **Hide** (teacher erases word.)
- **Write** the word on paper.
- **Seek** (teacher rewrites word.)
- **Check** spelling. If incorrect, rewrite word correctly.

4 Code

Have your students complete this activity to strengthen spelling ability and expand vocabulary.

1 Posttest

Test mastery of the spelling words. Challenge words are starred.

(Say) I will say the word once, use the word in a sentence, then say the word again. Write the word on your paper.

1. **better**   We'd **better** make a few extra cookies for the recital.
2. **dress**   Rosa will wear her red **dress** to the piano recital.
3. **funny**   Her piano piece is about a **funny**, fuzzy worm.
4. **guess**   Can you **guess** what song Carlos is playing?
5. **rabbit**   The children will feed the **rabbit** carrots.
6. **grass**   Pedro, the donkey, eats the **grass** in the yard.
7. **bell**   They ring a **bell** at lunch time at the ranch.
8. **pull**   Rosa likes to **pull** the rope to ring the bell.
9. **still**   Carlos and Maria **still** have to pack their things.
10. **mitten**   Rosa lost the other red **mitten**.
☆ **different**   She'll have to get a **different** pair of mittens.
☆ **letter**   Did a **letter** come from Aunt Mimi yet?
☆ **dinner**   The two families visited around the **dinner** table.

Progress Chart

Students may record scores. (Reproducible master in Appendix B.)

Personal Dictionary

Students may add any words they have misspelled to their personal dictionaries for reference when writing. (Cover in Appendix B.)

Inset (Appendix A — Lesson 29, page 392)

Hide and Seek

Check a paper for each word you spell correctly.

1 3 5 7 9
2 4 6 8 10

Code

Use the code to write the spelling words.

1	2	3	4	5	6	7	8	9	10	11	12	13
a	b	c	d	e	f	g	h	i	j	k	l	m

14	15	16	17	18	19	20	21	22	23	24	25	26
n	o	p	q	r	s	t	u	v	w	x	y	z

2 5 19 20
1. b e s t

6 21 14 14 9 5 19 20
2. f u n n i e s t

18 1 2 2 9 20 19
3. r a b b i t s

4 18 5 19 19 5 19
4. d r e s s e s

7 18 1 19 19 5 19
5. g r a s s e s

Word Bank

best	funniest	rabbits
dresses	grasses	

392

Lesson 29

I Game

Name _____

Rosa is getting ready to visit her uncle and aunt on their farm. Help her pack by moving one space each time you or your team spells a word correctly from this week's word list.

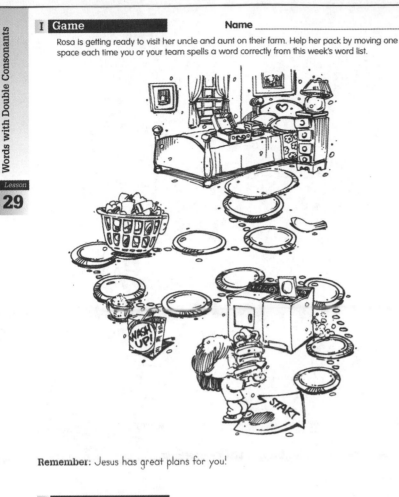

Remember: Jesus has great plans for you!

J Journaling

Write several sentences in your journal about a time you went somewhere special that you really enjoyed. Remember, being with your Heavenly Father will be very special!

248

---

2 Game

Reinforce spelling skills and provide motivation and interest.

Materials

- game page (from student text)
- flat buttons, dry beans, pennies, or game discs (1 per child)
- game word list (provided below)

Game Word List

Use of challenge words is optional.

1. **better**
2. **rabbit**
3. **funny**
4. **dress**
5. **grass**
6. **guess**
7. **mitten**
8. **bell**
9. **pull**
10. **still**
☆ **dinner**
☆ **different**
☆ **letter**

3 Journaling

Provide a meaningful reason for correct spelling through personal writing.

Review the story using discussion leads provided on the following page. Encourage students to apply the Scriptural value in their journaling.

 Take a minute to memorize . . .

Read the memory verse twice. Have students practice it with you two more times.

How to Play:

- Divide students into two teams, and decide which team will go first.
- Have each student place their game piece on Start.
- Have a student from team A go to the board.
- Read the spelling word two times slowly and clearly. (You may also wish to use the word in a sentence. Ex.: "cat — The cat climbed a tree. — cat")
- Have the student write the word on the board.
- If the word is spelled correctly, instruct all the members of team A to move their game piece forward one space on the game board. (Note: If the word is misspelled, correct the spelling immediately.)
- Alternate between teams A and B as you go down the word list.
- The team to reach Rosa's suitcase first is the winner.

Non-Competitive Option: At the end of the game, say: "Class, I am proud of your efforts to spell the words correctly. If you had fun and tried your best, you are all winners!"

355

Provide a meaningful reason for correct spelling through personal writing.

Say

- Where did Rosa and her brother and sister go each summer? (Sunrise Vista Ranch in New Mexico, their aunt and uncle's ranch.)

- What kinds of things did the children like to do there? (Ride horses, swim in the swimming hole, explore the barn, bottle-feed the calves, play with Pedro the donkey or the many baby animals, play with their cousins.)

- Have you ever spent time in a place you really enjoyed? What did you enjoy doing?

- Rosa spent the beautiful afternoon indoors packing her things to take to the ranch. Carlos and Maria thought she should wait to pack. What happened that changed their minds? (Uncle Mario and his family came a week early.)

- Do you think Rosa was glad she'd packed already?

- In your journal write about a time that you went somewhere special.

Quotables!

"Mastering spelling is a complex intellectual achievement, not a low-order memory task."*

*Watson, Alan J. 1988. Developmental Spelling: A Word Categorizing Instructional Experiment. Journal of Educational Research, Vol. 82, No. 2, November/December: 82-88.

Right or Wrong?

Rosa's honesty is tested when she doesn't remember how to spell a word.

"Three days. Just three more days till school will be out for the summer." Rosa sat back in her desk chair and looked around the familiar classroom.

Mrs. Morgan was leaning over James' desk helping him with something. Daniel swaggered across the room the long way to the pencil sharpener. Tommy frowned down at the math book open on his desk. The white airplane-shaped eraser on the end of Christopher's pencil swooped around as he wrote something on the paper in front of him. Kristin's forehead wrinkled as she concentrated on coloring something with a purple marker. Setsuko leaned over, straightening an already very neat desk.

"Setsuko must be finished with her math already." Rosa sighed. "Three days. I can't wait to go to Sunrise Vista and I can't wait for school to be over, but . . . I'm kinda sad that it's almost over at the same time. Most of us will be back next year, but maybe not everyone. And we won't ever be in Mrs. Morgan's room again." Rosa looked again at the teacher she admired so much. Mrs. Morgan smiled at something James said and patted his hand. "I'll sure miss Mrs. Morgan."

Rosa picked up her pencil and turned her attention back to the math book on her desk. "I'm glad this is our last math assignment." Her gaze drifted away from the math book to a butterfly fluttering past the window. "Just four more problems and the test tomorrow and I'll be through with math for the whole summer! Uh, oh, the spelling test is next today. Maybe I should practice my words."

"Please clear everything off of your desks, class, except for one blank sheet of paper and your pencil. It's time for our last spelling test." Mrs. Morgan's pleasant voice started a flurry of activity as Rosa and her classmates followed the teacher's directions.

"No time to go over those words again now." Rosa shrugged and wrote her name neatly at the top of the blank sheet of paper she'd placed on her desk. "I think I remember all of them pretty well, anyway."

When everyone was ready, Mrs. Morgan said, "I will say the word once, use the word in a sentence, then say the word again. Write the word on your paper. Number one. Rabbit. The rabbit hopped quickly away. Rabbit." Mrs. Morgan walked slowly around the room as the children wrote each word. "Number two. Finish. The girl will finish the race first. Finish."

"Finish! Is that f-i-n-i-s-h or f-i-n-n-i-s-h? It's probably f-i-n-i-s-h. That seems right." Rosa wrote f-i-n-i-s-h on her paper and stared hard at it. "Is it right? It doesn't look quite like it should. Maybe it's f-i-n-n-i-s-h after all." Rosa flipped her pencil over and rubbed the eraser across the word. She hurriedly wrote f-i-n-n-i-s-h just as Mrs. Morgan gave the next word. During the rest of the spelling test Rosa kept looking back at that second word. Was it right or not?

The next day Mrs. Morgan passed out the corrected tests. Rosa's palms got sweaty as Mrs. Morgan started her way. Was that word right or not? Mrs. Morgan placed the graded test on Rosa's desk with a smile and moved on to the next desk. Rosa stared down at the test without touching it. A+ 100%. IT WAS RIGHT! Rosa grinned at the second word.

"It still doesn't look quite right." Rosa thought. "But it's got to be or I would've missed it. Phew! That was close!"

"Psst." Kristin caught Rosa's eye from her desk across the aisle and one row up. "What'd you get, Rosa?"

Rosa tipped up her graded test paper just a little so Kristin could see her grade. "Wow!" Kristin mouthed. Then she held her paper so that Rosa could see it. The first thing Rosa saw was the bright red A on the top of it.

The next thing she spotted was the second word on the test. Kristin had gotten it right, too! But Kristin had spelled it differently than Rosa had. Rosa gave Kristin a thumbs-up sign, then she dug in her desk for her spelling book. Opening it quickly she looked for "finish." Had she spelled it right or not? "It has to be right! Here it is on this page." Rosa's smile dropped away. IT WAS WRONG!

Rosa flipped the spelling test over and nibbled on her fingernail. What was she going to do? She'd spelled that word wrong, but Mrs. Morgan hadn't counted it wrong. Rosa was usually really good at spelling. She hadn't missed any test words this year. If she told Mrs. Morgan about the misspelled word, her record would be ruined right at the end of the year. Rosa moved on to nibble on another fingernail.

That evening Rosa and her family, along with Uncle Mario's family, arrived at Knowlton Elementary for the school picnic promptly at six o'clock. Lots of other students and their families were already swarming over the playground and ball fields. Calls of greeting and shouts of laughter rang in the air as more families arrived. The picnic tables on the patio were covered with red and white checked cloths and loaded with good things to eat. There were hot dogs and burgers with all the trimmings, corn on the cob, carrot sticks, chips, and all kinds of cookies. There was a huge cooler of pink lemonade and another of punch. And there

357

were enough ice-cold watermelons to feed an army.

Lawn chairs popped up all over the playground, and colorful quilts were spread in the shade under the big trees by the fence. Toddlers explored under the watchful eyes of their parents and older children raced about with their friends. It didn't take long for most of the food to disappear.

Then it was time for the games. There were tug-of-wars and relays, three-legged races, human wheelbarrow races, and lots of other kinds of races. There was a giant game of freeze tag, followed by a game called "Blob." There was even a greased watermelon contest.

Later, Carlos, Dad, and Uncle Mario joined a softball game. Maria led Willie around and showed him to all her friends while Aunt Mimi sat in the shade where she could watch and visit with some of the other ladies. "Hey, you guys, they're going to start a game of Swim, Fish, Swim!" Kristin grabbed Rosa's arm in one hand and Alisha's in the other. "Come on!"

The field had been marked off in a huge rectangle. All the "fish" lined up along the line across one end. Mr. Valentino, the third grade teacher, stood alone in the center of the grassy rectangle. "Swim, Fish, Swim," he called and all the "fish" took off across the center of the rectangle trying to stay out of his way so that he couldn't tag them. But he was fast, and a few unlucky "fish" got caught. They had to stop right where he tagged them and keep their right foot in place. A few others ran out of bounds outside the rectangle. They had to stop and stay right where they had stepped out of bounds. The next time he called out, "Swim, Fish, Swim!" the "fish" had to run across without being tagged by Mr. Valentino or the "fish" that had already been caught. It got harder and harder to make it across.

Rosa ducked a flailing "fish's" arm and streaked across the line on the other side. Alisha hadn't made it this time. She was stuck

along with several others. When Mr. Valentino called again, Rosa took off. Just as she was about to step across the line, one of the "fish" players that had been caught grabbed for her. He was a big boy that Rosa didn't know and he had a long arm. Rosa dodged and he missed, but when she looked down she saw that she had crossed the boundary line. Glancing around quickly she saw that nobody noticed. She hadn't gone very much out of bounds. She could keep running and no one would ever know what happened.

"If I hadn't gone out of bounds that big boy would have caught me. It wouldn't be fair to him or to me to cheat, because I didn't really make it across." Rosa planted her right foot firmly into place right at the spot where she'd stepped out of bounds before reaching to try to catch someone running by her.

The next morning Rosa slipped into her desk chair when she arrived at school. "Two days. Only two more days of school." Rosa reached for her pencil and saw the spelling test. "If I tell Mrs. Morgan about the word I missed I won't have a perfect record. But it wouldn't be fair to her or to me to cheat, because I didn't really get it right." Rosa pulled the test out of her desk and raised her hand. Mrs. Morgan listened quietly while she explained it all. Rosa felt a whole lot better when she was done.

2 Discussion Time

Check understanding of the story and development of personal values.

- Did Rosa get all the words right on her last spelling test?
- Why was she tempted not to tell Mrs. Morgan that she'd missed the word?
- What game did Rosa play at the school picnic?
- Did Rosa cheat at the game when she had a chance? Why not?
- How do you think being honest about getting out during the game helped her decide to be honest about the spelling word she'd missed?

A Test-Words

Write each spelling word on the line as your teacher says it.

Name _____

1. another
2. both
3. wish
4. better
5. bring

6. hang
7. dish
8. fish
9. grand
10. sing

B Test-Sentences

The two underlined words in each of the sentences are misspelled. Write the sentences on the lines below, spelling each underlined word correctly.

Sevin men played trumpets in the badn.

1. Seven men played trumpets in the band.

We saw a wite rabitt in the woods.

2. We saw a white rabbit in the woods.

Mom maed this chewy candi.

3. Mom made this chewy candy.

☆ **Test-Challenge Words**

On a sheet of paper, write each challenge word as your teacher says it.

249

☆ **Test-Challenge Words**

On a separate piece of paper, challenge words may be tested using the sentences below.

4 Test-Sentences

Reinforce recognizing misspelled words.

Read each sentence carefully. The underlined words in each sentence are misspelled. Write the sentences on the lines in your Worktext, spelling each underlined word correctly.

Take a minute to memorize . . .

Have students say the memory verses from lessons 19, 20, 21, 22, 23, and 24 with you.

---

3 Test-Words

Test for knowledge of the correct spellings of these words. (See the instructions at the top right for challenge words.)

Say: I will say the word once, use the word in a sentence, then say the word again. Write the word on the lines in your Worktext.

1. another — Tommy began working **another** math problem.
2. both — **Both** Kristin and Rosa were glad they received A's on the test.
3. wish — "I **wish** I had spelled that word right," thought Rosa.
4. better — Rosa felt **better** when she saw the A+ at the top of her paper.
5. bring — Mrs. Morgan asked each child to **bring** a dessert to the picnic.
6. hang — They will **hang** red and white streamers on the tables.
7. dish — There was a big **dish** of strawberries on the picnic table.
8. fish — The girls joined a game of "Swim, **Fish**, Swim."
9. grand — All the students had a **grand** time at the school picnic.
10. sing — Rosa and her family like to **sing** in the car.
☆ short — Rosa chewed on her already **short** fingernails.
☆ different — Kristin's and Rosa's spellings of the word were **different**.
☆ letter — Which **letter** in the spelling word was wrong?

359

1 Test-Dictation

Reinforce correct spelling by using current and previous words in context.

(Say) Listen as I read each sentence. Then write the missing words in your Worktext. (Slowly read each sentence twice. Sentences are found in the student text to the right. The words **bend**, **thin**, and **end** are found in this unit.)

2 Test-Proofreading

Familiarize students with standardized test format and reinforce recognizing misspelled words.

(Say) Look at each set of words. One word in each set is misspelled. Fill in the oval by the misspelled word.

Test-Challenge Words

On a separate piece of paper, challenge words may be tested using the sentences below.

(Say) I will say the word once, use the word in a sentence, then say the word again. Write the word on your paper.

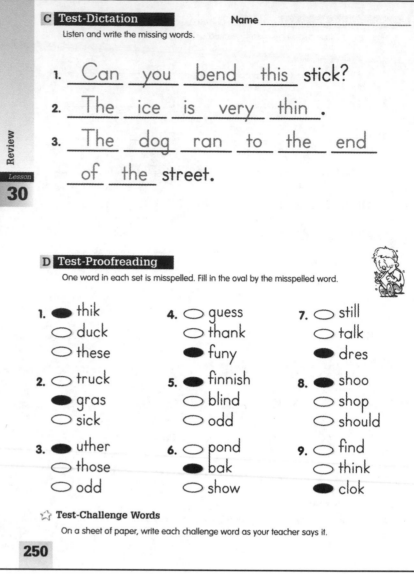

C Test-Dictation
Listen and write the missing words.

Name _____

1. Can you bend this stick?
2. The ice is very thin .
3. The dog ran to the end of the street.

D Test-Proofreading
One word in each set is misspelled. Fill in the oval by the misspelled word.

1. ● thik
   ○ duck
   ○ these

2. ○ truck
   ● gras
   ○ sick

3. ● uther
   ○ those
   ○ odd

4. ○ guess
   ○ thank
   ● funy

5. ● finnish
   ○ blind
   ○ odd

6. ○ pond
   ● bak
   ○ show

7. ○ still
   ○ talk
   ● dres

8. ● shoo
   ○ shop
   ○ should

9. ○ find
   ○ think
   ● clok

☆ **Test-Challenge Words**
On a sheet of paper, write each challenge word as your teacher says it.

250

☆ friend   Rosa's **friend** Kristin got an A on her spelling test.
☆ something Christopher wrote **something** on his paper.
☆ index   Setsuko has a stack of **index** cards in her desk.
☆ shelf   Mrs. Morgan straightened the books on the **shelf**.

360

E Test-Shapes   Name _____

Color each picnic food on which the word is spelled incorrectly.

251

☆ **Test-Challenge Words**

On a sheet of paper, write each challenge word as your teacher says it.

---

1 Test-Shapes

Test mastery of words in this unit.

(Say) Look at each picnic food. If the word is misspelled, color the piece of candy.

2 Action Game

Reinforce spelling skills and provide motivation and interest.

Materials
- container with folded cards (1 per student) numbered consecutively
- chalk
- chalk board

How to Play:

On the chalk board, write words tested on days 1, 2, and 3 leaving out 2 to 3 key letters, and numbering them consecutively. There should be as many words as there are students in your class. Pass the container around the room having each student draw a number. Call a student to the board. Have them fill in the missing letters of the word with the number they drew. Have students decide together if each word is spelled correctly. The game is over when every student has been to the board and all the words have been correctly completed.

Test-Challenge Words

On a separate piece of paper, challenge words may be tested using the sentences below.

(Say) I will say the word once, use the word in a sentence, then say the word again. Write the word on your paper.

☆ **brother**   Rosa has a younger **brother** named Carlos.
☆ **dinner**   They will eat **dinner** at the school picnic.
☆ **father**   Uncle Mario is Alisha and Willie's **father**.
☆ **shoes**   Rosa wore her tennis **shoes** to the school picnic.
☆ **block**   Rosa's dad didn't want to **block** the school drive with their car.

Game

1

Materials
- game page (from student text)
- stickers (13 per child)
- markers (1 per child)
- game word list

Game Word List

Use of challenge words is optional.

The Rainbow Trout

1. band
2. rabbit
3. candy
4. another
5. both
6. wish
7. better
8. bring
9. hang
10. dish
11. fish
12. grand
13. sing

The Wide-Mouth Bass

1. thick
2. grass
3. other
4. funny
5. finish
6. back
7. dress
8. shoe
9. clock
10. bend
11. thin
12. end
13. wash

The Pink Salmon

1. shop
2. pond
3. duck
4. those
5. guess
6. should
7. blind
8. sick
9. these
10. odd
11. show
12. find
13. shut

F Game

Name _____

At the school picnic, Rosa and other students played a tag game called "Swim, Fish, Swim!" Use types of fish as your team names for this game. Place a sticker each time you or your team spells a review word correctly.

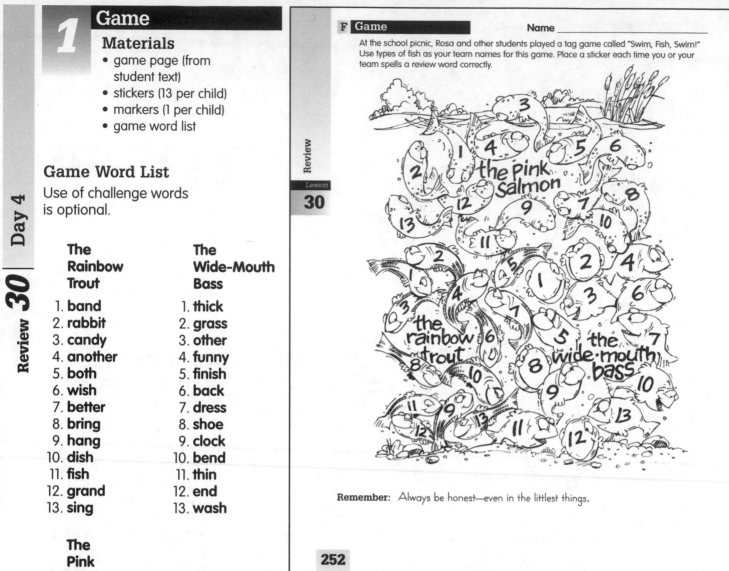

Remember: Always be honest—even in the littlest things.

252

How to Play:

- Divide students into three teams. Name one team **The Rainbow Trout**, one **The Wide-Mouth Bass**, and one **The Pink Salmon**. (Option: You may wish to seat students in groups of three, each child from a different team. They should share one game page.) Decide which team goes first, second, and third.
- Read the instructions from the student game page aloud.
- Have a student from the first team choose a number from 1 to 13.
- Say the word that matches that number (from the team's word list) aloud twice. (You may also wish to use the word in a sentence. Ex.: "cat — The cat climbed a tree. — cat")
- Have the student who chose the number write the word on the board.
- If the word is spelled correctly, have all the members of that team put a sticker on that number by their team name. If the word is misspelled, have them put an "X" through that number. They may not choose that number again. (Note: If the word is misspelled, correct the spelling immediately.)
- Repeat this process with the second team and then the third. (Be sure to use a different student from each team for each round.)
- When the words from all three lists have been used, the team with the most stickers is the winner.

Non-Competitive Option: When the game is over say: "Class, I'm proud of your efforts to spell the words correctly. If you had fun and tried your best, you are all winners!"

G · Test-Words

Name _____

Write each spelling word on the line as your teacher says it.

1. truck
2. thought
3. shut
4. pull
5. wash

6. think
7. still
8. talk
9. kind
10. thank

Review
Lesson
30

H · Test-Sentences

The two underlined words in each of the sentences are misspelled. Write the sentences on the lines below, spelling each underlined word correctly.

The <u>litel</u> <u>Indin</u> baby had brown eyes.

1. The **little Indian** baby had brown eyes.

At <u>scool</u>, the <u>bel</u> is very loud.

2. At **school,** the **bell** is very loud.

Do you drink <u>mutch</u> <u>mikl</u>?

3. Do you drink **much milk**?

☆ **Test-Challenge Words**

On a sheet of paper, write each challenge word as your teacher says it.

253

Test-Challenge Words

On a separate piece of paper, challenge words may be tested using the sentences below.

2 Test-Sentences

Reinforce recognizing misspelled words.

(Say) Read each sentence carefully. The underlined words in each sentence are misspelled. Write the sentences on the lines in your Worktext, spelling each underlined word correctly.

---

1 Test-Words

Test for knowledge of the correct spellings of these words. (See the instructions at the top right for challenge words.)

 (Say) I will say the word once, use the word in a sentence, then say the word again. Write the word on the lines in your Worktext.

1. truck	Rosa's Uncle Mario has a bright, red farm **truck**.
2. thought	"Only two more days of school," Rosa **thought**.
3. shut	Mrs. Morgan **shut** the lid so the ice wouldn't melt.
4. pull	In tug–of–war, the boys tried to **pull** hard.
5. wash	They had to **wash** their hands after eating the sticky watermelon.
6. think	Does Jesus **think** that any lie is little?
7. still	At the picnic Rosa **still** felt badly about the test.
8. talk	Rosa knew she had to **talk** to her teacher.
9. kind	Mrs. Morgan was **kind** as Rosa explained things.
10. thank	Always **thank** God for His faithful love.
☆ second	Daniel and Tony came in **second** in the race.
☆ along	Rosa ran her hand **along** the cold watermelon.
☆ together	Sarah and Katelynn entered the race **together**.

363

3 Writing Assessment

Assess student's spelling, grammar, and composition skills through personal writing.

(Say) • Rosa knew she spelled one word wrong. When, by mistake, Mrs. Morgan didn't mark it wrong, would it be cheating not to tell? (Yes. She got the word wrong. It wouldn't be fair for her to get it counted right when it was wrong.)

• What times do you find that it's tempting to be dishonest? (Maybe playing a game, on a test, answering questions, etc.)

• Why is it bad to be dishonest even in games and small things like that? (Because you get used to being dishonest and soon you won't be honest about anything, even very important, big things.)

• Write several sentences in your Worktext describing times you might be tempted to be dishonest. In the last sentence, write your promise to be honest all the time.

I Writing Assessment

Write several sentences describing times you might be tempted to be dishonest. In the last sentence, write your promise to be honest all the time.

Name _____

_____

_____

_____

_____

_____

_____

_____

Scripture
Luke 16:10

254

A rubric for scoring is provided in Appendix B.

---

4 Action Game

Reinforce spelling skills and provide motivation and interest.

Materials

• blindfold
• song (to the tune of London Bridge): "Who is going to spell this word, spell this word, spell this word? Who is going to spell this word? It is you."
• small prizes (erasers, pencils, stickers)

How to Play:

Choose one student to be **IT**. Have the other students form a circle around **IT**, holding hands. As you sing the song, have the students circle around **IT**, stopping at the end of the song. Instruct **IT** to point in any direction to choose a student to spell. Give the student to whom **IT** points a word to spell from today's test. If he/she spells it correctly, give him/her a prize and have him/her return to his/her desk; if he/she spells it incorrectly, have him/her be **IT**. Continue playing until every student has spelled a word correctly.

Spelling Is Fun!

ABC's

Spelling

This certificate is awarded to

_____

for practicing the following words, by doing terrific spelling activities and playing great spelling games!

Date _____

dish	band	back	another	bell
finish	bend	bring	both	better
fish	blind	clock	other	dress
shoe	candy	duck	thank	funny
shop	end	hang	these	grass
should	find	milk	thick	guess
show	grand	sick	thin	mitten
shut	Indian	sing	think	pull
wash	kind	talk	those	rabbit
wish	pond	truck	thought	still
☆ shelf	☆ friend	☆ along	☆ brother	☆ different
☆ shoes	☆ index	☆ block	☆ father	☆ dinner
☆ short	☆ second	☆ something	☆ together	☆ letter

Provide an opportunity for parents or guardians to encourage and assess their child's progress.

Say
- Write your name on the first line.
- Now I will write the date on the board for you to copy on the next line.
- Follow along as I read the certificate out loud.
- Be sure to show your parents or guardian all the words you've practiced spelling.

Take a minute to memorize . . .

Read the memory verse twice. Have students practice it with you two more times.

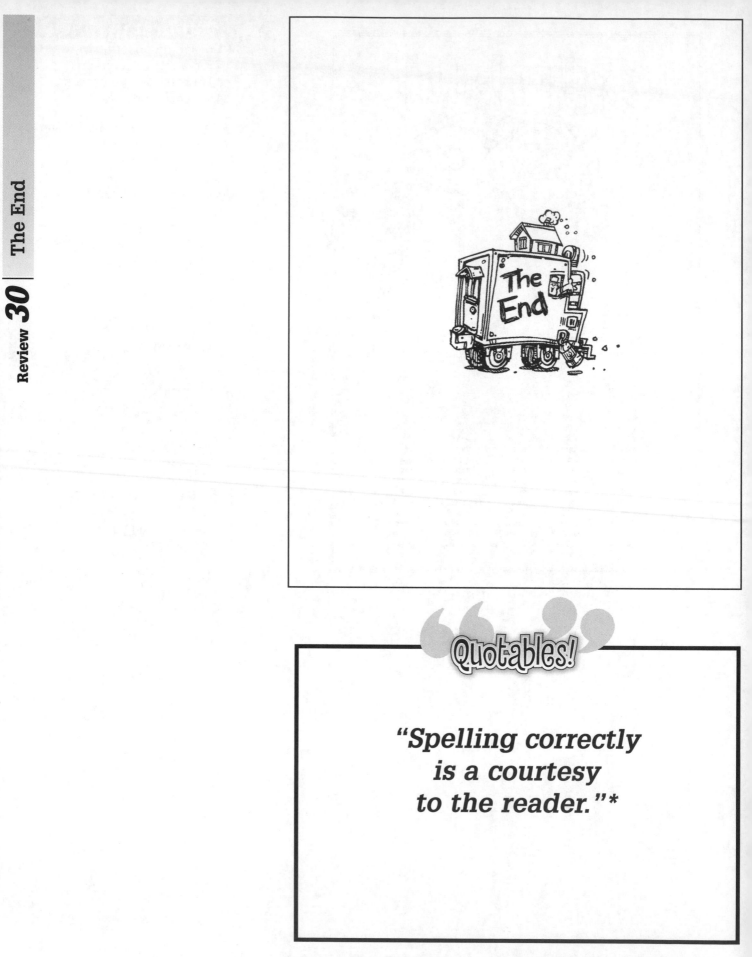

Quotables!

*"Spelling correctly
is a courtesy
to the reader."**

*Scott, Jill E. 1994. Spelling for Readers and Writers. The Reading
Teacher, Vol. 48, No. 2, October: 188-190.

PLEASE
PHOTOCOPY!*

The following pages contain Black Line Masters for use with the *A Reason For Spelling®* Student Worktext.

*Photocopy privileges extend only to the material in this section, and permission is granted only for those class-rooms or homeschools using *A Reason For Spelling®* Student Worktexts. Any other use of this material is expressly forbidden and all copyright laws apply.

Hide and Seek

Check a paper for each word you spell correctly.

Suffixes

Add **s**, **ed**, and **ing** to these spelling words. Write the new words.

	+ s	+ ed	+ ing
1. add			
2. ask			
3. camp			
4. last			
5. bath			

Double the final consonant before adding **ed** and **ing** to these spelling words. Write the new words.

	+ ed	+ ing
6. plan		
7. map		

368

Hide and Seek

Check a paper for each word you spell correctly.

Making Words

Add the endings to the spelling words. Write the new word in each sentence.

1. help + s
2. set + s
3. head + s
4. man → men
5. help + ed
6. leg + s
7. nest + s
8. help + ing
9. ever + y

The Red Cross _____ people.

Many _____ of hands made cleaning up easier.

Hard hats protect their _____.

Some _____ fixed food for them.

Tommy _____ find the dog.

The dog's _____ are hurt.

There were two _____.

Tommy had fun _____ others.

God cares about _____ person.

369

Hide and Seek

Check a paper for each word you spell correctly.

Secret Words

Use these clues to find the words that fit in the blanks.
Then use the boxed letters to discover the secret words.

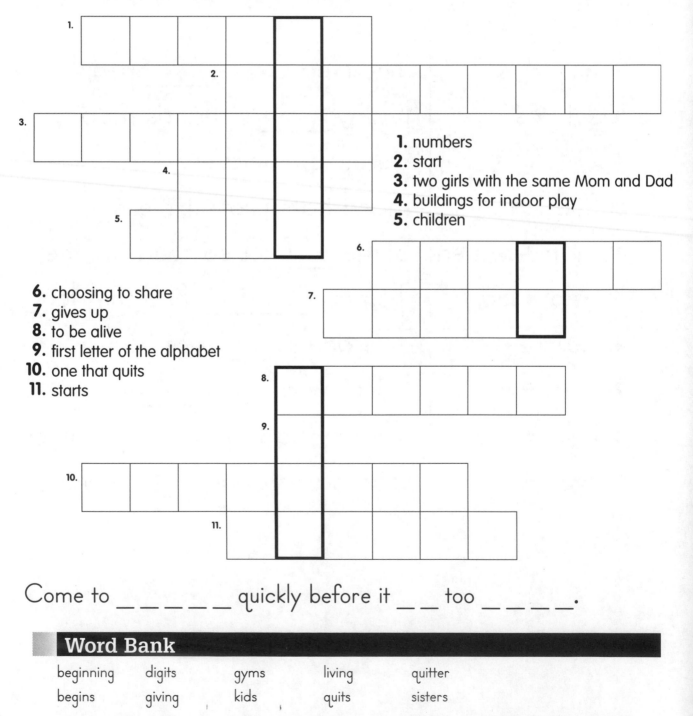

1. numbers
2. start
3. two girls with the same Mom and Dad
4. buildings for indoor play
5. children

6. choosing to share
7. gives up
8. to be alive
9. first letter of the alphabet
10. one that quits
11. starts

Come to _ _ _ _ _ _ quickly before it _ _ too _ _ _ _ _.

Word Bank

beginning	digits	gyms	living	quitter
begins	giving	kids	quits	sisters

370

Hide and Seek

Check a paper for each word you spell correctly.

Clues

Look at other forms of your spelling words in the word bank.
Use the clues to find the word that fits best in each blank.

1. cereal is packaged in these _____

2. little round marks _____

3. many _____

4. not loudly _____

5. let go of _____

6. land and water animals _____

7. chores _____

8. days after today _____

Word Bank

box + es   drop + p + ed   job + s   soft + ly

dot + s   frog + s   lot + s   tomorrow + s

Hide and Seek

Check a paper for each word you spell correctly.

Code

Mrs. Morgan's class likes to wear Knowlton Elementary's blue soccer jerseys when they play team games. Mrs. Morgan kept track of who used them on her clipboard last week. While she supervised recess one day, she made a spelling code with the names on her clipboard. Count over the number of letters indicated by the student's jersey numbers before their names and circle the letter. Write the letters you circled, in order, on the lines below each day to discover some other word forms of your spelling words.

Monday

13 Stephen Wilson
5 Setsuko Noma
4 Tommy Rawson
11 Rachel Jacobson
2 Beth Hill
3 Sarah
16 Katelynn Hatasaki
13 Stephen Wilson
15 Christopher Wright

Tuesday

13 Stephen Wilson
9 Rosa Vasquez
4 Tommy Rawson
11 Rachel Jacobson
2 Beth Hill
3 Sarah
6 Matthew Schilling
7 Daniel DeVore

Wednesday

1 James Thompson
9 Rosa Vasquez
3 Tommy Rawson
8 Christopher Wright
2 Beth Hill
7 Daniel DeVore

_ _ _ _ _ _ + _ _ _   _ _ _ _ _ _ + _ _   _ _ _ _ + _ _

Thursday

1 James Thompson
9 Rosa Vasquez
4 Kristin Wright
10 Tony Vanetti
12 Matthew Schilling
6 Katelynn Hatasaki

Friday

4 Kristin Wright
9 Rosa Vasquez
3 Tommy Rawson
1 Setsuko Noma

_ _ _ _ + _ _   _ _ _ + _

372

Hide and Seek

Check a paper for each word you spell correctly.

Suffixes

Add **s**, **ed**, or **ing** to make new words from your spelling words.

+ s

1. bake + s _____

2. cake + s _____

3. game + s _____

4. name + s _____

5. gate + s _____

6. grade + s _____

7. page + s _____

8. break + s _____

9. obey + s _____

+ ed

1. bake – e + ed _____

2. name – e + ed _____

3. grade – e + ed _____

4. page – e + ed _____

5. obey + ed _____

+ ing

1. bake – e + ing _____

2. name – e + ing _____

3. grade – e + ing _____

4. break + ing _____

5. obey + ing _____

Hide and Seek

Check a paper for each word you spell correctly.

Sentence Fun

Read each sentence. Write the missing words in the sentence.

1. Christopher was _____ selfish and unkind when _____ argued about setting the table.

2. Christopher _____ late the morning after he had _____ hurt.

3. Mom _____ him busy by _____ to him.

4. That _____ Mom _____ his face and combed his hair.

5. Christopher _____ making funny lines when he tried to write _____.

6. _____ can be fun to be around by _____ Jesus in our hearts.

Word Bank

being	cleaned	evening	keeping	kept	reading
been	eastern	he	kept	slept	we

Hide and Seek

Check a paper for each word you spell correctly.

Hidden Words

Using the word bank below, find the words in the puzzle. Circle and write each word.

m	k	i	r	I	a	p	l	s	t
i	g	b	c	s	p	h	i	p	a
g	u	b	u	y	s	k	g	u	f
h	f	c	r	i	e	s	h	o	y
t	l	r	n	g	s	e	t	g	d
y	e	i	c	m	i	k	s	n	r
m	w	n	i	g	h	t	l	y	i
c	h	i	l	d	r	e	n	l	e
e	n	s	w	l	a	m	q	w	d
a	d	u	r	i	g	h	t	s	p

Across

_____

_____

_____

_____

_____

Down

_____

_____

_____

_____

Word Bank

buys	cries	flew	mighty	rights
children	dried	lights	nightly	

Hide and Seek

Check a paper for each word you spell correctly.

Secret Word

Use these clues to find the word that fits in each blank. Then use the boxed letters to discover the secret word.

1. colder than anything else
2. houses that people live in
3. smooth paths to drive on
4. a ball or wheel does this
5. things you can sail or ride in on the water
6. not as young
7. to say
8. almost all

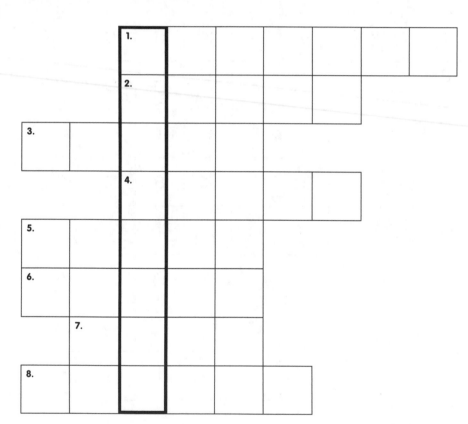

Kristin's class liked _ _ _ _ _ _ _ _ _ _.

Word Bank

boats	homes	older	rolls
coldest	mostly	roads	tell

376

Hide and Seek

Check a paper for each word you spell correctly.

Sentence Fun

Look at other forms of your spelling words in the word bank.
Use the clues to find the word that fits best in each blank.

1. Flowers are _____ in Grandpa's garden.

2. Jesus _____ when you are sad.

3. The wind is _____ the dust.

4. Grandpa _____ horses.

5. The _____ are crooked.

6. Beth is _____ the trash away.

7. Mom wasn't _____ down for the curve.

8. It hasn't _____ yet.

9. The big truck _____ the pickup back home.

10. It _____ in the winter.

Word Bank

blow + ing	know + s	row + s	snow + ed	throw + ing
grow + ing	own + ed	slow + ing	snow + s	tow + ed

377

Hide and Seek

Check a paper for each word you spell correctly.

Suffixes

Add **s**, **ed**, and **ing** to these spelling words. Write the new words.

	+ s	+ ed	+ ing
1. pray	_____	_____	_____
2. stay	_____	_____	_____
3. paint	_____	_____	_____
4. rain	_____	_____	_____
5. train	_____	_____	_____
6. play	_____	_____	_____

	+ s	+ ing
7. say	_____	_____
8. pay	_____	_____

Hide and Seek

Check a paper for each word you spell correctly.

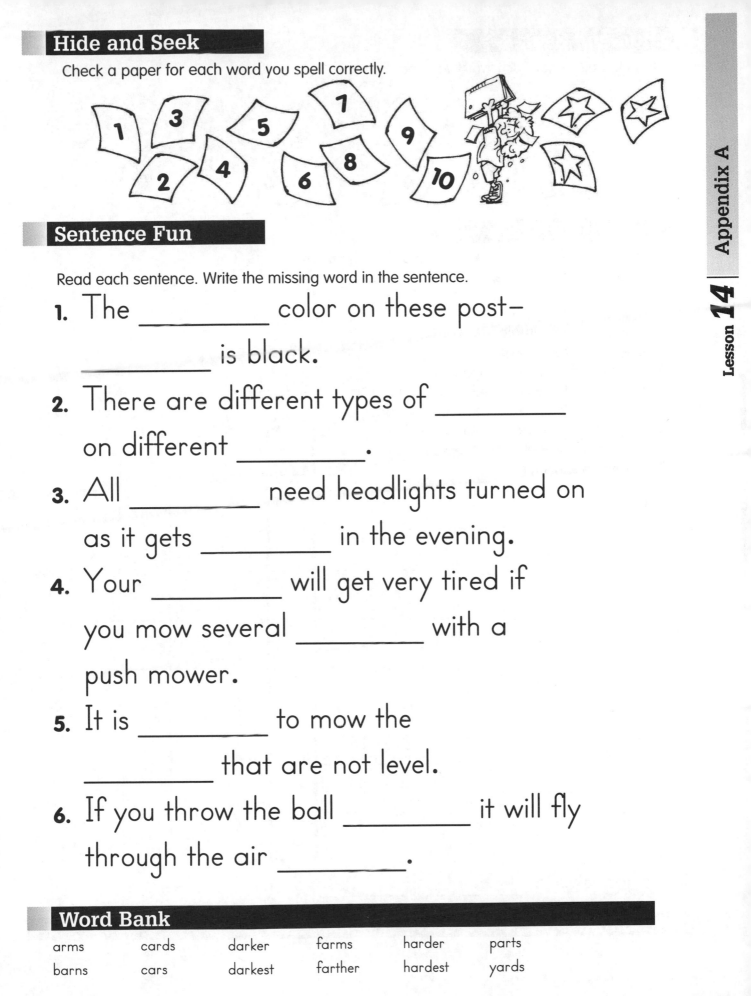

Sentence Fun

Read each sentence. Write the missing word in the sentence.

1. The _____ color on these post–
_____ is black.

2. There are different types of _____
on different _____.

3. All _____ need headlights turned on
as it gets _____ in the evening.

4. Your _____ will get very tired if
you mow several _____ with a
push mower.

5. It is _____ to mow the
_____ that are not level.

6. If you throw the ball _____ it will fly
through the air _____.

Word Bank

arms	cards	darker	farms	harder	parts
barns	cars	darkest	farther	hardest	yards

Hide and Seek

Check a paper for each word you spell correctly.

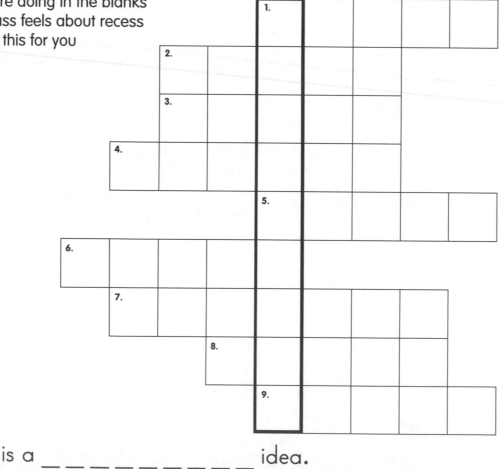

Secret Words

Use these clues to write the words that fit in the blanks.
Then use the boxed letters to discover the secret word.

1. are started with matches
2. cute but wild animals
3. overdue books will get you these
4. what the class does for Handwriting
5. Grandma did this to blankets on clothesline
6. there are lots of these on notebook paper
7. what you are doing in the blanks
8. how the class feels about recess
9. Jesus does this for you

Being honest is a _ _ _ _ _ _ _ _ _ _ idea.

Word Bank

| aired | cares | fires | lines | writing |
| bears | fines | likes | writes | |

Hide and Seek

Check a paper for each word you spell correctly.

1 3 5 7 9
2 4 6 8 10

Clues

Look at the endings added to the spelling words in the word bank.
Use the clues to write one of the new words in each sentence.

1. made up of letters _____

2. it does okay _____

3. animals that fly _____

4. shapes with no corners _____

5. what you did with crayons _____

6. what you are doing on this page _____

7. what you did to plants _____

8. can divide something this way _____

9. a name for far away planets _____

10. more than one shade of purple _____

Word Bank

bird + s	color + ed	third + s	word + s	work + ing
circle + s	purple + s	water + ed	work + s	world + s

Hide and Seek

Check a paper for each word you spell correctly.

Code

Use the code to write the spelling words.

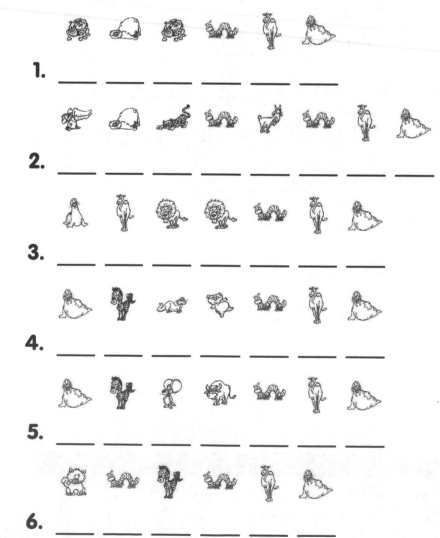

a b c d e f g h i j k l m

n o p q r s t u v w x y z

1. ___ ___ ___ ___ ___ ___

2. ___ ___ ___ ___ ___ ___ ___ ___

3. ___ ___ ___ ___ ___ ___ ___

4. ___ ___ ___ ___ ___ ___ ___

5. ___ ___ ___ ___ ___ ___ ___

6. ___ ___ ___ ___ ___ ___

382

Hide and Seek

Check a paper for each word you spell correctly.

Sentence Fun

Add the endings to the spelling words. Write one of the new words in each sentence.

1. You are my _____ friend.

2. The _____ loved dog sleeps on her bed.

3. Jesus always _____ you.

4. If you have _____, listen!

5. The _____ crashed to the floor.

6. The _____ stool was by the sink.

7. Stephen's glass was the _____.

8. The trail led through the _____.

9. Stephen is seven _____ old.

10. This jar is _____ than that one.

11. That loud noise hurts my _____.

12. I like _____ the birds sing.

Word Bank

book + s	dear + ly	ear + s	full + est	hear + ing	wood + en
dear + est	ear + s	full + er	hear + s	wood + s	year + s

Hide and Seek

Check a paper for each word you spell correctly.

Secret Words

Use these clues to write the words that fit in the blanks.
Then use the boxed letters to discover the secret words.

1. We have these in our house
2. The newspaper reports this
3. The letter after o
4. Is not new
5. Is opposite of later
6. My two front ones are missing from my mouth
7. People visit animals in them

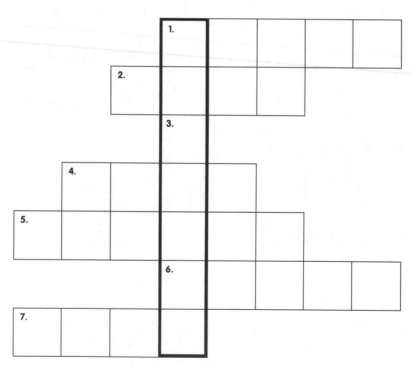

There is joy when one sinner _ _ _ _ _ _ _ !

Word Bank

news   sooner   used

rooms   teeth   zoos

384

Hide and Seek

Check a paper for each word you spell correctly.

Word Sort Suffixes

Write the spelling words with **ow**.
Write the spelling words with **ou**.

ow

1. _____

2. _____

3. _____

4. _____

5. _____

ou

1. _____

2. _____

3. _____

4. _____

5. _____

6. _____

7. _____

8. _____

Add **s**, **ed**, or **ing** to make new words from your spelling words.

	+ s	+ ed	+ ing
1. count			
2. bow			
3. round			
4. sound			

Word Bank

around	cloud	cow	flower	house	sound	vowel
bow	count	crown	found	round	south	

Hide and Seek

Check a paper for each word you spell correctly.

Suffixes

Add **s**, **ed**, or **ing** to make new words from your spelling words.

+ s

1. door _____

2. enjoy _____

3. form _____

4. horse _____

5. noise _____

6. orange _____

7. store _____

8. toy _____

9. voice _____

+ ed

1. form _____

2. enjoy _____

3. toy _____

4. horse – e _____

5. store – e _____

+ ing

1. enjoy _____

2. form _____

3. horse – e _____

4. store – e _____

5. toy _____

386

Hide and Seek

Check a paper for each word you spell correctly.

Secret Word

Use these clues to find the word that fits in each blank.
Then use the boxed letters to discover the secret word.

1. not as big
2. Run, runs. Walk,_____.
3. a person who is not yet grown up
4. a picture done with a pencil
5. moving slower than running
6. littlest
7. meals in a bag or box
8. would like to have

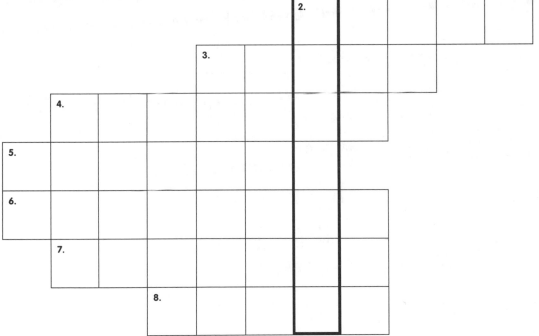

It is fun to play on a _ _ _ _ _ _   _ _ _.

Word Bank

child	lunches	smallest	walks
drawing	smaller	walking	wants

Hide and Seek

Check a paper for each word you spell correctly.

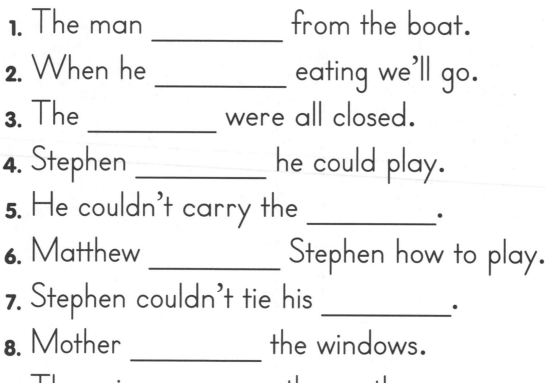

Making Words

Look at other forms of your spelling words in the word bank.
Use the clues to find the word that fits best in each blank.

1. The man _____ from the boat.

2. When he _____ eating we'll go.

3. The _____ were all closed.

4. Stephen _____ he could play.

5. He couldn't carry the _____.

6. Matthew _____ Stephen how to play.

7. Stephen couldn't tie his _____.

8. Mother _____ the windows.

9. The rain _____ the earth.

Word Bank

dish + es	fish + es	shop + s	shut + s	wish + es
finish + es	shoe + s	show + s	wash + es	

388

Hide and Seek

Check a paper for each word you spell correctly.

Suffixes

Add **s** or **es** to make new words from your spelling words.

+ s

1. band + s _____

2. bend + s _____

3. end + s _____

4. pond + s _____

5. blind + s _____

6. find + s _____

7. kind + s _____

8. Indian + s _____

9. friend + s _____

10. second + s _____

+ es

11. index _____

y to i + es

12. candy _____

Hide and Seek

Check a paper for each word you spell correctly.

Hidden Words

Find these words in the puzzle. Circle and write each word.

s	o	t	b	r	o	u	g	h	t
r	x	s	i	n	g	s	t	u	z
e	t	i	l	p	m	r	g	n	d
b	a	c	k	s	a	o	e	g	u
k	l	k	d	r	k	y	z	e	c
c	k	e	h	p	e	m	q	d	k
a	i	s	g	c	l	o	c	k	s
d	n	t	r	u	c	k	e	r	h
m	g	n	q	e	m	a	y	q	p
m	i	l	k	i	n	g	d	g	e

Across

_____

_____

_____

_____

_____

_____

Down

_____

_____

_____

_____

Word Bank

backs	clocks	hung	sickest	talking
brought	ducks	milking	sings	trucker

390

Hide and Seek

Check a paper for each word you spell correctly.

Clues

Look at other forms of your spelling words in the word bank.
Use the clues to find the word that fits best in each blank.

1. what you tell someone who
   has done something nice
   _____

2. two boys with the same mother _____

3. men who have children _____

4. how you spread something you like _____

5. someone who is more thin _____

6. the person who is the most thin _____

7. a sandwich that is more thick _____

8. the sandwich that has the most in it _____

Word Bank

brother + s	thank + s	thick + est	thin + n + er
father + s	thick + er	thick + ly	thin + n + est

Hide and Seek

Check a paper for each word you spell correctly.

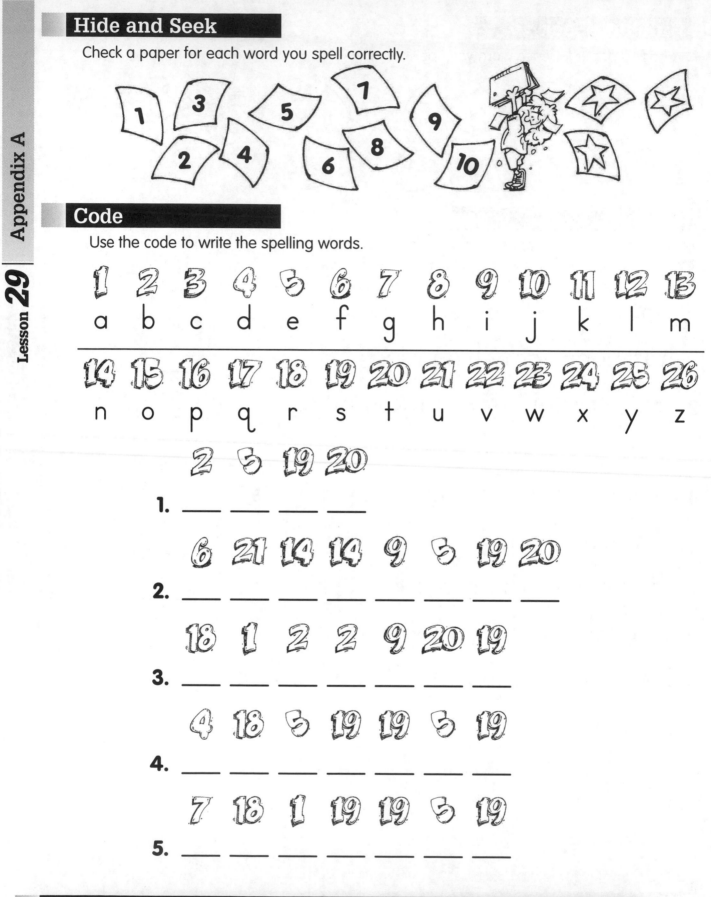

Code

Use the code to write the spelling words.

1	2	3	4	5	6	7	8	9	10	11	12	13
a	b	c	d	e	f	g	h	i	j	k	l	m

14	15	16	17	18	19	20	21	22	23	24	25	26
n	o	p	q	r	s	t	u	v	w	x	y	z

2 5 19 20

1. ___ ___ ___ ___

6 21 14 14 9 5 19 20

2. ___ ___ ___ ___ ___ ___ ___ ___

18 1 2 2 9 20 19

3. ___ ___ ___ ___ ___ ___ ___

4 18 5 19 19 5 19

4. ___ ___ ___ ___ ___ ___ ___

7 18 1 19 19 5 19

5. ___ ___ ___ ___ ___ ___ ___

Word Bank

best   funniest   rabbits
dresses   grasses

392

PLEASE
PHOTOCOPY!*

The following pages contain Black Line Masters for use with the **A Reason For Spelling**® Student Worktext.

*Photocopy privileges extend only to the material in this section, and permission is granted only for those classrooms or homeschools using **A Reason For Spelling**® Student Worktexts. Any other use of this material is expressly forbidden and all copyright laws apply.

Spelling Progress Chart

Fill in the five lesson numbers for the unit in the first row of blocks. Use the first half of the column under each block to record the score for the Preview, and the second half of the column for the Posttest. To record the score, begin at the bottom of the column and color the blanks to show the number of words spelled correctly. Use one color for Preview and another for Posttest.

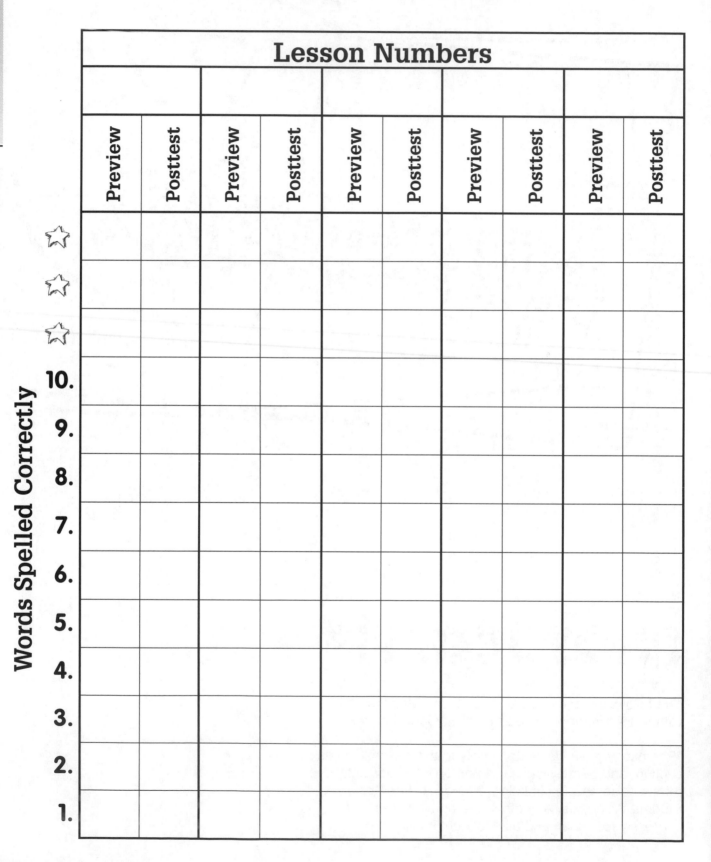

Words Spelled Correctly

Lesson Numbers

	Preview	Posttest	Preview	Posttest	Preview	Posttest	Preview	Posttest	Preview	Posttest
☆										
☆										
☆										
10.										
9.										
8.										
7.										
6.										
5.										
4.										
3.										
2.										
1.										

394

Rubric for Scoring

You may wish to use this rubric at the end of each unit to track student progress.

	Standard	Usually	Sometimes	Not Yet
1.	Writes all letters correctly and legibly (upper and lower case)			
2.	Uses correct spelling on words from current and previous lessons			
3.	Writes a paragraph in response to a prompt			
4.	Uses appropriate punctuation			
5.	Uses capital letters correctly			
6.	Writes complete, coherent, and organized sentences			
7.	Includes descriptive language			
8.	Forms plurals correctly			
9.	Subjects and verbs agree			
10.	Uses a logical sequence of events			

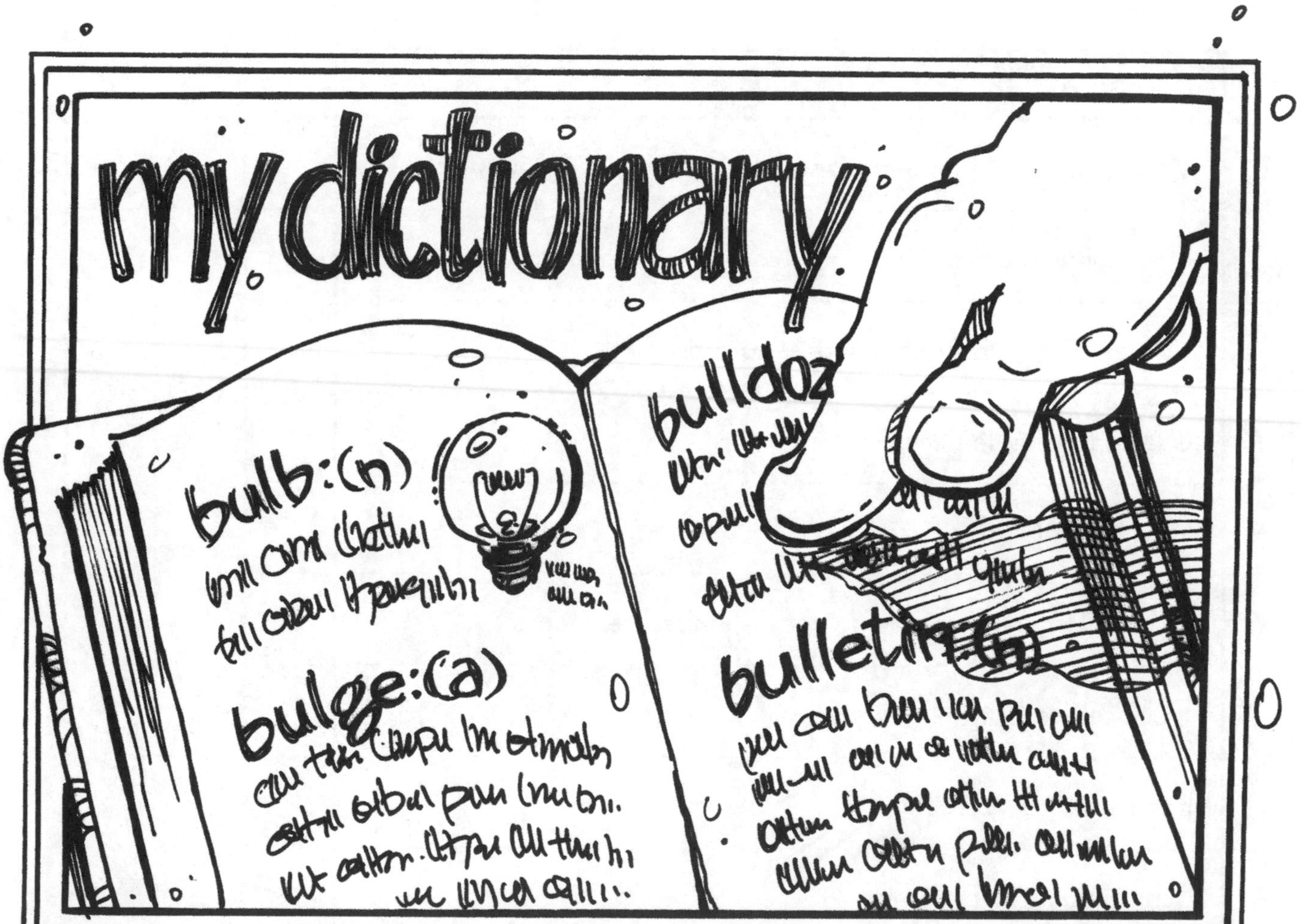
my dictionary
bulb:(n)
bulge:(a)
bulldoz
bulletin:(n)